ODYSSEY TO FREEDOM

ODYSSEY TO FREEDOM

George Bizos

*A memoir by the world-renowned human rights
advocate, friend and lawyer to Nelson Mandela*

For Della,

with my
best wishes

George Bizos
6·08·2008·

RANDOM HOUSE

Published by Random House (Pty) Ltd
Isle of Houghton, Corner Boundary Road &
Carse O'Gowrie, Houghton 2198, South Africa
in association with Umuzi
P.O. Box 6810, Roggebaai 8012
www.umuzi-randomhouse.co.za

First edition, second printing 2007
ISBN: 978-0-9584195-8-1

Photograph on cover © Gisele Wulfson 1996
Cover design by Mr Design
Text design and layout by William Dicey
Set in Minion 10.5 on 14 pt

Printed and bound by Paarl Print
Oosterland Street, Paarl, South Africa

For those who let me walk with them

CONTENTS

*Photographic inserts between pages 224 & 225
and pages 392 & 393.*

FOREWORD BY NELSON MANDELA

George Bizos and I have known each other well for close on sixty years. Over these years we have shared much and have grown to be close friends.

George came to South Africa with his brave, anti-Nazi father at the young age of thirteen – refugees, after a trying voyage of escape from the forces of fascism sweeping through their native Greece. We first met at the University of the Witwatersrand, and I am glad that what George records here includes his battle against the discrimination practised against black students at our alma mater.

George's identification with our struggle in defending victims of apartheid (often instructed by attorneys Mandela & Tambo), his acting for my former wife, Winnie, his general success in court became widely known, despite his status as a junior advocate. All of this assured me, early on, that George Bizos would continue to defend our people in their struggle for freedom with integrity, great dedication and complete commitment.

Perhaps it is George's tactical skills in matters of the law for which he is best known. It was this skill that led Bram Fischer, the leader of our defence team in the Rivonia Trial, to include George in that landmark event. Indeed it was George Bizos who warned us at our first consultation after the Rivonia arrests that Verwoerd's government was preparing the ground for the death penalty to be imposed on all of those arrested.

We were sentenced, instead, to life imprisonment and all of us appealed to George to continue defending our comrades and to assist our families, particularly by doing what he could to ensure that our children received a proper education during our incarceration.

While I was imprisoned on Robben Island and in other jails, George Bizos was one of my major lifelines. When I was hospitalised during my time at Pollsmoor Prison it was he, a wholly trusted confidant, whom I could send to assure Oliver Tambo in Lusaka of the preliminary negotiations I was conducting for the release of our comrades and plans to end apartheid.

Throughout my imprisonment, George unwaveringly shared our confidence that freedom for all and the dawning of democracy in our country was inevitable.

After my release from prison we were able to spend a great deal more time together. As a member of the ANC's Legal and Constitutional Committee, George played an important role in the writing of our country's Bill of Rights as well as in the shaping of its new constitution. He represented our government at the Constitutional Court to argue for the abolition of the death penalty and then represented us, too, when the country's new constitution was certified.

During my presidency of the Republic of South Africa, I often sought and received, always generously, George's counsel on many legal, constitutional and personal matters. He never once hesitated to assist where and how ever he was able and is considered a member of our family. Most of my children, grandchildren and great-grandchildren are rather partial, in fact, to their 'Uncle George'!

George's autobiography, *Odyssey to Freedom*, is not only a personal account of an extraordinary life but an invaluable addition to the historical record of our nation, captured here by a man whose contribution towards entrenching the human rights that lie at the heart of South Africa's constitutional values is impossible to overrate.

N.M.

PREFACE

For many years, friends and colleagues have been asking me to write this book. I started more than fifteen years ago, but as soon as the amnesty commission of the Truth and Reconciliation Commission began its hearing in 1996, I had to stop. I was asked to represent the families of those who had died in detention or who had been killed by the apartheid regime's death squads. Despite our efforts at the time, those responsible were exonerated by the courts. They now admitted responsibility for the deaths and torture of their victims in order to be granted amnesty. Also they admitted perjury, that they had suppressed evidence and had conspired with others to do the same, deliberately defeating the ends of justice. I felt strongly about the manner in which justice was cheated and that it should be written about in a separate book. I thought that it should be published as soon as possible because of denials by senior politicians, policemen, generals and other apologists of these injustices of the past. Among them were a few magistrates and even judges.

I chose five high-profile cases relating to the deaths of Ahmed Timol, Steve Biko, Neil Aggett, Simon Mndawe, Matthew Goniwe, Fort Calata, Sparrow Mkonto and Sicelo Mhlauli. When the magistrate at the inquest of the killers of Steve Biko said that no one was to blame for his death, his tearful widow, Nontsikelelo, exclaimed to me – 'What? No one to blame?' This was the title of the earlier book. I did not want the impact of that story to be diminished by autobiographical detail. I wanted it to be a record of what it was like to pursue justice during South Africa's apartheid years, a period when the conditions under which we practised were difficult to say the least. In the preface to that book Sir Sydney Kentridge QC wrote that in those years we were trying to do justice 'before an often hostile court, and an always hostile establishment'.

No one to blame? was noticed by Stephen Johnson of Random House and he told me that they would like to publish my autobiography. He was pleased to hear that part of it had already been written. He liked what I showed him and expected to publish reasonably soon. It was not to be. My involvement in the negotiations, the drafting of the Constitution, in constitutional litigation with the Legal Resources Centre, my defence of Morgan Tsvangirai and others in Zimbabwe on charges of treason as well as checking court records for those earlier cases I wanted to write about, all meant that it has taken much longer than anyone thought. I want to thank Stephen Johnson and the publishers for their patience and help. I also want to thank the editor, Mike Nicol, for his useful guidance and his arrangement of the chapters. Similarly, Annari van der Merwe for her assistance in putting the book together.

My gratitude is also due to my first editor, Carmel Rickard, a senior journalist legally qualified and well versed in the legal process.

Catrin Verloren van Themaat, the LRC's Bram Fischer librarian, is a most inventive Internet researcher who has unearthed useful information, something I, as a computer illiterate, was quite unable to do.

Early in the process Audrey Esser typed the script, then Julie Khamissa and finally the bulk of the work was done by Cyrenne Christodoulou. Each one in turn urged me to get on with it. Michelle Pickover and Carol Archibald in the department of historical papers at the University of the Witwatersrand, where some of the trial records were kept, helped me greatly. My daughter-in-law, Mary Beal, read the manuscript. I am indebted to all of them.

Thanks to all who have read the script for their helpful comments as well as all those who helped put the book together, particularly Gail Behrmann for searching for the photographs.

My wife Arethe and our sons and daughters-in-law, Kimon and Mary, Damon and Anna, Alexi and Monique, have been asking for years when was I going to finish. They kept on telling me how much better I would feel when I had done so. They were right. I thank them for their persistence.

G.B.

Part One: 1928–1953

CHAPTER 1

Mavrovouni – The Black Mountain

Mavrovouni – the Black Mountain – named for its dark, leaf-rich shrubs, separates the plain of Messinia: Pylos and Methoni on the west, Kalamata to Koroni on the east. On the mountain, you can count over thirty shades of green at any time and twice as many in spring. You can climb to the top along the winding footpaths made by goatherds and their flocks, by hunters and pickers of mushrooms, wild chicory and oregano. The mountain tapers off almost to the edge of Cape Akritas where the Ionian Sea ends and the Sea of Crete begins. Migratory birds from the north spend their last night at its foot before crossing the Mediterranean to find shelter along the banks of the Nile. And it was at its foot in the village of Vasilitsi that I was born and spent my first thirteen years, before setting off across the Mediterranean to take shelter in the land of the Nile.

Centuries before I was born, the village was known as Faneromeni. That is the name on the maps drawn during the Renaissance by the Venetians and the Genoans who built castles and observation towers to prevent the Ottoman Empire from invading their affluent cities.

But when *Moreas,* as the Peloponnese was then known, succumbed to the Turks, the new masters were not able to defend Faneromeni from pirates. The village was ransacked and the survivors fled behind a small hill where it is said there was a chapel of St Vasilios, near the edge of the sea. In the saint's honour they named the new village Vasilitsi. Most Greeks believe that their own village is better than any other.

On a clear day, from the top of the mountain, you can see the plain of Pylos with its remnants of the palace of Nestor, breeder of horses and wisest of all Greek kings. It was to Nestor that Telemachus, son of wily Odysseus, sailed from Ithaca seeking his long absent and adventurous father, who for over twenty years had been kept away from his home and his wife Penelope by the Trojan War, misfortune and a zest for pleasure.

To the west and south of the mountain looms the open sea, ending at Gibraltar and the coast of North Africa. Usually a calm light blue, the sea is filled with turbulent white horses when the winds blow, and if Poseidon vents his anger, it takes on the wine-dark hue of Homer's verse.

In some ways Vasilitsi, where my long journey started, remains my Ithaca.

What I learned in my first thirteen years there has influenced my whole life and work. And now, more than sixty years later in Johannesburg, a city unknown to me when we set off, I think it has been a worthwhile journey.

My father, Antonios, and my mother, Anastasia, were born in 1902. My grandfathers Yiannis Bizos and Panayiotis Tomaras arranged their marriage. But because the village records were burnt during the German occupation in the 1940s to prevent identification and recruitment to German factories, there is no record of the date or year in which they were married. All I know is that they married in their early twenties. Nor do I know the date on which I was born. The date of a saint's festival is more important in the Greek countryside than birthdays and anniversaries. My mother remembers that I was born on Saint Philip's day, 14 November. She remembers it because of the debate about whether I should be named Philip. The alternative was Yiannis after my paternal grandfather, the traditional custom unless the grandfather insisted otherwise.

It was a complex decision involving family and national politics. My grandfather's only child with Ekaterine Kranias, his first wife, was a George Bizos who was captured and killed by the Bulgarians during the First World War. A framed commemorative plaque in his honour, depicting the national coat of arms above two laurel branches, hung on the wall next to the olive-wood family icon. The votive lamp in front of this icon was lit every evening as the church bell rang for the short vespers service.

The great political divide among the Greek people at that time was between those who supported the liberal democrat, Elefterios Venizelos, and those who backed the kings of German origin, imposed upon the Greeks after the war of independence from 1821–1827.

My grandfather was a supporter of Venizelos, prime minister at the time George Bizos was killed. He mourned his son's death but proudly proclaimed that his son had not died in vain, that he had lost his life liberating a further portion of Greece from the Turkish yoke. He insisted that I be named after his dead son. As my mother had lost her first two children at birth, he was anxiously waiting for a grandson. I was his favourite, the only grandchild to whom he bequeathed a field on which he expected me to grow wheat when I was old enough.

When Ekaterine died, my grandfather married Nicolletta Koukos, a woman from a neighbouring village. 'Koukos' in Greek and 'cuckoo' in English have a similarly playful secondary meaning, and my father soon became known as Koukantonis. The rest of the family were given similar nicknames using the 'Koukos' prefix. In my presence, the villagers call me Kyrie Yioryo as a sign of respect, but behind my back I am 'Koukoyioryos'.

My father was a member of the *Laiko* – the Populist Party – one of the centre parties advocating agrarian reform. He was a close friend of the local member of parliament, and at election time I was roped in to help him. They bought a wooden box of Turkish delight and my task was to cut the matchbox-size pieces into four, then offer them to those who had gathered in the village square to throw their caps high and respond to my father's call: '*Zeto* – long live – Perecles Rallis' – the man who was seeking their vote.

My primary school was not unlike those the children of Soweto attended during the apartheid years. In the 1930s there were no fewer than a hundred and forty of us of different ages in one room with a single teacher. A blackboard, an abacus and a slate were the main teaching aids. A tattered reading book was passed on from one year to the next, while a new exercise book, a pencil and an eraser were all we had.

I began school in September 1935. My father had been elected mayor of the village and one of his duties was to oversee the education of the children. Very few girls were sent to school by their parents. When we asked our mother why she hadn't gone to school she said that her parents, like all the others in the village, believed that if you sent girls to school they would form relationships with boys – something which was frowned upon. My mother added with a smile, 'Little did they know how much easier it was to form relationships when you looked after sheep and goats in the fields.' It was also the mayor's function to appoint the teacher, find her accommodation, and welcome her and introduce her to the children and their parents.

Kyria Eugenia Kotsakis came to the village. She walked with a stick, dragging one of her feet, deformed at the ankle, for which she wore a specially made boot. In accordance with village tradition, rather than wanton cruelty, she was forever referred to as the *koutsi* – the cripple. But we called her *Daskala* – the teacher. She stayed in our house for a while with my grandfather, my grandmother Nicolletta, mother and father, my sister Vaso, brother Stavros and the infant Yiannis named after my grandfather and christened by Daskala. Having become the godmother of one of us, she was called *koumbara* (an intimate word for godparent) by our parents and grandparents and a special relationship developed between our families.

She was the mother of three children, a daughter Elvira and two sons, George and Frixos. She came from Kalamata, the provincial capital, some fifty kilometres away. Her husband, Costas Kotsakis, was a once-successful coffee roaster and merchant upon whom misfortune had fallen: a fire destroyed his premises and machinery and he never recovered from the catastrophe. He became a househusband

and remained with the children in Kalamata. Their sons George and Frixos, who became my best friends, visited her regularly, staying with her in the two rooms on the upper floor in a house near the school.

While she stayed with us or when she visited, Daskala would sit with us around the open fire in the lower part of our house, and tell us what life was like in the great city of Smyrna where she was born, where she had gone to school, and where she was preparing to become a medical student before polio led to her disability.

When the Greeks of Asia Minor were forced by war to flee in 1922, she was one of hundreds of thousands of refugees who settled in Greece. She told us how they had lived in wooden barracks on the beach at Kalamata, of becoming a teacher and meeting her husband, of living comfortably with her family until the financial disaster which made it necessary for her to return to teaching and take a post that separated her from her family.

She managed the school with ease and grace. We were not afraid of her. Before we arrived at school she wrote exercises on the blackboard for the older ones to do on their slates or in their books, then she read lessons to us, the younger ones. She set exercises then moved to another age group and more advanced work. The more precocious among us listened to what she was teaching our seniors and often attempted to answer the questions she posed the higher grades. She did not discourage us, but some of the older boys would glare and during playtime chased and threatened us for showing them up. During one of those chases I fell and broke my left arm which was set in a plaster made of a special soil and eggs to heal.

Daskala secured our discipline by appealing to our better natures. The worst physical punishment she ever imposed on anyone was three moderate smacks with a flat ruler on the palm of the offender's left hand – but she was capable of administering tongue-lashings which put us to shame.

One of our daily lessons was to read a prescribed section, taking it in turns from the front of the class to the back. One day I came late and wasn't there for my turn. I did not apologise but waited impatiently for the boy on his feet to finish, then sprang up, and read the lesson. Quietly she told me that I had read it well. I sat down full of self-satisfaction but it was very short-lived. She ordered me to stand. In a tone that I had never before heard from her, at home or in the classroom, she asked, 'Why did you not apologise when you came in late?' I had no answer. 'Who gave you the right to stand up and read when it was the turn of another? Don't you know that if you're the last to come in, you must be the last to take part?' I tried to fight back tears. She ordered me to the back of the class to stand until she gave me leave to return to my seat. Although my ordeal did not last too long, it brought home to me that the son of the mayor was not going to be treated differently from anyone else.

Women and children were not allowed in the *kafeneio*, where men gathered to smoke, talk at the top of their voices, play cards, blaspheme and tell inappropriate jokes. My tolerant father, who had the well-earned reputation of disliking manual work, spent a lot of time there. He had no objection to my standing by him while he and others played cards. I was even asked to keep the score on a small blackboard placed on the windowsill.

At that time, Greece was in a volatile state. The monarchist cause had suffered defeat in national elections, and in the *kafeneio* heated arguments would break out about the newly elected government. Venizelos, George Papendreou and Panages Tsaldaris were praised and the royalists generally condemned. But the dissident voices said that we Greeks were an ill-disciplined people, we needed a strong leader, a leader like the ones in Spain, in Italy and in Germany.

Daskala refrained from expressing views on this issue in public. She played the mandolin in her rooms and in our home, and sang songs that had not been heard in the village before, songs bemoaning the fate of the Greeks of Asia Minor, of loss of property and loved ones, of separation and unrequited love. Her favourite was a song praising Venizelos and condemning the king and his family. The king and the clowns around him were blamed for the 1922 catastrophe and the song predicted the return of Venizelos to sweep them away.

No one in the village had a radio, but occasionally someone brought in a couple of newspapers. Daskala regularly received newspapers from Kalamata and Athens. I eavesdropped on the conversations between her and my father. She predicted that the royalists would instigate a military coup, that the elected leaders would be pushed aside and that Greece would become a fascist state.

And so it happened. On 4 August 1936 Ioannis Metaxas seized power, restored the monarchy and detained many of its opponents. There were rumours of torture and of large doses of castor oil forced down the throats of those who would not denounce their left-wing tendencies. The dictator's supporters were singing a new song:

> *Why father is the world so happy?*
> *Why is everyone smiling?*
> *Because on this day my child*
> *This golden and joyous day is for you too*
> *The black tears have stopped*
> *The old wounds have healed …*

My father was a popular man. Not only was he expected to complete his four years as mayor, but was sure of being elected for a second term. The province's civil engineer regularly visited the village as my father's guest. He was known to us simply as Soumbli. With his help a road for vehicles had been built from Koroni to Vasilitsi, and there was running water – albeit from just six taps in different sections of the village. His only real opposition was from the few whose properties were cut up for the road, and the owners of the citrus groves below the source from where the water was piped to the village.

But now rumours reached my father that he was accused of being an ardent anti-royalist (in his later life he clearly showed that he was not) and that he would abuse his position as mayor if he was not removed from office. Furthermore, if he did not resign, the newly appointed *nomarchis* – the prefect – would not make funds available to the village for the completion of the works that my father had initiated, nor would new works be authorised. The advice of his friends, including Daskala, was that he should resign. He did so. However, in the eyes and minds of the majority in Vasilitsi he was their leader – a judgement proved correct when put to the test.

His decision to resign as mayor was welcomed by my mother and grandfather, who maintained that my father should show more interest in family affairs. My mother, in particular, was relieved that she no longer had to put up the numerous guests, who, in the absence of a hotel in the village, would stay with us, nor hurriedly prepare meals for those who came without notice.

Daskala's appointment to our village school came to an end after three years. Panayiotis Arnaoutis took her place. He was an old-style pedagogue, a strict disciplinarian freely administering corporal punishment favoured by most parents, but not by my father. Arnaoutis spent much time identifying the heroes of the 1821 revolution for Greek independence from the Ottoman Empire. We heard glowing accounts of their achievements, but little of the factionalism. Freedom songs and poems in their honour were rehearsed in preparation for 25 March, Independence Day, and for parents' meetings at the end of the term.

Every Sunday morning I accompanied my grandfather to the large new church, erected under the supervision of a talented refugee from Asia Minor who had settled in the village. Usually we arrived at the church before the village priest. Unlike my grandfather, my father was an irregular churchgoer and personified the anticlericalism of many Greeks which was considered not inconsistent with religious belief. As mayor, he had docked half a month's pay from the priest's salary when the cleric failed to turn up for his ten-day share of labour to build the road. The priest sued and, when he lost, made it known that he would refuse to give my father communion, traditionally taken just before the high feast days. The priest was not put to the test, however, as my father did not attend to receive it.

At my grandfather's request, I offered myself as an altar boy, only to be told by an older boy that I was not welcome. I was ordered to leave the sanctified area behind the *iconostasis*. I confess that I kicked him on the shin. A few years ago I received a message that he wanted to see me. Apparently he still had the mark from my kick.

In September 1938 I enrolled in the *astiko,* an intermediate school in Koroni, seven kilometres from the village. It was an ancient town fortified by the Venetians in the Middle Ages; a busy port, chock-a-block with fishing boats and *caiques* loading olives and olive oil, bags of blackcurrants and casks of wine, the cash crops of the area. I stayed with two elderly sisters close to the gate of the Venetian castle with a view of the harbour and snow-covered Mount Tyegetos, down the cliffs of which the Spartans threw their deformed children. At night across the bay shone the electric lights of Kalamata.

One day an Italian warship lowered anchor beyond the quay and a large rowing boat was dropped into the choppy sea. Eight oarsmen sat on either side with a helmsman at the back. Anxious curiosity – even fear – could be seen on the faces of those who gathered at the landing, not to welcome them, but to find out why they had come and what they wanted. The precision with which they handled the boat, their immaculate white, well-pressed uniforms, their round caps and ribbons impressed us all. The helmsman and two others came on shore. The port captain and an interpreter met them at the quayside. Hundreds of silent onlookers, including some of us schoolchildren, kept our distance, anxiously waiting to see what would happen. We could not hear what was said but soon the Italians smartly returned to the boat and with admirable dexterity turned it around and went back to their ship.

As the helmsman called the tempo to the oarsmen, the port captain told us not to worry. The warship was merely passing by, and their captain wanted to express his good wishes to Koroni, which his Venetian ancestors had endowed with a castle and a port. But this hardly put our minds at rest. Everyone knew that the Italians occupied the Aegean Islands of the Dodecanese and that their fascist leader, Benito Mussolini, aspired to combine all the countries on the shores of the Mediterranean into a reincarnation of the Roman Empire with himself, the *duce,* as emperor.

On the other side of the castle was the church of the *Eleystria* – the Saviour, the Virgin Mary, a holy shrine where on its festival day, 15 August, miracles were reputed to occur. Our school, in the middle of the town, had no place for physical training so we walked to the spacious park at the church for regimented exercises and folk dancing. We were expected to take turns at leading the dance. Those who faltered were given two strokes with a cane. When my turn came, I told the teacher that I could not lead the dance, and asked for the punishment to be administered. He delivered a short lecture to the class on my impudence and predicted my sure failure in life for not trying. He doubled the number of strokes and threatened to treble them if anyone followed my example. Unlike the village school, at the *astiko* there were different teachers for different subjects, and a gentle monk, who collected stamps and lived in a cell of the castle, taught us language, arithmetic and history and gave us religious instruction.

Soon after my entry into the Koroni school I was issued with a uniform – a pair of shorts, shirt and cloth cap – all of a blue so dark it was almost black. It was compulsory for every pupil to become a member of Metaxas' *Neolea* – Youth Movement. The physical training teacher taught us to march, salute and shout slogans praising Metaxas and his assumption of power. I later learned that the inspiration for the movement had come from Hitler's Nazi Germany and Mussolini's fascist Italy. To salute you raised the right hand above shoulder level with an open palm. If my father had any adverse feelings, he did not express them to me.

Shortly before a parade of the *Neolea*, the principal called in my father. The following Sunday, the *Neolea*'s march would end at Saint Demitri's Square in the centre of Koroni and my father and as many villagers as possible from Vasilitsi should attend. 'By the way,' he said, 'something has to be done about your son's shoes.' They were old and the heels had worn unevenly which made my walking unattractive. My shoes were certainly not good enough for such an important occasion as the march. Would my father see to it that I had a new pair of shoes before Sunday? There were no ready-made shoes to be had in Koroni but one of the four assistants of the shoemaker was persuaded to make me a pair in time. The march, however, left me with painful memories, as the new shoes, made of heavy leather, were too tight.

My father was also told that I was not living up to the school's expectations. My essay for the admission examination on Aesop's fable of the lion and the mouse had indicated to them that I had a proper understanding of patriotic and Christian values but my performance and behaviour since had indicated the contrary.

Despite these gloomy predictions, I passed. However, my father, after talking to Daskala who had now retired in Kalamata, decided that I should leave the village and the Koroni intermediate school, move into the Kotsakis home and enrol in the gymnasium on the beachfront of Kalamata. She enquired whether they would have me in the second grade of the gymnasium by recognising my year at the intermediary school. Not without an examination, they said. So I spent the early summer of 1939 in Kalamata being coached by Daskala in preparation for the exam. Despite her efforts I failed the examination and had to start in the first grade.

Kalamata was a new world for me: a city with tarred roads, electric streetlights, trams, motorcars, bicycles, horse carriages, a cinema, a large flour mill into which wheat was sucked up from ships berthed on the quayside, unlike other cargo, which was taken off by *chamals* in bags on their backs. For the first time I went to the cinema. As I entered the dark room in the company of George and Frixos, I was confused and frightened by the roaring lion of the Metro Goldwyn Meyer film studio.

The Kotsakis home was a comfortable one. I shared a room with the two boys. For the first time I could switch on an electric light, use an inside toilet, drink cool water from an ice box, water the orchard and vegetable patch by pushing and pulling a hand water pump. I could walk to the beach not more than a hundred metres away and go back to Koroni by a boat called the *Elpidophoros* – the Bringer of Hope.

My father would be waiting for me in Koroni. We would both mount our horse Psaris and ride the seven kilometres back to the village. There I would spend Saturday afternoon and Sunday and then be taken early on Monday morning to board the boat to Kalamata. I would board, laden with a large round loaf of whole-wheat bread as well as home-made pasta, pork sausage, eggs, raisins and almonds as a contribution to the household pantry for my keep.

Daskala not only coached her sons and me, but also gave private lessons to supplement her meagre pension. The father of the house, Costa Kotsakis, still suffering from the loss of his business, did the cooking and managed to retain his dignity. Life was not easy for the family. Once, when the grocer's assistant came to ask for payment at the end of the month, Daskala told him to tell his boss to read the papers. Had he not seen that pensioners would not receive their pension at the end of the month, but would have to wait into the following month?

Once again, I was inducted into the *Neolea*. Assembled on the road below the balcony of the principal's office, we were told that on Sunday after the church service we were to report at the regimental military headquarters in our *Neolea* uniforms. Every pupil from Kalamata and the nearby towns and villages had to be there for a grand parade. There would be serious consequences for absentees. Thousands turned up. The juniors dressed in shorts, the seniors wearing long pants, shirts and caps with a badge. In a high-pitched voice, the *Neolea* regional leader told us that the main purpose of the gathering was to celebrate the advent to power on 4 August 1936 of General Ioannis Metaxas, founder of the Youth Movement of which we should all be proud. But, he added, among us was a noxious weed that had to be separated from the mass of loyal and patriotic pupils. This pupil's father, a leftist and a traitor, had falsely alleged that it was compulsory to be a member of *Neolea*. We were to witness that this boy's father was lying. It was not obligatory to be a member of the *Neolea*.

A name was called out. The boy was marched to the makeshift podium on which the dignitaries sat. There he was ordered to halt and stand to attention. The fiery speaker took a pair of scissors and ripped the badge from the pupil's cap and the insignia from his shirt. 'About turn' – and the boy faced the thousands on the parade ground. We were ordered to march past and, upon the command of our platoon leader, to turn our eyes left, away from him in a show of contempt. As I approached, I saw the boy's lip quivering in a determined attempt to keep back tears. In unison with the others, I too turned my head away from him. We sang old freedom songs interspersed with songs of praise for the new regime and, at the end, the national anthem 'Hymn to Liberty', which the national poet said was born out of the very marrowbones of the Greeks.

Daskala was shocked to hear what had happened. She told us that such actions were not worthy of our people, although she had seen and heard of such cruelty organised by Turks against Greeks, Armenians and Jews in Smyrna during her student days. The removal of the insignia reminded her of what she called the 'Dreyfus Affair'. She was angry that her sons and I had been exposed to such an inhuman act. The parade-ground incident, coupled with Daskala's comments, became more meaningful to me a few years later when, as a teenage refugee in South Africa, I experienced the pro-Nazi apartheid regime taking power there.

Towards the end of the 1939–40 school year George Kotsakis asked his mother if he could return with me to my village for the long summer vacation. 'Who has invited him?' asked his mother. He said that I had done so, and she told him that I was in no position to issue such invitations.

Daskala's son then dictated a letter to me purporting to have been written by my father. He feared that his mother might more easily detect the forgery if it was in his own handwriting. We wrote that my father was in Kalamata, he was sorry that he could not call on Daskala personally but was in a hurry to catch the boat back to Koroni. He invited George to the village where he would be of help threshing corn, harvesting grapes, peeling almonds and, with me, shepherding the flock. There was of course no mention in the letter that our main purpose was to fish, swim, climb the cliffs and gather seagulls' eggs.

My father turned up in Kalamata a few days after we had given the letter to Daskala. She confronted him about being too busy to call on her and resorting to letters even when he was in Kalamata. 'What letter?' my father asked. We were caught out, but my father had no problem in extending the invitation. Daskala reserved judgement and said she would wait for the results at the end of the school year in mid-June to make her decision. But we had both done well, so George, his younger brother Frixos and I took the *Elpidophoros* to Koroni for the long holiday that would last until the end of August.

Of course by now the world had been at war for a year. Although over the months I had listened to snippets of conversation between Daskala and her visitors as they sat on her shady veranda, the war was of no immediate concern to me or her sons. Many feared that Greece would become involved, but the only local evidence of war was the presence of men in uniform in town. Neither the distant war and Germany's success over Czechoslovakia, Poland, France and the northern countries, nor the fact that our own country was ruled by a dictator sympathetic to Nazi and fascist ideology, nor detentions without trial were uppermost in our minds. During that summer of 1940, the Kotsakis brothers and I, together with other boys from the village, moved from one cove to the next, swimming, diving, splashing, all of us in the nude but mindful to keep a discreet distance from the freshwater pools where mothers and daughters washed and dried lengths of linen. This cloth was freshly off the loom and would be packed away as part of a dowry or cut up for sheets, dresses and shirts.

The Dormition of the Virgin on 15 August is the third most important religious holiday, after Easter and Christmas. For the two weeks beforehand, strict religious dietary laws deprived everyone in the village of cheese, yoghurt and milk, meat and eggs, and even fish. But stewed vegetables and *yemista* – stuffed tomatoes, peppers, marrows, potatoes, baked with rice in olive oil - were enjoyable enough. The day of the festival is keenly awaited. Then the fast is broken with lamb, goat or pig roasted on a spit at the chapel of the monastery outside the village, or in the spacious wooded park of Eleystria on the edge of the sea in Koroni. *Pasteli* – moulded sesame seed and honey cut into strips – is sold and everyone dances to folk songs accompanied by the *bouzouki* and *santouri*, the *klarino*, the high-pitched voices of women and the rhythmic clapping of hands. Many aspire to celebrate the festival at least once in their lives on the island of Tinos where thousands gather to pray. It is claimed that the sick, the disabled and the blind are cured at the climax of the divine service.

But that year, instead of heralding the joyous occasion, the village bell began to toll. Everyone rushed about, asking why? We heard that the Greek cruiser

Elli had been in the harbour of Tinos with many on board to take part in the celebrations. An Italian submarine fired a torpedo which struck the ship, killing and wounding many. Dirges replaced joyful songs and dancing. No one believed the Italians' denial of responsibility. Doubts were expressed about the safety of ships passing by Cape Akritas to Kalamata, Crete and elsewhere, and even of the *caiques* moored in Koroni's harbour. In retrospect, the earlier visit of the Italian ship to Koroni was seen as a bad omen.

As we boarded the boat to go back to school for the 1940-41 school year, other passengers expressed their fears about where the Italians might strike next. But the waters were calm and the captain relaxed. Once out of the Koroni harbour he let us steer the ship, and taught us to choose a peak far away on Mount Tyegetos on the right, then to keep the prow of the ship in line with the peak, to avoid zigzagging along the way.

As we approached Kalamata we saw armed men at the end of the pier and on the rooftop of the flour mill. There were notices on the wall that taking photographs was prohibited. Many more men than before stood about in uniform. We talked of war with our teachers at school. We listened to Daskala and her friends seriously discussing what Metaxas would do. After all, he had been against Greece entering the First World War. He had undergone military training in Germany and he had copied the German way of dealing with internal dissent. Would he surrender to the Germans as others had done, without even nominal opposition? Or would he follow the age-old Greek tradition? Since time immemorial, all would-be occupiers of Greek soil have been issued with the same challenge: we say *'Idou lavein'* – 'Come and get us if you can.'

Early on the morning of 28 October 1940, a small crowd gathered outside the *kafeneio* on our way to school. As we approached, the martial music playing on the radio became louder and louder. We heard a statement from the military high command being read out: early that morning, without any formal declaration of war, Italian forces in Albania had attacked the *Patrida* – the Motherland.

At school, our teachers ordered us to gather on the road below the balcony. There, the headmaster called on the senior mathematics teacher. He said that no matter what differences there may have been among us, they must be set aside. We would show the enemies of liberty that every metre of our soil would be defended even unto death. He was confident that victory would eventually be ours, that it would be a long and arduous struggle, that before it ended we would no longer be boys but men and that the new world emerging after the defeat of fascism would be better than the one into which we had been born. The school would close. Bombardment from the air was feared, as was the use of poison gases which the

Italians had used earlier in Ethiopia. We were to return to our homes and wait for the day when the call came for us to play our part in bringing about a new world. He himself had to join his regiment as a reserve officer in the artillery.

My father came to Kalamata to fetch me. There was no place for us on the *Elpidophoros*, nor were there seats on the buses; too many wanted to leave what had become an obvious enemy target. More than twenty of us boarded an old fishing boat made to carry five or six fishermen and their nets. A high wind came up shortly after we left the harbour. Most sat on the edge holding tight as the rising waves battered the boat. There were calls to the captain to turn back, but he shouted everybody down. He knew what he was doing. Holding fast to the tiller he moved us at once inshore and forward at forty-five degrees and then turned outward to avoid the force of the waves against the side of his boat. Drenched and shivering, we reached Koroni's harbour, and my father and I then walked the seven kilometres to the village. Never had the *tsaki* – the fireplace in the middle of the kitchen – and the hot meal served on the *sofra* – the low table around which my grandparents, my father and mother, my two brothers and sister sat either on the floor or on short wooden stools – been so welcome.

My grandfather, who would not sit down to a meal without a bottle of freshly drawn wine from the barrel, asked me to go to the cellar and fill the bottle from the barrel on the right, not the other that had been filled two months before and was still brewing. On my way I noticed that our horse Psaris was missing: always he would draw his head away from the straw kept back by the bamboo partition, and look at me, and I would stroke his mane. In answer to my anxious question, my father said that army officers had come and ordered that all the horses be brought to the church square. They looked them in the teeth, lifted their legs to examine their hooves and chose the best among them to be conscripted. The first to be taken was our Psaris, the preferred name for pure white horses. He was a hand taller than all the others.

I loved Psaris. He held his head high when I rode him in a canter or galloped him on the beach. Once, when I was asked to take him and the donkey to the enclosed field for the night, I was warned to ride the donkey and pull the horse behind. As soon as I was out of sight, I changed around and tied the donkey's lead around my waist. No sooner had I cajoled Psaris into a canter than the donkey put on the brakes and I fell on the back of my head. It left a depression which, to this day, reminds me of my foolishness and my love for Psaris.

Although my father could seek an exemption because his half-brother George had been killed in an earlier war or because he was thirty-seven years old or because of a defect in one of his eyes, he nevertheless volunteered. He was not sent to the front but to guard Italian prisoners of war at a place he would not disclose in his letter to us. The primary school teacher Panayotis Arnaoutis was called up and the village school closed. The mechanical flour mill outside Koroni was closed for lack of fuel.

My grandfather and mother loaded the donkey with two sacks of wheat and gave me careful instructions on how to get to an inland village to which I had never been before, where I was to use the watermill. On the way, the donkey got stuck in the mud; I lost my way and returned to the village dejected by my failure.

Because most of the younger men were in the army, hardly any were available to be hired as daily labourers. So during the day I was expected to help with gathering the olives, ploughing the fields and lightly covering the seeds of barley, wheat and oats. The vine prunings also needed collecting. During the winter months I was excused from the heavy work of hoeing. Instead I minded the animals grazing in the fields that were to remain fallow during that season. In the cottage my grandmother looked after my younger siblings.

Elderly men filled the *kafeneio,* listening to a radio. Standing in the cold outside, we strained to hear. In my father's absence, I had lost my earlier privilege of entering the premises. Every evening an announcement by the military high command was read out. The Italians were being pushed back day-by-day deep into Albania. With each announcement of the fall of a town to the Greeks, trumpets resounded over the radio. Almost simultaneously, the town crier would rush to the bell tower and the joyous sound of church bells would be heard in the scattered villages around Koroni. Letters from the front were proudly read out in public: they described the bitter cold but spoke triumphantly of successes against the enemy. Derisive comments were made about Mussolini, about his dress and headgear and the way he mimicked the Roman emperors. People improvised new lyrics with politically relevant words and sung them to the tunes of popular songs.

Ours were the first victories against the Axis powers. We heard of the praise heaped on our army, our national unity and our bravery. Even Churchill talked of us. He declared that henceforth it would not be said that Greeks fought like heroes, but that heroes fought like Greeks.

It was reported that the Italian soldiers had no stomach for such a war and that many took the first opportunity to surrender. We heard whisperings that the elements were our worst enemy; that many legs were amputated above the knee to avoid death from gangrene; and that doctors were too ready to amputate. It was said that the worst hit were regiments such as ours from the warmer southern parts. The colonel of the 9th regiment based in Kalamata was said to have agreed to put the troops under his command in the frontline immediately upon their arrival on the northern border. Letters coming through made no mention of such matters, which fuelled suspicions further, adding the fear that all references to difficulties or the deaths of others from the village had been censored.

The radio referred to battles fought in North Africa between the Italians and a combination of the British, Australians, New Zealanders, South Africans and Indians. Although the Allies had pushed the Italians out of Ethiopia and Somalia, they were holding their own in Libya and posed a threat to Egypt and the Middle East. Everywhere in the village people anxiously debated whether the Allies would come to Greece to help with its war effort. Even if they did, some asked, how much good would they do? Might it not have been better if they had not come at all, so that the Germans would not have an excuse to attack?

CHAPTER 2

The Beginning of the Journey

I will go to another land, I will go to another sea.
Another city shall be found better than this.

— CP Cavafy, *The City*

Metaxas died in 1940. And even his bitter opponents acknowledged the stand he had taken against Italy.

Towards the end of March 1941, the Germans made short work of Yugoslavia despite that country's heroic resistance. Next came the Bulgarians who had no problem capitulating. Early in April, Greece was attacked and within days the enemy was in Salonika. After just three weeks the fight was over, but the army in Albania was not prepared to surrender to the Italians and made an orderly retreat to north-western Greece. Many were left to their own devices and had to make their way home as best they could. Metaxas' successor, Alexandros Koryzis, however, committed suicide rather than surrender the country to the enemy. The king, the Greek government, sections of the Greek army and the British expeditionary force all made their way to Crete in the hope of continuing the fight.

Kalamata is the southernmost large, deep-water port of the Greek mainland. During the third week in April, many war and passenger ships moved into the Bay of Messinia to evacuate the retreating Allied expeditionary forces. These consisted of Australians, New Zealanders and the British as well as some Yugoslavs and Greeks. With the help of these ships, some eight thousand escaped to Crete before the Germans captured Kalamata on the morning of Tuesday, 29 April, taking seven thousand prisoners.

The evacuation of these seven thousand had been aborted the previous night, when the British naval command received a report, later established as incorrect, that the Italian fleet was on its way. Rather than surrender, more than two thousand stranded Allies took to the hills, hiding in the bushes and caves far from the roads and villages, which were now overrun by Germans in their lorries and sidecar motorcycles.

There was no welcoming party to receive the thirty Germans who arrived in Koroni, but neither was there anyone to oppose them. They took over the building in which the police were housed, lowered the blue and white Greek flag and raised their fearful banner, the swastika. They commandeered some of the best houses in Koroni, but offered to pay rent. They introduced food rationing but had their fill in the three restaurants where they paid for their meals and were served politely. People carefully avoided them, afraid that any show of hostility could lead to an adverse reaction, or that friendliness might mark one as a collaborator.

Vasilitsi, our village, was not on the map. Although the road built while my father was mayor could be used by vehicles, it was in a bad state after the winter rains and a couple of its turns on the river beds might have presented problems to unwary strangers. A young shepherd tending a large flock of goats on the uncultivated south-western side of Mavrovouni came to my father to report that strange men were hiding near the waterhole where his goats gathered for their late afternoon drink. The men crawled away into the thicker bush whenever he approached. My father, who'd returned home when the Germans invaded, told him to keep quiet about it.

The radio at the *kafeneio* had been hidden, and only a few trusted ones knew where. We whispered the brave words of Radio Crete among ourselves: there was a call to help those trapped on the mainland to get to Crete. Those who did so would be smuggled back onto the mainland if they wanted to return, but death would surely be the fate of those who were caught.

Towards the middle of May my father told me that the two of us would go to Faneromeni, the original site of the village. Just a couple of kilometres away from Vasilitsi, Faneromeni is a flat fertile area between the end of the mountain and the cliffs that drop down to the Ionian Sea. Before we left, my father packed food and he seemed to be taking more bread, cheese and olives than the two of us would need.

We set off on foot through the white, yellow and orange daisies and dark red poppies that covered the fallow fields. Those fields planted with cereals were changing from green to a biscuit tinge. Oleander bloomed and grape leaves of all colours covered the vines' short shoots. In other years, we celebrated the beauty of this season by gathering large bunches of flowers in the countryside on 1 May and bringing them back to our classrooms and our homes, where we would hang them on the lintel of the front door. But in 1941 we avoided all such expressions of joy, either to celebrate the beauty of the countryside in springtime or even in celebration of the resurrection on Easter Day.

On the way my father told me what the shepherd had reported to him and that he was specially taking me with him to instil some confidence in the minds of whoever was hiding: no one intending harm was likely to bring a young boy with him. We left the donkey track and followed the footpath leading to the watering hole where seven young men, looking half my father's age, emerged from the bushes. They wore old clothes no different from those worn by the peasants in the fields. They were light in complexion, one of them a redhead, and both they and their clothes looked freshly washed.

'*Kalimera*' – good day, said my father. *Kalimera*, they chorused in an unusual accent. My father pointed to himself and me, and gave our names. The first to introduce himself was Lewis, the only name I remembered. He introduced the others: their names were strange to us. Lewis, who had picked up some Greek, acted as the link. He told us that they were New Zealanders, and that they had abandoned their guns and their uniforms near Kalamata. Then they walked south at night, resting during the day. Along the way they had been given clothes and directions, but now they'd reached the end of the road, there was only the deep sea ahead of them.

They knew that Crete was somewhere to the south-east and they needed help to get there. My father took the *sakouli* – the homespun woollen bag – off his shoulder and opened up the pieces of cloth within it to spread out the bread, the cheese, the *pasto* – salted pork – and the olives. Though they must have been very hungry, they ate slowly and with dignity. One of them, by a gesture, asked for a cigarette but my father had none. We left them with a promise to return.

Back home, my father took some of his close and most trusted friends into his confidence and each of them contributed food, wine, cigarettes and a change of clothing. But few secrets can be kept in a Greek village. Many wanted to visit the strangers to give them what they could and assure them of their support. I was asked to accompany them, not to show them the place, but by my presence to reassure them that the visitor was a friend. One of the poorest in the village brought them mulberries with which they were obviously familiar. Another brought seven bunches of lentil plants laden with pods and ceremonially handed a bunch to each of them. They all bowed their thanks before sniffing the branches, apparently believing them to be flowers. I went up to one of them, opened a pod and put the sweet and juicy lentils into my mouth. The strangers quickly followed suit.

We feared that the longer they remained, the greater the danger that the Germans would find out, with disastrous consequences for the New Zealanders and the whole village. My father, therefore, concluded that he should try to get them to Crete. No boat could leave the harbour without a special permit from the Germans, so it was decided to approach the Armenian baker in Koroni whose hatred of the Germans was well known. His strong anti-German feelings arose because the Germans were allies of the Turks who had forced him to leave his home in Asia Minor thirty years earlier and flee to Koroni as a refugee.

The plan was for the baker to say that he wanted to buy a boat to send young men to chop wood for him on an uninhabited island. We hoped that this would work. After all, he had regular dealings with the Germans: they told him how much bread he was to produce and what rations he had to sell to each holder of a card. We gave the Armenian eight thousand drachmas which had been paid to us in compensation for our conscripted horse. If the application to leave the harbour was granted, the money was to be used as a deposit for a boat.

And it was granted. Another twenty thousand drachmas were then needed to pay the fisherman willing to sell his boat. It was six or seven metres long with two sets of oars and a sail. Not wanting us to deplete our savings completely, the baker asked for and received help from others, some of whom were to join us in paying off the boat.

The police commander of Koroni, a friend of my father's, had somehow heard of our plans. When he noticed one of the village shopkeepers, known for his sympathy to the Germans, enter the Germans' office, he suspected that my father's plans might have been revealed to the enemy.

Indicative of the paranoia of the time, when the police commander met my father in the square, he now sought to warn my father. He called out, 'Antoni, what are you doing here? It is known that you bought the rope. Have you come to buy the soap?' This was an allusion to the practice of soaping the noose of a hangman's rope so that the victim would strangle quickly. Despite his fears, the pro-German did not betray us to the Germans, and his warnings to my father were meaningless as the police commander was no friend of the invaders.

The deal to buy the boat was struck quickly and we found two loyal fishermen who were told of the ruse and agreed to sail to Crete. We arranged that a couple of days later the Armenian would report them to the police and to the Germans as thieves who had disappeared with the boat. When the plan was announced to my grandparents and mother, they tried to persuade my father not to do it, even though they must have known that they were unlikely to prevail.

But when they heard that I wanted to go with him, they were absolutely appalled. My grandfather told my father that he could go off and drown himself if he wanted to, but that he would not allow his thirteen-year-old grandson to suffer the same fate. I threatened that if I were not taken I would swim behind the boat. They would either have to take me and save me from drowning or that would be the end of me, I did not care.

I have often been asked why I wanted to go. There were a number of reasons. I had overheard Panayotis Arnaoutis, now returned from the front, saying that he intended reopening the primary school even though the education system no longer functioned and there would be no one to pay him. He argued that there was now no danger of bombardment or poisonous gases. He did not want the children of the village to remain illiterate, and expected my father to set an example: I should therefore go back to the village school and he would devise a special programme for me and a couple of others who had been attending higher classes elsewhere. The thought of returning to school with children six or seven years younger than me was unbearable.

There were also other reasons to make me want to go. On returning from the front, my uncle Niono reported that our horse, Psaris, had frozen to death in Albania. I missed the horse. One of the pleasures of my life in the village was gone.

Also, sometime previously, a friend and I had removed some lead from a fisherman's nets to make marbles. I'd heard that the fisherman had sworn to avenge himself against the young devils when he found out who they were. He was planning to see who was playing with newly moulded marbles.

Besides these reasons, my father was always good to me and had never raised a hand against me. Unlike my over-industrious mother, he did not expect me to do much manual labour. He always considered that education for me, my brothers and sister would be worth very much more than our contribution to the household needs. All in all, the option of leaving the village with him was most attractive.

Many years later my mother told me why she and my grandparents reluctantly accepted my going: my father told them of his fear that the Germans would follow the practice of the Turks. The Turks took young boys, converted them to their religion and then trained them as soldiers called *yanitsaris,* fierce fighters and relentless oppressors of the *rayiades*, the non-Muslim subject people of the Ottoman Empire. In the end, the Germans did not precisely follow this Turkish practice, but they ordered many people to provide compulsory labour in the munitions factories where death from hunger and lack of medical attention was commonplace.

A lamb was slaughtered for what turned out to be the last meal we would have as a family. My mother served my grandfather first. He asked for the portion covering the shoulder blade. He removed the meat, took the bone, wiped it clean and raised it up to the lamp in which olive oil was burning. He pronounced it clean of any blemish - a good omen for the success of our venture. While we prepared to leave, one squadron of Stukas after another flew alarmingly low over the village. Frightened by the great noise and, or so we children thought, by the square black cross under their wings, the animals in the field stopped grazing and the donkeys bolted, throwing off the women riding sideways on their backs.

As the planes crossed the bay they looked low enough to touch the sea. Despite the distance, we could hear the frightening roar of their upward ascent when they reached Mount Tyegetos. Then they disappeared over the mountain in a south-easterly direction. Although we did not know it then, the planes were heading for Crete and would drop their deadly cargo over the island. That was also our intended destination, but because of the successful bombing campaign, we would ultimately have to change our plans.

It was in the middle of the last week of May that we went to Kalamaki beach at Faneromeni (nowadays a favourite place for German tourists), our place of departure. It was out of sight of the Nazi occupiers in Koroni and the village. We gathered on the flat rock edging the beach, standing around the provisions to be loaded into the boat. I had been hugged and kissed by my grandparents and mother. My mother and grandmother were in tears, but for me, it was the beginning of an adventure.

While waiting there I learnt for the first time who else was coming with us and heard about a plan of my Uncle Vangos, with whom my father was not on good terms. This uncle, married to my father's sister, had arranged that a small, shallow boat would be tied behind ours, on which he would leave with a party chosen by him. As the sun set behind Mavrovouni, our boat emerged from a nearby cove and the two Koroni fishermen carefully brought her to the edge of the rock.

In the growing darkness the New Zealanders left their hiding place, smiling broadly when they saw the boat. We got in and set off at once into the dusk. The favourable north-west wind blew gently but the triangular sail was not hoisted for fear that it might attract attention, even in the failing light. It was decided that we would use the oars until out of sight of those, particularly in Koroni, who may have been looking for any movement towards the open sea.

We had not gone more than a few miles when a battle began between the south-east and north-west winds. This caused a choppy sea and made it impossible to raise the sail. It was decided to veer to the right, and land on the uninhabited island of Venitico, so named because the Venetians used it as an observation post to defend their interests against the Ottoman fleet and the pirates in days gone by.

We spent the night under the bushes on the island, but the New Zealanders were apprehensive and eager to leave, so before dawn we set off again with a good wind making it unnecessary to use the oars. We sailed due south instead of south-east to avoid passing the island of Kythera, where the Germans would surely have a presence. We made good progress until late afternoon, when suddenly gusts of wind swung the sail from side to side, quite out of control. The canvas tore and we had to duck to avoid being hit by the boom. I was told to crawl into the small cupboard in the prow.

For the rest of the journey I stayed there, unable to keep down food or drink. The others took turns at the oars throughout the night. Next morning conditions had improved, but the boat of my Uncle Vangos and his party had come untied from our craft. Ultimately, they made their way back to the mainland and returned home without the Germans ever knowing they had almost escaped.

On our boat, a blanket was tied across the sail to cover the gaping hole and, as we began the third night of our journey, we hoped that the late afternoon winds would not be as bad as they had been the evening before.

Just then the New Zealander holding the tiller pointed westwards towards the setting sun, where he had spotted a number of ships sailing in our direction. There were expressions of both hope and fear – were they British or Italian? Would they stop? Would our fishermen's disguise, and the bits of net and floats of coloured calabashes, fool them? Out of his pocket the helmsman took a small mirror. He held it high above his head to catch the sun, then suddenly brought it down again. He repeated this action a number of times, until one of the ships broke away from the convoy and headed towards us at top speed.

There were exclamations of joy from the New Zealanders when it came near enough for them to recognise the flag. As it approached, the ship reduced speed and many of the sailors on deck waved. We had to hold tightly onto the sides of the little boat, as it bobbed up and down on the massive ship's bow-waves. Comparative calm was soon restored; our boat was manoeuvred close to the side of the ship, to the applause of those above and ourselves below. We could not understand what the New Zealanders and the sailors were saying, but it did not matter. We knew that we were safe from the perils that the Sea of Crete may have held for us if we spent another night baling water.

One by one we climbed the rope ladder and, as we stepped on board, three or four officers shook each of us by the hand. We were given towels and taken to wash. A doctor examined me in the sickbay and gave me half a glass of sweetened water. My father came to tell me that our boat had been abandoned with all the provisions left in it. He and the others had gathered in the ship's dining room, where they heard that Crete was falling to the Germans. Clearly we couldn't go to Crete, but would be taken to Alexandria instead. The captain thanked my father for the help he had given the soldiers and said we should not worry; there were many Greeks in Alexandria who would look after us.

Nourished by the juice from tins of vegetables, pears and mashed fruit, I soon became well enough to join the others. The dining-room tables were used as beds at night and a hammock was also slung under each table. I slept in a hammock beneath my father.

We could not go to Alexandria directly. Our ship, like the others in the convoy, was off to Crete to help evacuate the Allied Forces as well as the remnants of the Greek army and government.

We remained around Crete for two or three days. Now the fleet no longer sailed in formation, but packs of two or three moved slowly beyond the mouth of the harbour in which many vessels of different sizes were moored. We were told that they were waiting to transport people out of Sitia, the only port not occupied by the Germans. The warships were there to keep at bay the German planes, laden with bombs. When the planes were heard or sighted, the ships moved fast in irregular patterns and fired at them from the deck guns.

I was anxious to see what was happening, but was not allowed on deck and instead had to stay in the dining room out of everybody's way. Disappointed at not being allowed to watch the war games, I stood at the door of the dining room watching one shell after another ascending on a conveyor belt, each hurriedly grabbed by a sailor who then ran out of sight towards the middle of the deck.

Only once did I feel that we were in danger when the ship made a sudden change of direction, its prow covered by waves with water rushing off the side. The manoeuvre was necessary to avoid a mine.

At first light one morning, the harbour was empty and the fleet withdrew since it had no further purpose to serve there. For some time, we sailed in convoy with the sun behind us until our ship, which I later learned was HMS *Kimberley*, once again broke away, turning south to take us to Alexandria.

Our trip to Egypt was uneventful: the sea calm, the crew relaxed; some were in earnest conversation with the New Zealanders, no doubt speaking of their experiences in Greece. In Alexandria we would be separated from the New Zealanders, who had to report to their army officers. For them, unlike us, the war was not over. They gave my father a note of their names, the name of their regiment and where they had come from.

CHAPTER 3

In the Land of the Pharaohs

Many vessels in Alexandria harbour flew the Greek flag. High-ranking officers dressed in khaki came on board and exchanged salutes with the captain and other officers. They shook hands with us and spoke to the New Zealanders. They smiled, and from their tone of voice and gestures, we assumed that they were thanking us, particularly my father, who Lewis had pointed to a couple of times while he was speaking with the officers. They promised to contact him and give him the money he had spent on the boat that we'd abandoned.

Below on the quayside a small group speaking Greek waited for us, wanting to know what Greece was like under German occupation. They told us they were proud that we had put our lives on the line for the benefit of our allies. They predicted that Greece would be free again and that, unlike other countries occupied by the Germans, there would be resistance to Nazi occupation. They said that a brave young man had torn down the swastika raised over the Acropolis in Athens and that many others had helped Allied soldiers to escape. It would not be long before the Greek army and its allies would liberate Greece and we would be free to return and join our families again.

The man from the consul-general's office spoke down to us. In more formal Greek than we were accustomed to, he told us we would be taken to his office to be issued with refugee permits and that my father and I would be separated. He and the others from the village would go to a refugee camp in Cairo. The official said nothing of what would happen to me, and it was left to the only woman in the group to put her arm around my shoulders and comfort me. I wasn't to worry, I would be looked after in a good and caring institution called Kanishereion, named after the communal benefactor who had built it and made sufficient funds available for its continued existence. They would take me there once the formalities were dealt with.

Birthdays are of no importance in village culture: the day one celebrates is one's name day, the feast day of the saint after whom one is named. Not surprisingly, therefore, my father did not know my date of birth. Asked by officials, he declared it was 26 December 1928. Many years later, I learnt from my mother that I was born on 14 November, and, judging from those with whom I started school, I was probably born in 1927. On the other hand it is possible that I may have been allowed to start school a year earlier because of my father's influence as a leading figure in the village. There is also a view that he did know the year I was born, but deliberately made me a year younger in his declaration to the officials in Alexandria: believing that the war could last for years, he wanted to delay my conscription into the army.

While the formalities were completed, I strayed off onto the balcony overlooking a small square. I found it strange that practically all the men wore red fezzes and long loose garments no different to a woman's dress, while the women had their heads and a part of their faces covered. I tried hard to make out what they were saying, but it was neither Greek nor anything like the language spoken by the New Zealanders.

A good woman, who later took charge of me, gave a note to my father as to where I would be and she assured me that my father would visit. Hugging and kissing was neither my father's way nor mine, and we took leave of one another without much fuss. I had thought of orphanages as places where children lived whose fathers and mothers were dead, who had no family to look after them, or who were born out of wedlock, and I had heard that the children in orphanages were kept in squalid conditions, that they went hungry and that those in charge often ill-treated them. But this woman's appearance and the loving way she spoke to me, the assurances she gave me – and the fact that she took me to one of the biggest pastry shops I had ever seen – foretold that the conditions at this place would be quite different.

It was an impressive building with large trees around a white marble facade which shone in the bright, hot sun. She rang the bell and a lanky, bearded man in a black cassock came to open the heavy iron gate. He welcomed me, and then the good woman lifted my school cap, caressed my crew-cut hair, promised to visit me and left. The man in the cassock took me to a dormitory and showed me a bed next to which was a small cupboard. He took out a change of clothing for me and, after I had taken off the clothes that I had worn for almost a week, said I should go to the bathroom to wash. He told me that there were over two hundred boys in the classrooms and that I should go down to the playground, sit in the shade and wait for the bell which would soon ring for the lessons to end. Everyone would then go into the dining room for lunch.

In the grounds there was a chapel of St George. As we approached it the man in the cassock asked me whether I went to church regularly. I told him that my grandfather and I were among the first in church every Sunday, getting there even before the priest. I did not disclose that for the almost two years I was in Kalamata I did not set foot in church except on high holy days when school was in session and attendance was compulsory. He asked me if I could recite Pater Ymon, the Lord's Prayer, the Pistevo – the creed of the Holy Orthodox Church – and the Kontakion in honour of St George. He started singing the first verse: *Os ton ehmaloton eleferotis ke ton ftohon yperaspitis* – the martyr who freed prisoners and supported the poor. He nodded that I should join him and seemed impressed by my effort though he smiled benignly when my breaking voice led to a false note. Perhaps he was satisfied that if I knew the saint's song of praise I would have no difficulty with the oft-repeated Lord's Prayer and the declaration of the true faith made at every service.

In the dining room, groups of about twelve children aged from five to eleven sat on benches at large marble tables. They all attended school in classrooms within the orphanage. The top table was for the teachers. Four or five tables were empty, waiting for the boys who attended the Hellenic gymnasium or commercial college nearby. Soon they noisily entered the dining room and took their places. The man in the cassock raised his right hand and everyone stood up. He crossed himself in the name of the Father, the Son and the Holy Spirit and gave thanks for what we were about to receive. We all crossed ourselves and sat down except those at one of the senior tables. These boys rushed to the hatch where the cook or his assistant passed them plates of food to be taken to each of us. The food that day, as on most other days, was good. But not many of us looked forward to the meals on Wednesdays and Fridays when *tahinosoupa* (a kind of peanut butter soup) and *foulia* (a strange blackish dried bean) was served with a quarter of a cucumber on the side. Watermelon was intended to make up for the dreary meal on those days when neither meat nor fish nor eggs nor milk was allowed. Nor were they served at home in the village, but at least then, if we children were desperate, we knew where to find the clay pots of pickled pork, smoked sausage and feta cheese.

As the school year would end a couple of weeks later, it was decided that I should go to the last grade of the primary school. I was given a set of books for history, geography, arithmetic and religion, as well as a reader and a few exercise books. The books were similar to the ones that I had had in the village school.

The teachers expressed their satisfaction with my abilities, pronounced me ready for the gymnasium and, believing that I was there to stay, suggested that I should sit for an exam at the end of August to skip into the second year. However, they foresaw a difficulty: I knew no English, no French, no Italian, no Arabic – all of which had been taught for two years at the primary school. I attended the language classes. The teachers did not utter a single word of Greek yet they seemed to be understood by the class. The pupils even understood the young man with the fez and the tidy suit who wrote on the blackboard, from right to left, at great speed, shapes which I was later told were letters. Italian was no longer being taught because it was the language of the enemy. The teachers staggered their annual holiday, some going off in July and others in August. On their return they would start me off in Arabic, French and English.

Kanishereion had a choir and a brass band, both under the direction of a teacher, a man in his mid-thirties with thick spectacles. He had entered the orphanage at the age of five and never left. He took me into the choir to sing in St George's chapel. There were no regular services. The man in the cassock was not an ordained priest. He was said to have been a monk who did not take easily to monastic discipline. Those who liked him said that he 'left' the monastery. Those who did not referred to him as the 'excommunicated one'. He had the title of Pedagogue. Not qualified to be a teacher, he was in charge of our discipline and occasionally our spiritual well-being. He spent most of his time sitting in the shade, but he would get up and chase us when we deliberately substituted lyrics of drinking and other secular songs in the sombre tempo and melody of well-known hymns or scripture, such as St Paul's Epistles:

> And the Lord then said unto his pupils
> Hey you fisherman
> Have you any fish?
> Have you any lobsters?
> Or any calamari?

The words, innocent enough at the start, became more irreverent as the song progressed.

Although there were no regular services at the chapel, many weddings and christenings were held there. They were quite unlike the weddings in our village which started on a Thursday and only finished the following Monday, beginning with the display of the dowry and the making of *diples* – egg and milk-rich dough, finely spread out, cut like the wings of a butterfly then deep-fried in olive oil, dipped in honey and sprinkled with crushed almonds. Several hundred were made and they would be the first offering after the wedding ceremony to which everyone in the village was welcome. A beast would be slaughtered on the Saturday and our families would go to the service on Sunday morning. Girls in their late teens would pass around the *mezedes* (a special kind of Greek snack); young men would serve the wine. By early afternoon the mood was exuberant. In the late afternoon, the two families would meet outside the church, the one group trying to out-sing the other in traditional songs. Her family praised the qualities of the bride, while his – the *levedi* – praised the manliness of the groom. They would enter the church in a boisterous mood. Hardly anyone took the priest or the cantors seriously. They were all waiting for the crowns to be exchanged on the bride's and groom's heads, and at the first words of 'Let Isaiah dance with the virgin' they threw rice and flower petals at the bridal couple while many of his friends aimed hard sugared almonds at his head as he held the bride's hand and tried to avoid the missiles.

At St George's chapel in Alexandria things were done very differently. There was a first-, a second- and a third-class wedding ceremony, and the number of lights to be switched on, the quantity of flowers to be placed before the altar and the number of teachers who would act as cantors depended on the class chosen and paid for. We in the choir attended irrespective of the class. We were sure of a *boubouneria* for a first-class wedding, would probably get one for a second-class wedding, but definitely would not for a third-class wedding. Sugared almonds decoratively wrapped in tulle were handed out to everyone. I was told that in a real first-class wedding there was sweet liqueur in addition to the peeled almond encased within a sugar coating.

A priest conducted a third-class wedding; a dean with a priest the second class, and a bishop with a dean, a priest and a deacon and the top cantors from the patriarchate officiated at a first-class wedding. There was much excitement when we heard that the patriarch himself would be there the following year on 23 March to celebrate St George's day. None of us doubted that I would be there to see His Beatitude but in the meantime we were not allowed to forget that there was a war on.

Although the Italians had been beaten out of Ethiopia and Somalia they were still in Libya. The Allies were said not to be doing well and were losing one battle after another. There were fears that now the Germans had conquered Western Europe and the Balkans, they might come to the assistance of the Italians in pushing the British out of Egypt and Palestine. They could also help take control of the Suez Canal and of the petroleum-rich Arab countries, not only to deny fuel to the West but also to oil their own war machine. It was said that Germany was not satisfied with extending its eastern border into Poland, Czechoslovakia, Hungary and Romania and could even, in time, invade Russia. That was the talk we heard of faraway places, but the war was not far away for us, and in Alexandria the sirens would warn of Italian bombers almost every second night. We were told that there was an understanding that neither Athens nor Cairo nor Rome would be hit for fear that their antiquities might be destroyed or damaged and lost forever. Cosmopolitan Alexandria, first built more than two thousand three hundred years ago, was not accorded that privilege. Its large harbour and trade centre made it a target not to be missed.

Kanishereion's lowest level was half below ground with windows at just about ground-level, the rooms originally intended to serve as storage and accommodation for staff. Sandbags were piled around the building to protect it from shrapnel and debris from bombs that would, hopefully, never fall directly onto it. If the worst did happen, it was hoped that the cement slabs above would afford some protection. We were trained to get out of the dormitories as quickly as possible and run to the basement until the sirens announced the end of the raid.

We took the attacks quite calmly. The Pedagogue monk would pray. The only woman in the orphanage, our nurse, would tremble from fear and crouch near the exit, to be the first to escape if there was a hit. I was invited to join the more experienced boys who slipped out of the basement into the dining room during an attack. We stood on the tables and watched through the high windows as the powerful searchlights raked the sky until one of them caught a plane in its beam. Then a couple of the other lights focused on the plane and soon the long-range guns fired one exploding shell after another until it was hit or somehow managed to escape from its illuminated trap.

Across the road from us was the Catholic cemetery full of elaborate marble sculptures, wrought iron and sometimes even bronze fences to mark out family graves. On our left, as we faced the cemetery, was an Egyptian army base. The enemy pilots who missed the desired target dropped many of their bombs on tombs in which people had been laid to rest in peace. Shrapnel hit our iron fence and opened some of the sand bags. The Pedagogue in his cassock declared that it was divine providence that turned the bombs away from us onto the graves of those of another faith. Together with many others, he held the view that the Catholics had chosen it as a place for their cemetery because the tomb of Alexander the Great was there: they had simply removed visible signs of it to deny the Greeks the glory of Alexander's achievements. For what other reason did the Catholics refuse to allow archaeologists from France, England, Egypt and Greece to dig in the cemetery in search of Alexander's tomb?

Sometimes we were taken to the beach before breakfast for a swim. Along the way we would seek shrapnel from both bombs and shells. There was keen competition among the three or four that had the most, and bullying of the younger ones who had picked up an odd piece of the deadly metal. No one explained why the shrapnel was collected or what was going to be done with it.

All in all, I wasn't having a bad time. I had not been away from my family and the village for long enough really to miss them. In the second week, my father came from Cairo. He said that there was a radio service into Greece sending cryptic messages to the relatives of those who had made it safely to Egypt. He had sent such a message – sufficiently vague not to be identified by the Germans, but clear enough to anyone who heard it and knew us. They would surely take the message home to the village. He was concerned about the occupants of my uncle's small boat. If they were caught, they might talk and endanger the family and those who helped us. As it turned out, neither happened: no clear message got to the family, nor did anyone give information to the Germans. In fact, no message got to the family until a Red Cross letter sent from South Africa towards the end of 1941 was delivered more than two years later.

In Alexandria, it looked as if I was going to get my education while living in Kanishereion. Because of my father's age and disability he was not wanted in the army and told to stay in the refugee camp until a job was found for him. I was beginning to settle down. French was considered the most useful language for me to learn during the school holidays and the bespectacled teacher asked me if I wanted to take up music. He needed a good trumpet player to take over in a year or two, when the present trumpeter finished his secondary schooling and left the orphanage. I never got to blow a single note, but there was much reading of do, re, me, fa, so, la, te, and I was taught how to write on ruled music paper. I was also taught breathing exercises: breathing in heavily through the nose while slowly counting up to seven and forcing the air out through the mouth with tight lips slightly opened in the middle of the mouth as if wanting to whistle. One of the most pleasant fantasies throughout my life, and more particularly when I watched the big bands on film during the post-war years, was that I had stayed at Kanishereion and become a great trumpet player like Harry James and 'Satchmo' Armstrong.

However, it was not to be. After six weeks at Kanishereion, my father was given the option of going to India or South Africa. He had decided on South Africa, where he had been told that gold and diamonds were there for the picking, even on the pavements.

The teachers and some of the boys saw me off, even a couple of those I had unwittingly hurt on the day after my arrival. At the time I had bragged that I could tell the difference between a Greek and an Arab. A dominant boy in the group, knowing that everyone there considered themselves Greek, challenged me to point out the Arabs. The laughter of the group increased with each pointing out. I had hardly got past the fourth when those whom I had wrongly classified pounced upon me. This incident had a strange adjunct. On our way to the railway station on the day of our departure, the chain and key my father was twirling on his fingers and thumb spun out of his hand and over a low fence, and landed on the lawn of an opulent house. A young Arab working in the garden picked it up and offered it to my father – the key in one hand, the other outstretched asking for baksheesh, a tip. A dialogue of the deaf ensued. Eventually a Greek passer-by jumped over the fence and forcibly took away the key, handed it to my father and directed a barrage of racist epithets and threats against Arab people in general and the young gardener in particular.

My first train ride, from Alexandria to Cairo, was hot and uncomfortable, and became ever more crowded, thanks to agile passengers who climbed through the windows and landed on our laps. The approach to the refugee camp was across the biggest bridge I had ever seen, over a wide river which I discovered was the Nile. Hundreds of trees, unlike any I knew, provided the shade under which many people sat on tidy lawns along the inner bank. Some had dozed off, or, half awake, fanned their hands over their faces to chase away the flies.

We arrived at the Gaziera showground, the exhibition halls of which had been converted to dormitories and dining rooms, and storerooms of used clothing to which one could help oneself. More than four thousand Greeks lived there, together with a small number from Eastern Europe who had fled the German occupation of their countries. These refugees travelled through Greece or Turkey, then on to Lebanon and Palestine, from where the British brought them to the camp. No one thought of showing me the museum, but I was taken to see the pyramids and sphinx. My request for a camel ride was refused. I was told it was too dangerous.

Many of the Greeks in Cairo came in their cars or horse-drawn carriages to the main gate of the camp on Sunday after the church service to invite people to lunch. They looked us over to decide who to invite, and those who appeared to demand an invitation almost as of right were deemed 'without pride' and often ignored. A well-dressed middle-aged man approached my father, who was sitting with me in the shade of a tree, and asked whether we would come to lunch. He said that he particularly wanted us to join his family, because his two sons were about my age. Their apartment was on the second floor and, for the first time, my father and I used a lift.

Never before, and rarely since, have I seen such thick and beautifully designed carpets, such striking pictures and such highly polished wooden furniture. A glass cabinet was filled with crystal and silver jugs and glasses of various shapes and sizes. We were not the only guests; a well-groomed couple and their two sons arrived shortly after us.

There were two richly laid tables, five places for the adults at a large table and five at the smaller table in the corner of the room for the children. Over lunch, my father was asked what part of Greece we were from and when we had left. They expressed amazement that we escaped from under the noses of the Germans. Their guests asked question after question in a strange Greek accent. What did the Germans look like? What did they do? How did people react to them? They listened enraptured and praised my father for his courage. Asked why he had taken me with him, he raised a laugh by saying that I was headstrong and insisted on coming.

The lunch was served by a woman who was too dark to be Greek, but obviously understood the instructions of the mistress of the house. These included a command that she remove the ice bucket from our table because we were putting too much into our glasses of water, which would do us no good. She always responded with a 'Yes, madam' in Greek. I had never known a house servant before, except that, because of her disability, Daskala in Kalamata had taken a young girl from the village to help her. But, despite being a servant, she would sit at the same table, though always the last to take her place and the first to get up to clear the dishes.

The two sets of boys spoke a language that I did not understand, but in any case my ear was tuned to the conversation of the elders. When they did speak to me it was to ask about my schooling. In response I asked what language they were speaking. It was French, said the elder of the two Greek-speaking boys. I asked why the other two were unable to speak Greek, our language. Because they were Jews, I was told. I had never met a Jew before but had heard much about them in church, particularly during the Thursday before Easter Sunday. Then, twelve lengthy passages from the New Testament were read, dealing with the betrayal of Christ by Judas Iscariot, the denial by the apostle Peter, the trial and visit to Pontius Pilate, the warning by Pilate's wife not to have anything to do with the death of 'that man', Christ's condemnation to die on the cross and the washing of Pilate's hands. The service on Good Friday and the funeral procession of the *epitaphios*, with lament and funeral dirges, all stressed the wrong done to the Lord by the Jews and the fact that their sins should be borne by their children and their children's children. I have often wondered how much less anti-Semitism there might have been throughout the ages if everyone, including the leaders of the Church, respected the humanity of everyone else.

At the end of July 1941 one hundred and forty-five of us, mainly from the refugee camp but with a few important persons who had been put up in hotels, set off by train across the desert from Cairo to Port Suez. When, at one point, the train stopped and reversed, anxious rumours spread among the already tense passengers that we were returning to Cairo. However, we soon stopped to pick up the body of an Indian military officer who, although handcuffed, had jumped from the window of the fast moving train to avoid a trial and a probable death sentence for killing one of his fellow officers. The soldiers who had been guarding the man got off the train. They took the handcuffs off his wrists, picked up his turban from the sand, dusted it and put it on his head. Then two of them solemnly carried the body back onto the train. This was the second time I had seen violent death. On the previous occasion, our school teacher had taken us to see the body of a police officer lying in state in the church of St Demitrios in Koroni. Half his face had been blown off by a shotgun. Our visit was part of the community's outraged rejection of the explanation put forward by the suspect that the gun had gone off by accident when the police officer tried to seize it from him for hunting without a licence.

Once the train arrived at Port Suez we were taken directly to the wharf and onto an enormous ship, the *Ile de France*. We were told that it was the second biggest ship in the world, with only the *Queen Mary* being larger. Our group shared the first-class section with a small number of soldiers who had contracted tuberculosis in the desert. They wore a special blue uniform and a red tie and were being taken to South Africa to recuperate. The rest of the ship was full of Italian prisoners of war. They were also headed for South Africa, where troops would embark and be taken to strengthen the Allied force in the Middle East. The Allies needed reinforcement, for the Italians in Libya were doing well against them and it was feared that if the Germans entered the arena, the situation might become even more bleak.

Despite the war, travelling first class on the *Ile de France* was luxurious, even if some of it was lost on us. My father and I were shown to a table in the dining room. The menu listed no fewer than sixteen items, none of which we could read. We had a tall Indian waiter to ourselves with whom we could not communicate, so we looked at the tables around us and pointed to plates placed before other passengers or randomly chose things on the menu in the hope that they would be to our liking. Invariably they were.

My father and I shared a cabin but I spent most of the time on deck watching the shoals of flying fish and the bigger fish chasing them. I watched the frothy furrow churned up by the massive propellers and how the prow cut a wide river into the apparently endless ocean. I played with the largest cat I had ever seen, teasingly moving my father's chain before her, as she tried to catch it with first one front paw and then the other. But we were not allowed to forget the war, and the alarm bells sounded regularly for us to don life jackets and stand next to the boats hanging on the side of the ship. We had to practise this exercise in case of a torpedo attack. It was a serious business and we, the twenty-odd children aboard, were warned not to give false alarms.

CHAPTER 4

In the Land of Gold and Diamonds

Eight days after we left Port Suez we approached the South African port of Durban, much praised by the seamen because it was so large and had so many ships berthed within it. Although we thought we had left the heat of Cairo and Port Suez behind, it had become hotter during the voyage, and we found that even the air blown into our cabin by the air conditioner was too hot to bear. But the nearer we drew to Durban the cooler it became, and the mid-morning sun, which we had tried to avoid in Egypt and for most of our trip southwards, was now as welcome as when we sailed to and from Kalamata on the *Elpidophoros* in early spring.

We entered Durban harbour on 8 August 1941. On the beach were swimmers and surfers, and fishermen casting their lines attached to long bamboo rods without reels. The fishermen and a sponge diver among us shook their heads. One of them said he had obviously made the wrong choice: he should have gone to India. Things didn't look too good here, he said. Poor as his island was, people could at least afford a stick or two of dynamite to blow up the fish they were after, then swim out to gather those floating on the surface. Clearly this was a much better technique than the primitive method used by these poor fishermen. He already regretted believing those who said that you could pick up gold and diamonds on the pavements of South Africa.

As the *Ile de France* was moored to the quayside, I looked below at dozens of tall black men, some of them with wooden discs in their ear lobes. They wore old and rather soiled sleeveless vests, exposing their muscular arms and their lean upper chests. Most of them wore short trousers and were barefoot, although some had sandals with soles made from used tyres and straps of rough leather. They pulled carts with two large wheels, which I later learnt were rickshaws. The men trotted over to one of the smaller ships, and stood patiently waiting in the sun, from time to time using the back of their arms to wipe the sweat from their temples and eyebrows. I remember feeling deeply distressed by the sight. I had never before seen a man doing work reserved for animals, and it shocked me greatly, making an impression that would never be erased.

Some twenty-five years later, on holiday in Durban, my sons Kimon, Damon and Alexi wanted to ride on a decorated rickshaw pulled by a man dressed in ornate headgear with horns, feathers and multicoloured beads. He, too, had large earlobes fitted with discs of carefully painted geometric designs in different colours. Parts of his body were covered with animal skins, and he wore no shoes. On his ankles, rings of some almond-shaped casts gave a rhythmic sound as the man pranced up and down pulling his cart. From time to time he raised himself into the air with the wheels screeching on the road, all the while performing a scissors movement with his legs to attract more attention from would-be customers. Once his fee was paid, he took people for a short ride, and if they paid extra, would give parents an opportunity to photograph their children on his rickshaw. Our three sons were excited and wanted a ride at once. Their loving mother had a camera ready to take their picture. But my mind went back to the morning of my arrival, and I refused. I did not want our children riding on the rickshaw nor did I want a photograph taken with them on it. Of course they asked why? But I could not, and did not want to explain. It appeared to me preferable to be thought of as an authoritarian and irrational husband and father than to relate how I had felt on the day I arrived in South Africa and first saw men pulling those carts.

Once off the boat, we were not allowed to look around Durban. Instead we immediately boarded a special train for the six hundred kilometre journey to Johannesburg. For a short while we travelled through lush semi-tropical hills; later through vast areas of grassland on which masses of cattle and sheep grazed, and later still through enormous tracts of ploughed land from which maize had been harvested.

We knew when we were approaching the big city because instead of just one railway line running in each direction, there were as many as ten. Our train had passed through a number of towns on the way, stopping at none. But even once we had reached Johannesburg, our train rolled on a couple of kilometres beyond the city's central railway station before finally coming to a halt.

There were hundreds of Greek-speaking men and women to welcome us, and they took us in their cars to our accommodation. My father and I were singled out for special attention. When the reception committee heard that we had actually lived under the Germans, albeit for only a month or so, we were taken to the Imperial Hotel in the centre of the city where we stayed for a couple of weeks. Then we were moved to Victoria Mansions, a block away from the grand entrance of the railway station. We soon found out why our train had not stopped there, and why we were taken to Braamfontein. It was feared that there would be a demonstration at the Johannesburg station against our coming, organised by people widely believed to be Nazi sympathisers, those who accused Prime Minister Jan Smuts of bringing the *vuilgoed* of Europe into *their* country.

The organisation *Philoptohos* – friends of the poor – together with the Hellenic community of Johannesburg and the Witwatersrand, took care of us. They paid for our room; they gave us a daily allowance for food. We regularly went to the Luculus Restaurant in Harrison Street, near Pritchard Street with its many Greek *kafeneia*, which served as social clubs. At the restaurant we were surrounded by familiar animated conversation. There was also a billiard table and a couple of private rooms at the back, said to be the venue for heavy gambling and illegal horse-race betting. We were also told about the stupid laws of South Africa which prohibited the *kafeneia* from selling liquor. Of course, they sold it anyway.

For a few months my father had no job. He and I hung around the *kafeneia*, as well as the University Café directly opposite the technical college, and, most often, the Petit Trianon, the cafe in the building adjacent to Victoria Mansions. My father sometimes helped to clear the plates from the tables, and the friendly café owner allowed me to stand behind the counter while he went into the kitchen to fetch food for me. It was there that one of our number, an elderly man, fluent in English and who had been a banker in Greece, introduced my father and me to a journalist. Neither my father nor I spoke English, and so the former banker acted as interpreter. Through him my father recounted the story of our escape from Greece and showed the journalist a letter written by the Middle-East Command to my father, thanking him for his contribution to the Allied Forces. The reporter disappeared and returned with a photographer. A few days later, a photograph of us appeared in *The Sunday Times* together with an article describing our escape as 'an odyssey'.

The publicity had an immediate beneficial effect for me – as well as a long-term impact which took some time to materialise. Customers would recognise me, pat me on the back, stroke my crew-cut hair and buy me slabs of chocolate. The fruit seller at a wooden stand outside the Jeppe Street post office gave me a banana and an apple every time I passed. Many, using the owner of the shop as an interpreter, would ask questions, wanting to learn more than had appeared in the newspaper.

My father valued education very highly, even though my mother was illiterate and he himself had not gone beyond primary school. (After we left Greece, my brothers and sister taught my mother how to sign her name so she could avoid the shame of admitting illiteracy when she had business transactions in our absence.) He was concerned about my schooling and discovered a Hellenic school in Malvern. Whereas the school year in Greece ended in June, here the school year came to an end in December, and he was told that it would be better for me to wait until the new year.

Nevertheless, we went to see for ourselves. It turned out that the school was

Greek in name only: the headmaster spoke no word of the language and had to call one of the Greek children to act as interpreter. Although the Hellenic community had built the school – complete with Corinthian columns – there was a lack of financial support, and the education authorities eventually took it over. The headmaster was kind but said I was too old. While this was a primary school, I was going on for fourteen and had already passed the equivalent of standard six in Greece. He suggested that we apply elsewhere. I then went to a school whose name made no impression on me, and to this day I do not know what it was. I lasted there only three days. I could not communicate, nor, as far as I remember, was I shown any sympathy, and I stopped going.

My father, meanwhile, had found a job in Pretoria at Iscor, working in the munitions section. We moved to Pretoria to live in a single room facing the backyard of a house. His new job raised the question of who would care for me. Friends advised him to look for a family with children that would be prepared to take me in, but at first this promised to be a difficult quest: I overheard one person saying that I looked the sort of boy who would be a bad influence on his children.

Then came some luck. George Marantos, the young shepherd who had reported the presence of the New Zealanders to my father, got a job at the Parkgate Café. He was asked by Ismene Caradas, wife of the owner, to bring the young boy they had read about in the newspaper to meet her family, particularly her two daughters, Poppy and Georgina, and her son John. When I arrived from Pretoria I was well received and invited to stay in a room at the back of the shop. Mrs Caradas, who had been a teacher in Greece, was particularly pleased with me and encouraged her children to spend as much time as they could with me in the afternoons after they returned from the nearby Catholic school, so that they could improve their Greek. They each had a bicycle which they rode on the footways of the park. Poppy, the eldest, taught me how to ride hers. After a couple of falls, I managed the balancing act and, to my great joy, it brought forth a radiant smile on Poppy's face for her achievement as a tutor.

My responsibility in the shop was to set the tables for breakfast and to help the other two assistants by handing up a loaf of bread, a pint of milk or a newspaper from the floor near the door as the customers requested. One day one of the assistants came to my room, called me a sleepy head, and tried to get me up. I groaned but couldn't move. He put his hand on my feverish forehead and called Mrs Caradas. My body was burning, I could hardly move my limbs. From time to time I went into spasms, moaning. Soon Mrs Caradas came. She stroked my face, neck and chest and asked if I was thirsty. She called for water even before I answered, pronounced that there was something seriously wrong with me and that she would immediately call the doctor. Dr Sarantos Tsalavoutas reached his diagnosis from the symptoms described by Mrs Caradas, and, after giving me only the most cursory examination, announced that I had malaria. He put his hand into his pocket and brought out two or three types of coloured pills. I recognised the quinine that we regularly swallowed in Kalamata where the marshy south-eastern side was a breeding ground for mosquitoes. The doctor visited me regularly after that and brought more medicine. He also suggested a diet including bananas, watermelon and pineapple.

The patriarch of the family was George Caratasis, who had changed his name to Caradas. He had come to South Africa from the mountains of the Peloponnese in the 1920s. Over the years he brought out more than a dozen of his nephews, training them to be good shopkeepers, and later helping them open shops of their own. He established Caradas Wholesalers to provide them and others who came from his home region with stock, often on credit, until they were established. Although stern and less friendly than his wife and children, he was easily influenced by them. He spoke to me only briefly and I got the impression that he was cautious about my presence.

One evening he asked me to fetch two tins of sardines from the storeroom. On my way I walked past a table on which lay two newly minted half-crown coins. As I came back, I picked up the half crowns and handed them to him with the sardines. Mr Caradas lowered his voice and said that he had put the half crowns there to test my honesty. He congratulated me and predicted that I would make good in life if I always remained honest. I saw the senior assistant, one of the nephews, suppressing his laughter. Later the same assistant congratulated me on passing the test, and in between chuckles told me that it was a test that every one of the nephews had to pass before he was taken into the fold. The old man, said the assistant, did not know that one of the cousins would always warn the new arrival of the test. He was a little apologetic for not having warned me, but, he said, he did not think that Mr Caradas would set his 'test' for me too.

Mr Caradas travelled from one shop to the other in a large sedan motorcar to deliver goods and take orders, always accompanied by Jim – a man whose surname and other names were not used by the rest of the people at the shop. Jim was tall, erect and self-confident, but, like all others of his race, was known by the staff at Parkgate as 'boy'. He had acquired some Greek and during his frequent trips with his 'master' would hum or sing Greek freedom songs in a rich baritone voice. He, too, lived in a room in the backyard, but it was even smaller than mine. And while I walked up the back stairs to a communal shower and toilet on the first floor, Jim had to use a derelict toilet in the yard. He washed himself in a galvanised iron bathtub hidden under the staircase and every Sunday afternoon he anointed his ebony skin with Vaseline. He brought me my food from the kitchen and spent time with me during the evening. We communicated as well as we could. While I recovered from malaria, we sang Greek freedom songs together.

Then Jim started to cough badly. His condition deteriorated and he ran such a high fever that he stopped working. I suggested that the considerate Dr Tsalavoutas be called, but was told that this was impossible. Basil Zachariou, a young chemist from Egypt, said that he had read in the paper of a black doctor who could be called. I was up and about in the shop by this stage, and on duty when a black man in a smart suit walked in. He wore a white coat over his suit and a stethoscope around his neck, and introduced himself as Dr 'Kouma' (as I would have spelled it then). I led him to Jim's room. The doctor instructed me to leave the room and I waited outside, then led him back to the shop when he had finished his consultation. Jim had pneumonia and for this he wrote out a prescription, also suggesting that Jim be given clean and fresh bedding. If the cough and fever became worse, he was to be called back. The kind Mrs Caradas carried out his orders. I did not know then that I had met a leader of the African National Congress. A few years later I recognised him in a photograph as Dr A B Xuma who had been elected president of the organisation.

For the next five years, even after I no longer lived with them, I spent Christmas Day and Easter Sunday with the Caradas family, either at their home or in their shop, which they closed for the day. Meanwhile my father, who remained in Pretoria, had left Iscor to become an assistant in what was called a 'native shop' next to a compound in one of Pretoria's black residential locations.

The arrangement with the Caradas family was not intended to be permanent, and eventually another family, this time in Germiston, agreed to take me in. They decided that it would be good for me to work in their shop for a year, as my exposure to the customers would help my English. They arranged for me to have an English lesson once a week at the home of a teacher. The only lasting memory I have of her is the explanation she gave me of a print on her wall of an ox wagon being pulled by over a dozen oxen. This was my introduction to the Great Trek, that significant moment in South African history when many Afrikaners moved away from the Cape into the interior.

I spent the better part of 1942 working a full day in the shop. I opened up early in the morning and worked long hours, but was given Wednesday afternoons off. I spent my free afternoon at a matinee and occasionally (when allowed) at Germiston Lake, where I would hire a boat and drift about with their son, who was half my age. Then I quarrelled with the boss. He paid me off with £9, and reminded me that he had given me a tailor-made suit with two pairs of trousers (as was the custom because the pants would last only half as long as the jacket).

With neither work nor accommodation, I took the train from Germiston to Pretoria to consult my father. He was upset because his wallet had been stolen one night while he slept. Finding his window open, the thieves had used a fishing rod and hook to snare his trousers, a common form of theft at the time. Along with his trousers and wallet had gone most of the £27 awarded to him by the Middle-East Command as compensation for the money he had paid for our escape boat from Greece. Even more sadly, the wallet also contained the piece of paper with the names of the New Zealanders. Thanks to this theft, we completely lost touch with those men. The only name I remembered was Lewis, the one who spoke some Greek. It would be sixty years before I established what had happened to them.

Towards the end of 1942 my father considered investigating the accommodation offered to the young people who had sailed with us on the *Ile de France*. They were put up at the YMCA in Jeppe, near the centre of Johannesburg. The nearest Greek shop was the Formain Café on the corner of Fort and Main streets. Angelos Karakatsanis, whose family had been trapped in Greece by the war, ran it along with a bachelor called by everyone Mr Bill, but whose real name was Vasilios Kosmopoulos. Mr Bill, a gentle and caring man, went with us to the supervisor of the YMCA, who, although sympathetic, said I was too young to stay there. The place was for young men, not for fourteen-year-old boys. At Mr Bill's suggestion I went to stay with him and his business partner. In return I would help them out in the shop until my father could make proper arrangements. For my father this was a happy arrangement, as he couldn't leave me alone in Pretoria while he was at work. For a while I shared a large single room with the two partners. A couple of months later, they found me a small, cheap room on the ground floor of a nearby building, facing the backyard. They paid the £5 monthly rental.

My experience in Germiston and in the Parkgate Café had taught me some English, but I was also a useful young assistant, fetching and carrying goods from the shelves at a time when self-service was unknown. I also managed the non-decimal pounds, shillings and pence system, the cold-meat slicing machine, which weighed in pounds and ounces, and I even operated the old cash register.

It quickly seemed that the temporary arrangement would become permanent. I made friends with a couple of the boys in the neighbourhood and occasionally played soccer with them in the nearby park during the early afternoon quiet period. Sometimes I asked Mr Bill for pocket money to attend a matinee at a nearby cinema or at a café bio in the centre of the city where the same film was played over and over again. You could enter at any time and be served with a bright-coloured cool drink from the soda fountain. Seeing the second half of the film before the first did not matter much to me as I understood only a little of the dialogue; it was the action that really counted. I looked set to become a proper shop assistant, earning £10 a month in the beginning but graduating to the £15 or even £20 that senior shop assistants earned. I thought of having my own corner shop one day, perhaps buying a place so that I would not have to pay rent. Sometimes I thought I might even start a wholesale business like Mr Caradas.

But chance would have it otherwise. One day, while serving a customer, I noticed a young woman in the middle of the shop staring at me. She was wearing a blue blazer with white and yellow stripes and a badge on the pocket with the head of a goat sporting long, upward-turned horns. There was a motto underneath but I couldn't read it, much less understand what it meant. As she waited her turn she stared at me. When I served her, she turned her head sideways, smiled, and asked, 'Are you not the boy whose photo appeared in the newspaper? With your father? The ones that escaped from the Germans?' I said I was. With an even broader smile she reached across the counter to shake my hand. 'What school do you go to?' I told her I didn't go to school. She asked to speak to my father and, when I said he worked in Pretoria, she waited for Mr Bill to finish serving a customer.

She introduced herself as Cecilia Feinstein, a teacher. Although the shop was busy – it was late afternoon and many people got off the tram at the nearby stop – she bombarded Mr Bill with questions about me and my father. Why was I not at school? How could she get in touch with my father? How old was I? How far had I gone at school before I came to South Africa? Would he get in touch with my father regarding my going to school again? Then she said she would come back in a day or two, by which time she hoped all would have agreed that she could take me to her school the following Monday.

The 1943 school year had already started, but she would arrange with the principal to have me admitted. We left a telephone message with the owner of the café where my father had his meals. He was only too happy for me to go to school, but asked if the two partners could keep an eye on me. He was now earning enough to pay for my room and would come every second weekend to give me money. Mr Bill was happy to pay for my room and give me whatever else was necessary. I could earn my keep by helping them in the shop after school.

The young teacher came back and was delighted to hear the decision. Would I put on my best clothes, including the cap that I wore when the newspaper photograph was taken, and be ready at seven the next morning? She would take me to Malvern Junior High, a school offering standards six to eight.

On the tram to Malvern, she questioned me about my early schooling. Had I liked going to school? What were my favourite subjects? She congratulated me on the amount of English I had picked up and asked whether I could read English. I said, yes, the Germiston teacher had taught me the alphabet. I also tried to read the news about the war in the newspapers and, whenever it was quiet, I read the comics we sold. She estimated that I had passed standard six but thought that it would be wise if I repeated that standard. She said she would ask the principal to place me in her class.

The principal appeared aloof and our interview was brief. He asked no questions, gave me no encouragement, and stopped the teacher short in her enthusiastic introduction of me. But he agreed that she could have me in her class, although she should see to it that I had a uniform as soon as possible. I was concerned about Mr Bredell's attitude. He was young, lean and blonde. I wondered why, in the middle of the war, he had trimmed his moustache in the style made famous by Adolf Hitler. Later I asked Miss Feinstein why Mr Bredell followed this fashion. She gave me a lesson in fair-mindedness, saying that I must not let appearances deceive me and that Mr Bredell was a good principal and a very nice man.

I joined Miss Feinstein's class of some ten girls and twenty boys, mainly from St George's Home in Bedfordview. The teacher introduced me to the class, explained my background and that I had escaped from the Germans. None of them seemed to be particularly impressed. Miss Feinstein taught most of the subjects but I went to other teachers for English and Afrikaans. I was given a set of textbooks and an exercise book for each subject. After school Miss Feinstein took me back by tram and told Mr Bill where to get a uniform and a school bag. We also arranged that I would make my way to school now that I knew where it was.

As part of our classes, the teachers often wrote a part of the lesson on the board for us to copy in our exercise books. As I had never been taught to write in English, my attempts to read what I had scrawled were not always successful. The teacher realised my problem was serious and took steps to remedy it. Two or three times a week I would go to her home in Kensington, a suburb between the school and the shop. She laughed when she saw my attempt to copy the Yeats poem 'The Lake Isle of Innisfree'. It was almost illegible. She brought a book and made me read the poem over and over again, which enabled me to make a brave attempt the next day to recite it in class. She would also sing with me the music teacher's favourite song for the Monday morning assembly: *What shall we do with the drunken sailor?* She helped me with my arithmetic and gently smacked me on the wrist whenever I muttered my multiplication tables in Greek. She stressed that for my own good I must think in English in everything I did and said.

Despite her encouragement and loving care, I almost left the school at the end of the first week. The stern and unfriendly woodwork teacher had prepared the drawing boards. He issued the drawing paper and instructed us to print the heading of the drawing of a wooden lamp stand we would eventually make. The main heading had to be in half-inch letters, the subheading in quarter-inch letters, and the date in one-eighth-of-an-inch letters.

I had never done any drawing, let alone worked in inches and their subdivisions before. Once he had issued his instruction, he slowly walked from bench to bench to inspect our efforts. His comments were confined to 'I have seen better' or 'I have seen worse'. When he saw my efforts he shouted at me without even allowing me to answer his many questions. 'What is the matter with you, are you deaf or something? Why didn't you use your T-square to faintly mark spaces of half an inch, and then a quarter, and then an eighth, so that you could write within them?'

I had to step onto the platform and bend down. He caned me, saying after each of the four strokes that this was to help me follow his instructions in future. I had only been caned once before, and for me this was a severe beating. I bit my lower lip to avoid crying out in pain. I had no sense of bitterness the first time I was caned when I had refused to lead the dance; I had brought the punishment on myself. But this was cruel and unjust. While the class continued drawing to scale the rough sketch on the board, I could hardly sit on the stool and did nothing for the rest of the period. The class was dismissed.

We were expected to march out of the workshop in military precision, but I moved slowly and left too long a gap between me and the boy in front. The woodwork teacher shouted, 'Move on! Otherwise I'll give you some more of the same.' In tears I reported my ordeal to Miss Feinstein. She was upset, wiped my tears and took some of the blame on herself. She had spoken about me to many of the teachers to prepare them, but had forgotten to include him. She was sorry about the incident and felt that it was partly her fault. I told her I would not leave the school; to do so would have let her down and I couldn't do that.

Soon I began to enjoy school. I was given a cadet's uniform including a cap such as soldiers wore and taught to march and salute. I was not good enough to take part in the school's sports teams, but earned some points for my house at the school's annual swimming gala. I made good friends with a boy called Ernesto Busscaglia. He and his mother had come from Italy to join his father just as the war started. That our countries were fighting on opposite sides did not prevent our friendship. The other pupils referred to us as 'the foreigners', which certainly helped cement our bond.

Whoever it was that taught Afrikaans gave me up as a hopeless case, but the elderly spinster, Miss Brown, who taught English, pushed me hard. She would ask me to read aloud passages from the set work, *The Prisoner of Zenda*, calling the class to order when they giggled at my pronunciation. She would patiently explain that English preferred the accent on the third last syllable of the word rather than the second and tell me that it was photógrapher and not photográpher, as I tended to say. She read passages to show the class how her fine language should be spoken. In a passage debating whether the claimant to the throne would succeed, Miss Brown, with a faint smile, read out, 'I bet a crown he will never be crowned.' She paused, hoping for some reaction. In the absence of any response she told us how disappointed she was and explained that a play on words such as this was known as a pun. It ought to have made us laugh, she said, but we were too dull to see what the words meant. 'All but one of you,' she said, and referred to me by name. 'I saw his face light up. He smiled and was about to laugh, but he checked himself because of your silence.'

This did nothing to improve my popularity with the others. As we left the classroom I heard one of the prettier girls, who I hoped to befriend, cuttingly remark that it was bad enough putting up with my being Miss Feinstein's pet, but now it looked as though Miss Brown wanted to make me her pet too. Pretty though she was, this was enough for me to give up on my classmate and look elsewhere.

At the end of the school year Miss Feinstein told me that despite some reservations, the teachers' meeting had decided to promote me to standard seven. She and Miss Brown had urged the others to agree. They said that as I was about two years older than the average it would make no sense to keep me back. My promotion was good news. Better still, Miss Feinstein was to move up with the class and would again be my class teacher.

My father came to Johannesburg to spend a part of his annual leave, and stayed with me in my room. There was only one bed, but we both slept on it, our heads at opposite ends. We talked late into the night, wondering when the war would end, what our future would be and what was going on back home.

He was pleased with my promotion, and told me that he had saved some money. We would go to the post office to open a savings account in my name. Some of the money would be needed for my education and some to send home for the education of my brothers and sister when the war ended.

It was the end of 1943, and we now felt more confident, since things were looking better for the Allies. The war was not expected to last forever. We agreed that when Greece was free again, we would decide what to do. In the meantime, I must work hard at school. I agreed, as I did not want to be a shop assistant all my life. If I learned to read and write properly, I could become a commercial traveller such as those who came to the shop to take orders. Then I would drive a motor car and work for just a few hours a day.

My father had other ideas. He hoped I would become an *epistimon*, go to university and qualify as a doctor. The next morning we went to the central Johannesburg post office, where he deposited £50 in my name. I wondered why. Was it because he was embarrassed that he could not read or write English? Or because he wanted to show his confidence in me? Or even to indicate that he was serious about finding some way to finance my further education? I think that he probably did it for all these reasons.

Of more immediate interest was the bicycle he bought me. It was a great joy and a welcome relief for Ernesto, who usually gave me a lift on the crossbar of his bike. Now I could pedal from one friend to the next to show off during the shop's quiet periods. I invited Poppy, her sister and brother for a ride. By now Poppy had matured and was in earnest conversation with Basil Zachariou, whom she later married.

I was full of confidence at the beginning of the school year; having jumped the first hurdle I thought nothing could stop me. My newfound freedom, my flippant attitude towards the customers and my frequently slipping away were not to the senior partner's liking. He would issue terse commands: 'Don't answer the telephone! Serve the customers! Be on time! Don't be later than four o'clock to tidy up the fruit and vegetable counter! Unpack the cigarettes onto the shelf so that we are ready for the five o'clock rush!' Mr Bill would surreptitiously give me a smile of sympathy, and shrug his shoulders as if to say, 'Bear it, I cannot interfere.'

During the mid-year school holiday, the senior partner caught me before an old mirror in the small kitchen brushing my bushy black hair. He took me by the wrist, led me to the barbershop adjoining the café, and told the woman barber to give me a severe haircut similar to his but even shorter. I tried to protest. He put his index finger on his lips and hissed, '*Ssshhh! – Siopi!*' – a warning not as sharp as 'shut up' but near to it. As I saw my locks succumbing to the barber's scissors and falling on the floor, I struggled to hold back the tears.

At school my classmates laughed at me. When Miss Feinstein entered the classroom, she too was amused and asked, 'Gosh, whatever happened to your beautiful hair?' I did not answer. When the bell rang for the first break, everyone else rushed out. Although my desk was the third from the front and the second row from the door, I was the last to leave. 'Come here, George,' said Miss Feinstein. 'You're not yourself. What is the matter?' I related my ordeal at the barbershop and how unhappy I was to be held on so short a leash and be shouted at. She asked if any alternative arrangement could be made to look after me. I could think of none.

She suggested that I spoke to my father. He might persuade the man responsible to treat me better. For once I did not take her advice. Back home, I continued sulking and said no more to my tormentor than formal greetings. I muttered to myself whenever he chided me, which made him angrier still.

One Wednesday afternoon Ernesto and I went to a matinee. We did some homework afterwards and chatted, oblivious of the time. Only when Ernesto said he must go did I look at his watch. It was nearly half past five. I was already an hour and a half late. When I walked into the shop, the senior partner asked where the hell I'd been. I did not answer that or his many other questions. Who do you think you are? Were you not supposed to be here at four o'clock? Did you forget how busy we are at the end of the month?

He went on and on as he served the customers. He stopped briefly to calculate the total, ring the cash register, and shout out, 'Next, please!' before continuing with his barrage of questions. When the clientele thinned out he asked in a more moderate voice what I had to say for myself? I told him that he had no right to speak to me as he had done. 'Listen to that,' he told Mr Bill. 'Listen to the thanks we get for looking after him. He expects to do as he pleases without even uttering a simple "thank you" to those who feed him, pay for his room and look after him so that he doesn't walk around like a loafer.'

Angry and remembering the money in the post office savings account, I said they did not have to do these things anymore: I was going and I would pay the rent for my room. After the shop closed at ten o'clock, Mr Bill came to me. He asked me to swallow my pride and come back. I thanked him for his kindness. I had no complaints against him but I could not stand his partner anymore.

After I left them, Mr Bill remained a close friend to me and my father and I often visited him in the shop when his partner was not there. He went to Greece and saw our family there shortly after the war, bringing us back an account of the tragedy that befell the village just before the German withdrawal at the end of 1944 and the horror of the civil war that raged after it. He was proud that I became a lawyer and, until his death in the late 1970s, he would visit my chambers from time to time to take tea with me.

When I told my father that I had left the Formain Cafe, he did not seem surprised and asked hardly any questions. I guessed that Mr Bill had spoken to him. Instead, he inquired about my schooling and seemed pleased that I was doing well. But who would look after me now? He appeared to accept my emphatic statement that I was old enough to look after myself.

At about this time, Miss Feinstein told me that she had become engaged to be married. By the end of the year she would be Mrs Smulowitz, and would no longer teach. I had told her of my father's wish that I become a doctor, and she said she believed I could do it. Such encouragement was new to me. When I had ventured to write about my dreams for the future in a class essay, my English teacher had added a note at the end saying that I was building castles in the air. Miss Feinstein said that she did not mean to criticise the school, but that for my dreams to come true I should go to a proper high school where I could matriculate. If my father and I agreed, she could arrange for me to start standard eight at Athlone High School on the other side of the hill. She made the same offer to Ernesto, but he had decided that after he had obtained his junior certificate at the end of standard eight he would become an apprentice plumber, which he did, and prospered.

I spent much time with Ernesto at his home next to the railway line. His father was an assistant in a bakery and brought home fresh white loaves not available to anyone during the war. His mother spoke no English, stayed at home, grew vegetables and cooked the tastiest dishes I had ever eaten. I often accepted her invitation to the kitchen table where she would pile large portions onto a plate exclaiming 'Mangia, Giorgio, mangia!' In return I helped in the vegetable patch and turned the hand-mincing machine when the year's stock of salami was made.

It was taken for granted that I would pass standard seven, but before I could leave Malvern I had to tell Mr Bredell that I was changing schools and ask for my transfer papers. When he inquired why I was leaving, I told him that my father wanted me to become a doctor. He said that my father and I, like most foreigners, knew how to make lots of money and that was why my father wanted me to become a doctor.

Mr Brett, the principal of Athlone High, received Miss Feinstein and me when we went for an initial interview. He showed some interest in my story as briefly told by Miss Feinstein, but spent far more time telling us about his role in the First World War. He showed us his book *The Makers of South Africa*, with its pictures of generals Louis Botha and Jan Smuts on the cover. This book had become recommended – if not compulsory – reading for standard eight pupils. He seemed glad to have me in his school and was obviously flattered that it was on the recommendation of another teacher.

Miss Feinstein was involved in Jewish affairs. The plight of the Jews in Germany and the countries under its occupation was seldom referred to in our conversations at school. There were hardly any Jewish pupils at Malvern Junior High and anti-Semitic remarks were heard from time to time. Miss Feinstein was no great disciplinarian: her favourite measure when the class got out of control was to draw a line on the top right-hand corner of the board and announce a five-minute detention. On a bad day there would be two or three strokes and the detention period would be correspondingly longer. During detention we would sometimes debate light-heartedly whether the behaviour of the class had been bad enough to warrant the second or third strokes. Then Miss Feinstein would defend her action and remind us of what we had done: there would be partial admissions and denials and promises to behave the next day. She would accept the assurances and good-humouredly say, 'Class dismissed and make sure that you don't misbehave tomorrow or for that matter, any other day' – a wish that both sides knew would not be fulfilled.

In one of these debates towards the end of Miss Feinstein's tenure, Thomas, the most troublesome boy, said, 'Oh Miss, why do you always Jew us with our time?' She slumped in her chair, covered her face with her long-fingered hands and, between sobs, said quietly, 'Get out, the whole lot of you. Get out!' This was towards the end of 1944 when incontrovertible evidence showed that millions of Jews had perished. None of this had brought home to Thomas and those around him the realisation that 'Jew' as a verb had a derogatory meaning.

I lost touch with Miss Feinstein. Her father's bicycle shop closed down and her brother's garage was sold. To my shame, it was almost thirty years before I took steps to find her. The Feinsteins are well represented in the legal and accountancy professions and eventually a senior attorney told me that he and she were distant cousins. He believed she was in East London. As chance would have it, I was having lengthy consultations with an engineer from that city. I asked the engineer if he knew of a teacher whose maiden name was Feinstein and who had married a pharmacist called Smulowitz. He said he knew of a Smulowitz who managed a pharmaceutical wholesale firm. He was almost certain that they were the people I was looking for.

Once I had her telephone number, I spent hours thinking what my opening words should be and how I should address her. I even wondered if she had forgotten me. After all, to her I might not have been anything more than one of many. But I had told my wife and later our boys about her and I was under pressure from them to do something about it. So I dialled the number. A high-pitched African female voice said a cheerful 'Hello'. The madam was out and would be back at lunch time.

After thirty years it did not seem proper to leave a message, so I said that I would phone again and did not mention my name or number. About fifteen minutes later, my office telephone rang. 'Hello, George, is it you? It's Cecilia speaking. Did you phone a short while ago?' 'Yes, I did,' I said, astonished. 'I have been waiting for your call since yesterday when I heard from my husband that you were looking for me. I thought that it must have been you who phoned earlier, but I just couldn't wait anymore. I so badly wanted to speak to you. I have been following your cases, and I am so proud of you.' 'And I am so grateful to you,' I said. 'If it had not been for you, I don't know what I would have done with my life.'

It was a long conversation. We spoke about our families and I asked if she would come to Johannesburg to stay with us and meet my family. She said she would. She had family she wanted to visit, but she also wanted to meet my family and particularly to tell my sons the sort of boy their father had been. When she came to Johannesburg, we spent the whole day together. Cecilia asked many questions. How did Arethe and I meet? Was I a good husband? What sort of father was I? She responded to many of the anecdotes by saying that my behaviour was exactly what she would have expected from the precocious schoolboy she had known. There was hearty laughter and more questions and exclamations, all in good humour but made mainly at my expense. We promised to keep in touch and I said that I would visit her when I went to the Eastern Cape. I did not keep that promise, but neither did I forget her.

Some years later, in 1996, when the University of Natal in Durban conferred an honorary doctorate of law on me, they asked who I would like to be invited to the ceremony. Cecilia Feinstein was top of the list and after more than fifty years I was able to make a public acknowledgement of her role, explaining that it was she who started me off on the route I had followed. I often wonder what I might have made of my life if she had not insisted that, refugee or not, I was entitled to the right to learn.

CHAPTER 5

Bad Times, Good Times

By the end of 1944 the Italian people had turned against Mussolini. Many of the soldiers he sent into Greece, believing they would make him a modern Roman emperor, had been tricked and butchered. When the Allied troops landed there, much of the country had already been liberated from the Germans by the resistance movement. Internal conflict then broke out. The king and government in exile insisted on returning, but the Left-inclined resistance demanded elections and a referendum, so that the people could decide if there was place for a king. Shooting occurred in Athens, and when Winston Churchill and Anthony Eden flew to the city at Christmas, Churchill's armoured vehicle came under fire. He was reported to have said, 'What a cheek!'

Photographs in the newspapers brought both joy and sadness: photographs of world-famous landmarks, now liberated, but also pictures of emaciated Greek children. We read that thousands had died of hunger or from illness because they lacked basic medicine. The Allied successes on the Western Front and the advance of the Soviet Union's army from the east made it look as if Hitler would suffer the same fate as Mussolini, but for Greece there was still the spectre of a civil conflict.

Our refugee permits entitled us to stay in South Africa until the end of the war. In the more than three and a half years since we'd left Greece, we had heard nothing of our family. There had been one telephone in the village but it was not worth trying to get through as telecommunications with Greece were dead. Finally we sent a telegram. For weeks there was no reply. Then, early in the new year, came a knock on my door by a man from the post office. He handed me an envelope without any stamp. It said 'Antonios Bizos' in Greek and 'Johannesburg, South Africa' in roman letters, the latter barely legible. The bearer of the letter was no mere postman but a rather more senior official.

I invited him to sit in the only chair in my room while I sat on the bed to open the envelope. The first page was torn from an exercise book and written in the handwriting of a semi-literate person. 'We are well. We learnt from the Red Cross letter we received more than a year ago that you too are well.' I quickly looked at the end to see on whose behalf it was written: 'Your loving wife, children and mother.' I went back to the beginning and found, midway down: 'Your father died last year, happy to have heard that you had survived your journey and that you are well.'

The postal official asked me if I was Antonios Bizos. 'No, I am his son.' 'I'm glad I found you,' he said. 'I took the letter from one shop to another around the post office and was eventually told that the people in the shop down the road would know how to find the right person.' He asked me whether the letter brought good or bad news. I said, both. It seemed our family had survived the war, except for my grandfather.

I could give the postal official no refreshment but offered to walk back with him to the tram stop close to the café where I had worked. Once there, I persuaded him to enter the shop, greeted Mr Bill and introduced him to the official. It was Mr Bill who'd sent him to me. He accepted a cream soda, and sipped it through a straw while I telephoned my father.

After I read my father the opening sentence he constantly interrupted me: Do they say when my father died? Did anyone inform the Germans of what we had done? Were no reprisals taken against the family? Were they left in peace? There were no answers to many of the questions. Later, when I took the letter to him in Pretoria, he read it over and over again. At times his face had a faint smile, but often, particularly in relation to the death of his father, he tried hard to keep back the tears.

Now letter followed letter. Though written in fear of the censor, as the war was going on elsewhere – not to mention the bitter civil conflict in Greece itself – these letters painted a gloomy picture. A year after the death of my grandfather, my grandmother had died of a stroke. My brothers and sister had not gone to school since the end of October 1940. The attempt by the teacher Panayiotis Arnaoutis to reopen the school was short-lived. One day, apparently acting on a tip-off, Italian soldiers arrived at his home, went straight to the bedroom and found the service pistol he had failed to hand in. He was publicly flogged outside the church of St Vasilios with many forced to watch, including his pupils, among whom were my brothers and sister. Arnaoutis was jailed and would have been executed had it not been for the intervention of highly placed people at the pleading of a young woman, whom he married upon his release.

But the worst incident began as the German occupation was drawing to an end. A band of partisans came to the village and asked for provisions, readily given to them by those who supported their struggle. The Germans had created security battalions to act against the 'communist bands', as the Germans and local right-wingers called the partisans.

After this visit by the partisans, a small group of these right-wingers, including

my Uncle Vangos, persuaded more than seventy men from the village to accept
the offer of arms from the Germans. They argued that they could use these arms
to protect the village from raids by the communists, who, they said, would otherwise loot their pantries, take away their horses and mules and rape their women.
Once armed, the recruited men hung around the village, untrained, undisciplined.
They turned their attention to those who disagreed with their assessment of the
motives of the anti-German partisans, among whom was my mother's brother
Vasili Tomaras, active in the resistance movement. In a small community, guilt by
association – if such it was – was readily accepted. Vangos claimed that my aunt
was not sufficiently provided for in my grandfather's will and demanded a division
of all the property. As the justice system had collapsed, his threats to take over the
property were alarming. He told my mother to move into a protected village –
guarded by the security battalions against the 'communist' partisans – with
her children. When she refused, he and his comrades believed that she must
be under the protection of her communist brother. In retaliation and on the
pretext that those in the protected village needed the provisions, they ransacked
the house.

Soon afterwards a band of partisans came to the village. They ordered my
mother to make sure that her children were out of the house as they were going to
burn it. She wanted to know why. They had orders, they said, which could not be
questioned. How could anyone give an order that the house of the sister of Vasili
Tomaras should be burnt? she asked. The group decided to spare the house.

Despite the fears and predictions of the right-wingers, no bands of partisans
descended to attack the village. Those who collaborated with the Germans warned
that a large force of communists was moving south from central Greece to take
control of the towns of the southern Peloponnese. Their intention was to form
the future government and keep the king out of the country. They urged their
comrades no longer to wait passively in the village. Instead they should go to
Kalamata, where the commanders of the security battalions would lead them
to face the ungodly traitors. Of the seventy-five men who set off for Kalamata
only three returned. The rest were slaughtered in an ambush. Among the three
who survived was Vangos. He returned to torment my mother and others with
renewed vigour.

After this tragedy, practically every woman in the village wore black for years
to come, signifying the loss of a husband, a son, or a father in the ambush. At
first their anger was directed at those who opposed – or even merely distanced
themselves from – the men who accepted arms from the Germans. Later most
of their anger was directed against those who had misled the poor, young and

ignorant men by influencing them to take up arms and deviate from the ancient tradition of non-collaboration with an occupying force.

When Vangos came back he threatened my aunt that, if she did not stop helping her brother by putting out food and clean clothing for him in the trees some distance from the village, she would be taken to the church square, stripped of her headscarf and sheared as if she were a sheep.

We discovered that whenever a village fisherman caught an especially large fish he would be asked by one of the right-wing collaborators to gut it and see whether it had eaten any portions of my father and me.

Despite news reports of hunger and people dying of starvation in the cities, concern for my brothers' and sister's lack of education was soon uppermost in my father's mind. As some form of normality appeared to be returning in early 1945, he insisted that they go to school and that tutors be engaged to make up for the lost years. He regularly sent money for this purpose.

In the meantime I had been received at Athlone High, then a co-educational school. Freda Greenberg, on the initiative of Cecilia Feinstein, was waiting for me and she helped me choose my subjects. In the class taking French, only three of us were not of Jewish origin. They had all heard my story and asked question after question about what the Germans looked like and how they behaved.

All the teachers but one were kind and helpful. Mr Scheepers, the standard eight Afrikaans teacher, asked whether I had seen the photographs in the newspapers of the starving children in Greece. I said I had. 'You look well fed to me,' he said. I ignored his remark, but he added, 'Don't you think that you are eating someone else's food?' 'Sir,' I replied, 'my father is working; he provides for me. I hope that one day I may repay society for the food I am eating.' 'Not only do we feed you,' said Mr Scheepers, 'but we have made you clever too.' I said nothing but my classmate, Solly Blecher, stood at his desk and said. 'Sir, you either apologise for what you have said to Bizos or I am walking out of this class and going to the principal's office to report you.' 'Ag man, Solly,' said Mr Scheepers, 'can't you take a joke?' The matter was left there, although no one laughed at any stage.

By way of contrast, Mr Combrink, the standard nine and ten Afrikaans teacher, was very helpful to me. To be accepted into university I needed at least an E in Afrikaans. He undertook to get me over this hurdle if I listened to him carefully and did what he said. In essays I should not use the past tense nor the double negative, which it seemed to him that I would never understand. I should rather write in the present or the future tense and that way I would give myself a chance. I did as he said and, no doubt thanks largely to his advice, I did get an E in Afrikaans in my matriculation examination.

As the war in Europe drew to an end in 1945, newspaper and newsreel reports gave ample proof of the holocaust against the Jewish people and the atrocities against others in the countries under German occupation. At school our outrage was expressed in daily conversations and in the questions we asked to debate during history lessons, while our essays dealt with the issue no matter what the prescribed subject. The Balfour Declaration on the independence of Palestine and the unfulfilled promise of the creation of an independent State of Israel led to strong anti-British feelings among my classmates. Freda Greenberg, though emotionally involved, urged us to be objective and to use moderate language. Restriction of entry into Palestine by holocaust survivors and the courage of some Greek captains in breaking the embargo indicated that we were on the same side.

Many of the boys and girls at the school were members of the youth branch of the Zionist Socialist Party and I attended some of their meetings. One of these was on the steps of the Johannesburg City Hall on a Sunday evening. At the same time as the speakers addressed us, there were three or four other small meetings taking place, with audiences varying between fifteen and fifty, sometimes applauding the speaker and sometimes jeering. Some in the crowd moved from one group to the next, apparently to avoid boredom. Given the prevailing laws and practices, these meetings were all white, but across the road, on the steps leading to the main entrance of the Rissik Street post office, sat a small group of black men. They were completely passive participants. When the clock struck half past eight that evening, they moved away, either alone or in pairs, to meet the nine o'clock curfew, which banned black people from city streets.

That evening was my initiation into South African politics. Over the next couple of years I often went to the city hall steps on Sunday evenings, where speakers on a variety of subjects put their views. I heard Hilda Watts (later Bernstein) extol the heroism of the Red Army, then pushing back the Nazis. I heard her expound the view that socialism was the only way forward after the war. A good-humoured elderly man wearing a workman's cap rode a horse to the meeting place. He advocated land reform by the adoption of a policy acknowledging that land was a gift from God and that no value should be placed on it, nor should it be taxable. Solly Sachs and Anna Scheepers waxed enthusiastic on the virtues of trade unionism and particularly its impact on the women working in the garment industry.

Then there was a team of two men, one black, the other white, who said that after the war against Hitler the demand by black people for equality would have to be addressed. The white man attempted to introduce the black man standing next to him but was interrupted by a loud and angry voice: 'Are you for or against Hitler?' 'We are against Hitler,' replied the speaker, 'but also against Jan Smuts' native policy!' Members of the small white audience booed as they left to join another group. With no one left to listen, the two speakers left as well; the black man hadn't spoken.

The Grey Shirts, a pro-Nazi group of Afrikaners, together with members of the right-wing Ossewa Brandwag, occasionally broke up meetings on the city hall steps. As South African soldiers who had fought in North Africa and Italy returned, some of them came to the city hall steps to speak of what they had gone through in battles and how they had survived in the enemy's prisoner of war camps. They spoke of being disappointed by what they found on their return. It was quite different from what they expected, with no sign of the better world they'd been promised. Inevitably, these soldiers clashed with people opposed to South Africa's participation in the war, and, because of these brawls, meetings on the city hall steps petered out.

Our refugee permits expired when the war came to an end in 1945 and we had to go to the department of immigration and Asiatic affairs from time to time for extensions. Given the news we were receiving from Greece, my father decided that it was not opportune to return just yet. When we were informed that we could apply for permanent residence, he decided to do so, planning to bring the rest of the family to South Africa. I welcomed the decision. I was well treated at Athlone High School, had formed good friendships and enjoyed my independence in Johannesburg with my father more than an hour's train journey away in Pretoria. Returning to Vasilitsi, Koroni or even Kalamata was not an attractive option.

Despite my father's decision, our application for permanent residence was stalled for another three years. Our precarious status, our lack of funds, the civil war in Greece and the need for a certificate of social *phronimotita*, without which you could hardly do anything with your life, kept members of our family apart for more than twenty years.

Phronimos is one who is prudent, quiet, well-behaved, virtuous and, particularly, obedient. In the eyes of the right-wing government's village informers, none of the members of our extended family merited such a certificate. If any proof were needed, my father's letter to my mother's brother detained on Makronisos, the Greek equivalent of Robben Island, was enough. Let alone my sister's visit to a distant relative detained in Kalamata and the difficult questions she asked during the religious instruction class in high school.

But life continued. In school, I was a below-average pupil, despite being almost three years older than the others. I had been appointed an officer in the cadets and wore the khaki uniform with three stars on both shoulders to school every Friday. Dressed in that uniform I looked old enough for the tram conductor to believe I was a real soldier, entitled to free travel, for he rejected my proffered coin. Probably at the request of Miss Smith, our class and maths teacher, the headmaster called me into his office and told me to shave off my moustache.

Most of the subjects bored me. I no longer had Cecilia Feinstein as my special personal tutor. Miss Greenberg scolded me for making no attempt to improve my illegible handwriting and for not using a dictionary to improve my atrocious spelling. The amiable senior teacher of history, a subject in which I had a particular interest, took us for English in Miss Greenberg's absence. On one occasion he gave us the heading, 'A visit to the park', and told us to write an essay on the topic. My work came back with a red line through its three pages. At the end was his one-word comment: 'inappropriate'. He must have expected descriptions of freshly mown and trimmed lawns, beds of roses, daffodils or azaleas and birds perched on flowering trees. Instead he was appalled to read my description of an attractive young woman sitting on a bench looking as lonely as I felt, and my hesitant and unsuccessful attempts to establish a liaison with her. He praised and criticised some of the essays during the course of the lesson but said nothing about mine. We looked at each other as I left his class and it was difficult to tell who was more embarrassed: the middle-aged bachelor, or me, seeking to outgrow my last year as a teenager.

English and history were my saving grace at school. I read not only the set works but also other books from the well-stocked library. I would recite to myself from 'The Rime of the Ancient Mariner', Anthony's 'Friends, Romans, countrymen ...' speech from *Julius Caesar* and Hamlet's 'To be or not to be ...' soliloquy. Eighteenth- and nineteenth-century European and American history fascinated me and I read about the American war of independence, the French revolution, the reign of terror and the Napoleonic wars, the march to Moscow, the defeat at Waterloo. I even tried to read Tolstoy's *War and Peace* but could not keep it out of the library long enough to finish. The restoration of the Bourbons who had forgotten nothing and learned nothing, the Paris Commune uprising in 1871 and the Communist Manifesto were matters of particular interest to me, and so was South African history.

I found it difficult memorising much of the detail we were required to know – governors from Jan van Riebeeck in 1652 until the invasion of the Cape by the British; the list of English governors afterwards and their wives; the 'kaffir wars' between the white settlers and the Xhosa. However, I found other sections of South African history even more fascinating – the reasons for the abolition of slavery, the Great Trek by the Boers. We were taught about the 'treachery of Dingaan', the establishment of the Boer republics, the greed of the English for diamonds and gold, and the Boer War itself. All these events made me ambivalent as to whose side I was on. The textbooks made brief reference to this issue and in class discussions our teacher dealt with the divisions in the country between Afrikaners and English-speaking whites as well as the 'native problem'. By contrast to English and history, my interest in science and mathematics was at a very low ebb.

Some of my teachers doubted that I would pass matric with a university exemption. I hung around the Parkgate Café after school, helping behind the counter during the evening rush hour for no other reward than a good supper. I regularly sat in the cheapest seats to watch forgettable films, spending hardly any time on revision in preparation for the important matric examination.

One day my father appeared at the café. He had come from Pretoria to see me because he had heard that I was not applying myself to my schoolwork. When I asked who told him, he, instead of replying, lectured me on the importance of taking myself more seriously and concentrating on my studies.

I had arranged to go to the cinema that night and hoped that he would leave early enough for me to keep my appointment. As the time neared, it looked as if he intended to stay, so I told him of the arrangement and asked if he would let me cancel it. Consistent with his tolerant attitude and my selfishness, he graciously said that I should keep my appointment, and I left him to find his own way back to Pretoria or seek accommodation with a friend. It did not occur to me to offer him the key to my room. But I took his advice seriously and after this visit I made some effort to catch up.

I remembered Mr Combrink's advice to write the matric Afrikaans essay in the present or future tense only, but ignored the advice given to the whole class that we avoid controversial subjects or venting our feelings by way of intemperate language in the English essay. Our teacher had reason to fear that opportunities would be sought in the exam that year to discuss the British presence in Palestine and calls for the establishment of an Israeli state – it was, after all, just a year before the State of Israel was recognised by the United Nations. Personal experience had shown her the strength of her pupils' feelings on the subject. Shortly before the exam, she took about a hundred of us to see *Henry V* at the Empire Theatre. The play's expression of fervent English patriotism so incensed some of us that we booed and jeered the end of Laurence Olivier's 'St Crispin's Day' speech.

There was a wide choice of English essay topics in the final examination, but I could not resist choosing 'Man is born free and everywhere he is in chains'. In the history class we'd held a heated debate on the subject and I strongly supported the proposition. When we discussed the paper with Miss Greenberg after the exam she correctly predicted that I had made a bad choice.

I obtained an E, only one notch above the dreaded F, in English, Afrikaans and science. This disqualified me from university, let alone getting one of the hotly contested places at the University of the Witwatersrand's medical school. A letter to this effect arrived from the dean of the faculty of medicine. Later, I had a sympathetic hearing from his secretary who suggested I sit for supplementary examinations in English and science. In the meantime I should provisionally register at the faculty of arts, subject to improving my marks and gaining a university exemption. She further suggested I choose four subjects for my first year at Wits, English being one of them. If I passed at the end of 1948, my application to medical school might be successful for the 1949 year, as the number of ex-servicemen who were being given priority would be reduced. I did not fully explain to my father the reasons for my failure to be admitted to study medicine, but instead rather overemphasised the ex-servicemen part. He agreed that I should pursue the course as advised by the dean's secretary.

The English supplementary paper was a gift. One of the essay topics was 'In the country of the blind the one-eyed man is king'. Having read H G Wells' story, I pondered whether to acknowledge that I knew his work. In the end, I apologised for any similarity between what I wrote and Wells, adding that I would try my best to write my own story. Similarly, I could not believe my good fortune with the poetry question. We were asked to discuss one of the poems we had analysed in my English tutorial at the beginning of the university academic year – Gerard Manley Hopkins' poem, 'Spring and Fall'. I simply regurgitated the tutor's exegesis. To my relief, when the results came out, I fared much better in English and did better in science than in the previous exams. As a result, my provisional registration came to an end.

For my main subjects in first year I had chosen English, history, psychology and ancient Greek, with classical life and thought, and history of art as supplementaries. In second year I decided, without consulting my father, that medicine was not for me; it was law I wanted to study. I justified the decision to my father by arguing that medicine was a long and expensive full-time course. For law, on the other hand, I could either become an attorney, taking a three-year course and serving five years' articles, or I could study six years to become an advocate, three years of which were to be full time in the faculty of arts and three years part time in the faculty of law.

Early in 1948, my father had happily announced the purchase of a shop in Johannesburg's Plein Street, for which it was necessary to withdraw the money in the savings accounts which had not grown much beyond £700. Sadly, his business venture was a disaster. The shop had neither a lease nor a licence. The attorney to whom my father was taken, either because of incompetence or because he favoured his client, the seller, did not incorporate in the agreement the usual conditions to protect the buyer. The municipal inspectors threatened to close down the shop if appropriate alterations were not made to the kitchen and other facilities. However, the landlord would not agree to the alterations, nor would he grant a lease. The money paid was lost and the shop was abandoned. My father had to start again from scratch by returning to his old job as a shop assistant in Pretoria. This was the point at which I told my father that I wanted to study law. Reluctantly he accepted my decision, but insisted that I go for the two degrees and strive for what was in his view the higher status of an advocate. When I asked where the money would come from, he said optimistically that the money would be found somehow.

At the time, a tension had developed between us, caused by my failure to gain entry to medical school, my criticism of him for making a foolish business decision without even discussing it with me, my decision to abandon his ambition that I become a doctor, and because we were still without permanent residence. Then, shortly before the shop was given up, we received a letter that our permanent residence certificates were ready for collection from the department of internal affairs.

The day the shop closed, all the tensions between us somehow came to an end and we sat for hours discussing the future now that we had our papers. We decided it was still not the right time to return home and that we should go ahead with our plan to get members of the family to South Africa.

My father's ill-fated shop was directly opposite the building in which the Afrikaans daily, *Die Vaderland*, was printed. Its staff often came across for coffee, lunch and sandwiches, attracted to the shop by the young blonde Afrikaner waitress. They were amused by the quaint, bookish way in which I spoke Afrikaans. When I talked to her she often corrected or finished my sentences, but always with a friendly smile or gentle laughter and never with derision.

A copy of the newspaper would be brought to her every afternoon, and on my return from lectures she would serve me lunch and sit closely next to me, reading out passages. She believed that her leaders D F Malan and J G Strÿdom would win the election, that South Africa would come back to the Afrikaner and that the blacks would be kept in their place. From time to time, my father looked furtively in our direction, no doubt wondering, as well he might, whether there was more between us than the almost over-friendly chats, but he never asked. I tried to be as discreet as possible, hoping that while my father and the woman's younger sister, with whom she lived in a room above the shop, might speculate, they would never know for sure.

On election day a public address system was set up outside *Die Vaderland's* premises, repeatedly exhorting residents as well as passers-by to vote for the National Party and ensure a white South Africa: '*Kom stem, dames en here, stem vir 'n wit Suid Afrika, stem Nasionaal.*' Cars with posters drove up and down and the shop had its busiest day ever. The waitress fully identified herself with the confidence of the jovial and optimistic customers, sure that they would win. She was cajoled and playfully dragged out of the shop. The only resistance she offered was a nervous giggle when taken onto the platform. She stood for a while and together with others applauded the oft-repeated slogan.

Despite our relationship I had no interest in dissuading her from her people's political views. In her room after she had sent her sister to the cinema, she confided to me that although not married she had a child being cared for by her mother in the small country town which was her home. Poverty had forced her to the city where she found a £15 a month job in the shop run by the man who eventually sold it to my father. When she came to town she had been faced with a terrible choice: who should she take with her, her sister or her baby? Eventually she brought her sister. Although she missed the child, she knew she couldn't hold down a job and look after the baby at the same time.

I have tried hard to remember her name, but to my shame I cannot recall it. However, I remember that she was paid off before we abandoned the shop. Afterwards, she did not know where I was living and I made no effort to see her. More than a year later we accidentally crossed paths in the centre of the city. I stopped and looked at her. She said, '*Waarom kyk jy so na my?*' – Why do you look at me like that? I didn't answer. She blushed in anger and turned her head away. We never saw one another again.

By the beginning of my third year I had to attend only two lectures a day in my major subjects, ancient Greek and psychology, to complete a Bachelor of Arts degree. I had became an avid reader, not only of the prescribed works but also of the great Russian and French nineteenth-century writers, and my enthusiasm for the courses led to my completing nine of the eleven required for the degree in the first two years. I also attended lectures on other subjects, particularly philosophy, and was a regular at lunch-hour meetings called by student societies.

During my third year – at my request, the two lectures followed one another so I was finished by ten o'clock – I found employment as a clerk for an attorney, Ruben Kahanovitz. He was a kind and generous employer, for not only was I receiving a salary but he also regularly took me to the best Italian restaurant, the Delmonico, for lunch. He had a general commercial practice, but never went to

court himself. He was also the Johannesburg correspondent for a number of lead-
ing firms of attorneys in Springs and Benoni, where he was born and brought up.
I regularly went to court with counsel and for the first time I enjoyed the work
I was doing.

I moved out of the cheap room into one with a private bathroom and passage
in Kenlaw Mansions, two blocks away from the university. I did not have to pay
much more because it overlooked the loading yard of the leading fish wholesaler,
Irvin and Johnson. It was furnished better than my previous room and even had
matching curtains and a bedspread chosen by my girlfriend, Arethe.

We had met two years earlier on the upper deck of a tram clanging along Main
Street towards Bezuidenhout Valley. I sat next to her even though there were many
empty double seats. She looked at me and blushed. I opened the conversation
by asking her how far she was going. She told me that she had not yet decided
whether to get off at her father's shop, the Subway Café, or to go home directly,
which would mean getting off at a stop farther along, in Dawe Street. 'Oh, I know
your father's shop. You must be Greek like me,' I said. Yes, she was. Her name was
Arethe Ekatharine (her grandmothers' names) but she was called Rita at school.
Her surname was Daflos and she was an art student. I told her who I was, and when
and why I had come to South Africa. She fixed her green eyes on mine, listened
with amazement and told me that her father, Basil Daflos, when my age, came
from Ipiros on the north-western border of Greece with Albania to join his uncle
in Stellenbosch and work in his café. Her grandfather Vassiliou had come from the
same area. He was the first confectioner in Johannesburg at the beginning of the
century. He married her maternal grandmother, Arethe Botsaris, who had come
from the island of Aegena. She thought that her grandmother was a descendant
of the great freedom fighter Markos Botsaris. She told me other details about
herself: for instance, that she had a younger brother, Niko, and sister, Aspasia. So
engrossed were we in our conversation that Arethe only realised the tram had
passed her father's shop when it turned left a few blocks beyond it. That was the
nearest tram stop to my room but I didn't get off. We continued talking and both
got off at the stop near her home. We walked the half-block up the hill and then
stood at the gate for a while.

In 1948, Greek mothers would not allow their daughters out on a date without
an escort, or, at the very least, not unless accompanied by well-known friends of
the family who could be trusted not to let the two out of their sight. In the coming
weeks I went to Arethe's parents' shop for some of my meals. Without disclosing
to them that I had met their daughter, I befriended them, particularly her mother,
Mary. Although born in South Africa she spoke Greek well but bemoaned the fact

that her children were not making much progress despite private lessons. Would I not come for lunch the following Sunday to meet them, she said, and could she ask me to insist on speaking to them in Greek? Would it be possible for me to help young Niko with his maths?

When Arethe and I were introduced, we remained silent about our earlier meeting through some kind of tacit mutual understanding. The first Sunday lunch, like many others that followed for over thirty years at the Dawe Street house, was an event not to be forgotten. Both the large walnut table, which could seat fifteen, and the top of the matching liquor cabinet were laden with dishes. The mistress of the house imposed her authority by making excuses for what she considered some minor failure in the preparation of a dish apparently in order to be reassured that it was as good as ever. She replenished one plate after another with a second and sometimes a third helping.

The door was opened for me to call on Arethe almost at will, particularly in the late afternoon and early evening when her parents were at the shop and her brother and sister were playing in the neighbourhood.

One hot day towards the end of the summer of 1948, I got caught in a thunderstorm as I trotted downhill to visit Arethe. I had barely passed the first of the four blocks when heavy drops of rain and hail came down on my bare head with increasing ferocity. By the time I reached the house I was drenched. My short-sleeved shirt and flannels clung to my body. My socks were like sponges squirting water out of my shoes with every step. The corrugated-iron roof covering the veranda was no protection, and the rain pounded Arethe's bedroom window. I rang the bell, she raised the edge of the curtain, saw me and rushed to open the front door. She pulled me into the carpeted entrance hall, and quickly fetched an enormous white fluffy towel. This she threw over my head, shoulders and arms and then hurriedly rubbed hard and energetically, tenderly calling me a silly boy for having allowed myself to be caught up in such a storm. I had never before been so sweetly caressed. When she was done she put the wet towel on the chair next to the telephone table. We looked deeply into each others' eyes. I put my hands on her upper arms, and drew her to me intending to give her a peck on each cheek in the traditional Greek fashion to express my gratitude. Instead, as I embraced her, we simultaneously closed our eyes and her lips met mine. It was the beginning of a loving relationship that has lasted over half a century, producing three sons and six grandchildren.

The pretence of my being a tutor to her younger brother was now abandoned and we became acknowledged companions. Together we spent many a late afternoon and evening in the backyard garage which had been converted into a studio.

About us was her work in progress in oil, still life in watercolours or gouache, copies of well-known Renaissance works, miniatures painted on ivory, charcoal drawings and sculptured heads in plaster of Paris.

There was a small carpeted area with an ottoman, on which I lay watching her work. I took a course in the history of art as an ancillary subject and we visited the Johannesburg Art Gallery and the Africana Museum housed in the Johannesburg library. Arethe listened with some amusement to my amateurish criticism of her work and tugged me along to lectures by local and overseas artists and academics to discuss what was then called 'modern art' and which explained how one could distinguish between the artist and the impostor who disguised by distortion an inability to draw. One of her still-life pictures won a prize at an art exhibition held in the foyer behind the massive Corinthian columns at Wits.

I lost no opportunity to tell even my casual friends that this was the work of my girlfriend. To this day the painting has pride of place in my office. When I am asked what my wife does, I show them the painting and recount her story that she gave up painting after she produced her three masterpieces – our sons. When pressed by one of our sons or daughters-in-law, however, she sometimes agrees to produce a picture to hang on their walls.

We went dancing regularly, as well as to the cinema, occasionally to the theatre, and enjoyed rowing boats on the lake. Transport was a problem, but Henry Panos and his wife Helen (Arethe's aunt) with their station wagon, and Peter Mentis who had free access to his father's Buick, with his companion Pamela Galatis, were all helpful friends.

Arethe's mother took me aside. She knew we loved each other and emphasised that I was welcome in their home. However, she had to deal with the criticisms of her relatives and friends who said that she and her daughter were flouting their traditions and that the impecunious student would drop Arethe as soon as he qualified. In despair she asked me to be more discreet. Was it really necessary for us to walk in the neighbourhood holding hands, for me to put my arm over Arethe's shoulders as soon as we got into a car and to dance cheek to cheek at the numerous twenty-first birthday parties of her friends? Could we not be more discreet? I said that we would try, well knowing that it would be difficult for me to keep my word.

I did not discuss my relationship with Arethe with my father, nor did I make mention of it in the occasional letter that I wrote to the family in Greece. I don't know what he heard, or from whom, but he broached the subject when I visited him in Pretoria, where he was working as a shop assistant for the Manolis family. He warned me against becoming committed before I qualified.

My relationship with Arethe ended eight years of loneliness, but this relationship – together with my thoughtlessness – also caused my father's attitude to me to change. The most important day on the Hellenic community's social calendar was the annual ball held at the Johannesburg City Hall. It was held shortly after Easter and as near as possible to 21 May, the feast day of saints Constantine and Helen to whom the orthodox cathedral in Johannesburg was dedicated. My father arranged for us to sit with a group from Pretoria, among whom was a young woman who I had never met and who seemed to be deliberately seated next to me. I found it difficult to speak to her during the long patriotic speeches. As soon as the band struck up the *kalamatiano*, the easiest and most popular of the Greek dances, my father nudged me with his knee and signalled that I should get up, offer her my hand and lead her to the ever-increasing circle of dancers. I did not take the hint, remained silent and looked straight ahead. Her mother, sitting opposite us, asked her brother to do the necessary. Everyone at the table except my father and me got up to dance. He told me that he did not know what was wrong with me. He expected me to behave properly during the rest of the evening.

Women had cards listing the forthcoming 'European' dances, including the waltz, foxtrot, quickstep and the tango. With a small pencil they filled in the names of the men who asked them to dance. I became detached and aloof and asked no one to dance with me. My father's anger increased, but he restrained himself because of the others at the table.

Long before the ball ended I walked out without saying goodbye and went home. When my father arrived, I pretended sleep. He grabbed my foot, shook me, and angrily asked for an explanation. I remained silent. He kept on shaking me, took my arm and dragged me upright. I pushed him and we almost exchanged blows. Then I dressed hurriedly and left, walking the streets until sunrise. I returned just as my father was leaving for work. We glared at one another in silence. For months I did not phone him. The ice between us was eventually broken when I went to Pretoria to show him a letter I had received from the immigration department, threatening prosecution because we had not notified them of our new address. We were asked to report at their office. That they had found my address was a worrying sign that I was not unknown to the police special branch.

Despite our estrangement, my father continued to pay my university fees in addition to sending the better part of his salary home to my mother. The fees were due at the beginning of the year, but we knew that we could wait until the end of August, when a registered letter of demand would arrive, calling for payment within seven days, failing which I would be barred from writing the final-year examination. When I graduated, I obtained two seats for the ceremony: one for my father and the other for Arethe, far apart from each other.

Graduation took place in the very hall where my stubbornness had so angered my father at the Hellenic ball. After my law degree was conferred three years later, I knew the time had come for Arethe and me to be formally engaged, with marriage following soon afterwards. I persuaded my father to come to the Daflos home for tea in preparation for the engagement party, but he was almost as sullen as I had been on the night of the ball. He came to neither the engagement party nor our wedding.

We continued at arms' length until he bought a second-hand Morris Minor for me after hearing that I was experiencing difficulty practising at the Bar without a vehicle. But it was only three years later that he softened towards Arethe and me. His change of heart was due to the birth of Kimon Anthony, his first grandson, and to the efforts of my late brother, Stavros, who had joined us from Greece.

CHAPTER 6

Student Days

There was not much excitement about the 1948 election on the Wits campus. It was widely assumed that the United Party, led by General Jan Smuts and his deputy Jan Hofmeyr, would be returned to power. While the general had acquired international status and had even played a role in the formulation and adoption of the United Nations Charter, Hofmeyr had been the principal of Wits and was said to be a liberal in favour of some form of qualified franchise for the African population.

During the pre-election period, Smuts busied himself with international and Commonwealth affairs and sojourned as guest of Queen Frederica of Greece. He left the election campaign to Hofmeyr, but his deputy's quiet academic style and the party's vague promises of reform were no match for the fiery nationalism of Malan, Strÿdom and Verwoerd, whose apartheid policies promised a white South Africa in which blacks would be kept in their proper – subservient – place.

The National Party's electoral victory, so unexpected and by so narrow a margin, led to vociferous political activity on the Wits campus. Among the student leaders in the National Union of South African Students (Nusas), the Student Representative Council and the cultural societies were men who had fought in the war and were highly politicised. Almost half the student body took part in a protest meeting on the steps of the Wits central block during which George Clayton and John Coaker, both of whom had fought in North Africa and Italy, addressed us. How could we accept being governed by people who had opposed and sabotaged the war effort against the fascists and the Nazis? Some of the Nats explained that their opposition to the war effort had been directed against British imperialism and to assert South Africa's independence, rather than support for the Axis powers. In addition, the Nats claimed to be democrats. Had they not won the election and come to power through the ballot box? In fact, fewer votes were cast for them in total than for the opposition. They had a majority of just four seats in Parliament and only a loaded rural white vote had helped them achieve even this slender margin. The vast majority of South Africans, of course, had no vote because they were black.

There were few Afrikaans-speaking students at Wits, and most English-speaking students supported General Smuts' United Party. Their leaders, Harry

Schwarz the most prominent among them, told us that South Africa's future lay in white unity. We were urged to rally behind them to ensure that the 1948 result was overturned at the next election in five years' time. The major policy difference between them was that the Nationalists would never allow black people meaningful participation in government, while the new official UP opposition reluctantly conceded that some form of qualified black franchise might have to be granted in the future based on educational qualifications and property ownership. However, after the 1948 election, a parliamentary debate clearly showed opposition thinking when Smuts stated: 'We have never been in favour of equal rights. We have always stood for social and residential separation in this country, and for the avoidance of racial mixture.' When it was suggested that he was moving nearer to apartheid, he replied, 'I do not see why the government should claim this, it has always been our policy.'

At Wits the small Labour Party and the even smaller Communist Party, liberals and religious groups, together with an ex-servicemen's organisation later to become known as the Springbok Legion, all advocated changes considered too radical by the vast majority of whites who supported the two main political parties. These small groups formed an amorphous body referred to as 'the Left'. I considered myself a part of it, though not a member of any particular group. Despite ideological differences among the groups, there was a consensus that student politics could not be divorced from what was happening in the country. Less than five per cent of the student body was black, but apartheid meant that even this small number should not be at the university and none should be admitted in future. Scholarships for African students to study medicine at Wits came to an end, while the acceptance of Fort Hare University College into Nusas led to the secession of Afrikaans universities from that student organisation.

Two student leaders in particular influenced the attitudes and values of many of us: Sydney Brenner, president of the Student Representative Council, a brilliant medical student who later became a distinguished molecular biologist and a Nobel laureate, and Phillip Tobias, president of Nusas, also a medical student who became a universally acknowledged professor of anatomy and human biology. More particularly, Tobias proved a worthy successor to Professor Raymond Dart, whose work he extended into the physical anthropology of the living peoples of Africa.

Brenner and Tobias condemned the government's policies, and criticised the principal of the university, Humphrey Raikes, as well as the council and senate for their failure to adopt a policy of non-discrimination against black students in all spheres of university life, including sport and other social activities. The authorities felt that we should confine ourselves to our studies, avoid controversy, and not advocate full equality on the campus. Above all, we should not protest. They feared our actions would lead the government to close the doors on black students. We did not heed their advice.

The government used the immigration laws, legislation restricting movement from one province to another and, finally, the euphemistically named Extension of University Education Act in 1959 to exclude blacks. But even then they did not succeed in excluding them all. The small number of African students at Wits included some who came from Basutoland (now Lesotho), Bechuanaland (Botswana) and Swaziland, then British protectorates. Even without official permission they had no difficulty entering and remaining in South Africa – a country where 'God Save the King' was still sung at the end of film shows, even though some bearded men and their wives would walk out in protest.

Neighbouring Mozambique was a Portuguese colony where Antonio Salazar's security police held sway. Eduardo Mondlane, a social science student at Wits on a scholarship from the Christian Council of Mozambique, spoke openly about the oppression of his people under Salazar. Soon after the Nationalists came to power, the Mozambican security police requested their ideological allies to expel Mondlane from South Africa. His permit to enter South Africa had been renewed regularly, until in mid-1949 he was given a week to get out. Hundreds of students attended a campus meeting in protest. Sydney Brenner outlined the facts, then Phillip Tobias argued that Mondlane's expulsion was part of the government's policy of excluding all black students, particularly those from the neighbouring territories. He called on every Nusas affiliate to support a campaign opposing the expulsion, a proposal almost unanimously approved.

Shortly afterwards, a security policeman approached Tobias and asked for a copy of the resolution. Tobias refused and reported the matter to the principal, who demanded to know of the chief of police what his agent was doing on the campus. Appeals to the government and the governor-general of Mozambique against Mondlane's expulsion fell on deaf ears, and so did other forms of student protest. After his expulsion from South Africa, Mondlane went on to become the leader of Frelimo, but he was murdered in a parcel bombing in Tanzania before his organisation liberated Mozambique. The University of Maputo is now named after him.

Mondlane's expulsion may have been relatively insignificant at the time, but it instilled a fear in me that I too would be deported if I supported radical causes. This fear remained for more than forty years. I was constantly anxious that if I spoke out or gave any sign of my views, it might provoke the authorities into deporting me. The intensity of this fear invariably increased whenever I was briefed to defend the 'enemies of the state', as the apartheid regime called many of my clients.

E M Forster's *Passage to India* was one of the set novels in my English literature course. The interracial relationships, the prejudices and political struggle described in the book attracted me to a meeting that dispelled any remaining ambivalence about whose side I was on and what career I should follow. Students of Indian origin were involved in celebrations following the recently granted independence of India. They had misgivings about the wisdom of dividing Hindus and Muslims, once united in the struggle against the British, into two separate states. The division was contrary to the wishes of Mahatma Gandhi, the Indian leader well known and revered in South Africa where he had spent some years and where his passive resistance campaigns had been intended to achieve the liberation of all black people.

The Transvaal Indian Congress called lunch-hour meetings addressed by Dr Yusuf Dadoo, Molvi Cachalia and others said to be related to Gandhi. They denounced the threats by Afrikaner nationalists against blacks in general and Indians in particular. Among these threats were remarks by a prominent cabinet minister, who had said that Indians did not belong in South Africa; that they should be deprived of their immovable property, and restricted in their business activities and job opportunities. And if they did not like this arrangement, they would be repatriated to India from where their grandfathers had come as indentured labourers to work on the sugar farms of Natal. Against such threats, speakers at the congress protest meetings called for action. They urged black unity and defiance of unjust laws and wanted newly independent India to initiate a campaign to isolate the apartheid regime, expel South Africa from the United Nations and other international organisations, boycott its products and impose sanctions.

It was at one of these meetings that Nelson Mandela was introduced as a part-time law student and a member of the African National Congress Youth League. He spoke to an audience of fewer than fifty, mostly Indian and African, and about a dozen whites. As I was to learn, the royal plural was his chosen form of address:

> Our chiefs and leaders ever since the arrival of the white man have fought wars to keep our land and protect our cattle. We have petitioned and sent delegations to colonial governors, to the kings and queens of England and their Parliament to protect us against the oppression of whites. The Union of South Africa was created against the wishes and the objections of our people

which led to the formation of our organisation the ANC in 1912. Ever since, our leaders have pleaded to prime ministers and governors-general, participated in advisory councils and boards in the hope of persuading the government to lessen the harshness of our oppression. We, in the ANC Youth League, are no longer prepared to knock on the door of the white man in the hope that he will open it for us. We will not put our hand out to ask for favours. We demand rights for all of us. No threat of imprisonment or other penalty will stop us. *Mayibuye iAfrika!*

There was no question time as Mandela had to rush off to work. But I overheard a student saying that Nelson Mandela was a staunch African nationalist, that he held a leading position in the Youth League and that he was a regular speaker in Sophiatown, Alexandra and Kliptown, as well as Lady Selborne in Pretoria. These places were among the few where Africans could own property and where political meetings could more easily be arranged. It was also said that he was suspicious of white communists and cautious of Indians, although he had come closer to them with India's independence.

There was a small but closely knit group of Greek students at Wits. Most of them were South African born but there were a number from Egypt who, had it not been for the war, would have gone to European universities. A few had come as refugees during the war, while others had come either from Greece or Cyprus at the end of hostilities. Arranging parties seemed to be their main objective and Arethe and I were invited to some of them. They also organised a float in the student Rag procession. The theme one year was 'Wishful Thinking'. As civil war was raging in Greece, I suggested that the theme of the float should be 'Peace in Greece'. This won support despite some reservations that it had political overtones and that we might be understood to support the anti-American contention that the civil war was being continued as part of the Cold War. Their fears proved unjustified. About thirty young women and men, some in ancient Greek dress, others in modern costume, danced to the music provided by the talented accordion player Michael Fasoulakis. The thousands lining the streets in the city centre heartily applauded us and threw coins and even pound notes into our float.

Aristidis Lagouros, a refugee who was with us on the *Ile de France*, was appointed lecturer in the classics department. He, like so many other Greek men of letters, did not accept that Greece made no contribution after the Roman occupation in the third century BC. He spoke to us about Byzantium; of the freedom songs and poetry from the centuries of Turkish occupation; of the Romantics – Byron, Shelley, Chateaubriand, Goethe and Schiller – and their contribution to the struggle for Greek freedom; and of the efforts by Greek poets and writers to gain acceptance of demotic Greek, of Solomos, Cavafy and Palamas in particular.

His fluent English, French and Italian enabled him to discuss comparative literature and a few of us tried to drum up interest among the Greek students, the classics department and the university administration to allow him to teach comparative literature as a recognised subject. Despite a little enthusiasm at first, the attempt was abandoned. However, he enhanced my knowledge and appreciation of modern Greek history and literature.

The Cold War replicated itself on the Wits campus, with ideological differences stretched from the far Right to the far Left – the latter being the most cohesive and well-organised section of students. During my first year of study the Students' Liberal Association (SLA) was formed on the initiative of Michael O'Dowd to resist the introduction of racial or political discrimination at the university. I attended its meetings and spoke in support of academic equality, political justice both on and off campus, and social and sporting equality within the ambit of the university. This commitment to equality by the SLA offended the government's policy as well as the policy of the university's council and its principal. There were also differences in the liberal Left coalition over such issues as students wearing their university blazers when participating in meetings and marches organised by black students in support of the proposed defiance campaign or in solidarity with students arrested on political grounds.

The greatest divide concerned Nusas. With the admission of Fort Hare, Natal and Rhodes universities threatened to secede from the organisation. However, they also questioned the introduction of quotas in admitting black students to universities, and, above all, the disaffiliation of Nusas from the International Union of Students, widely seen as a front organisation of the Comintern and manipulated by the Soviet Union.

Some powerful voices supported academic freedom, but did not insist on social and sporting integration as well. This group was even more cautious about the continued affiliation of Nusas to the International Union of Students. Included in this grouping were Michael O'Dowd and, to a lesser extent, Phillip Tobias. Vociferously supporting them were Patricia Arnett and John Didcott in Cape Town. Against them were Harold Wolpe, Lionel Forman, Godfrey Getz and David Holt. I associated myself with the latter at SLA meetings and in demonstrations together with black students.

In my second year Wolpe, who had replaced O'Dowd as SLA chairman, invited me to a caucus meeting of the liberal-left alliance. The intention was to choose candidates for election on a faculty basis to the Student Representative Council.

Wolpe had heard me speaking at SLA gatherings and once or twice in the Great Hall, and, as a result of the caucus meeting, I was given a slot on the ticket for which all progressive students would be asked to vote en bloc. The typical pattern was that less well-organised groups and individual candidates would split the vote among themselves and hardly ever be elected, while the liberal-left swept the board in all faculties except engineering. A further caucus meeting decided who would be put up as president and who as members of the executive. Some, particularly the medical students, preferred Godfrey Getz, also a medical student, as president. Matters were rarely put to the vote at caucus meetings, instead a consensus was reached. In the event, Wolpe became president, and, possibly as a trade-off, medical students filled important executive positions. At formal SRC meetings, our motions would invariably be carried by nineteen votes to three. By the same majority the other side lost whatever they proposed.

I was offered a position on the executive, but declined because of my work at the attorney's office. Instead I became a 'front-bencher', proposing and opposing motions as agreed upon at our group's caucus meetings. My election to the SRC made me bolder, even foolhardy. For instance, there was a heated debate in the Great Hall about the quota system which limited the number of black students to the medical faculty and excluded practically all black students from the dental faculty. During the debate, I proposed that an ultimatum be given to the university authorities: if they implemented the quota, we, the students, would go on strike. There was tumultuous applause for my proposal, but the matter was not put to the vote. The issue was, however, raised in Parliament. Prime Minister DF Malan told Parliament that he had information about troublesome leftist students but reassured the members that the level-headed majority would soon restore normality. Back in the Great Hall the next day I declared that if advocating equality for our black fellow students made me a leftist, I was proud to be one. My response to the prime minister was reported on the front page of *Die Transvaler* the next morning under the headline *Links-gesind en trots daarop* – Leftist and proud of it.

One of the elders of the Hellenic community approached my father and told him that I was bringing the community into disrepute. My father asked me for an explanation and nodded without any adverse comment when I gave it. Lionel Forman, editor of the student newspaper, gave me a lecture on strategy and tactics, saying that I should not have issued my ultimatum without consultation. My 'strike' proposal was quietly dropped and not raised again.

The electoral system served us well. I was elected for two further yearly terms and served until August 1953, the year I graduated from the law faculty. During my tenure, I was partly responsible for ending the system that favoured the candidates of the liberal-left.

The SLA had published a pamphlet too radical for some students and the university authorities. When the SRC failed to distance itself from the pamphlet, a meeting was called to pass a vote of no confidence. The SRC had also incurred some displeasure through its attempts to introduce sporting and social integration. In addition, the council and senate were worried about students involving themselves in radical political activities instead of being concerned with their studies. It was unacceptable to them that medical students, such as Harrison Nthatho Motlana, should have taken part in the Defiance Campaign; even more unacceptable that certain student organisations, funded by the SRC, should support students guilty of such unbecoming conduct.

The intervarsity rugby match between Pretoria and Wits was a festive event which we were expected to attend. Under the direction of a cheerleader we bellowed songs of support and praise for our team and applauded our cheerleader's jibes at our opponents. Then the SRC decreed that it would not tolerate the segregation of black students who were made to sit separately in the small stands on the south-western corners of Ellis Park and in separate stands in Pretoria.

When the SRC threatened that the event would not take place unless this practice was stopped, the Wits All Sports Council, consisting of the captains of the various sports, proposed the appointment of a committee to meet representatives of Tukkies. One of the three members of the Wits committee was Ismail Mahomed (later Chief Justice) who was on the executive as the minutes secretary. Pretoria refused to meet with the Wits committee if one of its members was a black student. They indicated that their decision might have been different if Mahomed represented only the black students. In accordance with apartheid policy, it was unacceptable for him to represent the general body of students, black as well as white. Together with a small bloc of their supporters on our campus they accused Wits of hypocrisy. Did the university intend having mixed teams, allowing blacks to use the swimming pool and permitting mixed couples to dance at our graduation ball? The majority on the SRC would have answered 'yes' to these questions, but we were ahead of most of our fellow students.

There had been an earlier motion of no confidence in the SRC moved by Michael O'Dowd because Harold Wolpe's executive acted contrary to the constitution. O'Dowd spoke to a largely hostile audience vociferously supportive of the SRC. The astute tactician on our side, Lionel Forman, then intervened. He accused O'Dowd of a lack of loyalty and said that a simple note or telephone call drawing Wolpe's attention to the provisions would have ended the matter. Calling for a motion of no confidence was inappropriate, Forman said, and the motion should be rejected. He called for closure. As if carefully orchestrated, a loud chorus of voices and enthusiastic applause led to the approval of Forman's proposal and a humiliating defeat for O'Dowd and his few supporters at the meeting.

Three years later, when Godfrey Getz was president, matters turned out differently. The hall was packed for the no-confidence debate, including a few rowdy engineering students and their bugler who interrupted proceedings. Applause for speakers in support of the motion appeared as enthusiastic as those opposing it. At the end more than a thousand hands were raised. The motion of no confidence was defeated by about thirty votes. Rhythmic hand-clapping and persistent shouts followed: 'Resign, resign, resign.'

On an impulse I rose and almost hit a high c: 'Fellow students, fellow students, fellow students …' The noise died down. I said that as a member of the SRC I did not want to continue unless we enjoyed the confidence of a substantial majority, and that this could only be determined by holding a referendum. The chairman put the matter to the vote, and it was carried. Many were critical of my initiative, which I tried to defend at the next caucus meeting. The importance of consultation was emphasised to me yet again, but in the end we all agreed to work hard to win the referendum.

Despite our efforts, it was not to be. There was a low turnout and we lost by a few hundred votes. A new election was held in May 1953. Godfrey Getz's SRC, in whom the majority apparently had no confidence, was re-elected almost to a man. Included in the new SRC was a woman, Irma Lief, and two black men, including Mahomed. When complaints were raised against the electoral system a commission was set up, which, as the senior law faculty representative, I chaired. The commission found that some of the criticisms against the electoral system were valid. As a result, Wits changed to a system of proportional representation and the influence of the organised liberal-left was greatly diminished.

Some of us brought our political activism into the lecture room, particularly in constitutional law. For ideological reasons and a desire to increase their slender majority in the 1953 election, the Nationalists enacted the Separate Representation of Voters Act to remove coloured people from the common voters' roll. The Nats claimed that Parliament had unfettered powers in such a matter, relying heavily for authority on the Appellate Division's 1937 *Ndlwana* case, which, ironically, pronounced that 'freedom once conferred can never be revoked'. Ellison Kahn, our professor of constitutional law, believed that Parliament had the power to deprive the coloured people of their vote with a mere simple majority. Some of us seized on a contrary article by Professor DV Cowen that argued against this notion. As first-year students we could hardly advance cogent arguments to show that the Appellate Division was wrong, but we were anxious to express our anger and felt superior when the minister of the interior lost the first round in the Appellate Division. This decision led to the packing of the Appellate Division and the subsequent validation of the legislation, with only Judge Oliver Schreiner dissenting.

There were fewer than a hundred students in the law faculty in 1951 when I began my legal studies. Despite the small numbers, the quarrel between the SRC and the university authorities relating to racial equality in all aspects of student life raged furiously within the faculty. For instance, at the annual law dinner the eight black students were not allowed to attend on the grounds that it was to be held at the Ambassador Hotel in Hillbrow. This injunction came from the dean, Professor H R 'Bobby' Hahlo. The hotel was licensed to sell intoxicating liquor and the law prohibited blacks from entering such establishments as guests. The eight wanted to come if for no other reason than to test the will of those in authority.

The SRC contributed £100 to subsidise the dinner for the non-paying guests, who included judges, the attorney-general and academic staff. During Sydney Brenner's presidency of the SRC, the use of student money for the entertainment of law students had been questioned. The faculty representative on the SRC eloquently explained that attending the dinner was part of a tradition inherited from England, and was necessary to expose students to the judges, the attorney-general and the leaders of the legal profession. This was seen as an essential part of their training for a successful career at the Bar.

Against this background, the opportunity to expose the contradiction and hypocrisy of the faculty was too good to be missed. I asked Harry Nestadt, assistant secretary of the Law Students' Council, to give the dean a message: if the black students could not attend or if any pressure were placed upon them to withdraw, I would move for the deletion of the £100 appropriation from the SRC's budget.

The following afternoon at the end of Professor Hahlo's lecture, mispronouncing my name and speaking in the third person, he called me to his office. He came directly to the point. Nestadt had conveyed my message. He had nothing against black students, but the law of the land prohibited them from coming to the dinner. Did my friends and I realise that they would be breaking the law in the presence of judges, the attorney-general and the leaders of the profession? What if the police intervened? He reminded me that I was a law student and that my first loyalty was to the faculty and – with some emphasis in his voice – to the brotherhood of the law. My duty was not only to vote for the item on the SRC agenda, but also to persuade my friends to do the same. I told him that I could not and would not do as he wished. He appealed to me to absent myself from the meeting, quietly withdraw from the situation and allow the elected law faculty representative to deal with the matter. When I refused he dismissed me from his office.

On the evening of the dinner, all the black students were present on the understanding that they would not 'partake of intoxicating liquor'. This did not prevent some of us from surreptitiously lacing their soft drinks. Acting Judge President of the Transvaal W H Ramsbottom, an acknowledged liberal, was far from embarrassed by their presence. He made a point of speaking to each of the black students, making it clear by his characteristic smile that he was pleased to see them there. Never once, for the next two and a half years, did Hahlo acknowledge my existence, either in the law library or the corridors. However, he behaved professionally towards me in the lecture room. Later he left Wits for Canada, saying that he was opposed to apartheid.

During his tenure at Wits, Hahlo refused to allow Nelson Mandela to write a supplementary examination to complete his LLB degree, despite a poignant written request by Mandela who had his sights on becoming the first black advocate at the Johannesburg Bar. Hahlo turned down his request and recommended that he drop his idea of becoming an advocate and became an attorney instead. Hahlo's refusal forced Mandela to do just that and he had to be satisfied with a diploma in law, entitling him merely to admission as an attorney. Ironically, during his imprisonment, Mandela was eventually able to complete his LLB.

While writing the history of Wits, Professor Bruce Murray unearthed the original letter written to Hahlo by Mandela, and sent a copy of it to Mandela in prison for his comment. When he received no reply, Murray, fearing that the letter had been withheld by the jailers, asked me to enquire whether Mandela had received it. Yes, said Mandela, he had, but as Wits was doing a good job he felt it would not be helpful to revive the matter by commenting on it, and asked me to explain and apologise to Professor Murray.

The SRC constitution stipulated that elections were to be held in every faculty in the same prescribed manner, but the law faculty did things differently. Candidates would be proposed and seconded as usual, but no ballot would be held. Instead a meeting of the faculty, under the chairmanship of the head of the Law Students' Council, gave each candidate an opportunity to make a short statement. They would then be questioned.

Two of us were nominated and during question time I was asked about my lack of commitment to the faculty's tradition of not being involved in wider political issues. Was I for or against the university authorities' view which favoured maintaining that tradition? Some questioners alluded to the law dinner incident.

Despite the practice that there would be no canvassing, it was clear that some were determined to keep me out. At the end of the debate a tall first-year student made the shortest and most effective speech of the meeting, and one which swung the vote in my favour. He said, 'Mr Chairman, we have for too long spoken about the university's tradition. The correct question to ask ourselves before we vote is surely: What is right and what is wrong?' I won by a narrow margin. When I asked who the last speaker was, I learned that he was Arthur Chaskalson, then one of the top first-year students.

In my third year and while employed by Ruben Kahanovitz, I discovered that in order to be registered as an articled clerk I had to be a South African citizen. My permanent residence status was less than five years old and my period of stay on a refugee permit did not count. I was simply not eligible. Although I continued to work as an attorney's clerk, I had no option but to go to the Bar for which there was no similar citizenship requirement.

Lectures in the law faculty started in the late afternoon and finished in the early evening. Most, if not all of us, had jobs. We would have a quick supper and return to the law library for the required reading. One evening, as I pushed open the door of the seminar room adjoining the library, I saw a fellow student, Duma Nokwe, hurriedly hiding a packet of fish and chips. He stopped when he saw it was me. I then realised that although black students could have lunch in the university cafeteria there was nowhere for them to have an evening meal anywhere near the university. We then arranged that he would come up to my room and we would order food from the Cypriot owner of Phineas Café, named after Phinny, the university's mascot. Over these meals, Nokwe told me about his family and his membership of the Youth League and participation in the Defiance Campaign. I learned that he and his wife were teachers, that they had been dismissed by the Bantu education department for taking part in politics. He was now a clerk to Harry Bloom. I also discovered that each evening he had to leave the library early to catch the nine o'clock train back to New Canada and then walk to his home in Orlando West.

We became close friends, and later unlawfully shared chambers in His Majesty's Building. Under apartheid legislation, Nokwe was not allowed to have chambers in a white area.

I continued as a member of the SRC when Getz was elected president. Again I had to refuse an executive post because of my job and the pressure of studying. Those of us close to Getz knew him as an ardent liberal, fully committed to student equality and bringing about a just and egalitarian society in South Africa. He annoyed Harold Wolpe and Lionel Forman with his criticism of the Soviet Union, particularly the excesses of Stalinism gradually being revealed. Nevertheless, as far as Humphrey Raikes was concerned, they were all communists. Chairman of the university council, PM Anderson, and the professor of social psychology, ID MacCrone, shared Raikes' view. They probably put me in the same category because I regularly moved motions supporting these 'communists' in the SRC and in general student meetings. MacCrone was considered a leading liberal, but according to Professor Murray's history, MacCrone wrote at the time:

> Nothing would please these people more than to expose what they consider the hypocrisy and pretension of a so-called liberal university and by so doing bring liberalism and its works into disrepute among the non-European intellectuals while at the same time enhancing the appeal of communism.

The Nationalists did not lose the 1953 election as many had predicted. The formation of the Liberal Party, the regrouping of the underground South African Communist Party, the launching of the Congress of Democrats (declared unlawful because it was thought to be an SACP front) and the defiance of unjust laws by the ANC all exacerbated the tensions within the student body. We missed the wisdom and tact of Phillip Tobias. Patricia Arnett, John Didcott, Michael O'Dowd and others from Pietermaritzburg, Durban, Rhodes and Cape Town were intent on putting an end to the hegemony of the Left in student politics. The affiliation of Nusas to the International Union of Students became a controversial issue during the organisation's congress scheduled for July 1953.

Almost invariably the president of the SRC would lead the delegation to the Nusas conference. Godfrey Getz was unable to attend and asked me to take his position, arguing that he would persuade the other members to accept my leadership. Even though I was not a member of the executive, I was among the most senior members of the SRC and was aware of the issues that would be raised. I had been granted a month's study leave for the final-year examinations. As I hoped these would be my last exams, I did not want to use my leave for any purpose other than revision. Nevertheless, I agreed to his request, and not only for political reasons.

It had been more than twelve years since I'd had a holiday and I yearned for the sea. I wanted to watch the waves breaking on long sandy beaches, remembering the coves where I'd swum in the calm waters of the Ionian Sea. I wanted to smell and taste water that was salty instead of chlorinated like that in the public swimming pools of Johannesburg.

The companionship of a group of like-minded students and their gentle and ironic respect towards me in the dining room and corridors of the train lightened the journey to Cape Town. Again I realised how vast and varied was my adopted country. Unfortunately when we arrived at Cape Town the clouds were dark and heavy, the visibility poor and a light drizzle prevented us from seeing the beauty of the fairest Cape. But there were brighter days to come.

It was the winter vacation and the students had gone home. We were accommodated in residences that had been hurriedly constructed to cater for the greater inflow of students after the war. These places had high-sounding official names but the students irreverently renamed them after Nazi concentration camps. I was warned that it would be cold but when I tried to buy a coat on credit before leaving Johannesburg, I was rejected. A couple of the African students from Lesotho wore colourful, neatly folded blankets over their shoulders, even to the student assembly. I caused a bit of a stir by following their example with a blanket borrowed from the bed.

I had not been to a congress before, and no one warned me that, as leader of the delegation, I would have to make a speech at the opening ceremony. Fortunately the universities were called upon in alphabetical order and when they reached Wits, more than half a dozen opening speeches had already been made. By then I had the drift of what needed to be said, and managed well enough, consistent with my habit of not speaking from notes even when I've prepared them.

Notice had been given that Nusas should disaffiliate from the international organisation. Those behind the motion had secured mandates from most of the affiliated SRCs and had more than enough votes to ensure success. The debate was both lengthy and heated. It was contended that the international organisation was an instrument of the Soviet Union and the Comintern, its congresses were used as platforms to extol the so-called socialism of the Soviet Union and to condemn the governments and people of the 'free world', and that its claim to represent a large student body was dependent on compulsory membership, not only for students at the tertiary level but also for pupils at secondary schools in the Soviet Union and its satellites. We were urged to vote for disaffiliation and told it would be preferable to join a democratic organisation, such as the International Student Conference.

In opposing the motion, it was difficult for me to defend some of the positions taken by the International Union of Students. Instead I attacked the motives of those who had already disaffiliated. I said that we should not help those who wanted to divide the world between East and West, capitalist and socialist, rich and poor; that we should remain non-aligned and that the International Student Conference was a creation of the Central Intelligence Agency of the United States. At the time, there was no hard evidence to support this but some twenty-five years later John Didcott, by then a judge, told me that among the CIA secrets exposed in *Time* magazine was the agency's formation and financing of the International Student Conference. He added that the American 'student leader' who had led him and a few others from South Africa on a tour of South East Asia now had a senior post in the Pentagon. Didcott was looking forward to similar disclosures from Moscow or Prague so that we could both admit that we had been manipulated.

So many votes were already committed to ensuring that Nusas left the International Union of Students that my intervention represented only a brave rearguard action by the Wits SRC. After this initial excitement, the 1953 congress trickled along uneventfully. As head of the Wits delegation, I proposed a number of resolutions already passed by our SRC for adoption by congress. They were agreed to without much meaningful debate or opposition and the chairperson more than once signalled to me to cut it short.

Cultural and social events and organised trips were scheduled to take place on what turned out to be a clear and warm day. I asked one of the organisers if there would be a trip along the coast and I told her what an important part the sea had played in my early life. I thought of it, dreamed of it and, having come so near to the coast, I wanted to walk barefoot on a beach, put my feet into the sea, however cold the waters, and let my eyes feast on it, all the way to the horizon. She had heard about my background and understood my need. More importantly, she had the use of her boyfriend's MG convertible and we drove to Cape Point along the seashore and came back on the road behind the mountain. Our conversation was limited to the names of the places we passed, and brief remarks about their historical significance. I silently compared and contrasted the size of the waves, the length of the beaches, the harbours, particularly the one where ships of the British navy were anchored, and, out at sea, the ships rounding Cape Point. I wondered if I might have been a junior officer on one of them. Had it not been for the war I might have pursued my ambition to become a ship's captain.

This was my last year as a student, and the congress the last event in my career of student politics. Unexpectedly, it ended at what was literally a high point, with a prank devised by a group on the train home. For some time they had been drinking beer and singing loudly, and when the train stopped for a while at de Aar, they woke the four of us in my compartment and we were ordered to join them. The carousers would not take no for an answer, dragged me from the bed in my pyjamas, pulled me out of the train and pushed me up the ladder onto its roof. Then they removed the ladder. I was accused of taking myself too seriously, and told I would only be let down if I made a speech so loudly that the residents of the sleeping dorp switched on their lights, thus proving that they had heard me. My captors vowed to applaud only if I said something amusing. I obliged as best I could.

Soon the driver, the stoker and the conductor joined us on the platform faintly amused, but did not interfere. Not so the infuriated Patricia Arnett. She ran towards us and in as loud a voice as I had used from the train roof, scolded me, 'Are you not ashamed of yourself? Is this the way for a leader of a delegation to behave? Do you not realise that what you have done could get into the newspapers as evidence of the irresponsibility of students in Nusas?' Pulling her flimsy dressing gown closed, she ordered me to get down. One of the jolly revellers suggested that they should put her onto the roof as well. She pointed her finger at them, shouting repeatedly, 'Don't you dare!' But she had made her point, and as she turned her back, they pushed the ladder against the train for me to climb down.

Part Two: 1953–1961

CHAPTER 7

Early Years at the Bar

As Ruben Kahanovitz's firm briefed Joe Slovo to do the occasional case, I discussed my forthcoming admission to the Bar with him. Joe felt that there were precedents for my particular predicament as he had been admitted without South African citizenship. Slovo, born in Lithuania, a country annexed by the Soviet Union, was stateless. We agreed, however, that whether a Greek national could take an oath of allegiance to the queen was an open question. He agreed to move my application for admission but cautioned that it might not sound convincing to two Waspish judges if a Lithuanian Jew – and a communist at that – argued that a Greek could take an oath to the queen. Instead he approached one of the top men at the Bar, the appropriately named Rex Welsh, to intercede on my behalf.

It was a worrying time. Rex assured me that there would be no difficulty unless we struck a judge more royalist in outlook than the queen herself. He prepared the argument, but the case he was doing lasted longer than anticipated and, in the end, he could not move my application. My papers went to an equally prominent member of the Bar, HC Nicholas. He correctly predicted that we would have no difficulty when he heard that judges Lucas Steyn and Frans Rumpff would be on the bench. They were both Afrikaner nationalists who probably believed that anybody could take an oath of allegiance to the queen – after all, they had done so themselves.

Barely a week after my admission I was in Motion Court with half a dozen briefs from Ruben Kahanovitz and his correspondents. Fred Zwarenstein, who would become a good friend, wondered how I got so much work and warned against my appearing too confident so early in my career. Nevertheless, he recommended to Ruth First, editor of the left-wing weekly newspaper called variously *The Guardian* or *New Age*, that I be asked to defend Eli Weinberg, who had been charged with contravening a banning order that prohibited him from attending gatherings. He allegedly attended an ANC protest meeting on Freedom Square in Sophiatown. At the time, Freedom Square was the hub of African political and cultural activities until its residents were forcibly removed a few years later and the area was resettled by whites.

Weinberg, once a leading trade unionist, realised after the passing of the Suppression of Communism Act in 1950 that he would inevitably be banned from taking part in trade union activities. In anticipation he upgraded his hobby of photography into a professional activity. Ruth had asked him to photograph the meeting, which he had done from the roof of a shack. At the consultation over his defence, I thought there was an argument that he had not 'attended' the meeting. But what if the security police claimed they had seen him in the crowd? Was I, the most junior member of the Bar, the best person to challenge their version? Vernon Berrangé, on the other hand, was considered the best cross-examiner at the Bar, particularly of policemen who had come to consider him their nemesis. I had seen and admired him in action but I hardly knew him. As both Weinberg and Ruth had been his comrades in the Communist Party before it was banned, Ruth undertook to approach Berrangé through her husband, Joe Slovo, with the request that he lead me in the case.

I consulted the dictionaries, the South African and English cases defining the various meanings of the word 'attend', as well as the cases arguing that, in favour of liberty, a statute should be restrictively interpreted. I handed the memorandum to Berrangé. He read it without comment to the last sentence in which I submitted that 'Mr Weinberg not only did not attend the gathering but he was conspicuously absent from it'. Berrangé nodded, said that he liked the turn of phrase and thought that we had a reasonable prospect of succeeding. However, we would have to prepare for cross-examination of the police witnesses who were likely to say that they had seen him in the crowd. My task was to take a careful statement from Weinberg. This was not confined to what he would say in the witness box, but included detail that would enable Berrangé to cross-examine the policemen about Weinberg's movements from the time of his arrival, including how he climbed onto the roof and precisely where on the roof he was when he took the photographs. We also needed the negatives to show the order in which the photographs were taken, and to ensure that none was taken from any place other than the roof. Weinberg was to identify the people on the platform and the order in which they spoke.

The purpose was to show the unreliability of any police witness who might claim that Weinberg was in the crowd, by demonstrating that he was on the roof throughout the meeting and that none of the photographs was taken from ground level. Berrangé's advice regarding how the statement should be taken and the further detail he extracted from Weinberg at the consultation (which lasted more than two hours) was the most useful tutorial I ever had on preparing for trial. It served me well throughout my practice at the Bar and was particularly helpful on how to use photographs and, later, television and video to discredit witnesses.

Our expectations that the police would lie proved incorrect. Their evidence placed Weinberg on the roof taking photographs and the prosecutor argued that this constituted a contravention. We submitted that he should be acquitted on the grounds set out in my memorandum. The magistrate agreed, found the accused not guilty and discharged him. My senior put his arm over my shoulder and thanked me for my contribution. I had learned much. If I had a regret it was being deprived of listening to his cross-examination. As it turned out I did not have to wait long to witness the man in action.

Berrangé became one of my mentors and had me briefed as his junior in a number of cases. In these matters I earned many times more than my daily fee when acting for the disadvantaged and the poor for whom there was no legal aid at the time. We did not charge a fee in short political cases such as Weinberg's, whose trial was among the first relating to a breach of a banning order. It attracted a fair amount of publicity and my reported association with Berrangé, coupled with my activism while at Wits, influenced the nature of my practice from the start.

For the first two years I did better than expected through criminal and civil cases in and around Johannesburg, charging the minimum fee prescribed by the Bar Council. I also appeared for African clients, briefed mainly by Nelson Mandela, Oliver Tambo and Shulamith Muller. My earnings, supplemented by Arethe's salary from an art studio, enabled us to move from our bachelor's apartment in the centre of the city to a three-roomed apartment in Emmarentia near the lake.

Until the mid-1950s, the 'pass' – that symbol of oppression – had, by law, to be carried by African men only. Attempts to introduce the pass for women years before had met with strong protest and failed. Then in 1953, the minister of native affairs, Hendrik Verwoerd, passed the euphemistically named Natives (Abolition of Passes and Co-Ordination of Documents) Act. Opposition groups and the press warned that the new law could be applied to women, forcing them to carry the hated document. It was not for nothing that Verwoerd, destined to become prime minister, earned the unofficial title 'architect of apartheid'. Angered by the criticism, he responded that agitators should not mislead the ignorant as there was no intention of extending 'passes' to women.

Despite his assurance, within three years the regime reneged. Those responsible for implementing the new policy thought it best to start in the apparently tranquil 'native reserves' and not the urban areas where the Defiance Campaign had shown that the ANC could quickly organise the masses. In the 'reserves' they anticipated the chiefs and tribal authorities would persuade the women to comply.

Implementation started in the Western Transvaal on the advice of ethnologists and commissioners that Setswana-speaking women were the most docile in the land. It was a serious miscalculation. These women had too often been deprived of the support and companionship of their husbands, fathers and brothers to acquiesce meekly. And then, to make matters worse, the regime's trigger-happy policemen galvanised opposition to the new policy when they baton-charged and fired on an anti-pass protest march in Lichtenburg in January 1956. Four men died and a number of men and women were injured.

During these troubles, Ruth First set me on a path that was to change both my practice and the pattern of my family life. She had been to Lichtenburg to investigate the incident and was convinced that the police action was cold-blooded murder. Claims that the police were in danger from stone-throwers she believed were false. Similarly, that the arrest of the men for public violence was a trumped-up charge. She wanted to speak to those detained, including the leader of the ANC in Lichtenburg, to confirm the story that she intended to publish in her paper the following week. She wanted Shulamith Muller to issue a brief for me to consult with the arrested men and apply for bail. Could we go the next morning, a Saturday?

We set off early through the mining towns of the West Rand and eventually turned onto a dusty road that for the next two hundred kilometres passed vast fields of maize and sunflowers, and large numbers of cattle grazing on the road verges. Invariably they were herded by poorly clad and barefoot men with wrinkled faces, some accompanied by fleet-footed boys who chased the cows out of the way. Ruth regularly had to slow down, swerving to avoid the cattle and, once or twice, guineafowl marching hurriedly across our path.

Judging by the steeples of its churches, the gardens of its well-built houses, the double-storey buildings with shops on the ground level and apartments on the first floor, the showrooms filled with Chryslers and Buicks, light and heavy lorries, tractors and harvesters, Lichtenburg was a town that catered for the needs of a rich white community.

As I did not know the names of most of my clients I had some difficulty getting access to them. There was no room big enough for a consultation so they were brought to the yard at the back of the police station. Ruth and I waited within the high walls of the bare parking place. The first man to come out of the holding cells greeted Ruth and introduced himself as Solomon Moseshe. Seventeen others followed, each introducing himself by his first name.

The two policemen accompanying them became quite hostile when I insisted that they move some distance away. The rule that, while they could be within sight, they should be out of hearing when a lawyer consulted with his clients was new to them. They watched us carefully from their vantage point.

My clients protested their innocence of any stone throwing or other act of public violence. They could not deny that some stones may have been thrown after the shooting when the crowd became angry. Moseshe said he had tried to stop the stone-throwing and get the crowd to disperse quietly to avoid any further loss of life or injuries. At the end of our meeting, I promised to be back on the remand date to apply for bail.

I left an almost full packet of fifty cigarettes as a parting gift. On my return, my clients told me that the packet had been confiscated. Some time later, Chris Plewman, honorary secretary of the Bar Council and later an Appeal Court judge, accosted me at lunch in the Bar common room. Trying his best to be serious, he told me and the others at the table that he had received a letter from the attorney-general stating that I was guilty of contravening a section of the Prisons Act promulgated more than fifty years previously. This prohibited the introduction into a prison of drugs, dagga or tobacco. I had breached the law by handing a packet of cigarettes to a group of prisoners. The attorney-general had decided not to prosecute but asked that the council inform all members that a more serious view would be taken if the offence were repeated. Everyone laughed, except me. I asked if the Bar Council wanted an explanation. Plewman countered that everyone on the council had burst out laughing at the letter. After this, I continued offering cigarettes to my clients until I stopped smoking about ten years later, but I avoided leaving packets behind without the consent of my clients' jailers.

During the preparatory examination, more than a dozen policemen gave evidence before the only magistrate in Lichtenburg. One after the other they described in Afrikaans and in almost identical terms how they had been attacked by a murderous crowd and in defence were compelled to open fire, causing the deaths and injuries. The cross-examination revealed that none of the policemen had been injured before the order to shoot was given by their captain. Had the captain threatened the crowd with violence? Each policeman indignantly denied that there was such a threat. The captain entered the witness box as a tail-ender. According to the provisions of the Riotous Assemblies Act, an order to disperse had to be given loudly and clearly in a language understood by the people in the crowd, warning them to move off within a given time or violence would be used to force them to move. The captain confidently asserted that this was precisely what he had done. Why then had so many of his men not heard his order? Nor did he mention that an interpreter repeated his order in Setswana, the language of the people in the gathering.

Then came a surprise witness – the elderly Afrikaner owner and driver of the dilapidated bus which ferried the people to and from the township. He confirmed the identity of a number of people in the dock, particularly Accused No 1. He knew him well and, immediately before the attack on the police, heard him shout, 'A re ye, a re ye, re ilo lolaya mapolesa' – 'Come, come, let's go and kill the police.' The witness said he knew Setswana as well as his own language.

The committal of the accused appeared to be inevitable so they reserved their defence, which would then be presented at the trial. The attorney-general decided not to indict them before a judge but remitted the matter to a magistrate for trial. Once their case began, the accused had the right to recall all the witnesses for further cross-examination and give evidence themselves.

When the trial started a few months later, it soon appeared that neither the investigating officer nor the prosecutor had given their witnesses a copy of the evidence from the preparatory examination. One after the other they contradicted not only what they had said but what others had said. Nor could they explain the contradictions. By the time they realised what was happening, it was too late. Worse was to come to subvert the Crown's case.

During the preparation of the defence case, Moseshe insisted that he and his co-accused knew the bus owner well. They were sure that he did not speak Setswana. He had never greeted them, never cajoled them, never made a joke or said anything to them except in Afrikaans. This was unlike other white people who spoke their language and wanted to show off. I asked for a book in Setswana and was brought a badly produced booklet of words and phrases with the verbs in the imperative mood to help the baas and missus give orders to their servants. As this was too elementary a text, I acquired a Bible in Tswana.

During cross-examination, I reminded the bus owner of his claimed proficiency in Setswana and, opening the Holy Book at random, placed it before him, and asked him to read. Without even glancing at the text, he said that while he spoke the language he could not read it. The interpreter was then asked to read a verse. The witness had no idea what it was about. The interpreter also read out two sentences each written on a separate piece of paper:

> A re ye, a re ye, mapolesa a tlilo re bolaya. (Come, come, the police are going to kill us.)
> A re ye, a re ye, re ilo lolaya mapolesa. (Come, come, let's go and kill the police.)

The bus owner was asked what each meant and confidently replied that they meant the same thing. When I told him of the fundamental difference between the two sentences, he replied, how could he possibly have known?

The accused's evidence was also unsatisfactory, mainly because they tried to minimise the anger of the crowd and the violent actions of some people. They also lost credibility by claiming that the police wantonly attacked a young woman, yet she never came forward to give evidence. In his judgment, the magistrate said the evidence of the police had been contradictory, improbable and unreliable. Despite the unsatisfactory features in the defence evidence, he found the accused not guilty and discharged them.

At the time and for many years yet, it was and would be unusual for magistrates to disbelieve policemen. When the judgment came to the notice of George Oliver, the *Rand Daily Mail*'s senior court reporter, he wrote a long piece on the trial, its unusual length and the significance of the court's finding. After the publication of Oliver's story, Berrangé, who was busy cross-examining witnesses at the preparatory examination that led to the treason trial, congratulated me on my success, as did Bram Fischer and other senior members of the Bar. One of my contemporaries, Ivan Stoller, said that if I wasn't careful, I would become known as the 'poor man's Berrangé'.

During the Lichtenburg trial, as with similar cases held in many other rural towns, it became obvious that counsel, particularly from Johannesburg, were not welcome. We were singled out for parking offences, for making u-turns or for the mud on our number plates. No local lawyer bothered to greet me. A doctor, who graduated from Wits the same year I did, criticised me for spoiling his practice with my probing questions. In court I had wanted to know why he refused to see female patients if they did not carry a pass. The local police charged me for not parking dead centre of the allocated space. Fortunately the magistrate had the charge withdrawn, presumably because he realised it was vindictive.

The magistrate also expected police officers to behave properly. Once, during the short adjournment, I had left my brief open on counsel's table. On my return I saw the sergeant I was cross-examining going through my papers. When he was back in the witness box, I asked if he had read my papers. He readily admitted that he had, adding that he had never seen a counsel's brief before and was paging through it out of curiosity. Although I thought that would be the end of the matter, I was invited subsequently to give evidence at an inquiry into the policeman's conduct. Obviously, the magistrate was concerned about the behaviour in his court, even during adjournments. As the policeman had already admitted the facts, I replied that I accepted his explanation. Nevertheless, the policeman was cautioned.

Not long after the Lichtenburg acquittal Shulamith Muller briefed me on a case to be heard in Zeerust. Government attempts to issue passes to women had led to a tribal revolt after the chief was deposed. A preparatory examination was to be held against twenty-two men and three women. These people, together with many others, had returned home from Johannesburg where they worked to deal with the situation. Four government collaborators were thought to be responsible for the unrest that had led the chief to flee into neighbouring Bechuanaland. The tribe, now without a leader, was called together by the people from Johannesburg, a court was constituted and the four traitors sentenced to death. A large police contingent arrived in time to save the four from being thrown into a deep hole on a nearby hill. This was how witches were dealt with in days gone by. Shulamith anticipated that the charges would be attempted murder, public violence and the burning of passes. She had already defended a number of women in Zeerust on charges of burning passes, and had found the police, the prosecutor and the native commissioner particularly hostile. Their attitude arose because most of her clients were acquitted, often because witnesses were reluctant to give evidence against their own people.

Shulamith spoke highly of the local Anglican priest, through whom she communicated with her clients. He had intervened on their behalf to secure the release of feeding mothers among the groups summarily charged and tried before she could get there to defend them. There was no local attorney who could act on her behalf. In any event, there would not have been enough money to pay him, just as there was not enough money for her to accompany me as instructing attorney. I expected to be away for a week at a time and promised to report to her on my return home at the weekends. Neither of us knew how long the trial would last.

Arethe and I were expecting the birth of our first child within a couple of months and I was much concerned about being away from home. My absence must also have affected Arethe, but neither of us said anything about it. After she had given up her job, Arethe occasionally accompanied me to these trials. She would sit at the back of the court with her drawing pad and sketch court scenes in charcoal. But going to Zeerust in her condition was out of the question.

I set off before dawn to ensure that I would have time to meet my clients, speak to the prosecutor and introduce myself to the magistrate before the case started. When I arrived the entrance to the court, the front door reserved for 'Europeans', the gate leading to the police parking ground and the back entrance to the court for 'Natives', were closed. Hundreds of men and women stood on the pavements of the narrow side street, their numbers growing by the minute. The street was lined with police vehicles. I slowly rolled downhill in my Morris Minor until I'd put some distance between my car and the last police vehicle before I parked. It meant walking back to court carrying a briefcase heavy with two volumes of

Gardiner and Lansdown's *South African Criminal Law and Procedure*, just in case they were needed.

From out of the crowd, Peter Magubane, then an up-and-coming photographer on *Drum* magazine, turned his concealed camera in an oil-smudged brown bag towards me. His wide-eyed expression signalled that I should not recognise him. Simultaneously, a well-built man emerged from the milling crowd, effusively greeted me by name, grabbed my bag, welcomed me, and congratulated me on my success in Lichtenburg. He was a Moiloa of the royal house of the Bafurutse. He no longer lived among them, having left during the war to join the army, serving in North Africa and Italy. This explained the unfamiliar singsong tone of his English.

While waiting with him, I noticed that the sturdy court building had been erected in 1912 and officially opened by Barry Hertzog, the minister of justice in the Union of South Africa. In the post-Boer War years he was the progenitor of Afrikaner nationalism against the policies of Louis Botha and Jan Smuts, his one-time fellow generals. Now an African man in an almost threadbare suit came from the side of the building onto the well-trimmed lawn with a neatly folded South African flag. He reverently unfolded it, tied it to the rope and slowly and deliberately hoisted it to the top of the flagpole. If this was intended to be a ceremony, the crowd paid no attention. The man went back the way he had come and a few minutes later opened the front door. He was the interpreter-clerk, and we often exchanged pleasantries during the course of the hearing. Later in the trial, I noticed he was no longer raising the flag. The lieutenant from Rustenburg in charge of the case had complained to the magistrate that hoisting the flag should be done by a white man. His clerk's faint, bemused smile indicated that he was not sorry he had been deprived of the honour.

There was another plaque in the courtyard between the façade and the row of offices overlooking the street and the courtroom. It recorded that the paving stones were taken from the laager of Kasper Coetzee, the Voortrekker who had founded Zeerust. What it did not record was how Coetzee and his men had conquered the indigenous people and pushed them off most of their land.

The courtroom was impressive: the bench, the lawyer's table, the original witness box, the doors and windows were built from heavy and well-seasoned wood. A second, makeshift witness box had been provided for 'non-European witnesses'. The dock, built for no more than five or six people, was pushed aside and three rows of benches had been placed in the well of the court for the twenty-five accused. The public area was segregated with separate doors: there was room for sixty white people but fewer than thirty black observers. Moiloa walked briskly over to say that the police would not allow the accuseds' relatives and friends into court. The 'non-European' section was being filled by those caught committing petty offences over the weekend.

I approached the prosecutor, a retired policeman, and requested that at least some of the relatives be admitted. There was no room, he said. What about the completely empty benches reserved for whites? No, he could not and would not allow black people to sit there.

My clients were brought into court, each wearing a large number on a piece of cardboard around their necks. The magistrate was called in, an older, placid Afrikaner, no doubt looking forward to his retirement and not accustomed to controversy. I immediately drew attention to the absence of the relatives of the accused and asked that proper arrangements be made to accommodate them. Remove those to be charged later with petty offences, and allow the relatives of my clients to sit in the section reserved for whites, I suggested. The prosecutor protested, emphatically repeating, 'The laws of apartheid must be obeyed.' Nevertheless, the magistrate ordered the petty offenders removed, although he did nothing about using the white section for the relatives.

Two people who did sit in the white public gallery were Sheila and Father Charles Hooper, both of whom had taught me English at Wits. They had much to tell me about the Bafurutse which proved useful in evaluating the differences between the Crown witnesses and my clients' version.

Dinokana, 'the place of little streams', was where Chief Abram Moiloa ruled, subject to the whims of the native commissioner in Zeerust. Some members of the kgotla, the tribal assembly, had complained to the commissioner about the chief's administration. These complaints did not receive serious attention from the authorities until it became clear that Chief Abram was deliberately delaying acceptance of the government's Bantu Authorities' Act – a law actively opposed by the ANC. The commissioner then summoned the chief and told him to gather all the women in the kgotla of Dinokana early the next Monday morning so that reference books could be issued. Chief Abram questioned the wisdom of this move, but was told to carry out the instructions.

Although colonialism denied the notion of kinship to smaller tribes, Chief Abram of Dinokana was pre-eminent among the other chiefs of the villages in which the Bafurutse had lived since time immemorial. He knew that, in the eyes of the women of his tribe, the will of the commissioner would be subordinate to his own. If he acted cautiously, he might achieve his purpose. He duly announced that a government unit would arrive and issue pass books to all the women. This was the white man's law which he as a chief had to obey and he produced his own reference book as evidence. He went on to say that the law was not a tribal law; he had had no part in promulgating it and he knew nothing about it. He concluded, 'I tell you only what I am bidden to tell you. The matter rests between you and the white authorities. Consider well how you intend to act.' The message was clear to the women, and to the authorities once the reports of their informers reached them.

The native commissioner again called the chief to Zeerust, and again ordered him to gather the tribe. When the chief regional commissioner from Potchefstroom and his man from Zeerust arrived at the village, they found Chief Abram sitting on the chair of office, a chair on which only the chief and his predecessors were entitled to sit. Around him, on the ground, sat the people of Dinokana. The senior official, as if he did not know, asked Chief Abram if he were sitting on the chief's chair. Then he ordered him to sit behind the other men, as he was chief no longer. He was to leave within a prescribed number of days and was not to set foot in Dinokana again without the permission of the Zeerust commissioner. The people were stunned. The officials explained that there were complaints against the chief made by some of his own people. The action they had taken had nothing to do with the Bantu Authorities law or the issuing of passes.

How the functionaries of the apartheid regime viewed the matter of chieftainship surfaced with the appointment of a successor. Custom decreed that Abram's uncle, Boas Moiloa, should be appointed. He was a dignified, elderly man who, during the troubles after Abram's expulsion, had come through necessity to be seen as the head of the tribe.

Without any notice, the regional commissioner and his entourage, accompanied by senior police officers from Rustenburg wearing their uniforms and all their decorations, came in convoy to Dinokana. They took over the school hall and sent messengers to bring Boas Moiloa to them. He was told that he was now the chief of the Bafurutse in Dinokana. They tendered papers, already signed and sealed. While they addressed him in Afrikaans, he chose to speak in Setswana:

With my own eyes I have seen three chiefs appointed to my tribe. Each one was appointed by being acclaimed by the tribe as a whole in the Kgotla, none in a school hall. My father and my father's father said that it was always so. I know that my people want our chief back. I will not become their chief unless the Kgotla acclaims me.

Incensed, the white officials stormed off, taking their pieces of paper with them.

The spontaneous action of Boas Moiloa was a good example of innate respect for democracy and love of freedom. Despite his lack of formal education and knowledge of the writings of philosophers and political theorists, he knew what was the right thing to do. But he paid dearly for it. He was banished to a place far away from Lefurutse where his language was not spoken and where he lived alone in a corrugated iron shack. He had no neighbours, no shop nearby where he could spend the £5 a month they gave him, and he had to walk miles to fill his can with water. He died a lonely death. The authorities kindly allowed his body to be brought back to be buried among his people.

The men I had been sent to defend were part of a group that decided to take action in response to the outrage done to their tribe and its leaders. They had filled two buses in Johannesburg and returned to Dinokana, concerned about the deposition of their chief, and about their mothers, sisters and wives being compelled to carry passes. They wanted to flex their muscles against the collaborators who they held responsible for the sorry state of affairs that had befallen their tribe. As their leader they chose Naphthaly Moilwanyana. They called a meeting at the kgotla.

Soon after dawn the tribe's bugle blared despite the absence of the chief – normally the only one who could call for its use. Moilwanyana was to be chief at least for that day. There were four people noticeably absent from the gathering. They were said to be against Chief Abram and to have given information to the government, thus betraying the tribe and responsible for the removal of the chief. Messengers fetched the four, and had to be stopped from assaulting the accused. Moilwanyana became the presiding judge, appointing a young Moiloa as prosecutor and another as registrar. The large crowd were both witnesses for the prosecution and members of the jury.

Where is the chief? the prisoners were asked. Why didn't you protect him? Why did you go to Zeerust and tell lies about him? Why did you invite the pass people to come to our village? Why didn't you chase them away when they came? Why did you force our women to take passes?

Their exculpating answers were drowned by a chorus of '*Marabela!*' – 'the traitors!' The unanimous verdict: guilty of treason. Sentence: death.

'Let us all go up the hill with them and throw them into the hole of Mamakgodi!' announced Moilwanyana. Some, particularly women, were said to have quietly expressed their abhorrence of what was about to happen.

Suddenly a posse of policemen arrived under the command of a police major from Rustenburg, responding to a telephone call from a local shopkeeper. The major saw the four men in distress and Moilwanyana in charge.

The major, a man called Wright, was in some ways different from the typical gun-happy South African police officer of the time and he engaged Moilwanyana in conversation. Moilwanyana remained defiant. This was a tribal matter and had nothing to do with the police. He challenged the major to shoot, saying they were not afraid of the police guns. The guns would shoot water, not bullets. While those around Moilwanyana advised caution, the major succeeded in extricating the would-be victims and withdrawing his men. The kgotla then called for the burning of the passes that had been issued to the local women. These had to be publicly thrown into a fire in the middle of the kgotla.

Major Wright, meanwhile, realising that those who had come from Johannesburg would be travelling back on the buses late on Sunday afternoon, set up a road block miles away from Dinokana and arrested them. Among those held were the twenty-five I had come to defend.

The victims easily identified the few that had taken a leading role in the 'trial'. I anticipated that they might find it difficult to identify all twenty-five and hoped that at least some of them would not be committed for trial. My first request was to have the number around the necks of the accused obscured until they were identified. The prosecutor objected but the magistrate overruled him.

While the evidence was led, I kept a tally. On a piece of paper I wrote one to twenty-five down the left-hand side with the names of the witnesses across the top. This I ruled into small squares and I put a tick whenever an accused was identified. The chart, which lay in front of me on the table, seemed to be of great interest to the lieutenant investigating the case. I noticed that he had even changed places with the prosecutor, possibly to see it more clearly.

At a point where I expected that the prosecutor would announce that he had no more witnesses, he instead asked for an adjournment until the next day. In the morning, a witness connected to the police was called. He slowly but surely identified eight of the accused, counting down the line before pointing a finger at each person he identified. At the end of his evidence, I found that as a result of his identification, I had filled in all the erstwhile empty squares. This was strange. Not only that he had identified those who had not yet been identified, but also that he had not tried to identify those identified by earlier witnesses.

During the adjournment I instructed the well-known and oft-identified accused among my clients to remain in their usual places. Similarly the women sitting prominently in the second row, but the rest were to shuffle themselves at random, keeping their numbers obscured when they entered the court and while I cross-examined the witness.

My first question to the witness was to repeat his identification and describe what he had seen them doing. The magistrate gestured impatiently but said nothing. The prosecutor and the lieutenant muttered that I was wasting everybody's time. The witness confidently identified the same number of people, once or twice with an irritated sigh, adding condescendingly that he would humour me to put an end to the matter.

At the end of his performance, I pointed out that he had identified the correct places but that they were now occupied by other people. The accused and their supporters burst into derisive laughter. The lieutenant blushed. The prosecutor accused me of improper conduct because I had not told him and the magistrate what I was doing. The magistrate simply asked the prosecutor to call his next witness.

Back in Johannesburg I found differences of opinion at the Bar about my tactic. Years later, an attorney was convicted of contempt of court for placing a look-alike in the dock. Criminal proceedings, so said the judges, had to take place in the presence of the accused. This matter was clearly different from my case. But I raise the issue lest someone gets into trouble for following my example – if indeed I was wrong.

Other witnesses were found to testify that each one of the accused was at the kgotla. Their presence in the bus corroborated the evidence. The argument that mere presence was not sufficient to prove either incitement to murder or the other offences was rejected by the magistrate, but eventually upheld at the trial. Even though they were all committed for trial, their bail was extended.

I hoped that the attorney-general, on a close study of the evidence, would not indict all the accused on charges of incitement to murder or other serious offences. When it was ready, Shulamith and I were surprised to find an indictment that included four counts against all my clients, including *crimen laesae majestatis,* in that the accused had usurped the function of the State by establishing and conducting a court. We went to the books as neither of us had heard of such a crime before. In times gone by, Roman governors and medieval princes had been charged in these terms for prosecuting crimes not in the name of the emperor or the king but in their own name. In addition to this rather exotic crime, my clients were also charged with incitement to murder, public violence and inciting persons to burn their reference books by way of protest against the law. Conviction on any of these charges would mean a lengthy prison sentence.

The trial was to take place in Pretoria before Judge Ramsbottom. During the months between committal and trial, many women were charged with burning their passes. I appeared in most of these cases, but when I could not, Shulamith sent the newly admitted Ismail Mahomed. We agreed that Ismail and I should appear for the twenty-five accused from Zeerust. We hoped to raise exceptions to the indictment and ask for detailed particulars, which, in our view, the Crown would not be able to supply. A new indictment might then be drawn against five or six of our clients but the others would be allowed to go. In the event our efforts failed, earning the judge's displeasure. In his view we were requesting particulars for the purpose of embarrassing the Crown rather than eliciting information to prepare our defence. The experienced prosecutor who was to deal with the case, EOK Harwood, was bemused by my having a junior to assist me, and, unlike the judge, was aloof and impatient towards Ismail.

The judge was obviously impressed by the evidence of the most prominent of the victims, Michael Moiloa, a senior tribal councillor, and a knowledgeable and dignified man. With pain and restraint, he described his ordeal before the 'court'. The judge asked many questions, not only about what happened on that day but also about what preceded it and particularly about the reaction of the tribe to the issuing of reference books to women. Some of the accused were discharged at the end of the Crown's case, others at the end of the trial, and only five were convicted on any of the serious offences. The *crimen laesae majestatis* charge was dropped when the judge asked what evidence there had been that, in their actions, any of the accused had purported to be an alternative government. Comparatively light prison sentences were imposed on the five, while a number of others were fined for participating in an unlawful gathering. The lenient sentences no doubt owed something to Father Hooper taking the stand in mitigation. He gave evidence of their personal circumstances, the provocative manner in which their chief had been banished, and the haughty behaviour of the police, who flouted the dignity of the women.

At subsequent trials, most of the women charged with burning reference books were acquitted, although mainly for reasons unrelated to our forensic skills. They escaped conviction because the prosecutor was unqualified and inexperienced, because the police work was sloppy (they were more experienced in harassing people than investigating cases), and because of the lack of sophistication of the elderly magistrate. That the native commissioner was trained in 'native administration' rather than law weighted the scales against the Crown. Also, statements taken from witnesses were often not adhered to in court. One after the other, the prosecutor's questions would be answered with '*Che a khitse, morena*' – 'I don't know, sir.'

Eventually, a senior magistrate was brought from Pretoria to deal with the situation. So was a prosecutor with the rank of magistrate who came from Johannesburg. They chose a case that they thought would be unanswerable.

Gertrude Mpekwa and two others were charged on nine counts of contravening the notorious section introduced in 1953 with the aim of ending the Defiance Campaign. This section provided for imprisonment of up to three years on each count 'committed ... by way of protest against the law or in support of any campaign against any law …' The prosecution team thought that they had a case in which sentences might be imposed that would put an end to pass burning, not only in Lefurutse, but elsewhere. They eventually failed in their purpose: the particulars they supplied at our request were in conflict with the offence and hardly any questions were asked in cross-examination of any of the witnesses. The accused did not give evidence and I asked for their discharge.

During the trial, the magistrate insisted on questioning me in Afrikaans and refused my request to conduct the debate in English. This was largely because, when I first met him, he greeted me in Afrikaans and I responded in English. He convicted the accused and imposed heavy jail sentences. On appeal, however, judges de Wet and Trollip set both the convictions and sentences aside.

Soon afterwards, Shulamith sent me a brief involving the defence of two hundred and thirty-three Gopane women in Zeerust. There was no charge sheet and no memorandum regarding the case, but as I knew that Gopane was a Bafurutse village I assumed they would be charged with burning their passes. I wondered how one would defend so many people, where the trial would take place, and how long I would be away from Arethe and our three-month-old son, Kimon?

In Zeerust, the street leading to the court was deserted, as was the court's backyard. I was welcomed by Major Wright and Mike Tucker, a senior member of the attorney-general's staff in Pretoria who had come with a special magistrate to conduct the trial, an indication of how seriously the prosecution took the matter. They informed me that the women refused to be bussed from their homes to court, nor would they pay the requisite bus fare.

Shulamith Muller had asked that buses be made available and undertaken to pay. The women disagreed. The police had brought them in buses when they were arrested; the police took them back to their village in buses when they were released, and the police should bus them to court. The conciliatory police major suggested that I accompany him in a police car and tell my clients to board the buses. They would listen to me and the question of bus fare could be settled later. I was not to fear the women as the police would protect me. He and the gentle, unflappable Tucker raised their eyebrows when I said that the duties and functions of counsel were well defined, and getting one's clients to court was not among them. Besides, what confidence would my clients have in me if I went with the police?

Father Hooper, who was standing a short distance away, invited me to the rectory for tea and on the way told me what he knew. A sergeant of the mobile unit had gone to Gopane to arrest a small number of women. They had probably been identified by the chief who, fearing the fate of Abram Moiloa, was cooperating with the police. The women refused to get into the police vehicles on the grounds that they were not the only ones who had burned their passes. The others also wanted to be arrested, and the first group of women said that they would show the sergeant who these women were. They started off in a small, singing procession that increased in size until they numbered more than two hundred. The sergeant then called for buses to take them to Zeerust under arrest. As the police had nowhere to hold them, the women spent the night on a piece of ground next to the police station, their songs and ululating keeping Zeerust awake. The young male policemen on duty were embarrassed at continually having to escort small groups into the nearby bushes. Little did they understand that none of the women wanted to escape, since their strength lay in their numbers. And they were strong. When the buses arrived early on the morning of the trial, they again offered to take the police to yet more women who wanted to be arrested. Charles Hooper advised me not to book into the hotel, offered me tea and toast, and suggested that I let my wife know I was likely to be home for dinner that night. Towards midday we strolled back to court. It was still deserted. The matter was withdrawn from the roll, although it was later reinstated with an additional charge of contempt of court. Eventually the whole matter was dropped.

In the other Bafurutse villages the women began to follow the example of those in Dinokana and Gopane. Lack of success in prosecuting the protesters led to harsh administrative action by the police and the complying chiefs, and the tranquillity of life among the Bafurutse came to an end. Everyone knew what lay behind the violence and the disruption of the people – everyone, that is, except the government, which appointed a native divorce court judge, Harry Balk, to head a one-man commission of inquiry into the origin of the troubles.

Balk believed that he would listen to the evidence in a semi-private hearing at the office of the native commissioner in Zeerust. Then hundreds of men and women, represented by Shulamith and me, turned up at the office, demanding a public hearing. The inquiry was hastily moved to the partly covered veranda outside the building, with a couple of chairs for senior police officers and ourselves. Reporters sat on the steps and the large crowd settled in the dusty courtyard.

The native commissioner, who was the first witness, spoke of the peace and tranquillity which had prevailed in his area until the ANC agitators came from Johannesburg to incite the women not to take passes. The agitators were joined by the Anglican priest, whose rectory was used as a gathering place to defy the law. The commissioner added that Shulamith and I were no less guilty in that we came from Johannesburg, secured the acquittal of the guilty, thereby encouraging others in their disrespect for the law. My angry response about the duty of lawyers in the courts was widely published in the media. I looked forward to cross-examining this native commissioner, but it was not to be. At the end of his evidence, the chairman ruled that cross-examination in a commission was discretionary. As we had not made it clear whom we represented and how the evidence could affect them, he would not allow us to cross-examine this witness. In response we declared that no useful purpose would be served by our remaining at the inquiry: we would get a copy of the record and all the evidence that was led, and we would come back to lead our own witnesses.

On the appointed day, as Shulamith and I were nearing Zeerust, special armoured police vehicles passed us at high speed. Military planes flew low, back and forth, as if the town were under siege. Father Hooper told us that, from the previous night, thousands had taken to the roads from all the surrounding villages to attend the hearing. Roadblocks had been set up. Many who did not have passes were arrested, and many were turned back with threats of being held for taking part in an unlawful march. The authorities were determined to show that the police, the army and air force were ready to protect the white residents of Zeerust from the black masses, even though they were mostly women and everyone was unarmed. It was obvious that our clients and our representations were not welcome. We soon abandoned the effort.

We had hoped to show that the native commissioner and his officials had no respect for legality and that vindictive action was planned. This intention was contained in a confidential letter written by the commissioner, a copy of which had come into Shulamith's possession. Early one Saturday morning a lieutenant from Rustenburg arrived at my office with a warrant authorising him to search my bag, my office and, if need be, my home. I assured him that I did not have the letter but had used it in compiling the memorandum. He said the letter had been stolen from the native commissioner's office, and how could we make use of stolen evidence? To his surprise I told him it was admissible if it established the truth, although this did not preclude those who had stolen it from being punished. While the lieutenant took me at my word, he wanted a statement that Shulamith Muller had shown me the letter. This would be placed before the attorney-general so that 'steps' could be taken against us. I gave him a statement; so did Shulamith to the effect that she had found it in an envelope in her office postbox. Nothing happened to us, but suspicion fell on an African clerk in the commissioner's office. There was no evidence against him but that did not deter the authorities. The clerk lost his job and was banished from his home and family for five years.

During the time of the Bafurutse revolt, the preparatory examination of the one hundred and fifty-six ANC leaders charged with treason was also in progress. The Crown wanted evidence that the ANC was responsible not only for the Bafurutse troubles but also for the violence that had broken out in Sekhukhuneland. The authorities viewed it as no coincidence that, as junior to Walter Pollock QC, I had also acted on behalf of the Sekhukhune paramount chief to set aside his banishment.

As it happened, the ANC was deeply concerned about the unbridled violence against the chiefs. Duma Nokwe brought Chief Albert Luthuli, the president of the ANC, to our chambers to ask why offers for peaceful mediation made by his organisation were being rejected.

When I first appeared in court in Zeerust, Shulamith Muller was already held in high esteem by the Bafurutse people for her commitment to their cause, for her successes in keeping women out of prison and because she was prepared to work for the little that they could afford to pay. Then she and her trade unionist husband were banned and harassed, and they sought refuge in Swaziland. In her absence, the Bafurutse tried to teach me Setswana. In addition, Boas Moiloa, who had taken on the mantle as leader of the tribe, presented me with a fine carved wooden spoon to stir the porridge of our baby boy. I was invited to become an honorary member of the tribe. To this day they tell that they realised I was on their side when I was ticketed for making a u-turn in front of the courthouse, but declined to accept the money they raised to pay the £2 fine.

During this period, I checked into the Groot Marico hotel from Monday to Thursday. It was not unlike many others in hostile towns, but there was a difference: a large portrait of Field Marshal Jan Smuts in full uniform with many ribbons and medals hung in the lounge. This was significant.

Over many evenings spent in front of the fire at the rectory with the Hoopers, I learned of the hostility against them, not only from the Calvinists, but also from their own Anglican Church council and their white congregation. Mostly this was because they refused to maintain apartheid in their ministry and personal relationships. Complaints were laid against them with Bishop Ambrose Reeves but he ignored them. When the bishop helped establish a fund for the defence of the people charged in the treason trial, many Anglicans in Zeerust left the church.

The Hoopers had never been invited to have a meal with any white family in the area. Once I asked them to have dinner with me at the hotel. When we entered, the whites in the lounge and dining room froze and remained silent for some time. Their faces asked what the Hoopers were doing there. By way of contrast, the owner, a larger-than-life Afrikaner, welcomed us, called on his headwaiter to pay us special attention and, at the end of our meal, offered us liqueur brandy. I later discovered that he was a *bloedsap*, a supporter of Jan Smuts. Both his grandfather and father had fought alongside Smuts in the Boer War and he had vowed never to join the National Party.

Charles Hooper was writing a book about their work in the church and the oppression of the Bafurutse. He asked me for some personal details that he wished to incorporate. An irrational fear prompted me to request that I not be named. He respected my wishes, and in his book *Brief Authority* I am referred to as 'the man Miss Muley sent' or 'the advocate'. It is a most significant, detailed account of the abuse of power and its consequences for ordinary people. The book was banned for possession. Radicalised by oppression, the Bafurutse became active opponents of Bantustan 'independence' and many took part in the underground struggle against the apartheid government. Their lands near the border of Botswana were used as escape routes for people leaving the country, and those who left were often given help by local men and women deeply alienated from the regime which had oppressed them so badly.

While resistance continued against the issuing of passes to women, the pass laws themselves were being applied with inhuman rigour during the late 1950s. Tens of thousands of pass offenders were sent to prison every year. Eventually, the departments of prisons and of native affairs decided to bypass the court system. A scheme evolved where those caught without papers were 'persuaded' to appear before policemen hastily promoted to the rank of assistant native commissioners. The unfortunate 'accused' would then sign a document that they freely and voluntarily 'requested' being sent to a farm for four months. There they would be paid a pittance, but for many this was preferable to being taken to court, convicted and sent to prison.

At this time, there was an emerging group of African reporters, among them Henry Nxumalo, Can Themba and Peter Magubane working for *Drum* magazine, and Joe Gqabi for *New Age*. These young reporters gained access to the prison farms in Ermelo, Bethal and Delmas, where thousands were held in abject conditions, supervised by the farmers and their sons on horseback and by their 'boss boys' on the ground. All carried sjamboks. Stories and photographs about farm conditions began to appear in *Drum* and *New Age*. A vagrant who had spent a term on a farm told Joe Gqabi how his uncle was beaten to death. Ruth First took an affidavit and the story appeared in *New Age*. The farmers of the area were outraged and approached Prime Minister JG Strijdom for protection. He ordered the deponent to be arrested and charged with perjury. I in turn was asked to act for him.

The regional court prosecutor had no fewer than twenty-six witnesses to prove that the allegations were false. He showed me a letter from the prime minister to the attorney-general instructing that the vagrant be prosecuted in order to clear the good name of the farming community. Having no fixed abode, the man was in custody.

The post-mortem report gave pneumonia as the cause of the uncle's death. I was asked to admit this 'fact', but refused to do so and called for the doctor, who read out his report. His cross-examination was brief.

BIZOS: Did you find the body of the deceased in the compound, which had been vacated by the few hundred other inmates?
DOCTOR: Yes.
BIZOS: Did you examine the body carefully?
DOCTOR: Yes.
BIZOS: Was there proper lighting?
DOCTOR: Yes, I had a torch.
BIZOS: Did you see any injuries on the deceased's body?
DOCTOR: No.
BIZOS: Did you, when you came to the door of the compound, ask the gathered workers who had had a fight in the compound with the deceased?
DOCTOR: Yes, I did.
BIZOS: Why?

Regional magistrate Louis Israel Cohen waited for an answer and asked the question again. 'Out of habit', the doctor replied.

The prosecutor argued that until the accused met Joe Gqabi and Ruth First in Johannesburg, he had not mentioned to anyone that his uncle had been killed by the farmer and his sons. We tried to find witnesses to contradict this but had no access to the farm. Would I admit, asked the prosecutor, that the deceased received no injuries between the time that he was loaded on the vehicle on the farm and the time he was off-loaded at the mortuary? No, I would not, I replied. The driver of the vehicle, a trusted employee of the farmer, was called, and I was able to question him about the heart of the matter.

BIZOS: Was the accused at the back of the truck with his uncle's body?
DRIVER: Yes.
BIZOS: Was he crying?
DRIVER: Yes.
BIZOS: Did you see injuries on the body?
DRIVER: Yes, I did.
BIZOS: Did you ask him how his uncle met his death?
DRIVER: Yes, he said that the boss boys beat him up.

The death had occurred on the property of a farmer named Hershowitz, who was mentioned in the media reports. Hershowitz was called to give evidence. Even before he took the oath he volunteered that no one had been assaulted on his or on other farms. It was all lies told by the English papers. The magistrate ordered him to keep quiet, put him under oath and told him to answer questions and not make speeches. The farmer soon got into trouble.

BIZOS: Do your boss-boys carry sjamboks, knobkieries or sticks?
HERSHOWITZ: No, nobody on my farm ever carried anything like that.
BIZOS: Do you employ night watchmen?
HERSHOWITZ: Yes.
BIZOS: Don't they carry sticks?
HERSHOWITZ: No, nobody does.

The magistrate took over.

MAGISTRATE: Why do you employ night watchmen?
HERSHOWITZ: To look after the place.
MAGISTRATE: How will they defend themselves if attacked?
HERSHOWITZ: I don't know.
MAGISTRATE: Why are you afraid to admit that your night watchmen carry sticks? There is nothing wrong with it. Night watchmen in Johannesburg carry sticks.
HERSHOWITZ: Well, if it is all right for Johannesburg, then my night watchmen do carry sticks.

It looked as if we were heading for an acquittal on the perjury charge, despite the number of witnesses still to be called. In a surprise move before the short adjournment, the prosecutor said that he had no objection if the accused were released on his own recognisance. My client came back almost half an hour late and while we waited for him I was more anxious than the prosecutor. If he absconded, what better proof of his guilt? I asked him where he had been. He had been looking for a shebeen to spend the two shillings I had given him. Despite his miserable condition, he gave clear and satisfactory evidence. By the time the court acquitted him, it had long seemed a foregone conclusion. But this did not stop the protests of the farmers, the statements in Parliament or the editorials in the Afrikaans newspapers about the bad name given to farmers by the liberal and leftist press.

The attorney Joel Carlson waged a further attack on prison farms by bringing a *habeas corpus* application on behalf of Dorcas Sadika, the wife of James Moses Sadika, a tailor of Alexandra township, against Petrus Johannes Potgieter, on whose farm near Heidelberg James Sadika was working. We asked Isie Maisels (who was then arguing an exception to the treason trial indictment) to move the *habeas corpus* application. Dorcas did not recognise her husband, guarded by two 'boss boys' in the lobby. Only when he greeted her, did she know who he was. They told him to keep quiet; no one was allowed to speak to him.

I reported this exchange to Joel who was also unable to resolve the situation. While I was helping Isie Maisels put on his gown, I related what had happened. Maisels was always master of the situation, and when Acting Judge Lamie Snyman took his seat on the bench, Maisels spoke up: 'M'Lord, the respondent runs a jail on his farm. But now he has extended his jurisdiction to the lobby of Your Lordship's court.'

Frikkie Eloff, later judge president of the Transvaal Provincial Division, had taken an affidavit from Sadika in his chambers in the presence of Potgieter, his client. In the affidavit, Sadika said that he was on the farm freely and voluntarily. To test this, Judge Snyman called the tailor into the witness box. He explained to Sadika that his wife had brought an application for his release. What was his response to the application? Did he want the court to adjourn so that he could speak to his wife's lawyers? When Sadika chose this course, Maisels had me see him privately in the robing room. Sadika started crying. At my concern, he raised his shirt: more than a dozen cuts raked the skin of his back.

Back in court, Maisels asked Sadika to show the judge and those in court his injuries. The judge quickly ruled that Sadika was free to go to his wife and that the case would be postponed for further affidavits to be filed.

Wide publicity was given to the case, and relatives of others held on the prison farms began queuing up at Joel Carlson's office and the offices of the Black Sash. Assisted by attorney Raymond Tucker and others we were soon bringing one *habeas corpus* application after the other. Once, when a farmer asked for a postponement in order to file affidavits, Judge Quartus de Wet impatiently wanted to know what the affidavits would say. That a signed document proved the applicant was there freely and voluntarily, came the reply of the farmer's counsel. 'Never mind about that,' said Judge de Wet. 'Show me what statutory authority there is to treat people the way in which they are being treated by this scheme.' There was no answer, nor could there be. The minister was ultimately forced to withdraw, and it took some time to devise a similar scheme with at least the semblance of statutory authority.

CHAPTER 8

And Who Are You?

... it is our determination to maintain such regulations as may suppress crime, and preserve proper relations between master and servant.

– Piet Retief, leader of the Voortrekkers
(in a manifesto explaining why they had decided to move out
of the Cape Colony after slavery was abolished, 7 May 1838)

Nelson Mandela has a weakness for smart clothes. I remember as a clerk seeing him in Alfred Kahn's shop being fitted for a new suit. Kahn was the tailor favoured by those who frequented the prestigious Rand Club on Loveday Street in central Johannesburg. At the time I was at Kahn's to collect a list of customers in default on their accounts. Nelson Mandela was there for a different reason – the final fitting of a suit that had been specially cut for him. Kahn was on his knees, measuring the length of Mandela's trouser leg. Kahn's customers might have raised an eyebrow at their tailor making suits for a black man, but they would probably have accepted that the tailor did it merely for the money and not as a challenge to the social order.

As a student I'd encountered Mandela, heard him speak and been introduced to him. He was a senior student and ahead of me in the faculty of law. He later started a partnership with Oliver Tambo and acquired a reputation for making his presence felt as soon as he walked into a courtroom. Prosecutors and magistrates complained that he was uppity. This may have been a political response conditioned by their own politics as much as his. Even whites who kept aloof from black politics were aware that he was one of the young Turks in the ANC Youth League that had pushed out the moderate leadership.

Mandela had hardly started work as a lawyer when, as volunteer-in-chief of the Defiance Campaign, he was convicted and sentenced to nine months' imprisonment, conditionally suspended. As a result, the Law Society wanted him removed from the roll of attorneys. Walter Pollak QC and Blen Franklin, two of the most prominent advocates at the Johannesburg Bar, successfully resisted this. Judge Ramsbottom declared that while in certain circumstances an attorney may be expected to observe the laws more strictly than other people, the fact that an attorney had deliberately disobeyed the law did not necessarily disqualify him from practising his profession or justify the court removing his name from the roll.

In a speech to the Law Society made in October 1993 Mandela alluded to this case:

I was pleased to receive your invitation to open the general meeting of my chosen profession. Mind you, this was at least the third time the Law Society thought of me. The two previous invitations were delivered by the sheriff. I was asked to show cause why I should not be struck off the roll of attorneys. My eminent counsel in the first application, Walter Pollak QC and Blen Franklin, persuaded Judge Ramsbottom that my conviction in the early '50s for being the volunteer-in-chief of the Defiance Campaign did not make me guilty of an offence involving moral turpitude.

I decided to ask the commanding officer on Robben Island to arrange for me to appear personally to oppose the second application brought soon after my conviction at the Rivonia trial in 1964. The thought of my being brought to Pretoria and being seen in open court must have convinced those who initiated the application to withdraw it. Here I am with my name still on the roll even though I have not yet got around to applying for a fidelity certificate to go into competition with you.

By the mid-1950s, Mandela was one of the most significant leaders of the ANC and seen as an obvious successor to the venerable Chief Albert Luthuli. By then the names of Mandela and Tambo were known throughout South Africa, and pictures of Nelson Mandela appeared regularly in the press. His leadership qualities were obvious whatever the activity, not just high-profile politics. By 1955 he was acknowledged as the leader of black lawyers. Years later on Robben Island, prisoners of all political tendencies regarded him in a similar light. Discriminatory practices in the legal profession hurt him: he was periodically asked for advice by his colleagues and he would often intervene on their behalf.

Soon after I became a member of the bar, I was told by Duma Nokwe (soon to become the first African member of the Johannesburg Bar) that the magistrate of Kempton Park was giving Nelson Mandela trouble. Duma wanted me to see Mandela and discuss his problems. Before this, I had acted for Mandela and Tambo in a couple of cases of no particular significance and I had dealt mainly with their clerks.

During the weekend Nelson Mandela arrived at the house that Arethe and I were looking after. He parked his sedan in the driveway and came to the front door. The two young daughters of my erstwhile employer, who was away on an extended overseas trip, were puzzled by the black man's behaviour. Nelson noticed this and, to alleviate my obvious embarrassment, told me that his children often asked him why he had white people visiting him.

I was appalled by the story I heard across the mahogany dining-room table. Nelson was acting for a government clerk, Elliot Setoaba, charged with accepting a bribe from a work-seeker, Elias Songwane, and issuing him a permit to work in the Kempton Park area. Such was the reputation of Mandela and Tambo, particularly in the black community, that people charged with offences not necessarily connected with politics also sought them out. They knew that they would get a spirited defence.

Setoaba's case came up in the Kempton Park court on 11 November 1955, before Magistrate Willem Dormehl. The accused was called upon to plead. Six foot two inches, broad-shouldered, immaculately dressed, Nelson Mandela stood up and in his strong voice said, 'I appear for the accused, Your Worship. My name is Nelson Mandela.'

The following exchange then occurred:

MAGISTRATE: Are you entitled to appear in this court?
MANDELA: Your Worship, I was admitted as an attorney by order of the above honourable court on the 27th day of March 1952. I am entitled to appear for the accused and have been duly instructed to do so.
MAGISTRATE: Where is your authority to appear?
MANDELA: I do not carry my certificate of admission with me, Your Worship. It is in Johannesburg.
MAGISTRATE: You must satisfy me that you are entitled to appear in this court. The court will adjourn.

No one within the legal profession could not have heard of Nelson Mandela. Either the magistrate was genuine or was being obstructionist. The court sat again early that afternoon and Dormehl resumed his questioning of Mandela.

MAGISTRATE: Are you now in a position to satisfy me that you are qualified to appear in this court?
MANDELA: I was unable during the luncheon adjournment to get to Johannesburg and return to Kempton Park in time for the hearing. I have been given to understand by the prosecutor that he was calling at least four witnesses and that there would be no reasonable chance of the matter being

completed today. May I suggest that we proceed with the case and on the resumed hearing of the matter I will produce my certificate entitling me to practise in the courts.

MAGISTRATE: I am not interested in that. I must remand. Mr Prosecutor, what date do you suggest?

When the prosecutor suggested 24 November, Nelson replied that he would be engaged in another court on that date. Dormehl retorted, 'I am not interested in you. The hearing is remanded until 24 November.'

In an aside, but within hearing of the magistrate, Nelson asked the prosecutor if he could postpone it to 25 November. The prosecutor nodded and turned to the magistrate: 'May I suggest we postpone the matter until the 25th?' 'Are you agreeing to a different date?' asked Dormehl. 'Your Worship,' said the prosecutor, 'Mr Mandela has suggested the 25th and I have no problem with that.' The magistrate shook his head as if he could not believe that the prosecutor had agreed to accommodate Mandela.

Having won a small victory Mandela continued: 'I would like the reasons why the case was remanded to be recorded, as well as my suggestion that I produce my certificate at a later date.' This idea incensed the magistrate. He turned on Mandela angrily: 'Sit down!' When Nelson repeated his request, Dormehl lost his temper. 'If you don't sit down I will ask the orderly to throw you out of court. I am giving you up to the count of three to sit down and if you don't sit down I will have you locked up.' Nelson slowly sat down. Dormehl said, 'You must be very careful otherwise I am going to get you into trouble.'

With that the case was adjourned. Mandela glared at the magistrate, picked up his file, put it under his arm, deliberately refrained from the customary bow of the head expected of legal practitioners and briskly walked out of the magistrate's court. In the corridor Dormehl caught up with him and said, 'I warn you that you will go to gaol if you are impertinent to the court.' Mandela informed him that he would find it very difficult to put him in gaol and walked off.

Mandela returned to confront Dormehl on 25 November. On my return from court that day there was an urgent message. Nelson wanted to see me at once. I sensed his anger and frustration as soon as he entered my office. He had gone to Kempton Park with his certificate early in the morning. Elliot Setoaba's case was called. Nelson produced the certificate. The magistrate looked at it, handed it to the young policeman acting as clerk of the court who gave it back it to Mandela. Elias Songwane gave evidence that he had been forced to pay the six pounds. Mandela stood up to cross-examine. 'In exactly what way did the accused force you to give him six pounds?' At this point Dormehl appeared to get agitated and interrupted Mandela angrily: 'That is irrelevant. I will not allow you to put that or any other irrelevant question to the complainant.'

Mandela tried to argue the relevance of the question, but was again interrupted by Dormehl: 'I warned you not to ask irrelevant questions and I won't have any nonsense from you. Proceed.' When Mandela hesitated Dormehl shouted: 'Ask your next question!' Instead, Mandela requested that his original question be recorded as well as Dormehl's ruling that it was not admissible. Dormehl, pointing his finger, glared at Mandela. 'I don't take any instructions from you.'

MANDELA: Your Worship makes it very difficult for me to proceed if I am not allowed to put questions and you refuse to record the questions asked and the rulings given.

MAGISTRATE: If that is the attitude you are going to take up I am going to record every question you put and every answer that the witness makes so that it can be shown how irrelevant your questions are.

Mandela agreed that they should proceed in this way. Soon Dormehl again interrupted Mandela's cross-examination of another witness, stating that the question was irrelevant. An argument ensued as to the merits of the question. Dormehl refused to allow it and Mandela insisted that this be recorded. The magistrate again lashed out: 'I don't take any instructions from you.'

Mandela tried to proceed but Dormehl intervened: 'Sit down!' Angered by the persistent interruptions, Mandela said he would not sit down until he had finished his cross-examination. This infuriated Dormehl. 'Hey you, I told you to sit down.' Then, to the orderly, 'Get this man to sit down.' Mandela sat. When asked if he had any more questions he insisted that his previous questions be recorded. Dormehl would have none of it. 'I have told you before I don't take any instructions from you. I am giving you a final warning. If you don't listen you will get into trouble.'

Mandela repeated his question. Dormehl made his threat again: 'I have warned you several times before about these irrelevant questions and if you persist in asking them I will discharge the witness.' When Mandela argued that the question ought to be allowed, Dormehl replied, 'Hey you, I have warned you before not to ask these irrelevant questions and if you persist I will have you thrown out of this court. Do you hear?' With that he adjourned the court until the afternoon.

Mandela repeated the question after the adjournment, at which Dormehl jumped up from his lofty chair on the bench and shouted, 'Hey you, sit down.' To the witness he said, 'You, go.' Mandela pointed out that it was irregular to dismiss a witness before cross-examination had been completed. Dormehl only repeated his command: 'Hey you, I told you to sit down. Will you sit down. I will count up to three and if you are still standing when I have counted "three" I will call the orderly to eject you from the court. One … two … three … Get this man out!'

Mandela did not sit down until the orderly had almost reached him. Dormehl then called the next witness, but before he entered the courtroom, Mandela stood up. 'In view of Your Worship's attitude I find it impossible to proceed with the case for the following reasons …' 'Are you withdrawing from the case?' asked Dormehl. Mandela replied, 'I do not think I have any other course open to me for the following reasons …' The magistrate interrupted, told him to sit down immediately and said that he could give his grounds for withdrawal later.

The magistrate then turned to Mandela's client and said, 'Your attorney has now withdrawn from this case. Do you want the case to go on or do you wish an adjournment to be granted to enable you to get another attorney?'

When the man insisted that he did not want to change his attorney, Dormehl said: 'You must get another attorney.' He was about to adjourn when Mandela stood up. He wanted the reasons he could not proceed recorded. Again he was forced to sit down when Dormehl once more threatened to throw him out of court. The case was hastily remanded until 10 February 1956.

Once Nelson had told me the whole story, we discussed various options. We could go to a senior reporter on the *Rand Daily Mail* to give the matter publicity. We could report the magistrate to the department of justice. Eventually we rejected both ideas. I suggested that Nelson's client sign a petition to the effect that he did not want to be defended by anyone other than Mr Mandela and that the magistrate's behaviour was racist. I recommended that the client petition the Supreme Court, asking that the magistrate recuse himself because he had objected to the client being defended by a black attorney. Nelson liked the idea. A few days later, together with Elliot Setoaba, we drafted the petition. Nelson attached his own affidavit along the same lines, adding that Dormehl

must find it offensive to mention my name because during the proceedings he preferred to use the word 'you' or more often 'Hey you' in order to draw attention to what [he] was saying. I say further that it is most unlikely that [he] did not know that I was practising as an attorney as my name has often appeared in the press and in the law reports. [His] requests that I should produce my authority was, in my respectful submission, made solely for the purpose of embarrassing me and not for the purpose of satisfying himself about the appearance of unqualified persons.

The petition was served on the magistrate as first respondent and the attorney-general as the second. In addition to asking that Dormehl be replaced as magistrate, we wanted the proceedings that had taken place before him set aside and that the costs of the application be paid out of his own pocket.

The attorney-general was quick to respond. He must have telephoned the prosecutor, a decent young man who probably told him that there was substance in the complaint against the magistrate. The Pretoria correspondents of Mandela and Tambo were informed that the attorney-general would not take part in the proceedings and would abide by the judgment of the court. However, the magistrate was not to be beaten so easily. He went to consult with the government attorney and it was arranged to brief a Pretoria barrister, AP Myburgh, later a judge of the Transvaal Provincial Division.

In his answering affidavit, Dormehl denied all the allegations against him. In addition, he questioned Mandela's interpretation of the events. He stated, among other things, that he refused to record Mandela's arguments because Mandela had not been accepted as the attorney of record. He also filed other affidavits in answer to our petition. This meant that on the set date we would have to seek a postponement to enable us to reply. As the matter was not going to be argued on that day, we asked a colleague in Pretoria to attend to the formalities.

Judge Quartus de Wet was to preside in the Pretoria Motion Court on the day initially appointed for the matter. He was known to be incensed by high-handed conduct, particularly by police officers and others connected with the administration of justice. He tended to be shy but abrupt with all who came before him.

As counsel gathered in the lobby of the court, the registrar told those in the recusal application that the judge wanted to see them in his chambers. His first question was, why had the application been put down on the Motion Court roll? Did those who brought it not know that such a case would have to be heard by two judges? Our colleague, who was only standing in for us, did not have a ready answer. And anyhow the judge's attention was on Dormehl, 'What is your client up to?' he asked Myburgh.

Myburgh replied that Dormehl denied all the allegations, and tendered a batch of affidavits. These had been drawn up by the magistrate, the prosecutor, the court orderly, the witness who had given evidence, and other witnesses waiting to give evidence. They had been served on us the previous day and we wanted a postponement so we could deal with the allegations. They referred to Nelson Mandela as '*die naturel*' – the native – who 'had his hands in his pockets on occasion'. This detail was apparently intended to support the statement by Dormehl that Mandela did not show due respect and insisted that everything should be recorded.

Judge de Wet did not even look at the affidavits. He angrily stuck them into the court file and turned on Myburgh. 'Which allegations does he admit and which does he deny? Did he or did he not ask Mandela to produce his certificate?' 'But Judge,' said Myburgh, 'he has put a version before you.' Judge de Wet cut him short. 'Tell me, Myburgh, why did he ask Mandela to produce his certificate? I would have thought that everybody knows that Mandela is an attorney.' What could Myburgh do but repeat his client's version? 'The magistrate says that Mandela came into court in such an arrogant manner that he could not believe that the person was an attorney.' Judge de Wet remained unconvinced. 'I don't think that many of my brother judges will believe him, Myburgh. You'll know what to tell the magistrate. The application is not properly before me. It should be before two judges. I do not want it mentioned in court. This is the sort of thing that brings the administration of justice in our country into disrepute. Myburgh, tell your client that the quicker he recuses himself from this case, the better for all concerned.'

We had hardly begun preparing our reply to Dormehl's supporting documents when the government attorney informed Mandela's Pretoria correspondents that the magistrate would recuse himself and that another magistrate would start the case anew.

In the meantime, Nelson had become involved in other matters and he asked me to present the clerk's case on his behalf. Nor could he be persuaded to see Dormehl recuse himself. We were happy that we had taught the magistrate a lesson. Whether we had or not was a moot point, for on more than one occasion in the years to come Dormehl showed that he was incapable of changing his spots. The case did, however, bring Nelson and me closer together. Unfortunately, we will never know whether the clerk was guilty or innocent. He was killed in a railway accident during the course of the trial.

CHAPTER 9

Separate Tables

The Dormehl incident was merely one of many during the 1950s. While Nelson Mandela and Oliver Tambo were appearing with the other accused in the pre-paratory examination of the treason trial, their two clerks, Godfrey Pitje and Douglas Lukele, had to cope with running the partnership as best they could. On this occasion Pitje had to pick up one of Tambo's cases being heard by Magistrate FAH Johl of Boksburg.

At the first hearing Tambo had run into Johl's racism when the magistrate instructed him to sit at a small table reserved for 'non-Europeans'. Tambo had responded as Mandela had with Dormehl and requested that the magistrate recuse himself on grounds of racial bias. The magistrate refused and Tambo approached me to submit an application similar to that made against Dormehl. But as the client, Stefaans Niekerk, was otherwise engaged we were unable to get his cooperation.

When Niekerk was due in court, the task of appearing for him fell to Godfrey Pitje. Although a clerk, Pitje was our senior in years. He had been a principal of a school and a university lecturer in anthropology before deciding that he could not bear the constraints of the Bantu education system imposed by the govern-ment. All his life, he had been involved in the struggle for the African people. He was not a timid man.

The court interpreter, Calvin Leboela, probably on the magistrate's instructions, approached Godfrey Pitje before court started and told him about the argument between Oliver and the magistrate. He hoped that Mr Pitje would occupy the table set aside for him in order to avoid further difficulties. In court Pitje sat at the large well-worn table reserved for 'European' practitioners and avoided the smaller, new table reserved for 'non-Europeans'.

Johl entered, fixed his eyes on Pitje and asked him to sit at the new table which was pushed up against the larger one.

PITJE: Why, Sir?

MAGISTRATE: I say sit there. This is my court and I am not going to argue with you.

PITJE: Is that an order of the court?

MAGISTRATE: Yes, this is an order of the court.

PITJE: But surely, Sir, I am entitled to an explanation.

MAGISTRATE: If you persist I shall fine you five pounds for contempt of court.

PITJE: Will you please note my protest, Sir?

MAGISTRATE: I shall not listen to you as long as you are standing there.

PITJE: Then I have no option but to withdraw from this case.

MAGISTRATE: You may do so if you please.

PITJE: May I be excused, Sir?

MAGISTRATE: Yes, you are excused.

Pitje was followed from the court by the court orderly who demanded the payment of a £5 fine. When he refused, on the grounds that he had not been fined, merely warned, he was taken to the cells. Initially he considered going to prison for five days to strengthen the protest but in the end the fine was paid on his behalf and he was released.

He and Oliver came to see me. Although there was some doubt about whether a person committed for contempt was entitled to place an affidavit before the Court of Appeal, we decided to follow this course because the magistrate hadn't given Pitje an opportunity to finish off his sentences.

In his affidavit, Pitje contended that he wanted to address the magistrate from the table at which all legal practitioners sat, adding,

> My intentions in attempting to ascertain from the magistrate the reason I was to be confined to what is referred to as a small table was because I had good reason to believe that the special treatment meted out to me was because I am an African. If the magistrate had told me that that was the reason, it was my intention to tell the magistrate that neither I nor my client would feel that he had been defended in his best possible interests if he was to be defended by me, and for that reason I was going to withdraw. I intended also to say that I was not aware of any statutory provision, or any other law which entitled the magistrate to order me to take a specific place or to compel me to assume such a place. I intended further to ask the magistrate to rescind the order he had made before he had given me an opportunity to address the matter.

When we eventually got to the Appeal Court in Bloemfontein, this passage was to be used against us by the panel of judges who heard the case.

In his reasons setting out why he had fined Pitje for contempt of court, Johl said:

The table I asked Mr Pitje to occupy is a brand new heavy kiaat table, clean and clear. On the larger table exhibits were strewn about. It is an exact replica of the larger table in a smaller size. The chair is a padded chair ...

He went on:

In this case, Mr Pitje has refused to occupy the table indicated by the court after an order of the court and surely this is a wilful refusal and must of necessity bring the presiding magistrate into disrepute. It would be intolerable and impossible to hold court if a defending attorney were to persist in excepting to a charge after his exception had been overruled by the presiding magistrate or judge. The same applies here ...

Had Mr Pitje occupied the smaller table at my initial request nothing more would have been said and to me it is indifferent whether the defending attorney is a European or a non-European. Both are accorded a deferential hearing. In fact, during his altercation I was calm and collected and never raised my voice.

This being a special case, it seems to me natural that Mr Tambo, when he instructed his junior Mr Pitje to appear, must have warned him what to expect and advised him on his course of action. His affirmation to my interpreter Mr C Leboela, viz. 'That he is well aware which table he should occupy,' lends substance to my assumption later on that the case must have been discussed with his senior. His protestations etc. must have been preconceived and in consequence his disobedience was most certainly wilful.

In conclusion I wish to add that Mr Pitje's version of occurrence is a very distorted one, and in confirmation of my version I attach hereto affidavits of the court orderly and the native interpreter.

Johl also acted as the commissioner of oaths on the affidavits he filed. No comment was made about this impropriety.

Appeals to the Transvaal Provincial Division were dealt with in a fairly summary manner. The two judges sitting as a Court of Appeal had from six to ten appeals per day and counsel was expected to be brief and to the point. We were fairly confident that the court would hold that Godfrey Pitje had not been given a proper hearing. On that very narrow ground, we expected that the appeal would be allowed and the conviction for contempt as well as the fine set aside. We could not have been more wrong. Unknown to us the case had assumed tremendous importance to those concerned with the administration of apartheid justice.

It was no accident that the matter had been set down before judges Piet Cillie and Wes Boshoff. They had both been hastily appointed to the bench soon after the Nationalists came to power in 1948. In later years, both were favoured with appointment as Judge President of the Transvaal Provincial Division of the Supreme Court and both were subsequently elevated to the Court of Appeal. Godfrey Pitje's case was the only one before them that day.

It was well known that Rudy Rein QC, the attorney-general of the Transvaal, hardly ever stepped into court. In this case, he appeared for the Crown together with a junior. I stood to argue two grounds of appeal: failure to hear Godfrey Pitje as to why he was not prepared to move to the smaller table, and the fact that the order was incompetent because it was based on racial discrimination. I referred to and read passages from the judgments in the Court of Appeal, particularly in the Rasool and Abdurahman cases, which I said supported the submission that it was unreasonable to deal unequally with practitioners equally entitled to practise in the courts. The junior but intellectually superior of the two judges, Boshoff, immediately took me up on both arguments:

BOSHOFF: But there is no evidence that the table set aside for the appellant was in any way inferior to the table set aside for European practitioners.

BIZOS: But M'lord, we are surely not concerned with the quality of the wood. We are surely concerned with the feelings, the perceptions of our colleagues and their clients who are parties to the litigation. They must surely feel offended by being treated differently.

BOSHOFF: Differently, but equally, Mr Bizos. Surely there is nothing wrong with that?

BIZOS: But M'lord, there is good authority that separate cannot be equal.

BOSHOFF: Authorities in our courts, Mr Bizos? I'd like to be referred to them.

BIZOS: No, M'lord, not in our courts, but in Brown v Board of Education of Topeka …

BOSHOFF: Well, if it's not in our courts, then it's no authority, Mr Bizos. The dicta that you rely on from Rasool and Abdurahman were made in 1934 and 1950. Has what was said in those courts any application now that our Legislature, in its wisdom, has passed the Separate Amenities Act?

BIZOS: M'lord, there is no suggestion that the magistrate acted in terms of the Separate Amenities Act. In terms of that Act notices have got to be put up. It can hardly be argued that powers given to local authorities and other public bodies to segregate parks and toilets should be used in a courtroom.

BOSHOFF: No, you don't seem to understand my point, Mr Bizos. The question is whether this was a reasonable order or not which had to be obeyed,
or was so unreasonable an order that it could be defied. The fact that a
democratically elected Legislature passed an Act authorising segregation
is surely more than adequate evidence of the reasonableness of separating
people on the grounds of colour?

While on my feet, I decided not to debate with His Lordship the use of the word
'democratic'. I realised that the stage had been set for an adverse decision and
feared that soon magistrates throughout the country would follow the example
of avant-garde apartheid, expounded by Willem P Dormehl and FAH Johl.

The attorney-general was prepared to persuade the court to dismiss the appeal,
always assuming persuasion was needed. He read the Separate Amenities Act to
the judges. He adopted the arguments so eloquently expounded by Judge Boshoff
and regretted that the appellant through his counsel sought to politicise a matter
which was nothing more than a convenient arrangement of the courtroom to
comply with government policy and the general practices of our community. He
saw no reason why the courts should be any different.

Except for Godfrey Pitje and me, no one in that courtroom saw anything wrong
with the attorney-general's sentiments. Judge Cillie, who wrote the decision, based
his conclusions on Johl's interpretation of events and said:

The court made a request to him [Pitje] which was, on the face of it, not an
unreasonable one. By saying that it was not unreasonable I do not wish to
convey that it was legally correct, but merely that it was a request which was
prima facie not ludicrous or insulting …

He concluded:

The appellant's conduct was, I think, calculated to bring the administration of
justice into disrepute and indicated his contempt of that order and of the court.
He was therefore guilty of misbehaviour which entitled the court to sentence
him in terms of Section 108 of the Criminal Procedure Act No. 56 of 1955.

The appeal was dismissed with leave to appeal, even though the learned judge
thought that there was no real prospect of success in the Appellate Division.
Judge Boshoff, together with Judge Lamie Snyman, who was appointed to the
bench shortly after he campaigned against the admission of Duma Nokwe to the

Society of Advocates, handed down the judgment on our application for leave
to appeal:

> It seems to me that if the whole case can be resolved on the facts then the
> applicant has no prospect of success on appeal but there is the important
> consideration that the case may have to be decided on the validity of the order
> which the magistrate made on this occasion. On that I cannot say that there is
> no reasonable prospect of success. In the circumstances the Court will grant
> the applicant leave to appeal.
>
> As the matter may be of some importance for the administration of justice,
> it [is] as well that the Highest Court should pronounce upon the case.

The matter only got there in September 1960. Chief Justice Lucas Steyn presided over appeal judges Hoexter, van Blerk, Ogilvie-Thompson and Botha. The
Crown was represented by JW Smalberger, himself later a member of the Court
of Appeal. The arguments advanced were similar to those advanced previously,
save that Smalberger did not repeat the attorney-general's remarks about politi-
cising the matter.

I thought to advance the argument by removing it from the racial arena to that
of the feminists, even though many did not know the movement by that name
at the time. I boldly submitted that if a judge wanted men and women counsel
to sit at separate tables, a woman advocate would be entitled to say, 'I want to
address you from this, the traditional position at the Bar as to why, as a woman,
you should not send me to a separate table.'

Chief Justice Steyn indicated that he could see nothing wrong with a judge
acting as in my example. Mercifully he indicated that he did not intend to separate
his court's benches either on the grounds of race or of sex. When I submitted
that a woman might feel aggrieved, as would her client, if counsel were treated
differently, Judge Hoexter said, 'Mr Bizos, similes are for poets. Let's get down
to the facts of the case.'

He made it clear that he did not accept that Pitje had been deprived of any
right to be heard. The judgment, written by the Chief Justice and concurred in
by the four other Judges of Appeal, was handed down six days later.

> A magistrate, like other judicial functionaries, is in control of his courtroom
> and of the proceedings therein. Matters incidental to such proceedings, if they
> are not regulated by law, are largely within his discretion. The only ground on
> which the exercise of that discretion and the legal competence of the order

might in this instance be called in question, would be unreasonableness arising from alleged inequality in the treatment of practitioners equally entitled
to practise in the Magistrate's Court. (Cf. *Minister of Posts and Telegraphs* v.
Rasool, 1934 A.D.167; *R.* v *Abdurahman*, 1950(3) S.A. 136 (Ad.).) But from the
record it is clear that a practitioner would in every way be as well seated at the
one table as at the other, and that he could not possibly have been hampered
in the slightest in the conduct of his case by having to use a particular table.
Although I accept that no action was taken under the 1953 Act, the fact that
such action could have been taken is not entirely irrelevant. It shows that the
distinction drawn by provision of separate tables in this Magistrate's Court, is
of a nature sanctioned by the Legislature, and makes it more difficult to attack
the validity of the Magistrate's order on the ground of unreasonableness. The
order was, I think, a competent order ...

From these facts and circumstances, it is apparent that the appellant, when
he went to court on this day, knew of the existence of the separate facilities
in the court, that he purposely took a seat at the table provided for European
practitioners, that he expected to be ordered to the other table and intended
not to comply with any such order. He further had in mind eventually to
withdraw from the case after having informed the magistrate that the interests of the accused would be better served, and that he would by implication
have a fairer trial, if he, the appellant, were to refrain from defending him.
It follows, I think, that his failure to comply with the order was deliberate
and premeditated. It cannot, therefore, avail him to contend that he did not
intend to insult the magistrate and was not motivated by contempt. It is true
that the insulting statement which he intended to make, to the effect that the
magistrate would not give the accused a fair trial if defended by him, he did
not make, but that does not alter the fact that, in spite of repeated warnings,
he wilfully disregarded the order. That was contempt of court.

Although the appeal was dismissed, administrative instructions must have
been given to all magistrates not to behave as Johl had done. But no one in what
is generally referred to as the organised legal profession raised a voice in protest
when the magistrate convicted Godfrey Pitje. Nor was there any word when he lost
his appeal to the Transvaal Division, nor even when the appeal to the Appellate
Division was dismissed.

I have often wondered whether I was not partly to blame for the unfortunate
outcome. What would have happened if instead of the appeal being argued by
me – then counsel of only six years' standing – the incorporated Law Society and

the Bar Council had taken it upon themselves to brief one or more of the leaders of the Bar? They would then have been able to submit more forcefully, by virtue of their institutional backing, that the dignity of our black colleagues was being insulted by magistrates providing separate tables for them.

Godfrey Pitje later became the president of the Black Lawyers' Association. In September 1987, a number of South Africa's then still all-white judiciary and a cross-section of the legal profession were invited by the American Bar Association to its annual conference held in Washington DC. Pitje was called upon to thank our host. He said, 'We want to thank the ABA for inviting us to its conference. It gave us an opportunity to meet some of our judges.'

There is an unfortunate personal postscript to this story. Chief Justice Steyn said in the Appellate Division that he would not require legal practitioners to sit at different tables, but his comments apparently did not reach the town of Bethlehem, a few hundred kilometres away. Douglas Lukele, now no longer a clerk but an admitted attorney, appeared in a criminal matter there. The magistrate ordered him to sit at a separate table. Lukele refused. The magistrate warned that if he did not comply, he would be removed from the court by force. When Lukele still did not obey, the court orderly was told to remove him – which he did, using force.

The matter came to my attention and Lukele insisted that he wanted to sue the magistrate and the court orderly. Summons was served. But Douglas Lukele had been born in Swaziland and although nobody had bothered about his immigration papers in the past, he was now summarily arrested, kept in custody and served with a deportation order. He applied to have it set aside, claiming that it was invalid because he had not been given an opportunity of being heard. The argument did not prevail and he had to leave South Africa, which put an end to his action against the magistrate and the court orderly.

CHAPTER 10

A Stranger at the Door

Let us in turn ask the question whether the Bar Council is properly concerned about the administration of justice if it wants to overturn the policy, tradition and ambit of the legislation of the country for the sake of an individual.

– Editorial, *Die Transvaler* 18/9/56
('The Bar Over the Top Again')

The first African to be admitted to the Johannesburg Bar was Philemon Pearce Duma Nokwe, my fellow student who had sometimes slept on the couch in my room when he needed to work late at the library. He had studied law after he and his wife, Tiny Nokwe, were dismissed by the education department because of their involvement in politics.

At first Duma had worked for Harry Bloom as an articled clerk, an arrangement initiated by Joe Slovo. Bloom was an accomplished attorney with wider interests than usual. He had been a newspaper correspondent, had covered the Nuremberg trials, and he had written a fairly successful and topical novel, *Transvaal Episode*. His firm was known as Bloom and Warner. There was no Warner, but Bloom thought the name gave his practice a Waspish sound.

Bloom held out the prospect that Duma could even become a partner – an unheard-of proposition at the time. It was an attractive offer. Duma was torn between the security Bloom offered and the speculative prospects of an African man making a living as an advocate. Nelson Mandela was particularly keen that he take the plunge, promising that there would be plenty of work from Mandela and Tambo.

Duma was duly admitted to the Bar, and in one of the stranger ironies of apartheid South Africa, the department of foreign affairs published, with some pride, an article trumpeting Duma Nokwe's achievement. There stood Duma in his black robes, white wing-collar and bib, the photograph accompanied by a short biographical note. No doubt this was intended to boost the country's image abroad. *Die Transvaler*, on the other hand, saw the matter differently. The newspaper reported that advocates were divided 'over the question of whether a native should be allowed to become a member of their Society'. And would this member be allowed, in terms of the Natives' Urban Areas Act, to rent chambers with the other advocates in the city centre?

Being admitted to the Bar and joining the Society of Advocates was not an issue, as membership was not restricted to whites. By way of contrast, advocates in Pretoria were sharply divided on the same issue in the early 1980s when Dikgang Moseneke wanted to become a barrister and a member of the Pretoria Bar.

At the time of Duma's admission, the Bar was accustomed to conducting its affairs quietly. Certainly contentious issues were never leaked to the press. The Nokwe affair changed this, to the consternation of the conservative old guard.

No more than ten days after Nokwe's admission *Die Transvaler* was reporting on the dissension created by the African advocate. A hostile group were objecting to his use of the library, the common room and the robing room. The question of his legal right to rent chambers in a white area kept raising its head. Even worse, there was a prospect that an Indian would soon join him. News of the brilliant student, Ismail Mahomed, who was about to come to the Bar, had travelled fast.

At the time, the Bar had not reserved enough rooms in His Majesty's Building for every member to have an office. About thirty junior members shared offices. When they needed to consult, they used the library, the common room or a nearby coffee shop. Among those forced to share was Balthasar John Vorster. He had given up his attorney's practice in Brakpan and become a member of the Bar, no doubt in preparation for higher political office. Eventually he became minister of justice, then prime minister and finally state president. Vorster shared a small fourth-floor office with hardly any facilities.

I had managed to get a foothold in what was probably the most prestigious group. Walter Pollak QC was about to go on a long overseas trip and he asked if I would move into his room, look after his books and try to index his opinions while he was away. It was an offer I could hardly refuse. Shortly before he came back a vacancy occurred in the group. Over twenty members applied, but I was fortunate enough to be selected. By the time Duma arrived I had had my own room for more than eighteen months. Consequently I invited him to hang his robes behind my door and to put his few books and papers on one of my shelves.

What *Die Transvaler* referred to as 'the protest group' was led by JH 'Lamie' Snyman and George D Anderson Munnik. Many thought that their close cooperation with the government over the Nokwe issue probably helped to secure their elevation to the bench.

The Bar Council appointed a commission to hear the objections of the protesters and other proposals for resolving the conflict. I appeared before the commission and explained my relationship with Nokwe.

Their findings recommended that Nokwe be regarded as a fully-fledged member of the Bar. He should have chambers in His Majesty's Building and use of the library. The commission's other recommendations were less clear. It felt that Nokwe was at liberty to use the common room but wondered whether he wanted to take the risk. This referred to a threat by the protesters that if he did so they would lodge a complaint that he had committed a criminal offence under the Group Areas Act.

Duma was upset that the onus had been put on him. So were many of us, his friends, but we could not prescribe to him. He consulted with Mandela, Tambo, Walter Sisulu and others. They hated the racist overtones but felt that the right to occupy premises and to practise at the Bar was of such fundamental importance that Duma ought to swallow the bitter pill. Walter Sisulu had the last word: 'Are we to lose an opportunity to break the barrier for lack of a cup of tea?'

A general meeting of the Bar was called to discuss the commission's recommendations. Isie Maisels QC presided and Munnik, Snyman and Vorster spoke. They believed it would be illegal for Nokwe to occupy premises in a white area and that he should seek assistance from the department of native affairs for office space in one of the black locations around Johannesburg. Maisels responded that the intention was to apply for permission for Duma to occupy the premises. The owners of the building had agreed that Duma could take an office if he had the necessary permission. Vorster, slowly and deliberately, in his usual guttural voice, assured us that no such permission would be granted.

'Are we going to have reverse discrimination?' asked Munnik. Everyone knew that there were no rooms available and that all newcomers had to share. 'Was Nokwe to be given a room of his own ahead of many others who had already been waiting?' asked Snyman. 'Well, let us ask,' retorted Maisels, 'who would be prepared to share with Nokwe?' I raised my arm. 'There you have it,' said Maisels, 'Bizos is prepared to share with him.' He sounded as if he had no prior knowledge of my willingness, indeed of the existing arrangement.

An application was made for a permit and in anticipation of gaining permission, the signwriter was called in to put Duma's name under mine on the door.

As Vorster had predicted, the permit was refused. The letter to Nokwe from the native commissioner of Johannesburg gave as his reason merely that it was 'contrary to policy'. Nokwe was urged to obtain an office in one of the municipal native residential areas. The controversy raged on in the newspapers but Duma remained in chambers at His Majesty's Building.

Cases for Duma came in from Mandela and Tambo, Harry Bloom, Jack Levitan and a number of other attorneys whose clients were invariably Africans. Duma could not charge high fees but was soon earning enough to justify his decision to come to the Bar.

Then a different sort of brief arrived and threw him into turmoil. It was from a leading firm of attorneys acting on behalf of a prominent mining house. Duma was asked to accompany the attorneys and their client to a tribal meeting to negotiate the sale of the tribe's mineral rights to the mining house. He recognised the political and ethical questions involved and asked his political colleagues and more particularly Nelson Mandela and Walter Sisulu what he ought to do about this brief. They had no clear answer. What was my view? I deferred to Walter Pollak, who had been chairman of the Bar Council and was generally considered the guru of ethical problems at the Bar. When he saw the brief he smiled faintly.

Without saying anything directly, he assumed that we all knew why the brief had been sent to Duma. He explained the cab-rank rule and indicated that Duma was obliged to take the brief if he were not booked for another case. He suggested that Duma tell the tribe that he was acting on behalf of the mining house, that he was representing the interests of the company and that members of the tribe were free to make up their own minds about what they ought to do. He might also suggest, hinted Pollak, that the matter was of sufficient importance for the tribe to take independent legal advice. In fairness to the client, Duma was to tell the attorneys how he intended handling the matter. Once Duma had outlined his strategy, he never heard from the firm of attorneys again.

Some three months later, Duma was arrested on a charge of treason. His name remained on the door of our shared chambers but his practice was erratic. He could only work on cases when the preparatory examination and trial were adjourned. Our office was regularly used for meetings after working hours. Those prohibited from attending gatherings felt safer at the advocates' chambers.

But in reality it did not matter if you were an advocate. If you were black and the police stopped you, you were in trouble if you didn't refer to them as 'baas'. Calling them *meneer* was just not good enough. Duma Nokwe discovered this when he was stopped while driving his small, smoky two-stroke Auto Union car. He was questioned and badly beaten up for no apparent reason other than that he did not acknowledge the two white policemen as his 'masters'. The three of us, Isie Maisels, who was defending Nokwe on a charge of treason in Pretoria, Duma and I decided that both a criminal prosecution and a civil trial for damages should be instituted.

I was briefed by the attorneys handling the treason trial, A Livingstone and Co, to monitor the criminal proceedings in relation to the police assault when they stopped Nokwe in his car. Nokwe's evidence was straightforward. The only

possible reason for the vicious assault emerged when the senior of the two policemen, obviously exasperated, exclaimed in Afrikaans, the equivalent of, 'You still
call me 'Sir' and not 'Master'!'

Dirk O Vermooten led the defence of the two constables. They denied the charge
of assault, and seemed intent on ruining Nokwe's career at the Bar by testifying
that his story was fabricated. They produced perjured evidence that a policeman,
someone other than the two accused, had seen him several hours earlier drunk
and beaten up. The two constables, so they said, far from assaulting him, had been
attempting to assist him. They complained that they had been kind and helpful to
Nokwe and their reward was the false charge he had laid against them. They had
been in a completely different part of town and had police witnesses to prove it.

I sat near the prosecutor and suggested one or two questions to him during
the course of his cross-examination of the accused and their witnesses. Eventually,
Vermooten loudly objected to my 'interfering', although the prosecutor did not
appear to mind. I was asked by the magistrate to move away.

The two constables were backed by some of their superiors who gave evidence
in support of their scandalous defence. But they were still convicted and fined.
The civil claim was settled on the basis of a comparatively small sum to be paid as
damages and costs. As it turned out, we had to battle to get our costs. The taxing
master decided to disallow the costs of a copy of the proceedings in the criminal
trial. We had asked for this to enable us to prepare for the civil trial.

Eventually we had no option but to bring an application for review before
Judge Simon Kuper to overrule this decision. Setting aside the taxing master's
decision, the judge held that the attorney would have failed in his duty if he had
not obtained a copy of the record. During the course of the argument, when he
realised how small the amounts involved were, the judge suggested to counsel for
the policemen that the government attorney appeared to have acted churlishly.

Not long after this, Ismail Mahomed arrived. We had become good friends
during our student days on the SRC and he asked me to move his admission to
the Bar. A separate robing room and toilet had been set aside for Duma Nokwe
at the Pretoria Court, but Ismail and I decided that we would not use the little
room provided for 'non-white advocates'. Instead, we walked together into the
robing room established for counsel at the beginning of the century.

Those in the room fell silent as they watched me struggling to get the studs
through the holes of the over-starched white-winged collar on Ismail's double-
cuffed shirt. A senior member of the Pretoria Bar asked me if I knew that there
was a separate robing room for non-whites. I muttered something but neither of
us took the matter any further. Then a senior member of the Johannesburg Bar,

with a reputation as a teller of awful ethnic jokes, launched into a story using a hopelessly inauthentic Indian accent. His story fell flat. At least the judges who admitted Ismail wished him well.

For years Ismail moved from office to office until he eventually found permanent chambers. Despite this handicap, he developed one of the busiest practices at the Johannesburg Bar and even the most fashionable attorneys and their clients sought his services. For over fifteen years, however, there was one privilege that he could not enjoy. He did not take tea or lunch in the common room. The fiction was that he chose not to. In reality he feared the threat made by the protesters against Nokwe, that if he joined his white colleagues in the common room, he would be reported to the Group Areas inspectors.

Towards the end of 1973 Joan Mostert, a teacher of Afrikaans literature, was bemoaning the way in which her people, the Afrikaners, treated black people. I told her not to be too hard on them. 'Had the members of the Johannesburg Bar been any better?' I asked. Ismail Mahomed and the other black advocates who had joined the Bar still didn't use the common room. She called over her husband Anton. He was influential with the government of the time, and was regularly briefed to act for the State. How could he and his colleagues tolerate this state of affairs? Anton, with his usual confidence, announced that he would guarantee to the chairman of the Bar Council, Sydney Kentridge, that no action would be taken by the government or any of its officials if black members of the Bar made use of the common room. And so the situation changed.

Ismail Mahomed came to be recognised as one of the most outstanding constitutional and administrative law practitioners in southern Africa. He was elevated to the bench, eventually becoming Chief Justice in Namibia and later South Africa.

One of the most calculated insults I ever witnessed was directed against the well-mannered, gentle Oliver Tambo. It took place in Pretoria in the period between the preparatory examination and the treason trial itself. He telephoned me one Saturday morning to say that he was with the parents of a young man due to be hanged that Monday. His defence to charges of robbery and murder had been rejected in the absence of his alleged accomplice, who had escaped. Now the alleged accomplice had been rearrested. The parents and Oliver hoped that in the new trial evidence would emerge that would absolve the condemned man. Could we bring a stay of execution? Both Oliver and I knew that the courts frowned upon such applications. It was considered an act of mercy, or at least a kindness, not to delay such matters. I was hesitant. Nevertheless, I telephoned Sydney Kentridge for advice. In matters of life and death, he said, one does not have to weigh up the strength of one's case too carefully.

We lodged the application and met with the registrar of the court, the attorney-general's representative and the secretary for justice, who held the execution warrant, at the home of Judge Simon Tos Bekker. The registrar had informed Oliver that the applicant required only one legal representative. Both of us understood the registrar's remark.

When we arrived at the judge's home, Oliver, without a trace of bitterness, said he would stay in the car. The nature of the matter was such that anything smacking of protest against the norms of white practice towards blacks might have endangered the success of the application.

While Mrs Bekker made tea and crumpets for all but one of us, the humane judge persuaded the secretary of justice not to hand over the execution warrant to the sheriff until the new trial was over. Oliver jumped out of the car and happily embraced me when I emerged from the house and gave him the thumbs up sign. He never did say how he felt while waiting in the car. Unfortunately the story does not end on a good note. The trial of the accomplice did not, ultimately, help the condemned man.

CHAPTER 11

Jeremiah's Lamentations

Mandela and Tambo had a varied and busy practice. They seemed to take on every case that came in. Local ANC officials, members of advisory boards and clergymen would send distressed people for help. The two lawyers could not possibly cope with all their clients and newly qualified advocates did much of their work. The advocates, however, charged fees for which the partnership became responsible and the firm was not always able to collect the money charged by counsel. Despite the great activity in their offices, little was left for them at the end of the month.

A typical case in which I helped was that of a small farmer in the Eastern Cape, a Mr Qhaka. He was charged with ploughing his land against the contour. He knew it was best to plough along the contour to avoid erosion but told me he couldn't do so because that would mean obeying the new regulations. 'We do not, in our tribe, recognise the chief appointed by the government against our traditions and our will,' he told me. 'I cannot recognise and obey his regulations.'

Mandela and Tambo then briefed me to attack the validity of the regulations.

I went off to some occasional court that would have been impossible to find had not one of Mandela and Tambo's clerks driven me. The magistrate was surprised to see counsel from Johannesburg. The legal training of rural magistrates was often limited to a couple of law examinations set by the civil service. They would start out as clerks, be promoted to prosecutor, then acting magistrate, and eventually assistant native commissioner for the area. Or they might have been banished to remote areas, considered unsuitable for judicial service in the cities. Inevitably the magistrate would be Afrikaans and have difficulty in understanding the language of the concept we were trying to explain. Seldom would they have dealt with a challenge that the regulations were invalid. In these instances our arguments either held that the regulation was invalid or did not give sufficient guidance regarding what was prohibited and what was enjoined.

One thing they did understand was that declaring the regulations invalid would expose them to numerous difficulties. The judgment would have to be brought to the attention of the senior public prosecutor. The decision would have to be backed by reasons. The senior public prosecutor might recommend an appeal to set aside the magistrate's decision. A conviction, on the other hand, would lead to even more trouble. We would appeal and the magistrate would have to file reasons for conviction and deal with arguments we had presented which often made no sense to him.

Sometimes the bemused official decided on a polite approach and the court orderly would be sent to invite the young white counsel to tea during the adjournment. This would cause the same young counsel a dilemma because the invitation would not be extended to the clerk from Mandela and Tambo's office. The clerk would urge acceptance. He would shrug his shoulders and say that it would not be in the interests of the client to snub the magistrate. To our shame, we often accepted these invitations.

On this occasion, the contrary ploughman, wearing his Sunday best, seemed pleased from his seat in the dock. His counsel was putting the inspector of lands through his paces. The accused did not understand the language, but listened intently and smiled from time to time as the interpreter translated. The slower pace gave the magistrate the opportunity to write down the question and answer.

The courtroom accommodated the magistrate on a long bench, a large solid desk for the prosecutor on the side and a long desk separating the dock from the bench for defence counsel and attorneys. Two witness boxes, one for whites and one for blacks. Up to the early 1950s there was only one witness box but with the advent of apartheid the situation changed.

Signs on two entrances were clearly marked: EUROPEANS ONLY/SLEGS VIR BLANKES and NON-EUROPEANS/NIE-BLANKES. A door in the middle was reserved for officials. Some of us thought that we were making a small point by walking through the section reserved for blacks. The looks we got from white policemen and the prosecutor betrayed their thoughts: what sort of white man is this that has no pride in his own race?

Generally the courts would be packed with middle-aged to elderly men neatly dressed in worn suits kept for church and occasions such as this. The public gallery for blacks would be crammed, with five or six whites on the other side. Standing was not allowed so those that couldn't find seats were ordered out. Court procedure was to deal with the whites first. These were minor matters: the theft of a chicken or a sheep. Little evidence was led. The accused black man would plead guilty. The white section would be empty by the time the black cases were called.

As far as the magistrates and native commissioners were concerned, we were a curious group of young advocates. From time to time, we had the temerity to question why people vitally interested in the outcome of the case were not allowed into the court. The whites-only section was empty, we pointed out, why can't they sit there? The presiding officer would be astounded that an officer of the court could seriously make any such proposal. They found it just as strange that we insisted on calling black witnesses 'Mr' or 'Mrs', coupled with their surnames and not, as was the custom, 'Jim' or 'Martha'.

More often than not, we won our cases. Not because the regulations were invalid – that would have been too complicated and risky for the magistrate – but by virtue of some minor omission in the evidence. In the long run, the victory was short-lived. In future, when others were charged with the same offence, the prosecution's case would be better prepared. It became more and more difficult, even for Mandela and Tambo, and the half-dozen or so young counsel briefed by them, to stem the number of prosecutions and fines that eventually subjected the community to the will of the newly established tribal authority.

Gradually, ANC talk of freedom and an end to oppression filtered back to the rural areas. People joined the organisation. They would hold meetings to speak of the struggle of their ancestors to keep the land. In due course reports of this activity reached Pretoria. The governor-general was the supreme chief of all the African people in South Africa. He could make laws for them without consulting his subjects, he did not even have to ask the whites-only Parliament to pass legislation. Consequently, a law was passed banning meetings of more than ten natives in the reserved areas unless the native commissioner had first given permission. Exceptions were made. If a meeting was to be presided over by the government-appointed chief to discuss the affairs of the tribe, no such permission was required. Nor was permission required to hold any religious gathering. However, chiefs and headmen were required to report any unauthorised meetings, especially if they involved people from the cities. Once a report was made, a large contingent of policemen would arrive, surround the crowd, order them to disperse and warn that a refusal would be met with force.

Usually the organiser of the meeting and the guest speaker would be arrested. Inevitably a call was put through to the offices of Mandela and Tambo. It had become accepted practice in many rural areas not to pay admission of guilt fines. Typically such cases would end up as a brief to one of us at His Majesty's Building. In trying to establish a defence I would invariably be told they were holding a religious gathering. 'What made it a religious meeting?'

'Well,' I would be told, 'I am a lay preacher in my church and as such can preach the gospel. I can read the Bible. This meeting was also held on a Sunday morning. Therefore it was a religious gathering.'

'Did you have a Bible with you? Did you read from it?'

'Oh yes,' I was assured. 'But it was not necessary to read from it. Everyone knew chapter five of the Lamentations of Jeremiah by heart. How strange that Mr Bizos doesn't know the passage!'

I asked to be reminded. The elderly man stood, adopted his lay preacher's pose, raised his head towards the ceiling, closed his eyes and intoned:

> Remember, O Lord, what is come upon us: consider, and behold our reproach.
> Our inheritance is turned to strangers, our houses to aliens.
> We are orphans and fatherless, our mothers are as widows.
> We have drunken our water for money; our wood is sold unto us.
> Our necks are under persecution: we labour, and have no rest ...

Eventually I interrupted that, according to the charge sheet and the further particulars, he was condemning the issue of passes to women. Also that there was insufficient land. On top of this he had demanded a pound a day as a minimum wage.

My client, the lay preacher, agreed, arguing that a good lay preacher not only quotes from the Bible but speaks about the burdens of the people.

My defence of a religious gathering did not succeed. Perhaps because it was difficult explaining the sale of left-wing newspapers, the distribution of pamphlets and the shouts of '*Africa Mayibuye!*' at the meeting. Fortunately the magistrate was amused by the defence and imposed the lightest possible fine on our lay preacher.

CHAPTER 12

Cultural Clubs

*The Bantu must be guided to serve his own community in all respects.
There is no place for him in the European community above the level
of certain forms of labour.*

– Dr Hendrik F Verwoerd
Minister of Native Affairs, 1953

The purpose of the Bantu Education Act No 47 of 1953 was:

To provide for the transfer of the administration and control of native education
from the several provincial administrations to the government of the Union,
and for matters incidental thereto.

By 1955 the government effectively had control of African schools. The minister
of native affairs had the power to close down schools if he believed they were not
in the interests of the Bantu people or any section of such people or were likely to
be detrimental to the physical, mental or moral welfare of the pupils or students
attending or likely to attend such schools.

The Act further provided that any person who admitted a Bantu child or any
person or who established, conducted or maintained any Bantu or native school
without proper authority would be guilty of an offence and could be fined or
imprisoned. Some parental participation in school boards was allowed, but these
boards comprised both appointed and elected members. The latter had to be vetted
by the department so that undesirable elements could be excluded.

Separate education for African people was nothing new. There were some fine
schools, particularly in the Cape, Natal and Transvaal provinces, established and
run by the churches, which produced educated and independently minded young
people, such as Oliver Tambo, Duma Nokwe and many others. The Anglican and
Catholic churches were thought particularly guilty by Verwoerd and his Bantu
Education Commission of producing 'little black Englishmen' who would not fit
into the government's apartheid ideals.

In April 1955, a pupil boycott of the schools was called by the ANC, but it was
poorly planned and Minister Verwoerd warned that any students absent after

the end of the month would be expelled. Teachers who stayed away would have their employment terminated. At the end, more than seven thousand children were left in limbo, prevented from admission to any school in the country. Over a hundred teachers lost their jobs. For the government this was of no great concern and people defined as suitable in accordance with official criteria took over and administered the Bantu schools.

In response the African Education Movement was formed to sponsor 'cultural clubs' which pupils and schoolteachers could join. They dared not use the words 'teacher' or 'pupil' as this might provide evidence of a crime and lead to prosecution on charges of running an illegal school. In and round Johannesburg, the Anglican Community of the Resurrection under Father Trevor Huddleston took an active part in this movement.

Groups of 'club members' and a 'leader' would meet in homes, garages or under trees, not to be 'taught', but to participate in 'cultural activities'. Invariably the police would raid these cultural clubs and those who appeared to be over the age of sixteen and did not have a pass would be arrested. Often an admission by the 'leader' that he was a dismissed teacher was grounds enough to arrest him and charge him with unlawfully conducting an unregistered school. His 'pupils', to use the police word, were told to disperse and warned that they should not be caught again attending an illegal school. Despite the warning the 'cultural club' would reconvene at a new place.

Nelson Mandela, Oliver Tambo, Shulamith Muller and I helped those who fell foul of the law. We searched in legal and ordinary dictionaries and looked for decided cases that dealt with the proper legal meaning of 'school', 'institution' and 'education'. These were the words used in the Act so we needed to know the defined limits of each. In the end, the primary meaning of 'school' in *The Oxford English Dictionary* served us well for some time. According to that definition, a school is an 'establishment' in which boys or girls, or both, receive instruction.

We advised those who provided the programme for the 'cultural clubs' not to call it a syllabus. Merely imparting information was not a contravention of the law. The Crown could hardly describe an informal gathering – in a home, a disused garage or on the veld – where a group leader read stories to an audience, as a school in the dictionary sense. We also advised against the use of text and exercise books and even makeshift blackboards.

The first case to be heard involving a 'cultural club' concerned a group in Alexandra township. Representatives of the African Education Movement attended court along with Father Huddleston. So did a number of foreign and local media correspondents. Prosecuting people for imparting knowledge was obviously a newsworthy event. The magistrate was not unaware of the presence of these people.

As in all magistrate's courts, he first had to deal with what were referred to as the 'petties' – cases involving people arrested overnight on pass offences or for being on the streets after the nine o'clock curfew. They might also have been arrested on suspicion of being 'foreign natives' from the British colonies surrounding South Africa. The punishments for these offences could be anything from one pound or a month in prison to five pounds or six months' imprisonment.

The cases were usually dealt with quickly. But before such a distinguished and probably hostile audience, the magistrate was particularly careful. Most offenders were cautioned and discharged. A couple were fined a mere five shillings. The magistrate made a short speech after each sentence commenting on how chaotic the urban areas would be if people entered them freely. Your place is on the farms and mines where you are needed, he said.

The journalists did not show much interest in these cases. They were waiting to see if a former teacher would be sent to prison for doing nothing more than keeping youngsters off the streets.

The case was called. The police officer took the witness stand, then slowly and deliberately related in Afrikaans what he had seen under a tree in the veld on the outskirts of a township. The local journalists whispered a translation to their foreign colleagues.

Under cross-examination the policeman confirmed that there were no blackboards, desks, books or other educational aids. How then could this be described as a school? The magistrate found the accused not guilty and discharged him. The small group of parents and members of the teachers' families were pleased and excited that their school could carry on.

Prosecutions pending in Benoni, Soweto, Nelspruit, Kliptown and elsewhere were dropped. The African Education Movement thought that it could now proceed unhindered, providing alternative education to that envisaged by Verwoerd. The 'cultural clubs' served a real need – but it was increasingly clear that they faced serious difficulties. They had no money to pay the teachers or 'leaders', there were no suitable premises, there was a lack of discipline and, understandably, no long-term planning.

Then came an even more serious setback. What, in our youthful enthusiasm, we had considered a triumph for education was short-lived. A case was brought in Benoni a few months later where it quickly became clear that ingenuity was not our prerogative alone. The first witness was a youth. The 'teacher' immediately recognised him as one of the club members or pupils. We believed he must have been coerced into giving evidence. We were wrong.

The youth was eighteen, although he looked several years younger. He had been at police training college for several months before he was ordered to join a club under false pretences. He was to prepare daily reports. Dressed in an old shirt, short trousers and a tattered pair of tennis shoes, he was welcomed. No one had any reason to check his story.

His reports in court gave a graphic account of the unconventional teaching methods employed – the cyclostyled sheets distributed surreptitiously at the end of the day, the essays delivered to a neighbour of the teacher from where they were picked up, corrected and marked. The young police recruit's neatly written notes were handed in as exhibits, as were some of the cyclostyled sheets that he referred to as 'lessons'.

We were taken by surprise and requested an adjournment to establish if the evidence could be challenged. The accused was a political activist as well as a teacher. Before he would answer any of our questions, he wanted an answer to his own: Did the police have the right to teach a boy to lie about who he was, where he came from and why he attended the club?

We told him there was nothing that said they couldn't. He lowered his head, turned his eyes upwards and in a subdued, angry tone said there was no part of the evidence that he could challenge. Timid efforts to test the memory of the witness worsened our case.

But there was another unpleasant surprise in the offing. A portly, bespectacled man stepped into the witness box. He was an inspector of education. He had read the young policeman's notes and the lessons that were handed out. He had also heard the evidence.

The inspector then quoted at some length from one of the documents headed, 'The Story of the Pharaoh and his Daughter', which was geographically explicit, described the Nile's fauna and flora and the river's economic benefits. The inspector believed this constituted the systematic imparting of information and that it was presented in a particularly appropriate way to educate young people. He would, in fact, recommend to the next inspectors' circuit conference that some of the material be introduced into the curriculum of Bantu schools. That the copyright might lie with the hard working teachers and students of the African Education Movement was not something he considered.

The case for the Crown could not be contradicted. The argument, so well received in the previous case, could hardly be repeated now following the cogent evidence led by the policeman and the inspector of education. The magistrate convicted the accused and imposed a fine which he coupled with a stern warning that if the accused ever ran a school again he could be sent to jail.

One after the other the cultural clubs closed down. The expelled teachers and pupils had to find other ways of earning a living or receiving an education. A few of them went to Lesotho and Swaziland where they completed their education at various church schools. Some of the younger teachers became professionals, some of them lawyers. Others had to be satisfied with jobs as filing clerks or messengers.

In the late 1980s, I was about to deliver a paper at a seminar when a young attorney assigned to chair a later session insisted that he should preside at my presentation instead. He told me that I had defended his father who ran an illegal school. Now he wanted to write to his father, who was in exile, and tell him that he had chaired a meeting at which I spoke.

CHAPTER 13

Urban Agitators

In the late 1950s I took on another case for Mandela and Tambo. The client's name was Timothy Fefo Rampai, and he had the dubious distinction of being declared an 'undesirable' person in his home area of Germiston. The local authority had tried to evict Rampai from his house in terms of the recently amended Urban Areas Act 25 of 1945. He was, they said, an agitator. Two weeks after the eviction notice he was arrested and sentenced to three weeks' imprisonment with compulsory labour. On completion of the sentence he was to be removed from Germiston.

Nelson Mandela was concerned not only for Rampai, but for many others, vulnerable because of their membership of ANC local committees. To the white municipal councils they were troublemakers. To the ANC leadership they were important organisers, because they worked at grass-roots level among the people.

Rampai had received letters from the council accusing him of being an agitator. Mandela requested details of his client's wrongdoing. The council said Rampai had 'shown opposition to the law' and that he had organised a campaign to defy legislation. Rampai's denials of these allegations prompted the local authority to hold a special meeting.

During the first case in which we defended Rampai, the town clerk gave evidence that the council had ordered Rampai to leave. We asked for the minutes – not only of the decision itself, but of the debate. The magistrate expressed surprise at the request but let the case stand down so that the minutes could be produced. The *Rand Daily Mail* had reported that the council was divided on the issue of Rampai's expulsion. The minutes confirmed this. In fact the meeting had split down the middle – five National Party councillors supporting the eviction, five members of the United Party opposing.

Despite the strength of the opposition, the mayor cast his deciding vote to banish Rampai.

At the end of the trial we put up a notice of appeal which meant that the magistrate had to produce written reasons for his decision. He couldn't have been paying attention during the trial as he telephoned me and asked that I repeat our argument very slowly. This argument came back to us word for word in his written reasons supporting the judgment. Finally he added a single sentence: 'There is no substance whatever in this argument.'

On appeal we contended that the order made by the council was invalid because the local authority had not understood the legislation they were administering. Otherwise they would have or at least could have come to a different decision.

The minutes of the crucial meeting demonstrated that the councillors were ignorant of the Urban Areas Act. We submitted that whether the presence of an individual was detrimental to the maintenance of peace in the area was subjective. The onus rested on the local authority to establish the merit of the allegations. But no investigation was carried out. No notice was served on Rampai concerning the impending eviction and he was given no chance to reply to the allegations. The local authority's only defence was that the councillors believed that their decision was not final. This belief was based on the assessment of a supposed legal advisor. They had also been assured that Rampai had committed other offences.

Judge Bekker presided at our appeal. Along with Judge Steyn, Judge Bekker set aside Rampai's eviction on the grounds that the local authority 'misunderstood the legislation which it was administering' and, therefore, its decision was invalid. Not much use was made of the iniquitous provision afterwards. But the authorities found many other ways to deal with those who did not accept the established racist order.

Another case that I took on appeal for the Mandela and Tambo practice concerned Tanci and four others.

The five men had been convicted of attending or presiding at a meeting where more than ten natives were present. The meeting had been held to protest against the Peri-Urban Areas Board taking over the administration of Alexandra township. Unfortunately they hadn't requested permission to hold the meeting. Tanci was fined £20 (or two months' imprisonment with compulsory labour) for having presided. The other four were fined £3 (or ten days with compulsory labour) for having addressed the meeting.

We had two grounds for appeal. The first was that the government notice gave authority to a native commissioner or magistrate allowing him absolute discretion in whether to ban or allow a meeting. We contended that this was an invalid delegation of authority. Had the official been given guidelines as to how and under what circumstances the notice should be implemented, it would then have been a proper delegation. We supported our arguments with past cases in which guidelines had been given to the official concerned. These guidelines enabled them to carry out their duty properly.

The second ground for appeal was that the notice did not prohibit gatherings or assemblies 'of natives', but rather gatherings at which more than ten natives 'were present'. We contended that there was a fundamental difference. The Native Administration Act of 1927 prohibited gatherings of natives, but the notice under which they had been convicted had a different meaning. We submitted that, properly construed, it meant that as soon as ten natives joined a meeting of whites, it became illegal.

The presiding judges, Oscar Galgut and Charles Theron, agreed that our first line of attack had to fail. In their view sufficient guidelines had been provided for the official to make a proper decision. The regulation permitted the prohibition of a very limited kind of gathering and the official's discretion was therefore to be employed in a specific, limited field.

On the second point we were successful. The judges discussed the different meaning and scope of the Native Administration Act and the government notice. They agreed that the Act provided for the prohibition of gatherings of natives, whereas the notice prohibited any meeting at which more than ten natives were present. The Act was clearly intended to refer to meetings consisting of natives only. They concluded that since the regulation was not limited to meetings of natives it exceeded the powers conferred by the Act and the appeal should therefore succeed. Obviously the thought that the rights of whites could be affected by as few as ten natives must have weighed heavily on the minds of the judges. That Tanci benefited was probably incidental to them, though most welcome to us.

CHAPTER 14

Vark and Banda

A criminal case handled by Mandela and Tambo, and on which they briefed me, concerned two resourceful young men nicknamed Vark and Banda. The first bore an unfortunate resemblance to a pig; the second looked like the then president of Malawi.

The incident that got them into trouble concerned an armed robbery of a concession storekeeper on a mine.

The last weekend of the month would always be particularly busy for such stores and, come the Monday morning, concession store owners would deposit thousands of pounds into the bank. On one such Monday, two young black men robbed a storekeeper on his way to the bank at gunpoint and fled with the cash into a nearby reedbed. The robbery was reported to the police and Detective Warrant Officer van der Linde jumped to conclusions and ordered his most trusted native detective constable to 'Go and get Vark and Banda!'

They weren't apprehended until the middle of the next day, despite a careful police watch over their likely drinking places and their girlfriends' homes. Then the constable spotted the men in town and arrested them. They offered no resistance or protest and were told that when they got to the police station Warrant Officer van der Linde would explain why they'd been picked up.

The lanky van der Linde had the two men handcuffed to one another. He didn't tell them why they were under arrest, or that they had a right to remain silent. He was an old-fashioned, practical detective. He came quickly to the point. 'Where's the money?' 'What money is the baas speaking about?' the two suspects answered. Vark and Banda were both smart enough to know that you did not refer to Warrant Officer van der Linde as '*meneer*' or 'sir'. 'Don't try and be clever with me,' said the policeman. 'Where's the Jew's money?' 'No, we don't know, baas,' replied the duo. 'Can the baas please explain?'

Van der Linde sprang up. Towering over them, he banged their heads together. 'I won't stand for your nonsense,' he shouted. 'Either you tell me where the money is or I'll break your bloody necks.' Vark and Banda stuck by their story: 'We don't know about any money, baas.'

Van der Linde established that they had less than £30 between them when they were detained. A search of their pockets revealed a receipt for £50 from Mandela and Tambo. The receipt was made out to Vark and Banda in their proper names. Purpose of payment was given as Regina v. Selves.

Van der Linde lost his temper. 'You bloody kaffirs,' he yelled. 'Not only do you rob a Jew of his money but then you go and give it to kaffir attorneys. You say you know nothing about the money yet you go and pay to be defended even before we arrest you.' Vark and Banda maintained they knew nothing about robbing anyone. They said they had borrowed the £50 when they heard that the police were looking for them. They had given the money to Mandela and Tambo so that the attorneys could bail them out if they were arrested. Van der Linde placed them in separate cells and predicted that the two suspects would soon talk.

Vark was beaten but insisted he knew nothing about the money. Banda's treatment was less severe. After a few blows he said he wanted to talk to the baas alone. Banda then told van der Linde that they had given the money to Mr Mandela. 'When?' asked the policeman. 'This morning,' Banda replied. 'And the gun, where's the gun?' 'No, baas, we handed that to him as well.' 'Why hand it over to him?' 'No, baas, they do that at the offices of Mandela and Tambo,' said Banda. 'They put everything in a small room next to their offices. There is a lot of stuff in it. I saw exactly where he put the money. I can show the baas. He also put the gun in another place. All mixed up with plenty of things. I can show the baas as well.'

Van der Linde knew enough to protect himself against smart attorneys, so he asked Banda to make an affidavit. Banda agreed. Then he and van der Linde went to the offices of Mandela and Tambo.

There van der Linde told Mandela that, according to an affidavit he had, money stolen during a robbery was hidden on the premises, as was an unlicensed handgun used during the robbery. Mandela asked who had received the money and the firearm. 'You did,' said the policeman.

Before Mandela could say anything there was a commotion in the reception area, and he went out to investigate. He returned leading Banda by the hand. Banda apologised for bothering the attorney but said it was the only way he could stop the police from torturing his friend and himself.

Mandela ordered the detective out of his office, said he would be sending a doctor to examine the two suspects, and that they had better appear in court within forty-eight hours of their arrest.

For a white man to be spoken to in this way by a black man, even though he was an attorney, was insulting enough. But to be tricked by Banda must have been unbearable for the policeman. A chuckling Nelson telephoned me soon afterwards. Did I know a doctor who would be prepared to rush out and see the two suspects? He also asked me to hold myself available for the trial.

Percy Yutar enjoyed a reputation as a zealous prosecutor. Most judges liked him and it was not difficult to tell who they were: they referred to him as 'Dr Yutar', in recognition of his qualifications. As we were to discover, Judge Joe Ludorf, before whom the 'Vark and Banda' case was to be tried, particularly admired Dr Yutar.

Those of us in private practice who were Yutar's less experienced juniors held him in awe. He was attentive, courteous and considerate to Crown witnesses and the opposite to the accused and defence witnesses. He was quick-witted, articulate and hard-working. Irony, and at times sarcasm, punctuated his cross-examination. Without using a single note, he would rattle off a list of the contradictions and improbabilities in the evidence of a defence witness, all this to the amazement and joy of the regulars at Johannesburg's Court One.

Nelson was not usually able to sit with counsel during the conduct of a trial, but his interest in this particular matter was such that he spent some time helping me prepare and then assisting me in court. On the day of the trial I had not faced the combination of Judge Ludorf and Yutar before and did not know the judge's attitude towards the famous prosecutor. We didn't have long to find out. 'Silence in court,' called the orderly. The packed courtroom rose; Yutar and I bowed to the judge. As soon as the judge had taken his seat we all sat down except Yutar. 'Yes, Dr Yutar?' said the judge.

Not a good sign. In a somewhat obsequious manner, Yutar indicated that he appeared for the Crown. The charge was read out. A plea of not guilty was entered and I stood up diffidently to say that I appeared for the accused. I had hardly sat down before the judge again said, this time with a smile, 'Yes, Dr Yutar?'

The prosecutor began a speech. 'This is a very simple case, M'lord. The complainant, a weak and frail gentleman, set off on a Monday morning. It was his habit to deposit the weekend's takings at the bank. The two accused, M'lord, without any regard for his age or the condition of his health …'

Rising, I registered an objection and began a sentence indicating that it was not proper for a prosecutor to comment in his opening address. He should merely set out the main facts which the Crown intended to prove and indicate how the Crown intended to prove these facts. With a degree of patronising benevolence, the judge stopped me. He knew it should be done as I had indicated, but I should not worry about any deviation from standard procedure as this was not a jury case.

(Strangely, I was to hear almost the same words in response to a similar objection I made during the Rivonia trial some years later. The Vark and Banda case was the first of a number of occasions on which I appeared against Yutar during the 1950s. They all provided me with useful experience when I needed to advise my colleagues on tricky issues relating to Yutar in the Rivonia trial.)

Even though Judge Ludorf made no ruling against Yutar, my interjection was of some assistance and Yutar restrained himself a little. He informed the judge that a properly constituted identification parade had been held at which three witnesses positively identified the accused. The first witness would be the storekeeper himself, the victim of the robbery. While the witness was going up to the witness box the judge, an experienced presiding officer, asked me whether he could reasonably infer that the identity of the accused would be put in issue. I said this was indeed so.

The concession storekeeper gave his evidence about what had happened on that morning. Yutar led him very ably. The storekeeper made no reference to visiting the police station or to any subsequent events except that he attended an identification parade a few days after he was robbed. To Yutar's questions he said he had pointed out the two accused in the dock. As I was to learn, Yutar could never resist over-elaboration.

> YUTAR: Are you absolutely certain that these are the right men?
> WITNESS: Yes, I am absolutely certain.
> YUTAR: You have taken an oath. Are you a religious man?
> WITNESS: Yes, M'lord, I am a religious man.
> YUTAR: Had you any doubts whatsoever about the identity of the two persons who robbed you, would you have told His Lordship about this doubt?
> WITNESS: Oh yes, most certainly, M'lord, I would have done so.

Looking at the three newspaper reporters sitting directly opposite him, Yutar smiled and sat down. The judge, who had been making a note of the witness's evidence, looked up and, with the customary nod, indicated that my cross-examination could begin.

> BIZOS: Did you give a description of your assailants to the police officer?
> WITNESS: Yes, as best as I could.
> BIZOS: Please tell us what description you gave.
> WITNESS: That the one was stout and the other one was thin. The one was about as tall as I am and the other shorter.
> BIZOS: Could you give the investigating officer any distinguishing features about their appearance?
> WITNESS: No, I could not.
> BIZOS: Did the investigating officer say anything when you gave him this very brief description?

WITNESS: Yes, he said to the other policeman, 'Go and get Vark and Banda.'

BIZOS: Did you drive to the scene of the crime in the investigating officer's car?

WITNESS: Yes, I did.

BIZOS: Were you not interested in ascertaining from him who Vark and Banda were?

WITNESS: Yes, I was. I asked him about it.

BIZOS: We would only like to know what he said about their appearance.

WITNESS: Well, I was asking him and he was telling me. I don't remember exactly how it came about but he would say, 'Didn't one have a big round head and face?' And after he said so, I said 'Yes, yes, that is so.' And he would say: 'Didn't one have longer hair than the other?' And I said, 'Yes, yes.' And so it went on.

BIZOS: Would it be correct to say that the description given by the investigating officer to you was more detailed than the description you gave the detective?

WITNESS: You could put it that way if you like.

BIZOS: On the description given by you to Warrant Officer van der Linde, there was hardly enough detail to identify your assailants?

WITNESS: I would say so, but Mr van der Linde knew who had done it.

BIZOS: Before you went to the identification parade, did you see Warrant Officer van der Linde?

WITNESS: Yes, I was waiting in his office for about half an hour.

BIZOS: Did he tell you why you had come to the police station?

WITNESS: Yes, he told me that I was there so that I could point out Vark and Banda.

BIZOS: Did he tell you that Vark and Banda would be on the identification parade?

WITNESS: Oh yes, that was the whole purpose of my coming to the police station.

BIZOS: When the officer actually conducting the parade asked you to go and put your hand on the shoulder of the persons that had robbed you, you already knew from Warrant Officer van der Linde that they were, in fact, on the parade, didn't you?

WITNESS: Yes, I did.

Yutar knew the judicial decisions relating to identification all too well. He would have realised that much of what had happened was in conflict with what the courts would allow and he sat uncomfortably ruffling his papers during the cross-examination. He came close to interrupting at one stage, but restrained himself. My next question upset him and he could keep quiet no longer. 'Did you see any injuries on the faces of one or other of the accused on the identification parade?' I asked the witness.

Yutar immediately jumped up to object. The judge asked whether it was being suggested that there were such injuries – for his part, he could see none on the photograph of the people on parade. 'Yes,' I replied. 'There were still bruises on their faces at the time as a result of an assault by the police which led first to the intervention of Mr Mandela, my instructing attorney who is sitting here in court, and then to a visit by the district surgeon and a private doctor.'

Yutar lost his self-control. In his high-pitched voice he assured the judge that the police would deny any improper conduct. Moreover, he trusted that His Lordship would not allow the court to be used to besmirch the good name of a fine officer who had so competently, so efficiently and so fairly conducted this investigation.

The judge looked at me and, realising that I was about to make a speech in reply to Yutar, a speech which the judge obviously did not want to hear, said, with all his judicial gravity, 'What was your question to the witness again, Mr Bizos?' 'Did he see any injuries on the face of one or other of the accused, M'lord?' The judge turned towards the witness and invited him, by gesture, to answer the question. The witness said that he had seen no injury on either accused.

When the judge took the customary fifteen-minute mid-morning tea adjournment, Yutar waited until he was out of the court and then turned on Nelson and me. 'Why do the two of you want to introduce this sort of irrelevant matter into this case?' he demanded. 'I warn you there may be serious consequences if you persist in playing to the gallery and the newspapers by making false and unfounded allegations against the police.'

At that moment the storekeeper passed us, and Yutar, who I came to learn was a professional showman, loudly congratulated him on the fine manner in which he gave his evidence. He did so even though he knew that the witness's disclosure about what had happened at the scene and before the identification parade, could well endanger the conviction he had so confidently expected.

Two other witnesses had pointed out the accused at the identification parade, with each witness identifying only one of our clients. Nelson and I felt confident that our clients would probably get off on the grounds of unreliable identification.

The following day Yutar closed the case for the Crown without calling van der Linde. Yutar had apparently decided it would be safer not calling the policeman and risking what he might say in answer to our questions.

I began the case for the defence by calling Banda as the first witness even though he was the second accused. He denied that he had anything to do with the robbery. He admitted his lifelong friendship with Vark and described where they had been on the day of the robbery.

He said he and his co-accused had heard that the police were looking for them and so had taken the precaution of paying a £50 deposit to Mandela and Tambo for which they had obtained a receipt. The judge looked puzzled and stopped making notes. When Banda spoke of the police taking this receipt and of the threat of violence that followed, Yutar jumped to his feet and appealed to the judge to stop the irrelevant evidence. In response the judge asked what the evidence about the receipt had to do with the issues before him. I explained that the evidence would show that the investigating officer had assaulted the accused. The judge interrupted me, saying such an allegation was 'irrelevant'.

JUDGE: What has that got to do with it? The Crown has not attempted to lead evidence of any statement made by them, which you contend was not freely and voluntarily made. Why must I listen to their evidence complaining of an assault? Why don't they lay a charge against the policemen they allege assaulted them? Why must I be bothered with it in this trial?

BIZOS: Well, M'Lord, the investigating officer has a special relationship with the witnesses. If he is prepared to act unlawfully by assaulting the accused, it is more likely that he might have improperly tried to influence the witnesses to point out the accused. Besides, M'Lord, there is authority for the proposition that the manner in which an accused person has been dealt with should be of concern to the trial court even though it may not be strictly relevant to the main point in issue.

Without calling Yutar to reply, the judge impatiently advised me to continue expeditiously as he did not consider it particularly relevant.

Banda spoke of the assaults and of the trip to Mr Mandela's office. As he listened to the story, the judge looked at Nelson and me and betrayed a measure of amusement by allowing a faint half-smile. Yutar conducted his cross-examination on Banda's alibi with proper decorum. He asked only a few questions about the assault and none at all about the trip to the offices of Mandela and Tambo. After that, Vark and the alibi witnesses were quickly dealt with. Once the defence case was closed, Yutar said that he would not be long in argument. His main contention was that there was enough cogent evidence of identification. They should be convicted.

Nelson and I had prepared an argument that began with reference to various cases dealing with the dangers of mistaken identification where there were no distinguishing marks on the exposed parts of the suspect's body. These judgments held that identification was valueless if the witness was influenced, wittingly or unwittingly, to point out the accused in court. As the storekeeper himself admitted to the court, he had pointed out the persons described to him by Warrant Officer van der Linde rather than anyone he remembered through his own observation.

The investigating officer had emerged as someone with no respect for legality. Once he had unduly influenced the storekeeper, why should it not be held that he had similarly influenced the other witnesses? Van der Linde should have taken detailed descriptions of the perpetrators from the witnesses before he came to the conclusion that Vark and Banda were to blame. The fact that he had not done so made conviction problematic.

Yutar wanted more than the last word, although he was only entitled to reply on questions of law. In his shrill voice he told the judge he should disregard the infamous allegations made against the fine officer who had investigated the case. He had before him a docket opened when the accused and their attorney, Mr Mandela, had decided to lay a criminal charge against van der Linde. He would like to show His Lordship the endorsement of the attorney-general of the Transvaal himself, who had said that after careful consideration of the contents of the docket he refused to prosecute. I could not resist saying in a stage whisper that this was not the way to prove facts. Anyhow, I added, what did the attorney-general's opinion have to do with the matter? Yutar exclaimed: 'Did Your Lordship hear that? Did Your Lordship hear my learned friend say that the attorney-general's opinion is of no relevance to this matter? I would venture to suggest that Your Lordship would always be guided by the opinion of the attorney-general rather than that of my learned friend. The opinion of the attorney-general is ten times, nay a hundred times weightier that his!'

The judge adjusted his papers. He was a veteran of many years at the Bar and of almost five years on the bench. He didn't require time to consider his decision, or even to formulate it. He proceeded to give judgment there and then, concluding that the evidence of the storekeeper could not be relied on to convict the accused.

On the evidence and in the absence of contradictory testimony from van der Linde, he assumed the correctness of the allegations made by the accused, although he made no finding that what they said was true. The fact that the accused, on their respective versions, were inseparable created a strong probability that if one was involved, so was the other. His Lordship was satisfied beyond any reasonable doubt that they were guilty of the offence of robbery as charged.

A number of other judges in the division would no doubt have acquitted the accused. Judge Ludorf thought he had a nose for guilt and innocence and was a great believer in not articulating the premise upon which his judgment was based. During a trial, no one may refer to the previous convictions, if any, of an accused. But our judge would have drawn certain conclusions right at the start when he heard that Warrant Officer van der Linde ordered Vark and Banda's arrest.

He would have assumed that the investigating officer not only knew them, but knew them because of their previous criminal activities. The judge was not a man who would have convicted a person unless he was satisfied that the person was guilty. The only criticism one could make of Judge Ludorf would have been that he was not guided by the evidence alone, but shrewdly read between the lines and allowed what he found there to influence his decisions.

Once the two had been found guilty, the court could be informed of their previous convictions and Yutar appeared to relish the moment when he handed up this information. They had come out of prison only a few months before the concession storekeeper was robbed. The judge again smiled, no doubt at the thought that his hunch had proved correct.

A comparatively short sentence of six years was imposed on both men. Yutar walked off triumphantly, but Warrant Officer van der Linde was deeply hurt. Holding the docket that Yutar had waved about, he complained to Nelson and me that he had been a police officer for over twenty-five years and had never been the subject of an investigation. He referred to Vark and Banda as 'rubbish'. Why did they have to spoil his name by laying a complaint against him? Had we put them up to it?

Nelson and I had mixed feelings about our clients and Warrant Officer van der Linde. But we were quite clear about our feelings in relation to Yutar and the way he operated. Nelson and I were to appear against Yutar and before Judge Ludorf on a number of occasions, one of which also involved Nelson as an accused. Judge Ludorf was one of the three judges appointed to hear the treason trial in which Nelson and other leaders of the Congress Alliance were charged. He recused himself at the beginning of the trial on the grounds that he had been counsel to the police special branch whose members had unlawfully seized documents intended for use in the treason trial.

CHAPTER 15

The ANC and the Defiance Campaign Trial

It has been said that I have done more political trials than anyone else. However, in most of the high-profile trials I appeared not on my own, but with one or other of the giants of the advocates' profession, briefed by a small number of committed attorneys and with invaluable help from a handful of top-class academics.

If South Africa had been a completely totalitarian regime, none of us would have been able to make a contribution. Where there is not even a semblance of judicial independence or freedom of expression, and where the rule of law has been completely abrogated, then neither judges, nor lawyers, nor the media can help in any way. In South Africa, despite many impediments, there was at least lip service paid to these principles. Most whites were not concerned about the majority of the people, but for themselves they wanted democracy and justice administered by an independent judiciary, appointed from within their own ranks.

We were a small group of lawyers, making use of those few procedural safe-guards which were in place for everyone's protection. In our work, we defended many black – and some white – men and women who the regime wanted executed, imprisoned or discredited as terrorists. The dice were loaded against our clients. Many were wrongly accused of serious, even heinous crimes. Confessions were often extracted from them under torture, although torture was routinely denied and often coupled with an allegation that we, their lawyers, were engaged in a campaign to besmirch the good name of the South African Police.

Illegitimate regimes frequently use political trials to discredit their opponents, simultaneously denying that they are political trials. These governments contend that those on trial, who just happen to be their opponents, are common criminals. By adopting this strategy, South Africa was no different from other illegitimate regimes. The accused in such show trials also behaved as their counterparts do and have done elsewhere, using the court case as a forum to speak out. And the courtroom often was the last forum available to condemn oppressive policies and the deprivation of fundamental rights, to demand their right to meaningful citizenship, free and fair elections, dignity, equality and a fair distribution of goods and honours in a democratic state. Although the judiciary was not representative of the population and many judges were ideologically aligned to the regime, a few made use of the narrow space available. These few bravely maintained their independence by interpreting the law in favour of innocence and disbelieving high-ranking police officers and compliant witnesses whose statements were taken under duress.

I was often struck by the courage, integrity and commitment of most of our clients, both young and old, men and women. They loved life no less than anyone else and yet they were prepared to sacrifice their freedom and even their lives to achieve the liberation of all South Africans. Ironically, their lawyers had to face criticism on two fronts. The wrath of the regime was at least not unexpected. However, we also had to deal with those who should have been allies or friends, but who accused us of doing nothing more than lending legitimacy to the regime. Our answer was that for those facing death or long-term imprisonment and for their families who asked us to act, it was not a matter for academic debate. We would give up only if and when those involved in the struggle asked us to stop our legal work. They never did. Nor did they criticise us for helping them by appearing in court. Even now our former clients judge our role more kindly than those who often wrote their criticisms without consulting the main victims of the political injustice in our land.

Although some of the people we defended were members of the Liberal Party, the Pan Africanist Congress (PAC), students in Nusas, supporters of the Black Consciousness Movement and the United Democratic Front (UDF), the vast majority were part of the Congress Alliance headed by the ANC. For the proper defence of our clients it was necessary for us to become familiar with the ANC's history and policies, particularly from the early 1940s to the end of 1961. By then, the organisation had decided that it could no longer keep knocking on the door of the deaf. It began to challenge the authority of the regime by using violence against symbols of apartheid (at the same time taking care to minimise injury and loss of life). The organisation also lobbied to ensure the isolation of the regime from the international community and mounted protests which would render the country 'ungovernable'.

The vast majority of whites knew little about the history or policy of the ANC. It suited them to portray the organisation as a small group of agitators, agents of the Soviet Union, bloodthirsty revolutionaries, bent on destroying a white and Christian democracy. Politicians, prosecutors and their witnesses repeatedly referred to the cataclysm that would ensue if the barbarians were not checked.

In 1912 the South African Native National Congress was formed and renamed the African National Congress in 1923. It was to be a political organisation representative of the African people that sought to use constitutional means to advance its struggle but specifically reserved the right to 'passive action'. From its founding until the early 1940s, the ANC was primarily a suppliant organisation, politely – even humbly – asking for the amelioration of the grievances of the African people, using neither harsh words of protest nor threats of defiance. Then, in the 1940s, the demands became more strident.

Nelson Mandela, Oliver Tambo, Walter Sisulu, Ashby Mda, Anton Lembede and others started to question the policy and tactics adopted by their organisation. Their questioning led to the founding of the ANC Youth League in April 1944, and by 1949 the league had become sufficiently strongly rooted to influence the decisions of the ANC annual conference in Bloemfontein. It pushed through a militant programme of action which resulted two years later in a letter calling on the prime minister to abolish a range of oppressive, discriminatory legislation by the end of February 1952. If the government failed to act, the ANC would implement a plan for the 'defiance of unjust laws', a plan that would become known as the Defiance Campaign.

I did not take part in the trials which resulted from the Defiance Campaign but I spent time in court as a spectator. I also had lengthy discussions with Duma Nokwe, who took an active role in organising and participating in the campaign and who was a close associate of Mandela, Sisulu and other members of the Youth League. What was said in and out of court in these cases laid the foundation on which our defence was built in most of the political trials for almost forty years afterwards. And the echoes of those statements resounded down the decades in the statements of many subsequent accused.

Those charged in the Defiance Campaign trials said, for example, that they were not content to remain mere spectators at events organised by whites, for whites, to mark milestones in the history of South Africa. The Defiance Campaign was probably the first time that Africans and other black people were heard to say that this was not only a white man's country, and certainly it had not been said by such great numbers before. An estimated forty thousand people took to the streets in protest, while white gatherings elsewhere were enjoying pageants in seventeenth-century costume, presided over by members of the government.

The protesters did not expect much sympathy from the courts, which religiously applied every apartheid law and regulation whether passed by the highest or the lowest structure of government. In most cases magistrates imposed a jail term with the option of a fine. However, part of the plan was to fill the jails to the limit. By creating public awareness among white people and hopefully arousing public sympathy, the government might be forced to change. In each court case, defiers refused to pay either bail or the fine option. As the courts were filled by campaign supporters, the spectacle often attracted media attention, and the campaign gained fame and momentum. It quickly spread to more than thirty centres around the country and managed to make some inroads in the rural areas.

As the campaign gained momentum, men and women filled the jails. In Mafikeng the magistrate freed twenty resisters that he had just found guilty because the jail was full. To lessen the pressure on the prison system, magistrates imposed corporal punishment on young defiers and repeatedly told them that they were being misled by people who were not prepared to go to jail themselves. Others ordered that defiers found in possession of money were to have their funds seized and used to pay fines, even if the person had chosen to go to jail. This strategy was easily countered by volunteers appearing penniless in court.

By August 1952, four ANC leaders had already been convicted under the Suppression of Communism Act. Soon after their conviction, raids took place across the country in an attempt to find evidence of treason, sedition and other offences. In one of these raids Mandela, Sisulu and other senior members of the ANC were held under the Suppression of Communism Act for leading the Defiance Campaign, whose aim, the government claimed, was to 'bring about a change in the industrial and social structure of the country through unconstitutional and illegal methods'.

I was among a group of law students and attorneys' clerks who, led by Duma Nokwe, went to court to follow the proceedings in this trial. The spacious, lengthy corridor with its high ceilings supported by Doric columns was packed by people pushing and shoving to get nearer to the courtroom in the hope that they would see Bram Fischer, Vernon Berrangé and George Lowen, a refugee from Nazi Germany, in action. Lawyers and their clients involved in matters due to be heard in the twenty-odd other courts battled to get through. Our path was made easier because many in the crowd recognised Nokwe, and eventually we gained entry to the courtroom.

The din of the crowd made it impossible for Magistrate Johannes to start the proceedings and he asked counsel to send a couple of their clients to appeal to the crowd to keep quiet, or better still, to disperse. Proceedings were adjourned for some of the leaders to address the crowd. The wide corridors of the court were decorated with large murals by Pierneef, glorifying the Boers in their trek northwards to escape the effects of the abolition of slavery and English colonial power. I wondered what the Voortrekkers and Pierneef thought of the scene below them. The crowd held a day-long meeting outside the court building, chanting freedom songs and shouting slogans of support for their leaders.

Inside the court, many documents were produced by the prosecution: the 'threatening' letter to the prime minister, minutes of meetings, draft speeches, pamphlets, copies of statements sent to newspapers. Vernon Berrangé and George Lowen, both flamboyant cross-examiners, were in their element and they took to task policemen and informers who came to give evidence, in a manner intended to embarrass them and delight the crowds:

- On whose instruction did you join the ANC?
- I followed my heart.
- I am not interested in your heart. Did you join the Congress at someone else's instructions?
- I can't answer that question.
- You were paid for and instructed to spy on your own people. Did you resign or were you expelled from the ANC?
- My membership was cancelled when they knew I was an informer.
- During your 15-month membership did you realise you were a traitor to your people?
- No, I did my duty.
- Did you become a member of the defiance organisation too? I put it to you that you were one of the first defiers.
- I took an oath to carry out duties to defy the unjust laws.
- And from the start you were prepared to break your oath and report to the police? Having twice broken your oath, how can we believe you now?
- I broke the ANC oath.
- Did you get any special reward from the police?
- No, I was on duty.
- None of the speakers referred to any violence?
- They spoke only of non-violence.

Witnesses who tried to discredit any of the volunteers or leaders were quickly and effectively dealt with. Invariably they conceded what was put to them. Berrangé was not known for his restraint or his use of moderate language. When the prosecution closed its case, he indicated that no evidence would be led by the accused as the evidence led by the Crown did not support the charges and none of the accused should be committed. He lashed out at the Suppression of Communism Act under which the charges against the accused were framed, arguing that the government believed that by 'jumping onto the anti-communist bandwagon it [would] recapture some of the reputation which it [had] lost amongst the nations of the world – but in its desperation it [had] taken steps to prosecute the accused under an Act, which although supposedly intended to suppress communism,

[was] now being used in an endeavour to suppress the legitimate aspirations of the non-Europeans'.

What a pity that Berrangé did not see the end of the regime that he so courageously and eloquently condemned in this and other trials that followed. The red-faced Magistrate Johannes could hardly sit still during Berrangé's address. Yet he committed the accused for trial on the grounds that the campaign aimed at bringing about 'political, industrial, economic and social change by unlawful acts alternatively encouraging feelings of hostility between whites and blacks, and in so doing wrongfully and unlawfully advocated, defended, advised or encouraged the achievement of the aims of communism'. To which Mandela commented, 'Today we are charged; tomorrow it may well be parliamentary opposition and everybody who dares to criticise the Nationalists. The same thing happened in Nazi Germany. I am, however, convinced that the people have learned what they can do and no power can stop their forward march to freedom.'

During the Supreme Court trial, presided over by Judge Frans Rumpff, attempts were made to elicit evidence from police witnesses, who had infiltrated the ANC and become Defiance Campaign volunteers, that violence was envisaged. These witnesses were turned around in cross-examination to say that the ANC had not advocated violence at any meetings. They also conceded that, far from encouraging feelings of hostility between the races, speakers had stressed a policy of acceptance and cooperation between African, coloured, Indian and white people as evidenced by the members of all these groups that had taken part in the Defiance Campaign.

The accused had decided on a change in counsel for the trial: Berrangé's rhetoric, so effective at the preparatory examination, would not be as well received by the Supreme Court as would the scholarly argument that could be presented by Harold Hanson and Rex Welsh. The former was considered the most persuasive of advocates and the latter the most jurisprudentially sound – between them the best team to persuade the court that, however wide the terms of the Suppression of Communism Act, they did not cover the conduct of their clients. At one stage there was even some hope of an acquittal when Judge Rumpff asked if 'a party of European women who had sat down in the street and refused to leave when ordered to do so because they had decided on a plan to obtain a change in regard to the rules of jury service, would be guilty of communism?' The Crown responded that the wording of the Act was wide enough to cover such conduct.

When the case went against the ANC, it went to the Court of Appeal before Acting Chief Justice Leopold Greenberg and four other judges, all of whom had rejected the government's arguments in other important cases and from whom some relief was hoped. Hypothetical cases were again raised, until Judge Greenberg dismissed those arguments by stating that the court had found correctly by finding the appellants guilty.

That decision was a licence for the apartheid state to use the Suppression of Communism Act to squash non-violent political campaigns, for few ordinary protesters would be prepared to risk a ten-year jail term. The sentences imposed by Judge Rumpff were wholly suspended, but there was a clear warning that future planners and participants in similar campaigns would face sentences of up to ten years. The conviction also led to Mandela and other leaders being served with banning orders by the minister of justice under the Suppression of Communism Act and the Riotous Assemblies Act. These bans prohibited them from attending any gatherings, and confined them to their city of residence for two years.

To ensure that there would never again be a defiance campaign of this nature, Parliament passed the Criminal Law Amendment Act of 1953, which dramatically increased the penalty for minor offences committed by way of protest against any law and included a whipping of up to ten strokes as part of the punishment. For those who incited others to take part in such a campaign the fine was increased and also included whipping. Increased penalties would be imposed on anyone who solicited, accepted or received any monies for such a campaign. Needless to say, hardly a single provision in its ten sections would have survived in any constitutional state. This and other legislation passed in the early 1950s severely restricted those who wanted to bring about peaceful change and made the task of defence lawyers even more difficult.

The regime was no doubt pleased that it had crushed the Defiance Campaign and it was not the last time that it tried to solve its problems by the introduction of draconian legislation. But though the Defiance Campaign had not produced the results hoped for by the ANC, it had served the organisation well nevertheless. Thanks to the campaign, the ANC's membership had increased from seven thousand to a hundred thousand and the organisation went into the next phase of its struggle against the government with a boost in numbers as well as in confidence.

CHAPTER 16

The Treason Trial

At the end of the court term in December 1956, I was arguing a case before Judge Joseph Francis Ludorf in the Western Circuit at Klerksdorp. He called me to his chambers and pointed at the lead story of that day's *Rand Daily Mail*, which reported that early-morning police raids were likely to lead to a charge of treason for those detained. It was rumoured that Nelson Mandela, Oliver Tambo and Duma Nokwe had been arrested. The judge asked me what my friends were up to. Surely there must be evidence of a plan to overthrow the government by force? To his disappointment I could only shrug my shoulders. I had been away from Johannesburg, so I did not know much more than he did. I resisted suggesting that he ask his friends both in and out of Parliament for details, as they were spreading alarming stories that the ANC planned to poison the water reservoirs.

During conversation, Judge Ludorf recalled that he had been counsel for one of the accused in the case of Robey Leibbrandt, the Nazi sympathiser tried for treason. Leibbrandt had decided not to be represented by counsel, thus freeing himself to say what no counsel would have been able to say before the judges. Judge Ludorf hardly needed to remind me that Leibbrandt claimed that the Third Reich would be the salvation of the Afrikaner people from British imperialism and from the 'international Jewish conspiracy'. The judge believed he had special knowledge of the law of treason, but as he was about to expound on this issue he stopped himself and said with a smile that he had better not say more, after all, he might be appointed as a member of the special court set up to try those arrested.

South Africa has had more than its fair share of treason trials. For those of us involved in political trials, history books and the law reports were essential tools of our trade. In 1815, Dutch frontiersmen revolted against British rule and were sentenced to death. The injustice of that trial, at least in the minds of many Dutch settlers, contributed to the Great Trek, which in turn led to the subjugation of most of the African people in southern Africa. Later, the African chiefs Langalibalele and Dinizulu were convicted for refusing to register their peoples' guns and taking part in the Zulu rebellions of 1874 and 1909 respectively. Generally the sentences handed down were fairly lenient, even though the death sentence could have been imposed. Some white Afrikaners in the British colonies of the Cape and Natal helped the Boer forces against the British in the Boer War of 1899–1902, and were later convicted of treason. During 1914, South Africa's participation in the First World War led to a rebellion headed by General Christiaan de Wet which resulted in many Boers being convicted of treason. Both the general and the burghers were sentenced to short terms of imprisonment, but there was one notable exception – Jopie Fourie was court-martialled, sentenced to death and executed. General Jan Smuts, then a field marshal, was forever blamed for his death and was branded as a traitor to the Afrikaner people.

In 1922, white miners went on strike to prevent blacks from performing semi-skilled jobs on the mines, and Smuts was again blamed for the heavy-handed manner in which he broke the strike. Charges of murder rather than treason were brought following violent clashes during the miners' revolt. Death sentences were imposed and carried out on key figures, which radicalised white workers despite their privileged position in relation to black fellow workers.

In 1944, Leibbrandt, trained by the Nazis as a saboteur and propagandist, was tried, convicted and sentenced to death. He was captured while on a mission to assassinate Smuts. By this time, Smuts, who was then prime minister, a field martial of the British Empire and a member of Churchill's war cabinet, had learned his lesson. He did not want Leibbrandt to become yet another great Afrikaner hero and so he commuted his sentence to life imprisonment.

Frans Rumpff, one of Leibbrandt's counsel, later became chief justice. Once, while hearing argument from counsel as to how long a prisoner would spend in jail if sentenced to 'life imprisonment' (generally a minimum of fourteen years), he asked, feigning ignorance, whether Leibbrandt had not been released after just a couple of years. Did counsel agree? the chief justice asked, and could he explain why there had been an early release? When counsel suggested that Leibbrandt had been released with the change of government in 1948, the chief justice responded with a degree of self-satisfaction, 'Oh, I see. He was not imprisoned for the period of his life, but for the life of the government.' Little did he know that history would repeat itself and that hundreds sentenced to life imprisonment would be released at the end of the life of the very apartheid government that had appointed him chief justice. Parallels such as these were used by our clients, our expert witnesses and by us in argument. The arguments were often not well received, but in many cases they had the necessary effect and the death sentence was avoided.

Although I was not one of the counsel briefed to defend the accused in the treason trial, the preparatory examination and the trial itself had an effect on both my professional and my personal life. I had been sharing chambers with Duma Nokwe for almost a year and, in his absence, had to attend to his desk. In addition I was assisting the clerks at Mandela and Tambo, and had been asked by Vernon

Berrangé and John Coaker, who were conducting the preparatory examination, to scan those documents which had been seized by the police special branch but which were not tendered in evidence by the prosecution. I was to ferret out documents that were inconsistent with the allegation of a conspiracy to overthrow the government by violence. They also needed examples of provisions in democratic constitutions throughout the world similar to those in the Freedom Charter. I was also to assist the members of the families of the hundred and fifty-six appearing in the preparatory examination and, later, the relatives of the smaller number who actually stood trial. Duma Nokwe, together with the other lawyers charged, was a member of the defence committee that liaised between the clients and the attorneys and counsel appearing on their behalf. As they were on bail most of the time, Duma discussed with me the issues, the options available to them and the best tactical course to take.

The hundred and fifty-six accused made up the leadership of no fewer than forty-eight organisations representing a wide range of political views. Most were members of the ANC, but even this did not mean that they knew each other and it was reported that some of the co-conspirators had to be introduced to one another as they had not met before.

Political trials of the oppressed in South Africa had, up to this point, usually been conducted on a shoestring by attorneys and counsel. They agreed to a reduced fee either because they were sympathetic to the cause, or because they believed that everyone had the right to be different, particularly those who sought to bring about change. Often, if a trial was not long, neither attorneys nor counsel charged a fee at all. In this instance, however, because of the extraordinarily large number of accused, the long period covered by the indictment and the complexity of the legal and factual issues involved, it was absolutely necessary for resources to be made available for the proper conduct of the trial. Christian Action in London took the initiative, while in South Africa church people, MPs and other eminent citizens set up what became known as the Treason Trial Defence Fund. Among the contributors was a former judge of the Court of Appeal, Richard Feetham; the Transvaal Supreme Court's Frank Lucas; the Archbishop of Cape Town, Geoffrey Clayton; the Anglican Bishop of Johannesburg, Ambrose Reeves and the celebrated writer Alan Paton, along with his fellow founders of the Liberal Party, William and Margaret Ballinger.

The international community took notice. Gerald Gardiner QC, later the Lord Chancellor, arrived to observe the preparatory examination on behalf of the Bar Council in London, as did various groups of lawyers interested in the protection of human rights. The South African foreign minister, Eric Louw, thought this to be an impertinence. He and his successors often recorded their displeasure at such visits to monitor political trials. They proclaimed that the judiciary did not need watching and that the presence of observers was an insult to the judges, whose honour and impartiality was universally accepted. The International Commission of Jurists lent its support and in a public statement drew attention to the terms of the Suppression of Communism Act, under which some of the charges had been framed, apparently in the hope of discrediting the organisations involved. The commission said that legislation in such terms was far removed from both the theory and the practice of the rule of law.

Later, when the treason trial proper began, Dean Erwin Griswold of Harvard University and other prominent lawyers arrived to observe the proceedings. Although they always behaved with propriety, calling on the prosecution, the judges and the defence, it was difficult for them to suppress their feelings, and they were accused of identifying themselves with the defence. In many cases, this was true and it became a matter of grave concern to the prosecution and the government. Applications for visas by such observers were often either refused or inordinately delayed in the hope that the trial would finish before a decision had been made on whether to allow them into the country.

Judge Rumpff, who headed the special court that was to try the accused, together with his judicial colleagues on that court, was scrupulously correct in his reception of the American delegation. He offered them tea in his chambers and indulged in small talk. While he obviously did not want to discuss the charges of treason, he could not resist the temptation of asking whether, on their way back to the United States, they would stop over in Cuba to observe how Fidel Castro's regime was summarily trying its opponents on charges of treason and putting them against the wall within days of their arrest. That things may have been much worse elsewhere was often enough to salve the conscience of supporters of apartheid.

The American Committee on Africa started to play an important role in providing finance and using its influence with members of the UN to support the oppressed against the government. Support also came from the British Labour Party, Holland and some of the Nordic countries. Summing up their attitude were these remarks, made by the *Daily Telegraph* almost immediately after the arrests: 'The outside world tends to assume that there is something fundamentally rotten in a state which has to defend its constitution and its policies against whole sections of its own citizens.'

The preparatory examination commenced before the chief magistrate of Bloemfontein, FCA Wessel, at the Drill Hall within the army's headquarters near the centre of Johannesburg. Leading members of the Bar offered their services, the most senior among them Maurice Franks QC. He enjoyed the reputation of being the most gentle of the giants of the Bar and yet the most effective cross-examiner. He rose to speak, and, although accustomed to being patient, polite and softly spoken, he could not control his anger in describing the conditions in the court: 'Your Worship confronts this unprecedented scene which we see before us today: the accused caged, as Your Worship sees. Caged, one almost said – I am most anxious not to allow my indignation to get the better of the language I use but I think I am justified in submitting to Your Worship that they appear before the court caged – like wild beasts. I state on behalf of every member of the Bar and Side Bar engaged by the defence in this case, that if these are the conditions upon which it is proposed to hold the preparatory examination, then the whole body of us propose to leave this court and take no further part in the proceedings.'

He was speaking on behalf of, among others, Isie Maisels, Bram Fischer, Vernon Berrangé and Sydney Kentridge. Inside the courtroom, conditions were chaotic. The accused could not hear the magistrate or the prosecutor, let alone their own counsel. The cage had to be removed and a more effective loudspeaker system brought in. Outside the courtroom, conditions were no less chaotic. The courtyard and the streets had been filled by thousands of the accuseds' supporters and the police decided to disperse the large crowd. Tension mounted. Stones were thrown and the police opened fire. Due to the joint efforts of the deputy commissioner of police, Colonel P Grobler, and Bishop Reeves, the shooting stopped and order was restored. Meanwhile, inside, the accused were admitted to bail and remanded to January 1957 for hearings that were to go on for months.

Now freed on bail, Duma came to chambers early in the morning and late in the afternoon to open his post, deal with the odd brief, draft a summons or a plea and make telephone calls. He also gave me a blow-by-blow account of court highlights and of what plans were being made by the defence for the upkeep of the hundred and fifty-six families. The defence fund made some contribution, but it was hardly enough for those who did not have their own means, and most of the accused fell into this category.

Nelson Mandela and Oliver Tambo could not attend to their legal work after their arrest, although they tried to keep themselves afloat by instructing their clerks and junior members of the Bar when they could. Some of us at the Bar held briefs on behalf of Nokwe who had been instructed by Mandela and Tambo and other friendly attorneys. We did so relying for precedent on the wartime practice of holding briefs for advocates away on active service. The guardian of professional ethics, Walter Pollak QC, advised us that we could do this for Duma but that we need say nothing about it, unlike wartime protocol, when a formal statement was required to be made in court. Pollak further showed his support when he regularly handed me a sealed envelope containing his personal cheque to help Duma maintain his family.

Duma related what had happened from the day of their arrest until they were released on bail. Nelson had behaved as though imprisonment was a blessing in disguise. The restrictions of his banning order had severely curtailed his meetings with colleagues to discuss the policies and strategies of the liberation movement. The time spent in the overcrowded cells and in the exercise yard was used as if they were all at a conference. Nelson would not relax. He would wear his suit and tie the whole day, every day. Unlike many of his co-accused he was concerned about the common-law prisoners. He readily talked to them and, when asked, gave advice about their defence and family problems. This brought him into conflict with the warders, who insisted on keeping the treason trial accused apart from common-law prisoners, and warned him of disciplinary action. He ignored their threats. Later, he continued a deep concern for his fellow prisoners, both political and common law, throughout his stay on Robben Island. His conduct and influence, coupled with the exposure of appalling prison conditions by Laurence Gandar and Benjamin Pogrund in the *Rand Daily Mail*, together with the intervention of the Red Cross, led the authorities to recognise that some respect had to be shown for the dignity of the prison population as a whole and particularly of political prisoners.

The government, meanwhile, was assembling its legal forces to wage the battle of the treason trial. Determined not to be outdone by the eminence of the defence counsel, they called on Oswald Pirow QC to lead the prosecution team. As minister of justice in the late 1920s and early 1930s he was responsible for introducing the Riotous Assemblies Act, often regarded as the first piece of anti-communist legislation in South Africa. He was also a long-standing supporter of Hitler. After visiting Hitler in 1933, Pirow astounded everyone by announcing that he thought that South West Africa, which had ceased to be a German colony at the end of the First World War, should be returned to Germany by South Africa, then a trustee appointed by the League of Nations to administer the territory.

Pirow made only rare appearances towards the end of the preparatory examination and during the initial period of the trial itself, when the defence successfully attacked the indictment. Although he was semi-retired, he was engaged at enormous cost, not only for his ability and experience, but also because he was ideologically attuned to the policies of the government. Moreover, he both understood and aligned himself with its fervent desire to crush the liberation movement by removing many of its leaders from the scene. He died long before the trial had finished, leaving the prosecution to a legal team of mixed ability. Although the team was not necessarily committed to the ideology of Pirow or the government, its members seemed to have had no reservation about using their forensic skills to secure a conviction.

At the preparatory examination JC van Niekerk QC from the attorney-general's office spent more than eighteen hours outlining the case. In short it showed the accuseds' intention to 'incitement and preparation for the overthrow of the existing state by revolutionary methods involving violence and the establishment of a so-called people's democracy'.

More than a hundred witnesses produced and read out documents they had seized from the homes of the accused and their alleged co-conspirators. Some gave evidence of what was said at meetings. Almost half of them conceded under cross-examination that the speakers had stressed the non-violent policy of the ANC and that calls had been made for a non-racial, democratic state at all their meetings. Those witnesses who maintained that violence was advocated were discredited by Vernon Berrangé, who revelled in establishing that their scrappy and semi-literate notes did not correctly reflect what was said at meetings. At times he was able to show that the evidence was fabricated. His persistent and humiliating style is illustrated by the following typical exchange:

- Do you write notes consecutively or do you leave gaps and then fill things in?
- I write consecutively.
- You have the time 2.30 noted?
- Yes.
- All the names of the people who arrived are written below the line on which the time 2.30 appears?
- Yes.
- But some of those people actually arrived before 2.30?
- Yes.
- So you could not have written everything consecutively?
- I filled in the time afterwards.
- But did you not say you wrote everything consecutively?
- No.

The magistrate intervened, 'You did say it.' 'Well, then,' said the by now desperate witness, 'I did say it.' When practically all those in court guffawed, the embarrassed witness retorted to the court in general, 'There is no need to laugh.'

Berrangé was even more devastating with another witness:

– You say a speaker said: 'It is time to shoot Malan'?
– Yes.
– How do you spell 'shoot'?
– s-h-o-o-t.
– Now read the letters you have written down in your notes. Is it not
  c-h-e-c-k?
– Yes.
– Does that spell 'shoot'?
– No.
– In fact your notes show that the speaker said: 'It is time to check Malan'?
– Yes.
– Then why did you say 'shoot'?
– It was a mistake.

As one witness after the other was ridiculed, the magistrate became impatient of both Berrangé's ironic, even sarcastic, style and of the irrelevancies introduced by the Crown. These included posters seized at the Congress of the People where the Freedom Charter was adopted. 'Soup with meat', said one poster, while another proclaimed, 'Soup without meat'. At one stage, Joe Slovo, who was both an accused and also his own lawyer, was fined for contempt of court for not readily accepting a ruling by the magistrate. Sydney Kentridge appeared for Joe Slovo on appeal and the conviction was set aside. Sydney, in explaining to us his success on appeal, said that he understood why the magistrate had gone wrong: his patience had been exhausted by Berrangé. He may have been on better ground if he had held Berrangé in contempt rather than Slovo, said Sydney, adding, 'but as we know it would take a particularly brave man to convict Vernon of contempt'.

A long Christmas break was taken to enable the defence to study the documents and evidence and come to a decision about whether to lead any evidence in rebuttal. According to Duma Nokwe, serious consideration was given to finding expert witnesses to contradict the 'expert' evidence of Professor Andrew Howson Murray of the University of Cape Town philosophy department. He claimed that he could tell the difference between documents and speeches advocating communism and the violent overthrow of the State on the one hand, and those calling for peaceful democratic change on the other. After he was called by the prosecution during the preparatory hearings, Murray had been ridiculed by Berrangé and Slovo for unwittingly identifying some of his own early writings as belonging to the former category. They soon forced him to concede that he would have to know the background of the speaker or writer before he could determine the correct interpretation of a document. The Crown was bent on using his evidence to prove its thesis. Although logic and common sense suggested otherwise, the prosecution made the wrong decision. Murray was called at the trial where he not only exposed himself as irrational, but also made important concessions under cross-examination which were destructive of the prosecution's case.

The Attorney-General of the Transvaal, AJ McKenzie QC, announced that charges against sixty-one of the hundred and fifty-six would be dropped as there was no case against them. Nevertheless, they were unashamedly named as co-conspirators in the indictment charging the rest with treason. Among those against whom charges were withdrawn were Chief Albert Luthuli and Oliver Tambo, respectively the president and secretary-general of the ANC.

In discussing the motives that influenced the prosecution's sifting process, Murray said he thought that the prosecution chose to continue prosecuting those considered to have leftist leanings. Those with a track record of religious beliefs, or who tended to be pacifists, were let go. This explanation accommodated Murray's view that in order to interpret what is said, you must first know who said it. The prosecution must have felt that few would believe that Luthuli, a devoted Christian, was an advocate of communism. Tambo had a similar religious profile and was known to have wrestled with whether to become a lawyer or a priest. The failure of the prosecution to charge these two would cost them dearly. They probably did not realise how difficult it would be to persuade a court that there was an organisational conspiracy when the president and secretary-general had the charges against them withdrawn. At this stage, Pirow condescended to come to the Drill Hall, not to argue the matter on the evidence, most of which he had not heard, but to say glibly: 'The Crown case was based on the Freedom Charter whose objects were intended to achieve the setting up of a communist state by other than peaceful and legal means. All the accused subscribed to the Freedom Charter and were pledged to carry it out. They were all communists or communist sympathisers.'

The defence submitted that there was insufficient evidence to commit any of the ninety-five remaining accused for trial on charges of high treason, an offence which carried the death penalty. Berrangé added, 'The Crown has established nothing more than a desire to put an end to any form of effective opposition to the government of this country.'

Despite these efforts, however, they were all committed for trial. Most of the accused had in the meantime lost their jobs and those in private practices or in small businesses were also adversely affected.

The government's expectation that the arrests and lengthy court proceedings would cripple the various organisations was wishful thinking. Instead, the organisations grew. Helen Joseph, one of the leaders of the Federation of South African Women, was among those arrested and committed for trial. The federation to which she belonged organised twenty thousand women to march to the Union Buildings in 1956. The people of Alexandra township organised one of the most successful bus boycotts in South African history, protesting against an increase in fares. Passes for women were rejected; rural communities resisted the Bantu authorities' structures; the prison farm system was successfully challenged in the courts; the trade union movement was flexing its muscles and calling for a minimum wage of a pound a day. The call for 'freedom in our lifetime' was changed to 'freedom now'.

Against this political background, the trial of the people's leaders began in earnest. For more than three years from August 1958 the prosecution tried to convict a progressively diminishing number of the original one hundred and fifty-six arrested in December 1956. The gravamen of the main charge of treason was the involvement of the accused in the adoption of the Freedom Charter. The preamble of the charter, accepted by the Congress of the People held at Kliptown on 26 June 1955, says, essentially, that the country belongs to all its people and that it cannot be prosperous or free until it is a democratic state based on the will of the people without distinction of colour, race, sex or belief.

None of the accused was alleged to have committed an act of violence. The charge sheet also listed offences under the Suppression of Communism Act. Although the accused had chosen to be tried by a jury their decision was overridden and a special court was set up consisting of three judges, Frans Rumpff, Alexander Kennedy, and, as he had predicted to me earlier, Joseph Francis Ludorf. Pirow led a team of seven others, three of whom had been appointed Queen's Counsel. On the other side, the highly qualified Michael Parkington was appointed full-time attorney for the trial. He briefed Maisels to lead a team of eight, including Bram Fischer, HC Nicholas, Rex Welsh, Vernon Berrangé and Sydney Kentridge. Nelson Mandela, Duma Nokwe and Joe Slovo were appointed to liaise between the team and their fellow accused. The trial was to be held in the Old Synagogue in Pretoria, which had been converted into a courtroom.

When the accused, now fewer than a hundred, took their places, the overcrowded courtroom saw Maisels rise and ask for the recusal of Judges Rumpff and Ludorf. Ludorf caused the defence concern because, four years earlier, he had acted as counsel for the minister of justice and the police when an application was made to exclude his clients, the police, from a conference called as part of the preparations for the Congress of the People. Speeches made at that conference would form part of the Crown's evidence, and the accused feared that Ludorf's involvement in the earlier case might prejudice him against them. They also feared his active membership of the National Party (he had unsuccessfully opposed General Smuts in the 1948 election). He recused himself on the first ground, but rejected the second, saying there was no validity to it.

The call for Judge Rumpff's recusal was based on a statement made by Justice Minister CR Swart that Rumpff had chosen Judge Ludorf as an additional judge in the case. Choosing who would sit on the special court was not one of Judge Rumpff's functions, but was, rather, the prerogative of the minister of justice. Rumpff denied the accusation and refused the application for his recusal. The minister did not contradict the judge, attributing the conflict to a 'misunderstanding'. Judge Ludorf's place was taken by Judge Tos Bekker. Helen Joseph said of him, 'Bekker has emerged as the judge-who-wants-to-know. He wants to know everything, the meaning of every phrase, the factual background to every situation ... His persistent quest for knowledge has never ceased as the months and years go by.' Many felt later that Judge Bekker might have made a vital difference to the final outcome.

The first of a number of successful attacks on the indictment was argued soon after the recusal issue was resolved. By the end of August the bench had quashed one of the charges under the Suppression of Communism Act and ordered the Crown to prepare further particulars on the other charges by mid-September. The court also directed that each of the accused be informed how the different allegations of conspiracy and common purpose affected their individual liability. Again the indictment was found wanting. Pirow withdrew the second charge under the Suppression of Communism Act and presented an amended indictment with further particulars on the charge of high treason but removing the 'acting in concert with common purpose'. The defence team chipped away until they received a clear acknowledgement that if the prosecution failed to prove a conspiracy, there would be no case against the accused. When there was yet another attack on the amended indictment, the court gave the Crown another opportunity to put its house in order. The new concessions meant that a substantial portion of the allegations against the accused were dropped, and the defence then contended that there had been a misjoinder, where the allegations were unreasonably linked, and complained of other obscurities as well. Pirow announced that he would withdraw the indictment and yet again serve a fresh one.

The difficulties experienced by the prosecution in framing the indictment were not brought about by lack of expertise. At least two of the prosecution team,

John Trengove and Gus Hoexter, were leaders of the profession and later became judges in the Court of Appeal. The problem was lack of direct evidence that the accused intended to use violence to overthrow the State.

The repeated attacks on the indictment caused inordinate delays, but led to substantial gains for the defence. At one stage, all the charges were temporarily suspended against all the accused until a fresh indictment could be presented to the court months later. Then a further sixty-one names were removed from the indictment, although the threat of arrest remained. By this stage, only thirty were left in the dock, among them Nelson Mandela, Walter Sisulu and Helen Joseph. Of this group, the eminent Professor Tom Karis, who closely followed the trial, wrote: 'all that distinguished the thirty was "the more violent tone of their rhetoric"'.

Once what became the final version of the charge sheet was put to the accused, the defence again presented a detailed and vigorously argued attack. During the course of this argument Judge Bekker asked Sydney Kentridge whether the time had not come for the trial to begin. His response was characteristically sharp and short: 'For our clients, My Lord, the trial started more than six months ago.'

The court rejected most of the arguments advanced to quash this indictment but asked for certain particulars. In a last attempt to avoid a long trial, the defence sought leave to appeal against the special court's judgment. The proceedings were adjourned to enable them to argue the following issues on appeal:

Since treason requires an element of violence to overthrow the established government, are the words alleged in the indictment capable in law of constituting treason? The defence submits that no court could ever find the words alleged in the indictment are treasonable.

Since not more than one or two or three of the accused can be linked with any particular meeting or speech, can they, in the circumstances, all be joined together in one indictment? The defence maintains that there is no link between the overall allegations.

The Court of Appeal ducked the issue and held that it had no jurisdiction to pronounce on points of law arising from an ongoing trial.

During the adjournments Duma Nokwe and Nelson Mandela met regularly in our office. They discussed some of the cases they were doing together, and briefed ANC leaders on the trial. They also talked about the affairs of the ANC. The office was considered a safer place for these discussions than other venues. I participated in some of their briefings, but would go to the library when I realised that they wanted to discuss sensitive political matters. They were well pleased with the preliminary skirmishes initiated by their defence team. The Crown's apparent inability to put together a proper indictment led many an editor, diplomat, academic and political analyst to doubt the disparaging assertions made by the regime against the ANC and its leaders. It also persuaded the West to join with the majority at the UN and vote to condemn apartheid.

The engagement of its leadership in the trial prevented the ANC from dealing effectively with the internal disputes that emerged among the second tier of leadership. This in turn led to the first serious split in the organisation and the formation of an Africanist congress under the leadership of Robert Sobukwe. Sobukwe and Nokwe had been close friends in the early days of the ANC Youth League, and were destined for high office in the ANC. According to Duma, Sobukwe fell by the wayside when, for personal reasons, he did not take part in the Defiance Campaign. As an office bearer of the Youth League while at Fort Hare, and a staunch supporter of the Programme of Action afterwards, Sobukwe was temporarily suspended as a teacher. However, he was reinstated after deciding that he would not take part in the campaign. Sobukwe was subsequently not invited to the Congress of the People that adopted the Freedom Charter. Instead, he aligned himself with an Africanist group, which he eventually led as its president when the Pan Africanist Congress was formed in April 1958. Duma believed that Sobukwe's call to defy the pass laws in March 1960, a call ultimately leading to the Sharpeville massacre, may have been partly inspired by a desire to purge his failure almost ten years earlier, to follow the road that led to freedom via the prison.

It was during an adjournment that Oliver Tambo confided to me the difficult financial position he and Nelson Mandela were in. Their flourishing practice had diminished. Although Tambo was relatively free to work, the restrictions on Mandela made it impossible for him to practise. Despite the lack of income, their clerks had briefed counsel without obtaining cover to pay them which put pressure on the partnership's financial resources. Oliver asked me to convey this situation to my colleagues at the Bar, and to ask them please to be patient if the fees were not paid on time.

In the midst of all this Nelson had fallen in love. He was divorcing his wife and planning a traditional wedding in the Transkei to marry Winnie Madikizela. At about this time, Albertina Sisulu and a group of other women from Soweto were protesting against the issue of passes to women. It was reported that Nelson was arranging bail for them and planned to handle their trial. Winnie was one of the accused. One day I answered the telephone to hear Nelson's familiar booming voice: 'George, I have married trouble.' He chuckled. 'Winnie is charged with assaulting a policeman. Will you defend her?' I asked for a copy of the charge sheet and said they should come and see me. Nelson reminded me that he was on trial, adding that he was happy to leave his wife's fate to me.

Winnie came to the office in the late afternoon directly from work. She was as striking as she appeared in the wedding photographs Duma Nokwe had shown me, though now in sombre mood. She was shy and could not bring herself to call me by my first name – nor has she ever done so in the many years since. Once she chided her teenage daughters for daring to do so and ordered that I be called 'Uncle George'.

That afternoon she articulated her defence clearly and with conviction. The police had come to arrest her for taking part in an anti-pass meeting. She told the constable to wait outside until she had dressed properly and packed the things she would need in jail. Ignoring her request, he followed her into the bedroom, grabbed her by the arm and tried to pull her out. A struggle ensued. Somehow her elbow connected with his chin. He lost his balance and fell.

She records a more dramatic version in her autobiography *Part of my Soul* and adds:

> Then they said I was resisting arrest. George Bizos, our lawyer – I would listen to him as I would listen to my father. He treats me in the same way as Nelson does. He weighs the same authority with us. So he says to me outside court, 'I want you to behave like a lady in front of the magistrate and not like an Amazon!' Nelson always said to me – one of the things George and Nelson agree on – 'Zami, you are completely and utterly undisciplined! You need a great deal of training!' I don't think I am undisciplined. But you have to use the language they understand: to have peace you must be violent.

Partly because of the policeman's embarrassment at having to admit that he was floored by a woman, he was not a good witness. His explanation of why he went into the bedroom and why clothing and toiletries had to be brought by a relative to the police station made Winnie's version sound the more probable. The well-dressed, politely charming young woman who, to the magistrate's surprise, refused the services of an interpreter, must have impressed him. He found her not guilty, and I became the couple's counsel of choice, a professional relationship that has lasted more than four decades.

Meanwhile the treason trial dragged on. More than a hundred and fifty police witnesses gave evidence based on more than four thousand documents seized during the raids. Much of this evidence had been broken down during cross-examination and the inaccuracies and contradictions revealed.

The cross-examination of Professor Murray by Maisels was based on information gathered by the indefatigable Parkington. This was put together for Maisels primarily by Rex Welsh and Sydney Kentridge, with some assistance from Nelson Mandela and Duma Nokwe. It is regarded by many as an example worth following.

Murray was led by the prosecution in a lengthy and circuitous manner on his expertise in communism. When asked a question about the policy of the Soviet Union, Maisels was quick to object, saying that he did not recall Murray qualifying himself as a witness on that subject. Counsel leading Murray tried to remedy the omission in a roundabout way. One of the judges turned to Maisels and asked if his objection still stood. 'Yes,' was the curt reply. Judge Bekker, wanting to get on with the case, asked Maisels what he expected the witness to be asked and what Murray would have to say to satisfy him. Maisels, not one to lose an opportunity to dominate the scene, asked with great emphasis, and in his usual imperious style: 'Professor-do-you-consider-yourself-as-an-expert-on-the-policy-of-the-Soviet-Union?'

The by now somewhat intimidated witness uttered a hardly audible 'No'. 'I thought so,' said Maisels.

This was just the start of the demolition of Professor Murray. I was in Pretoria to do a short appeal and spent the rest of the day watching the masterly performance by Maisels. By lunch time Murray had given up any attempt to defend his theories and opinions, and it could hardly be called cross-examination any longer. Maisels would read lengthy paragraphs from his notes, adjust his spectacles, fix his eyes on Murray and ask, 'You agree, don't you, Professor?' The answer was almost always 'Yes.' On the rare occasion when Murray seemed to want to qualify or disagree with the proposition, Maisels would merely say, 'Come, come, Professor', and the affirmative answer would follow.

During the afternoon, Murray again fell into the trap of describing some of his own writings and the writings of others of undoubted democratic provenance, as advocating communist doctrine. He also unwittingly made a concession in favour of the defence, saying that the use of violence to overthrow the State was fundamental to communist doctrine. Therefore if violence was not called for or had not taken place, there could not have been a communist conspiracy to overthrow the State.

Murray also had to concede that the activities of the accused in calling for fundamental change was not to further any ideological commitment. Rather, it was aimed at putting an end to both the political and personal injustice committed against the vast majority of South Africans. Murray was hardly in a position to deny the obvious. Finally he agreed that the Freedom Charter was not a 'communist' document but was, in fact, similar to many religious and political documents produced over the centuries. He also admitted that the charter could be the natural reaction of oppressed people to prevailing conditions. The notes used by Maisels for this part of the cross-examination deeply impressed Duma Nokwe. Afterwards he acknowledged that, although himself a victim of government policy, he had not fully realised how bad things were until he heard Maisels.

The defence now led its witnesses, including Chief Albert Luthuli, in a systematic analysis of the ANC's history, organisation, and policies.

Luthuli's evidence was interrupted by the events of 21 March 1960, when, at Sharpeville near Johannesburg, police shot and killed sixty-nine and wounded a hundred and seventy-six in anti-pass demonstrations organised by the newly formed PAC. There was worldwide condemnation of the regime and the ANC called for a stay-at-home. The State's answer was to declare a state of emergency in terms of the Public Safety Act No 3 of 1953. Despite claims of real and imminent danger at the time of its enactment, its provisions had not yet been used. Many of the accused were again wakened at dawn, arrested and taken to Pretoria Central Prison; others were arrested as they arrived at court. In addition, some two thousand people throughout the country were detained. Those taken into custody were not allowed to communicate with people outside prison. A few weeks later, on 8 April 1960, the ANC and the PAC were declared unlawful organisations, a ban the government kept in place until 2 February 1990.

The treason trial defence team felt that conditions imposed by the emergency regulations made it impossible for them to defend their clients properly, and they withdrew. Duma Nokwe took over the defence.

The emergency regulations were then amended to accommodate the accused in detention and to facilitate the return of the defence team.

Sydney Kentridge spent a long time in preparation with Nelson Mandela before he called him to the witness box. It is apparent from the hundreds of pages of the record that they both knew the contents of the documents and the other evidence before the court particularly well. Sydney carefully directed Nelson to the page and passage on which each of his questions was based, and Nelson appears to have known precisely how to formulate his answer to advance the defence case. No important or difficult question was left for the cross-examiner.

By the time Nelson went into the witness box the issues had become fairly clear. There were to be no surprises. Where short direct answers were called for they were given. When history and policy were to be explained it was done concisely. Questions by the judges seemed to have been foreseen. When the witness occasionally strayed, he was brought back to the issue at hand. When questions were put by the cross-examiner or even one of the judges based on some incorrect premise, Nelson would politely but firmly draw attention to the correct premise. His evidence dealt with the development of African nationalism in the late 1940s through the ANC Youth League, his acceptance of the non-racial policies of the ANC in the early 1950s, his cooperation with other groups on preparing and running the Defiance Campaign and acceptance of the Freedom Charter, as well as the formation of his M-Plan for communicating through a network of underground cells.

Sydney Kentridge's re-examination of Nelson is yet again a textbook example. Those points made during cross-examination by Hoexter and the judges which appeared to lend some support to the Crown's case, were explained, either by reference to documents or by the introduction of other facts or circumstances which removed any inference in favour of the Crown. So comprehensive and well thought out was his evidence in the treason trial, that Nelson was able to condense and incorporate it into his famous statement from the dock in the Rivonia trial.

In the end, the judges stopped the defence counsel before they finished their closing submissions, a sure sign of an acquittal. The most comprehensive of the three judgments was that of Judge Bekker. He held that the Crown had not disproved the evidence of the leaders of the ANC, in which they denied a conspiracy to overthrow the State by violence. It was a long and costly affair, but victory was no less sweet.

Nelson Mandela believes this trial was important in enhancing the reputation of the ANC and turning many nations against the apartheid regime. I believe the treason trial should not be seen in isolation, but is, rather, the second part of a trilogy, coming between the earlier Defiance Campaign trial and the Rivonia trial that lay in the future. In many ways the treason trial was the last of the political trials in which some of the normal legal procedural safeguards to ensure a fair trial were observed. In its wake, the rules were changed and acquittals made even more difficult.

CHAPTER 17

A Personal Footnote: the 1950s

The 1950s saw many changes in my life. My youngest brother Yianni came to live with us in our Emmarentia apartment and eventually (after I'd arranged private English lessons for him) went on to study at the University of the Witwatersrand. My other brother, Stavros, who had been drafted into the army during the civil war in the late 1940s, was so taken with the country when he first visited us that he applied for permanent residence and returned to live here.

Having my brothers in the country was comforting even though the family remained divided. I hadn't seen my mother in twenty years and, because I have never been a good letter writer, my contact with her was sporadic. Occasionally she would ask her youngest brother, Pavlo, to write and then I would respond. But her circumstances were tough: she received an income from the two main cash crops of olive oil and blackcurrants, and my father, then working as a shop assistant in Pretoria, sent her the better part of his salary. But her circumstances weighed heavily on me.

Stavros was more steeped in the traditions of family life than I was and was particularly concerned about our sister, Vaso. According to tradition it was the duty of the brothers to provide her with a dowry. While he worked as a salesman of dairy products he contributed a large part of his salary to purchasing an apartment in Athens for her. At his request I made a contribution to this.

One of the issues that was of persistent concern to me was the separation of my mother and father. I wanted them to be reconciled. Together with Stavros, I persuaded my father to return to Greece, partly on the excuse that he should help Vaso find a husband. He went, but was neither reconciled with his wife nor found a husband for his daughter.

My relationship with him remained strained and he kept his distance although I called on him from time to time. I suspect he was proud of my achievements, although he never said so. With the birth of my first son Kimon in 1957 and Damon fourteen months later, he started visiting us in Emmarentia and I have fond memories of walking on the grassy banks of Emmarentia Dam with Stavros and my father, pushing the pram. Perhaps our relationship eased somewhat.

Earlier my father had helped considerably by buying me a car, a Morris Minor. It had been a great asset; in fact it made it possible for me to practise as an advocate. In that car I'd covered many thousands of dusty miles through the Transvaal, Free State and Northern Cape to courts where I defended the clients of Mandela and Tambo. Somewhat curiously the car came to the attention of the security police. I had never registered the vehicle in my name so it remained in the name of the original owner, a close friend of my father's. One day he was approached by the security police wanting to know what he had been up to the previous Sunday night. Nothing, he replied. As usual he had closed his shop at nine o'clock and gone home. Nevertheless they wanted to know why his car had been parked outside a house in Yeoville where a known communist lived. Nor would they leave until he supplied a statement confirming that I was using the car. Then he telephoned me. Of course I had been at the Yeoville house, not to attend a communist party meeting but to play poker with, among others, Joe Slovo and Harold Wolpe. I never heard from the security police about this matter.

Although most of the work I did through the 1950s was for minimum fees, when those were coupled with Arethe's earnings from her paintings, we felt flush enough to trade in the Morris Minor and buy a new version on hire-purchase. With that we took a holiday on the Cape Peninsula in a cheap hotel at the seaside town of Fish Hoek. I had so missed the sea that I immediately went to the beach and fell asleep on the sand. The resultant sunburn was bad enough to make my skin blister and peel.

At about the same time we decided to buy a house although we ended up acquiring a pan-handle property of three quarters of an acre in Parktown North. The stand was a subdivision and had originally been an orchard. When the deeds were signed we possessed a piece of land covered by khaki weed, neglected peach, plum and apricot trees, as well as some huge oak and plane trees. The cost had been a steep £1500, some £500 of which we'd borrowed from a friend. The rest had been raised on two bonds: one through a building society, the second from a firm of attorneys to pay the Dutch builders. The building society's instalments were always met, although I have to confess that occasionally the builders had to be patient. Because we couldn't afford an architect, Arethe and the builders designed a long three-bedroomed house with large windows and stable doors in front and at the back.

We moved in shortly before Christmas 1958. Together with a young gardener from Zimbabwe, Martin Mangwandi, I set about clearing the khaki weed, pruning the trees and planting flowers in preparation for a New Year's party. It was a party that ended with breakfast. In many respects that party signalled the end of the 1950s. While from a personal point of view I had much to be sanguine about, it was clear from the Defiance Campaign trial and the treason trial that politically we were entering troubled times.

Part Three: 1961–1971

CHAPTER 18

Black Man in a White Man's Court

Celebrations after the acquittal of the treason trial accused continued late into the night at the home of Joe Slovo and Ruth First. Among the revellers were members of the legal team who had been lifted onto the shoulders of their clients at the announcement of the verdict. Some of our colleagues at the Bar, strict and strong defenders of the unwritten ethical code, questioned the propriety of senior members of the Bar attending a party with treason accused, even if they had been acquitted, and especially a party at which races mixed.

The party was also attended by a posse of policemen, determined to show that while they may have been beaten, they were not to be forgotten. The police said they were looking for evidence that the hosts were 'selling or supplying intoxicating liquor to natives' in contravention of the liquor laws. Within seconds of their arrival, all the glasses were empty and every drop of evidence had disappeared.

A few of days later Duma Nokwe came into the office. We embraced and jovially chatted about our families. I pointed to his robes hanging behind the door, the unbound volumes of the monthly law reports and the wooden tray overflowing with correspondence, accounts and briefs for which I would now no longer have to bear any responsibility. I confidently predicted that his acquittal would enable him to concentrate on his legal work once again. He said we would talk about this issue later, but that his immediate priority was to call on the leaders of our group, particularly Isie Maisels, to thank him for leading the defence team, and Walter Pollak to express appreciation for his help.

He and many others considered their acquittal a pyrrhic victory rather than a judicial triumph. More than a year earlier, the ANC had been declared an unlawful organisation. The Communist Party had disbanded itself in 1950, believing that this would protect its members from prosecution. The ANC, by contrast, had built up a large membership over fifty years and its leaders were not going to follow the same route. Instead, Oliver Tambo left the country to organise the organisation in exile while Mandela and other members of the leadership went underground, while Chief Albert Luthuli and other remnants of the national executive carried on as best they could with anti-government activities.

Even before the treason trial verdict was handed down, Duma allowed neither the banning of the ANC nor his own banning to prevent him from helping convene the December 1960 Consultative Conference of African Leaders. He was elected to the continuation committee charged with organising the 'All-in' African Conference. From me he wanted to know if it would be a contravention of the Unlawful Organisations Act if the resolutions and actions of an amorphous body such as the 'All-in' conference, at which dozens of organisations would be present, were similar to those of the ANC before its banning. I looked carefully at the wording of the Act and concluded that provided it was not done for and on behalf of the ANC and that it was not predominantly in its special interest, there would be no contravention. The magistrate who later tried Duma Nokwe and others on precisely these charges, did not agree, however. They were sentenced to twelve months for furthering the objects of the ANC, but their conviction and sentence were set aside on appeal.

Nelson Mandela was not among the accused in Nokwe's trial, even though he had made the most of the opportunity offered by the expiry of his banning order to deliver the keynote address at the 'All-in' conference. He had given up his practice, and accepted separation from his family to continue the struggle underground. His first task was to organise a three-day strike, starting on 29 May and continuing until the day the government and its supporters celebrated the first anniversary of the declaration of the Republic of South Africa. The strike was not successful. The government's show of force, the PAC's open dissociation from the strike, threats of dismissals by employers and disapproval by even the small number of newspapers not unsympathetic to the liberation cause, coupled with a hastily-taken decision to call the strike off, enabled the government to claim victory. To the ANC leadership it was a clear signal that changes were needed in their strategy if the struggle were to continue.

Detective Sergeant Carl Johannes Dirker, for many years a special-branch policeman, had repeatedly failed the examination to become a lieutenant because of his lack of intelligence and formal education. However, his zeal, tenacity, disregard for the rules of due process and lack of respect for the truth made him a useful member of the covert security police. Although a wide, turned-down hat covered the upper part of his head, his height and the breadth of his shoulders made him easily recognisable to those who attended political meetings and to those of us who often saw him in the court corridors or in the witness box. At about this time he was frequently seen watching, by turn, the east and the west entrances of His Majesty's Building. Those he knew to be involved in 'black politics' he stopped and searched. If challenged to produce a warrant he would usually say that it wasn't essential as he had just received 'reliable information' that the suspect possessed documents about a serious crime that had been or was about to be committed. Although he gave some of us dirty looks, he didn't stop or search advocates.

Then one afternoon the unthinkable happened. Duma had been gone fifteen minutes when he returned and slumped into an easy chair, covering his eyes and temple with his hands, obviously in great distress. Dirker had searched him and found a document headed 'v must be met with v'. The security policeman did not have to read beyond the first paragraph to believe that he had found what he was looking for. 'Is this what you want, Nokwe?' he demanded. 'To meet violence with violence?' Dirker unleashed a tirade: 'Whose violence are you going to meet? How are you going to do it? This is what you wanted all the time. It proves that everything that you and your bloody Jewish lawyers said at the treason trial – that you wanted peace – was a lot of bloody lies. I would have arrested you right here and now but my officers say I mustn't before they have seen the documents I find. We will be watching you. Don't go out of Johannesburg. One false move and you will be behind bars.'

Duma explained to me that the pressure for violent action was increasing. The younger leadership was more militant, while those steeped in the non-violent ANC tradition were resisting. Duma had been on his way to a meeting of regional leaders to argue for a change in policy. Now he dared not go to the meeting for fear of being followed and exposing his colleagues to charges that, at the very least, would be of contravening their banning orders. Instead, he found a trusted office messenger, not known to the police, who alerted the meeting that it would be unsafe for Duma to attend. Meanwhile he and I discussed the charges that could be brought against him. Putting thoughts to paper could at worst be an act of preparation. Yet despite his fears, no charge was ever brought against Duma arising out of this incident.

Although Duma was careful not to compromise me, our discussions enabled me to infer what was happening. For example, would some members of an unlawful organisation be liable for the acts of violence committed by others? Could there be a political wing and an armed wing of such an organisation, as existed in Northern Ireland? In other words, what would be the consequences for the top leadership, such as Chief Albert Luthuli, if some members became involved in a policy of selective violence? And what would the political consequences be if Luthuli's nomination for the Nobel Peace Prize succeeded?

Some of these questions were answered in the early hours of 16 December 1961 when homemade bombs exploded in various parts of the country. They targeted buildings that had come to be regarded as symbols of apartheid. Simultaneously, a pamphlet was distributed announcing the formation of Umkhonto we Sizwe (MK), which declared in its manifesto: 'The time comes in the life of any nation when there remain only two choices: submit or fight. That time has now come to South Africa. We shall not submit and we have no choice but to hit back by all means within our power in defence of our people.'

Understandably, the document did not disclose those in MK. However, the statement that the organisation 'fully supports the National liberation movement, and our members, jointly and individually, place themselves under the overall political guidance of that movement', made it clear that the ANC and its leadership, particularly Nelson Mandela, were responsible.

The first victim of a planned act of sabotage was a man named Molefe who, together with Benjamin Ramotse, was about to place a bomb when it exploded prematurely. Ramotse was Duma's neighbour and had informed him shortly after the explosion of the tragic consequences. Soon Ramotse was arrested. Duma feared that Ramotse would be tortured and confess, implicating members of the ANC leadership. I was asked to appear for Ramotse.

In the holding cells below the courtrooms, I found my client in a bad state, partly because of the death of his friend Molefe, and partly because of a lengthy interrogation by a Lieutenant van Wyk who had allowed him no rest or sleep. Before the formal appearance I approached this lieutenant, hoping that he would agree to bail. No, he would oppose bail, so I raised Ramotse's complaints with him. Although he admitted that he had interrogated Ramotse at some length, van Wyk denied that he had in any way exceeded reasonable bounds. I reminded him that now Ramotse had come before the court and was legally represented, he had no right to approach my client and that I would ask the court to make an order to that effect. Van Wyk balked at this and undertook not to approach Ramotse again. As soon as his investigations were complete he would agree to Ramotse being released on bail. I accepted his assurance.

Ramotse was held in the Fort, originally built by the Boers to defend Johannesburg against the British. In the late afternoon following my conversation with van Wyk, the superintendent of the jail phoned to tell me that Ramotse was behaving strangely, threatening to commit suicide and repeatedly asking to see me. I rushed to him. In the consulting room he burst into tears. His sobbing turned to hyperventilation and for a while he was unable to speak. Eventually he told me that he had been threatened by van Wyk. The policeman spread coloured photographs of Molefe's mutilated body on the table, and said, 'Benjamin, look what happened to your closest friend. You know who is behind all this. If you do not want it to happen to you, your wife, your children and many others, why don't you tell me? It will be a secret between you and me.'

Even the prison superintendent was moved by Ramotse's condition. I asked for an assurance from him that he would not allow van Wyk or anyone else from the special branch to see my client, not only because it was against the rules, but also because, in my view, Ramotse was on the brink of suicide. I added that if Ramotse were to kill himself, then he could be held responsible. I suggested that a contact visit by his wife was essential. Reassured that the superintendent would contact Ramotse's wife, I left.

I tracked down van Wyk and warned him that if he went near Ramotse again, he and his colonel would be respondents in an urgent application to court. Wasn't he ashamed to have broken his express undertaking to me? How could I or any of my colleagues at the Bar ever trust him again? He did not deny his assurances to me or that he had spread out the pictures on the table hoping to induce a confession. Then he said, 'My country is in danger and I will do anything to protect it.' He nevertheless agreed to Ramotse being freed on bail. Some years on this lieutenant led the raid on Lilliesleaf Farm that resulted in the arrest of Walter Sisulu, Govan Mbeki and others and culminated in the Rivonia trial.

Before he was granted bail, Ramotse's wife visited Benjamin with photographs of their newborn baby, which he showed me. He grabbed my little finger and squeezed it hard saying that his baby was strong and could squeeze his small finger with equal strength.

Ramotse was admitted to bail but soon afterwards left the country. Later he was caught in Ian Smith's Rhodesia, brought back to South Africa and detained for months on end, before being convicted and sent to prison on Robben Island. On his release twelve years later he sought me out. Nobody would give him a job and his wife's earnings were not enough to maintain the family. He was also too closely watched to continue with any political activities. Eventually he succumbed to depression and committed suicide before the demise of apartheid.

The government capitalised on the liberation movement's decision to commit acts of violence. This fulfilled the official prophecy that the ANC's Defiance Campaign and Freedom Charter would inevitably lead to violence. The change in ANC stance effectively nullified the treason trial verdict acquitting the ANC leaders and with it the finding that the organisation was neither violent nor communist. According to the government, the ANC's decision justified the extraordinary powers adopted by the executive from 1950 enabling it to ban organisations, issue banning orders on individuals, declare states of emergency and hold people in detention. Now it strongly chided those who accused it of abrogating the rule of law. The government knew better. Allegedly peaceful mass action, strikes, boycotts and protests were preparatory to an overall plan to overthrow the State by violence. The highest law, said its ministers, its broadcasting corporation and most of the newspapers, was the safety of the State. And now even more powers were needed to protect it.

Given the prevailing political climate, the cumbersome law requiring two or more witnesses for every act of treason was regarded by the government as an impediment. So a law was passed equating sabotage in the broadest sense as treason punishable by death. Convictions on charges of sabotage rather than treason would, so the government thought, make easier a comparison between the ANC and MK on the one hand, and the German Baader-Meinhof gang, the Italian Red Brigades and even the PLO on the other, all of which they called 'terrorists'.

The courts did not remain immune to the climate created by the government and its supporters. Walter Sisulu was convicted by a regional magistrate and sentenced to a term of imprisonment. As the law stood, the magistrate had no jurisdiction to refuse bail pending an appeal as a Supreme Court ruling to this effect was binding on all lower courts. Their only power was in the amount of bail to be paid. This magistrate refused Sisulu bail on fatuous grounds. An urgent application for review of the decision was set down for the afternoon session in the higher court. The magistrate's ruling aroused the concern of members of the Bar, even among the apolitical: would the judge hearing the application for review sanction the lower court's disregard of a Supreme Court decision?

The court was packed to capacity with advocates, both seniors and juniors. Judge Oscar Galgut took his seat on the bench and scanned the faces before raising his eyebrows as if to say there was no need for our demonstration. Galgut was not known for his patience. Before counsel for Walter Sisulu had finished he stopped him in mid-flight, called on counsel for the State and castigated the prosecution for opposing bail in the court below and for persisting in opposing the application for review. He ordered Sisulu released on appropriate conditions. The judge had been a senior member of the Pretoria Bar and although politically conservative would not sanction such a brazen breach of the rule of law.

The State's fears that Sisulu would go underground to lead the ANC struggle were well founded. Walter was to quip later that had he been imprisoned for just a few years, he would not have faced a capital offence, nor spent twenty-five years on Robben Island. For its part, the regime was determined to remove the granting of bail in political cases from the jurisdiction of the courts. It lost no time in changing the law. In future, if the prosecution produced a certificate from the attorney-general refusing bail, then the court had to abide.

The government and the Minister of Justice John Vorster, in particular, threatened to smash the underground soon. The sabotage, said Vorster, was inspired and directed by white agitators, known to him and his security police. Parliament gave him even greater powers. For example, to bypass the courts when issuing house-arrest orders, and to close down newspapers. Later he was empowered to detain people for ninety days, then for a hundred and eighty days, and eventually he could hold detainees for an indefinite period.

Nelson Mandela led the ANC from underground and Duma shared responsibility for finding safe houses, for arranging his meetings with regional and local branches, and discussed the new policy and tactics and how to avoid detection. His arrest was the main occupation of the special branch. Duma often despaired because Nelson exposed himself to many people, including friendly journalists, and was constantly at risk.

Although Nelson had no passport, both the internal and external leaders of the ANC insisted that he should lead their delegation to the Pan-African Freedom Conference in Addis Ababa. There he met with other African leaders, many of whom pledged their support and gave an undertaking that MK soldiers would be welcomed and trained in their countries. In mid-June 1962 he arrived in London to meet Oliver Tambo and other ANC leaders in exile. He also met with the leadership of the Labour and Liberal parties.

Nelson's sense of history prevailed over concern for his personal safety. He couldn't help but record these meetings in a diary which was found at Rivonia by the security police. In fact, a reason he did not give evidence at the Rivonia trial was to avoid cross-examination on these meetings and the discussions with the various leaders. In retrospect, his arrest after returning to South Africa seems almost inevitable. Although some attempt was made to keep his movements and meetings in London secret, it was not difficult for the South African security police, probably with the assistance of their British and American counterparts, to monitor his journey back to South Africa early in August 1962. Soon afterwards, dressed as a chauffeur and driving the theatre producer Cecil Williams who was sitting in the back, Nelson was captured at Howick. Banner headlines announced the arrest of the 'Black Pimpernel'. It was a triumph for the regime and a sad day for its opponents. Nelson was charged with inciting workers in essential occupations to act illegally by staying away from work, and leaving the country without a valid permit. He was convicted and sentenced to five years imprisonment.

During the trial, dressed in African regalia, Mandela addressed the court for more than an hour. To him the aspirations of the African people were on trial and that was why he had conducted his own defence. Most importantly he said, 'Why is it that in this courtroom I am facing a white magistrate, confronted by a white prosecutor, escorted by white orderlies? Does anybody honestly and seriously suggest that in this type of atmosphere the scales of justice are evenly balanced? Why is it that no African in the history of this country has ever had the honour of being tried by his own kith and kin, by his own flesh and blood? I will tell Your Worship why: the real purpose of this rigid colour bar is to ensure that justice dispensed by the courts should conform to the policy of the country, however much that policy may be in conflict with the norms of justice accepted in judiciaries throughout the civilised world … Your Worship, I hate racial discrimination most intensely and in all its manifestation. I have fought it all my life. I fight it now, and I will do so until the end of my days. I detest most intensely the set-up that surrounds me here. It makes me feel that I am a black man in a white man's court. This should not be.'

His address prefigured what he would say at the Rivonia trial eighteen months later.

Nelson was not the first person whose statements could not be published. In protest the press left blank spaces in their reports where words had to be omitted. Eventually, general permission was granted to publish what was said in court, 'as long as it is not abused by creating a forum for such persons'. Immediately the press was informed that by printing Mandela's statement they would be creating precisely such a forum. As a result very little meaningful was published. The only exception was *New Age*, which carried a full report under the banner headlines: White Court Cannot Dispense Justice. The government closed down the newspaper a few weeks later.

Fear of house arrest and detention without trial led many an activist to leave South Africa surreptitiously, among them Duma Nokwe and Joe Slovo. For some time before he left, Duma kept away from the office. He refused briefs which would have lasted any length of time. He did not even bother to open the monthly law reports.

Then, late one afternoon, when most of the members of our group had gone home and I was about to leave, Duma walked in. He was wearing a cap and, despite the autumn chill in the air, a pair of sandals, a coloured shirt and an old pair of corduroy trousers – hardly the garb a member of the Bar would normally wear to chambers. He gestured for me to leave the office, a sure sign that confidential matters, not for the ears of the special branch, were to be discussed. We went to the end of a passage where he told me that the liberation movement had decided he should leave the country. Rumours suggested he was about to be picked up under the ninety-day laws and detained for interrogation. As Oliver Tambo needed a senior ANC office-bearer, Duma had been selected for the job. He had no option but to leave his family behind, but he feared that his wife might be detained and interrogated about his disappearance. Would I do what I could if she or his mother needed help? And would I do the same for Walter Sisulu's wife, Albertina, and for the wives of others who were underground, in exile or in prison? I stood silently watching him as he emptied his drawers, then we hugged. It turned out to be our final goodbye.

Fear prevented any communication between us during the years that followed. He went to Zambia and then to London as a member of the national executive of the ANC-in-exile. Later he represented the ANC at the United Nations in New York. However, his movement was restricted to his hotel and the nearby UN building. This was a reflection of the Cold War and the inimical attitude of the United States to the ANC, an attitude which the Rivonia trial managed to dispel. Duma's family joined him later, but he died prematurely, in exile. Fear again prevented me from writing a letter of condolence to his wife and their children.

I had to wait more than thirty years for a proper meeting with his family, this time at his mother's funeral when I gave the family Duma's 1963 diary that he had left behind in our office. In paying tribute, then Deputy President Thabo Mbeki, who had stayed in the Nokwe home before going into exile, praised Duma's contribution to the struggle. Nor has he been forgotten in post-apartheid South Africa. A prestigious Human Rights Award annually honours his memory when it is conferred as closely as possible to 10 December, to coincide with International Human Rights Day.

CHAPTER 19

A Small Farm Called Lilliesleaf

*Impartiality in political trials is about on the level with the Immaculate
Conception: one may wish for it, but one cannot produce it.*

– Theodor Mommsen
German philosopher and Nobel laureate, 1902

Early in the afternoon of 11 July 1963, a fine winter's day, the telephone rang in
my chambers. I heard a coin drop into the call box and then the muffled voice
of Harold Wolpe. He named a corner in the city centre and asked me to meet
him there. Our meeting place was outside a bookshop and I found him staring
intently into the window at the books on display. He didn't turn round when I
greeted him but pointed at a book. We stood side by side, facing away from the
pedestrians while he whispered that the leadership of the ANC had been arrested
at its Rivonia headquarters and that he was going into hiding. He handed me a
file, asked me to find some excuse for his absence from court, and to report what
had happened to his brother-in-law and partner, James Kantor. I was not to see
Wolpe again until he returned from exile almost thirty years later.

Official confirmation of Wolpe's news broke during the day. The police triumphantly announced that Walter Sisulu, Govan Mbeki, Ahmed Kathrada, Raymond
Mhlaba, Dennis Goldberg, Rusty Bernstein and Bob Hepple had been arrested at
the Rivonia home of Arthur and Hazel Goldreich on a small farm called Lilliesleaf.
Rivonia, a peri-urban area of Johannesburg, was usually regarded as a 'mink and
manure' suburb where the rich rode their Irish and Arab thoroughbreds and
enjoyed a lavish lifestyle. It was an unlikely place for African revolutionaries to
hide. Chaplinesque photographs were published of Sisulu, Mbeki and Kathrada,
still in heavy disguise just after their arrest. The labourers on Lilliesleaf were also
detained lest they have information relating to the traitors. Police gave details of
the raid and said more arrests were expected.

Predictions were made that sabotage and terrorism would now come to an
end. A massive treason trial was in the offing and death sentences were expected.
Those arrested would be interrogated and held incommunicado for ninety days
before they were brought to court.

Police raids on the offices of Kantor and Wolpe uncovered the purchase agreements of Lilliesleaf Farm. Arthur and Hazel Goldreich were arrested as were Wolpe and the nominees who had bought Lilliesleaf cheaply in the aftermath of the Sharpeville massacre, an event that had greatly depressed the property market. When Wolpe and Goldreich escaped with two others from Marshall Square, police also detained Kantor even though he was known to be apolitical. Joel Joffe, who had left the Bar to become an attorney and was waiting for an emigration visa to Australia, was asked to step in and take care of the Kantor/Wolpe partnership.

In this crisis, Hilda Bernstein, Albertina Sisulu, the parents of Ruth First (who had also been detained), and the relatives of other detainees turned to Bram Fischer for help and advice. Bram called Joel and me to a meeting in Arthur Chaskalson's office, as his was likely to be bugged. We were asked to act for those arrested. Initially Bram was hesitant about leading us, but Arthur was adamant that as an Afrikaner, Bram was best placed to say with confidence, to the judge and to the world, that those we were defending had acted no differently from Afrikaner patriots such as General Christiaan de Wet. Such patriots had not only escaped the death penalty, but received comparatively light sentences of imprisonment.

At that time none of us knew the extent of Bram's involvement in the underground movement or that this was the cause of his hesitation. The question of who would lead the legal team was deferred until Vernon Berrangé returned from overseas. But the request from the families and our insistence left Bram wrestling with his conscience. He could possibly save his comrades' lives by appearing for them, yet in doing so he would break the ethical rules applicable to the legal profession in a normal and just society.

As the ninety-day detention period neared its end, rumours started that the show trial planned by the State would be held in Pretoria even though the accused were arrested in Johannesburg. Johannesburg was also where their families lived, their attorney and counsel practised and where the other side, the security police and prosecuting team, were based. This was not the first time, nor the last, that a trial was moved out of Johannesburg to make it more difficult for everyone concerned. The main reason was to reduce the number of people who would protest or go to court in solidarity.

During the afternoon of 7 October 1963, Joel telephoned the leader of the State's prosecuting team, Dr Percy Yutar, to find out if the accused would appear the next day, as was rumoured. They would, said Yutar, without explaining why we had not been informed.

Bram was not available the following day. This wasn't of great concern, as senior counsel usually didn't attend a formal hearing when the case was bound to be postponed. So Joel, Arthur and I set off early in the morning in the hope of seeing our clients in the courtroom cells before the case was called in open court. We found neither the special security arrangements nor the large number of reporters inevitably associated with such an event – both clear signs of a change of plan. The spacious lobby of the court house, officially named the Palace of Justice, was bare. The lights and overhead fan of Court C, the main criminal court, were off and the door of the main holding cell below was wide open. The court's registrar knew nothing about the case and Yutar was not in his office.

We asked to see the attorney-general, Rudolf Werner Rein QC. He politely listened to our tale of woe, barely concealing his contempt for Yutar, his deputy. We later learned that the previous day Yutar, obviously considering it a mere formality, had put the indictment before Rein to sign. Rein refused, pointing out defects and slovenly draftsmanship. This sharp criticism by his superior was obviously something Yutar preferred to keep to himself. He was hardly likely to disclose it to us as the reason he had not kept us informed of the delay.

We went next to the jail in search of our clients. As we did not know who would be charged, we wrote on the requisition form, 'Walter Sisulu and others charged with him', fearing that otherwise officials would bring only those we named. Then, a senior warder arrived and raised a difficulty that we had not anticipated. Our clients included both blacks and whites. In accordance with prison practice they would let us see the white clients first. We baulked and our arguments prevailed, but only after we obtained the authority of the commissioner of prisons. They first brought in Dennis Goldberg, Rusty Bernstein and Bob Hepple. Some time later Walter Sisulu, Govan Mbeki, Raymond Mhlaba, Ahmed Kathrada, Andrew Mlangeni and Elias Motsoaledi arrived. Later still, to the surprise of us all, who should be brought in but Nelson Mandela wearing prison short pants, a tunic and sandals.

It took some time for our clients to reorientate themselves after their lengthy solitary confinement. The warders stared in amazement at the sight of black men and white men jovially embracing one another. We gave them information about their families and the others who were detained. Goldberg, Mlangeni and Motsoaledi were unknown to us, while most of the others didn't know Joel and Arthur, so I bridged the gap.

I told them we didn't know much more than they did except that the State was planning a show trial. This would eclipse all others including the earlier, mammoth treason trial. We also told them that the State was preparing the country and the world for the death sentences that it predicted would be imposed. Our clients confirmed that there would be a common defence although we felt that James Kantor should seriously consider separate counsel.

Then, to everyone's surprise, Bob Hepple said that he had been offered indemnity from prosecution if he gave evidence for the State, an offer he was still considering. We were stunned. For the rest of the meeting we avoided discussing our clients' defence and confined our conversation to practical matters regarding families and fresh clothing for the first court appearance.

As newspaper reports suggested that Ruth First would be one of the accused, we next visited the women's jail. The matron insisted that her orders from the security police were clear – she was not to allow anyone to see or speak to Ruth. I had earlier asked Yutar if she would be one of the accused, to which he replied, why did I think she might be? I ignored the jibe.

The day the trial started, we found the street leading from the prison to the court, which lay almost two kilometres away, partly closed off and teeming with heavily armed policemen as if a major attack was imminent. The intention was to reassure the white spectators on the pavement and those looking out of their office windows along the route that their government was in control. The massive cast-iron gates leading to the back entrance of the court and the cells were wide open. The courtyard was empty, whereas usually it would be filled with the judges' cars. As we entered the robing room overlooking the courtyard, I heard a cacophony of sirens. Below, three police cars screeched in, followed by a Black Maria and another three or four cars. Policemen leapt out holding Sten guns. They hurriedly took up position and saluted the officers alighting from the other vehicles. Our clients, meanwhile, deliberately ignored gestures and commands that they move quickly from the van into the large cell under the building.

Our consulting room was a poorly lit cell with two large wooden tables and long benches, its walls scratched with graffiti protesting innocence or threatening revenge. I also noticed prayers for redemption written by some of those sentenced to death in previous trials. Our clients were delighted to see Bram. He warmly embraced each one except Bob Hepple. The two men shook hands, Bram glaring at the embarrassed Hepple.

We had yet to see a copy of the indictment, though we learned from a friendly reporter that it had been distributed to the media, embargoed until the judge received it that morning. Full publication was expected that afternoon. Our strategy was to ask for a postponement of three months.

Led by Bram in his silk gown we climbed the dark concrete stairs to the well of the court where a new, much larger dock had replaced the original. The left half of the public gallery was packed with black spectators. On the right were some familiar, friendly white faces, while others, judging from their appearance, were security policemen. No barriers to separate black and white had been erected in the superior courts as was the situation in the lower courts, but the policemen acting as court orderlies directed spectators according to their skin colour. Relatives and close friends waved tentatively at us, particularly at Bram, who crossed the barrier to assure them that their loved ones were in the cell below.

At least fifteen uniformed policemen took up position in the gap between the dock and the wooden partition separating the public gallery from the well of the court. When the eleven accused (then including Bob Hepple) entered the dock, relatives and friends stood on their toes, straining to see them above the caps of the policemen.

A few minutes before ten o'clock, Yutar entered with considerable brio. He led an entourage of counsel, senior officers in uniform, the head of the security police and the team of investigating officers and interrogators. Special seating arrangements had been made for them. At a nod, one of his assistants distributed copies of a document to the large group of journalists and some of the VIPs in the jury box, and then, as if as an afterthought, a single copy was handed to the four of us and our clients.

It was common knowledge that the Judge President of the Transvaal Provincial Division, Quartus de Wet, would preside at the trial. No one knew whether he would sit with two assessors as was customary, but not obligatory, in serious cases. Bram, who knew his fellow Afrikaner's background and the circumstances under which he had been appointed a judge shortly before the Nationalist victory in 1948, believed that while he might not have been the best judge for us, we could have done much worse. That he came into court without assessors was, we hoped, an indication that he might not impose the death sentence.

Yutar stood to call the case of the State against the National High Command and Others. Bram announced that he was appearing with Arthur and me for the accused. Before he could say anything more, Yutar was on his feet declaring that he was ready to proceed with the trial. Could the registrar now put the charges to the accused?

Bram in his usual polite, quiet manner interrupted him, indicated that a postponement was being sought and asked if he could motivate the application. Judge de Wet nodded his approval. Bram said that his clients had been in solitary confinement for ninety days and needed as much time as the State had enjoyed to prepare their case, especially as they had only now seen the indictment. Yutar replied that he feared for the safety of his witnesses and that the case should proceed immediately. Despite his fears, a postponement of three weeks was granted.

Any hope that the accused and their relatives would be allowed to speak to one another was dashed as our clients were hurriedly removed from the dock. A tight formation of uniformed policemen rushed them down the stairs, preventing them from even stretching out to touch the fingers of their loved ones.

I asked Yutar for more copies of the indictment. Loudly enough to be heard by my colleagues, he thanked me for greeting him (which the other members of the team had not done) and asked his junior to give me whatever copies were available. Then we followed our clients to the cell below. But our consultation was short. For security reasons, they had to be rushed back to prison as soon as possible.

Some supporters stood at the back of the court building holding placards that read, Stand by Our Leaders. They waited patiently to salute their comrades. Standing apart, a small group of whites had gathered with a solitary makeshift placard: *Laat hulle vrek* – let them die like animals. Even before the gates opened, the sirens of the lead cars and motorcycles wailed. And as the Black Maria emerged, some faces could be seen at the round ventilation holes. With raised fists, the crowd shouted, '*Amandla! Amandla! Amandla!*'

Before we left the Palace of Justice, we were surrounded by the relatives and close friends of our clients. When and where could they see their loved ones? What were the allegations in the indictment? What defence were we going to present? There was little we could tell them but we promised to urge the prison authorities to arrange visits as soon as possible.

James Kantor, who was separately represented by H C Nicholas Q C, applied for bail. Nicholas was one of the leaders of the profession, and an outstanding lecturer in the law of evidence at Wits university, known for his high ethical standards. During the bail application his eloquent plea came close to assuring the judge that James Kantor was innocent, and that his arrest after the escape of Harold Wolpe was no less than persecution. Nicholas was so confident of his client's innocence that he took the unusual step of handing in the statement extracted from James during his ninety-day detention, a statement which would otherwise have been inadmissible in court. This showed that there were hardly any specific allegations against him personally, but focused instead on his partner Wolpe. Nicholas was heard without interruption and sat down confident that his client would accompany him back to Johannesburg.

The judge asked Yutar if there was any evidence to implicate Kantor in the acts of sabotage alleged in the indictment. Yes, James Kantor was fully involved, an assurance subsequently shown to have been made recklessly. The judge, accustomed to accepting such assurances, summarily dismissed the application for bail. He also dismissed a second application some time later. When it became clear towards the end of the State's case that Kantor's acquittal was inevitable, Yutar tried to save face by offering to withdraw the charge against James if he gave evidence for the

State. The evidence would relate to side issues as James was clearly not party to any conspiracy. James had in the meantime been released on bail. In an act of revenge, when he refused to testify for the State, the police procured hearsay evidence one Saturday afternoon and his bail was cancelled. James Kantor was an innocent victim. He and his family suffered, but despite that he retained his dignity and humanity. Eventually James was acquitted. By then he had had a nervous break-down from the solitary confinement, and his attorney's practice had collapsed. He died young in exile.

Joel Joffe and I spent days with our clients in the absence of Bob Hepple and James Kantor. The charges used various sections and subsections of the Sabotage Act, including recruiting numerous named and unnamed co-conspirators for military training, performing acts of sabotage, training people in the preparation, manufacture and use of explosives, guerrilla warfare and raising funds within the country and outside to finance their plans. The dates on the indictment implicated Mandela from the time he went underground and during the period he was out of the country. He was listed as Accused No 2. For reasons we couldn't understand, Yutar charged the National High Command as the first accused as if it were a corporate body, without any regard to the provisions in the Criminal Procedure Act relating to corporate liability.

Although the charges were general and lacked specific allegations, we were able to assess the situation in broad terms. Nelson Mandela, Walter Sisulu and Govan Mbeki would not deny that they had gone underground. Nor would they deny that the struggle against apartheid involved controlled violence, with spe-cial care to avoid loss of life. What had they actually told the authorities while in detention? We discovered that Nelson had not made a statement. Walter refused to answer questions, insisting that he would only speak to the political bosses, not the police. Govan Mbeki had adopted a similar attitude.

Dennis Goldberg, with his engineering background, had been tasked with acquiring parts from different manufacturers. He did not know their end pur-pose. These parts would only have been used had the movement embarked on guerrilla warfare.

Ahmed Kathrada and Rusty Bernstein would deny planning or commit-ting acts of violence, as would Raymond Mhlaba. Andrew Mlangeni and Elias Motsoaledi would admit their membership of MK, but only to the extent that they transported to the borders people intending to further their education or receive military training.

The end of solitary confinement and the prospect of seeing family eased the strain our clients were under and our consultations became more focused even if they remained constrained. To enable us to discuss their defence, we assumed that the room was bugged. Two warders in the passage watched us through the open door. To frustrate any eavesdroppers we communicated by pointing to key words on a piece of paper, words such as 'judge', 'prosecutor', 'witness box', 'statement from the dock', 'cross-examination', the names of individual witnesses. These words were never spoken aloud. A nod, a shrug of the shoulders, or a gesture filled in many nuances.

We made our clients aware that the prosecution would be seeking death sentences and told them how the government-supporting media had created an almost hysterical bias against them. We speculated about those who might have broken in detention and given evidence. We also discussed the documents found at Rivonia and other places, and whether these would enable the State to prove its case.

Each day Joel and I returned to Johannesburg, numbed by the seriousness of the situation. I recall stopping at Bram's home late one afternoon and being joined under a tree in the garden by him and Arthur Chaskalson. There we sadly reported that it looked as if most of our clients would have no defence.

While we consulted with our clients, Arthur analysed the indictment, drawing attention to ambiguities and inconsistencies. He predicted that the indictment might be excipiable and suggested that a comprehensive application for further particulars should be served so that each of our clients would know what specific acts he performed to make him guilty.

We agreed to meet regularly for progress reports. Joel was also dealing with the personal problems of our clients and their families. He needed to get assistance for their upkeep and the education of their children as well as funds for the trial. I gave up most of the other work I had accepted, and refused new briefs. I usually went to Pretoria alone, but was occasionally joined by one or more of the other members of the legal team.

A few days after the postponement I was working in my garden before sunrise, turning the soft soil following the spring rains, when I heard the splutter of the Fischer family's Volkswagen Beetle driving down our long pan-handle driveway. This was an unusual event at that time of the morning in our quiet neighbourhood. The car stopped at the side of the patio and Bram, in shorts and sandals, walked briskly towards the front door. He hadn't seen me in the garden. I called his name and he turned and unfolded the front page of the *Rand Daily Mail*. The headline read that the UN General Assembly had demanded the abandonment of the Rivonia trial. He shoved it in my direction and with great excitement said: 'Take this to them and tell them that they will not dare to hang them after this!'

We embraced and then I read that the UN General Assembly had passed a resolution by a hundred and six votes to one, declaring that the apartheid regime was persecuting its political opponents and that the trial should be stopped.

Bram refused my offer of coffee. He said that the UN decision was a boon to be taken up locally and internationally as a matter of urgency so that it could have maximum effect. Clearly he was intent on playing an active role in such a campaign.

In Pretoria, I bought a number of copies of the paper and spread them on the table in the consulting room for my clients to see as they were brought in one at a time. There was immediate joy, and then doubts that the UN decision might prove counterproductive. The regime had often thumbed its nose at the UN, contemptuously referring to it as a 'talking shop' dominated by the communists and the Afro-Asian group led by India. The UN had dedicated 10 October to a call for the release of political prisoners. (Somewhat to our irritation, we learned that during the debate a delegate from a small tyrannical regime had asked what sort of justice could the Rivonia accused expect if they had lackeys of the Verwoerd government appointed as their lawyers.)

The consultations continued but they were slowed by the surreptitious manner we had been forced to adopt and many issues remained outstanding. How were they going to plead? What facts were going to be denied? Would any admissions be made to curtail the proceedings? What documents were found at Rivonia and who would they implicate? None of these questions could be finally answered. Nelson Mandela admitted that he had been at Rivonia before and after his overseas trip. At the time of his arrest more than a year previously, his books, writings and diary were at the farmhouse. He had given instructions for them to be removed and put in a safe place away from any underground political activity. But this hadn't happened. And these manuscripts alone proved his legal responsibility. He would not deny the facts, but neither would he plead guilty. He asked for a transcript of his lengthy evidence at the treason trial, his statement from the dock and some of his banned writings. Again he planned to deliver a statement from the dock.

Walter Sisulu would deny that he was an active member of the National High Command, but admit that he was the head of the ANC underground. The police had found a document entitled 'Operation Mayibuye' on a table at Rivonia. Nor would he deny that a couple of weeks before the arrests he had acknowledged his leadership of the underground movement over a clandestine radio and that he had also called for action by the oppressed. He would also say that, as MK had put itself under the guidance of the national liberation movement, he occasionally attended meetings of the National High Command to discuss strategy.

One of the matters scheduled for discussion during the meeting interrupted by their arrest on 11 July had been this very document 'Operation Mayibuye'. Walter knew that this document dealt with a proposal by Goldreich and others for guerrilla warfare. He was opposed to the idea. Dennis Goldberg then said he had made a statement under duress about the foundries and other manufacturers that he approached regarding the components of landmines, hand grenades and other arms of war. Individually, the manufacturers would not have known the eventual purpose of the components, but collectively it would have become obvious to the police. Also, he had made inquiries about some unusual fertilisers that could be used as explosives. This information was compiled at Arthur Goldreich's request and, although Dennis's family had already left the country, he remained behind to complete the task. Now Dennis offered to take full responsibility and plead guilty to help the others even though he was not a member of the High Command, nor had he attended the meeting where 'Operation Mayibuye' was to be discussed. He had driven Walter to Rivonia and should have dropped him and left. Instead he stayed at the farmhouse, waiting for Hazel Goldreich to come home after fetching the children from school. When the police raided he was sitting in the lounge. Although he used pseudonyms when making his enquiries of the manufacturers, he had not disguised himself, and felt he had been positively identified. Nevertheless, the police would not have evidence that he was a member of MK, much less serving on its High Command.

Govan Mbeki told us that he would not deny that he had spent most of his fifty-three years in the struggle. He was the leader of the ANC in the Eastern Cape, where the organisation was stronger than anywhere else, and where many of its leaders had been nurtured, particularly at the black university of Fort Hare. A number of the acts of sabotage charged in the indictment were committed in his area. Despite his banning he continued to work underground, endorsed the decision to violence and was a senior member of the National High Command. He had written extensively on the plight of black people. Govan had a dual reputation: as an intellectual with university degrees, and as an activist who inspired many others by personal example.

Raymond Mhlaba worked in close cooperation with Govan Mbeki, but for most of the period covered by the indictment had been out of the country receiving military training. He was in disguise at Lilliesleaf Farm, but doubted there'd be evidence implicating him in sabotage, or evidence of his membership of the National High Command. With a smile he would brush aside a searching question, and made it clear that he was not afraid of any punishment, even the death sentence.

Both Kathy Kathrada and Rusty Bernstein denied that they were members of MK and the High Command. They had been invited to the meeting because they had participated in the struggle from a young age. They were members of the Transvaal Indian Congress and the Congress of Democrats respectively, both lawful organisations. They had been members of the Communist Party before its banning in 1950 and joined again after it re-emerged in the early 1950s. They were staunch supporters of the ANC and occasionally attended meetings to discuss political policy and tactics. As there was no charge covering such acts, they had a defence which might possibly succeed.

Andrew Mlangeni and Elias Motsoaledi continued their membership of the ANC after it was declared an unlawful organisation. While they were not members of the High Command, they had associated themselves with MK by arranging transport for young recruits leaving the country for military training. They were extensively interrogated but knew of no witnesses giving evidence against them.

We agreed that Nelson would spend the time in his cell working on the speech he would give from the dock. The rest of us would work on the history of the ANC's struggle. Whether this evidence would be given by our clients or historians was left open. Its purpose was to explain the actions of the accused as politically justifiable as all other means had failed.

The consultation room was directly opposite the office of Chief Warder Breedt. After a few days the wooden door was replaced with an iron grille door and locked while we worked. Breedt occasionally glanced in, but Colonel Aucamp, chief of security for political prisoners, would regularly stop to observe us, as would the notorious and brutal interrogator 'Rooi Rus' Swanepoel with his large tape-recorder.

They objected to Joel and me bringing home-grown salad, fruit, cheese, cold cuts and loaves of French bread. We were told that in terms of the regulations, convicted prisoners were not allowed food brought from outside. Nelson responded by refusing to eat our food. Walter had no such qualms even though he, too, was officially a convicted prisoner. When Breedt saw the food spread out on the table, Nelson spoke to him in Afrikaans: '*Meneer Breedt, wat doen a man wanneer hy honger is, en daar is kos op die tafel?*' – Mr Breedt, what does a hungry man do when there is food on the table? Breedt, turning his back as if to avoid seeing what was happening, said softly, '*Hy eet, Mandela*' – He eats, Mandela.

By this time, local and overseas reporters wanted details about the accused and their families, particularly the less well-known ones. To promote the international campaign for their release they wrote autobiographical notes. These were edited by Nadine Gordimer, who had already made her mark as a writer. Bram and Molly Fischer and their daughters, Ruth and Ilse, Hilda Bernstein and other members of our clients' families duplicated and distributed these biographical sketches, hoping to dispel the negative image created by the press sympathetic to the apartheid regime.

At the start of each visit we had to wait for our clients to be brought to the consulting room. I often stood by the window looking onto the deserted courtyard a few metres below. Bram, steeped in Afrikaner history and folklore, pointed out the spot where Jopie Fourie was put against the wall after the 1914 rebellion and shot. If our clients received the death penalty they would be taken to the gallows less than a kilometre away. Jopie Fourie's yard was a constant reminder that we were involved in a life-and-death struggle.

Bram and Arthur had completed their task. They believed the indictment was 'vague and embarrassing' and that if their requests for further details were not addressed, it would be excipiable. Those details would have to explicitly implicate each one of the accused. Without them, a motion to quash it would be made. None of us thought Yutar and his team could furnish those particulars before we were due back in court.

We also believed that the extra time was to our advantage. Although our clients remained in custody, the hysteria would die down. Increased pressure could also be brought to bear on the regime by the UN. Telegrams from trade unions, NGOs and human rights organisations intensified calls for boycotts and sanctions. Messages of support were sent to the registrar of the court.

Yutar believed that he had an unanswerable case. He was impatient to deliver his opening address and lead evidence. The accused would be proved guilty and discredited in the eyes of the world. His impatience and certainty led him arrogantly to ignore well-known principles of criminal procedure. His hurried answers to their request for further particulars allowed Bram and Arthur to draft a notice of exception as he had failed to state precisely what each accused had done or even who had represented the ANC and the Communist Party in the conspiracy.

Not giving the information was bad enough, but his answer that the facts were 'known to the accused', or that the facts were 'peculiarly within the knowledge of the accused' and occasionally with an added emphasis, that the facts were '*blatant and peculiarly within the knowledge of the accused*' affected his indictment.

We returned to court on 29 October 1963. Once again the sirens of motorcycles and motorcars blared, but this time there were many more spectators, at both the front and back entrances of the court. In the cell below the accused were cheerful, buoyed by their mutual companionship and by visits from family members. They dressed in their best suits, shirts and shoes.

First to enter the dock was Nelson Mandela. He turned to the packed gallery as if he had simply climbed the platform on Freedom Square, and threw up his boxer's fist, shouting, '*Amandla!*' Most of the black and some of the white spectators jumped up and in unison responded '*Ngawethu!*' This ritual was repeated as each one – except for James Kantor and Bob Hepple – took his place in the dock. The practice, so irritating to the authorities, was brought to an end with the decision that the judge would come into court before the accused.

The first draft opinion that I wrote for Bram Fischer QC was a tutorial for me. At the outset he wanted all the adjectives, adverbs, 'wherefores' and 'aforesaids' removed, along with every ambiguity. It was to be as laconic as possible. Many judges and colleagues would say it is a lesson I did not learn or take to heart. Although most of the accused were his friends and, as it subsequently transpired, his close comrades in the struggle, Bram controlled his emotions throughout the trial. Once proceedings were under way, he delivered a devastating and clinical attack on both the indictment and the further particulars. He drew attention to many inconsistencies and *non sequiturs*, none more telling than that Nelson Mandela had committed a hundred and fifty-six acts of sabotage – all of which had occurred while he was in jail. By saying that the accused had 'personal knowledge of what they had done' and did not require particulars, Bram submitted that the State had effectively decided that since the accused were guilty they did not have a defence to the charges. Hardly any questions were asked of Bram, and the judge showed impatience when he read passages from the decided cases.

Bram was followed by counsel for James Kantor, George Lowen, who likewise contested the validity of the indictment and the particulars it contained. Lowen had left Nazi Germany in the early 1930s. He used one pejorative adjective after the other to describe the indictment against his client and the further particulars. For his climax he drew attention to an answer provided by the prosecution in reply to a particular question. This answer consisted of three dashes and an exclamation mark. Judge de Wet was not known for his sense of humour, but with the faintest of smiles, said, 'In my copy there are four dashes, Mr Lowen.' It was a small but encouraging sign.

Now we had to see how the judge would deal with Yutar. If he gave Yutar a difficult passage we would feel more confident. Unexpectedly the judge didn't call on Yutar but asked Bob Hepple if he wanted to say anything about the indictment. Before Bob could reply, Yutar jumped to his feet and triumphantly announced that he was withdrawing all charges against Accused No 11. Hepple would be the State's first witness against the accused. Yutar looked at us for some response but got none. It hadn't come as a surprise for we had already heard that Hepple had consulted counsel and members of his family and had decided to give evidence. For the same reason none of the other accused, whatever their feelings may have been, responded to the announcement. Despite this, Yutar must have been pleased with the excitement shown in the jury box where top police officers and members of the diplomatic corps sat. There was a sigh of disbelief as Bob was escorted down the steps. His mother and father were staunch supporters of the struggle.

Many did not know the pressure placed on Bob during his time in solitary confinement. Both the police and Yutar pressed him relentlessly. Yutar because he wanted Hepple as a witness to show that not all Jews (Bob's mother was Jewish) were 'traitors' like Slovo, Wolpe, Goldreich, Bernstein and others named as co-conspirators. Bob got his own back. He was released from custody after Yutar's announcement and left the country before he could be called to give evidence.

Back in court, Yutar dealt with Bram's argument by simply ignoring it. Instead he questioned the integrity of the accused and, by implication, our integrity as their lawyers. He asserted that there was nothing wrong with the indictment, that the request for further particulars was unnecessary and that it was intended to embarrass the State. He produced a neatly bound document in a cover held together with ribbon resembling something ready to be filed in a Notary Public's protocol. This was his opening address and contained all the information we wanted, and more. Bram was about to object to the document being handed in, when the judge said he saw no reason to allow Yutar to hand it up and asked if he had any authority for his actions. Yutar was flummoxed but said that our refusal to accept the document demonstrated that we did not really want further particulars.

Yutar was directed to confine himself to legal argument and told not to introduce irrelevant material. Undaunted, Yutar went off on another tangent, telling the judge what evidence he was going to lead. Bram objected and the judge decided he had had enough from Yutar: 'I regret I must uphold that objection, Mr Yutar. This is not a political meeting. This is a legal argument, and this is a court of law. I don't know anything about any of these organisations you have mentioned. If the State wishes to make allegations like that they should be made in the proper manner.'

Yutar then listed the documents he would hand in and the expert witnesses he would call. These documents would show that Nelson Mandela had planned to escape from jail while awaiting trial in his previous case. Again the judge stopped him, and pointed out that he had to deal with the matter as the law required when arguing a preliminary matter: 'That is the correct approach and once you adopt the correct approach you are in difficulty with your argument.'

Realising he was in trouble, Yutar 'begged', 'implored' and 'craved' the judge not to quash (in his excitement he used the word 'squash') the indictment. He undertook to furnish within a week all the particulars which the bench required. But the judge would not be drawn into playing such a role and told Yutar that it was not the judge's responsibility to tell the State what particulars were required to make a good indictment.

In desperation, Yutar offered to furnish summaries of the evidence that he planned to lead. The judge would have none of it. He gave his decision immediately, in the main adopting the argument advanced by Bram. His concluding words did not flatter the experienced deputy attorney-general: 'The accused are assumed to be innocent until they are proved to be guilty. And it is most improper in my opinion when the accused ask for particulars in regard to an offence which is alleged to have been committed, to say to them: "This is a matter which you know all about". That presupposes that he is guilty and he will not be told anything about the offence.' With that he threw out the indictment.

The accused knew that they would be rearrested and charged. Some of their relatives and supporters, though, thought that this was the end of the case. They rushed forward to embrace the accused but were stopped even though our clients had not yet been properly rearrested. When Joel tried to intervene he was threatened with arrest for preventing a policeman from carrying out his duty. Joel angrily told the officer to learn what his duties were.

Judging by the telegrams and the newspaper reports and editorials, the decision to quash the indictment was equated with an acquittal. Many referred to the continuation of the trial as 'persecution' rather than a prosecution.

Both the legal team and the accused knew that a fresh indictment would be put together and that a long and difficult trial would follow. Confident that there was no cogent evidence against Rusty Bernstein, we had prepared an application for his bail. Jimmy Kantor's lawyers had done the same. Yutar, wounded by his humiliating defeat, submitted that the court had no jurisdiction to grant bail as there was no indictment before it. The judge curtly rejected Yutar's submission and pointed out that the court could release anyone from custody at any time.

Kantor's counsel was sympathetically received and he was already making submissions on an appropriate sum to be fixed as bail, when a senior police officer made a stage-managed entry and handed a document to Yutar. This sealed the fate of both Kantor and Bernstein. Yutar declared that the document was top secret and could not be placed before the court. It dealt with a plot to spirit out of the country any of the accused granted bail. Our objections to its admissibility were rejected after a senior police officer made an affidavit assuring the court that he knew of such a plot.

The judge thought it inconceivable that a police officer would make such an affidavit without good grounds, so bail was refused. Yutar later complained that our colleague, Denis Kuny, had been overheard by a policeman telling his client, James Kantor, that the authorities would do anything, including commit perjury, to keep him behind bars. Although Denis denied saying this, he added that he should have done so, a view shared by our clients and the rest of the legal team.

Two days later, without any notice to us, our clients were taken to court and remanded to a date not arranged with us, contrary to practice. Shortly before the scheduled remand date, a second indictment was served, this time excluding the National High Command and Bob Hepple from the list of accused. The main allegations were the same as the first time but even though greater particularity was given, the accused were not told which of them were alleged to have committed which of the hundred and ninety-three acts of sabotage set out in a schedule, nor were we told what each of the hundred and twenty-two named co-conspirators had done to further the conspiracy.

Bram and Arthur again submitted detailed argument, challenging the validity of the second indictment, but the judge was not interested. Nor was he moved by the forceful argument presented by Harold Hanson QC, one of the most senior and flamboyant advocates in the country. Hanson was probably the only one who could speak to a judge president so forthrightly: 'My Lord, look at the seven alleged acts set out in the further particulars against Kantor. Not one of them supports the allegation that he is guilty of the conspiracy.'

'Mr Hanson, even though each one of the individual allegations might not amount to much, the cumulative effect may be sufficient.'

'My Lord, the cumulative effect of seven noughts is nought.'

'You will have great difficulty in convincing me that this indictment does not implicate Kantor.'

'Is Your Lordship inviting me to sit down? My application is made seriously and I am not here to play the fool.'

Hanson's words were spoken in anger. He crossed his arms and stared at the judge, hardly mindful that he might have overstepped the mark. It was clear that he would say nothing more until the judge responded to his outburst. In a conciliatory manner the judge said that although Kantor's involvement was not expressly stated it was obvious that it was implied. As he was sitting down, Hanson could not disguise his anger, despair even: 'I have yet to hear, My Lord, that an indictment is made good by implication.'

We hoped that the trial proper would not start until early in the new year. However, Judge de Wet ordered that it begin in November. This would allow Yutar to call witnesses who, said the leader of the prosecution, feared for their lives at the hands of the accused and their supporters 'whose threats had forced his witness Bob Hepple to leave the country'. November was difficult for us. Vernon Berrangé was not expected to be back until Christmas. Bram, due to prior engagements, would not be available to lead us. Copies of documents found at Rivonia and elsewhere had not been given to us and the lack of particularity made it difficult for us to prepare cross-examination. The judge was adamant. If we required time before questioning any particular witness, that witness could stand down.

Arthur and I were comparatively junior members of the Bar, and both of us were anxious about what we and our clients would face.

The next day came a statement by Bob Hepple from Dar-es-Salaam. He had been under threat, not from the accused or their supporters but from the police. His statements to them were made under duress and they failed to keep their promises. Nor had he ever intended giving evidence against the accused. He identified with their struggle.

The escape of Bob Hepple was a blow to the dramatic opening scene in the script devised by Yutar. The simple truth that he was not ready to proceed in view of Hepple's flight would have been more than sufficient for the granting of a postponement. But the straight and narrow path was always more difficult for Yutar to follow. He informed us that he would ask for a week's postponement to assist Kantor's counsel, a generous gesture not extended to us. That it was a ruse to give himself more time was obvious: he could have accommodated Kantor's counsel by simply not calling any evidence implicating Kantor during the early days of the trial.

Only later did I learn of Yutar's burning desire to 'rehabilitate' the Jewish community which in his view was sullied by the comparatively large number of Jewish accused and co-conspirators. What better proof of Jewish rehabilitation than that a Jew should take the stand against the traitors? Once Bob Hepple slipped out of the trap and was no longer available to play the role of the 'patriotic Jew', Yutar's attention turned to James Kantor.

He put an offer to Kantor's lawyers. If James gave evidence against his brother-in-law, Harold Wolpe, and if he told the court about his conversations with Dennis Goldberg and Rusty Bernstein in the exercise yard, then the charges against him would be withdrawn. James Kantor did not even consider the offer. He believed that his honesty and integrity would better serve himself, his family and his community. He maintained his innocence and refused to perjure himself on behalf of a self-appointed saviour of the Jewish community's good name. He was in good company. Others of his community, such as Isie Maisels QC, steadfastly disassociated themselves from Yutar's activities.

CHAPTER 20

Rivonia: Trial of the Century

Not until the day Yutar was to deliver his opening address in the Rivonia trial had a radio transmitter and microphones entered a South African courtroom. When we arrived that December morning we found technicians from the South African Broadcasting Corporation, the apartheid regime's main voice, installing a microphone on the bench and another on the bar in front of the distinctive chair reserved for the attorney-general or his senior representative. Any forlorn thought we might have had that microphones would also be placed before us and before our clients vanished when the technicians packed up their tools and left without coming near our side of the court.

A few moments later the judge entered the court before the accused, clearly a strategy to prevent the slogans that would otherwise be exchanged between our clients and the crowd. Then the court registrar rose, held the indictment before him and, looking at the dock, addressed one accused after the other as they stood up to respond:

- Accused Number One, Nelson Mandela, how do you plead to the indictment served upon you?
- The government should be in the dock, not me. I plead not guilty.
- Accused Number Two, Walter Sisulu, how do you plead?
- It is the government which is guilty, not me …

The judge intervened. 'I don't want any political speeches here. You may plead guilty or not guilty. But nothing else.' Walter Sisulu went on as if the judge had not spoken:

- It is the government which is responsible for what is happening in this country. I plead not guilty.
- Dennis Goldberg, how do you plead?
- I associate myself with the statements of Mr Mandela and Mr Sisulu. I plead not guilty.

All the accused followed suit except for James Kantor. He observed the legal niceties, saying merely, 'I am not guilty, My Lord.'

The judge wisely ignored those who disobeyed his stern order, but Yutar was livid, while a senior police officer sitting behind him said, 'Skande!' – disgraceful!

Senior diplomats sitting in the jury box and the journalists alongside them furiously scribbled notes. We were not surprised by our clients' defiant statements, for we had discussed the nature of our defence and planned to give notice of it at the earliest opportunity.

Yutar quickly stood up, ready to counter any effect that our clients' remarks may have had. He held two ornately bound and ribboned copies of his opening address, one for the judge and one for himself. Ordinary stapled copies were handed to us and others.

As Yutar switched on the microphone, Bram rose to speak. Quietly and politely he asked on whose authority the radio transmission had been arranged and if, since Yutar was permitted to read his opening address over the air, an assurance would be given that the defence would have an equal opportunity to do the same. The judge looked embarrassed. He had granted the SABC leave to broadcast the proceedings, believing that no one would have any objection. In view of Bram's attitude he ordered that the apparatus be removed immediately.

Even ignoring Yutar's rhetoric and hyperbole, his opening address contained such startling allegations, coupled with a promise to lead evidence in support of them, that, if proved, the ANC leaders in the dock would surely be sentenced to death. The accused, said Yutar, 'deliberately and maliciously plotted and engineered the commission of acts of violence and destruction throughout the country, directed against the offices and homes of municipal officials as well as against all lines and manner of communication. The planned purpose thereof was to bring about in the Republic of South Africa chaos, disorder and turmoil which would be aggravated, according to their plan, by the operation of thousands of trained guerrilla warfare units deployed throughout the country in various vantage points. These would be joined in various areas by local inhabitants as well as specially selected men posted to such areas. Their combined operations were planned to lead to confusion, violent insurrection and rebellion, followed at the appropriate juncture by armed invasion of the country by military units of foreign powers. In the midst of the resulting chaos, turmoil and disorder, it was planned by the accused to set up a provisional revolutionary government to take over the administration and control of this country.'

Our main task during the period before the trial resumed had been to discuss with our clients the facts to be admitted and the allegations to be denied.

One of the first issues decided was that Nelson Mandela, as an ANC leader, would acknowledge that he, Walter Sisulu, Govan Mbeki and others in the ANC had taken the initiative in forming MK. To protect the rank-and-file members of the ANC,

MK was to be a separate organisation, open to the South African Communist Party and the trade union movement as well as to the ANC. MK would undertake a campaign of sabotage against selected targets, exercising care to avoid the loss of life. It was hoped that the government would respond and negotiate with the liberation movement, but if it did not, guerrilla warfare would be considered.

During our discussions on this issue, Nelson made it clear that he would take full responsibility, even though he was in prison when most of the acts of sabotage were committed. Almost from the outset it was agreed that he would not enter the witness box. Instead he would deliver a statement from the dock.

During the postponement, he mentioned that the small table in his cell was rickety and unstable while he wrote. Later, when Colonel Aucamp crept up to the grille door of our consulting room, Nelson asked in Afrikaans if the table could be replaced with one suitable for the homework the lawyers had assigned to him.

The colonel's reply came quickly. 'Mandela, you forget that you are a prisoner and not a lawyer. I am in charge here and I will decide what you get.'

Nelson stared at Aucamp and asked in an exaggeratedly polite manner, 'Have you finished, Colonel?' 'Yes,' said Aucamp in anger. 'Thank you, Colonel,' said Nelson in an even more exaggerated manner as he executed an about-turn in a military fashion that appeared to incense Aucamp. When he returned to his cell Nelson found a sturdy, almost new, recently varnished table.

Yutar's request to have the trial start on a Friday at the beginning of December was unusual. Presumably he wanted the Friday start to catch the weekend newspapers. The judge ignored this ruse assigning the trial to begin on a Monday. The choice of December meant that the long summer vacation would adjourn proceedings until February 1964. Nevertheless, Arthur and I entered court with trepidation, relative juniors in a major trial.

On the way to Pretoria we anticipated eventualities, finally agreeing that we would neither say nor do anything to betray our fears to our clients. But as we entered the cell below court in our junior counsel's robes, starched double-cuffed shirts and winged collars, Nelson came between us, put an arm over our shoulders and assured us that he and his colleagues had absolute confidence in us. He thanked us for all we had done, and then singled out our attorney Joel saying he had gone beyond the call of duty in assisting members of their families.

The first witnesses called by the prosecution were the Goldreich family's helper, Edith Ngopane, the supervisor of the farm labourers, Thomas Mashefane, and his son, Joseph. They had been detained during the initial raid. There was no suggestion that they knew of any conspiracy, much less that they were party to it. They had seen Accused Number One, known to them as David, staying at Rivonia.

They also identified Govan, Walter, Raymond Mhlaba and Goldberg as occasional visitors. This was evidence we would not dispute. Young Joseph identified Rusty Bernstein as the man he had seen one Saturday afternoon putting up wires for a broadcast which he had said would be made from the farm.

The only other 'incriminating' evidence given by the elder Mashefane was that he had seen 'David' walking in the grounds with an airgun, shooting at birds in the trees. This was the only evidence throughout the trial that anyone had used a firearm for any purpose. Nelson didn't deny it, but said he was put to shame when Goldreich's young son asked why he was shooting birds. Mortified, he took the boy's criticism to heart and changed to target practice.

Walter vehemently denied that his 26 June speech, using the underground transmitter, was made from the Rivonia farm. He thought that the young man must have been mistaken, because although there was a brief experimental broadcast before that date, Rusty had had no part in it. Walter refused to disclose where the actual broadcast had been made from, nor would he disclose the identity of the man who had helped in the earlier experiment. For his part, Rusty Bernstein confirmed that he had not been at the farm at the time. He was under house arrest during the weekends and was closely watched. Getting involved in such an activity would have been foolhardy. Eventually the mystery of the young man's mistake was solved. In a subsequent trial, an expert radio technician called as a State witness said that he had been involved in the pre-broadcast experiment – his build and the colour of his hair were similar to Rusty's.

Arthur and I took turns cross-examining the witnesses. To the chagrin of Yutar and the indifference of the judge, we asked whether reasons had been given for their detention or if they had asked to be released. We wanted to know if they knew of any wrongdoing that had occurred on the farm; had they been held in solitary confinement; why had their detention continued? Yutar, mindful of the growing national and international criticism of detention without trial, made no formal objection to our questions but simply burst out, 'They were not in detention, they were in protective custody', a concept unknown in our law at that stage.

During the adjournment I suggested to Walter that if he was going to admit that he had participated in the broadcast it did not really matter where it had been carried out. He came close to taking me to task. 'No, it must be challenged,' he replied. 'I am not so interested in the legal aspects but politically it is very important for the ANC. Many of our people know that the police can trace where a broadcast is taking place. Our people will ask what sort of leaders we have who broadcast from their regular hiding place. It could be very damaging to us.'

In the cells at the end of the day, Nelson put his arm around my shoulder and

These photographs of the small fishing vessel that carried me, my
father Antoni and the seven New Zealand soldiers were taken from
HMS *Kimberley* in 1941. *Courtesy Imperial War Museum, London*

we bought a sail-boat, we will go together, the boat is big enough, it needs a little repair and it will be ready soon, do not worry and don't be afraid, we will take care of you until we will leave together, all expenses of food boat etc. is ours, because we think is our duty and o-obligation.

good luck
sincerely yours.
anthony Bizos.

My father did not speak English and dictated this letter to the New Zealanders, assuring them that their escape was being planned.

Courtesy New Zealand Herald

Six of the seven soldiers who escaped from Greece, photographed in Alexandria. Back, from left to right: Mick Karup, Tom Freeman, Don Gladding and John Lewis. Front: Sid Hey and Peter Martin.

Courtesy New Zealand Herald

Greek Who Saved Anzacs Works In Rand Cafe

Thrilling Story of Flight From Greece In Small Boat

SAVED SEVEN ANZACS: This Greek, Antonios Bezos, and his little son, George, saved seven New Zealand soldiers from the Germans during the Greek campaign. Both are now in Johannesburg.

ONE of the unsung heroes of this war is a Greek farmer now in Johannesburg. He is exiled from his country and his wife. He has lost all he possessed because he and his 13-year-old son defied the Germans and smuggled seven New Zealanders out of Greece to safety.

He is 38-year-old Antonios Bezos, who knows no English. He is working in an Eloff Street cafe, near Johannesburg station, to learn the language of this country.

Bezos told his tale to the "Sunday Times" through an interpreter. He regards his deeds as something which most Greeks were prepared to do to "help the saviours of our country."

In May last, said Bezos, British troops were fighting desperately in the Peloponnesus. A party of New Zealanders and Australians, weary and dusty, came to the outskirts of a town. They were told by Greeks that the Germans were already in occupation. They were advised to take to the mountains. Seven of the New Zealanders did, and were fed and sheltered by Greeks until Bezos found them. He took them to a farmhouse on a high hill near the sea, and for 11 days fed them and hid them while the Germans scoured the countryside.

He hoped to get a boat and sail the soldiers to Crete. But all boats had been commandeered by the Germans by this time; he finally obtained permission to charter a small sailing boat, little larger than a row boat, on the pretext that he was to fetch food for the community. Finally he had to buy the boat outright and paid £35 for it.

Bezos and his small son put to sea one day, sailed out of sight and then, with nightfall, put back to a small bay where, by previous arrangement, seven New Zealanders were hiding. Before he sailed Bezos had given to one his overcoat, to another a cap, a third a scarf, another a jacket, to disguise in some measure the battledress from the German aviators who were constantly overhead.

The party of eight men and a boy set out for Crete, dodging aeroplanes and sailing far to the south before putting back in the direction of Crete. They were forced to put into a small island, and here they were stopped by the British warship Kimberley. They were asked where they were going and were told that they could not carry on to Crete as it was already occupied by Germans. The destroyer took the party aboard, but Bezos had to leave his tiny craft behind.

The Kimberley took them to Alexandria, and the New Zealanders there parted from Bezos. He afterwards met some of them in Cairo, where he had been taken in preparation for evacuation to South Africa.

Friendly Greeks, among them K. Kinoglou, the Greek artist in Johannesburg, are looking after Bezos and his little son, and Bezos, when he has mastered English, hopes to obtain a job until the war is over and he can return to his wife.

He tells, with amusement, that the Germans put out orders that Greeks sheltering British soldiers would be put to death. But "the Greeks took no notice of that," said Bezos. One of the New Zealanders, Private Fraser, knew a few words of Greek. This was the sole means of conversation in the party.

All Hope for
M
A

A report of our escape from Greece appeared in the *Sunday Times*, 5 October 1941. Courtesy *Johnnic Communications Library*

My father Antoni, 1941, Johannesburg. *Bizos family archive*

Standing, second from left in the middle row, among the cadet officers and student officers at my school. The photograph was published in the school annual, *The Atholonian*, in 1947.
H. Marks/Athlone High School

Cecilia Feinstein, the teacher who was responsible for getting me back to school. She took a special interest in my education and arranged places for me at both Malvern Junior High and Athlone High. *Feinstein family*

With Mrs Crystelis of the Philoptochos, an organisation that helped refugees who arrived in South Africa in 1941. The photograph was taken at Gerekomio, the Greek old-age home, circa 1970. *Photographer unknown*

With Arethe on our wedding day, 1954. *Maurice/Bizos family archive*

With Arethe at a Wits University dance, 1955. *Dennis Dolly/Bizos family archive*

Joel Joffe, circa 1964. Joffe was part of our team on many of the human rights cases. In 1965 he emigrated to the UK, and was raised to the peerage as Baron Joffe of Liddington in the County of Wiltshire in 2003.
Courtesy Johnnic Communications Library

Duma Nokwe and I had a long relationship that started in the Wits library during our student days. Many a night after working late he slept on a couch in my flat. Later he shared my chambers at His Majesty's Building because he couldn't have chambers in a white area.

Baileys African History Archive

Bram Fischer and Vernon Berrangé, who led the defence team at the
Rivonia Trial, outside the Palace of Justice in Pretoria, 1964.
Photographer and publication unknown

With Sydney Kentridge, co-counsel on a number of human-rights cases, including the Biko inquest in 1977, outside the Old Synagogue in Pretoria circa 1970. Sydney was knighted in 1999 for his service to human rights. *Baileys African History Archive*

With the family: Kimon, Arethe, Damon and Alexi, 1971.
Eli Weinberg/Bizos family archive

Dancing with Arethe at a club in Athens. *Bizos family archive*

Dressed in style, Johannesburg, late 1970s. *Peter Ucko/Bizos family archive*

said, '*Ungadinwa nangomso*' – don't get tired even tomorrow. He explained that it was an expression to say thank you for a job well done. I greatly appreciated the encouragement.

Later in the week when he had completed his evidence, Thomas Mashefane requested permission to speak. His question would have made a more concerned judge sit up. Did the police have the right to assault him if he had done no wrong? Mashefane asked. The judge made no comment. If we had been more experienced or had had the confidence of a Vernon Berrangé, we would have questioned Mashefane. Had Yutar objected, the reason for our intervention would have been that improper means were used to procure evidence against the accused. Instead, the witness was curtly dismissed by the judge who simply asked Yutar to investigate the complaint.

Some newspapers reported prominently on the allegation of ill-treatment. Yutar soon gave an assurance that he personally had investigated the complaint fully, adding that he was satisfied that it was without substance. Thomas Mashefane did not want the matter taken any further.

Bram's absence from court did not go unnoticed. Reporters from the pro-government media as well as policemen wanted to know where he was. Then a rumour spread that he wasn't in court in case he was identified by the farm servants as a regular visitor to the Rivonia hideout. We dismissed the gossip but it persisted.

Before the adjournment at the end of the 1963 session, most of the time was taken up by Yutar calling witnesses whose evidence was not seriously disputed. He read into the record documents found at Rivonia and at the homes and work-places of some of the named co-conspirators, even before the authenticity and provenance of these documents had been established by admissible evidence. Portions influenced by or alluding to Marxist ideology were read with the aplomb, emphasis and variations in tone and voice we had come to know, all synchronised with glances towards the press corps. Of course they had been given advance copies in the hopes that these would be published.

His most theatrical performance was reserved for extracts or paraphrasing of the writings of Mao Zhedong and Ernesto 'Che' Guevara on the virtues of guer-rilla warfare. Our objection to this unusual procedure the judge brushed aside. In turn this was seized on by Yutar as a licence to damn the men in the dock and their organisations as dangerous terrorists and agents of the Comintern and a threat to Western democracy.

For the year-end break, none of us went on holiday. We assumed that all the accused, except Nelson, might have to give evidence and each of them would need to prepare a comprehensive statement. Everyone agreed except Walter. He quipped that the reason there was so little evidence against him was because he had learned of the dangers of putting pen to paper. Written notes the police could seize and use as evidence.

As he was likely to be the first witness I took his statement in the presence of the others so that they could model their own along the same lines. During this process I was struck by how reluctant he was to speak of his personal background and circumstances during his younger years. It was almost as if his life began only when he joined the ANC. For more than a month we worked on his statement.

Sisulu, who had spent more than thirty years as one of the leaders of the organisation and, during an important period, as its secretary general, was the best person to give evidence under oath about its non-violent history. The aim of his testimony would be to rebut the State's contention that the ANC was a terrorist organisation. During the preparation process I would occasionally pose as Yutar to give Walter experience of being cross-examined. His crisp and telling answers persuaded us that he would be more than a match for the chief prosecutor. His memory, sincerity, lateral intelligence and sharp mind would, I thought, make him an excellent witness. I had a similar view of Govan Mbeki, whose academic training and intellectual prowess would make him slower and more deliberate than Walter, but an equally effective witness.

For instance, I would ask in my Yutar impersonation: 'You say that your peaceful protest and the selective targets you chose for sabotage would bring the government to the negotiation table, yet you described the government as granite-like?'

The answer came back: 'The collapse of granite columns often starts with small fissures.'

Govan was writing his own statement but appeared to be bored by the process. He asked for a copy of Tolstoy's *War and Peace* and I dropped it off with Chief Warder Breedt. Breedt withheld the book and passed it on to the security police. Annoyed, I contacted the investigating officer to reassure him it was a classic novel, not a manual for guerrilla warfare. Would he like a certificate from a professor of literature to that effect? He nodded, and then as an afterthought I asked if he would allow me to give the professor his name. He understood the innuendo, for he smiled and promised that he would get the book to Mbeki without further delay, and without a certificate.

There were differences of opinion between Walter and Govan in relation to the status of the document 'Operation Mayibuye'. Although Nelson had made arrangements for military training while out of the country, he had been in prison for about a year before the document was compiled. It appeared that the leadership of MK had authorised Joe Slovo, Arthur Goldreich and others whose names were not disclosed to us to draw up the document. While it had the support of the MK leadership, those within the leadership of the ANC and the Communist Party were opposed to the strategy.

Joe Slovo had taken the document to Tanzania in the hope of having it approved by the ANC's mission-in-exile. The main item on the agenda of the meeting of 11 July 1963 at Rivonia was to resolve the hesitancy about adopting the plan. Walter Sisulu strongly rejected the proposal on political grounds. Even were it possible to get the grandiose plans for a guerrilla war off the ground, the concept was so foreign to the ANC's policy of mass action and selective sabotage that he could not accept it. Rusty Bernstein reported that the central committee of his party rejected it on two grounds. There was no hope of successful implementation and it was counterproductive to the movement's efforts to isolate South Africa from the rest of the world politically and by economic, cultural and sporting boycotts.

Kathy Kathrada agreed with Walter and Rusty. Govan Mbeki, who was privy to the discussions in MK, was unclear about its ratification within the liberation movement. (Years later, when Bram was charged, we learned that he too had been opposed to the plan when it was discussed by the Communist Party. In his statement from the dock he described the document as 'an entirely unrealistic brainchild of some youthful adventurer'.) Consequently, our clients believed that the plan had not been adopted and our defence was conducted on that basis.

We would take issue with the State on four main questions. First, Goldberg, Kathrada, Bernstein and Mhlaba were not members of the National High Command of MK or indeed of MK at all. We reserved the position of Walter Sisulu, as it might be arguable that he was an ex-officio member by virtue of his position as head of the ANC.

Secondly, membership of the ANC did not automatically mean membership of MK. The leadership of both organisations had taken clear and deliberate steps to act independently and keep the two bodies distinct, even though there were lapses due to the difficulties of operating underground.

Thirdly, we denied that the ANC was a tool of the Communist Party. The ANC was a broadly based national movement whose main object was equal political rights for all, black and white.

Fourthly, although MK was formed to undertake sabotage if and when it was considered that there was no other way, MK and the national liberation movement had not adopted the military plan called Operation Mayibuye. Consequently there was no intention of embarking on guerrilla warfare during 1963 or in the near future. To prove this, detailed evidence had to be gathered regarding the histories and cultures of the organisations so that we could make the denial more effective.

We knew that even if we proved the correctness of our version, most of the accused would not escape legal liability. But then the main purpose was not to secure an acquittal. Rather it was to present a case in which the grievances of the disenfranchised people of South Africa were articulated; in which it was demonstrated that the violence used and under consideration was carefully planned to avoid loss of life, and that those on trial were the legitimate leaders of the majority of the country's people who at some future date would need to talk with their oppressors. Forlorn as that hope may have appeared, at least we had mapped out what we hoped to achieve.

For almost two months we studied and discussed documents found at Rivonia, and prepared statements. Vernon Berrangé had returned with news that the trial was of keen interest outside the country. We brought him up to date, relieved that we could return to court under the leadership of Bram and Vernon.

For our clients, the thought of the death sentence was ever present, but visits from family members, lunches with special foods prepared for the festive season, and apricots, peaches and plums picked in my orchard by our young children lightened the atmosphere. We indulged in family talk, photographs, amusing stories about the pranks of our children. The most poignant stories were told by Dennis Goldberg and Elias Motsoaledi, the two most seriously affected by the separation from their families.

On a writing pad and the back of his empty cigarette boxes, Dennis drew greeting cards and pictures, some of which he cut into small pieces of various shapes and sizes as puzzles for our children. His inventiveness served him and his fellow prisoners well for many years.

During the adjournment Joel and I had other duties too. Members of the diplomatic corps and visitors from their countries were anxious to meet us, and some also wanted to talk with the wives of our clients. These arrangements fell to us and provided a welcome break from the intensity of the preparatory work.

On the day the trial resumed, Vernon Berrangé lost no time in making known his feelings towards Yutar. He came into court shortly before the judge and heard Yutar complaining to me about our clients' lack of cooperation with the policemen guarding them in the cell below. Loudly enough for everyone to hear, Berrangé said, 'George, why do you allow this silly little man to talk to you in that way?' Yutar muttered, 'Did you hear that? Did you hear that?' It was the first of many clashes between them.

Part of the court was packed by the most senior uniformed policemen, their chests adorned with ribbons, and security policemen in their Sunday suits, topped by dark glasses. The witness box had been moved to the prosecution's side so that the witnesses would have their backs to the media and look directly towards the jury box. No explanation was given for this rearrangement of the stage on which Yutar and his main witness were to dominate.

Yutar, in his most solemn and theatrical manner, asked the judge to invoke a section of the Criminal Procedure Act and clear the court of all except the journalists. They could report on the proceedings but would not be allowed to divulge the name of the witness or other information which could lead to his identification. 'He is definitely in mortal danger,' said Yutar. 'I assure this court that the State fears for the safety of this witness.' Vernon objected but not vehemently, wishing to show that we were unconcerned about the safety of witnesses. Our clients knew the witness. He had nothing to fear from them or their supporters.

The reason the prosecution did not want witnesses who had been detained incommunicado to give evidence in open court was obvious. If they saw friends, relatives and other people from the 'outside world', they might be less inclined to repeat the untruths which they had been programmed to deliver before the judge. If the court were closed, then the fear instilled in them by their interrogators would continue.

Vernon drew the judge's attention to the solitary occupant of the jury box, Detective Sergeant van Rensburg of the security police, whose appearance and reputation as a brutal torturer made him a figure to be feared. He was instructed to leave his vantage point. Also the press was told to refer to the witness as 'Mr X'. Our clients had told us the identity of 'Mr X' some time before, proof that, hard as jailers may try, not many secrets are kept from those behind bars.

'Mr X' – Bruno Mtolo – was called to the witness box. Yutar was accustomed to addressing Africans either by their first name or their surname. He would never use an honorific. So it didn't come as a surprise when, in a loud clear voice, he called out: 'Bruno, are you a saboteur?' The speed and confidence with which his witness answered, 'Yes, I was!' clearly indicated a well-rehearsed dramatic opening to his lengthy evidence. Yutar could never resist the theatrical.

'Did you blow up pylons and other government property in Durban?' Yutar continued. 'Yes, I did,' Mr X promptly replied.

He remained in the witness box for days on end. Part of his testimony implicated Mandela by reporting at length what Nelson had said at a Natal regional MK meeting before his arrest in 1962. At this meeting Nelson disclosed that he was the leader of MK, gave details of his travels in Africa and elsewhere, and reported on the assistance promised by the leaders attending the Addis Ababa conference. In convincing circumstantial detail Mtolo described committing a number of acts of sabotage with other MK members. He had met Joe Slovo, been at the Rivonia farm, discussed MK activity with Govan Mbeki and others among the accused. He was a member not only of MK but also of both the ANC and the Communist Party.

Much of what Mtolo said we could not and would not dispute, but there was other work for Vernon Berrangé in cross-examination. Mtolo claimed that he was disillusioned with MK: he had not been paid, yet the leadership lived in luxury outside the country, unconcerned with the rank and file. Sisulu not only had lots of money to pay bail but lived in a luxurious home and even had a car of his own. For these reasons Mtolo had cooperated with the security police. He had no regrets for deserting the cause. Mtolo clearly enjoyed his VIP status as well as the praise of higher-ranking policemen heaped on him during adjournments while he lounged in the passage, accepting cigarettes, beverages and food from his new-found friends.

Nelson Mandela gave us details of the Natal regional MK command meeting, while Walter and Govan told us what was discussed with Mtolo at the Rivonia hideout. None of them had information about Mtolo's background and activities. We asked that the witness stand down while Joel Joffe went to Natal to gather what information he could from Billy Nair, one of the leaders of the regional command. Many of them had also been detained and were awaiting trial on charges of sabotage. Joel brought back useful details.

Unbeknown to those who recruited him, Mtolo had spent a number of years in prison for theft. He was an active MK member and served on the regional command but his membership of the ANC and the Communist Party couldn't be confirmed. Despite his apparent enthusiasm for the struggle, once caught he quickly made a deal with the security police. In exchange he was given indemnity from prosecution. Mtolo even gave them incriminating information about his own brother who he had recruited and smuggled out of the country for military training. Also, Mtolo had provided a bomb for an attempted revenge killing. This collaboration led to the collapse of MK in Natal.

Vernon Berrangé was a master of the art of cross-examination, but he was not given much room to manoeuvre in view of Nelson Mandela's commitment to the truth and his preparedness to take full responsibility for the formation and activities of MK. Hoping that he might subtly induce the witness to remember or regain some of the dignity he enjoyed when he joined the struggle, Vernon pointedly referred to him as 'Mr Mtolo' before asking his first question. It had no visible effect. Mtolo was an old lag, and the many weeks spent in preparation and his commitment to his new masters kept him steadfast. No matter what improbability, contradiction or demonstrable lies were put before him, Mtolo stuck to his version.

Vernon questioned him on his attitude towards the leadership in exile.

BERRANGÉ: You said that the leaders had left the country and that was why, when you were arrested, during that night, you decided that you were going to give evidence for the State. I am asking you what leaders had left the country at that time when you came to that decision?

MTOLO: Joe Slovo, Michael Harmel, Jack Hodgson.

BERRANGÉ: They all left the country at that time?

MTOLO: They had left.

BERRANGÉ: Really? And Nelson Mandela?

MTOLO: Talking about Nelson Mandela, I want to tell you that he is the only one of the leaders that I have respect for.

BERRANGÉ: But you were talking about a lot of leaders leaving the country. You see a lot of men in the dock here, don't you?

MTOLO: Yes.

BERRANGÉ: Tell me, other than going to jail for theft, breaking into railway coaches and that sort of thing, have you ever been banned? Have you ever been put under house arrest?

MTOLO: No.

BERRANGÉ: Have you ever been prohibited from attending meetings?

MTOLO: No.

BERRANGÉ: Have you ever been sent to jail for your political beliefs?

MTOLO: No.

BERRANGÉ: Though that is what happened to most of these men here. But you, Mr Mtolo, prefer to give evidence against these men because you say the leaders had left?

MTOLO: I said one of the reasons. But these people, referring to these people sitting here, there are some of these also that I realised were playing the fool with us. I haven't suffered the sufferings they have suffered, but the deeds they have done are almost the same as the deeds of those who have fled.

Then there was an exchange about his evidence that the people and their organisation, the ANC, were not being looked after:

BERRANGÉ: So in order to ensure the safety of the ANC you decided to make the statement?

MTOLO: In the interests of the ANC. Not the ANC alone, all the people in South Africa.

BERRANGÉ: They would all benefit? And you regarded yourself as a benefactor?

MTOLO: Every person on this earth ought to think of other people.

BERRANGÉ: Don't you think that that is just a bit of sheer hypocrisy?

MTOLO: No, I am saying that for it is true, from the bottom of my heart, My Lord.

When Vernon wondered if Mtolo had ever been to the Sisulu home to see that family's non-existent opulence, Mtolo invented a story. He had been taken there by a friend, Levi Seloro, on the way to a party. This, although Mtolo was in hiding at the time and would have exposed himself to danger had he gone to a house that was under rigorous surveillance.

BERRANGÉ: Did you go inside the house?

MTOLO: Yes.

BERRANGÉ: Who was there?

MTOLO: There were some children sitting in the door. We went in and enquired for his wife. She was not there.

BERRANGÉ: Why should Seloro want to show you Sisulu's house?

MTOLO: He was just going to show me the house of one of the leaders. He was one of the leaders.

BERRANGÉ: But why?

MTOLO: So that I should just know.

BERRANGÉ: Know what?

MTOLO: Know my leader's house.

BERRANGÉ: But why?

MTOLO: It was just incidental.

BERRANGÉ: What parts of the house did you go into?

MTOLO: We went through the kitchen; we went to the dining room.

BERRANGÉ: Yes. Anywhere else?

MTOLO: We sat down in the dining room.

BERRANGÉ: In the absence of Sisulu or his wife. What for?

MTOLO: Seloro then asked where Mrs Sisulu was and the boy said that she was not at home. Then Seloro said it was alright, we would see him at the party in any case because he would be there.

BERRANGÉ: So that was your only reason for going to his house?

MTOLO: That is all.

BERRANGÉ: When was this?

MTOLO: Towards the end of April 1963.

BERRANGÉ: But by that time you had already become disillusioned with your leaders?

MTOLO: That does not mean to say that I would not agree to go to their house.

Nelson Mandela denied Mtolo's version on a number of issues, particularly concerning what he had said at the Natal regional command meeting. Mtolo would not budge.

Yutar had not asked Mtolo anything about the MK policy of choosing targets that would avoid loss of human life. Vernon cautiously broached the subject and led Mtolo into admitting that those were his instructions and that these instructions had not changed up to the time of his arrest – an important concession in support of our case that there was no decision to embark on guerrilla warfare. Although we made some headway by successfully challenging portions of his evidence intended to smear the accused and their movement, most of his evidence establishing the legal responsibility of Mandela, Sisulu, Mbeki and Mlangeni remained unchallenged.

The prosecution was justifiably pleased with Mtolo. He earned his complete indemnity from prosecution and a low-profile job under an assumed name from an employer closely connected with the regime. Van Wyk, the investigating officer, snidely asked me later what I thought of the witness. I gave a non-committal reply and he commented, 'Your side's big mistake was to recruit a criminal into your ranks', identifying us, the defence team of lawyers, with our clients.

Van Wyk was not the only one to blur the distinction between the lawyers and the accused. Before the trial I had played bridge with a regular partner, Dimitri Roussos. We played socially on Wednesdays and competitively on Mondays at the Johannesburg Bridge Club. Some four months after I stopped playing because of pressure of work, Dimitri urged me to be his partner again for an evening at the home of a well-known society lady called Evang. The wife of one of the other players, Doreen, pulled me aside at teatime. 'George,' she said, 'I was worried about you, seeing your picture and name in this big case. I was so worried that I phoned Evang and asked her, "Is George a Red?" She told me not to be silly, "George will do anything for money," she said. And I said to Evang, "Oh, I am so relieved."'

After the testimony of Mr X, the prosecution wanted to prove that Dennis Goldberg had conducted a camp for MK during December 1962 on a farm called

Mamre near Cape Town. The aim was to train about thirty young men in guerrilla warfare. They called Cyril Davids as a witness. Dennis maintained that those who attended the camp were members of the ANC Youth League and the Coloured People's Congress. The camp was actually a weekend outing to enjoy various activities.

Some of these activities were to be led by Davids who, quite coincidentally, was knowledgeable about electrical circuits, telephones and other devices. Because it was a non-racial group someone called the police, but they were told that the camp was held for 'health and spiritual purposes'. Suspicions aroused, the police called in their security arm. Statements were taken from the camp leaders, but there was no evidence that an offence had been committed. No follow-up occurred for more than nine months.

After the Rivonia arrests, Cyril Davids was detained for ninety days. Solitary confinement and long interrogation sessions followed until he made a statement 'to the satisfaction of his interrogator'. In this instance, the interrogator was satisfied only when the 'outing' was changed into 'a guerrilla warfare training camp', despite the statements originally taken from Davids.

Vernon led the cross-examination.

BERRANGÉ: How long was it after you were first arrested that you were interrogated?

DAVIDS: Five days.

BERRANGÉ: And you persisted with your assertion that this camp was for health and spiritual purposes?

DAVIDS: Yes.

BERRANGÉ: And I suppose you were laughed at?

DAVIDS: Yes.

BERRANGÉ: You were told that you weren't telling the truth?

DAVIDS: Yes.

BERRANGÉ: You were told that unless you did tell the truth you would be kept there for ninety days and a further ninety days and a further ninety days?

DAVIDS: Yes, I realised that.

BERRANGÉ: You were told that?

DAVIDS: Yes.

BERRANGÉ: But despite that fact you insisted that the camp had been run for health and spiritual purposes?

DAVIDS: Yes.

BERRANGÉ: So, thereafter, when were you next interrogated?

DAVIDS: A week after that.

BERRANGÉ: And I take it you again insisted that the camp was run for health and spiritual purposes?

DAVIDS: Yes, I did.

BERRANGÉ: And again you were told that they didn't believe you? And they told you that unless you came out with a different story you were going to be kept there?

DAVIDS: Yes.

BERRANGÉ: When was your next interrogation?

DAVIDS: Three weeks after that.

BERRANGÉ: And did you again persist in your statement?

DAVIDS: Yes, I did.

BERRANGÉ: We come then to the fourth interrogation. How long was that after your third?

DAVIDS: I can't remember the exact period, but it must have been about two weeks.

BERRANGÉ: Did you again persist in your attitude?

DAVIDS: Yes, I did.

BERRANGÉ: And again you were told, 'Well, you will be kept here indefinitely'?

DAVIDS: Yes.

BERRANGÉ: Not told that you would be charged, or could be charged?

DAVIDS: I realised that. I can't remember having been told.

BERRANGÉ: Is it possible?

DAVIDS: It is possible that I could have been told that.

BERRANGÉ: But you had a distinct feeling that you might be charged?

DAVIDS: Yes, I had an idea that I might be.

BERRANGÉ: And the fifth interrogation – how long was that after?

DAVIDS: It was about three weeks afterwards.

BERRANGÉ: Who interviewed then?

DAVIDS: Lt Sauerman.

BERRANGÉ: I suppose he was friendly again?

DAVIDS: Not exactly.

BERRANGÉ: Well, what was he, if he was 'not exactly friendly'? Was he angry with you?

DAVIDS: Yes, he was. That time he must have been very angry with me.

BERRANGÉ: He now got to the stage of threatening you?

DAVIDS: Yes.

BERRANGÉ: What did he threaten you with?

DAVIDS: A further ninety days.

BERRANGÉ: Yes, but you had been told that before. On every previous occasion as I understand it, you had been told that you would be kept for a further ninety days, as you said on previous occasions. On this occasion you say he was very angry and threatened you. How did he show his anger?

DAVIDS: He only threatened to leave me in prison for a further ninety days.

BERRANGÉ: Well, then how did his anger show itself on this fifth occasion?

DAVIDS: Because he refused to see me again.

BERRANGÉ: Did he call you a liar?

DAVIDS: Yes. He did that often.

BERRANGÉ: What was going to happen if he didn't see you again?

DAVIDS: I would stay for another ninety days, I should imagine.

BERRANGÉ: Now, you would just be kept there for the rest of the time by yourself without even having the privilege of visitors from the special branch, from the security police. Is that the idea?

DAVIDS: Yes.

BERRANGÉ: What did you do on this occasion? Again adopt your earlier attitude?

DAVIDS: Yes.

BERRANGÉ: Were you interrogated again?

DAVIDS: Yes, I was, another three or four weeks – possibly four weeks after.

BERRANGÉ: Now, did you still persist?

DAVIDS: No.

BERRANGÉ: Who came to you on this occasion?

DAVIDS: Lt. Sauerman.

BERRANGÉ: That was the occasion on which three weeks had elapsed between that and the earlier occasion?

DAVIDS: Yes.

BERRANGÉ: What did he ask you?

DAVIDS: He asked me what the camp was all about.

BERRANGÉ: Did you say for health and spiritual purposes?

DAVIDS: No, I did not.

BERRANGÉ: What did you say?

DAVIDS: I told him it was a camp where young guerrillas would be trained.

BERRANGÉ: Now you were prepared to assist in the training of young guerrillas?

DAVIDS: Which Lt Sauerman knew.

BERRANGÉ: Did he tell you that?

DAVIDS: Yes. No.

BERRANGÉ: Now, please, why did you say 'yes'?

DAVIDS: It slipped actually.

BERRANGÉ: A very significant slip. I want to suggest to you, Mr Davids, that Lt. Sauerman came to you and said to you: 'I know that you were one of those training young guerrillas, because I got that evidence from other people'. And that was why you said 'yes' when I asked you the question.

DAVIDS: No.

BERRANGÉ: Well, why did you say so?

DAVIDS: It was a slip.

BERRANGÉ: I see. Now, Mr Davids, you said that you weren't particularly affected by this ninety-day imprisonment. You weren't feeling lonely. You weren't feeling depressed. You had been well fed. You didn't miss your wife, though you had missed your children. You did not mind being alone, because you are not a man who likes a lot of people around you. And you had adamantly persisted in what you say was a lie on at least five earlier occasions – there were actually six including the occasion when this matter was discussed with you three weeks after the camp. What made you change your mind?

DAVIDS: I felt that I had had enough of ninety-day detention.

BERRANGÉ: Were you by that time getting very depressed?

DAVIDS: Yes, I was.

At this point Davids had forgotten his earlier attempts to convince us that his confinement had been something of a lark. Earlier on, he had been asked:

BERRANGÉ: You weren't feeling lonely?

DAVIDS: No.

BERRANGÉ: Were you enjoying yourself?

DAVIDS: To an extent, yes.

BERRANGÉ: You like being alone?

DAVIDS: If it is possible.

BERRANGÉ: You welcomed this ninety-day imprisonment?

DAVIDS: To an extent.

But later in the cross-examination, Vernon's questions were exposing the witness's real feelings, not those so carefully prepared to prove his bona fides to his police captors, which had been trotted out earlier:

BERRANGÉ: You told us on the last occasion that the reason why you told your interrogators on so many occasions what you now say is not the truth was because you were concerned to save your own skin, and to a lesser extent to protect your companions. You remember telling us that?

DAVIDS: Yes, I do.

BERRANGÉ: And that was why you kept telling your interrogators that the object of this camp was quite an innocent one?

DAVIDS: Yes.

BERRANGÉ: You say you did that to save your own skin?

DAVIDS: Yes.

BERRANGÉ: I am therefore asking you what made you decide that you were no longer interested in saving your own skin?

DAVIDS: Because I was getting fed up with the ninety-day detention.

BERRANGÉ: Yes, but you might have done more than that. You might have had not only ninety days' detention, but you might have had years and years and years in jail. You realised that, didn't you?

DAVIDS: Yes, I did.

BERRANGÉ: So what was it that decided you to risk these years in jail?

DAVIDS: I wanted to get the whole thing over with.

BERRANGÉ: Was it that you preferred jail to ninety days' detention?

DAVIDS: That's one way of putting it.

BERRANGÉ: No, no. I don't want to put words into your mouth. Is that what you really felt?

DAVIDS: Yes.

BERRANGÉ: You felt that jail as a hard labour prisoner would be a very much easier life to you than to be detained as a ninety-day detainee?

DAVIDS: That is correct.

BERRANGÉ: Had the police told you that you won't be prosecuted?

DAVIDS: No, they did not.

BERRANGÉ: Never?

DAVIDS: Never.

BERRANGÉ: Had they told you that you would be released from your ninety-day detention as soon as you had given your evidence?

DAVIDS: Yes.

BERRANGÉ: You are still under ninety-day detention? You are still in custody?

DAVIDS: No ... Yes, I am.

BERRANGÉ: And have you been told that when you have given your evidence you would be let go?

DAVIDS: Yes.

BERRANGÉ: So you don't expect to be charged, do you?

DAVIDS: Yes, there is a charge against me in Cape Town.

BERRANGÉ: But you have been told that you would be released as soon as you have given evidence here?

DAVIDS: That's right.

BERRANGÉ: You realise perfectly well that if now you were to go back on the statement you made to the police and were to tell this court what you had originally told the police, namely that this was an innocent camp, you would again be detained. You realise that?

DAVIDS: Yes, I do.

For over a quarter of a century many of the witnesses in political trials distorted the facts to please their interrogators, much as Davids did. Some of us adapted Vernon Berrangé's techniques and they helped us in our efforts to show up the dangers of accepting evidence obtained by the security police from isolated detainees in their interrogation rooms.

During this part of the trial, another witness illustrated the problems encountered by those trying too hard to please their police interrogators. A less sophisticated participant at the camp had been called and was asked to identify the leader of the camp. By that time Vernon's cross-examination of Davids had made it clear that the leader was Goldberg, so we fully expected the witness to indicate Goldberg or one of the other accused in the box. When, without any hesitation, the witness pointed his finger at me even the surly judge laughed. For my part, I thought it an accusation there was no need to deny.

CHAPTER 21

Never Bet Against a Greek

Vernon Berrangé relished any opportunity to cross-examine policemen. Dozens of them gave evidence about acts of sabotage committed throughout the country, what explosives were used and what damage done. From research by Arthur Chaskalson it was clear that most of their evidence was inadmissible as proof that our clients were responsible for those acts. When such a policeman was called, we would ask a few questions to establish that their evidence was hearsay and could not be used.

Vernon could not resist taking on Lt du Preez from the security police in Port Elizabeth. Du Preez had identified by name and rank dozens of MK members throughout the Eastern Cape alleging that they all had committed acts of sabotage. Bram in his usual polite manner established from du Preez that he had no personal knowledge of the matters but that he relied on confessions and admissions made to him and on written statements contained in the police dockets. Lt du Preez's memory as to who had done what, when and how was quite remarkable.

As Bram finished his questioning and the judge was about to thank and discharge the witness, Vernon sprang up and audibly cleared his throat. Did he want to put any further questions? the judge asked.

BERRANGÉ: Yes, if Your Lordship pleases. Lt du Preez, you have told us of the many ANC and MK members who confessed to you their membership and the acts of sabotage they had committed? And I take it that each one of them did so freely and voluntarily and without any inducement offered by you?

DU PREEZ: Yes, that is so, My Lord.

BERRANGÉ: It was all as easy as that, was it?

DU PREEZ: No ... it was not that easy, My Lord.

BERRANGÉ: Oh, do tell us of the difficulties that you had in extracting the confession from the first one, and then the second, and thereafter the third and so on ...

There could be no satisfactory answer to that question or others like it. Through his persistent and probing questions, Vernon established how the security police made use of informers to detain people for ninety days or more. The police would then tell those in solitary confinement what they had learned from their inform-ers. Eventually the detainee would confirm the information.

The same Sergeant Dirker who had found Duma Nokwe in possession of incrim-inating documents was among the group of policemen that raided the Rivonia farm. He was deliberately untruthful. We decided that most of these untruths would make no material difference to the guilt or innocence of our clients with the exception of a lie told against Rusty Bernstein. Despite our efforts not to disclose any details of Rusty's defence, the prosecution, probably by bugging our consultations, knew that Rusty would contend that he arrived at the Rivonia meeting shortly before the police pounced. Dirker wanted to contradict Rusty's evidence to strengthen the State's case against him. The prosecution claimed that he was a member of the high command and that he must have been at the farm for the better part of the morning discussing the document, Operation Mayibuye, which Dirker said he found on the table. So the policeman made up a story that immediately after the arrest of the accused he went to Rusty's car, opened the bonnet, and felt that the engine was almost ice-cold. He reckoned without Vernon Berrangé.

BERRANGÉ: Do you know how long it takes an engine to cool off?

DIRKER: Yes, a number of hours.

BERRANGÉ: Not within half an hour or so?

DIRKER: Certainly not, I know from my personal experience.

BERRANGÉ: Did anything unusual happen when you lifted the bonnet?

DIRKER: No.

BERRANGÉ: Did an alarm go off at any stage?

DIRKER: No.

BERRANGÉ: Tell us again what time the raid took place?

DIRKER: Shortly after two.

BERRANGÉ: Did you know that Mr Bernstein's house-arrest order compelled him to report to Marshall Square, the central police station in Johannesburg, between one and two every afternoon?

DIRKER: Yes.

BERRANGÉ: How long would it take to drive from the police station to Rivonia?

DIRKER: About half an hour.

BERRANGÉ: Did you check at what time Mr Bernstein might have reported on that day?

DIRKER: No.

BERRANGÉ: You should have. Have a look at a photostat copy of the page of the occurrences book specially kept for restricted people to sign and the time confirmed by the police officer on duty. Do you see Mr Bernstein's signature and the time? Read it out.

DIRKER: About a quarter-to-two.

BERRANGÉ: Do you agree that you deliberately lied?

His answer did not matter. Nor could he deny that Bernstein's car alarm went off automatically as soon as the bonnet was opened. Dirker also made a last-ditch attempt to implicate James Kantor, who was not at the farm on the day of the arrests, but came in a few days later. Dirker said he had spotted him feeding the chickens. This led him to believe that Kantor was so familiar with the place that he must have made numerous visits there in the past, and that he must be a co-conspirator. The judge, who had by that time decided to acquit Kantor, commented to his counsel, John Coaker, that Kantor was not likely to have returned to the farm if he had been a co-conspirator and that bags of chicken feed are usually kept near a fowl run. Dirker's observation of Kantor's chicken-feeding activities proved nothing.

Among the many diplomats, academics and political scientists who came to observe the trial were Gwendolen Carter and Thomas Karis. They were ushered to seats in the jury box just as Yutar was completing the examination-in-chief of a witness. That day Vernon was in great form and the visitors were enthralled by his performance.

Thomas Karis I knew from the treason trial, where he had been a regular observer on behalf of the United States embassy. We had a common bond in that his father and I were born in the same province. The connections went further. His mother-in-law was born in Koroni, a member of the Lahana family, and the sister of a monk who had taught me. He and Gwendolen Carter had come to South Africa to assess apartheid policies and more particularly the move to prepare the Transkei for 'independence'. The end result of their trip would be a book – *Transkei: An Experiment in Domestic Colonialism* – that was hardly an endorsement of the government's policies.

Tom knew Nelson Mandela and Bram Fischer. At a dinner that evening I confided to them that the three leaders had no defence and that the best we could hope for was to avoid the death sentence. They undertook to lobby decision-makers in the United States in our cause.

Gwendolen was intrigued by Bram. I sketched his background, but she couldn't understand how he could be a communist. Again I provided a context, suggesting that at a time when no other political party or group advocated political rights and equality to the African people, the Communist Party did. Also Bram valued the sacrifices made by the Soviet Union in the war against the Germans. I went so far as to say that if the Labour or Liberal parties had adopted a policy of granting universal franchise, Bram might not have joined the Communist Party.

The next evening Bram invited Gwendolen and Tom to dinner. The following morning on our way to Pretoria he was unusually quiet. When I asked him how the dinner had gone, he said curtly, 'Fine,' and then after a long pause he added, 'George, do not ever again apologise to anyone for my political beliefs.'

By the time the prosecution's case looked as if it was nearing an end, Nelson produced the first complete draft of the statement he was to make from the dock. I was shocked by his closing words: that he was ready to die for what he had done. Surely this would be viewed as a challenge, irresistible to the prosecution, the judge and the government? I also feared it might alienate some of the movement's more tentative supporters. Nelson remained adamant. Arthur agreed with him. Walter was supportive but cautious. He reminded us that during the Defiance Campaign, he and others had said that they were prepared to sacrifice their lives. It would be wrong to say anything that might sound like a plea for mercy, or a retraction of the earlier position. I argued that surely Nelson wanted to live and accomplish what he and his organisation strove for.

We turned to Bram. He was ambivalent. I proposed that Nelson say he hoped to live and achieve his ideals but *if needs be* was prepared to die. On this we agreed. What influenced me here was an argument that Socrates might have saved his life if he had not challenged the Athenian jury in so resolute a manner.

With Nelson's permission I took a copy of his statement to Nadine Gordimer. It so happened that Anthony Sampson was staying with her; he had edited *Drum* magazine in the early 1950s and had known Nelson well. In fact they'd remained in close contact when he returned to England. In the intervening years he had acquired an international reputation as a writer and journalist. I asked him to look at the statement and suggest any improvements.

He withdrew to Nadine's small study. Nadine's husband, Reinhold Cassirer, was a refugee from Hitler's Germany. He was of the opinion that South Africa could be compared with Nazi Germany in the 1930s. Many would have agreed. Reinhold had brought with him some of the family's Impressionist works of art, several of which were hanging on the lounge walls. I gazed at them for what seemed like hours while we waited for Anthony, who eventually returned, obviously moved by what he had read.

He prophetically judged Nelson's statement an important historical document but said that to gain maximum impact, some of the paragraphs should be rearranged. Journalists, forever against deadlines, would hurriedly scan the first three or four pages and then just a page or two at the end. He suggested that the paragraphs dealing with the nature of the struggle, the ANC's democratic tradition, its independence and the fact that it was not committed to any particular ideology, dogma or any foreign power should be set out at the start. He renumbered the paragraphs accordingly. However, he was pleased with the concluding paragraphs.

Our decision not to call Nelson Mandela into the witness box was a well-kept secret. If the prosecutors had any thoughts to the contrary they would have dismissed them when we took a number of volumes of the treason trial records to the chief warder. These he was requested to give to Mr Mandela who needed them to prepare his case. Within days, similar copies were seen on Yutar's desk. He was no doubt studying them carefully in preparation for the cross-examination which he anticipated.

During the adjournment after the State closed its case, we had to finalise our preparations. Considerable effort was devoted to the statements of those giving evidence. I spent much time preparing with Walter Sisulu and Govan Mbeki.

Then, almost on the eve of the trial's resumption, Joel Joffe called a crucial meeting in the Fischers' shady garden. He felt that some of the accused should not give evidence under oath. By giving evidence, our clients could only worsen the case against them. He predicted that Yutar's cross-examination would seek to establish that the loss of life had been foreseen and that there was no difference between MK, the ANC and the Communist Party. In addition, if Yutar obtained an admission of membership from any accused, that would be sufficient to convict all of them, including Raymond Mhlaba, Rusty Bernstein and Kathy Kathrada. Arthur Chaskalson tentatively agreed with Joel's argument. He had done considerable work on the law and in analysing the evidence had concluded that much of what had been said or handed into court was inadmissible. If any of our clients gave evidence, careful cross-examination could fill in the gaps to the disadvantage of the three who had a chance of being acquitted.

Bram Fischer and Vernon Berrangé turned to me. I predicted that Yutar would not conduct the careful cross-examination envisaged by Joel. In the main he would challenge Walter Sisulu and Govan Mbeki on their political beliefs and actions. His motivation being to discredit them and their organisations while simultaneously justifying the government's apartheid policies. I thought that our clients would be more than a match for Yutar on this score.

I took the argument further: If we did not give evidence denying that guerrilla warfare was an agreed option, then the judge could draw an adverse inference against us. If we gave evidence denying an agreement on guerrilla warfare, and the judge wanted a reason not to impose the death penalty, then this evidence might influence him to hold in our favour. Above all I was aware that the judge had never had any meaningful contact with black people, particularly Africans, except at the level of master and servant. I believed that if our clients testified for days on end, he might still not be satisfied enough to let them go free, but the justice of their cause, their deeply felt sense of grievance, their intelligence and courage would become clear and could lead him to spare their lives. Further, since their organisations had been banned, their leaders maligned, their freedom of expression denied, the opportunity to use the witness box as a platform to speak to the people of South Africa and the world at large was too good to be missed.

In their subsequent books Joel Joffe, Hilda and Rusty Bernstein, Stephen Clingman, Glen Frankell and others have written in approval of my intervention at this point. And, after their eventual release, the convicted men spoke from public platforms honouring me as the tactician who saved their lives. But the views I expressed at that crucial meeting were not mine alone. They were also the opinions of Walter Sisulu and Govan Mbeki and the other accused.

By the end of the meeting, we had reached consensus. Despite the dangers articulated by Joel, we felt we should respect our clients' views: they should go ahead and give evidence under oath.

During the adjournment Colonel Aucamp had made our work more difficult by rearranging the consultation facilities. Yet despite these impediments, we were ready to present the defence case on the arranged date. Bram began by explaining in broad terms what would be admitted. When he said that an agreed policy of guerrilla warfare would be denied, the judge showed particular interest. Yutar, who was making notes, raised an eyebrow as he looked back at a group of security police officers behind him, indicating that he was confident he could deal with the accused and their advocates.

For all his self-assurance, Yutar was visibly astounded when Bram said, 'The defence case, My Lord, will commence with a statement from the dock by Nelson Mandela who personally took part in the establishment of Umkhonto, and who will be able to inform the court of the beginnings of that organisation and of its history up to August 1962 when he was arrested.'

In a frenzy Yutar jumped up. 'My Lord!' he exclaimed, 'My Lord, I think that you should warn the accused that what he says from the dock has far less weight than if he submitted himself to cross-examination!' 'I think, Mr Yutar,' replied the judge, 'that counsel for the defence have sufficient experience to be able to advise their clients without your assistance.' The judge's way of showing displeasure with Yutar was persistently to call him 'Mr' rather than 'Dr', a title Yutar cherished.

The prosecutor's outburst provoked Bram into a moment of rare irony. He thanked his learned friend for his advice and assured the court: 'Neither we, nor our clients are unaware of the provisions of the Criminal Code.'

VIPs in the jury box, dozens of journalists, some of them standing for lack of seating, were all focused on Mandela. Most of the spectators in court, seated behind the dock, stared at the back of his head. His co-accused and we, their lawyers, half turned to the right to watch him. But the judge managed not to look at him, nor did Yutar or any of his team turn around as Nelson Mandela spoke of his early life, his political development, his participation in various campaigns and other forms of struggle, as he claimed the moral high ground and castigated the government. He denied many of the allegations intended to discredit him and his organisation, particularly that it was a 'terrorist' or 'communist' organisation.

Poignantly he articulated the claims of the vast majority of the people of South Africa.

And immediately before he delivered the last portion of his statement, he set out the fervent belief in political equality. These views were considered tantamount to treason by the apartheid regime and its supporters who boasted that their republic would last a thousand years. Finally he came to his last powerful declaration:

> During my lifetime I have dedicated myself to this struggle of the African people. I have fought against white domination, and I have fought against black domination. I have cherished the ideal of a democratic and free society in which all persons live together in harmony and with equal opportunities. It is an ideal which I hope to live for and to achieve. But if needs be, it is an ideal for which I am prepared to die.

As predicted by Anthony Sampson, newspapers published just brief selected passages of Mandela's statement. But there was one important exception: The *Rand Daily Mail* published it in full despite the prohibition against quoting restricted persons. The paper's editor, Laurence Gandar, and senior political reporter Benjamin Pogrund decided it was essential that the whole text be carried. For this and other acts of courage, such as exposing the ill-treatment of prisoners, police brutality and abuse of power in many other respects, they paid dearly, eventually having to face criminal charges, then being convicted and losing their jobs.

Mandela's statement was widely circulated. Many a carefully folded printed copy of it was found by the security police hidden between the pages of textbooks belonging to students arrested for taking part in the 1976 uprisings. The statement served as a model for many charged with political offences. Often, when young or old were asked what their defence would be to charges arising out of their participation in the struggle, their answer would reflect their admiration for their jailed leader: 'The Nelson Mandela Defence', they would reply. Later the law was changed to prevent speeches such as these, and the right of an accused to make a statement from the dock was removed.

After the drama of Nelson's statement, our first witness, Walter Sisulu, was called. During our consultations, Bram had carefully gone through his statement with him. He would write a question in the margin of Walter's statement and Walter would point to the relevant passage in the statement to indicate the answer he would give. This was an arduous business but a necessary precaution to beat the bugging devices.

From the witness stand, Sisulu spoke of his early years and how from the mid-1940s as a member of the ANC he had espoused the cause of the African people. Even though its policies and programmes of action employed non-violent means, they still at times infringed unjust laws affecting every aspect of the daily life of all Africans. Walter repeated under oath what Nelson had said from the dock, particularly the difficulty encountered in deciding to use 'controlled violence' after the blows dealt by the Sharpeville massacre, the declaration of a state of emergency, the detention of many anti-apartheid activists and the banning of the ANC. Asked for his attitude to the ANC's banning, he replied: 'We could not accept the ban on the African National Congress because it was the mouthpiece of the African people. It was the only hope that the African people had for liberation from oppression.' He denied formal membership of the National High Command of MK, although he admitted to attending some of its meetings as a senior member of the ANC. He had done so because the ANC had to agree to any fundamental change in the policy and tactics of MK. He stressed that he and his organisation were against the adoption and implementation of Operation Mayibuye.

Anticipating that Walter would later be asked questions which would expose persons not before the court, Bram gave him the opportunity to clarify where he stood on this issue.

FISCHER: Mr Sisulu, you have chosen to give evidence under oath so that your story can be tested by cross-examination in the ordinary way.

SISULU: That is correct, My Lord. Except that I would like to make my position very clear. My Lord, I would find it difficult to testify or to answer any questions relating to my organisation which might lead to the prosecution of my people. I would not do anything which would lead to revealing the workings of my organisation's confidential matters. I would not be able to testify in so far as that aspect is concerned. I am aware that by doing so I might worsen my position but I find that I cannot do otherwise.

Vernon Berrangé had made a great point of addressing African witnesses as 'Mr'. The implied criticism was not lost on Yutar. He stopped using their first names, calling them by their surnames but still unable to bring himself to use the polite 'Mr' when addressing a black person. Yutar had been deprived of the opportunity of cross-examining Nelson Mandela. Now he rose to question Walter, confident that he would get admissions to secure a conviction (admissions that were hardly necessary in view of the concessions already made during the trial). He also wanted to discredit him and his co-accused as untruthful opportunists, terrorists who had no respect for human life, lackeys of international communism, impostors who represented a tiny minority of the otherwise docile and happy 'Bantu peoples'.

Yutar must have expected that because Sisulu had limited formal education and because as a black man he was, by Yutar's definition, not very intelligent, he would be no match for a deputy attorney-general: a man with a doctorate in law; a man, moreover, whose thoroughness, rich vocabulary, literary witticisms and not-so-gentle irony had served him so well for so long in exposing the petty perjuries of the accused and their witnesses. Little did he know that he was about to cross swords with an honourable and honest man possessed of a phenomenal memory and a well-developed lateral intelligence. In short, a man with a worthy set of values, who was a dedicated husband and father and who, as a leader of the ANC, enjoyed the love and respect of a vast majority of the people of South Africa.

The cross-examination began and soon Joel Joffe whispered in my ear that my predictions about Yutar's intentions were coming true. After an hour, another of my colleagues, Harold Hanson, doyen of the legal profession at the time, who had entered the court to observe the cross-examination, felt that Yutar had not scored a single point.

During the lunch adjournment we usually ate at what was commonly called a Greek café directly behind the rear entrance to the court. In gold-leaf letters the establishment advertised, 'Grills at all hours'. The black relatives and friends of our clients could not join us, as that would have been a contravention of the Group Areas Act. Most certainly they could not sit down with us. At times one of the braver ones, Winnie Mandela among them, came up to ask how things were going. Inevitably the other customers, including some of our legal colleagues in their black jackets or waistcoats, wing collars and bibs, squirmed uncomfortably, hoping that the intruders would leave. Above all they stared at Bram Fischer, one of their own, wondering how he could tolerate the approach of a black person, shake hands, put his hand on a shoulder, embrace some of them and even kiss Albertina Sisulu on the cheek.

On this particular day, we had ordered our food when Joel Joffe rushed in, fuming. Loudly he announced that Yutar had ordered Walter to be isolated from all the others. Had anyone ever heard of this happening in any other case? Some of the sympathetic members of the Bar glanced at us and shook their heads in disbelief. What were we going to do?

We hurriedly finished our lunch and went back to speak to our clients. Most of them demanded the strongest possible protest. Nelson, however, advised caution lest it be suggested that we wanted to protect Walter against his cross-examiner. Knowing Walter better than any of the others, he thought that his friend could handle the situation. This view prevailed and Nelson was proved correct.

Judging by the way he dealt with his cross-examiner, Walter proved that however unpleasant the extra days on his own may have been, he did not require our protection. When Joel was able to control his anger, he said to me, 'By the way, you don't have to pay for your own lunch anymore. You have already won the bet you took with us that Yutar would not behave as an ordinary prosecutor would.' And Vernon reminded us that one of Damon Runyon's characters had said that you must never bet against a Greek.

Back in court, Yutar asked Walter about Operation Mayibuye: 'So, despite your fifty years of trying to persuade the Bantu of this country that they were being oppressed you only had in 1960 a total enrolment of about a hundred and twenty thousand out of twelve million?'

Sisulu replied: 'Yes. The reason is obvious. There is no country which conducts greater intimidation against political movements than South Africa. And yet that does not mean that because we have a hundred and twenty thousand we do not represent the aspirations of the African people. The point you are making is this: that we are not representative of the African people, that we don't have a following. Political organisations don't get everybody. The organisations themselves are smaller in numbers yet they represent the aspirations of the people.'

Asked whether he thought there would be support for the armed struggle and particularly guerrilla warfare, Sisulu responded: 'If the masses knew that we were leading them and there was a real possibility of success they would respond in overwhelming numbers. The reason for this is that the people do want to have a vote in this country.'

At this point, the presiding judge struck a blow against judicial impartiality, betraying the fact that his beliefs were no different from those of the average privileged white South African. He interrupted the cross-examination: 'Would they really? Is that correct, Mr Sisulu? You think they should have the vote, but how do you know that the ordinary Bantu-about-town wants the vote? You think that he ought to have it, and you are telling him that he ought to have it. But how do you know that he really wants it? You only know that you think he ought to have it, but how do you know that he wants it?'

These questions and comments caused us some concern as they revealed his political attitude and prejudices. They could even be regarded as indicating his attitude towards the death penalty. His ignorance of the aspirations of the African people was starkly revealed. It seemed obvious too that he had not heard of the UN Declaration on Human Rights in 1948, or of Harold Macmillan's 'Wind of Change' speech in 1960. The judge's views were those of the vast majority of his fellow Afrikaners, namely that the relationship between white and black should be that of master and servant, and that was the end of the matter.

Sisulu's answer to the judge's comment was direct and to the point, based upon his own experience: 'Well, I have not come across meetings where I have heard people saying, "No, we don't want the vote!" People always support the idea of the vote.'

Later in the cross-examination, the judge questioned whether the accused were concerned about the safety of their followers.

JUDGE: I think some of your clever colleagues like Dennis Goldberg would be able to tell you that if they don't know beforehand that a broadcast is taking place, they wouldn't be able to trace the place?

SISULU: Well, that's what they suggested, My Lord.

JUDGE: If the technicians are so clever that they can trace the origin of a broadcast within a few minutes then it doesn't matter where you hold the broadcast, they will catch you red-handed?

SISULU: We would still take the risk. There was no doubt that those who were there were taking a big risk. But the point is that we were in hiding and that is the reason it was not done at Rivonia. We were staying there, and we would have been exposing it to the police.

JUDGE: So you don't mind the people who were working on the broadcast and putting your recording over the air – you wouldn't mind their being caught so long as you are not caught? Is that the position?

SISULU: No, that is not what I am trying to say. One does take the risk. But you would not put all your eggs in one basket. Those who were to do it were there. That is why we were not there – and not that we didn't care about any particular person who might be arrested.

JUDGE: Isn't that rather typical of politicians? That they are always prepared to let the rank and file take the risk, and see that they don't put themselves in danger. Isn't that the position?

SISULU: I don't think that that interpretation is correct. Take the case of war. The generals are not very exposed, not because they want to expose others.

JUDGE: But exactly the same thing happens with people who are plotting a rebellion or revolution. They look forward to being the government in due course. And they see to it that they preserve their own skins, not so?

SISULU: My understanding, My Lord, is that we, to the best of our ability, want to preserve everyone.

Whatever basis there might have been for the judge's generalisation about politicians, it could hardly be true of those before him who were risking their lives in their struggle for freedom against a powerful and ruthless foe.

The issue of risk and respect for life was also raised by Yutar when he queried the assertion that MK and the ANC respected the value of human life and that MK operatives were expected to behave in a responsible manner to avoid killing or seriously injuring anyone. Yutar derisively asked how much care was taken and what training was provided to avoid injury and death. Did they perhaps ask their recruits to produce a school-leaving certificate? Sisulu hit back by asking how much care the government took to ensure that the guns put into the hands of white school leavers would not be used irresponsibly and be turned on innocent people in the black townships. He said that the MK manifesto made clear its commitment to respect life. Next he referred to the evidence that the choice of targets showed there was no intention to injure anyone.

Again the judge intervened:

JUDGE: There was a trial during the last war that I remember in which a bomb was placed next to the Benoni post office. Some unfortunate passer-by came to post a letter, the bomb exploded and he was killed. If you were going to start bombing buildings, is it possible to avoid that type of accident? Can you ever be sure that you have avoided killing or injuring people?

SISULU: My Lord, an accident is an accident. But the intention in fact is the intention, and the method used – for instance at night, when people are not there. These are some of the things we take into consideration, that it should not be done just at any time in any manner, in order to avoid the loss of life.

JUDGE: Your argument is that as long as you have not got the intention to kill people, it does not matter if you kill people. Is that your argument?

SISULU: No, Sir. I am saying that the precautions are taken in order to avoid such a thing. I am not saying that it can't happen. But I am saying that precautions are taken that it should not happen.

We considered these exchanges as ominous. On this reasoning, the judge might find that deaths could have been foreseen; that the acts of sabotage were committed recklessly. This would be a reason to impose the death sentence. Bram and Vernon remembered the Benoni post office case and told us that two members of the Ossewa Brandwag, which opposed South Africa's entry into the war, were convicted of murder and sentenced to life imprisonment. They were released after their side had become the government in 1948, by which time they had served about four years. Arthur Chaskalson quickly pointed out that we could use this as a precedent in our argument against imposing the death sentence.

Nelson Mandela's statement that white people feared democracy because the majority of voters would be Africans did not prevent the judge from asking questions clearly showing that he shared that fear. Sisulu said that one task of the ANC was to 'educate people in this country and the people abroad that the only solution in South Africa is living together as black and white'.

The judge immediately continued his questioning:

JUDGE: Living together? But doesn't that involve – according to your ideas – control by the non-white element because they have more in numbers?
SISULU: My Lord, we have always maintained that because of historical conditions in this country the mere fact that the Africans are in the majority would not mean black domination.
JUDGE: No, but black control! Won't it mean black control?
SISULU: Only in the sense that the majority of rulers will be black.
JUDGE: That necessary involves control, not so?
SISULU: Well, it might be that control can be exercised by both races together. We have in the history of this country, an example in the Cape Province where the Africans themselves elected a European.
JUDGE: You would never agree to that, would you?
SISULU: Why not?
JUDGE: You being represented by a white person?
SISULU: No, not to be represented, My Lord. We don't want to be represented. But we say if the people of South Africa elected Dr Verwoerd by all means let him come to Parliament – if he is elected by the whole lot. We are not fighting the issue on the basis of colour.

The judge's questions in relation to Operation Mayibuye showed that he was sceptical about whether guerrilla warfare had been agreed upon. Yutar asked Walter to clarify the written injunction 'for insurrection by the guerrilla units, armed invasion, whether by sea or air, leading eventually to open rebellion'.

SISULU: We were not planning any armed invasions.
JUDGE: Was it not discussed?
SISULU: Yes. I am saying that a plan like that could not possibly be adopted. Certainly the National Executive of the African National Congress would not take a matter like this lightly. It is a serious matter, a serious matter of war.
YUTAR: Of course it is. It is high treason.
SISULU: I know, but I am not talking about the legal liabilities. I am talking about the seriousness, even to embark on a thing like this. It requires serious consideration. It would involve the lives of people.

Yutar instead of leaving well alone would almost invariably take up the judge's interventions at length, giving Walter an additional opportunity to deal with the issue. For five days, during which he was kept in isolation overnight and during court adjournments, Walter calmly endured repeated attacks on his credibility, dignity and the just cause of his organisation. On only two occasions was he anything less than completely controlled. Once he moved towards Yutar saying he wished Yutar was an African so that he would be able to understand the plight of the people. The second event occurred when he asked Yutar how he would feel if his teenage son was arrested and held in a police cell. The reference was to news that Sisulu's son had been arrested for not having a pass, even though he was under the prescribed age of sixteen.

Eventually the judge had heard enough and asked Yutar how much longer his cross-examination would take. One more day, was the prosecutor's answer. Later that afternoon Arthur Chaskalson and Joel Joffe, who unlike me kept a handwritten record of what was said, listed a number of important aspects of Sisulu's evidence-in-chief that had not been tested properly. In particular he had not been asked what was said about Operation Mayibuye before the police raid; what the view and the degree of participation was of each one of the accused present; what time Rusty Bernstein had arrived; why he, Kathrada and Mhlaba were at the meeting; why Goldberg had not been there, and a host of other relevant matters. A further day was hardly enough.

While Walter, alone in his cell during the weekend, must have wondered what further questions he would be asked, we spent hours preparing Ahmed Kathrada as our next witness. This also gave us an opportunity to consult with Govan Mbeki about the matters raised by the prosecutor and the judge. Much to our surprise, on the Monday morning Yutar announced that he had decided to curtail his cross-examination in the light of the admissions made by the witness and would take only another hour.

There were no ambiguities or contradictions to be cleared up in the re-examination of Walter. But we felt it necessary to deal with the judge's accusation that while the ANC leaders were not prepared to risk their own lives and liberty they expected their followers to do so. Bram took Sisulu through his political history from his conviction as Accused Number One in the Defiance of Unjust Laws Campaign in 1952, through his arrests and punitive restrictions afterwards. Merely by leading the ANC after it was declared unlawful, Walter had exposed himself to many years of imprisonment, something he spelled out in answer to Bram's questions.

> FISCHER: And when you were detained for ninety days (that is to say, from the day of the arrest at Rivonia) were you approached and interrogated in any way?
>
> SISULU: Yes, I was interrogated by members of the special branch several times. They said that they believed I was in possession of vital information which would help the State, and that I was facing a very grave charge, the penalty for which is death. They told me I could escape if I was prepared to give evidence, or rather to give them information confidentially. They said it would not be known by anybody. And they told me that some of the Europeans had already spoken and given information about me. They repeated examples of the rebellion of 1914 when Jopie Fourie was [executed]. I however said that I would never give information about my colleagues and that they could do what they wished.
>
> FISCHER: So you did not accept any offer though it may have saved you from the death penalty?
>
> SISULU: Yes.

His time in the stand over, Walter was allowed to join us and his co-accused during the short adjournment in the dimly lit basement cell. We hugged and congratulated him on his forbearance. I had watched the judge carefully throughout Walter's evidence and felt that he was bemused by Walter's manner, memory and directness in answering the questions. My hope was that the judge's long first encounter with such an impressive man would help ensure that Walter was not deprived of his life.

CHAPTER 22

'Let Us Forget about Moral Guilt'

Ahmed Kathrada's first political home was the Transvaal Indian Congress, an organisation inspired by the teachings and activism of Mahatma Gandhi. By the time Kathrada joined, the famous 'Doctors' Pact' had been agreed upon by the leaders of the ANC and the congress, Dr AB Xuma and Dr Yusaf Dadoo respectively. They pledged that their two organisations would participate in a common struggle for the liberation of all the people of South Africa.

Kathy had formed friendships with senior members of the ANC Youth League, including Mandela, Tambo and Sisulu. He left his rural home in Schweizer-Reneke and moved to Johannesburg. He cut short his formal education and became, effectively, a full-time political activist. He lived on meagre commissions from a printer and stayed in a conveniently situated small apartment not far from the key places he frequented – the ANC offices, the Congress of Trade Unions, the weekly left-wing newspaper (its name changed from time to time) and the law offices of Mandela and Tambo. Many clandestine meetings were held at his flat under the guise of social events and he invariably served tasty curry dishes and other delicacies at these gatherings.

Rarely would a protest meeting be held in his absence. He was usually responsible for organising the venue, printing pamphlets and, when necessary, arranging for a public address system. He helped resist the eviction of members of the Indian community under the Group Areas Act and the expropriation of their properties. 'Indian' homes and shops in practically all urban areas were under threat as they were designated for white ownership and occupation. Almost half a century earlier, Mahatma Gandhi had resisted policies with a similar aim, and the Transvaal Indian Congress was determined to continue his political work.

Kathy was frequently arrested and charged with contravening various regulations and for breaching his banning orders. He was usually acquitted, except for his conviction in the Defiance Campaign trial.

At the end of the four-year treason trial, Kathy was freed, but placed under house arrest. Fearing further detention, he went underground disguised most effectively as a Portuguese businessman. He hid in a number of places, remaining in touch with the underground ANC leadership and the central committee of the Communist Party, of which he had been a member since its resurgence in the early 1950s.

Despite his arrest at Rivonia, the State had almost nothing on him. The circumstantial evidence against him could easily be explained away. And an attempt by the State to implicate him in the transport arrangements of MK recruits was based on evidence so improbable and given so badly that we thought it would never be accepted.

Kathy was thoroughly prepared for the witness box by Vernon. We all knew the hostile policy of the apartheid regime towards South African citizens of Indian origin. The government and its supporters deeply resented these descendants of indentured labourers, brought to Natal to work in the sugar fields. They thought of these immigrants as a noxious weed imported to South Africa by the British Raj. As soon as it had the power, the government restricted freedom of movement for Indians, the right to own immovable property and to any meaningful political expression.

Senior National Party politicians would proclaim that despite these restrictions, Indians in South Africa were nevertheless much better off than their kith and kin in India. They also made much of India's opposition to the repatriation of South African Indians, even while Delhi complained to the UN about the treatment meted out to this group.

Not that South Africa's English speakers were much better in their attitude to people of Indian descent. Once I asked Walter Pollak, a leader of the Johannesburg Bar, what he meant by referring to a particular lawyer as a 'Natal liberal'. He replied, 'One who says that compared to the coolie the kaffir is not bad.' On another occasion, in the mid-1970s, when my opponent asked a Natal judge to give us time to settle a matter that involved Indian litigants, the judge replied that we could have all the time we wanted to 'sort out these coolies'. He appeared oblivious of Ismail Ayob as my instructing attorney or that I had taken over the matter from a colleague, Ismail Mahomed. Obviously my white skin was all the encouragement this judge needed to indulge in racist remarks.

Under Vernon's masterful cross-examination we thought Kathrada was doing well in his evidence-in-chief although we were concerned that he wasn't making a favourable impression on the judge. He hardly looked in Kathy's direction, nor was he noting Kathrada's explanations for why he was at Rivonia – to make a tape-recording and improve his disguise.

Like Sisulu, Kathrada made it clear that he was not prepared to implicate others. Yutar asked why not.

KATHRADA: I am honour bound not to.
YUTAR: Honour bound to whom?

KATHRADA: To my conscience, to my political colleagues, to my political organisation, to all of whom I owe loyalty.

YUTAR: What about being honour bound to the Almighty?

KATHRADA: I am not telling any lies.

YUTAR: You are not honour bound to that, are you?

KATHRADA: Well, I don't know if the police are doing the Almighty's work! But I am not prepared to give the police anything that might implicate other people.

Asked whether it was not highly irresponsible to place bombs on railway lines and signal boxes as an Indian child might have been killed, he answered that his sorrow would be the same if any child were killed.

An issue Yutar was keen to deal with was a note written by Mandela on his return to South Africa mentioning that he was met by 'K', who he embraced. He had gone to K's home where his host prepared a tasty meal. There they talked until the early hours of the morning, K briefing him about what had been taking place in the country.

YUTAR: Are you sometimes referred to as 'K'?

KATHRADA: I am not referred to as 'K'. I don't know of anybody who refers to me as 'K'.

YUTAR: Do you know anybody else who goes under the initial of 'K'?

KATHRADA: Yes.

YUTAR: Who?

KATHRADA: Mr Khrushchev.

YUTAR: So you are trying to be funny at my expense?

KATHRADA: I wasn't. You asked me if I knew of any 'Mr K' and I told you.

Yutar's attack now switched to Kathrada's involvement in a campaign in the late 1950s to stop the forced removals from Sophiatown, a suburb then on the outskirts of Johannesburg, and one of the few places in the country where black people could acquire freehold title for building homes, churches and some shops. The presence of a land-owning black community on the doorstep of white Johannesburg was unacceptable to apartheid theory and practice. Worse, Sophiatown had become a cradle of urban African culture, music and theatre, and its Freedom Square was a symbol of protest. The government's plan to remove Sophiatown – the Western Areas Removal Plan – was vigorously opposed by the Congress Movement in which Kathrada was active, the churches led by Father

Trevor Huddleston and the residents. Yutar asked Kathy about his involvement in the campaign, something Kathrada readily admitted. But that was not enough for the prosecutor. He accused Kathrada of misleading the people. Would Kathrada prefer to live in the squalor of Sophiatown than in 'beautiful Meadowlands' to which people had been removed? Kathy's immediate response was, 'Sophiatown', where his mother could visit without a permit.

Unlike Sisulu, Kathrada was not isolated during his cross-examination. This followed an objection by Vernon and upheld by the judge, who agreed that the procedure adopted against Sisulu was unprecedented. Kathrada's sharp and witty replies pleased the spectators and his co-accused who occasionally laughed, but they irritated the judge. True to form, most of the cross-examination was no more than an angry political debate and Yutar conspicuously failed to cross-examine on the matters in issue. Despite the judge's apparently negative attitude, we still hoped to persuade him to acquit Kathy. True, he had admitted membership of the unlawful Communist Party. But this was not covered by the indictment, although it might have led to a new charge being laid against him after any acquittal.

Raymond Mhlaba followed Kathy. He had been a leading member of the ANC and was closely associated with another prominent figure, Govan Mbeki. Raymond was known for his energy as an organiser and for his loyalty and dedication to the ANC. The Lilliesleaf domestic workers had given evidence of his presence at Rivonia for a short period before his arrest. The only other evidence against him was that given by a single witness who had taken part in the first acts of sabotage committed by MK on 16 December 1961. The witness said that Raymond had orchestrated various acts of sabotage committed in Port Elizabeth at that time. Raymond denied that he was in the country when MK was launched and said he was on a mission assigned to him by the ANC, details of which he would not disclose in the witness box.

The circumstantial detail provided by the witness persuaded us that he was probably speaking the truth about his own participation and that of others. But it seemed obvious that solitary confinement and interrogation brought about his false implication of Raymond. Vernon's cross-examination brought out improbabilities and contradictions in the evidence of the witness. Enough we thought, for us to argue that a credible denial from Raymond and an explanation of why he was at Rivonia was sufficient to secure his acquittal.

Yutar asked Mhlaba to identify the members of the ANC in Port Elizabeth. Mhlaba refused. Next, Yutar acknowledged that he and the security police knew that Mhlaba had been out of the country by asserting, 'I want to put it to you that in December 1961 you were either in Port Elizabeth or in Leipzig.' Vernon leapt to his feet. If the witness answered the question he could incriminate himself in offences with which he was not charged. The judge agreed. Yutar quickly offered a limited indemnity. This, too, Mhlaba refused.

Although the judge had tolerated Sisulu and Kathrada's refusal to name any-one not before the court, he indicated that he would draw an adverse inference from Mhlaba's silence. 'The position is, Mhlaba, that you say you were not in Port Elizabeth on 16 December, but you refuse to tell the court where you were on that date. Is that the position?' Raymond's confirmation, coupled with the hesitant and faltering manner in which he answered questions, did not augur well, and we feared that our submissions for his acquittal would not be well received.

A debate among academic lawyers and medical doctors current at the time of the trial concerned the acceptance of evidence from people held in detention without trial and obliged to make a statement to the satisfaction of their interroga-tors. Inevitably, detainees were also threatened with perjury if they later repudiated their statements in court. Prominent among the South Africa academic lawyers involved in this debate were John Dugard and Barend van Niekerk of Wits and Tony Matthews of Natal university.

When we tendered to lead the evidence of professors Danziger and Ronald Albino, psychologists at the Universities of Cape Town and Natal, Yutar accused us of attempting 'to make political capital out of the provisions of the ninety-day detention clause.' For his part, the judge said he had no need of doctors to tell him how to assess the evidence of a witness. This view persisted among judges and magistrates throughout the thirty years that the draconian security legisla-tion remained in force.

Evidence on detention and its effects would have had a direct bearing on the testimony of Lionel (better know as Rusty) Bernstein. He too had been well prepared for the witness box by Vernon. The factual issues in contention were clear enough. Was he on the roof the day that the radio aerials were erected? Why did he go to Rivonia from time to time and more particularly on the day of the arrests? Had he gone to Durban to start a branch of MK? Had he arrived shortly before the raid or hours earlier as suggested by Dirker's evidence that the engine of his car was cold?

He explained that he was engaged by Goldreich to carry out architectural work at the farm, including the design of outbuildings to double as living quar-ters, and to supervise the building operations. During that period he had met Nelson Mandela, who was living there. He denied that he was on the roof and said he had nothing to do with MK. Berrangé, in asking for Bernstein's acquittal at the end of the case, said: 'The cross-examination of Bernstein covers a hundred and fifty-three pages of transcript. This is not remarkable in itself. But what is remarkable is that, in that hundred and fifty-three pages there is not one word of cross-examination as to the facts deposed to by Bernstein.'

Yutar's further desire to discredit Bernstein, the liberation movement, and more particularly Bram Fischer as one of its leaders, led him to a most elementary mistake. A mistake neither expected nor forgiven even when made by the most junior and inexperienced prosecutor or member of the Bar. Yutar badgered Bernstein to admit that he was a member of the illegal Communist Party, something Bernstein refused to concede for fear of incriminating and exposing himself to charges not covered by the indictment. Yutar's offer of an indemnity was rejected on our advice. We told Rusty that even if he were to accept the indemnity, the agreement was not binding on the minister. More importantly, accepting Yutar's 'deal' would lead to a string of other questions and answers which might incriminate many more people.

Yutar appealed to the judge to instruct Bernstein to answer the question about party membership. Instead of the usual curt command and threat of imprisonment if his order was not complied with, the judge gently informed the witness that he was required to answer the question. Failure to do so would result in a recurring sentence of eight days' imprisonment until he had answered. Knowing that Rusty had been in custody for more than nine months, he smiled benevolently at him, saying, 'I don't suppose that threat of imprisonment will make much difference to you under present circumstances.' At the same time the judge made a clear gesture to Yutar that he should proceed to some other topic. This practical, even sympathetic, approach indicated that Rusty was making a good impression on the judge.

Unbeknown to us Rusty had written a letter to his sister, telling her of the unfair methods that the police and the prosecution used to obtain evidence from people in detention, how detainees were coerced into making statements to please their interrogators and how the police even procured false evidence. Rusty did not know that a copy of this letter had been handed to Yutar. He was asked questions without reference to the letter, no doubt in the hope that he would contradict what he had written. Not only did he repeat his accusations in the letter, but after Yutar produced it and read passages, Rusty elaborated. He referred to the experiences of detainees, exposed by Vernon during his earlier cross-examination of State witnesses, and used the evidence to give weight to his own comments in the letter.

Another of Yutar's tactics during cross-examination and one he used with Bernstein, was to associate people with the accused. For instance, during Sisulu's cross-examination, he tried to associate Chief Albert Luthuli with the formation of MK and the planned acts of sabotage. The trick was to besmirch the person's good name. All he hoped for was that the press would report the question. He now tried to implicate Bram and associate him with the Communist Party. Under the privilege afforded to judicial proceedings, he produced an article that Bernstein had written ten years earlier praising Bram as an example of a white person and an Afrikaner committed to the liberation of all the people of South Africa. He was, said Bernstein, living proof that not all whites were racists. The article was published in a magazine called *Fighting Talk*. This magazine was not put in evidence, nor was there anything in the article relevant to the charges. Yet suddenly, and apropos of nothing in particular, Yutar pounced:

YUTAR: Who was the secretary general of the Communist Party?
BERNSTEIN: I am not prepared to answer that question.
YUTAR: Well, since you are unable to answer that question, perhaps we may conclude that it was the gentleman referred to in the exhibit before you. Will you please hand it to the judge?

That exhibit was *Fighting Talk*. We later discovered that a police informer had infiltrated the ranks of the most senior members of the Communist Party and Yutar was privy to this information. His desire to smear Bram was so great that he was prepared to risk betraying the existence of an informer, and even his identity. As the vast majority of white South Africans held strongly negative views about white communists, Yutar was keen to trade on this sentiment. But we believed that the spontaneous, articulate and erudite answers given by Bernstein might persuade the judge away from this prejudice.

There was no need to re-examine Bernstein, except on the deleterious effect of solitary confinement on the human mind and body. He gave eloquent testimony, explaining how he was haunted by irrational fears and was unable to distinguish between what was important and what was trivial. He developed a nervous tremor of the hands which persisted long after his solitary confinement ended. And for some time after his release from solitary confinement, he was unable to concentrate, despite the companionship of Dennis Goldberg in the exercise yard and the interaction with his co-accused during consultations in the early part of the trial.

While cross-examining Walter Sisulu, Yutar attempted to play down the suffering of black people in South Africa and questioned the justice of the cause espoused by the ANC. In response we decided to prepare Govan Mbeki to drive home to the judge and the rest of the world that the actions of the ANC were inevitable and unavoidable given the intransigence of an illegitimate regime. We had more time to prepare him than the earlier witnesses and I wrote a lengthy statement from which Bram led him.

After outlining Mbeki's background and career, including his rise in the ANC to a senior position, Bram asked him if he had good reason to continue playing an active role in the ANC after it was banned.

> MBEKI: Yes. The ANC after a number of years, a number of decades, has been [in] the vanguard of the struggle of the African people for national libera-tion. And it [the banning] was something that I just couldn't accept. At the time thousands of people looked up to the ANC to lead them in the struggle against the laws which were threatening practically every right that the African people had enjoyed before. As I say, I just could not accept the fact that the government should destroy the ANC. I therefore continued to be a member of the ANC under conditions of illegality.

He eloquently corroborated and augmented descriptions already given by Nelson Mandela and Walter Sisulu about the sufferings and aspirations of the African people. He recounted the derogatory remarks with which their appeals were rejected by successive prime ministers, who seemed to think that by changing the name of the policy from segregation to trusteeship, *baasskap*, apartheid and finally separate development, they would appease not only their victims within South Africa but international opinion as well.

Asked by Bram whether there had been any change apart from the name, Mbeki answered, 'No. Apart from that, the leopard has not changed its colours at all.'

Bram thanked the witness and bowed to the judge, indicating the end of this part of Mbeki's evidence. He had hardly sat down when Yutar sprang up and sur-prised us all with his remarks: 'I want to remind you that this court is trying issues of sabotage and other offences, and it is not a court of enquiry into grievances of the Bantu. So I hope you will forgive me if I don't even attempt to challenge the correctness of some of your complaints.'

What, I wondered, led Yutar to this decision. Possibly the bugging devices had picked up our relief that he had done precisely the opposite when cross-examin-ing Sisulu. But we need not have worried: this was another leopard incapable of changing his spots. His cross-examination rattled off questions usually found in manuals defending apartheid. If things were so bad in South Africa, why did so many 'foreign natives' from neighbouring countries flock here? How could he say that hospital services were not free? Did he not agree that South Africa had eradicated ritual murders? Did he know that South African medical research assisted neighbouring countries?

Mbeki dealt with the questions well enough, but it was even better when someone sitting behind Yutar tugged his gown to tell him that hospital services were not free, but that on admission the patient had to pay half a crown. Yutar turned to Mbeki and said half a crown was nothing to speak of. Mbeki quickly retorted that half a crown might be nothing to Yutar, but it was not nothing to those without any money at all. Yutar appeared stunned by the thought and quickly moved to another topic.

Govan Mbeki's quiet and dignified manner must have infuriated Yutar. At one stage the prosecutor said he had a tape of a speech made by Mbeki and broadcast over Radio Liberation. He began to probe Mbeki's demeanour in the witness box by comparing it with what he had heard on the tape.

YUTAR: You have given your evidence here in a calm, quiet voice. To make certain I was listening to the same person, I had your tape played back. You don't always speak that way, do you? You can raise your voice?

MBEKI: If I must raise it, yes.

YUTAR: And you speak a little faster than you have spoken here?

MBEKI: If I must speak a little faster, I do.

YUTAR: And not so sanctimoniously as you have tried to speak here?

MBEKI: That is your opinion.

YUTAR: A newspaper wrote of you that '... beneath his quiet charm and gentle smile, [there is] a ruthless determination to reach his goal – the emancipation of his people.' Is that a fair description of you?

MBEKI: I think so.

YUTAR: A 'ruthless determination'! And in some of your speeches you could be ruthless, not so, and in fact you were in speeches when you attended meetings throughout the country, do you deny that?

MBEKI: I spoke the truth and exposed what was the hardship of the Africans. If you call that ruthless – speaking the truth – then I was ruthless.

YUTAR: No, I am just trying to convey, not the subject matter, but the way in which you put it across. You were not the gentle, quiet, sanctimonious human being that you are now showing in the witness box.

MBEKI: No, that would have to be the opinion of whoever was listening to me.

Then Yutar switched to Mbeki's membership of a Communist Party group in Port Elizabeth.

YUTAR: Which group?

MBEKI: The Communist Party group.

YUTAR: I know. Which group? I am asking you which group?

MBEKI: The Communist Party group, I say.

YUTAR: But how many groups were there in Port Elizabeth?

MBEKI: I don't know. I was only concerned with my group.

YUTAR: That is the group I want. What was its name?

MBEKI: The Communist Party group has no name. It is not like a football club.

YUTAR: And who were the members of your group?

MBEKI: That I am not prepared to say.

YUTAR: You are not prepared to tell us? Why not?

MBEKI: Why should I do so? I am not prepared to incriminate anybody.

Cross-examination directed against Mbeki had already elicited admissions sufficient to convict him on all four counts, but that was not enough for Yutar:

YUTAR: Well, Mbeki, I will put it to you in very brief form. Four charges against you, and you have replied to all of them. You have replied 'Yes' to all of them. Can you tell His Lordship why you have pleaded not guilty to the four counts?

MBEKI: Yes. I did not plead guilty to the four counts for the simple reason firstly that I should come and explain from here under oath some of the reasons that led me to join Umkhonto we Sizwe. And secondly for the simple reason that to plead guilty would to my mind indicate a sense of moral guilt to it. I do not accept that there is any moral guilt attached to my actions.

YUTAR: All right, let us forget about moral guilt. Having now admitted, after making some political speeches, that you were on the National High Command, have committed sabotage, that further acts of sabotage had been conspired to be committed, and that you furthered the aims of communism, that you and your colleagues solicited money both here and abroad in order to advance these campaigns, do you now plead guilty?

MBEKI: I am not pleading guilty!

YUTAR: No, you don't. You don't even admit you are legally guilty?

MBEKI: I have explained my position.

We had felt some trepidation about Mbeki's cross-examination because we expected probing questions about whether Operation Mayibuye had been adopted by the MK National High Command and the constituent bodies that had brought it into being. Govan Mbeki admitted his involvement in all of them, so he was the obvious witness to be questioned thoroughly.

In our opening address, we made the proposed adoption of the new strategy an issue, so we felt Mbeki would be in the firing line over this crucial point. Our instructions from our clients were not clear: their opinions differed.

The suggestion that Joe Slovo, Arthur Goldreich and Harold Wolpe may have jumped the gun in implementing the policy was plausible. But a skilful cross-examiner could have thrown doubt on such a theory and raised the likelihood that these three were 'blamed' because they were out of the country and beyond the reach of the security police. Instead of concentrating on this potential vulnerability by questioning Mbeki, Yutar spent days on books and documents hardly relevant to any of the issues before the court.

Over and over again we debated whether to have Dennis Goldberg give evidence under oath. The evidence by Davids of the 'guerrilla camp' was so highly improbable that we felt the court would reject it. But that was not the only evidence against Goldberg. There was little doubt that during his short stay in Johannesburg Dennis had worked for the National High Command. In the State's version he was amassing tons of materiel to be used in the imminent guerrilla war. According to Dennis, he was exploring the possibility of clandestinely manufacturing hand grenades and other weapons in South Africa. To that end, in the guise of either a 'Mr Williams' or a 'Mr Barnard', he inquired of a number of foundries about casings and other explosives used in the mining industry. We hoped to persuade the court that his actions were acts of preparation and that he was not privy to the conspiracy or any attempt to commit the crimes charged.

But matters did not look good for Dennis from the moment the judge referred to him as 'Sisulu's clever friend'. At that stage there was nothing before the court but untested allegations. Clearly the derisive expressions pulled by Dennis when a prosecution witness contradicted himself, as well as his persistent though muted remarks to his co-accused had not escaped the judge. During our consultations with Dennis, his answers were quick, flippant and humorous which earned him many a rebuke from Berrangé. Such behaviour would not go down well in court. But not even Vernon could handle him. After one such rebuke, Dennis jumped off his chair, stood to attention, saluted, and said, 'Yes, Sir'. We all laughed. How could you be cross with such an amiable man?

Once Dennis was called to the witness box, Vernon pointed out that though the accused was arrested in the main house, he was not in the room where the leaders conferred. This showed that although Dennis was trusted to drive the vehicle that brought them to Rivonia, and although he had been asked to gather information about the availability of materiel, he was not involved in the decision-making structures of MK or other organisations. We expected the cross-examination to be particularly scathing because Dennis was a Jew. Yutar expected all Jews to be loyal to the regime, yet here was a man who misled the police by promising to cooperate but telling them nothing they didn't know. On top of this, he had almost escaped from custody.

Yutar again took us by surprise. This time he called on his senior assistant, AB Krogh, to cross-examine Goldberg. Krogh was an experienced prosecutor who had conducted innumerable criminal trials, mostly in Afrikaans. His limited English vocabulary minimised the effect of his questions, especially when he tried to mimic Yutar's flamboyant oratory, mean irony and heavy sarcasm. To our relief, Dennis was a satisfactory witness. He successfully avoided any witticisms and controlled his expressions. But the judge's lack of interest in his evidence was clear from his body language. We did not hold out much hope that he would be acquitted.

Honest men charged with political offences are often proud of their actions and prepared to abide by the judgment of the court and its punishment. But they resent false evidence being given against them, particularly if it is extracted under duress from friends and comrades held in solitary confinement. Their resentment is strengthened when they themselves have been tortured in detention.

Andrew Mlangeni and Elias Motsoaledi were disciplined and loyal members of the ANC and of Umkhonto we Sizwe. They admitted recruiting young men for military training outside South Africa and other activities of the regional command. The two would inevitably be convicted. Giving evidence under oath would serve no useful purpose. We thought that their degree of participation was less than that of the leaders and that their sentences would likewise be lighter. For these reasons, we agreed that they make short statements from the dock.

Mlangeni constantly denied the charges against him, because he was out of the country during 1962. With great difficulty we persuaded two of his neighbours to corroborate this. In his statement, Mlangeni said:

> The court can now see that some of the evidence given against me is true and some false. I have chosen not to give evidence, My Lord, because first of all I do not want to be cross-examined about people I have worked with and places I have visited in case I might give these people away. Also, My Lord, I have frankly admitted that I have assisted Umkhonto we Sizwe. I want to say that I joined the ANC in 1954. I did it because I wanted to work for my people.

I did this because of the treatment my people have received from the rulers of this country. In the ANC I found a political home where I was free to talk against the government.

South Africa, My Lord, is a very rich country. The resources could be exploited for the benefit of all the people who live in it. The government and the previous governments have exploited not the earth but the people of various racial groups whose colour is not white. But the government daily makes laws in its white Parliament, which laws are aimed at suppressing the political aspirations of the majority of the people, who have no say. I know that you, My Lord, have to administer the law, but when you do so, I ask you to remember what we, the Africans and non-white people, have had to suffer. That is all I have to say except to add that what I did was not for myself but for my people.

He also described being subjected to electric shocks at the security police headquarters as they attempted to coerce him into making a statement.

The statement of Elias Motsoaledi, a short, amiable man, was poignant because of its delivery and its content. He, too, described his upbringing and the poor conditions of his family of ten in a Sekhukhuneland reserve. Like so many others he sought work in the city, first in a boot factory earning a meagre wage. Later he joined a trade union and then the ANC. Elias continued:

There was nothing left for us to do except suffer. Then Umkhonto we Sizwe was formed. When I was asked to join it, I did so. There was nothing else I could do. Any African who thought the way I did about my own life and the lives of my people would have done the same. There was nothing else.

I did what I did because I wanted to help my people in their struggle for equal rights. When I was asked to join Umkhonto we Sizwe it was at a time when it was clear to me that all our years of peaceful struggle had been of no use. The government would not let us fight peacefully any more and blocked all our legal acts by making them illegal. I thought a great deal about the matter, but I could see no other way open to me. What I did brought me no personal gain. What I did, I did for my people and because I thought it was the only way left for me to help my people. That is all I have to say.

Except, he also related how he had been assaulted by the security police, in their efforts to force a statement from him. Finally, before sitting down, he said in a trembling voice:

More than three months ago they arrested my wife and detained her for ninety days. And when she finished her ninety days, she was arrested again. As it is she is still in jail. I consider this disgraceful on the part of the police, My Lord, that a woman with seven children should be punished because of offences committed by me.

His last words affected most if not all those who sat silently in the courtroom. I put my arm around his shoulders as he was leaving the dock and almost in a whisper he said: 'Please help Caroline to bring up and educate the children.' Despite persecution, poverty and loneliness, Caroline did well to keep the family together during the twenty-five years that her husband Elias was imprisoned on Robben Island.

CHAPTER 23

Because I Love My Country

It is high time that the world realised that the South African judiciary is independent and its judges are not amenable to pressure from government, public or any other source.

— The Hon Frances Napier Broome, Natal's judge president
(on the outcry over Mandela's life sentence)

By April 1964, our evidence had been led. The trial was seven months old, the interest inside the country had lessened. Beyond the borders the accused were regarded as 'the accusers' and their forthright manner had garnered them sympathy and support for the ANC. And this support came not only from Eastern European countries but from the UN, the Non-Aligned Movement and Western countries as well.

Yutar, with his four expensively bound volumes labelled 'argument', copies of which he handed to the judge and selected members of the media, acted as if his eloquence would turn the tide against the accused again. In his 'argument', however, he made no real attempt to analyse the evidence on the disputed issues. For days he summarised the evidence, periodically adding rhetorical flourishes he believed might make good headlines. Thus:

Although the State has charged the accused with sabotage, this is nevertheless a case of high treason par excellence. It is a classic case of the intended overthrow of the government by force and violence with military and other assistance of foreign countries. The acts have been corroborated by the accused themselves. Nevertheless, for reasons which I do not have to detail, the State has preferred to charge the accused with sabotage.

And further:

At the outset of my argument I said that this case was one of high treason par excellence. Because of the people who have lost their lives and suffered injury as a result of the activities of the accused it is apparent that this case is now one of murder and attempted murder as well.

That there was no such allegation in the indictment did not appear to matter – hyperbole and alliteration were more important:

An aggravating thought is that a man like Goldberg, having created a Frankenstein monster and put it into action, would have gone abroad to join the band of brothers; this included the great and glorious guerrilla, Goldreich, the heroic Harmel and Hodgson, Slovo the soldier and the wise Wolpe. From a safe distance of six thousand miles or more they would behold the tragic works of their handiwork.

He went on, in what we felt was extremely bad taste, particularly since none of the accused was able to reply to his insults:

My Lord, for the edification of Your Lordship, I have decided to nominate a shadow cabinet for the provisional revolutionary government. Because Goldberg was alleged to have run a camp for spiritual and health purposes, I name him Minister of Health. But he will have to learn the truth first, which he will find difficult if one takes into consideration the lies he told in court.

There is evidence before the court that despite appearances of solidarity all is not well in relations between Africans and Indians. It is clear therefore that there will still have to be a Ministry of Foreign Affairs in the proposed revolutionary state – who but Kathrada could be minister of this department? As Minister of European Affairs I nominate Govan Mbeki. Bernstein will be nominated as Minister of Information, Raymond Mhlaba as Minister of Foreign Affairs. Elias Motsoaledi has told the court that he had to live on four acres of land while thousands of acres of white-owned land lay fallow. I accordingly name him Minister of Lands so that he can correct these disparities. Andrew Mlangeni [I name] as Minister of Transport and Duma Nokwe as Minister of Justice. From the information that Bob Hepple has given the police I would like to make him Minister of Information. But because Bernstein already occupies that post I name Bob Hepple Minister of Informers instead.

I wish I had the pen of a Pope and a Dryden to describe the infamy of Slovo who, with Goldreich, was one of the worst traitors to infest South African soil. Goldreich [I name] as Minister of Munitions, Sisulu Minister of the Interior, Nelson Mandela, Defence and Deputy Prime Minister and Albert Luthuli as President. I have not been able to find portfolios for all the men involved. But if they run true to form, then if and when they come to power there will be a lot of internal strife resulting in many casualties, and they will be able to fill the vacancies which will inevitably arise.

The significance of Nelson Mandela's words, echoed by the other leaders who had given evidence of their vision for a united democratic and non-racial democracy, was lost on Yutar. He envisaged different ministers for different ethnic groups and could not accept the idea of a harmonious government led by Africans. That the judge did not interrupt Yutar as he abused his position to hurl insults at the accused was a matter for concern.

However, the judge and Yutar were soon involved in an exchange which we found more than welcome. Carried away on the stream of his rhetoric, Yutar proclaimed, 'The day of the mass uprising in connection with the launching of guerrilla warfare was to have been May 26, 1963.' The judge immediately intervened: 'You do concede that you failed to prove guerrilla warfare was ever decided upon, do you not?'

We tried hard to suppress our joy, while Yutar, disconcerted, mumbled that 'preparations were being made'. 'Yes, I know that,' said the judge. 'The defence concedes that. What they say is that preparations were made in case one day they found it necessary to resort to guerrilla warfare but they say that prior to their arrest they never considered it necessary, and took no decision to engage in guerrilla warfare. I take it that you have no evidence contradicting that and that you accept it?' By clear implication, the judge accepted this as an accurate statement of the situation. 'As Your Lordship pleases,' Yutar replied in a barely audible voice.

Arthur Chaskalson, although the youngest member of our team, had already become known at the Bar as a lawyer's lawyer. Bram asked him to prepare argument and he was the first among us to address the court. His manner was the very antithesis of Yutar's. Arthur's height, his demeanour, use of language and logical analysis made him a formidable presence. Vernon and I would not have resisted the temptation to launch an attack on Yutar for his misrepresentation of the evidence and for gratuitously insulting our clients. Arthur for all practical purposes ignored him:

May it please Your Lordship, the State has told Your Lordship that this trial is a trial for murder and attempted murder. The indictment alleges military training and sabotage. But despite this the accused have been subjected to cross-examination on murder, incitement to murder and attempted murder. The evidence presented to the court on these claims is all hearsay, and the existence of these claims has never been substantiated in this court. There has been a mass of inadmissible evidence which bears no relation to the indictment.

The defence will not even deal with these allegations as they have nothing to do with the case. The defence concedes that Umkhonto we Sizwe recruited men for military training and that members of Umkhonto committed acts of sabotage. The defence denies however that they committed all the acts of sabotage with which they are charged. I will demonstrate to Your Lordship, from the evidence, that there were other organisations in South Africa committing sabotage at the time in question.

The judge interrupted. 'Mr Chaskalson, there is no need to pursue your argument on this aspect. I accept that there were other organisations committing sabotage at the same time and choosing the same targets.'

Arthur's next point was also crucial. When an act of sabotage occurred, even if a security policemen had an admission that it was performed by a member of MK, this was not admissible against the accused under any circumstances. Arthur was armed with a number of cases in support of his submissions, and the judge listened carefully when extracts of these decisions were read to him:

Even if the State had succeeded in proving that certain acts of sabotage were committed by Umkhonto, that is not the end of the matter. The accused, who the State said were the leaders of Umkhonto, are only responsible for acts falling within the designated policy of Umkhonto. The evidence is that Umkhonto's policy was only to commit acts of sabotage against government and public property which it labelled symbols of apartheid. The evidence further shows, and stands corroborated by the evidence of State witnesses, that the clear policy of Umkhonto was sabotage without loss of life. The authorities show that if one member of the conspiracy goes out and commits an act falling outside the ambit of the conspiracy, his fellow co-conspirators are not legally liable for such acts. On this basis the accused, who adhered at all times to a policy designed to avoid danger to life, were not responsible for acts of sabotage committed even by proved members of Umkhonto against their instructions. The accused accordingly disclaim any responsibility for bomb attacks on private houses.

On a painstaking analysis of the evidence, Arthur showed that of one hundred and ninety-three acts of sabotage, no more than thirteen were proven by proper evidence to have been committed on behalf of the High Command of Umkhonto we Sizwe. More importantly, none had been proved in which there was loss of life.

Bram Fischer worked for weeks on the two main arguments that formed his section of the final address. First, he urged the judge to accept that guerrilla warfare had not been agreed to and, secondly, that membership of the unlawful ANC did not make one responsible for the acts of Umkhonto. The judge stopped him. He accepted that no decision had been made about guerrilla warfare, nor had any date been fixed for such a change in strategy. Moreover, the evidence had established that the ANC and MK were separate organisations, albeit with some overlap.

The first point made by the judge was important to us as we tried to determine his view on sentence. The second point was important to thousands of members of the ANC. Without the judge's clear distinction they could have been charged with treason rather than with furthering the objects of an unlawful organisation. The former charge could be punishable by death, while the latter drew a maximum of ten years in jail.

Vernon argued for the acquittal of Bernstein, Kathrada and Mhlaba. He believed that the case for Dennis Goldberg's acquittal was almost unarguable. Unlike Arthur, Vernon could not pass up the opportunity to comment on Yutar's behaviour:

> During his address, Dr Yutar delivered himself of what he was pleased to term a number of 'observations' concerning the accused, the relevance of which we have found difficult to ascertain. On the assumption that these so-called 'observations' which have consisted of sarcastic and satirical attacks upon the accused, are relevant, we have consulted with out clients for the purposes of replying thereto. With the dignity that has characterised the accused throughout this trial, they have instructed us to ignore these remarks.

He argued the case for the acquittal of Bernstein and Kathrada with greater confidence than that of Mhlaba who wasn't as good a witness as the others. Finally, Bram, Arthur and I argued a number of other, less important issues in the trial.

Yutar had a right to reply only on questions of law. He tried to re-argue the case against Bernstein, but the judge cut him short. Then, contrary to Yutar's undertaking that he would not rely on presumptions, he mentioned a proclamation promulgated during the course of the trial. This proclamation, the government said, would operate retrospectively. It had the effect of equating the ANC with Umkhonto. Yutar tried using it to buttress the case against Kathrada. Again the judge cut him short. He would not at that late stage listen to an argument which could prompt the defence to request that the case be reopened. True to form Yutar withdrew this argument. His case was so strong that he did not need any presumptions, he said.

The court was adjourned for three weeks, when the judge would deliver his verdict.

Knowing that a conviction was certain for Mandela, Sisulu and Mbeki, we discussed leading evidence in mitigation of sentence. Who could be asked to testify?

Bram and I visited a few religious and political leaders not closely connected to the ANC, but with credibility among the majority of the people of South Africa. Although we were received with sympathy, they declined with regret. Some felt they were not prominent enough, or did not know enough about the accused or that their organisations would be compromised. Others were prepared to sign a petition for clemency if a death sentence were imposed.

When Bram canvassed author Alan Paton, whose novel *Cry, the Beloved Country* had given him an international reputation, Alan asked only one question: were their lives in danger? When we told him there was a serious chance that the death penalty would be imposed, he agreed at once. Although members of the Liberal Party were unreservedly opposed to apartheid, they shied away from the Congress Movement campaigns for a number of reasons. For instance, they were not prepared to work with communists, they did not fully support the one person, one vote policy, and because most, including Paton, were opposed to any form of violence. The differences between the Liberal Party and the ANC did not prevent Paton and Luthuli from making a joint public appeal to Harold Macmillan, before he came to South Africa, not to say a single word that could be construed as praise of apartheid. In another development, a few of the leading members of the Liberal Party had identified themselves with a breakaway group from the ANC when it established the Pan Africanist Congress, and they queried their party's policy of non-violence. This was a matter of great concern to Paton, who abhorred violence.

Witnesses called to give evidence in mitigation tend to fare badly if they are not conversant with the issues in the case and the findings made by the court. I was deputised to meet Paton a few days before judgment was due, at the home of the British Consul General, Leslie Minford, to brief him. Periodically during the trial, the consul general had invited me to brief him and important visitors from the United Kingdom on the trial. On those occasions I told them we feared that death sentences could be handed down. I would also argue for government pressure to avoid such a result.

Shortly before my meeting with Paton I visited the Minfords. As I was leaving Leslie put his arm around my shoulders and said, 'George, there won't be a death sentence.' I did not ask him how he knew. For one thing, he had downed a number of whiskies. Certainly I felt I could not rely on the information, nor could I tell the team or our anxious clients. With the publication of Anthony Sampson's biography of Nelson Mandela in 1999, I read that Minford was thought to have had intelligence links and may have had reliable information about the case.

Security arrangements along the streets and in the squares of Pretoria were as tight as they had been more than eight months previously when the trial began. Police set up roadblocks and turned back buses full of supporters but about two thousand managed to gather on Paul Kruger Square. Some of them hoped to gain entry to the courtroom. The entrance was blocked to all except wives and friends of the security police. The wives and close friends of the accused would have been kept out if Joel Joffe had not protested to a senior officer.

In the cell below, Nelson Mandela made a defiant announcement. Speaking for himself, Walter Sisulu and Govan Mbeki, he said that irrespective of the verdict there should no appeal. We urged that no final decision be made until we'd heard the judgment and the sentences.

We anticipated that after so lengthy a trial, judgment would take the better part of a day. Judge de Wet dispensed with it in two minutes:

I have very good reasons for the conclusions to which I have come. I don't propose to read these reasons. The verdict will be: Nelson Mandela is found guilty on all four counts; Walter Sisulu is found guilty on all four counts; Dennis Goldberg is found guilty on all four counts; Govan Mbeki is found guilty on all four counts; Ahmed Kathrada is found guilty on count two and not guilty on counts one, three and four. Lionel Bernstein is found not guilty. He will be discharged. Raymond Mhlaba is found guilty on all four counts; Andrew Mlangeni is found guilty on all four counts; Elias Motsoaledi is found guilty on all four counts. I do not propose to deal with the question of sentence today. My reasons will be made available in the statements. The defence will be given an opportunity to study these reasons and if so required, to address me on the question of sentence. I will deal with the question of sentence tomorrow morning.

Despite the verdict, Rusty Bernstein expected to be rearrested. However, he made sure that the dozens of news reporters in court would publish the fact that the law in South Africa protecting its citizens against double jeopardy had been abrogated by the recently enacted Sabotage Act. He did not follow the others down the steps to the cell but wrestled his way against one policeman after another, attempting to reach us. Perhaps he hoped that our white shirts, winged collars, starched bibs and long black robes might be an effective shield. We all knew that there was nothing we could do. The brutish pair, Captain Swanepoel and Detective Sergeant Dirker, arrested him. Vernon Berrangé taunted Dirker: 'After your disgraceful exhibition in the witness box, I take it you will not oppose bail when we apply for it.' The policeman muttered a non-committal reply.

Our request for Rusty to be brought to the cell to say goodbye to his colleagues was refused. We had copies of the judgment but were told that for security reasons we would have to consult with our clients at the prison. The most unexpected aspect of the judgment was the conviction of Kathrada. But he didn't want to be singled out and agreed with his comrades that the correct political decision was not to appeal even if death sentences were imposed.

Behind the court building supporters filled the street and pavements singing freedom songs, chanting slogans and expressing support. As the vehicle taking the convicted men to prison emerged from the yard and the first of the clenched fists appeared through the van's air vents, a deafening roar of 'Amandla! – Ngawethu!' was repeated over and over. The sound was so loud that it cowed a small white group, predominantly students from the nearby University of Pretoria, an institution attended almost exclusively by the sons and daughters of the most vociferous supporters of the apartheid regime.

Bram Fischer could not be persuaded to deliver the plea in mitigation. He was under great stress because he thought the leaders of the African people, his comrades and friends, might be sentenced to death. He had high regard for the advocacy of Harold Hanson and had already asked him to deliver the plea. In the prison consulting room, Nelson Mandela in particular remained defiant. Speaking for all the convicted men he said that neither Hanson nor Alan Paton should say anything on their behalf which could be construed as suggesting that the accused regretted what they had done, nor should they make an abject plea for mercy.

The real possibility of the death sentence was on our minds and infected the atmosphere. What, we were asked, happened when a death sentence was passed? The usual process was for the judge to ask if there were any reasons why the death sentence should not be passed. None of us on the legal team knew of anyone's life being spared by a trial judge as a result of a statement made by an accused at that late stage. Nevertheless, Nelson said that if the judge asked such a question, he should be the one to answer. He would tell the court so that their supporters and the world could hear, that the liberation movement could not and would not be suppressed by sentencing them to death; their deaths would inspire others to take up the struggle. When we pointed out that such a defiant approach might be counterproductive, he drew attention to something he had written in one of the exhibits: 'There is no easy walk to freedom. We have to pass through the shadow of death again and again before we reach the mountain tops of our desires.'

Our clients wanted no help in drafting such a statement. We left them contemplating the shadow of death.

While my colleagues conferred with Hanson at his chambers, I took a copy of the judgment to Alan Paton at the consul general's home. We chatted for a while and I agreed to take him to Pretoria early the next morning, 12 June 1964.

It was a sombre author that I gave a lift to the next day. But then neither of us had much to say on the drive. The first roadblock occurred outside Alexandra township. Cars and buses were being stopped but we were waved on. As we approached Pretoria the security arrangements became tighter, almost as if an attack were expected.

Despite the road blocks and security checks, there were twice as many black people in the square and around the court as the previous day. Similarly the number of Pretoria university students had also doubled, as had the number of even more heavily armed policemen.

Paton and I had no difficulty in getting into the court, but Vernon Berrangé had to produce his driver's licence to be admitted. Joel Joffe was abused and threatened at the main entrance for attempting to secure places in the court for the wives and close relatives of the accused.

The possibility of a death sentence throws a solemnity onto the court. The judge took his seat and looked straight ahead as the eight accused filed into the dock. Harold Hanson called Alan Paton to the witness stand. Yutar made it obvious that he had Paton's security police file and he did not bother to make a single note of what Paton said.

Paton spoke of the plight of the African people and of their aspirations which could only be achieved if they acquired political rights. He knew Mandela as a leader of the ANC and as the man who was regarded as the likely successor to Nobel Peace Prize winner Chief Albert Luthuli. He knew Walter Sisulu and Govan Mbeki by reputation as men of commitment and ability. 'I have never had any doubt about their sincerity,' he said, 'their deep devotion to the cause of their people, and their desire to see that South Africa becomes a country in which all people participate'. Asked why he had come to give evidence he replied:

Because I was asked to come. But primarily because having been asked, I felt it was my duty to come here – a duty which I am glad to perform, *because I love my country*. [My emphasis.] And it seems to me, My Lord, with respect, that the exercise of clemency in this case is a thing which is very important for our future.

He stated that he was opposed to all forms of violence but understood why people who had tried to bring about change by peaceful means for so long would adopt violence as a last resort. The judge was irritated by Paton's reference to the history of the Afrikaner people and his point that they used violence against the British first to maintain their rights and then, when these were lost, to regain them. He interrupted Paton. 'There were many cases where people resisted and were convicted of high treason and executed. I have in mind the famous gunpowder plot in England. In the light of subsequent history, these people had legitimate grievances. But they are not entitled to break the law by force. And what happens to people like that historically is that they get convicted of high treason and are condemned to death.'

I looked at our clients. Like me, they thought this might be a warning that the judge would impose death sentences. Bram whispered that the judge need not have gone back so many centuries and so far away for a precedent. The court had conveniently overlooked the short prison sentence imposed on General Christiaan de Wet, the leader of the 1914 rebellion in which hundreds lost their lives. Anger and despondency were written into the faces of our clients. Nelson took a piece of paper from his pocket, put on his glasses and repeatedly looked at it during the rest of the proceedings.

When Nelson handed over his file to Joel Joffe at the end of the trial, I saw the notes he had made the previous night. That he must have been under tremendous stress is evidenced by the marked difference in his otherwise legible handwriting. He has never been able to decipher the fourth sentence. He wrote:

1. Statement from the dock.
2. I meant everything I said.
3. The blood of many patriots in this country has been shed for demanding treatment in conformity with civilised standards.
4. [Of the five words under this heading, the first three appear to be] 'coming is being ...'. [To this day he does not remember what he wanted to say, nor does he want to speculate. The context suggests that he might have predicted that bloodshed would ensue.]
4. [used again instead of '5'] If I must die, let me declare for all to know that I will meet my fate like a man.

(Recently, Professor Tim Couzens deciphered the fourth point as: 'The army is beginning to grow' – a reading with which Mandela concurs.)

When it came to cross-examination, Yutar once again showed his lack of respect for ethical legal practice. Instead of beginning by asking Paton a question, he made a most insulting statement:

I do not usually cross-examine witnesses who give evidence in mitigation, but I propose to cross-examine this witness with Your Lordship's leave. And I don't do so in order to aggravate the sentence, but in order to unmask this gentleman and make perfectly clear that his only reason for going into the witness box, in my submission, is to make political propaganda from the witness box.

Paton turned to the judge with a pained expression, but the judge appeared unperturbed. The author then turned to us. But we could do nothing except glare angrily at Yutar.

Alan Paton enjoyed an unblemished reputation as a devout Christian and lay-preacher of the Anglican Church. He had a strong sense of justice and compassion. He was a writer of international repute, a close friend of the former deputy prime minister, Jan Hendrick Hofmeyr, whose biography he had published that year. His best known work, *Cry, the Beloved Country*, dramatised the injustices done to Africans in South Africa and had been read by millions throughout the world in many languages.

Paton had given ample proof of his courage and transparency as one of the leaders of the Liberal Party. Under his leadership the party espoused a policy of full political rights for Africans in a united South Africa. Although some leaders of the Liberal Party were banned, the party itself was a lawful organisation. So what 'mask' did Yutar believe he was going to remove?

McCarthyism had been on the way out for a decade but even its most ardent devotees would have been upstaged by Yutar:

YUTAR: Mr Paton, are you a communist?

PATON: No.

YUTAR: Are you a fellow traveller?

PATON: I don't understand what a fellow traveller is, but I understand your implication. No, I am not a fellow traveller.

YUTAR: Your understanding of my implication is correct. Do you share the aims and objects of the Communist Party?

PATON: Some of their aims I would share.

YUTAR: Such as?

PATON: Such as a more equitable distribution of land and wealth, better economic opportunities.

YUTAR: What don't you approve of the Communist Party?

PATON: I would disapprove entirely of the totalitarian methods which they adopt to bring about such changes.

YUTAR: You disapprove of that?
PATON: Entirely.

Yutar knew that to be a communist in South Africa was a serious offence punishable by ten years' imprisonment. He must have known from the security police file in front of him that Paton was neither a communist nor a 'fellow traveller'. Yet he wanted to smear Paton as a victory for the side that he so fervently espoused. Having failed to get an admission from Paton, he tried to prove guilt by association. He put to Paton that the ANC was dominated by communists. Paton denied it. Looking through the police file, where no doubt Paton's movements were recorded, Yutar asked him whether 'he moved a lot with communists in this country', such as Roley Arenstein.

When Paton said he had met Arenstein through the organisation Defence and Aid, Yutar attempted yet another smear.

YUTAR: That is another organisation with a high-sounding name which assists the saboteurs in this country, isn't that so?
PATON: No.
YUTAR: No? Well, what did it assist in?
PATON: It assisted in defending people who were brought before the courts so that they might get a fair and just trial.

Defence and Aid was a lawful organisation founded by the Anglican Bishop of Johannesburg during the 1960 emergency after Sharpeville and for which Canon Colin Collins in London collected and transmitted funds. It was declared an unlawful organisation in the mid-1960s, but only after the Rivonia trial. The government resented the organisation for helping people with their defence in political trials, but also found unacceptable the help provided to wives and children of prisoners to visit their loved ones on Robben Island and elsewhere.

Yutar believed he could get Paton to admit that things were not so bad in South Africa because he, Paton, was free to speak. Selecting one of the many newspaper cuttings in Paton's police file, he read out a plea from Paton to Scandinavians to concern themselves with the injustices of apartheid. Paton admitted the entreaty.

YUTAR: Campaigning even from this country?
PATON: Yes.
YUTAR: Against your country?

PATON: Against my country? No, no! Against certain policies that are followed in this country, yes, but against my country, no.

YUTAR: You have spoken openly against the government?

PATON: I have.

YUTAR: That is not treason, is it?

PATON: I trust not.

YUTAR: Have you spoken against apartheid?

PATON: I have.

YUTAR: And that is not treason?

PATON: Not yet.

YUTAR: Do you think it will be?

PATON: I think it might become so.

YUTAR: You have spoken against the policies followed in this country with perfect freedom?

PATON: Not perfect freedom by any means.

YUTAR: Why, how are you …?

PATON: It is extremely difficult for one thing to get a hall to hold meetings. It is extremely difficult because the security police often make it impossible to hold the meeting. We have actually had cases where people bringing people to the meeting in trucks and lorries have been stopped by the security police and advised not to go on. I call it intimidation.

He could have added that his high profile might have afforded him some protection. But that similar protection was not available to many thousands of others whose organisations were declared unlawful, who were banned and whose statements could not be quoted, whose newspapers were closed down, whose writings were censored, whose unions were harassed and who could be charged under various acts that defined incitement, conspiracy, furthering the objects of communism or even terrorism. And above all who could be detained for ninety days without trial and whose detention could be repeatedly extended for a similar period.

In an interview with the Canadian Broadcasting Corporation in 1960, Paton predicted that the peaceful methods adopted in South Africa might be abandoned in favour of violence. For Yutar there was no distinction between prophecy and conspiracy. Over and over again he suggested that Paton knew of the ANC's plans to use violent means and that he lent support to them. This would have made him guilty of the very charges the accused were facing, but it was obvious such charges could never have been proved or he too would have been in the dock.

Yutar's scurrilous cross-examination may have pleased many of the supporters of the minority regime. But it went down very badly with the vast majority of the people of South Africa, and with millions more throughout the world for whom the unsullied reputation of Alan Paton was enhanced by his ordeal. The judge's reputation would also have been enhanced had he curbed the cross-examiner's style.

Harold Hanson, whose presence invariably attracted attention, delivered the final address. He spoke of the function of a political trial and particularly pointed out that it was the last forum of those who were otherwise silenced. He reminded the judge of earlier political trials, particularly those of Afrikaner nationalists who had risen up against oppression, whose actions were both illegal and violent, but who were not harshly punished. They had lived to become the fathers of the Afrikaner nation. He emphasised that understanding and compassion had always formed part of the basis of judicial decisions in South Africa. In his peroration he said, 'Man will not be deterred from being grieved about his position in life, or for hoping for betterment, or for expressing his views and hopes ... It is not a reprehensible thing – far less an immoral thing – for leaders to desire the advancement of all people in their country.'

Judge de Wet not only took no note of what was being said but he appeared not to be listening. Certainly he didn't consider the words of Paton or Hanson. Immediately Hanson was done, he signalled to the accused to stand:

The function of this court, as is the function of the court in any other country, is to enforce law and order, to enforce the laws of the State within which it functions. The crime of which the accused have been convicted, that is the main crime, the crime of conspiracy, is in essence one of high treason. The State has decided not to charge the crime in this form.

Bearing this in mind and giving the matter very serious consideration, I have decided not to impose the supreme penalty which in a case like this would usually be the proper penalty for the crime, but consistent with my duty that is the only leniency I can show. The sentence of all the accused will be one of life imprisonment.

The judge turned around and hastily disappeared. Although we had achieved our primary objective – to avoid the death sentence – we could not do more than direct a faint smile to those in the dock. We silently took Bram's hand and pressed it in gratitude for his leadership. The rush of journalists to the side door prevented us from speaking to or touching our clients as they were hurriedly removed.

In the cell below, Nelson thanked us for what we had done. We felt that Kathrada had a reasonable prospect of being acquitted on appeal or of having his sentence substantially reduced. We also told Mlangeni and Motsoaledi that there was a possibility that their sentences could be reduced on appeal. Our meeting was cut short by the police in a hurry to take them away, citing security concerns.

More than two thousand people gathered behind the courthouse in a defiant mood, again singing freedom songs and shouting ANC slogans. They declared their loyalty, vowed that their leaders would not serve their sentences in full, and promised 'freedom in our lifetime'.

Before the prisoners were taken away I appealed to Colonel Aucamp, the officer in charge of political prisoners, to grant the families an opportunity to see the prisoners. He assured me that arrangements would be made for the early afternoon at the prison. Yet when we got there I learned that they were being taken directly to Robben Island from a military base outside Pretoria. The families were bitterly disappointed. We were told that if we wanted to discuss matters with our clients we should go to Robben Island.

I took Alan Paton back to the consul general's house. He hardly spoke. The Minfords had heard the outcome on the one o'clock news. Paton summed up his feelings, using much the same words that appeared in a newspaper a few days later:

> In our preparation of the plea in mitigation neither of us had foreseen that Yutar would attack me as a person and would impugn my integrity. It is not my nature to be secretive; on the contrary I rather pride myself on the openness of my political life and actions. It was almost as though Yutar had some bitter personal animus against myself. I can only describe his attack as vitriolic … His attack was so virulent that I looked up to the judge to indicate that I thought he should intervene. But whether he saw me or not, he did nothing. I am inclined to think that he enjoyed it, and that he thought the 'unmasking' to be well merited.

The almost universal condemnation of the convictions and sentences was unexpected by the government. *The Daily Telegraph* reported that 'this is not the end, rather the beginning of debate on the larger moral issues … Whenever and wherever government rests on any other foundation than the general consent of the whole people, the patriotism of those repressed tends to appear in the eyes of the rulers as treason.'

The New York Times said, 'Most of the world regards the convicted men as … the George Washingtons and Benjamin Franklins of South Africa, not criminals deserving punishment.'

Judge de Wet thought otherwise: 'I am by no means convinced that the motives of the accused were as altruistic as they wished the court to believe. People who organise a revolution usually take over the government, and personal ambition cannot be excluded as a motive.'

The department of foreign affairs called on the Honourable HHW de Villiers, the recently retired judge president of the Eastern Cape Division, to write a booklet entitled *Rivonia: Operation Mayibuye*. Judge de Villiers had a history of supporting government causes: he had been chosen as one of the additional judges appointed to the Court of Appeal in the mid-1950s to ensure that coloured voters would be removed from the voters' roll. Another recently retired judge president, the Honourable Francis Napier Broome, wrote the foreword, commenting: 'Two recent overseas comments on the Rivonia trial indicate the need for a book such as this. Both related to the sentence of (life) imprisonment imposed by the presiding judge instead of sentence of death. One ascribed the judge's leniency to government policy, the other to the pressure of public agitation.'

He went on to praise South Africa's judiciary in the words set out at the beginning of this chapter. He reassured readers that they could rely implicitly on everything written by Judge de Villiers, who had high praise for the impartiality and competence of Judge de Wet. A senior political correspondent, Margaret Smith, with the help of Joel Joffe and me, wrote an article pointing out a number of serious errors and misrepresentations in the book.

The draft of her article was sent to Judge de Villiers. He responded that he was not responsible for the text relating to what happened at the trial. This rejoinder was included in the full-page critique published in Smith's paper. According to Judge de Villiers, the text for which he took no responsibility had been prepared by counsel in the foreign affairs department. As a judge he was accustomed to counsel presenting the facts accurately to the court. We were told that the counsel was 'Pik' Botha – later minister of foreign affairs. He was to be seen occasionally during the trial sitting among the spectators.

Some thirty-five years later, on the threshold of the twenty-first century, legal journalist Carmel Rickard described the Rivonia case as 'the trial of the century'. I would agree with that assessment. It overshadowed the lives of those involved, mine included, both personally and as counsel. For more than thirty years it hung like a dark cloud over all who followed in the footsteps of Nelson Mandela, Walter Sisulu, Govan Mbeki and their colleagues who had sat in the dock of the Rivonia trial.

CHAPTER 24

The Worst of Times

Bram and Molly Fischer invited the lawyers involved in the Rivonia trial and our wives to join them at their home in Beaumont Street. There we found a few political activists not yet banned from attending gatherings. Although they congratulated and thanked us for saving the lives of the eight ANC leaders, their brave stand and that of their supporters within and outside the country had been invaluable. As had Bram's expert leadership.

Everyone knew that Bram and Molly were absolutely committed to the struggle. Their deep love for one another was also legendary. Bram would often caress and squeeze Molly's hand as she put down a tray of refreshments on the table. They were also devoted parents to their daughters, Ruth and Ilse, and their son, Paul, who required special attention for a chronic illness.

The day after the celebratory gathering, Molly and Bram planned to drive their old grey Mercedes to Cape Town, returning along the Garden Route, where they had spent many a holiday with their children. This time they were anticipating being with Ilse, a student at the University of Cape Town, to celebrate her twenty-first birthday. While in Cape Town, Bram would be joined by Joel Joffe. The two were to visit Robben Island to discuss with our clients the matter of an appeal.

The next day Hilda Bernstein telephoned the tragic news that Molly had drowned in an accident. Arethe and I went to Beaumont Street. The house was full of people, men and women, young and old, political friends, members of the legal profession, members of the two families. Bram was withdrawn, almost sullen. He uttered a muted 'thank you' for the condolences, and looked into space. Stricken with grief, I heard him mutter, '*Wat het ek gedoen … My arme vrou.*' – What have I done – my poor wife. Ilse, as ever the strong member of the family, sat next to him and held his hand.

Nor would he speak about the accident. We learned some details from Elizabeth Lewin, who had been in the car. Bram braked and swerved to avoid a cow frightened by an oncoming motorcyclist and their car left the road, plunging into a deep pool below a bridge. She and Bram, sitting in front, managed to get out but Molly was trapped at the back. Bram, fully clothed, dived in repeatedly, desperate to save her. Eventually he was stopped by helpful strangers who feared that he would drown.

Bram wanted a quiet family gathering at the crematorium as soon as Ruth returned from abroad. However, his comrades and friends, particularly the women, eventually persuaded him that Molly's contribution to the struggle had to be acknowledged. She had been a role model for thousands. On the day, funeral orations of the kind that sometimes led to criminal charges of incitement were delivered, to the perceptible alarm of some relatives of the Krige and Fischer families sitting in the front pews, strangers to most of us. They were distinguished by their formal dress, particularly the women, who wore hats.

Both Bram and Molly had distanced themselves from any religious observances, yet the thoughtful Bram knew that for both their families there could be no closure without the Lord's Prayer. He habitually carried a piece of paper or a used envelope in his jacket pocket, and now wrote a note to his brother Paul. Paul took the microphone and, struggling to keep the tears back, solemnly commenced 'Onse Vader ...'

The next day Bram called a meeting of the five Rivonia lawyers. Although he was deeply affected by Molly's death, he wanted to do what was expected of him. We gave our views on the prospects of success on appeal. The consensus was that Ahmed Kathrada might succeed and had the best chance of having his sentence reduced. After all he was found guilty on only one count.

Regarding Raymond Mhlaba, Andrew Mlangeni and Elias Motsoaledi, the Court of Appeal might be persuaded that their degree of participation in the conspiracy was less than that of Nelson Mandela, Walter Sisulu, Govan Mbeki and Dennis Goldberg. We felt the convictions and sentences of the latter group were unassailable.

Bram took off his jacket and covered the telephone on his desk, perhaps hoping to muffle the ever-present bugging device. He was concerned that the flood of editorial support for those convicted and the calls for their release would stop if an appeal was pending. Even the *Rand Daily Mail* questioned the wisdom of the ANC in resorting to violence and not persisting in peaceful methods. In response the underground movement posed its own question to the editor, Laurence Gandar: 'Do you sincerely believe there is any other way that is effective? We are held in a fist of iron and only force can prise it open.' This sort of debate was valuable and we were keen to have it continue.

However, an important decision had to be made: were we to appeal? This could only be decided by our clients.

Joel believed that only two of the team should visit the prisoners on Robben Island. Though we charged only nominal fees, the demands on Defence and Aid in other cases, particularly in the Eastern Cape and Natal, were such that even our travelling expenses weren't covered. As previously arranged, Bram, as the leader of the team, and Joel, as the attorney, would go.

They returned with the instruction that there would be no appeal. However, Nelson wanted to see me: he was anxious about Winnie and their children and concerned about the education of the children from his first marriage. The prison authorities required good reasons to grant a visit even by counsel. It took some months – and a good deal of Winnie's ingenuity – before I was allowed to visit Nelson Mandela.

Meanwhile, Joel had arranged that I charge R500, half the monthly fee, for the work done up to 12 June. Precious little had come in for the second half of the month. I had taken over a trial in the magistrate's court for which I charged R25. In total, apart from his R500, I had earned just over R100. July looked better. Joel was taking on some cases from the Eastern Cape, including that of Washington Bongo, who had been sentenced to death for the murder of an informer. Despite protesting his innocence, Bongo was convicted, sentenced to death and refused leave to appeal. Joel instructed me to prepare an application for leave to appeal to the chief justice.

It was a difficult case to argue. The condemned man's allegations against the investigating officer were rejected by the judge. Our suspicions that the State witnesses were tortured had not been probed at length. In any event the witnesses would not have implicated the police. Any departure from their statements would have landed them in jail. The judge found no extenuating circumstances and was, therefore, bound to impose the death sentence. It did appear from the record that killing had a political objective during troubled times in a divided society. These factors, according to numerous writings and decided cases, could extenuate the seriousness of the crime. The authorities on this argument had been collated by Arthur in the Rivonia trial and I used them again in the written application to the chief justice.

Oral argument is not called for when a petition for leave to appeal is filed, nor are reasons given for refusal. A two-line letter to Joel from the registrar of the Appellate Division of the Supreme Court in Bloemfontein, refusing leave to appeal, sealed Bongo's fate. Nevertheless, Joel's strong sense of justice led him to bring an action for damages against the investigating officer. The action failed, and, as the trial judge had ordered, Bongo was hanged by the neck until he was dead.

I never met Washington Bongo but Joel saw him regularly and was impressed with him. I was not asked, nor did I volunteer, to visit him in the death cells. I had defended a number of accused facing death sentences, but up to then it had never been imposed on any of my clients, although a couple had been narrow escapes. The strain of such a prospect affected me deeply and I hoped that I would never witness a judge handing down so cruel and inhuman a form of punishment. Visiting a client in a death cell awaiting execution was not a thought I wanted to contemplate. Yet within a month I faced this reality.

While I was preparing for Bongo's appeal, Joel put a lengthy record on my desk. Three members of the Port Elizabeth command of MK, Zinakile Mkaba, Vuyisile Mini and Wilson Khyingo had been convicted of sabotage, housebreaking and theft. They were also found guilty of the murder of Sipho Irwin Mango in that they instructed five others to kill him. Mango was to be a witness against other members of MK charged with burning down the house of a representative of Kaizer Matanzima. This official was collaborating with the government in accepting independence for the Transkei, which would deprive millions of their South African citizenship. Not surprisingly, the ANC and MK vociferously and violently opposed Transkei's sham independence.

Mini was a co-accused with Mandela, Sisulu and Kathrada in the treason trial. He took part in the Defiance Campaign and was active in the trade union movement. There was some incongruity that members of MK's High Command charged in the Rivonia trial had avoided the death penalty, while members of the regional command were sentenced to death. Govan Mbeki, who had worked closely with Mini, felt strongly that this anomaly be addressed.

I spent days analysing the judgment and the evidence, listing contradictions and improbabilities, seeking any significant misdirections that might overturn the judge's findings on appeal. The evidence against the appellants on the sabotage and other counts was overwhelming. At best, I reported to Harold Hanson, we might get some of the convictions set aside, but it wouldn't influence the sentence imposed for this group of offences. On the other hand, the evidence on the murder charge was that of a single witness, an informer whose identity was not made public but recorded as 'BB'. I suggested that we abandon the appeal on all charges except murder. By persuading the court to set aside the murder conviction, it would be difficult for the prosecutor to press for the death sentence on the sabotage counts, especially given the Rivonia trial sentence. At the end of my assessment, Hanson looked hard at me over the rim of his reading glasses. Apparently Bram had discussed the importance of the case with him and suggested that I be his junior. He believed I lacked neither ingenuity nor optimism. However, he was emphatic that we could not adopt my strategy without discussing it with our clients. Joel and I were delegated to brief them and ensure they understood the consequences. We were to leave a copy of the record and my notes.

Mini and his colleagues were not alone on death row. At that time more than a thousand were sentenced to death every year, but most had their sentences commuted to imprisonment. There were about two hundred in the death cells at any given time and between eighty and a hundred were executed each year.

At the central prison we filled in the necessary forms. Three or four steel gates opened and we climbed the stairs to the first floor. With each step deeper into the prison, a faint dirge became louder and more mournful. The key-keeper opened the door of a small waiting room where the chief warder was on the telephone, speaking in animated Afrikaans. He was the selector of a local rugby team and his conversation concerned the up-coming Saturday game. We waited patiently. How strange it was to hear such a mundane conversation in a section of the prison were so many people awaited their execution.

The chief warder checked the forms and ushered us through the last gate. As soon as the thick steel key clicked in the lock and the gate was pushed open, the singing stopped. It was as if the singers were led by a choir conductor. In reality they were in separate cells and could hardly communicate with one another.

Our clients were brought to a single cell which doubled as a consulting room. We sat on two fixed benches since there were neither table nor chairs. Never before had I seen faces like these – drawn, matt-grey skin with a tinge of dark blue on their cheeks, their eyes sunk in their sockets, their pupils dilated. No grip in their handshake. Their voices but whispers. The months they had spent on death row had almost snuffed out their humanity.

Mini had seen the best lawyers at the Bar in action in defence of himself and his colleagues – Vernon Berrangé and John Coaker at the treason trial preparatory examination; Isie Maisels, Bram Fischer and Sydney Kentridge when they successfully challenged the first indictment in Pretoria leading to charges being temporarily withdrawn against him and others. After a while, he asked how they all were.

When we explained the reason for our visit they were devastated. Mini believed that once the judge had given leave to appeal he would walk out a free man. We explained that this was an unrealistic expectation. At best we hoped to set aside the death sentence.

Resigned, Mini left matters in our hands, taking some comfort in Harold Hanson arguing the case.

Hanson's view of the hopelessness of any appeal on the sabotage charges was more firmly held than Joel's and mine. He directed us to prepare heads of argument aimed at persuading the Court of Appeal to overturn the murder conviction. If that failed, we would rely on the political motive as an extenuating circumstance to set aside the death sentence.

In court, Chief Justice Steyn was careful not to disapprove of the trial judge's decision granting leave to appeal. But he appreciated our approach of not pursuing an appeal on the sabotage convictions. 'In my view,' he said, 'there is every justification for counsel's attitude, as the evidence relevant to those convictions offer scant prospect of a successful appeal against them.' As to our forceful argument that there was insufficient evidence to prove beyond reasonable doubt that the appellants were responsible for the murder, that the single witness was not satisfactory in all material respects and that there was no adequate corroboration of his evidence, it became apparent that the three judges were not impressed. In their view, proof that the accused were members of MK's regional command and responsible for acts of sabotage corroborated the informer's evidence that they had planned and ordered the killing. The judges rejected, even as a reasonable possibility, that the informers might falsely have implicated Mini and his colleagues precisely because of their membership of MK.

Most judges found it easy to distinguish between the leniency of the courts in dealing with Afrikaner patriots and their tough policy on MK cadres. These latter they regarded as terrorists, even though the conduct of the two groups was similar. Afrikaner patriots took part 'in open conflict arising from political dissension', while MK cadres were involved in 'a cold-blooded decision taken in the comparative security of seclusion'.

The appeal was dismissed two weeks later. When the men were executed in November it had a devastating effect on us all, particularly those on Robben Island.

Eventually I was granted a permit to see Nelson. I was warned to be there before seven in the morning, when the ferry brought in the children of the warders attending schools in Cape Town. While some non-political prisoners loaded provisions onto the ferry, the captain, wearing a prison warder's uniform, inspected my permanent residence permit issued in the early 1950s and the letter from the commissioner of prisons in Pretoria. Without a word, he indicated that I walk down the plank onto the ferry. I was the only passenger. I sat on a wooden bunk facing the stern, but due to the mist and the cloud covering the mountain with its famous tablecloth, the fabled view was obscured.

Beyond the harbour wall, the ferry pitched and tossed on the choppy sea. I feared that my self-esteem would be lost forever if I succumbed to seasickness. I held fast to the elbow rest and remembered the advice given to me during my childhood to look at the horizon. Mentally, I prepared myself for what lay ahead by imagining what sort of meeting this would be. Would they allow us to write key words on a piece of paper as we did during our Rivonia trial consultations?

How much of the day could we spend together until the ferry sailed back in the afternoon to fetch the schoolchildren?

As we neared the island, the mist lifted. Thousands of penguins clambered on the rocks, but not a single seal, even though the island was named after these mammals by the early Dutch settlers.

I was met by a uniformed warder with three stripes and a star on his upper arm. He took me to a small L-shaped building near the quayside consisting of cubicles rather than rooms. There I signed a form, and was told to stay put and wait for the prisoner. The warder disappeared in an open bakkie. About ten minutes later the vehicle returned. Six warders rode on the back and two in the cab. They leapt off with military precision and formed a square into which Nelson was ordered to jump. Dressed in a comparatively warm tunic, a pair of khaki shorts, no socks and roughly made leather sandals, he held his head high and waved at me. The warders, accustomed to prisoners falling into step with them, started a quick forward march, but Nelson would have none of it. He acted as if he were an official taking part at a military parade and set the pace. I rushed towards them and Nelson and I embraced. Shocked by such an unusual scene, the warders stopped. Nelson said, 'George, let me introduce you to my guard of honour.' He did so by rank, then by first name and surname. Each one reluctantly and rather lamely shook my hand.

In the building, Nelson closed the door of the cubicle, silently claiming the right to privacy. The guards took turns to watch us through the small panel of glass in the door. Throughout the interview, Nelson sent a clear message: though he was their prisoner and they could deprive him of his freedom, neither the island, the prison walls, the iron bars nor the degrading clothing would deprive him of his humanity or his dignity or the right to consult counsel of his choice in private.

Of course his first questions were about Winnie and the children, and then the lawyers involved in the trial, naming each one except for Bram. When Bram and Joel saw Nelson those many months previously, Bram had been unable to mention Molly's death. The emotion was too much for him. Nelson had subsequently heard of the tragic accident. Now he pulled my writing pad towards him and reached for my pen. He wrote *'Unqaphele'* – the title conferred upon short, elderly and respected persons – and by gesture asked after Bram. I gave the thumbs-up sign, and Nelson nodded relief. We continued our discussion in this laborious, cryptic manner. By the brevity of his answers to my queries about prison conditions, I realised he was more interested in knowing what was happening outside. What was the reaction to their conviction? Were there any signs that the liberation movement was still active? Had there been further arrests? They were most effectively isolated. They had no access to news or other prisoners and the warders were prohibited from talking to them.

In the same cryptic way I told him that a few acts of sabotage had been committed for which MK claimed responsibility. A bomb had exploded on the concourse of the Johannesburg railway station which injured more than twenty people, including a grandmother who died of her wounds and her granddaughter who was badly burned. Police almost immediately arrested John Harris, a member of the African Resistance Movement, not connected to MK, but an offshoot of the Liberal Party. Nevertheless, Minister of Justice John Vorster attributed the new wave of subversion to 'white South African communists' who would soon be crushed. Shortly afterwards some MK High Command members were detained, among them Wilton Mkwayi, David Kitson, Mac Maharaj, Laloo Chiba and John Matthews. At Bram's suggestion, Joel Joffe briefed me to defend them in what became known as the 'Little Rivonia trial'.

Nelson was saddened by the news, especially as Wilton was one of his co-accused in the treason trial. But he was pleased to hear that Rusty and Hilda Bernstein had successfully crossed the border into Botswana.

At one point, the senior warder interrupted us to say that the prisoner had to be returned to the cells for lunch. I would be escorted to the warders' canteen. After lunch we could continue our interview. It was made clear that traipsing around the island was strictly prohibited.

Our afternoon session was more relaxed. We talked about the others and I told him about Dennis Goldberg, who was kept in Pretoria. (Even in jail, apartheid laws and practices had to be maintained, and the island was for black prisoners.) Nelson requested that I come regularly to see them, and that I report to their families. They were all concerned about their families and the education of their children.

Our time together ended, and Nelson was taken away. I was escorted to the quay. Once again I was the only outside passenger. The wind was up and I took shelter in the cabin. Spray covered the small panes blocking out the late afternoon light. As the vessel tossed and jumped to and fro, the smell of engine oil and diesel fuel contributed to making that one of the worst days of my life.

Winnie, Albertina, Caroline and family members of the others applied for me to visit the island again. Their applications were either refused or ignored. We were told later that letters written by prisoners to me were not posted. No reasons were given at the time, but I learned later from Nelson and Kathy that Colonel Aucamp was responsible. Shortly after that first visit, Aucamp told Nelson that he would never see Bizos again as a lawyer – next time it would be as a prisoner in a cell near his. When Kathy asked Aucamp for permission to see me, the colonel said that it was not necessary because Kathy would see me soon – in a cell next to his.

Joel and Venetta Joffe's application to emigrate to Australia was turned down, no doubt thanks to the security police. They decided on the United Kingdom instead, but not before a few important cases were heard. One of these concerned the defence of Wilton and his co-accused, about to be tried on charges similar to those faced by Mandela and the others. But now some of the offences post-dated the Rivonia trial. Joel believed that the State would have witnesses from among the accused's former comrades. Also that none of our clients could put up a defence on the merits. In addition he feared that another judge might view matters differently to Judge de Wet and hand down death sentences. Life sentences might not be regarded as sufficient deterrent. Such an argument could point to the continued operations of MK as proof, adding that the time had come to impose the extreme penalty to put an end to such acts of terrorism.

Wilton Mkwayi, the first accused, was the son of a poor peasant family in the Cape and the eldest of thirteen children. He left school after finishing the sixth grade to work as a labourer, later becoming a union organiser and a senior official in the South African Congress of Trade Unions. A prominent activist during the 1950s, he left the country to undergo military training, returning to lead MK.

Mkwayi circulated through the African townships, especially Soweto, recruiting and forming MK cells. He taught his comrades how to make bombs, how to recruit others to print and distribute pamphlets and how to work within lawful organisations to support the struggle for freedom. Most of this was known to the security police. It was clear that there would be no shortage of witnesses against him and his co-accused.

Visible public support for the ANC and MK was at a low ebb, so low that the State felt no need to hold the trial in Pretoria to avoid demonstrations. The judge was WG 'Wes' Boshoff, a National Party supporter from the Pretoria Bar, appointed over the heads of his seniors soon after the party came to power. He was a good lawyer, a polite and patient trial judge, with the useful ability to write judgments considered appeal-proof. There was no doubt about his political sympathies, as I'd experienced in arguing Godfrey Pitje's appeal.

Although our clients were circumspect in revealing how they became involved in MK activities, it became apparent that the Rivonia trialists, together with Bram Fischer, Hilda Bernstein and others from within the liberation movement were implicated. They predicted that the main witness against them would be Lionel Gay, a lecturer at the University of the Witwatersrand and a friend of David Kitson. Kitson believed that Gay would not disclose all he knew. He asked Joel to brief

Fred Zwarenstein to cross-examine in the hope that he, Kitson, and one or more of his co-accused might be acquitted. Mac Maharaj, who knew Gay, was much less optimistic. He privately confided to me that despite Gay's technical and other skills it had been a mistake to recruit him into the movement at such a high level. They felt he would only have implicated them under pressure.

Gay was a difficult witness to cross-examine. He, like many others after him, salved his conscience by not telling the security police everything. He kept back vital information to retain some credibility among his comrades, and to convince himself that he had not totally betrayed the struggle. Having made a deal absolving himself from prosecution if he stuck to the statement, he resented the cross-examiner for probing too deeply or asking questions about what prompted him to betray his friends. He could not admit to being tortured, for this would break the contract between himself and the investigating officer. And this officer sat directly opposite the witness box.

I gently reminded him of his dedicated services to the liberation movement, his belief in the just cause and of his oath of loyalty to his comrades. This line of cross-examination occasionally succeeded. Details of savage behaviour by interrogators would pour out, and cause outrage among a sympathetic audience. The prosecution and the security police would glare at the witness in anger and he would realise he had lost his chance of gaining his precious freedom.

During my cross-examination I almost got Gay to reveal the circumstances behind his evidence. But as I put the last question, which might have led him to speak the truth, Judge Boshoff suddenly adjourned the court almost half an hour before lunch.

After lunch, my advantage had been lost. Gay's interrogator, Lieutenant Johan Jacobus Viktor, retained his deal. This policeman rose to the rank of general by the mid-1980s, no doubt because of his success as an interrogator. A number of detainees vouched for his cruel and inhumane methods. Interestingly, he was less successful with women: he flirted with Ruth First and Stephanie Kemp, but failed to persuade them to betray their friends.

There was more than sufficient evidence to convict the accused, so they decided to follow Nelson Mandela's precedent and make a statement from the dock rather than face cross-examination. The tenor of their statements echoed his, although Mac Maharaj also spoke of the unspeakable methods of torture used by Lieutenant DJ Swanepoel. As he listened, Judge Boshoff tightened his thin lips and nervously adjusted his spectacles. Blood rushed to his face. He was angry about what was being said in the packed courtroom and carefully noted by journalists.

After an adjournment, the judge produced a well-crafted judgment. As expected, the accused were found guilty. But Boshoff went further, relying on snippets of hearsay evidence to implicate Bram Fischer in the MK conspiracy, even though he was neither named in the indictment nor given an opportunity to be heard. Lieutenant Viktor correctly predicted in a stage whisper as the judge was leaving the bench that Bram's name would be banner headlines in the afternoon papers.

The finding was the sole topic of discussion in the Bar common room. Many wondered in hushed voices what would happen to Bram. At a couple of the tables where his fellow Afrikaners sat, there was neither sorrow nor restraint. But they were a minority. Many of the Afrikaners, pre-eminent among them GPC 'Gee' Kotze, the chairman of the Bar Council, considered Bram an honourable but tragic figure and refused to disassociate himself from him.

Joel and I sought guidance from our colleagues, including Bram, regarding our approach to the question of sentence. We agreed that there was no point in finding witnesses to give evidence in mitigation, but should use cases dealing with the length of imprisonment in political cases. Also, we assumed that since the leaders of MK had not been sentenced to death, such a penalty was not a possibility. We would also urge the court to differentiate the length of imprisonment according to the accused's participation.

I had hardly begun my argument when the judge remarked that the penalty for the offences committed by the accused was death. I tried hard to suppress my abhorrence of the death penalty. Judge Boshoff lost no opportunity in questioning my attitude.

Did I not agree, he asked, that the security of the State was the highest law? Mkwayi had not gone into the witness box to deny the evidence that he was busy teaching many in Soweto how to make gun powder, 'Molotov cocktails' (petrol bombs) and other bombs. Surely he must have foreseen that these deadly weapons were to be used to commit acts of terror by fanatical terrorists like himself?

After these comments, the judge allowed me to finish my prepared argument with barely concealed impatience. Then he adjourned the court to consider sentence. Wilton, sensing that his co-accused and Joel and I were in a state of shock, tried to comfort us, saying that, like the leaders before him, he was prepared to die.

As it turned out, the judge's strongly stated views were intended not for those then on trial but as a warning that death sentences might be imposed in the future. He sent Wilton to jail for life, imposed twenty years on David Kitson and twelve years on each of the others.

Despite this low point for the liberation movement, the optimism of Wilton and his colleagues had not waned. They thanked Joel and me and felt they would not serve the full term of their sentences. Liberation was not far away.

CHAPTER 25

Bram Fischer's Trial

He chose the road that had to pass through the jail. He travelled with courage and dignity ... He challenged his own people because he felt that what they were doing was morally wrong ... I fought only against injustice, not against my own people.

– Nelson Mandela
(delivering the Legal Resource Centre's first
Bram Fischer Memorial Lecture, 1995)

During the latter half of the Rivonia trial, it became apparent that the security police had documentary and other evidence that Bram Fischer was one of the senior leaders of the Communist Party and actively involved in the underground movement. They did not dare arrest him during the trial as they feared the outcry. The prosecutor and the police semi-cryptically suggested that he would soon be behind iron bars.

After the trial and the death of his wife, Bram did hardly any legal work. He rarely came into the Bar common room. Since many of his comrades and close friends were banned, there was no longer a steady stream of late afternoon visitors to his home in Beaumont Street, Oaklands. For the few of us who visited him, the void created by Molly's death and the heavy blows struck by the regime against the liberation movement were mirrored in Bram's face. He rarely smiled but stared into space as we sat on the veranda. His son Paul would occasionally join us. Ruth had married Anthony Eastwood, a lawyer practising in Salisbury in Ian Smith's Rhodesia. Ilse was in Cape Town. Arthur Chaskalson, Joel Joffe and I visited Bram regularly on the way home. He would ask about our families, remembering not only the names of our children, but also their progress at school and even the sports they played.

Once, he had met my mother at a lunch where our boys took turns to rotate a lamb on a spit, proudly watched by their grandmother. Bram greeted her with a broad smile, took her by the arm and led her around the lawn patting her hand. She spoke no English and this gesture was the only way he could communicate the affection and admiration he felt for her, having been told by me what she endured during the German occupation and the civil war. My mother assumed that everyone in the whole world spoke Greek. She asked him questions about his family, his work and how he and I became friends. Bram nodded, smiled and gave her a hug. When Bram, Molly and Paul had left, my mother asked me to tell her about this good Christian gentleman who had accompanied her around the lawn.

Bram rarely accepted invitations after Molly's death. He claimed he was too busy preparing an important case to be argued before the Privy Council in England on behalf of a large international pharmaceutical company. He had no passport, although he had applied for a temporary travel document. The government was in no hurry to respond, but he was hopeful that embassy pressure and requests from some leading members of the legal profession might have the desired result.

We knew that he had charged no more than a couple of thousand rand for the nine months' work on the Rivonia trial and even that sum Joel Joffe had to insist he take. The hefty fee he could charge in England would be welcome. Then he was detained for a couple of days without being charged, and his plans seemed in jeopardy. He was released and received a passport. Two days later, on 23 September 1964, Bram was arrested and charged under the Suppression of Communism Act.

Although it appeared that there might have been a lack of communication between the security police and the ministry issuing passports, this was thought unlikely. Prime Minister John Vorster held a tight grip over such matters. He, his government and their functionaries considered Bram a traitor who had turned his back on his people and their brand of Afrikaner nationalism. Was it a Machiavellian plot to let him go after his arrest, hoping that he would not return? Was that not the best way to get rid of him and simultaneously discredit him in the eyes of his supporters? He was to be the first accused of the six women and five men scheduled to appear before senior regional magistrate, S C Alan. It was this same Alan who, some eight years earlier, had disbelieved the group of policemen in Lichtenburg. He was one of the few English-speaking magistrates and he was thought competent and fair.

An application for bail was made before Magistrate van Greunen, an Afrikaner with a reputation for impartiality. Harold Hanson Q C, spoke of his close friend's patrician background, and of his grandfather, Abram, a lawyer, advisor and confidante of President Steyn of the Orange Free State, particularly during the Boer War. After the republic was vanquished by the British, Bram's grandfather had become prime minister of the Orange River Colony. His father was the judge president of the Orange Free State Provincial Division of the Supreme Court of South Africa. Hanson reminded the court that Bram himself was a most respected senior member of the Bar, had been elected to the Bar Council on a number of occasions and had served as the Bar Council's chairman.

And indeed Bram had the support of most people at the Bar. Though many did not approve of his politics, they admired him for his courage, professional integrity and impeccable manners. A number of us were at court to hear him say, 'I have no intention of avoiding a political prosecution. I fully believe I can establish my innocence. I am an Afrikaner. My home is South Africa. I will not leave South Africa because my political beliefs conflict with those of the government ruling the country … I assure the court that if I am allowed to go to London, I will return in good time to stand my trial.'

In a short judgment the magistrate described Bram as 'a son of the soil', adding he was satisfied that Bram would return for the trial. The prosecutor had opposed bail, but found it difficult to reconcile the government's granting of a passport with a genuine fear that Bram would abscond. He wanted bail fixed at R50 000, while the defence requested R5 000. The magistrate set it at R10 000. There was no shortage of volunteers to pay it. Vernon Berrangé then made an application for bail on behalf of Eli Weinberg, the trade unionist turned professional photographer. His application was refused. One other of the accused was granted bail. The rest remained in custody throughout the trial.

Bram went to the Privy Council and won his case. Before returning home he spent time with Ruth and Anthony Eastwood. He saw his friend Mary Benson, and also Joe Slovo and various leaders of the Communist Party in exile. Some tried to persuade him against returning. Although he later acknowledged that there were more complex reasons for his return, he articulated only one at the time: 'I will go back because I said I would.'

By the time the trial began in mid-November, Ivan Schermbrucker and Lewis Baker had been added as accused. They faced three separate counts: membership, participation in the activities of, and furthering the aims of the Communist Party. The magistrate's jurisdiction was limited to three years on each count. Harold Hanson, Vernon Berrangé, Denis Kuny and Ismail Mahomed from the Bar, along with Joel Joffe and other attorneys, undertook the defence.

Piet Beyleveld, a senior member of the liberation movement, was in detention without trial. Rumours spread that he was cooperating with the police and had disclosed vital information about the Communist Party, implicating Bram and most of the accused. Bram was confident that Beyleveld would not give evidence. He expected him to follow the example of Vuyisile Mini. Mini had been sentenced to death, but refused the State's offer to commute his sentence if he gave evidence against Wilton Mkwayi. Bram was devastated when Beyleveld entered the witness box to betray the secrets of the movement and particularly the Communist Party. His pain was exacerbated because Beyleveld was a fellow Afrikaner.

From the evidence of spies within the organisations, conversations clandestinely taped and documents seized, the conviction of most, if not all, the accused was inevitable. Even more devastating for Bram, the liberation movement had been dealt a savage blow.

During the 1964 year-end recess and in early January 1965, Bram appeared more sullen and withdrawn than ever. One Friday we walked back and forth in the long passage outside his office while he told me that he had come to say goodbye. For my own protection he would give no further details. He was worried that his actions might place his children in danger and asked me to help them if they were detained. We embraced. And he hurried off. I guessed his intentions but had to wait for confirmation on Monday morning when Harold Hanson handed into court a letter written to him by Bram:

By the time this reaches you I shall be a long way from Johannesburg and shall absent myself from the remainder of the trial. But I shall still be in the country to which I said I would return when I was granted bail.

I wish you to inform the court that my absence, though deliberate, is not intended in any way to be disrespectful. Nor is it prompted by any fear of the punishment which might be inflicted on me. Indeed I realise fully that my eventual punishment may be increased by my present conduct.

I have not taken this step lightly. As you will no doubt understand, I have experienced great conflict between my desire to stay with my fellow accused and, on the other hand, to try to continue the political work I believe to be essential. My decision was made only because I believe that it is the duty of every true opponent of this government to remain in this country and to oppose its monstrous policy of apartheid with every means in his power. That is what I shall do for as long as I can.

In brief, the reasons which have compelled me to take this step and which I wish you to communicate to the court are the following:

There are already over 2,500 political prisoners in our prisons. These men and women are not criminals but the staunchest opponents of apartheid.

Cruel, discriminatory laws multiply each year; bitterness and hatred of the government and its laws are growing daily. No outlet for this hatred is permitted because political rights have been removed, national organisations have been outlawed and leaders, not in gaol, have been banned from speaking and meeting. People are hounded by pass laws and by group areas controls. Torture by solitary confinement, and worse, has been legalised by an elected Parliament – surely an event unique in history.

It is no answer to all this to say that Bantustans will be created nor that the country is prosperous. The vast majority of the people are prevented from sharing in the country's wealth by the colour bar in industry and mining, and by the prohibition against owning land save in relatively small and grossly overcrowded parts of the country where, in any case, there exist no mines or industries. The idea that Bantustans will provide any solution would deceive no-one but a white South African.

What is needed is for white South Africans to shake themselves out of their complacency, a complacency intensified by the present economic boom built upon racial discrimination.

Unless this whole intolerable system is changed radically and rapidly, disaster must follow. Appalling bloodshed and civil war will become inevitable because, as long as there is oppression of a majority, such oppression will be fought with increasing hatred.

To try to avoid this becomes a supreme duty, particularly for an Afrikaner, because it is largely the representatives of my fellow Afrikaners who have been responsible for the worst of these discriminatory laws.

These are my reasons for absenting myself from court. If by my fight I can encourage even some people to think about, to understand and to abandon the policies they now so blindly follow, I shall not regret any punishment I may incur.

I can no longer serve justice in the way I have attempted to do during the past 30 years. I can do it only in the way I have now chosen.

Finally, I would like you to urge upon the court to bear in mind that if it does have to punish any of my fellow accused, it will be punishing them for holding the ideas today that will be universally accepted tomorrow.

In a postscript he thanked Harold Hanson for all he had done for him. The prosecutor, JH Liebenberg, described Bram's commitment as 'the desperate act of a desperate man'. Banner headlines announced his disappearance. Justice Minister Vorster publicly challenged the legal profession to condemn Fischer and take appropriate action against him if it were sincere in claiming the role of guardian of the rule of law. Within two days the Johannesburg Bar Council chairman, Melville Festenstein, called an urgent meeting of the council. The upshot was to apply to court to have Bram struck from the roll. John Coaker, a member of the council and of my group on the eighth floor of Innes Chambers, was quick to tell me that for him and a couple of others it had not been an easy decision, but they felt duty bound. In particular Bram's breach of his oath of office was viewed seriously and his failure to honour his word to stand trial.

I was stunned and shook my head in anger but remained silent. I declined his invitation to Dawson's around the corner, a bar frequented by some of our colleagues, because I was anxious to get home. What worried me was that Ilse might be detained for interrogation about her father's disappearance and likely hiding place.

The next morning the press reported Ilse's ignorance of her father's plans or whereabouts. He had left while she was asleep. It was a story plausible enough for journalists, but unlikely to be accepted by the security police without testing her. Fortunately for Paul, whose ill health made him more vulnerable, he was in London with his sister Ruth.

I came across a member of the special branch, Lieutenant Fourie, sitting on a bench outside the entrance of the court where I was to appear. 'Where's your friend Bram, George?' he asked. Irritated, I retorted, 'In my backyard!' I could not resist adding, 'We are advocates Fischer and Bizos to you.'

On reflection I thought that my provocative words might lead to a raid on our house, but Fourie understood my facetiousness. Fourie's presence outside court was just the start. Those in charge of the manhunt for Bram were convinced that I knew where he was. Surely if they bugged my telephones and watched every movement I made, I would sooner or later lead them to the fugitive's hideout.

Bar Council's decision was to apply to the court to disbar Bram. Arthur wrote to the council asking for reasons. They replied that they don't give reasons for their decisions. Harold Hanson blamed Melville Festenstein for lack of leadership, and my friendship with some of the members of the council became strained. Unexpected support for Bram came from Leslie Blackwell QC, who had joined the Bar in 1910, and who took an active part as a member of Parliament in the United Party led by Jan Smuts. Smuts had appointed him a judge of the Supreme Court. He wrote an article published in *The Sunday Times* setting out historical examples of Afrikaners at the Bar who had not been disciplined, although guilty of serious crimes committed to achieve political objectives. Among these he listed the minister of justice, who, as a member of the Ossewa Brandwag, engaged in pro-Nazi activities.

Some of us thought of requisitioning a special general meeting of the Bar to reverse the council's decision. Our seniors, among them some of Bram's close friends, strongly advised against it. They predicted an overwhelming majority would rally behind the council. Bram wrote letters to Harold Hanson and William Aronsohn explaining his motives in greater depth. He also complained about the council's indecent haste and its failure to let him put his case.

In the media Bram became a phantom. He was 'seen' in various places both within and outside South Africa. Letters posted supposedly by him lent credence to the reports. As weeks and then months went by, senior police officers also gave weight to the stories that he was out of the country. Otherwise their thorough investigations would have led to his arrest. For the majority of whites he was a traitor. But for the vast majority of the country's people he was a hero, a worthy successor of Nelson Mandela and Walter Sisulu to lead the underground struggle for freedom.

When I visited Nelson one of the first questions he asked was whether 'the short one' was still at large? We were using our usual cryptic method of communicating. I gave the thumbs-up sign below the level of the table out of sight of the vigilant warder. Nelson, assuming that I must have some contact with him, wanted me to convey the support of those on the island and their gratitude. There was no doubt that Bram was repairing the pre-Rivonia structures, fractured by the arrests and subsequent trials.

In the meantime the Bar Council's application to strike him off the roll was taking its course. Notices were published, calling upon 'Abram Fischer, male, Queen's Counsel, formerly residing at Beaumont Street, Oaklands, Johannesburg, but whose present whereabouts are unknown ...' and inviting him to appoint attorneys, indicate his intention to oppose the application, and file documentation.

Astonishingly, Bram did all three by writing letters and surreptitiously having them delivered. His case was argued by Arthur Chaskalson and Sydney Kentridge sc. Judge President Quartus de Wet heard the application. Bram was struck off the roll early in November 1965, for 'dishonourable and deplorable' conduct. The judge said, 'We are concerned with the laws in force at the present time and with the structure of the society as it exists in this country at the present time'.

Bram remained underground almost nine months. His arrest was not the result of conventional methods of investigation, but rather the torture and interrogation of his comrades. Although detention without trial for ninety days had been of great assistance to the State, it was not long enough. In addition, the charade of releasing and re-detaining detainees on their eighty-ninth day of detention was clumsy. The Act was amended, increasing detention to a hundred and eighty days. To quieten critics who complained that there were no regulations to protect detainees, provision was made that the minister would promulgate regulations in the *Government Gazette*.

Issy Heymann was a dedicated communist. He had given undetected assistance to many people who had to flee the country and was an invaluable contact for those who came back to work underground. Heymann was deliberately excluded from Bram's plans and he chose to remain ignorant of Bram's whereabouts lest he be detained, break down under torture and unwittingly lead the police to Bram, a man he considered a close friend and a hero of the struggle.

Issy was detained after the arrest of Michael Dingake, a senior member of Umkhonto. Issy's wife Anne came to my office with her attorney Ruth Hayman, to whom Joel Joffe, by then in self-imposed exile, had left the remnants of his practice. We looked at the newly promulgated hundred-and-eighty-day detention clause. Anne was anxious about her husband's safety, given the notorious practices of his captors. People – even those who were politically aware – still often found it difficult to accept that the jurisdiction of the courts had been ousted and that lawyers could do little to help in such matters. Despite his assurances about the protective regulations, the minister had never published them. This gave us the basis for a habeas corpus application for Issy's release.

I approached Namie Phillips, a senior member of my group, to lead me the next day in our application, hoping that his stature and unquestionable professional integrity would persuade the court. His pessimism and reluctance to become involved in controversial cases were legendary, but once he agreed, his enthusiasm often surpassed that of those emotionally committed to the cause. He had been hurt by a regional magistrate's criticism when he successfully defended the own-ers of the property where Arthur Goldreich and Harold Wolpe lived after their post-Rivonia escape. Consequently he was reluctant to be involved in yet another case in which the conduct of the police and their minister would be questioned. Nevertheless we took the draft application to his home.

Sitting in his study, he questioned the prospect of success, repeatedly testing various responses to possible questions. His wife Joan, who was reading in the lounge, could hear our discussion. When he asked for the umpteenth time what to say to a particular question, Joan loudly answered, 'You must say what he has been telling you for almost two hours!' Namie, with a faint smile, said, 'Very well, let Anne sign it; serve it as soon as you can tomorrow morning and set it down for two p.m.'

It occurred to me in the small hours of the morning that the application should be served as early as possible to avoid a postponement. Any delay would allow the police to publish regulations which would defeat the application. I telephoned Ruth at five a.m. with my suggestion. (In due course it became clear that the security police were taping my conversations. From this one they inferred that I was trying to prevent the capture of Bram Fischer. They were convinced that I knew where he was and was actively involved with him.)

We arrived in court at two p.m. The application was to be heard in Court A, reserved for appeals and reviews, and heard by Senior Judge Bresler and the recently appointed Judge Gee Kotze, who'd vouched for Bram's integrity at his bail hearing. That there were two judges implied that the matter was considered of importance and in the public interest. The minister, the attorney-general, the commissioner of police and the station commander were represented by Henry Moll, soon to be appointed a judge of the Supreme Court and later the judge president.

Namie Phillips asked Moll if the government conceded that no regulations had been promulgated. Moll agreed that they had not. Namie briefly but forcefully outlined the nature of the application and submitted that there was no answer to an order being granted for the immediate release of Heymann. Indeed Moll couldn't answer our attack on the validity of Heymann's detention without trial, so he sought his argument elsewhere. He informed the court that Bram had been arrested, that Ruth Hayman and I had been told of this at the police station, that the police had invited both of us to see our client, but that we had refused. I was outraged and I blurted out, 'That's a lie!' I had not even gone to the police station. Moll told the judges that it was not proper for me to interrupt him. The judges agreed, but asked if affidavits supporting Moll's submissions would be filed. An adjournment was called.

During the break, the enormous Colonel van Niekerk, head of the security police interrogation and investigative unit, put his outsized hand on my shoulder. I should be careful what I said about the police and I should control my temper, he advised. After the adjournment, Moll informed the court that there had been a 'misunderstanding'. No offer had been made, nor had such a conversation taken place. He offered no apology, nor was there an explanation as to how the mistake had come about.

The judges made an order that Heymann be released immediately. This was hurriedly prepared and given to the sheriff to serve on the commander of the police station. Neither the senior police officers nor their counsel offered to phone to secure his release.

When the sheriff arrived with the order, he learned that Heymann had been transferred for investigations. No one knew the destination. He would be released on his return, the sheriff was assured. That evening, Heymann's wife Anne was told that regulations had been promulgated in an extraordinary *Government Gazette*. Consequently, the moment he returned to the police station with the investigating officer, he was detained for a hundred and eighty days in terms of the Act and the regulations. Later, the court expressed disapproval of the process and ordered the police to pay attorney and client costs, a pyrrhic victory. We had no answer to their chicanery or their lies, although these were reported in the media. Then again, few cared about the way the police abused power and brought the administration of justice into disrepute.

On the morning of 12 November 1965, as I approached the first set of traffic lights no more than a kilometre away from my home, the posters of both the *Rand Daily Mail* and *Die Transvaler* announced the arrest of Bram Fischer. I stalled the car. Those behind hooted while I beckoned a newspaper vendor. On the front page of the *Rand Daily Mail* was a large photograph of Bram in disguise being held firmly on the elbow by the most notorious torturer in the security police, Captain Swanepoel. A report gave the police account of the arrest, together with praise for the hard work and effective methods of investigation used by the investigating officers.

Four days earlier, instructed by attorneys Hayman and Aronsohn, I had started the case of Fuzile and others in the main criminal court in Johannesburg. It was a trial garnering publicity and required my focused attention. I needed badly to talk with friends about Bram's arrest but there was no time. In the cells where I consulted with my clients, I placed the two newspapers on the rickety table and Fuzile and his co-accused shook their heads in despair. None of us felt inclined to discuss their case.

Eventually the white court orderly announced that the session was about to start. I folded the newspapers, put them in my bag and followed him up the stairs into the courtroom through the dock. The investigating officer, the interpreter and a number of black spectators had already taken their seats.

I spotted Arthur Chaskalson alone in a corner at the back of the court and we were able to talk briefly about Bram's arrest. He urged me to continue with the case and to control my sadness and despondency. Along with senior members of the Bar, he believed that Bram would be detained incommunicado and tortured. The security police would want to know his underground contacts. Arthur had been briefed by William Aronsohn to visit Bram at Ilse's request.

Shortly before the mid-morning adjournment a triumphant Captain Swanepoel entered the court. He took a seat directly behind me while I conducted a cross-examination. The moment the judge announced an adjournment, chief interpreter van Wyk rushed across the court, took Swanepoel's hand and shook it vigorously, saying, *'Mooi werk, Kaptein. Ons land Suid Afrika is nou weer skoon'* – Nice work, Captain. Our country South Africa is clean again.

Arthur Chaskalson was summoned to see General Hendrik van den Bergh. From him he learned that Bram was not being detained for interrogation. As an awaiting-trial prisoner, he was being held at the Pretoria Local Prison and would appear on Monday in Johannesburg, then be remanded for further investigation.

Although the general was curious how Arthur knew that Bram wanted to see him, he sanctioned the visit. Bram was as well as could be expected, and wanted to see me as soon as possible.

Chief Warder Breedt, with whom I had a reasonably good relationship, wasn't pleased when I arrived to see Bram on the Saturday morning. I would have to wait as Bram was in the exercise yard. I walked into the room where the Rivonia trial consultations had taken place. I looked into the yard, the yard where Jopie Fourie was executed. Bram was under the shower, still sporting the goatee of his disguise. I felt embarrassed watching him and moved away from the window. When I glanced out again, he was trying to wipe himself dry with the palms of his hands before he used a prison 'towel', not twice the size of a handkerchief.

Soon afterwards Breedt brought him to the room, and stood in the doorway to observe us. We knew that somewhere a tape-recorder was running. In my list of distressing meetings, beginning with my first visit to Nelson on Robben Island, that Saturday morning with Bram features near the top. There is nothing worse than seeing a friend in distress. To this day I am amazed at my lack of understanding of Bram's feelings.

In typical fashion, he asked after Arethe, my mother and our children. Then he mentioned that his greatest worry was Paul's health. He hoped that Paul's stay in England with Ruth and Anthony had been beneficial despite the English weather. Had I seen Paul? How was he? I told him that the English doctor had inferred that Paul's health had been neglected. Bram coloured with anger. 'Neglected? What does he know?' Didn't the doctor know how much time Molly spent with Paul? Did this doctor know how much love and care the whole family gave Paul? How did he think Paul had lived so many more than the ten years originally predicted? 'Neglected indeed!'

When his indignation subsided, Bram asked about Ilse and Pat Davidson. He had missed them during his nine months underground, and said so loudly for the benefit of the tape-recorder. This would also corroborate their protestations that they had no contact with Bram, should it be necessary.

Understandably, Bram was bitter about the Bar Council's decision. How could they have applied to court to have him removed from the roll of advocates? Their actions baffled him. However, he was grateful for the efforts of Namie Phillips and Ruth Hayman, for our attempt (albeit unsuccessful) to have Issy Heymann released. He knew how much torture Issy had withstood before breaking down. And although Issy didn't know where Bram was hiding, he put the security police onto Violet Weinberg. Under torture, Violet cracked before Bram could change his hiding place. In the aftermath, Issy attempted suicide as he battled with having disclosed Violet's key role. Bram asked me to tell them all that he admired their integrity and loyalty. He fully understood what had happened and would never blame them. Their dedication to the struggle was well known and no one was responsible. That he had managed to stay at liberty for nine months was a bonus as he had expected the police to find him within three months.

Then, thoughtlessly, I asked him if giving up his family, his practice and his freedom had been worthwhile? He stared at me in anger, hurt and disappointed. 'George, did you ask Nelson Mandela the same question? He too had a practice, a family and loved freedom. Did you ask Walter Sisulu or Govan Mbeki?' 'No Bram,' I replied, 'I had not thought of asking them that question.' 'Well, then, don't ask it of me.' I bowed my head in shame.

Bram quickly changed the subject: 'How is your practice? Has it suffered as a result of the political work?' Surprisingly it had not. Not only were most of the attorneys who briefed me before the Rivonia trial doing so again, but large, reputable firms were offering me well-paid work. I was earning more than R1 000 a month.

After a long pause Bram hesitantly asked if I would take his case. I put my hand on his wrist. Yes, of course I would, but surely he deserved more senior members of the Bar? I would insist on being led by Harold Hanson. 'No, not Harold,' protested Bram. 'He has done more than enough for me, and he may be embarrassed that I wrote the letter to him to be handed up to the magistrate.' Did I think that Sydney Kentridge would be prepared to lead? I knew that he and Arthur Chaskalson were livid at the Bar Council's actions at striking Bram from the roll. I left him with the assurance that I would ask Arthur to speak to Sydney.

The short visits allowed to members of Bram's family and Pat Davidson, who had grown close to him, were frustrating. For one thing they were too brief for meaningful discussions, and there was always the presence of the prison warder. In the hopes of filling a void, I visited the family regularly, both before and after my visits to Bram.

Meanwhile I called on JH Liebenberg, the prosecutor, to ascertain the process. The evidence led at the trial from which Fischer absconded was to be converted into a preparatory examination. I also learned that they required time to investigate the additional crimes of sabotage and other offences that Bram had committed while underground. Consequently, they wouldn't be ready until mid-January 1966.

For the summer holiday break, I had booked a house at Plettenberg Bay and seats on the train. In those days Plettenberg Bay was not the fashionable playground of the rich it has become. It was a small village to which Bram, Molly and their children had often gone for their summer holidays. Bram and Molly introduced us to the resort town and we'd holidayed there with them four years previously. Lookout Beach reminded me of the beach near my home village where I had swum twenty-five years earlier. It was on Lookout Beach, too, that I met Bram's brothers, Paul and Gustav, and their families. In return for their hospitality, we had prepared a lamb on the spit. For them it was a novel treat and for a few years the Plettenberg holiday became an annual event. The Rivonia arrests and their aftermath prevented us from taking a holiday at the end of 1964, and with the current circumstances I was inclined to cancel my arrangements. Bram would have none of it. I was to go there on holiday.

While walking on the beach a few weeks later, I was startled to hear Bram's voice behind me. Various possibilities flashed through my mind. Had he escaped? Had he been admitted to bail? Was I hallucinating? I spun round. It was one of his brothers speaking with an accent and tone common to the three of them. He did not notice me as I stood, almost numb, my head half turned away, my eyes focused beyond the breaking waves.

Every day of that holiday I was reminded that Bram was in prison. Before I'd left for the coast he had asked for a copy of Nelson Mandela's Rivonia statement, some of the notes made by us of the evidence and arguments in that trial and a few of the exhibits. He also had at his disposal a senior articled clerk from the firm of Friedland, Mansell and Lewis who would also liaise with Ilse and Paul. I should also mention that a number of senior attorneys offered to act for him, including Bell, Dewar & Hall and Willy Aronsohn – all without charging a fee.

Arthur would also have been in the case had he not been defending Chief Warder Theron, who faced numerous charges arising out of a lengthy statement he had made under oath and published in the *Rand Daily Mail*, exposing serious malpractices in jail. Arthur offered to give up Theron's trial, but Bram felt it important that he continue.

I felt easier going on holiday once I knew Arthur would be available during the court recess to visit Bram regularly and discuss aspects of his defence. He also took an active part during the preparation appearance in court when the Theron trial was not in session.

I returned from holiday at the end of the first week of January. Most of my time was now spent with Bram. He appeared at peace with himself. He had had good visits with members of his family, a few colleagues and particularly Arthur. Much of the time he read various accounts of the Boer War, as well as commentaries on the rise of fascism after the First World War. He had also been rereading Karl Marx's *Das Kapital*, the Communist Manifesto and the Programme of the

Communist Party of South Africa, subtitled The Road to South Africa's Freedom. This document had been handed in as an exhibit at the Rivonia trial. He was pleasantly surprised that the security police allowed such material into prison. He had clearly spent time poring over Nelson's statement and the notes of Walter Sisulu and Govan Mbeki, and underscored portions of these.

Bram found it painful discussing his case. He had been arrested on the eve of moving to a new secret house and the documents the police found, the evidence already led before he went underground and his public statements would be enough to convict him of sabotage. He had decided against going into the witness box, but would follow Nelson's example and make a statement from the dock. This statement he wanted to discuss in detail. A major point, I felt, was for him to explain his intentions in delivering a statement, which would forestall any criticism from the judge.

This section eventually read:

And I wish to emphasise that I [speak] from the dock and not from the witness box, not because I fear cross-examination on these matters. I would in fact welcome nothing more than to discuss the subject, but I know that cross-examination must go further and must involve others who may or may not have been associated with me in my work. In the long series of political trials which this country has experienced in recent years, brave men and women have refused to testify against their friends and have accepted long prison sentences rather than do so.

In this very case, Mrs Lesley Schermbrucker, whose husband is already serving a five-year sentence for his political ideals, provides an outstanding example of that courage. She was prepared to sacrifice herself and the happiness of their two young children rather than give evidence. I ask the court to consider my position in the light of such conduct.

I will not go into the witness box and prevaricate or lie. I cannot go into the witness box and answer questions that might implicate others. There is only one alternative therefore which is open to me. That is to make my statement from the dock. I know that it is possible for this court to draw adverse inferences from my failure to go into the witness box. In the circumstances I cannot avoid that possible consequence. In no circumstances, whatsoever the consequences to me personally may be, would I myself be a State witness. I cannot even allow myself to be put in the position of informing on others, whether directly or indirectly, whether by answering or by refusing to answer questions.

We spent hours debating the morality of civil disobedience and revolt. Bram was still deeply wounded by the Bar's action and the court's judgment that his conduct was dishonourable. He wanted assurance that he was right and they were wrong. Was Mahatma Gandhi wrong? What about George Washington? Cromwell? Those who sacked the Bastille, who revolted against the Tsar or conspired to kill Hitler? What about the Xhosas, the Zulus and the Boers who fought against British colonialism?

What did the ancient teachers of ethics say about this? He knew that I was fond of quoting the Greeks. We discussed the case of Socrates. The philosopher had accepted his conviction and death sentence and had refused an offer by his pupils to help him escape. His reasoning had been that they lived in a constitutional state (although this was cold comfort to slaves in that society) and he had been convicted by a majority of his peers in a public trial. Of course we do not know what Socrates might have said had he lived under a tyrannical government and as far as I knew he had never pronounced upon the morality of a revolt by slaves against their masters.

Bram pressed further. Did any of the ancients have anything to say about the use of violence or other serious crimes? Yes, Aeschylus considered the case of Prometheus and concluded that he had committed the first just crime in stealing the splendour of fire from the gods for the benefit of the mortals.

In his final statement Bram argued:

I accept the general rule that for the protection of a society laws must be obeyed. But when laws themselves become immoral and require the citizen to take part in an organised system of oppression – if only by his silence or apathy – then I believe that a higher duty arises. This compels one to refuse to recognise such laws. The laws under which I am being prosecuted were enacted by a wholly unrepresentative body, a body in which three-quarters of the people of this country have no voice whatever. These laws were enacted not to prevent the spread of communism, but for the purpose of silencing the opposition of the large majority of our citizens to a government intent upon depriving them, solely on account of their colour, of the most elementary human rights: of the right to freedom and happiness, the right to live together with their families wherever they might choose, to earn their livelihoods to the best of their abilities, to rear and educate their children in a civilised fashion, to take part in the administration of their country and obtain a fair share of the wealth of their produce; in short, to live as human beings.

Bram wanted to explain not only to the judge but to the rest of South Africa and beyond, that there was no inconsistency for one born and bred into Afrikaner nationalism to become a communist. His grandfather, a lawyer, legal advisor and confidant to the president of one of the Boer republics, had fought against great odds to save his country from British imperialism. Finally, after a scorched-earth policy destroyed their farms, and their women and children had been interned in concentration camps, the Boers capitulated. Conflict within the Afrikaners did not end there. Some accepted British rule, others remained rebels at heart. With the advent of the First World War, a rebellion occurred that led to arrests, imprisonment, and for Jopie Fourie execution. In turn, he became a hero of Afrikaner nationalism.

Bram was seven years old when the revolt occurred. His father, a member of the Bar, held the rebel leaders in great esteem. Although he did not actively take part in the revolt, he acted as counsel for many of them. Bram remembered going with his mother to the Bloemfontein prison to take food to the awaiting-trial prisoners. He recalled his father's anger that a judge could send burghers to prison for three years or more for doing what they considered their patriotic duty.

Towards the end of January, Bram was brought from Pretoria to Johannesburg for the preparatory examination in the magistrate's court. Some of his friends, those not yet jailed, banned or forced into exile, and some students from the university filled the segregated public gallery. The entrance for the prosecutor, lawyers and witnesses was congested by well-dressed security policemen sporting trendy hairstyles. They glared at me. I ignored them, entered the empty dock and went down the stairs to see Bram.

I gave him the morning newspaper, although his guards queried my right to do this. I brushed them aside. Bram scanned the headlines. We engaged in small talk, avoiding any speculation about what new evidence the prosecution might lead. Shortly before the hearing began I returned to the court and took my place. Then Bram climbed the stairs from the cells to the dock, and as his head appeared, most people in the gallery stood up. Uniformed policemen lined the gap between the dock and the spectators' barrier. No one was allowed to speak to him or shake his hand, not even his daughter Ilse.

The prosecutor handed in a glossy album of photographs of co-conspirators and others who would be identified by the witnesses. His assistant placed a copy in front of me. Anxiously, I flipped through the pages and came across a post-card-sized photograph of myself. Mindful that I was probably being watched by the security policemen now sitting on the side benches in the well of the court, I kept on turning the pages.

I waited until the mid-morning adjournment before revealing my discovery to Bram. He was furious. We should take up the matter with the magistrate and demand an explanation from the prosecutor. He predicted that some witness must have been compelled to make false statements that we had met while he was underground. Clearly their intention was to embarrass me and other lawyers who defended those committed to the struggle. In the end we left the matter in abeyance until I could gain further advice from our friends at the Bar. Ultimately I let the issue rest. No witness referred to me, nor did anyone ask or explain why my photograph was in the album. I decided it was intended to increase my stress, and it succeeded in reactivating the duodenal ulcer for which I regularly sucked antacid tablets, even while court was in session.

The State regularly called close friends and relatives of an accused into the witness box, even though their innocuous evidence was unnecessary for the purposes of the case. This strategy was devised in the hope that relatives would refuse and thus earn themselves a few years of imprisonment under newly enacted legislation. I feared that Violet Weinberg, Lesley Schermbrucker, Issy Heymann and others who'd assisted Bram in his underground work could be called, as well as those such as Ilse, her close friend Sholto Cross and Pat Davidson. These three had met with Bram while he was in hiding, not to 'further the conspiracy' in the words of the prosecution, but because they were his family or friends.

The former group were expected to refuse to give evidence. This was partly out of loyalty and partly because the prosecution's ploy was to make public the names of others involved. If confronted by any statement they might have made in detention, their plan was to tell of the brutal methods used by the police to extract such statements. As to the second group, what purpose would be served if they disclosed that they surreptitiously met for coffee, a picnic in a park or a ride in the countryside?

Bram accepted the distinction, but was concerned that some members of the struggle might not understand why those close to him gave evidence. Sholto Cross was expected to be called. I told him that although the decision was his own, no one would blame him for giving evidence. Whatever he said did not advance the case against Bram, nor would it betray anyone else in the struggle. He later told me that the investigating officer had asked whether he would keep to his statement. His affirmative answer upset the officer. 'Then come with me, you fucking coward,' he shouted, thrusting Sholto into the courtroom. He no doubt hoped that the insult would change Sholto's mind and send him to prison. Although obviously uncomfortable, Sholto related what had been said at a couple of meetings with Bram. Their conversations had been entirely of a personal and social nature.

The police had a particular reason to hate Sholto. He withstood a rigorous interrogation, insisting that neither he nor Ilse had had any contact with Bram. This led the police to believe that Bram was out of the country. For surely he would have contacted his daughter otherwise? Sholto told the magistrate that he had no relevant evidence and that he was convinced he was called merely because he was Ilse's fiancé. He believed the police wanted to embarrass him and hurt her and her father by getting him to give evidence. In answer to a couple of loosely formulated questions, he said Bram had gone underground as a service to his country. When asked why he did not contact the police about Bram's planned meetings with his daughter, Sholto replied that he had no moral right to inform on them.

Lesley Schermbrucker's counsel told me she refused to give evidence despite facing imprisonment and risking charges for sabotage and furthering the aims of communism. Her decision was final, but would I ask Bram for his opinion. Bram was almost reduced to tears. The liberation movement's policy was clear: there would be no consent for those involved in the struggle. If he said yes and Lesley decided to give evidence, she would regret it for the rest of her life, as would her husband, Ivan, who was already serving a term of imprisonment. He felt for both of them and their children, but the decision had to be Lesley's. Bram added that if she did give evidence he would understand.

She walked into the witness box in a determined and defiant mood. Her detention in solitary confinement had not affected her courage or her radiance. She looked neither at the magistrate, nor the prosecutor, nor at her interrogator who sat behind the prosecutor and directly opposite her. Instead, she faced Bram in the dock, acknowledged Ilse, Pat and other friends sitting behind him. Her face lit up with the broadest of smiles. She told the magistrate she would not give evidence. 'I don't wish to be disrespectful and I don't want to go to jail, but it is a question of principle. I am prepared to take the consequences.'

She was sentenced to three days' imprisonment. If she changed her mind, her sentence might be remitted. Lesley looked at the gallery and audibly told her teenage daughter, Jill, sitting next to Ruth and Ilse, not to worry. Then she smiled again at Bram. She never did come back to testify. Violet Weinberg later followed the same route.

Even generally truthful and honest people sometimes distort the facts in political trials taking place in unjust societies. June Middleton had a farm near the semi-rural town of Rustenburg. From time to time she took in lodgers and had taken in a Mr Thompson, who was brought to her farm by a young man she did not know. The young man told her that Mr Thompson wanted a quiet period as his wife had recently died. He had kept to himself. Neither she nor her domestic helper, nor her gardener had ever heard of Bram Fischer. She did not see Mr Thompson behaving in a strange way and he left after six weeks without telling her where he was going. In those six weeks she somehow managed not to notice that Mr Thompson's appearance was completely transformed. Nor could she see Mr Thompson in court. Nor could one of her assistants, despite repeated prompting from the prosecutor. When the witness left the box would he carefully look around to see if the man who had come to the farm was in court? I objected: 'Your Worship, there comes a time when a person leading a witness has to give up.' Although the prosecutor was alone in not being amused, he called it a day.

To support the fraud charges against Bram, many witnesses were called to give evidence and produce documents that Bram had opened bank accounts in the false names of Douglas Black and Peter West. Bram passed me a note not to cross-examine them. The police gave evidence of documents found in the house where Bram stayed, including correspondence in easily decipherable cryptography. These contained sufficient information to convict him of taking part in the activities of Umkhonto we Sizwe and the central committee of the Communist Party, both within South Africa and outside its borders.

The structures and rules of the underground movement were designed to limit the number of people exposed should there be an infiltration or breach of security. It was considered well-nigh impossible that regional or national leaders would betray each other, or that the structures could be infiltrated. Bruno Mtolo and Abel Mtembu in the Rivonia trial and Piet Beyleveld and Gerard Ludi clearly showed that both assumptions were wrong. Detention, solitary confinement, torture, greater security police efficiency and electronic surveillance made practically everyone vulnerable at all levels.

When the prosecutor announced that the next witness would be Bartholomew Hlopane, Bram was devastated. It demonstrated the disintegration of the party. Hlopane had been a member of the party for many years and was on its central committee from 1962, yet he was now to give evidence of its inner workings.

Bram's disillusionment turned to anger when it emerged that some of Hlopane's evidence were no more than a repetition of what Bruno Mtolo had said in the Rivonia trial. The essence of this was that the Communist Party was in control of both the ANC and Umkhonto we Sizwe. Hlopane also gave details of incidents intended to cast Bram as a supporter of unbridled violence, intemperate and foul tongued. Although Bram would not deny his membership of the central committee of the Communist Party, he challenged the correctness of sections of Hlopane's evidence, and denied any involvement in the activities of the Christian Institute and its director Dr Beyers Naude, the Defence and Aid Fund and the Institute of Race Relations. These were innuendoes the State was keen to put about.

We decided that since Bram would be committed for trial irrespective of what he might say in his intended statement from the dock, that statement would be reserved for the end of his trial. At the time, an accused had the right, at the end of a preparatory examination, to opt for trial by a jury or a judge. Such a jury would have consisted of nine white men picked by the sheriff from the all-white electoral roll. I always thought that, no matter how bad some judges might be, nine 'first class' citizens would be worse. Under these circumstances we did not elect trial by jury. Bram was duly committed for trial. He faced a main count of sabotage and fourteen other charges.

During the course of the preparatory examination a senior colleague, Fred Zwarenstein, came to my chambers and, to escape the bugging devices, we took a walk in the passage. While with clients in the cells of the magistrate's court he learned that a small group of white awaiting-trial prisoners were making arrangements for Bram's escape. They were desperadoes probably collaborating with the security police to discredit Bram or even to kill him in the attempted escape. From Bram I discovered that he had been befriended by a man charged with fraud. This man had talked of helping Bram escape. It was curious that the security police rule of contact between common-law prisoners and political prisoners had suddenly been broken. We agreed that it was probably a trap.

We had about a month to work on Bram's statement before the trial opened in Pretoria with Sydney Kentridge leading me. Incensed by Hlopane's derogatory propaganda against Marxism and communism and at the distorted picture he painted of the Communist Party's role in South Africa, Bram decided to put the record straight, even though it would neither influence the trial nor mitigate his sentence. He added the words:

In my mind there remain two clear reasons for my approach to the Communist Party. The one is the glaring injustice which exists and has existed for a long time in South African society; the other, a gradual realisation as I became more and more deeply involved with the Congress Movement of those years (that is, the movement for freedom and equal human rights for all), that it was always members of the Communist Party who seemed prepared, regardless of cost, to sacrifice most; to give of their best; to face the greatest dangers, in the struggle against poverty and discrimination.

He described his early years playing with African children on the farm without regard to the difference in the colour of their skin. Then how later his attitude changed as he subconsciously developed an antagonism towards black people for which he could find no rational basis. When he and a few friends started literacy classes in the locations, he came to understand that:

> … colour prejudice was a wholly irrational phenomenon and that true human friendship could extend across the colour bar once the initial prejudice was overcome. And that I think was lesson number one on my way to the Communist Party which has always refused to accept any colour bar and has always stood firm in the belief, itself 2 000 years old, of the eventual brotherhood of all men.

He spoke of sacrifices made by communists, black and white, who lost their jobs, their homes, their freedom of movement and who were separated from their families. He reminded the court that:

> … at that stage, and for many years afterwards, the Communist Party was the only political party which stood for an extension of the franchise. To this day, the elimination of discrimination and the granting of all normal human rights remain its chief objective … It is the objective for which I have lived and worked for nearly 30 years. But I have to tell this court not only why I joined the Communist Party when it was a legal party … I must also explain why I continued to be a member after it was declared illegal. This involves what I believe on the one hand to be the gravely dangerous situation which has been created in South Africa from about 1950 onwards and, on the other, the vital contribution which socialist thought can make towards its solution.

Bram had written lengthy paragraphs on Marxist principles and the role of capitalism in South Africa. Sydney and I had some misgivings – we were concerned that the judge might interrupt Bram on the basis that his speech was furthering the aims of communism, expressly prohibited by the Suppression of Communism Act. We asked what he would say to the judge in this instance. His ready answer came in the form of a question:

> Is one not entitled to defend oneself and one's party when both are insulted, defamed and accused of false motives, as the prosecution, aided and abetted by the turncoat Hlopane, is doing?

Bram had obviously not lost his sharp legal mind.

Applying the principles he had set out, he concluded that fear and racialism were the main causes of the grave situation that the country was facing.

Damningly he blamed his fellow Afrikaners for the situation in the country, warning that it was creating a 'deep-rooted hatred' of Afrikaners. He concluded poignantly:

> It was to keep faith with all those dispossessed by apartheid that I broke my undertaking to the court; separated myself from my family; pretended I was someone else; and accepted the life of a fugitive. I owed it to the political prisoners, to the banished, to the silenced and those under house arrest, not to remain a spectator but to act. I knew what they expected of me and I did it. I felt responsible not to those who are indifferent to the sufferings of others, but to those who are concerned. I knew that by valuing above all their judgment, I would be condemned by people who are content to see themselves as respectable and loyal citizens. I cannot regret any condemnation that may follow me.

Sydney Kentridge, having read the preparatory examination record, spent time with Bram identifying the evidence in contention. He concluded that there was sufficient evidence to convict Bram on the fifteen charges, particularly the main count of sabotage. This being the case, he faced life imprisonment. None of this was news to Bram. Clearly there was no need for a lengthy trial. What he wanted to put in issue was the false evidence led at the preparatory examination. Whatever our innermost fears, no mention was made of the possibility of a death sentence.

The trial opened towards the end of March 1966 in the court where Bram had appeared as lead counsel for Nelson Mandela and the others. Uniformed policemen stood on the street corners and in Paul Kruger Square, although they were fewer in number than at the Rivonia trial. The court was packed with more spectators than could be accommodated.

I found Bram sitting alone in the large, dimly lit cell below the court. Once the trial started, he sat alone in a dock specially built for twelve. He waved to family and close friends. The prosecutors, JH Liebenberg and Klaus von Lieres und Wilkau sat where Percy Yutar had sat during the Rivonia trial. Sydney Kentridge, Arthur Chaskalson and I were in the seats once occupied by Bram Fischer and Vernon Berrangé. Justice Wes Boshoff presided. He entered the court, and Liebenberg opened the proceedings, giving the impression that this was the beginning of an ordinary trial. Bram pleaded not guilty.

Bartholomew Hlopane was intended to outdo Bruno Mtolo, the 'Mr X' of the Rivonia trial. It soon became clear that the security police had programmed

Hlopane to contradict the evidence of Walter Sisulu and others in the Rivonia trial. In particular, he was to challenge the testimony that Operation Mayibuye was contentious. This would allow the prosecution to argue that Judge President Quartus de Wet's finding was wrong. Hlopane said that the plan was presented to the Communist Party central committee by Joe Slovo, and approved. The National High Command of Umkhonto we Sizwe had also approved it. As treasurer, Bram's task was to find money to fund Operation Mayibuye. He also suggested targets, implying that precautionary measures to avoid loss of life had been discarded.

Then I was struck by a most disturbing thought. Either this was part of a propaganda campaign to discredit the liberation movement, or it was more sinister? Was this evidence being led to allow Judge Boshoff, much closer to apartheid ideology than Judge President de Wet, to impose a death sentence? The thought was so frightening that I dared not speak of it.

Sydney Kentridge is a great advocate and cross-examiner, and although handicapped by Bram's decision not to give evidence in the witness box, he nevertheless showed that Hlopane's newly contrived evidence was false. Hlopane's explanations about why it had not been mentioned in the preparatory hearing were unbelievable. Much of the evidence, particularly the allegation that the Communist Party controlled the ANC, was denied by Piet Beyleveld. He gave evidence in the original trial and was again called after Hlopane. Sydney skilfully established one important contradiction after another. We were confident that an objective judge would reject Hlopane's evidence. We did not dispute seriously the evidence of other witnesses. Mostly they were confined to such technical details as contraventions of statutory provisions relating to the opening of bank accounts and obtaining a passport and a driver's licence in a false name. Gerard Ludi's evidence about Bram's membership of the Communist Party was not challenged, and the State's case was over after a few days.

In the meantime, Bram changed his statement, specially to deal with Hlopane's false evidence. In delivering it, he was also at pains to state that he wanted democracy for South Africa, and real equality and justice for all. And he fervently believed it could be achieved non-violently.

All the conduct, My Lord, with which I have been charged, has been directed towards maintaining contact and understanding between the races of this country. If one day it may help to establish a bridge across which white leaders and the real leaders of the non-whites can meet to settle the destinies of all of us by negotiation, and not by force of arms, I shall be able to bear with fortitude any sentence which this court may impose on me. It will be a fortitude,

My Lord, strengthened by this knowledge at least, that for the past 25 years I have taken no part, not even by passive acceptance, in that hideous system of discrimination which you have erected in this country, and which has become a by-word in the civilised world.

Once Bram had given his statement, Sydney conceded the main charges against our client but argued that the counts of fraud and forgery were ancillary, probably intended to discredit and belittle him. Hlopane's evidence was disposed of as contradictory and improbable, particularly as it was contradicted by another State witness, Piet Beyleveld. It was further suspect as it had been extracted from him in detention.

We thought that the judge might reserve his decision for a day or two to formulate his judgment. Inexplicably, he wanted six weeks to study the evidence and the documents.

Bram's statement from the dock made headlines throughout the world, despite attempts by the authorities to prevent its distribution. Declarations of protest and support poured in to the family and others. Pressure grew for his name to be included in the UN's October 1963 call for the release of all political prisoners.

We regularly visited Bram to buoy up his spirits. He had come to terms with his situation, and his main concerns were now about his children. Eventually the six weeks ended. Again we went to court, this time to hear Bram convicted on all counts. His Lordship had reasons for accepting Hlopane's evidence. This was not surprising, considering that Boshoff had technically already convicted Bram in the Little Rivonia trial. (Three days earlier, and much to his elation, Bram had been awarded the Soviet Union's Lenin Peace Prize.)

In mitigation of sentence, Sydney emphasised aspects of Bram's speech from the dock. Judge Boshoff took another four days to formulate a learned judgment on the purpose of punishment before sentencing Bram to life imprisonment for sabotage, twenty-four years for his participation in the affairs of the Communist Party and small fines for the other counts. Shortly before sentence was passed, Bram gave me a letter:

Pretoria Prison
3/5/66

Dearest George,

I know I shall be seeing you tomorrow and probably on other occasions thereafter, but I should like to spend a moment this evening saying one or two of the things that are normally reserved for the end of a man's life when it is no longer possible for him to hear what is being said.

Perhaps I can best explain what I really want to say by telling you what the children say – if you'll keep it to yourself. They are deeply grateful to many friends who have rallied round and helped them through this trying period. And they say so. But they add: George is the man with real understanding.

And George, that's how you've helped me most in all this case. In saying this, I'm not overlooking the fact that the one truly masterly paragraph was yours – the paragraph that will live if any single one does. But all through it you've always understood the whole field of battle and you have not only controlled that but also found time to nurse the pain of my family with such skill and sympathy.

There are a few events that happen to one and that one carries through life. I shall never forget your offer to give up your Xmas holiday in order to be able to visit me!

You must look after yourself and keep fit. You have so much important work to do. From the place of safety which I have now reached I shall be holding thumbs for you all the time.

My love to the children, but especially to Arethe and your mother.

Bram

As his counsel I was allowed to see Bram in prison. Of course the warders insisted on their right to listen to our conversations confined to family matters. I visited his family regularly and brought him their news. He was particularly concerned about Paul, who was chronically ill. Shortly after the trial Ilse married Tim Wilson and the couple came to see him, as did the Wilson family. Yet he wanted my reassurance that Ilse would be happy. To my positive response, he said, 'George, I know you only too well. You sometimes say things to comfort me. I want you to tell me why you think that it is a good marriage.' I thought for a moment. 'Bram, do you think a lesser man would have led your Ilse down the aisle to the altar of an Anglican Church?' He put the palm of his hand on the glass separating us and so did I. Bram shed a tear of joy.

I kept this incident secret from Tim and Ilse until the writing of this book. But at the time I told Helen Joseph. She believed God had inspired my answer.

In the beginning of 1975, Bram was terminally ill with cancer. Ruth, Ilse, Helen Suzman and Bram's brothers urged Jimmy Kruger to release him. Kruger prevaricated, fearing that even on his deathbed he would inspire his supporters to continue the struggle. Instead of releasing him to his daughters, Kruger eventually agreed to release Bram to his brother Paul Fischer in Bloemfontein. The strict conditions almost turned the home of Paul Fischer and his family into a prison. The authority of the prisons department was needed before anyone could go to the house or gather outside it.

In May, at the age of sixty-seven, he died. The prisons department removed his body and had it cremated. His ashes were not given to the family.

Isie Maisels, Arthur Chaskalson, Lewis Dison and I went to the memorial service in Bloemfontein. The funeral oration was to be delivered by André Brink, who had sat at the back of the court during Bram's trial. Unfortunately, he was unable to travel and Arthur Chaskalson spoke in his stead.

The prophecy by Chief Justice Rumpff to Isie Maisels that Bram would be long remembered has been fulfilled. His school, Gray College, has honoured him: Most Afrikaners now consider him a patriot. His name has been restored on the roll of advocates by a non-racial bench of judges. In the words of Judge President Bernard Ngoepe, Bram would have been happy that the General Bar Council of South Africa and the Johannesburg Bar supported his daughters' application for his reinstatement.

The Legal Resources Centre has arranged a Bram Fischer Lecture, which over the years has been delivered by President Nelson Mandela, Chief Justice Ismail Mahomed, Chief Justice Arthur Chaskalson and Deputy Chief Justice Dikgang Moseneke. A building overlooking Gandhi Square in the centre of Johannesburg is now known as Bram Fischer House. His biography, written by Stephen Clingman, *Bram Fischer: Afrikaner Revolutionary*, won the Alan Paton Prize for literature. Steps are being taken to name a major highway after him.

His legacy is acknowledged. He contributed to establishing a non-racial democracy in South Africa.

CHAPTER 26

The Namibians

My Lord, we find ourselves here in a foreign country, convicted under laws made by people we have always considered foreigners. We find ourselves tried by a judge who is not our countryman and who has not shared our backgrounds.

– Andimba Herman Toivo ja Toivo

A few months after Bram Fischer's trial ended, I was offered more work than I could manage by large firms of attorneys representing clients able to pay a reasonable fee. As there were no major political trials pending, I settled down to predominantly civil cases that enabled me to pay off both the second bond on the house and an Austin Marina. Then I was put to the test by Joel Carlson. He had briefed Isie Maisels and me during the late 1950s when we brought a series of *habeas corpus* applications against farmers using prison labour on their farms. Although Joel and I were close family friends, relations between us soured when I cautioned him that the Law Society might take steps against him for his immoderate language in public statements, and his persistence in commenting to the media on his cases. He retorted by saying that I was no longer the man he had known at university, that political cases had to be handled differently and that I had turned out the same as the mainly conservative lawyers at the Bar. The unjust accusations stung.

Despite this hiccup, Joel approached me when London solicitors asked him to act for thirty-seven South West Africans, mainly from Ovamboland on the Angolan border. They had been detained for months – a few for almost two years – in South African jails. They were charged with terrorism in terms of a recently promulgated act, which abrogated every principle of the rule of law. The act authorised the police to detain any person thought to have committed an act of terrorism or who might have information regarding the commission of such an act. This law passed through Parliament with the concurrence of the official opposition, the sole dissenting voice being that of Helen Suzman. It was to operate retrospectively to 1962, its provisions were extended to South West Africa, and, worst of all, the death sentence could be imposed. As I scanned the indictment I saw that a number of the thirty-seven were specifically charged with the murder of chiefs and headmen who they considered collaborators with the Pretoria regime. Joel had no experience in cases involving so many accused facing such serious charges. My experience in the Rivonia trial, as well as other major cases, was needed.

For the first and only time in my legal career, I hesitated about taking on a matter such as this. I feared not being able to handle the renewed pressure. On the face of the indictment and the circumstantial detail set out in it, as well as Joel's tentative conclusion that many would have no defence, more than ten of them could be sentenced to death. The men had been tortured by the same police team that I knew from past cases. Under torture, the accused made statements implicating themselves and others. In addition, they were isolated from their families. Their only garments were the clothing they wore when the police arrested them. The provisions of the Terrorism Act had been applied long before it was enacted.

The more Joel spoke, the greater grew the conflict within me. I said I'd think it over and let him know in the morning. Taking on this case would mean shedding some of the work I was committed to. Before I made a decision I needed to discuss matters with Arethe, as I knew that I became difficult to live with when the shadow of death loomed over those I defended. Actually, I made up my mind less than an hour after we parted.

In a phone call to him I suggested he ask for all the statements made by the accused, adding that I would prepare a request for further particulars as well as a questionnaire relating to their activities and interrogation. I took this decision without discussing it with anyone. How could I live with myself if I had opted out? How would my friends in jail, under house arrest, or in exile, have felt about me?

The first accused was Eliazar Tuhadeleni. He was a peasant farmer to whom the young guerrillas, infiltrating from Angola into Ovamboland, had turned for help. He assisted them in establishing a camp in the bush, in the recruitment of young men and the provision of food. When the camp was attacked by South African helicopters and ground forces most of the accused were arrested, but Tuhadeleni escaped. For almost a year he roamed the countryside, earning himself the nickname 'General de Wet', after the elusive Boer leader.

Tuhadeleni knew the Bible in Ovambo by heart. As there was no Oshivambo dictionary he would point out the verse, or at times the very word, to the two teachers among the accused, Jason Daniel Mtumbulua and Johnny ja Otto, whenever they found it difficult to interpret his words or thoughts. He was steeped in the oral history of the Ovambo people and produced a genealogy of the Ovambo kings going back three centuries. He wanted to plead guilty and be put to death on condition that all the others were freed.

The chairman of the internal wing of the South West Africa People's Organisation (Swapo), Emmanuel Gottlieb Nathaniel Machuriri, and the two teachers who were on the executive, couldn't understand why they were charged with terrorism. They were in Windhoek, not in Ovamboland. They had publicly opposed incursions by armed guerrillas. After I explained the doctrine of common purpose to them, Machuriri, a lay preacher, uttered an unprintable expletive.

Jason, the maths teacher, and the most articulate and intelligent among the accused, quietly spoke to us about Herman Toivo ja Toivo, Swapo's Ovamboland leader. (The use of African first names was not yet in vogue. Such first names were not even mentioned in the indictment.) He feared that Herman had been permanently affected by the physical and mental torture he had undergone in detention. We told him that others had been cured of a similar affliction slowly but surely by the companionship of their co-accused, by interaction with their lawyers and by visits from their families. Of course, in the case of our clients, no such visits were allowed. We advised against calling in a psychiatrist, as there was a danger that Herman would be sent to a mental hospital. There he would again be isolated and under police control. Happily, within a couple of weeks his condition improved.

As one of the founders of Swapo, Herman was well versed in the country's political history. In brief, after the First World War the League of Nations directed South Africa to govern the territory. Since then there had been breaches of trust and from the 1950s, the United Nations regularly passed resolutions challenging South Africa's right to deal with South West Africa as one of its provinces. In keeping with this knowledge and background, the accused wanted us not merely to claim their innocence, but to challenge the validity of the Terrorism Act. The final section of this Act provided that the law would also apply to South West Africa.

By now Denis Kuny and Ernie Wentzel were part of the legal team. None of us knew much about public international law. And our clients argued that they were not South Africans but Namibians. They found it difficult to accept that parliamentary sovereignty applied. We asked John Dugard, then professor of public international law at the University of the Witwatersrand, for an opinion. He advised that a plausible argument could be made that the resolutions passed by the United Nations had terminated South Africa's mandate. He felt our clients could not be indicted under a law passed by South Africa's Parliament.

In terms of the Bar rules, John Dugard could not join our legal team. On the other hand, we felt too junior for such an audacious argument. Without a senior member of the Bar to argue the point, we might be accused of a gimmick to embarrass the government. It was left to me to persuade Namie Phillips to lead the defence team. I convinced him that his stature, integrity and apolitical profile would be helpful in persuading Judge Ludorf not to sentence anyone to death. But when he saw John Dugard's opinion he said the point wouldn't succeed, and doubted if the argument was appropriate.

Subsequently the five of us met in the Wits law library for more than five hours trying to persuade him to challenge the Act. Eventually, long past midnight, we agreed to leave the final decision to him. We were to meet in his office the next morning at nine.

I was at his office before eight and asked him to take one final question into consideration. If some of our clients were sentenced to death, what would our colleagues throughout the world say if we had not raised the key point uppermost in the minds of our clients? A point also debated at the UN and in articles published in learned journals.

He was clearly upset by my audacity and didn't invite me into his office. As he was closing the door, he said that he was sure no reputable academic would put his name to an article advocating such an outrageous view.

An hour later we met as arranged. He asked John if he would write an article in support of this view and if a reputable law journal would publish it. Without hesitation, John said yes to both questions. Namie sighed in despair. While I had a private word with John, we were to draft the notice to the registrar and the attorney-general informing them that the point would be taken.

That South African lawyers were prepared to argue in a South African court that South Africa had no right to try Namibians brought some joy to our clients, but none to the prosecution, judge, court officials, and the government. Nor did it please the vast majority of whites in South Africa. Even some of our friends at the Bar were critical of us, as was the government-supporting sector of the media.

As the prosecutor, Piet Oosthuizen, knew as little as we did about international law, a senior government law advisor came to argue the case against us. The reaction at the United Nations and in the media throughout the world, particularly the Nordic countries, the United States and the United Kingdom, was strongly adverse to the South African government, and they called for the Namibians to be released and returned to their country. Save for the support it received from Salazar's fascist government in Portugal, South Africa stood alone. Again, in the eyes of many, the accused became the accusers at a time when the regime thought it had crushed its opponents. In this, the case of the thirty-seven Namibians was reminiscent of the treason and Rivonia trials. There were other similarities.

The accused were tried in the same Old Synagogue where Mandela and the others had sat for almost three years, charged with treason. The security arrangements were as elaborate as they had been for the Rivonia trial. A small corrugated iron structure was erected to serve as a cell. It was not big enough for a single table or chair to use for consultations. We insisted on our clients being brought to court as early as possible so we could consult before proceedings started. Senior correspondents from the media and observers from universities and human rights organisations vied for the few available seats in a building whose acoustics were designed for the rabbi, the cantor and the choir, not for lawyers.

Namie Phillips was above average height, straight as a rod, his bearing that of the officer he had been during the Second World War. In a firm voice and without gestures, he kept close to his prepared argument. Although most of the thirty-seven could not follow the detail, they knew the effect of what he was arguing – let these men go, we have no right to try them nor to punish them in Pretoria.

Sitting on Namie's left was John Dugard, who had prepared the argument. He had a row of books in front of him with the relevant pages marked, ready to pass them to Namie the instant he needed to read the appropriate quotations. Although this was John's day in court, the archaic rules prevented him from robing or presenting argument himself. Sitting on Namie's right, facing the judge with the thirty-seven behind us, I half turned to look at them and saw their faces relaxed for the first time. I saw there a hope that something good might come out of this.

The judge appeared to be taking the argument seriously, was almost differential to Namie and asked only the occasional question. I started hoping that our bold step might induce the judge not to pass the death sentence. He was known for his support of the government, but he was also a politically sensitive man.

The State's argument was expected: Parliament was supreme; the courts had no jurisdiction to pronounce upon the validity of legislation – propositions for which there was ample authority in the South African courts. No serious attempt was made to deal with our arguments. If the South African government could thumb its nose at the world, it was probably too much to expect that one of its judges would say that this was wrong. Our application failed, but fortunately without adverse comment by the judge. No doubt the stature of Namie Phillips saved us from such an embarrassment. Judging by the worldwide support we received during the rest of the trial, we would have been acquitted if we had been tried by a jury of honest men and women drawn from the world at large.

A number of notorious security policemen from Johannesburg and Pretoria, repeatedly accused of extracting information through torture, came to give evidence. They referred to the accused as terrorists who had established a terrorist camp in the bush. This the South Africans had kept under observation before they executed their carefully planned military attack. They described how they had pounced on the terrorists using helicopters and heavy weapons. They did not make it clear whether they regarded this as a battle or as police action aimed at effecting arrests. They found weapons and ammunition and documents issued by Swapo. Because the tall grass had been flattened, they inferred that a platoon of recruits had been drilled on this 'parade ground'.

Some of those detained gave evidence of the camp routine and said that their objective was to get rid of South Africans from their land. They also described their months of interrogation, the sleep deprivation, serious assault, electric shocks, and verbal abuse they'd suffered. Their interrogators had taunted them as no longer being 'big men', with no chance of lawyers, priests or doctors coming to their assistance. They were under the authority of the South African Police who knew how to treat 'kaffirs'.

At that time, only a few judges would receive evidence or allow cross-examination regarding the treatment of an accused after arrest. Judge Ludorf did not fall into that category. The moment the cross-examiner approached this subject, he would stymie the line of argument. Judges knew, or must have suspected, that some of the allegations of police torture were true, but many would claim they saw no relation between this and the evidence before them.

Most of the accused, with the assistance of ja Toivo and the schoolteachers, had written lengthy statements concerning the unspeakable torture they had suffered. Our team was divided on whether to cross-examine the policemen on the treatment of the accused. Namie Phillips was against this strategy and his view eventually prevailed.

As most of the accused had no defence to the charges, there was no reason for them to give evidence under oath. If they went into the witness box, the cross-examination would be nothing more than allegations unsupported by evidence. However, if they didn't, we risked criticism from the judge and might further diminish our slender chance of avoiding the death penalty.

The most serious evidence was against the young men who had openly carried their AK47s through the villages along the border and in the northern town of Oshakati, the regime's outer administrative post. It was in one of the many Cuca bars in the region that a chief accused of collaboration had been shot and some of his followers injured by one of these young men, Tall Herero.

Tall Herero's grandfather had been a rare survivor of the German army genocide campaigns against the Herero some seventy years earlier. He had fled to the then Bechuanaland protectorate. Tall left school to join Swapo and undergo military training partly to avenge the wrong done to his family and people, and partly in the hope that he would one day return to an independent Namibia to claim the ancestral lands his grandfather spoke of, which were now occupied by the Boers. He had also joined other armed attacks where lives were lost. There were many witnesses to prove his guilt. However, he would not deny what he had done.

While we were consulting in the courtroom with the political leaders I looked over my shoulder and saw Tall sitting on a bench alone, staring into space. I went over and sat down, apologising that we had not paid much attention to his case. I said that we would argue that the grievances of the people of Namibia were well founded, that his actions were of a political nature and that he should not be sentenced to death. Tall said he knew that he was going to die. He understood that it would be freedom or death when he joined the struggle. Having lost his freedom it was better to die than be jailed for life. He knew his case was hopeless, but he thanked us for what we were doing and asked me to go back to work on the cases of those who had a chance of being acquitted or receiving lighter sentences.

The evidence against the three leaders of the internal Swapo concerned publishing a cyclostyled news-sheet, referred to as the *Swapo Times*. Written mainly in Oshivambo, it repeatedly spoke of the wrongs done by the *moordlustige* – bloodthirsty – Boers and of the justice of the Swapo cause. The indictment alleged that their broadsheet promoted hostility between the races, an offence under both the Terrorism and Suppression of Communism Acts. It was also alleged that in praising Swapo they were responsible for the organisation's actions, including the armed struggle in Ovamboland.

When we refused to accept the translations into Afrikaans produced by barely literate policemen who distorted the meaning of important passages, the court was presented with a problem. There wasn't a sufficiently competent Oshivambo/Afrikaans interpreter in the department of justice in South West Africa. A senior clerk in a mining house reluctantly agreed to become the court interpreter, but refused to translate the documents as he did not want to become a witness against his own people. The judge was prepared to postpone the trial until the translation issue could be resolved.

Then one of the high-school teachers, Johnny ja Otto, offered to redo the translations, submit drafts to the prosecution and favourably consider any changes suggested by them. And this is what happened. Soon a strange friendship developed between the prosecutor Piet Oosthuizen and ja Otto. Neither regarded the other as the stereotypical enemy. When Piet asked, '*Johnny, hoekom is jy so maer?*' – Johnny, why are you so thin? – he received a playful answer. '*Dit is my onskuld wat my so maak, Meneer*' – It is my innocence that makes me so, Sir.

Oosthuizen knew that we were preparing the three from Windhoek to give evidence. And he knew the thrust of our argument. That they would deny associating themselves with the acts of violence that had taken place. That they would deny provoking hostility between the races. That they would claim to have written the truth about the grievances of the people of Namibia. He must also have known that we were consulting with Professor John H Wellington, who had written a scholarly chronicle of the injustices done to the people of Namibia, first by the Germans and then by the South Africans. Oosthuizen had to assume that, with the assistance of John Dugard, we would introduce the evidence placed before the World Court in an attempt to prove that the apartheid laws and practices were contrary to internationally acceptable norms. He knew that the only way to avoid the court being used as a platform to condemn his government's policies was to make a deal with the defence.

Although plea-bargaining sanctioned by the court was foreign to our criminal procedure, he was confident that the judge would privately approve of any deal we made. After some hard bargaining, we agreed to an offer that our clients from Windhoek would change their plea to one of guilty under the Suppression of Communism Act and that an effective sentence of imprisonment for no longer than three months would be imposed. They sought the blessing of their co-accused, which was readily given.

The State closed its case and we announced that we would not be leading any evidence. We argued that there was insufficient evidence to convict some of the more elderly, whose degree of participation was minimal. In one instance nothing more than giving some dry spinach to the insurgents.

The judge took time to write his judgment. He acquitted a couple more than we had asked for, but found it necessary not only to convict ja Toivo, but to attempt to discredit him as a political leader. He also found it necessary to praise the security police, saying that they had acted in a responsible manner and that the security of the State was in safe hands.

When Namie Phillips stood up to say 'As Your Lordship pleases' at the end of the judgment, the judge announced that, after due consideration, and without hearing any evidence in mitigation, he would not impose death sentences because the accused had been misled by agitators.

I looked at the young Tall Herero. He was smiling and hugging his comrades. When our eyes met his smile broadened and he gave me the thumbs-up sign. So much for those who, in support of the death penalty, contend that it is preferred by those likely to face life imprisonment. We thought the presence of international observers, including Richard Falk of the Woodrow Wilson Institute of Foreign Affairs at Princeton University, the dozens of ambassadors, correspondents of leading newspapers and television stations, and the trenchant editorial condemnation throughout the world, must have played a part in persuading the judge to make the announcement.

In the light of the judge's announcement, our intention to lead evidence in mitigation by some of the accused, Professor Wellington and international law experts who Joel Carlson had seen in America and the United Kingdom, had to be revised. We decided that ja Toivo would follow the example of Nelson Mandela and read a statement from the dock, speaking not only for himself, but also for his co-accused and the Namibian people. He insisted on answering the judge's criticisms of him in strong terms, even though we warned that his sentence was likely to be increased. He didn't care, he was going to have his say. After he had read the first two paragraphs about being tried in a foreign country, the judge interrupted him, saying that it was his duty to judge them. Ja Toivo ignored this and continued:

We are far away from our homes. Not a single member of our family has come to visit us, never mind be present at our trial. The Pretoria jail, the police headquarters where we were interrogated and where statements were extracted from us, and this court, is all we have seen of Pretoria. We have been cut off from our people and the world.

The State has not only wanted to convict us but also to justify the policy of the South African government. We will not even try to present the other side of the picture because we know that a court that has not suffered in the same way as we have cannot understand this. This is perhaps why it is said that one should be tried by one's equals – we here are being tried by our masters. Had we been tried by our equals it would not have been necessary to have any discussions about our grievances: these would have been known by those said to judge us.

He could not be persuaded to leave out the paragraph in which he took the judge to task for having called him a coward:

In the last war I joined the army to fight for this country while this judge was a traitor and belonged to the pro-Nazi underground organisation which committed sabotage as I stood guard at military installations facing the bullets of his colleagues. Now I am called a coward and he is the judge.

The prosecutor was most upset, so much so that he threatened to reopen the case. He wanted to contrast this aggressive statement with the one ja Toivo had made to the police. We reminded him that he would have to convince the court that the statement had been made freely and voluntarily. Oosthuizen swallowed his indignation.

After ja Toivo's statement from the dock, the judge listened to the pleas we presented in mitigation. According to our arrangement, the internal Swapo leaders were sentenced to an effective three months. Life imprisonment was imposed on most of the rest, with lesser sentences for those who had not undergone military training but who had assisted the guerrillas.

Ja Toivo was sentenced to twenty years in jail and his statement eventually led to an amendment of the Criminal Procedure Act which deprived an accused of the right to speak from the dock. The judge let it be known that people like me had abused the right to speak from the dock to make propaganda against the State and insult the judges. He also told Margaret Smith of *The Sunday Times* that he knew that I was Bram Fischer's successor as leader of the Communist Party.

Some years on, Professor Barend van Niekerk, a keen researcher on judicial independence in South Africa, asked Judge Ludorf whether the government had ever tried to influence any aspect of a case where he presided. Yes, he said, but only once. The then prime minister, John Vorster, had phoned to ask that he not impose death sentences in the South West Africa terrorism trial. The prime minister wished to avoid further pressure on the South African government. Judge Ludorf told the professor that he regretted having listened to Vorster: he should have followed his instinct. Had he done so, he would have sentenced about a dozen of them to death.

The judge had a serious drinking problem and took early retirement.

Namibia became independent in 1980 with Sam Nujoma as its first president and ja Toivo as one of his senior ministers. None of those sentenced to long terms of imprisonment served their full sentence.

CHAPTER 27

A Personal Footnote: the 1960s

The opening years of the 1960s, before the treason trial, were good years. As a family we were happy and content. Together with my brother Stavros and my friend Henry Panos, we'd started a catering equipment company that Stavros was to manage. Yianni had a good job and was engaged. His fiancée, Dionysia, had been orphaned during the war when her parents were killed by British bombs under circumstances that have become known as 'friendly fire'. She had been brought up by an elder sister, aunts and uncles and cousins, but had never called anyone *mitera* – mother. But once she and Yianni were engaged, she made numerous phone calls to my mother in Greece, only too happy to call her *mitera*. Those phone calls and the impending marriage helped Stavros and me persuade our mother to make a trip to South Africa.

Of course we planned a party to welcome her and daily expected a telegram advising us of her travel arrangement. But my mother had her own way of doing things. Unexpectedly one morning a Greek-speaking South African Airways hostess phoned to say that my mother was at the airport. I rushed there, appalled that we hadn't been on the spot to welcome her. I hugged her as I'd hugged her when I said goodbye as a thirteen-year-old. We both cried with heartache and joy. All the way home she kept touching my hand on the steering wheel or caressing my cheek with her calloused hand.

At home the family gathered to meet her. She couldn't kiss Arethe or the children enough. She was quite overcome. I introduced her to our domestic helper, Eileen, (whom my mother referred to as Eleni) and she embraced the woman and kissed her on both cheeks. Later she asked me if she had done the right thing as she had felt Eileen stiffen but I assured her that she had, explaining that most black South Africans were not accustomed to being embraced by whites.

The soil has never been far from my mother's hands and she could not understand why we did not use a section of the garden as a *perivoli* – a vegetable patch. Was she expected to sit on an easy chair the whole day? She chose the northeastern corner of the garden, where I had planted a fig tree, for her *perivoli*. Soon she was supervising Martin in digging up the lawn and transplanting the fig tree. She bought seeds and in the coming months home-grown vegetables and spices became part of our meals.

My mother spent a lot of time in the vegetable patch weeding, hoeing, removing snails and slugs, spraying, with a diluted vinegar solution, the aphids and the fungus that attacked the tomato, brinjal, bean, marrow and cucumber plants. She was happy that she had created a *perivoli* which duplicated the one she cultivated a few kilometres from her home at Vasilitsi. Equally importantly, her fresh vegetables went into the dishes she prepared, especially during Lent, and on Wednesdays and Fridays, when the rules of the Greek Orthodox Church forbid the consumption of meat or dairy products.

My mother's presence in our house brought with it a connection to Greece, and Greek traditions and customs. She spoke in Greek to her grandsons, she sang them lullabies and folk and freedom songs, she told them the fairy stories that she had once told me.

In the village she would not miss vespers, the liturgy on Sunday morning and the services on many of the saints' days. At home she had only two hundred metres to walk to the large village church, but in Johannesburg I had to drive her ten kilometres to a church. I was only too happy to do this, but on every occasion she felt obliged to apologise. Fortunately she never asked why I dropped her and did not attend the service myself.

The reception for Yianni's marriage to Dionysia was held at our home and I wanted the occasion to resemble a village wedding. We had home-made *mezedes*, a variety of meats and fish, and traditional confectionary. In every respect it was a memorable day, not least because Johannesburg experienced its heaviest snowfall on record. We had to temporarily roof the patio with canvas, and kept the champagne cool in the thick snow. My mother sat the young bride on her knees and sang traditional wedding songs, praising her youth and beauty. We danced, we sang. But what I did regret was that matters between my parents were unresolved and my father did not attend the wedding.

While she was with us my mother expressed no wish to see my father, and after a couple of years became restless to get back to her daughter and property. Much as she would miss her grandchildren, she wanted to go home. I was sad to see her leave, more so because I did not have a South African passport and was reluctant to apply for a Greek one in case I was not allowed back into my adopted country.

Although the catering equipment company took a little time to get on its feet, Stavros was able to offer my father a 'commission' so that he could stop working as a shop assistant in Pretoria. He resigned and moved into an apartment in Joubert Park. The commission was more to protect his dignity than of any practical benefit, although his support of the Greek cafés in Johannesburg created much goodwill for the business.

During 1967 Stavros married Eleni Perivolaris and this time my father attended the engagement party and the wedding. He developed a close relationship with his new daughter-in-law and socialised with Eleni's parents and relations. He also visited us from time to time and was particularly proud of his two elder grandchildren, Kimon and Damon, who had delighted him with their guitar playing at Stavros and Eleni's wedding.

Unfortunately, a decade that began well for the family ended in tragedy.

In 1969 my father was knocked down in a motorcycle accident, his leg smashed in two places. The breaks were so bad that the doctors refused to operate and instead my father's leg was encased in plaster of Paris in the hope that this would bring some relief from the pain. My father became convinced that the accident was deliberate, part of a revenge conspiracy by people he had quarrelled with in Pretoria. That quarrel concerned his attempts to prevent a developer from buying church property. In the end he had gone to court and lost. Now he did not trust the doctors and seemed to have little faith in me. When I took him to hospital for a check-up, he flared angrily and rushed off down a corridor until his crutch slipped and he fell. He then blamed me and the doctors for the incident.

As he found comfort with Eleni, she became his succour in his last months. Actually, thanks largely to her, for the last two years of his life my father knew again the intimacy of family life and the embrace of people who cared for him. His last Sunday was spent at Stavros's home, playing cards with Eleni's family. He went home after a happy relaxed day.

The next morning I was at court when I learnt of his death. It appeared that he had fallen in the bathroom after putting his morning coffee on the gas stove to boil. Unable to move, perhaps unconscious, he had lain there while the coffee boiled over, extinguishing the flame. He succumbed to the leaking gas. For this accident Stavros and I were harshly criticised by the police for not looking after our father, a criticism we both had to live with. At his wake, one of his closest friends commented that my father had done much in his life for others and very little for himself.

Part Four: 1971–1985

CHAPTER 28

A Taste of Freedom

Wherever I may travel Greece wounds me still.

– George Seferis

In 1972 I was involved with Isie Maisels on the inquest into the death of Ahmed Timol, who'd died after falling from a tenth-floor window of police headquarters at John Vorster Square in Johannesburg. We were also acting on behalf of the father of Mohammed Essop. Essop had been arrested with Timol and later found comatose in a Pretoria hospital.

I was extended and needed a holiday. Jules Browde, a senior member of the Bar and a good friend, believed I was made of steel as I never took a break. He wondered why I didn't visit my home country. I confided that I'd been refused South African citizenship and that I feared this might lead the minister of justice to have me struck from the roll of advocates.

I also fretted that I'd had to lie to my mother when she returned to Greece by promising that I'd visit her. Yet I had no passport. The pressure to obtain travel documents was mounting but I could do nothing about it. Arethe's father had died. He had come as a young boy to South Africa from a Greek village near the Albanian border, and now she wanted to visit the village where he was born. Our boys were keen to see the country of their ancestors and they kept asking when we'd be travelling to Greece.

Jules shook his head in disbelief at my story. Less than two weeks later I answered the phone and had an astonishing conversation.

'George, this is Judge Galgut. What the hell is the matter with you?'

Somewhat tentatively I asked, 'What have I done wrong now, Judge?'

'Jules spoke to me,' he said. 'Why didn't you come to me yourself much earlier to ask for help? Listen, this is what I have done. I raised the matter at a judges' conference. Twenty of the twenty-two said that they had no right to treat you this way; the other two – you probably know who they are – disagreed, but they don't matter. I went to the prime minister to ask him to rectify matters as soon as possible. John Vorster asked me why you don't take a Greek passport. I refused on your behalf. I asked John what he thought lawyers here and overseas would think if it came out that the man who had done some of the most important political trials in our country had to travel on a foreign passport because our government had refused to grant him citizenship even though he had been here for more than thirty years. He told me to tell you that the question of citizenship might take some time but that you should immediately go to the regional representative for the department of home affairs in Johannesburg with two photographs. There you will be required to fill in a form for a temporary travel document.'

Hardly believing my ears, I thanked him.

'By the way, even though I think you and Isie Maisels are crazy to accept briefs in practically all the political matters that come before our courts, I told John not to expect you to change your ways.'

A few days later I went to the department of home affairs where a senior official was expecting me. Having heard from friends for whom special representations were made that they had been interviewed by the security police as to where, when and for what purpose they were going overseas, I feared that I too might be subjected to such treatment. But no questions were asked. The official said I would be notified by phone when the document was ready. Early the next morning the same official was on the line. Could I send a messenger to collect my travel document? I replied that I'd come myself. I ran all the way. He handed me the document as well as application forms for citizenship. Neither he nor I said anything about who was responsible for dispensing with the customary bureaucratic procedures.

Elated at the prospect of travelling abroad, I asked the principal of the school attended by our boys whether they could stay away for a couple of weeks longer than the winter school holidays. I couldn't help mentioning that this was their first overseas trip, and my first return to Greece after thirty-two years. Although he didn't have the authority to grant such permission, with a smile he wished us a good trip.

There were still two matters of concern that I did not want to discuss with the family. Instead I sought the advice of Arthur Chaskalson. During April 1967, a coup was staged in Greece by a group of army colonels and by the time of our planned visit they'd been in power for over five years. Prisons on various islands were full of detainees. Melina Mercouri and other Greeks in exile had called for a boycott of their country, particularly by tourists. How would it look if I did not heed that call? Arthur had a quick and simple answer – our family was going on a pilgrimage.

My second problem concerned my military training. Or rather my lack of it. Greeks of my age living abroad could be exempted from conscription on payment of a relatively small sum of money provided they had not left Greece for the purpose of avoiding military training. However, the colonels were a law unto themselves. What if one of their ardent supporters in South Africa – by definition, such a person would be both a racist and an enthusiastic supporter of the apartheid regime – were to collude with some security policemen to confine me to Greece? Arthur waved aside my anxiety. Any funny business would result in an outcry against both the colonels and the South African regime.

Somewhat mollified, I undertook the pilgrimage.

As the plane approached the mainland of Greece, we took turns in gazing at Crete through the window. I pointed to the westernmost cape of the southern Peloponnese and told the children that Vasilitsi, my village, lay in that direction. They were enthralled.

We landed at Athens airport – a significant moment, yet the sight of plastic bags and other debris blowing about in the fresh breeze was disappointing. At the passport cubicle I carefully put the four newly issued light-green passports on top of my smaller black-covered travel document. The officer looked fleetingly at the passport photographs and the four members of the family standing behind me. Then he picked up my travel document with the tips of his thumb and index finger, waved it at me and asked, 'What is this? Why haven't you got a proper passport? What wrong have you done?' I thought that the less I said the better. I shrugged. This was the document I had been given. He shook his head, opened a drawer on the side of the cubicle, and asked me to spell my name in Greek. He looked on the list for *Mpizos*, and having satisfied himself that my name was not there, stamped the document and pushed it back across the counter.

Come to welcome us was Anthony Christopoulos, the son of Vangos and my aunt. (I carefully avoided discussing with Anthony the actions of his father, regarded by many of the family as a collaborator.) He gave us a wonderful welcome. Soon we were indeed a party of pilgrims paying our respects at the Parthenon, the Acropolis, the Athens Museum and particularly at the Temple of Poseidon at Sounion where Aegeus, the king of Athens, had waited for his son, Theseus, to return from Crete. According to mythology, before Theseus left, he had agreed that on his return he would raise a white sail if he had killed the monstrous Minotaur. When Aegeus saw the black sail flown by his victorious but forgetful son, he jumped off the cliff in despair. I had read that Lord Byron engraved his initials on one of the columns and asked the children to find it. A middle-aged English woman who overheard me protested that no Englishman would do such a thing and that their search would be in vain. In that case, I asked her, was the Lord Elgin who had chiselled off the Parthenon marbles (now in the British Museum), not an Englishman? She muttered that he was different and walked away. The children quickly grew bored looking for Byron's initials and gave up their assignment. To this day I don't know if the story of Byron's vandalism is true.

From Athens we took the overcrowded, noisy bus for what was then a six-hour drive to the village. Nowadays new multi-lane highways and tunnels almost halve the time. I remember it as a hard, nauseous trip that affected all of us except Arethe.

Before she came out to South Africa to visit us, my mother had sold our ancestral home and built a small three-roomed house for herself. We managed well enough in that house, particularly as there was a leafy pergola over the veranda. It was so warm that we could sleep uncovered, the only disadvantage being the playful cat and its love of human toes.

One of our first visitors introduced himself as the son of my godfather. His father had been killed in 1944 by the Left in an ambush of those who had taken arms from the Germans. He tried hard to keep back the tears. His father having died, would I now consider him as my *nouno* – godfather? I embraced him, we kissed each other on both cheeks and to this day I have called him my *nouno*. The next evening we took up his invitation to dinner. We found the table set on the small veranda next to an open clay oven. On the table were two round pans filled with meat baked with potatoes, tomatoes and peppers and sprinkled with oreganum, and freshly baked bread. His wife, daughter, son, my mother and my family sat around the table hardly able to contain our appetites.

The children had heard that the favourite meat in the village was goat and vowed never to eat it. During the meal, however, the boys had more than their fair share of the meat. On the short walk back I asked how they had enjoyed the meal. Kimon wondered why I asked. Just because, I said. He had suspected that the meat was goat, but didn't want to ask. Almost in chorus they said they'd like more of it.

My mother took us to see the family fields, the boundaries of which she had demarcated by planting trees as markers. She pointed out that the greedy neighbours encroached on our property while she was in South Africa, planting trees to claim the land for themselves. She exacted a promise from the boys that they and their cousins would see to it that the fields remained our family's forever.

Much had changed. The road to the village was tarred. There was running water and electricity in every home. A new primary school stood on top of the hill. Instead of just one teacher, there were now four teachers for fewer than half the number of pupils there'd been in my day.

In mid-June, when the school year was about to end, we were invited to attend the prize-giving ceremony. Although the classrooms were new and had been well decorated for the occasion, the poems, the songs and dances were no different from those I remembered.

There were no fewer than six *kafeneia* in the village, each with a television set. Television wasn't yet available in South Africa and our sons loved it. Children were generally not welcome in the *kafeneia* but an exception was made for ours. They went from one to the other to watch outdated cowboy films screened in English with Greek subtitles. Each *kafeneio* had its own political and social identity, from the far Left to the far Right. Not all were politically defined: one was a place for soccer fans, another was a dance venue with American pop tunes sung in Greek translation.

I visited them all, avoiding only the one blasting out pop songs. At each, attempts were made to put me in a political pigeonhole. I was asked obscure questions to which my answers were equally obtuse and vague. Eventually I would be challenged about the situation in Greece. Except for making clear that a dictatorship was an insult to our democratic tradition, I avoided identifying myself with any of the political parties that had been active prior to the colonels' takeover. To their credit most of my fellow villagers shared my view of the colonels. But they were cautious. No one wanted to condemn them outright and so they sought safety by reminding me of the imperfections of democracy.

But some members of the family seemed as determined as the people in the *kafeneia* to know my political stance. My mother's youngest brother, for instance, who had been held as a political prisoner on Makronisos (Greece's Robben Island) during the civil war, took me aside. There was an urgent task which was mine alone. I was the only one who could restore the honour of my grandfather's first son, George, the man after whom I'd been named. The fascists had erected an obelisk in the churchyard in honour of fallen heroes. Almost at the top of the list was my uncle's name.

Of course it was not true. He was not a fascist sympathiser. They'd also assigned his fate to the wrong war. Below George's name were the names of collaborators who'd fought with the Germans against their fellow Greeks. My uncle did not belong in such company. A sort of postscript on the obelisk recorded the names of two patriots executed by the Germans. I should demand either that the obelisk come down or that my uncle's name be removed.

My argument that such action would reopen the wounds of the past fell on deaf ears. So did my view that it would delay the reconciliation taking place, particularly among the children and grandchildren. The issue was left unresolved.

Relatives and friends went out of their way to make our stay pleasant. The children rode horses and donkeys and were taken down to the sea. We visited different beaches, including Kalamaki, where I showed everyone the very rock from which I had stepped onto the boat with the New Zealanders all those many years ago. Everyone gathered round to touch the rock. The secretary of the village council showed me a letter written by the prime minister of New Zealand thanking the villagers for their efforts. On a sadder note, I learnt that after we left, another group of New Zealand soldiers was found by the Germans and executed.

We joined family and friends in following the parish priest from one chapel to the next, celebrating the various saints' festivals. Lamb and pork turned on spits, *souvlakia* were grilled, and for those with a sweet tooth there were *pasteli*, a *sesami* slice dripping with sesame and honey. At some of these festivals we had music from a traditional band – violin, guitar, clarinet and *santouri* – and no excuse was needed to dance.

At one such happy occasion I alarmed my cousin, who was our driver for the day. There was a long queue at the toilet. A captain in army uniform appeared and briskly walked to the head of the queue. I went up to him, touched him on his upper arm, pointed out the queue and asked him to join it at the back. He said that he would not delay us for long. I told him that at the back of the queue he wouldn't delay us at all. Embarrassed by such temerity he went away. My cousin warned me to be careful. The captain knew I was not a local man or he would have dealt with me quite differently. For instance he could have trumped up an assault charge because I touched him. He could have said that I used insulting language. Those were grounds for taking me into custody, until I'd been 'persuaded' to sign an admission of guilt, pay a fine and apologise. I shook my head in disbelief. How could they be so terrified of an army uniform? The implications could go further, said my cousin. The officer might stop us when we left. He could charge my cousin with using his vehicle to transport people other than members of his immediate family. There would then be court cases and my family could be warned to appear as witnesses. I was fortunate to have a foreign passport.

That unsettling incident aside, we returned to happier events. Such as harvesting grapes which were spread out on the drying lawns and would eventually be sold as raisins. We also collected figs for drying and almonds for family consumption. When our holiday in the village ended, my mother overloaded us with olive oil, olives, dried fruit and *diples* – thin pastry fried in olive oil and covered with honey and crushed nuts – which she had made. She insisted that we take noodles and even a head of *mitzithra* – a special cheese that is grated to eat with pasta.

From Vasilitsi we returned to Athens and Arethe's relatives, then on to her father's village. This entailed flying to Yiannina in the north-west, and reporting to the police and the army for a special permit entitling us to travel to the village on the Albanian border. At Yiannina we hired a sturdy taxi as the roads were notoriously bad.

Fortunately at Yiannina a fellow guest at our hotel was able to help me sort out the permits. He knew the authorities' office only too well, as he had escaped from Albania's tyrannical regime in 1946 and had spent three days in that office being interrogated. Finally he satisfied them that he was a Greek and had been allowed to join his uncle in America. Now he was back with his wife and three children, intent on visiting the village where he was born. Unfortunately, the border was closed and there were no diplomatic relations between Albania and almost the whole of the rest of the world. To overcome his disappointment he had arranged with a Greek army patrol to take him to the top of a mountain so that he could show the family his village in the valley below.

The Second World War and the civil strife that followed had devastated Arethe's paternal family. An uncle had lost both his legs to frostbite during the 1940 Albanian Campaign. An aunt and her daughter spent eight years in a refugee camp in then Czechoslovakia.

The family village of Lia was put on the literary map when the novel *Eleni*, written by Nicholas Gage (Gatsoyiannis to the Greeks), and a rebuttal, *The Other Eleni*, were published. The first book claimed that his mother was executed on trumped-up charges, the second that she and her father collaborated with the Germans. The remnants of the village were still sharply divided.

During our evening out in Yiannina, I found a driver with a fairly new model Volvo to take us to Lia the next morning. The man's name was Sotiri, and the road turned out to be hardly worthy of the name. We proceeded slowly, periodically having to remove rocks before we could drive on.

The village was almost completely deserted, but an elderly man pointed out a narrow path next to a stream that led to the house. As we approached, voices could be heard from behind a tall walnut tree. Arethe tried hard to subdue her sobbing and wiped her tears with the back of her hand. The four of us – the three boys and I – realised that it was not a time for words. Kimon and I each took her by a hand and led her towards the voices ahead and the relations she had never met. The meeting was emotionally draining on everyone.

Arethe's Aunt Anthula wailed for the brother she had not seen since the late 1920s and who had died so far away from home. She wailed for him as a father whose place of birth his eldest child was only now seeing for the first time.

Anthula was the head of the house: her husband suffered from Parkinson's disease, his mother was nearing a hundred years old and exceedingly frail, while her daughter and two granddaughters had little to say. Back at their home, a young goat was slaughtered and cuts from the legs and shoulders threaded onto wooden skewers, and cooked over a slow fire. Arethe asked to see her grandfather's home, but a cousin had appropriated the house and the aunt had no key. We could look at the well-weathered stone and the untidily repaired slate roof, but we couldn't get inside.

On our walk we stopped at the school built with funds repatriated by John Costa, the first person from the village to emigrate to South Africa. He had fought with the Boers against the English and was imprisoned on Saint Helena. After the war he prospered as a café owner in Stellenbosch. Over the years Costa sent enough money home for them to build a school for more than three hundred children. It was Costa who had enticed Arethe's father to South Africa sixty years before, and so in a sense Costa played a significant part in my life too. The civil war, the lure of the cities and the drain of emigration to America, Australia and Canada had rendered the school redundant. It was now used as a home crafts centre in which only seven girls had enrolled for that year.

Arethe's aunt was penurious, dependent on the occasional cheque from a relative in the United States. Some twenty years later I met her again outside Boston in the US. She had left the village and was living there with relatives.

The village has not been completely abandoned: Nicholas Gage built a guesthouse there in memory of his mother and it is visited by readers of his poignant book and fans of the movie based on it.

Our return journey from Lia to Yiannina was no easier. The next morning our plan was to travel by bus to the nearby harbour and from there by ferry to Kerkyra, better known as Corfu. I asked Sotiri if he would drive us to the harbour. I thought he might want the business, especially as he had told us the car was on hire purchase and he was finding it difficult to pay the instalments. My offer was enthusiastically accepted.

In the morning neither Sotiri nor his car arrived. Instead another driver with a jalopy said he had taken over as Sotiri's car was damaged. My family pounced on me. It was my fault that Sotiri's vehicle was damaged. It must have happened on our trip, and so I was duty bound to phone him, apologise and offer to pay for the damage. But when I phoned I discovered that Sotiri had left in the early hours of the morning for Athens with a seriously ill customer. I didn't know which story to believe.

The year before our first visit to Greece, Professor Constantine A Trypanis edited *The Penguin Book of Greek Verse*, with selections from Homer to the Nobel Prize winner George Seferis. The book ran to more than six hundred pages and included the best of Greek poetry from almost twenty-five centuries, with English translations.

In the late 1960s I had been elected chairman of the South African Hellenic Educational and Technical Institute, Saheti, established some ten years earlier, for the purpose of building a Greek school, encouraging the learning of Greek and promoting Hellenism. Following the publication of his book, we invited the eminent Professor Trypanis to visit South Africa and deliver a number of lectures. He declined because of age, suggesting we ask Vasilios Mandilaras. Mandilaras had been a student of Trypanis at Oxford and was by then teaching classical literature at the University of Athens. Vasilios and his wife Soula accepted our invitation.

Vasilios was a cousin of Nikiphoros Mandilaras, a leading Greek human rights lawyer. Nikiphoros had been the first victim of the colonels, and his battered body was found floating in the sea. Hardly anyone believed the story advanced by the colonels to explain his death. In their version, a naval patrol craft had ordered the captain of a ship taking Mandilaras to Cyprus to stop for a routine check. Mandilaras then jumped off the vessel to avoid arrest. No plausible explanation was forthcoming for the injuries to his body so clearly visible in a set of photographs his widow kept in her bag and showed to whomever she met. I had seen the tears of the mother of Ahmed Timol; I had heard her cries for justice. The widow's lament was no different.

After his cousin's death, Vasilios' academic promotion was delayed. He was under police surveillance. On one occasion he was visited by the police demanding an explanation for an assignment he had given his senior students. The students had to complete a fragment written by Solon more than two thousand five hundred years ago as to what prize should be bestowed on the *tyranoktonos* – someone who killed the tyrant intent on subverting the democratic constitution of Athens. Vasilios brought out his files to show the police that he and his predecessors had set this assignment frequently over the years. What was the concern? Did anyone the police served think of himself as a tyrant? They advised him to be careful.

Vasilios and I became close friends and over the years he introduced me to the works of writers and poets I had not yet read, to painters and musicians, to ancient and modern Greek theatre. He travelled with us to most of the important sights in Greece, a knowledgeable and fascinating companion. He correctly predicted that the time of the colonels would not last, that freedom and democracy were in our blood. Their regime collapsed two years later, in July 1974.

By way of contrast it is worth noting that we in South Africa have preserved Robben Island as a monument to the struggle for freedom. But in Greece, following the overthrow of the colonels, the concrete and steel cages they erected on a number of islands were blown up so that they could never be used again.

Despite their illegitimacy, the colonels tortured and imprisoned thousands without due process, killed unarmed demonstrating students and proved to be deeply corrupt. They nevertheless found favour and support from President Richard Nixon and his administration. Once democratic government was restored, the colonels were charged with treason. Although the death penalty had almost been abrogated by disuse, the five judges sentenced some of the colonels to death, finding them guilty of treason in the worst degree. The new president, Constantine Karamanlis, together with his all-party government, commuted these sentences to life imprisonment the very next day and won international praise for an action so striking in its lack of revenge.

Karamanlis had been prime minister in a government before the colonels' coup and had gone into exile for the intervening years. At their trial, the colonels argued that their actions were not a coup but 'a revolution of historical necessity'. This argument was demolished by Panayiotis Kanelopoulos, the acting prime minister when the colonels took over. On 21 April 1967 he was frogmarched to a military camp as the colonels took swift and brutal action to halt the election which George Papendreou appeared bound to win.

Kanelopoulos had stern words for the overenthusiastic young lawyer defending the colonels. Under cross-examination by this advocate, Kanelopoulos challenged the concept of a 'revolution of historical necessity'. True revolutionaries proclaimed their aims in declarations that promised to respect the human rights of the people, said the old democrat. They marched down the streets followed by large crowds. The lawyer's clients on the other hand had rolled tanks down the streets of Athens; the people had taken cover and locked their doors. As if this were not enough, said Kanelopoulos, the first act of the new leaders was to forge his signature on a document stating that they had taken control of the country at his request.

When Kanelopoulos was asked why there were no security men at the entrance of his home (implying that the State was too disorganised to protect its prime minister), he snapped back: 'Those who rule by the will of the people do not require machine guns or bravos to protect them.'

Fortuitously the trial was under way while I happened to be in Athens and I managed to view the closed-circuit television broadcast for foreign correspondents in a public lounge of the Grande Bretagne, a leading hotel on Constitution Square. As I watched Kanelopoulos, this elderly, frail gentleman, testifying in so dignified a way before five civilian judges conducting the trial with great decorum in a hall within a prison, I began to sense that we could all, once again, feel proud of being Greek.

Shortly after my return from our first trip to Greece, I applied for South African citizenship and, as promised, it was granted without delay. With about thirty others, Arethe and I took the oath of allegiance in the library of the magistrates' courts before the chief magistrate. Afterwards his clerk called us to his office. He privately congratulated me and asked Arethe why persuading me to become a South African had taken her so long. I didn't enlighten him.

Throughout the centuries Greeks living outside Greece have established schools for their children. I was present in 1945 when Prince Paul, in exile with his family in South Africa during the war, laid a foundation stone on a farm near Heidelberg for such a school. The stone was supposed to be laid jointly with General Jan Smuts, then prime minister, but he failed to make the ceremony. The planned school was to cater for children of Greek origin living in southern Africa. But the community became divided, and the money promised at the grand inaugural function was not forthcoming. The proposal was scrapped and the land sold. With the proceeds a seventy-two acre site was bought about ten kilometres from the centre of Johannesburg.

Some time later, one of the members of the original 'farm school' committee, the wealthy baker Charalambos Constantinides, informed me that the school project had been abandoned. A section of the land was used as a sporting club and a scout hall, but the rest lay neglected. It was time to revive the original initiative. He felt that his daughters were being deprived of their right to learn Greek. And if it was now too late for them, then he wanted to ensure that his grandchildren could enjoy their heritage. He promised moral and financial support if I formed a committee to drive the project. I was reluctant, largely because community affairs can be complex. He retorted: 'For the sake of your children, their children and many more, it is your duty to become involved to remedy the situation.'

Close to a hundred people turned up for the special meeting I arranged. Almost inevitably there was a slanging match as old factions surfaced but by the end of the meeting eight board members had been elected. With tears in his eyes, Constantinides said that for the first time in more than twenty years he believed a school would be built. The board voted six to one against me for the position of chairman but was unanimous in electing me vice-chairman. I did not hold the vice-chair for long, as the chairman soon resigned and I was left to chair the committee, a position I held for nineteen years. During that time the Saheti School was built and established by Morgan Ellis and Mini Janks as head of the high school and primary school respectively. Their work was developed by Malcolm Armstrong and Martha Cavaleros. Today the school has almost a thousand children, all of whom learn Greek irrespective of their gender, race, colour or religious belief. The head is Soula Krystalides. As an aside it should be noted that the buildings won Myra Kamstra an architectural award.

There were many hurdles along the way. The 1951 constitution provided that the school was for children of European decent. I objected to this clause and it was deleted. Nevertheless, there were dissenting voices, all of them supporters of the apartheid regime and almost invariably also of the colonels. They were unhappy with the leading role I played, because of my attitude to the governments in Pretoria and Athens. Although the Greek ambassador, the consul-general and the archbishop were supportive, they received reports that I was involved in the project to cover up my political activism. Under pressure from the board, I reluctantly agreed that the minister of education could unveil the new foundation stone. But I was stretching a principle.

Another trying moment came when the thoughtful and gentle chairman of the community, Stamatis Lagoudes, received an order from Greece via the embassy that a doxology was to be celebrated to mark the 21 April accession of the colonels to power. The chairmen of all Greek organisations should attend. I firmly told him that I would not attend any function in honour of the colonels. Lagoudes said he would make my excuses to the ambassador. I told him to say that I was working in my garden. My absence was not because I had something else to do; I would deliberately not attend. Exactly three months later the colonels' regime capitulated.

In 1988 I didn't stand for re-election. I was off to Columbia University in New York as a visiting scholar for five months, and besides the committee needed new blood. In subsequent years, the institute's attempt to establish a chair of Modern Greek at Wits unfortunately failed, but happily there is a vibrant department at the University of Johannesburg.

Regrettably, the school came too late for my own children, but it is there for our grandson and two granddaughters. Undoubtedly, without the overwhelming support of the Greek community both here and in Greece, it would never have been built. To this day, Greece pays the seconded teachers to teach Greek language, history, geography, dancing and singing. Contrary to the fears of the older generation that our children and grandchildren were not likely to support the school, the enthusiasm of younger parents has exceeded all expectations. Individual and collective efforts have built more classrooms, a laboratory, a chapel and a music centre. Scholarships and bursaries worth millions of rands have enabled those who couldn't afford the fees to attend the school. Accumulated funds ensure the school's continued success. A substantial percentage of the learners are not of Greek descent, but they all become Philhellenes. Saheti's graduates are welcome at South Africa's leading universities and many have excelled in medicine, engineering, architecture, law, education and the arts.

Soon after my retirement I was appointed one of the institute's life-vice-presidents. Occasionally I attend board meetings where I have a voice but no vote. Of my own accord, I have appointed myself one of its honorary gardeners and my task is to help fill its spacious grounds with trees. My seventy-fifth birthday was made especially memorable by the school – I was handed seventy-five roses by seventy-five toddlers from the nursery school. They formed a guard of honour down the middle of the hall that has been named after me, as has the scholarship and bursary fund.

In speaking to the teachers and pupils over the years I have often quoted the words of George Seferis:

> *Just a little more*
> *And we shall see the almond trees in blossom*
> *The marble shining in the sun*
> *The sea, the curling waves.*
> *Just a little more*
> *Let us rise just a little higher.*

Though we are far from the shining marbles and curling sea of Greece, still Seferis speaks to us, for there are enough almond trees that blossom here at the end of each September to herald the beginning of South Africa's spring.

CHAPTER 29

Winnie Mandela's Trials and Tribulations

They will never succeed in building a wall around her. It does not matter where they banish her ... This woman is so dynamic, she will make the birds sing and the trees rustle wherever she goes.

– Sally Motlana

During the late 1960s and early 1970s, I appeared for Winnie Mandela on a number of occasions. As her political activism increased, so the State retaliated by detaining her, placing her under banning orders and severely curtailing her movements. At first the legal defences we mounted were accepted by the higher courts, but not long after my return from Greece our luck ran out.

If there is a beginning to the harassment, it was probably in the early hours of 12 May 1969, when more than a hundred people were detained throughout the country, most prominent among them Winnie Mandela. Like the rest she was held under the Terrorism Act. Joel Carlson represented her, but his letters to the security police were ignored.

Unbeknown to us, the police were concocting an elaborate act of chicanery involving an attorney, Mendel Levin, a Mrs Kay and Moosa Dinnath. The two women had criminal convictions and were paid police informers. These details were unknown to Winnie. She thought their friendship was genuine.

Mrs Kay and Moosa Dinnath pretended to be supporters of the freedom struggle and initially persuaded Winnie's relatives that they could arrange prison visits and would raise funds for her defence. They engaged a man called Mendel Levin as her attorney.

Levin was a strange choice. When he became a member of the National Party, he publicly announced that he was the first Jew to be accepted by the party, proof that it was not anti-Semitic. Some years earlier, he had avoided a long prison term for fraud by giving evidence against his co-accused. His sharp practice in insolvency matters had earned him judicial criticism. No sooner had he started 'acting' for Winnie – by making a public statement that he had organised for her to see a private doctor – than a colleague of mine in the United States received a request from him for funds. Perturbed, Professor Gwendolyn Carter forwarded me a copy of Levin's letter. He claimed that he had been appointed Winnie's lawyer and retained Vernon Berrangé, Fred Zwarenstein and me as counsel. He asked for a substantial sum of money as a first instalment on our fees. I lost no time in telling Gwendolyn that Levin was not to be trusted.

Five months later, twenty-two of those arrested were remanded to a court set up in the Old Synagogue. Their trial date was 1 December 1969. Levin, who had been given access to Winnie, was confident that he would be accepted as attorney for the whole group. He didn't know that Joel Carlson had obtained a power of attorney from the relatives, and he outwitted Levin by asking for a short adjournment so that the relatives could speak to the accused.

The inevitable happened. Winnie confirmed that initially she had given a power of attorney to Levin, but that subsequently she had been instructed by her husband on Robben Island to entrust her case to Joel Carlson. The other accused followed suit. The bizarre plot hatched between Levin and the newly promoted Major Swanepoel, chief interrogator of the detainees, fell apart, although it cast a shadow over the trial.

Joel came to see me with a copy of the indictment. The twenty-two were not charged with terrorism but with contravening the Suppression of Communism Act and the Unlawful Organisations Act, which prevented furthering the aims of organisations such as the ANC. All the accused were charged with conspiring with a number of others, most of whom were still in detention. Among these were Winnie's younger sister and Shanti Naidoo, whose large family were involved in the struggle. The detail in the indictment about the time, place and purpose of various meetings, as well as the printing of pamphlets, told us several things. It meant that the group had been under close police surveillance. It also indicated an informer. Suspicion fell on one Skosana, reputed to have played an important part in the conspiracy. He had no struggle credentials. Inadvertently, the interrogators let slip that they had obtained detailed information about the conspiracy because one of the plotters reported on the activities. My instructions from Joel were to consult with Winnie and the accused, and to see Nelson Mandela.

The first accused was Sampson Ndou, a leading trade unionist. His co-accused included Rita Ndzanga, a prominent activist in bus boycotts and anti-pass campaigns; Joyce Sikakane, a journalist and pamphleteer; and photographer Peter Magubane. Also Elliott Goldberg Mhlangu, a stalwart ANC member, known as 'the chairman' because of his insistence on chairing meetings. His second name honoured the owner of the farm where he was born. Mhlangu complained that the name did him no good in detention. He was called a 'bloody Jew' and given an extra punch in the stomach during interrogations.

Joel asked Arthur Chaskalson and David Soggott to join the legal team. Our preliminary assessment was that most of, if not all, the accused would be convicted. Although the maximum sentence was ten years, there was no provision for a minimum sentence as was the case under the Terrorism Act. No one was charged with an act of violence, although the prosecution informed us that there was sufficient evidence to charge them with terrorism. Apparently being charged with a lesser offence was thanks to the interventions of the good attorney Mendel Levin. Or so we were told. And if they pleaded guilty, as Levin had arranged, the prosecution would request lenient sentences.

Without being allowed consultation among themselves, the three women and nineteen men apparently accepted this deal, believing they were following Winnie Mandela's lead. Once they were able to discuss the matter, literally on the steps into the courtroom, they quickly rejected it.

We had less than three weeks to prepare. It was unusual to start a major trial at the beginning of December and then, after just two weeks of hearings, adjourn for the long summer vacation. The State claimed this was to facilitate a number of witnesses who were in detention and due for release once they had given their evidence. It was a good enough reason for both Judge Simon 'Tos' Bekker and the defence team.

By the time we got to court, Winnie had not seen Nelson for more than a year. At her request I'd been to see him, partly to reassure him that she was well, despite her ordeal during interrogation, and partly to discuss the sort of defence we should conduct. As he was named a co-conspirator, he could be called as a witness for the defence.

Nelson was concerned for Winnie's health. He was relieved that she had withstood the pressures of detention, and grateful that Levin had been replaced by Joel Carlson. That Arthur Chaskalson and David Soggott were on the case further eased his anxieties. After studying the indictment, and using our usual cryptic methods, we discussed the strength of the State's case. Although he was saddened at the prospect of Winnie's being imprisoned, he was proud of her bravery in rekindling the spirit of resistance. He wanted her and the others to use the trial to become the accusers. Their aim should be to mitigate sentence, rather than proving their innocence.

Nelson had developed a rapport with Judge Bekker during the treason trial and spoke of the man with affection. He was certainly prepared to give evidence. The government had no right to declare the ANC an unlawful organisation. On a more personal note, I was to tell Winnie that he was at last allowed a picture of her in his cell. He wanted me to convey his deep love for her, and how her heroism sustained not only him but all his comrades on the island.

Winnie was not one to listen: she wanted to be heard. At the start of the trial, she did not respond with a simple 'not guilty' when asked to plead. Instead she said that after the suffering inflicted on her and others and more particularly Caleb Mayekiso, who had died in detention, she felt she had been convicted already. When she said, 'I find it difficult to enter any plea because I regard myself as already having been found guilty,' the judge said, 'I think you are wrong in that assumption; I will enter a plea of not guilty on your behalf.'

That Winnie's smart attire was a mix of the ANC's colours could not have gone unnoticed by Judge Bekker – not on the first day or throughout the trial. But he said nothing. And certainly no proclamation of illegality would deter Winnie from wearing black, green and yellow.

The keen interest shown in the trial by the governments of the UK and the US soon became apparent. The first witness was Philip Golding. He was so frightened of Major Swanepoel standing nearby that he could hardly be heard. He was a trade unionist from the UK who had made contact with the ANC and its trade union movement. He wanted to assist in the establishment of trade unions in South Africa. He helped financially and with advice, and had contact with Sampson Ndou. Golding had been detained and held in solitary confinement. Clearly he got more than he bargained for when he arrived in South Africa.

However unimportant his evidence, David Soggott slowly and carefully probed Golding's statement to the interrogators about matters that were commonplace in the egalitarian, free society in which he lived and worked. Soggott wanted to establish how Golding was treated in detention. Obviously, he had been told by the security police not to speak about the interrogation, but eventually and reluctantly he admitted being made to stand for two days. He described this as 'not a particularly painful procedure'. He also admitted being kicked and hit on his back 'only four or five times'. He would say no more. He earned his release and permission to leave the country. He was escorted away by Her Majesty's representative.

The next witness was Mohalie Mohanyele, an employee of the United States Information Agency. He had allowed Winnie, Joyce Sikakane and Rita Ndzanga to use the agency's cyclostyling and other machinery to print ANC pamphlets. He was also a conduit for overseas mail intended for the accused. Judging by the detail he supplied so readily and the political discussions he held with Winnie – matters which she would not deny – we decided not to question him about his treatment in detention. Even if he had been tortured, Mohanyele would probably have denied it. The assistance he gave a banned organisation, with which the United States government was not then particularly friendly, was an embarrassment to that country. When he left the witness box he too was accompanied from the court by consular officials – presumably to debrief him and discuss his future.

Statements made under duress adversely affected their weight as evidence. Often judges would dismiss this line of cross-examination, but Judge Bekker was of a different mould. Another witness in this trial was so fearful of the police that he tried hard to suppress the truth. However, as a result of patient probing, allowed by Judge Bekker, important details emerged:

> COUNSEL: How long have you been in custody now?
> WITNESS: Seven months.
> COUNSEL: And you were kept at a little police station called Addo, were you not?
> WITNESS: That is correct.
> COUNSEL: And Accused No 22 was brought there by the police once?
> WITNESS: Yes.
> COUNSEL: What was your condition when Accused No 22 was brought there?
> WITNESS: There was nothing the matter with me.
> COUNSEL: Didn't you have injuries on your face?
> WITNESS: No.
> COUNSEL: You needn't be afraid before His Lordship.
> WITNESS: I am not afraid.
> COUNSEL: Did anybody tell Accused No 22 to tell you to make a statement?
> WITNESS: I beg your pardon?
> COUNSEL: Did anybody tell Accused No 22 to tell you to make a statement?
> WITNESS: When he was brought there he was accompanied by two policemen and he asked me to make a statement.
> COUNSEL: And did he [do so] in the presence of the policemen?
> WITNESS: In their presence, yes.
> COUNSEL: And was it clear that it was at the request of the two policemen?
> WITNESS: I don't know.
> COUNSEL: Nonetheless he was in their company?
> WITNESS: Yes.

The court intervenes:

> JUDGE: Had you by then not made a statement yet?
> WITNESS: I had not.
> JUDGE: And how long had you been detained by that time?
> WITNESS: I was arrested on May 14 and they came and saw me on June 4.

Counsel continuing:

> COUNSEL: And on how many occasions had you been requested to make a
> statement?
> WITNESS: On seven occasions.
> COUNSEL: And wasn't your lip cut when Accused No 22 saw you?
> WITNESS: No.
> COUNSEL: And didn't you have bruises on your face?
> WITNESS: No.
> COUNSEL: What were the people who were asking you to make a statement
> doing when you refused?
> WITNESS: Nothing.
> COUNSEL: Were they just nice, polite requests?
> WITNESS: I was standing. I was asked to make a statement. They spoke to me.
> COUNSEL: And for what period of time were you standing?
> WITNESS: From Monday to Thursday.
> COUNSEL: All the time?
> WITNESS: Yes.
> COUNSEL: Night too?
> WITNESS: Yes.
> COUNSEL: Were you kept standing from Monday, Monday night, Tuesday,
> Tuesday night, Wednesday, Wednesday night and Thursday?
> WITNESS: Until Thursday, yes.
> COUNSEL: Without sleep?
> WITNESS: Without sleep.

Judge Bekker turned his head towards the prosecutor and the security policemen sitting behind him and sadly shook his head.

Princess Madikizela, Winnie's younger sister, was threatened with a long term
of imprisonment if she did not give evidence against Winnie. She knew little that
would help prove the State's case, but it was important for the State to show it could
and would call fathers against sons, mothers against daughters, brother against
brother to embarrass and hurt, to split families and to have them proclaim loyalty
to the apartheid state. When she took the box, we did not challenge her innocuous
evidence. Instead our questions concerned how she had been treated.

> COUNSEL: It can't be pleasant to stand in a witness box and speak about what
> your sister and her friends were doing?

MADIKIZELA: That is so.

COUNSEL: And you must have made a statement to the police?

MADIKIZELA: I was practically forced to. They said, 'You are not going to leave this office until you make a statement.'

COUNSEL: Who said this, Miss Madikizela? I want to give you this assurance that you can speak freely before His Lordship and as far as the court is concerned, at any rate, I don't think that you have anything to fear anymore.

MADIKIZELA: I understand.

COUNSEL: How did [the police officer] come to say that you would not leave that office unless you made that statement?

MADIKIZELA: I told this person that it is difficult for me to talk about my sister.

COUNSEL: And what did he say or do about that?

MADIKIZELA: He then remarked that even a male person cannot leave here unless he makes a statement and this applies to me too.

COUNSEL: And for how long did you hold out?

MADIKIZELA: Well, I was brought there during the early hours of the morning and in the afternoon I made my statement.

When Shanti Naidoo was called to the witness box she refused to take the oath. She would not give evidence, as Winnie Mandela was her friend. JH Liebenberg, the prosecutor, read the Act providing for imprisonment of up to five years for anyone refusing to give evidence without good cause. Judge Bekker turned to Shanti and explained the provision. He must have noticed that she looked at me while he spoke. She knew me, and I knew her and her family's contribution to the struggle. The judge said:

JUDGE: Mr Bizos, what am I to do in these circumstances?

BIZOS: My Lord, as counsel for the accused we think that we should keep out of this, lest it be thought that we are encouraging the witness not to give evidence.

JUDGE: I am not asking you in your capacity as counsel for the defence. I am asking counsel to assist me.

BIZOS: Well, My Lord, as my learned friends for the State no doubt know, it was held in the Heymann case by the Appellate Division that it was irregular to punish one who has indicated that he or she was not prepared to give evidence, without giving them an opportunity to consult a legal representative to represent them, both on the issue of what may be just cause and the appropriate punishment to be imposed.

JUDGE: Is that so, Mr Liebenberg? (The judge bristled. Why had he not been told this by the prosecutor?)

LIEBENBERG: Yes, it is, My Lord, the reference is … (Judge Bekker could barely conceal his anger at not being referred to the case earlier.)

He then asked Shanti if she wanted a lawyer. Yes, she did and was sure that her family would arrange for one. After consulting attorney and counsel she was called back to the witness box.

Now she told the court that she had been interrogated for five days and nights without sleep. She was threatened with indefinite detention and with the detention of her whole family. As a result of the long period of sleep deprivation and standing, her '… mind went completely blank and I went to sleep standing … I had a sort of dream in which I was actually speaking to the officers who were interrogating me, in my sleep, and afterwards when I had sort of regained my senses I was interrogated on this dream I had which was complete nonsense. I had absolutely nothing to do with any …'

Judge Bekker intervened. 'I am afraid I am not with you at the moment. You fell asleep standing and you had a dream?'

NAIDOO: My mind went blank, I had a sort of dream … and in this dream I was speaking with the officer that interrogated me. When I regained my senses I was interrogated on this dream.

COUNSEL: Can you tell His Lordship, if it is at all possible, by way of estimate or otherwise, how long this interrogation was?

NAIDOO: The interrogation went on for five days without any sleep.

She told the judge that her conscience did not allow her to give evidence against her friends. Her statement was made against her will. Judge Bekker ruled that she had not advanced good and sufficient reasons why she should not give evidence. (Interestingly, for many years until apartheid was at its end, no judge said what would be good and sufficient reasons for not giving evidence.) He imposed imprisonment for a period of two months. This was a sort of blessing for Shanti. It meant her solitary confinement and further interrogation would end and she could enjoy the minimal rights afforded to convicted prisoners.

The next witness was Presina Nkala. She, too, would not give evidence. She was from the Eastern Cape, had been kept in solitary confinement for months and prohibited from contact with her family. She neither had a lawyer nor knew how to approach one. The judge told her she was obliged to give evidence or face punishment. He offered to appoint a lawyer for her at the State's cost. How strange, said Presina Nkala, that the government that arrested her, kept her in solitary confinement and tortured her, would now pay a lawyer to represent her.

In the event her family arranged a lawyer for her. Her reasons for not testifying were similar to Shanti Naidoo's and she was duly sentenced to a similar term of imprisonment.

The court then adjourned until mid-February the following year. As our clients remained in custody, Arthur Chaskalson, David Soggott and I visited them regularly to prepare their defence.

The small plot of subdivided land Arethe and I had bought more than ten years earlier on which to build our home was the orchard at the back of the original house. Apricot, plum and peach trees produced more than enough fruit for our extended family. Our three boys enjoyed climbing the trees and regularly filled a large basket which I took to our clients. But before they ever saw the fruit, Chief Warder Breedt would help himself. A perk of his job.

On one occasion, Breedt opened the grille gate of our cramped consulting room with a message that Colonel Aucamp wanted to see me. Standing in front of Breedt's desk, the colonel announced that he was putting an end to consultations involving both men and women. A love letter had been found in a woman's cell, written by one of the men. Why not charge the people concerned according to prison regulations? I suggested. But in the meantime we were preparing for a trial and a separation of the accused would delay us. We would have to explain to the judge why we were not ready. Aucamp grabbed a peach and squeezed it until the juice ran through his fingers. He raised his pulpy fist to my face. Was this my duty too? To pick fruit? Yes. I considered it part of my duty to ask my sons to gather fruit for the prisoners. He stormed off, livid, but never made good his threat.

Attempts to establish who would give evidence when hearings resumed met with no response from the prosecutor's office. On the day the trial resumed, and mere minutes before the judge's entry, Attorney-General Kenneth Donald McIntyre Moodie entered the courtroom wearing his silk gown. He greeted no one, walked straight into the judge's chambers without observing the normal protocols. This was unusual behaviour from the top law officer in the country. Although known for his aloofness and stern in his relationship with members of the Bar, Moodie did not have a reputation for rudeness, or for ignoring procedural rules. Eventually Moodie returned and silently took his place as the new head of the prosecution team.

Judge Bekker, inexplicably red faced, took his seat, then nodded at Moodie to speak. The attorney-general said that in terms of the powers vested in him, he withdrew all the charges against the accused. This left the judge with no discretion but to find them not guilty. Our clients were discharged. But before anyone could move the security police hurriedly escorted them out of court, announcing that they were detained in terms of the Terrorism Act.

Stunned by these events, I appealed to Moodie to accompany me to the judge's chambers, which he reluctantly did. I complained about the behaviour of the prosecution and the police. More particularly, my clients had copies of their confidential statements, outlining our defence. I wanted to see our clients to get back the statements and discuss matters concerning their families. Neither the judge nor the attorney-general had any power to intervene: no one had the right to communicate with a detainee.

Later I learned the reasons for the attorney-general's extraordinary behaviour. The ministry of justice and the security police were unhappy with the trial. They were angry that, led by Winnie Mandela, the accused had breached the agreement struck between attorney Mendel Levin and the security police. They were most unhappy that Judge Bekker gave us a free hand to examine witnesses on the harsh treatment in detention. Consequently they approached the attorney-general, urging that the charges be withdrawn and the accused charged with terrorism instead. Moodie was reluctant. In response, the head of the security police, Liebenberg and others flew to Cape Town on a military jet and persuaded the deputy minister of justice to order Moodie to obey. It was an order the authorities would soon regret.

Our efforts to have the crucial documents returned to us failed. So did our attempts to interdict the police from unlawfully interrogating and ill-treating them. Judges Theron and Curlewis found no urgency in the application, nor any legitimate concern by our clients' relatives that their loved ones would be ill-treated. Others saw things differently. Protests both national and international radicalised many young people, who became activists against the apartheid regime.

Our strategy of eliciting information about police interrogation methods had had unexpected results, but at least it exposed the terrible suffering that our clients had undergone. This, in turn, gave impetus to the campaign for their release and the validity of their acquittal.

More than three months later, our clients were charged with terrorism. The authorities had added a new accused, Benjamin Ramotse. In 1962, I'd represented Ramotse when he stood charged with sabotage. He had estreated his bail, gone into exile and received military training. Subsequently he had been abducted from the then Rhodesia into Botswana and detained in South Africa. His inclusion among the accused meant the prosecution could lead evidence about the activities of MK. They hoped to persuade the court and the public that the other accused were as guilty as Ramotse. But matters were about to take a new turn.

We'd no sooner realised the strategy when Isie Maisels called me to his office. He wanted to know the differences between the old and the new allegations against the original accused. I said they were similar. Had I read the judgment of Lord Morris of Borth-y-Gest in the latest All England Weekly Law Reports? It appeared that the plea of *autrefois acquit* – we have been previously acquitted – might be available to us.

A closer analysis of the charges revealed that the order of the paragraphs and sub-paragraphs of the original indictment had simply been reshuffled. As I was busy in a trial, we asked David Soggott to prepare comparative schedules and Michael Kuper, one of the brightest new members of the Bar, to follow up Lord Morris' judgment and research the South African law. The schedules and memorandum were soon ready. It looked as if we could try the special plea. We suggested to Joel that Sydney Kentridge review the argument and the schedules.

We met on a Saturday morning in his tastefully furnished chambers. Sydney paced up and down, wringing his hands and trying hard to contain his excitement. The proposition was unanswerable, he declared. He would be happy to argue the matter. I questioned Sydney's optimism. The judge scheduled to hear the case was Gerrit Viljoen, not someone of Simon Bekker's mould. But I had never heard Sydney so confident. It didn't matter who heard the case, the argument was unanswerable.

In September we put in a special plea on Ramotse's behalf. This claimed that he was not properly before the court because he had been kidnapped by the Rhodesian police and unlawfully handed over to the South Africans.

By that stage, two of our clients had been released from detention and were not recharged. Sydney, arguing on behalf of the remaining nineteen, was at his best. Over two days he analysed the fifty-eight-page indictment and compared it with the old one on which there had been an acquittal. The older one was two pages shorter. The difference was the allegations against Ramotse.

Sydney carefully compared the indictments. Occasionally he would turn the knife by assuring the court that we were not suggesting that it was done deliberately to confuse. After lunch on the second day, I offered to take over the reading but Sydney felt this would lessen the intensity of the argument. And soon the judge was satisfied that the allegations were the same. If there was an answer to our argument, the State didn't make it. The judge reserved his decision.

When his court reconvened, the judge announced in relation to Ramotse: 'I have therefore come to the conclusion that his seizure was lawful and his trial should proceed.' Regarding the others he said: 'I am handing down my judgment as I do not intend to read it out but for the last sentence which reads as follows: "I have, therefore, come to the conclusion that the plea taken on their behalf is a proper one and they were acquitted. All nineteen for whom the plea succeeds may go."'

As they had been acquitted before, then re-detained in court, the accused did not know what to do. Unaccustomed though Sydney was to exhibiting any emotion while in his robes, he said to us loudly enough for our clients to hear: 'Let them go! Let them go!' Leaving the dock, they gathered outside the court and were warned to disperse. Joel Carlson, fearing brutal police action, advised them to move away quickly.

The State appeal to the Appellate Division failed. Whatever skill Joel may have lacked as a trial lawyer he more than made up for as a most caring attorney. No other lawyer devoted as much time and effort to his clients' needs. And no one was despised as much by the security police. Members of his staff were induced to become informers or they 'would be dealt with'. His office and home were shot at. He received death threats, the lives of his wife and children were in jeopardy. Eventually they could take no more, and emigrated to the United Kingdom and later to the United States. With his departure, I once again had to seek the services of another attorney for Winnie Mandela.

Winnie's acquittal only made the authorities more determined to get her behind bars. She was constantly under surveillance as they waited for her to break her restrictions. It was virtually impossible for any banned person to live and work without falling foul of the banning order's many and ambiguous conditions. Winnie was first banned in 1962 under the Suppression of Communism Act and restricted to Johannesburg. She could not attend any gatherings, communicate with any persons under a similar order or take part in a political organisation. Less than a year later she was charged with attending a gathering. A conviction would have carried an imprisonment sentence but she was found not guilty and discharged. In 1965 she was again banned for a period of five years and restricted to the Orlando township where she lived. As a direct result she lost her job with the Child Welfare Society.

That was not enough for her tormentors. Additional restrictions were imposed on her, preventing her from 'preparing, compiling, publishing, etc any document, book, pamphlet, record, poster or photograph'. Under her banning orders, she required special permission from the magistrate of Johannesburg to visit Nelson on Robben Island. On one occasion she was charged with violating these conditions as she had flown to Cape Town instead of travelling by train. Also she failed to give a policeman, who she thought a reporter, her Cape Town address. For this she received a twelve-month jail sentence, suspended for three years. A technicality meant she had to serve four days.

Worse was to come. The authorities served another five-year banning order on her, drafted in the most severe terms possible. She was under house arrest every night and at weekends, and forbidden to receive visitors. Of this condition she immediately fell foul and was charged with receiving five visitors. Her sister, Nobantu Mniki, with her husband and two children, as well as her brother-in-law, Gilbert Xaba, had gone to the house to fetch a shopping list for Winnie. The State's case was put simply. The order prohibited her from 'receiving any visitors other than her doctor and her children' and it was contravened. The magistrate accepted the argument. He found her guilty and sentenced her to six months' imprisonment, suspended for three years.

To avoid the patent injustice of such provisions, we indulged in a combination of Talmudic and Byzantine hair-splitting, using many a dictionary and whatever relevant case law we could find. We contended that to 'receive' was 'to shelter or harbour' and that a 'visitor' was a 'person who stays with one for a period of time as a guest'. We pushed the argument to its limits. Xaba made nothing more than a business call. This was no different to calls made by the postman, the refuse collector or the light and water meter reader. On the State's argument even the policeman checking her movements would be committing a prohibited act. We scorned the suggestion that the safety of the State was threatened by a nine-month-old baby and a two-and-a-half-year-old toddler. As for her sister and brother-in-law, there was no evidence that she even spoke to them. The judges on appeal were embarrassed by such minutiae and set the conviction and sentence aside.

Winnie was again acquitted on appeal in 1971. This followed a conviction for communicating with another banned person, Peter Magubane, for which she was sentenced to twelve months' imprisonment, suspended for three years. The four acquittals probably gave Winnie confidence in the integrity and impartiality of superior court judges. They might also have led to the erroneous belief that with my help she would always get out of trouble.

Our luck finally ran out in 1973. Winnie was caught lunching with her daughters, Zenani and Zindziswa, and Peter Magubane. He had driven the children close to Winnie's work so that she could see them while they were in Johannesburg on holiday from their Swaziland school. The zealous prosecutor elevated the case to one of great importance. He cross-examined Winnie and Magubane at great length to prove that this was not a chance encounter. Rather it was a deliberate subterfuge by two banned people to arrange a meeting. The magistrate was of like mind. He sentenced them both to a year's imprisonment.

Our appeal to the Provincial Division failed, but we were given leave to appeal to the highest court in Bloemfontein. Our argument was both complex and difficult and only partially successful. The sentences were reduced to six months, which Winnie served at the Kroonstad Prison. On her release in April 1975 her banning order had expired and for the first time in thirteen years she was comparatively free.

A year later came the Soweto uprising on 16 June 1976. After the shooting of the pupil, Hector Petersen, unbridled violence erupted, spreading from Soweto to many townships throughout the country. This was a spontaneous reaction to an order by the deputy minister of Bantu education that certain subjects should be taught in Afrikaans at black schools. During the uprising the security police detained a number of community leaders in Soweto, including Winnie Mandela, under Section 6 of the Terrorism Act. She was held at the Johannesburg Fort for over four months. No charges were laid against her or any of the other detained community leaders. When the judge president of the Transvaal Provincial Division, Piet Cillié, investigated the causes of the Soweto riots, Percy Yutar attempted to lay the blame on Winnie.

Yutar produced lengthy statements from three young activists claiming that the night before the riots they and others had gone to the home of Winnie Mandela. There they'd received instructions on how the march and riots were to be pursued. This 'evidence', read out by Yutar for the activists to confirm, hit the headlines. The *Rand Daily Mail* questioned the veracity of the statements, considering that the young men were still in detention and under the control of the security police. Besides, these allegations were contrary to the growing mountain of evidence showing that the unnecessary and brutal killing of Hector Petersen was the immediate cause of the violence.

The *Rand Daily Mail* went further and criticised the conduct of the commission. It was being used as a platform to defame and condemn people who had no opportunity to respond. Moreover, the judge had given Yutar freedom to place untested evidence before the commission. In reaction to these claims, the judge's registrar telephoned Ismail Ayob, Winnie's new attorney, to invite both Winnie and her legal representatives to the commission. The witnesses would be recalled for cross-examination and she could respond to the evidence. The judge also conveyed this arrangement to the newspaper.

I was busy before Judge Eloff at the time, defending two young men on a charge of murdering the first victim of that day's violence, prominent social scientist, Dr Melville Edelstein. However, I was given leave to attend Judge Cillié's commission for Winnie's appearance.

Yutar called his first witness and asked if the evidence he had given the commission was true:

> No, Dr Yutar, it was not true and you knew it. We told you so when you consulted with us at John Vorster Square. We told you that the statements had been forced out of us. But you persuaded us to come and allow the statements to be read to the commission for 'information purposes' saying that no one was to be adversely affected by our evidence, and more particularly not Mrs Winnie Mandela. But what do we see today – Mrs Mandela sitting there and Mr Bizos in front of her ready to cross-examine us. That is not what we agreed to.

Once again the tables were turned on those wishing to make serious allegations against political leaders. The other witnesses made similar declarations and it was hardly necessary to cross-examine them. At the end of their evidence the judge asked whether I would call my client. We confidently submitted that it was not necessary. However, if some finding was made against her eventually, we should be given notice. The judge agreed with the proposal.

When the court adjourned, Yutar patronisingly congratulated me. In a subdued voice he mentioned that he felt sorry for the young men and would do all he could to avoid a charge of perjury being brought against them. I said that I hoped his efforts would be successful as the last thing I wanted was to end up cross-examining Percy Yutar. With a sour face he turned to Winnie and asked, 'Winnie, how is dear Nelson?' 'We are Mr and Mrs Mandela to you,' she said. 'My husband is well.' Twelve years had not been long enough for either of us to forget Yutar's role in the Rivonia trial.

In the wake of the Soweto uprising, the regime felt that whatever her role might have been, Winnie's continued presence in the area was undesirable. She was an inspiration to the young and this alone inspired rebellion. At least that was their thinking. However, they could not keep her in detention for too long lest the worldwide protests become even louder. The usual restrictions of banning orders and house arrest had proved ineffective. Their efforts to convict her had failed. But they still had an untried weapon: banishment. Although rarely used and confined mainly to dissident chiefs in the rural areas, this was now brought into play.

Mid-May 1977: During the early morning hours, Winnie was taken to the Protea police station and informed that she was being removed from Soweto. She was given no information about where she was going. She and her daughter were piled onto a lorry and taken to Brandfort in the Orange Free State. Winnie managed to get a message to Ismail Ayob about this sudden development. At that stage, I didn't even know where Brandfort was. In the legal diary we found an attorney in the town named Piet de Waal. Ismail appointed him as his local correspondent to look after Winnie's interests, to be of whatever assistance he could to her and to report back as soon as possible. Like most Afrikaners in the Orange Free State, de Waal was a loyal Nationalist. He was also a friend of Kobie Coetsee, then a member of Parliament but later to become minister of justice. De Waal and his wife Adele, despite their background and political beliefs, were both decent human beings, for they not only observed the professional rules but courageously stood by Winnie, often to the extreme annoyance of the security police.

At the earliest opportunity, I went to Brandfort. I found Winnie and her daughter Zindzi in what was no more than a shack. It was a cold winter's day. Winnie was trying to light a fire in a little coal stove, breaking pieces of coal too large for the stove's opening. She was on her knees blowing into the stove. Smoke filled the 'room' that was curtained off as a kitchen. Mother and daughter had no more than a few eggs, a tin of baked beans in tomato sauce and three-quarters of a loaf of bread. This was lunch for the three of us. Outside in the warm sunshine we discussed what had happened and what was to be done. Winnie angrily questioned the legality of her banishment. Was this justice? Could they take her away from her home and dump her here? I had to put an end to it. I should seek Nelson's advice. In the meantime, she would not surrender. The people expected her to be strong and she would be.

By the time I visited her, Winnie had already started planting trees and flowers in the yard, giving notice that she could take whatever treatment might be meted out. As we spoke, some of the older toddlers passing by gave her a broad smile and saluted her, fists in the air. I thought to myself that Winnie Mandela would not change, but Brandfort would never be the same again.

Predictably, the white people of Brandfort could not understand why the government had chosen their quiet town for her banishment. It was rumoured that representations were being made to the prime minister to take her somewhere else. Whatever the case, she was followed everywhere by a hostile Sergeant Gert Prinsloo. In the beginning he helped her erect her washing line, brought her coal and told her where she could get fresh water, but he soon turned nasty.

Once, while waiting in de Waal's office for a telephone call from Cape Town, Winnie suddenly declared that she had to leave or she would break her restrictions by getting home late. Adele de Waal urged Winnie to wait for the call. She would drive her home. Which she did, taking her son along for the ride. The following day Prinsloo served a summons on both Adele and her son for entering a 'Bantu location' without a permit. Piet de Waal was furious, his wife even more so. He phoned Minister of Justice Jimmy Kruger in protest and the summonses were withdrawn. The experience started a close friendship between Winnie and Adele, and Zinzi and the de Waals' daughter.

Eventually I was permitted to see Nelson. I told him that Arthur Chaskalson and I felt there was nothing that could be done through the courts to challenge Winnie's banishment order. Why not ask the de Waals to intervene with the government on her behalf? he asked. I agreed to try, but didn't believe de Waal would exercise any influence over the minister.

In the meantime, dozens of prominent people began making the trip to Brandfort. Desmond Tutu, then Dean of the Anglican Cathedral in Johannesburg, Helen Joseph, Helen Suzman, the ambassadors of almost all the countries that had maintained diplomatic relations with South Africa, congressmen and senators of the United States, members of Parliament and shadow ministers from the United Kingdom. She met most of them next to the telephone booth outside the post office. Some she met in semi-clandestine conditions, with Gert Prinsloo hiding behind the bushes. The stream of pilgrims grew and many South Africans travelling from and to Cape Town would stop to pay their respects.

Eventually Colonel Johan van der Merwe, the head of the security police in the Orange Free State, could stand it no longer. He contrived with Gert Prinsloo to bring a number of charges against Winnie for contraventions of her banning order. The case was to be heard in the regional court in Bloemfontein and likely to last a week. Ismail Ayob arranged for Winnie, Zindzi and the legal team to stay at the President Hotel for a few days to consult. We were booked in there for the duration of the trial. Our presence caused concern among the white guests, particularly when we sat together in the dining room and were visited by the venerable former president of the ANC, Dr James Moroka.

One of the most serious charges brought against Winnie was that she had received her sister and her sister's three-year-old child as visitors, despite the refusal of the magistrate to grant a permit. Winnie couldn't let her sister sleep in the veld, and had told the magistrate this but it didn't soften his heart. How about if Zindzi received the visitors? she suggested, promising not to talk to her sister while she was in the house. This cut no ice either. Winnie had no option but to break the ruling. And no sooner had the sister entered the house than Prinsloo arrested Winnie. She called de Waal and he negotiated a settlement with Prinsloo. This allowed the sister to overnight but she had to leave early in the morning. Prinsloo released Winnie, following her repeated undertaking not to speak to her sister.

All this had been described to me and confirmed by Piet de Waal. He was prepared to give evidence, and was outraged that she had been charged.

Another charge related to a 'gathering' with two post office workers. This chance meeting occurred while she was looking for a place to buy small lumps of coal. During her discussion with the workers she had also asked them to buy her a chicken from a farmer who came into town every Thursday. Another charge concerned receiving Priscilla Jana as a visitor. Winnie regarded Priscilla as an attorney. While she had been held in the Johannesburg Fort, Priscilla had visited her regularly, and only attorneys were given access to the Fort. Strictly speaking, Priscilla was awaiting admission, having completed her studies and training. The rest of the charges were insignificant matters, which Winnie either denied or easily explained.

I was confident of a favourable result, but I did not want to stay in Bloemfontein for the scheduled week. To expedite matters I approached the senior prosecutor the day before the trial started and disclosed my defence to the various charges. This included the appearance of Piet de Waal. The prosecutor told me he was withdrawing the charges against my client, but would do it in open court the next morning. Winnie was delighted, and I arranged to return to Johannesburg the following day.

The next morning there was no sign of the prosecutor or the State's star witness, Gert Prinsloo. Nor could anyone tell us where they were. Finally, at 11.30 a.m., the prosecutor arrived, embarrassed and apologetic. Although his decision to withdraw the case had been approved by the provincial attorney-general, Colonel van der Merwe insisted that the case should proceed, or be postponed until the colonel had the minister overrule the attorney-general's decision. Before this pressure, the attorney-general had given in. The trial would commence. No explanation was given to the magistrate, the foreign journalists or the courtroom packed with an almost exclusively African audience.

Gert Prinsloo was a shocking witness, contradicted by the accused and by de Waal. He could not be believed. Regarding the Priscilla Jana charge, Winnie would say that she did not believe her rights in Brandfort would be less than those she had enjoyed as a prisoner at the Fort. She couldn't resist adding that actually she had enjoyed more rights in prison than in Brandfort. Under cross-examination she confirmed that she had told the magistrate she was not there to defy his authority, although she had done so. 'Then could you explain why you come to court every day dressed in the colours of the ANC?' the prosecutor asked. Without a moment's hesitation Winnie replied: 'Of the very limited rights available to me, the choice of wardrobe every morning is still mine.'

The prosecutor, whose heart wasn't in the trial, also had an awkward time outside court when the *New York Times* reporter asked, 'Sir, I don't want to be impertinent, but don't you feel silly asking so many questions about a chicken?' Stung, he ignored the question. (Eventually he resigned as a prosecutor and joined the attorneys' profession.)

The magistrate convicted Winnie on two counts. He took the view that a child could not receive a visitor, only the head of the household. And no matter how trivial the conversation may have been regarding the coal and the chicken, it nevertheless constituted an unlawful gathering which she was forbidden to attend. He suspended the whole of the sentence. The convictions were subsequently set aside by the Provincial Division of the Orange Free State Supreme Court.

As time passed, pressure grew from the people of Brandfort to get rid of Winnie. She had started a number of projects making use of her training and experience as a social worker. Local white people complained that their serv-ants had become uppity; demanded higher wages and even the formation of a trade union. Ultimately, General Johan Coetzee, by now commissioner of police, paid a 'friendly visit' on his way to Cape Town for the opening of the parliamentary session. He made Winnie an offer: he could get her appointed as a social worker at the Oppenheimer Hospital in Welkom. Her answer was brief. 'My home is in Soweto. You brought me to Brandfort against my will. I will only leave it to go home to Soweto.' She remained in Brandfort until June 1984. Of her own accord she left the town and returned to Johannesburg following an attack on Zindzi. In her absence the house in Brandfort and the clinic she had built were destroyed.

Winnie remained in Soweto, effectively unbanning herself. In Cape Town, Nelson had undergone surgery and she travelled there to be near him and insisted on visiting him daily. This alone broke all the prohibitions in her banishment and banning order. Correctly she assessed that the authorities had lost the bat-tle against her and she could ignore their restrictions. She spoke her mind. At a funeral in Mamelodi she addressed a crowd of more than fifty thousand. There were no repercussions. Those who seek the origins of her later behaviour point to that funeral as the beginning of her belief that she was above the law, that she could say what she liked, even though her views sometimes contradicted the policy and practices of the liberation movement.

During the formation of the United Democratic Front in August 1983, Winnie was stuck in Brandfort. Because of her banning order she could not take part in the comparatively open political activity then possible through the UDF. In any event, she tended to act independently. On her return to Soweto she became involved in the Release Mandela Campaign. She raised funds on her own, avoiding the UDF, whose patrons were all the leading ANC prisoners. Nor would she heed requests by Nelson and Oliver Tambo to work in close cooperation with the movement. She refused to take my telephone calls.

Her penchant for the dramatic led the media to follow her everywhere. She stage-managed events to achieve the maximum effect. At the end of January 1985, President PW Botha offered Nelson Mandela a conditional release, dependent upon his not planning any acts of violence for the furtherance of political objectives. Winnie and Ismail Ayob received Nelson's response and this was studied by Arthur Chaskalson and me to ascertain the legal implications.

The four of us with Zindzi met in my office to discuss matters. Winnie's trip to Nelson had been prominently reported, and speculation was rife that Nelson would accept the offer. The telephone rang incessantly, with journalists asking if we were preparing a statement. But Winnie was firm. The leader of the people would speak to his people the next day, through her, at a rally called by the UDF in Soweto's Jabulani Stadium to honour Archbishop Tutu on his return from Oslo as the Nobel Peace Laureate.

We cautioned her. There was uncertainty about her banning order, it might still be in operation. Speaking at a rally would be a risk. Winnie had a ready answer: Zindzi would speak. No one would dare do anything to her. Botha's offer was seen as part of a strategy to divide the ANC.

The statement read out by Zindzi next day had the thousands at the stadium on their feet. She said that her father should be there to speak for himself or, failing him, at least her mother should speak since she had heard his words. But she was not allowed to address them. Zindzi then punctuated her speech with the electrifying phrase, 'My father says'.

My father says:

Let [Botha] renounce violence.

Let him say that he will dismantle apartheid.

Let him unban the people's organisation, the African National Congress.

Let him free all who have been imprisoned, banished or exiled for their opposition.

Let him guarantee free political activity so that the people may decide who will govern them.

My father says:

> Prisoners do not make contracts with their jailers. I cannot and will not give any undertaking at a time when I, and you the people, are not free. Your freedom and mine cannot be separated. I will return.

Winnie's inspired decision to have Nelson's answer read to thousands of people by his daughter had its effect. From then on, no one needed to speak about the ANC in hushed tones anymore, and Winnie was hailed as the 'Mother of the Nation'. Unfortunately, from this high point, her lack of judgment progressively diminished her stature and sullied her reputation. For Nelson, her family, the movement and the nation it was a serious embarrassment. For Winnie, it was nothing less than a tragedy.

CHAPTER 30

The Foes from Abroad

The early 1970s were good years for the apartheid regime. Such opposition as there had been by whites was rapidly dwindling. The *Rand Daily Mail* had spent over R250 000 in an unsuccessful legal defence of its editor Laurence Gandar and its senior political reporter Benjamin Pogrund, and this encouraged further self-censorship in the media. The black leaders of the liberation movement were on Robben Island and the comparatively few whites convicted of political offences were in a special section of Pretoria Central Prison.

The government's Bantustan policy was taking root: there was no shortage of compliant chiefs willing to consider the quasi-independence on offer. The student movement was divided and its leaders hounded. Inspired by the success of McCarthyism and the House Un-American Activities Committee, a parliamentary commission was established to discredit Nusas, the Christian Institute and other church bodies, the Institute of Race Relations and similar organisations that had sometimes done no more than voice dissent.

Lesotho, Bechuanaland (later to become Botswana) and Swaziland harboured a small number of regional leaders of the liberation movement. They directed many of the young people who escaped from South Africa into the ranks of MK. But it was highly dangerous work. The landlocked countries were vulnerable and apartheid agents operated freely within them, often successfully infiltrating ANC ranks. Ian Smith's Rhodesia and the Portuguese colonies of Mozambique and Angola proved comfortable cushions preventing any incursions into South Africa. Calls by the United Nations and others for an economic and cultural boycott were mainly ignored. The far more successful sports boycott was an irritant, but worth the price of maintaining the 'South African way of life'.

Against this background, it came as a shock and a huge embarrassment to the zealous security establishment when an enormous, elaborate ANC banner was mysteriously found hanging on a tall building in Durban. The banner celebrated the adoption of the Freedom Charter on that day in 1955.

An Australian citizen, Alexander Moumbaris, was arrested in connection with the banner and was about to be charged with terrorism. I was asked by the Australian embassy to defend him. Moumbaris was an ANC courier who'd been operating between London and South Africa.

I found a conquered and disorientated man in the death row section at the Pretoria Central Prison. The security police had assured him that as the death sentence was inevitable he might as well become accustomed to death row. The incessant singing prevented him from sleeping and the horror of the heightened activity on execution days was driving him mad. His cell was next to that of Dimitri Tsafendas, who had fatally stabbed Prime Minister Hendrik Verwoerd. The two prisoners spoke Greek and Tsafendas told Moumbaris of the unspeakable violations he had suffered at the hands of the police and prison staff. Moumbaris was desperate. He wouldn't be able to speak to me about his case until he had been moved from death row.

The head of the prison informed me that Moumbaris' detention was in the hands of the security police. He could not help us. I went to the investigating officer. Moumbaris was being held in the securest part of the prison because of the serious charges against him. That decision had been made by the prison officials. Finally, I knocked on the door of the leader of the prosecution team, Cecil Rees, who was worse than Percy Yutar. He told me it was none of his business. I visited my client several times over the next few days, helping him through the wait until we came to court where his case was to be heard by Judge Boshoff.

Once the matter was called I wasted no time:

My Lord, we wish to raise a matter which Your Lordship may not consider to be within Your Lordship's province. Our client is being held in a death cell. He cannot bear it. He is unable to give us instructions on his defence. Whenever we see him he wants to know when his ordeal will come to an end. We approached the prison authorities, the security police and our learned friend for the State. They have all adopted a Pontius Pilate attitude.

The judge interrupted me:

You are quite wrong, Mr Bizos, in thinking that this is a matter beyond my province. The accused is entitled to a fair trial. Part of it is the manner in which he is being held outside my court. I order that his circumstances change immediately to your reasonable satisfaction. Report to me if this is not done immediately.

Headlines that day proclaimed 'Awaiting-trial prisoner kept in death cell'. Rees, furious, accused me of a lack of patriotism for raising the issue in open court. I reminded him of my visit to his office. Perhaps his patriotic love of his country should have led him to act differently. Almost stamping his feet in a petty rage, he said he had fought in the last war. And as the matter was now to be raised in the

Security Council of the United Nations, the ambassador wanted an explanation. All this was clearly my fault. Our acrimonious discussion ended when I suggested that he report to the ambassador that the matter was 'none of his business'.

Moumbaris was born of Greek parents in Egypt. When they separated, his grandmother in Australia brought him up. As a result, he could validly claim three passports. When in London he visited the office of Greek exiles opposed to the colonels' regime, which was in the same building as that housing the ANC. As it happened, his Australian and Greek passports were good for South Africa while his Egyptian papers were accepted in most of the rest of Africa. One of his first missions was to bring in the large ANC banner that had so infuriated his interrogators. He later regularly brought trained MK operatives into South Africa through Swaziland and Botswana. At the time of his arrest he was travelling with his *compangnon* who lived in France. (He told me that I should not use the word 'girlfriend' but rather 'companion' or 'partner' when referring to her.) She was shortly to give birth to their child. He loved her dearly, and was grateful that the authorities had deported her.

At about this time, the honorary Irish consul asked me to undertake the defence of J W Hosey. Hosey was also at the maximum security central prison in Pretoria, but not on death row. The jail authorities would not allow a joint consultation between us and our two clients in the prison. Unfortunately, Hosey did not trust us. He avoided all questions about his background, why he was arrested and why he was in Natal. Instead, he wanted to study the Terrorism Act and asked questions about South Africa's criminal procedure.

The turning point came when a warder brought a tray of tea with two cups. I pointed out that there were three of us. The warder replied that the regulations did not allow him to give tea to prisoners. I told him to take the tray away. He returned a few minutes later with three cups on the tray. When the warder was out of sight, Hosey grinned. 'I'd say this is our first victory, sir, let's hope for more to come.'

(The incident had a counterpart some years later. The treatment of prisoners was gradually improving. On this occasion, a lieutenant interrupted my consultation with Nelson Mandela to ask if I would like tea or coffee. 'Coffee', I said, 'provided Mr Mandela is also offered refreshment.' 'Surely, Mr Bizos,' he replied, 'you would never have thought it of us that we would offer refreshment to you and not to your client?' Not only did he bring coffee for us both but he also produced a stainless steel platter with assorted sandwiches. I had not breakfasted before the early departure of the ferry to Robben Island, and thought that I was perhaps having more than my fair share of the food. When I apologised to Nelson, he said he was deliberately not eating much because he had been beaten at tennis and wanted to get fit for the revenge match. Things were beginning to change.)

Back in Pretoria Central, Hosey spoke more freely and explained that he had brought money to South Africa for oppressed trade union members. Unknown to him the person who received the monies was an MK member. In fact, Hosey's original contact had been detained and had broken under interrogation. With knowledge of the transaction, the security police sprang a trap at the rendezvous and arrested Hosey and several members of MK. They were charged with my two clients. The attorney acting for Moumbaris, fearing a conflict between Moumbaris and these MK members, did not want us to defend them. Defence and Aid was by this stage banned and its London office had lost its contacts in South Africa, so the MK group was defended by *pro Deo* counsel from Pretoria.

Moumbaris had made a lengthy statement to his interrogators under duress. He realised that he had been under surveillance for some time and some of the people he had brought into the country had made statements implicating him. Although his statement was inadmissible, it enabled the investigating officers to find witnesses who could testify against him. His orders included reconnoitring the Transkei coast as part of an ambitious plan to disembark larger numbers of MK fighters. Even the friendly Xhosa gillie Moumbaris had hired as a fishing companion was called as a witness. The man was bewildered by everything he saw in Pretoria's main criminal court. Before he took the oath he insisted on smiling broadly at Moumbaris, and greeting him.

Others Moumbaris had brought into the country gave evidence against him – evidence which we couldn't challenge. Finally Moumbaris insisted on giving evidence under oath. Rees cross-examined him at length from the information in his statement. The prosecutor was confident that a conviction would inevitably follow on all the charges, including the main one of conspiring to overthrow the State by violence. Rees laboriously tied the evidence to the numerous charges. I learned that he intended asking for the death sentence on the main count.

I began our argument by submitting that the Accused Number One couldn't be found guilty on the first count.

JUDGE: How can you say that, after all the evidence that I have heard?
BIZOS: My Lord, the evidence shows that he joined the conspiracy in London.
JUDGE: So what?
BIZOS: In terms of Section 4 of the Terrorism Act no person may be charged with terrorism for any act committed outside the country unless he is or was a South African citizen or a permanent resident.

JUDGE: Let me have a copy of the Act. I think that before we go any further I
  should ask Mr Rees if he has an answer to the point you raise. Mr Rees?
REES: My Lord, we submit that there is no substance whatsoever in the argument and that it should be rejected with the contempt it deserves.
JUDGE: Mr Rees, I think that you need an adjournment to find an answer, if
  there is one, to the point raised by Mr Bizos. The court will adjourn.

Rees glared at me and stormed out of court. The next day he had an augmented
team with a library of books. In his argument he equated terrorism to treason,
mentioned that both carried the same penalty, and compared treason to a polluted stream. It was a 'continuous offence' of which you were guilty irrespective
of when you might have become involved. Judge Boshoff appeared bemused by
the argument, and as Rees paused to pick up yet another book he intervened.

JUDGE: Mr Rees, are you married?
REES: Yes, My Lord.
JUDGE: When were you married?
REES: In 1948, My Lord.
JUDGE: Are you still married?
REES: Yes, My Lord.
JUDGE: But on your argument you could have told me you were married
  yesterday?

The subtlety of the judge's questions didn't occur to Rees, who went on reading cases.

Moumbaris' mother attended the trial, but she did not come alone. She brought
the *battonier* of the Paris Bar, not as a mere observer but to assist in her son's
defence. The *maitre*, through an excellent interpreter provided by the French
consul-general, studied the Terrorism Act. He pronounced it 'an abomination'.
How could such a law have been passed? Did the South African Bar denounce
it? Did we protest to the court that justice could not be done to anyone charged
under it? He came close to telling me that we merely lent legitimacy to a completely
unjust system. He was incensed about the conditions under which our client had
been kept before the court's intervention.

When I explained the possibility of an acquittal on the main charge, he shrugged
his shoulders, conceding that perhaps there might be some useful purpose served
by having a lawyer even though so little could be done.

He was a *bon viveur* familiar with South African wines. I understood some of his

French and he some of my English; the interpreter filled in the gaps. Unfortunately he had to leave before the end of the trial, but he invited me to visit Paris.

Hosey's mother had also come, comforted by our reassurance that her son might be acquitted. No direct evidence contradicted his version. We were cautiously optimistic that he might go free. In the event, Judge Boshoff acquitted him on one of the two counts. On the remaining charge he was convicted because his explanation was deemed so far-fetched and improbable that it couldn't reasonably be believed.

Moumbaris was acquitted on the first count and convicted on most of the others. Rees called for the longest term of imprisonment to deter other foreigners. After the judge sentenced Hosey to the minimum of five years with leave to appeal, I wondered what he would find an appropriate sentence for Moumbaris. The penalty for assisting trained MK activists varied between ten and fifteen years. The judge suggested that the degree of Moumbaris' participation over a lengthy period was an aggravating factor, but he did not accede to the State's request for the longest possible prison term. He sentenced Moumbaris to twelve years. And so Moumbaris and Hosey joined Bram Fischer, Dennis Goldberg, David Kitson and all the other white political prisoners. They fell under the authority of a Captain Schnepel, who was capable of unimaginable acts of inhumanity, the worst of which were reserved for Bram.

Hosey's appeal to the Appellate Division in Bloemfontein failed. During argument Chief Justice Ogilvie Thompson indicated that Hosey was lucky to have been acquitted on the other count.

We empathised with the mothers of the two men when they parted from their sons. South Africa had only recently introduced television. On that Christmas Eve I was watching a sentimental programme on the Afrikaans channel eulogising peace on earth and happiness to all mankind. I knew that most prisoners would get a special festive visit from their families, but I also knew that the two mothers back in their homes far away would not be able to visit their sons in Pretoria. Might Captain Schnepel allow me to visit them instead? I wondered.

I hurriedly put on a suit and tie and rushed to Pretoria. Captain Schnepel and I wished each other well for the festive season. Then I explained my business. A special visit, no more than a couple of minutes, so that I could phone their mothers afterwards? The captain grew angry. Why did I choose to see these two prisoners? Did I not know that there were over a hundred thousand prisoners in South Africa? Why was I not concerned about them? 'I won't let you see Moumbaris and Hosey,' he said. 'You can tell their mothers that I told you they are all right.' He stormed off before I could speak.

Dejected, I returned home and rushed to the telephone every time it rang in the forlorn hope that Captain Schnepel had changed his mind. I waited on edge until I knew that the prisoners would have been locked up for the night. Then I phoned the two mothers to wish them well and to assure them that their sons were fine. I did not tell them of the captain's refusal. I feared that such a story would raise doubts in their minds about the safety of their sons. And yet Captain Schnepel considered himself a good democrat. We'd had a discussion about the government's overwhelming success in an election. Did I not think that the opposition's loss of seats would damage the country's image? Without an opposition, people could say South Africa wasn't a democracy. There was no point in telling him that the leaders of the real opposition were in jail and that the millions of their supporters did not have the vote.

Morris Zimmerman, one of the most senior attorneys in Johannesburg, had occasionally briefed me to defend his clients in labour disputes. Although he acted for trade unions, he occasionally acted for the accused in political trials and made sure that his anti-apartheid voice was heard. He was popular among policemen, prosecutors, magistrates and judges because he had been a rugby Springbok. Hardly any trial in which he was involved would start or resume on time. There were always discussions about the great games he had played, his opinions of the present team, and who was going to win the next test. His enthusiasm for his client's cause was boundless and he was the dominant member of any defence team. Morris came to brief me about one of his clients, Quentin Jacobsen, a British citizen of Danish origin, who was to be charged with terrorism.

The chief investigating officer was security policeman Johan Coetzee, who was to rise to head that branch and eventually become the national commissioner of police. Coetzee told Morris that Quentin's friends had turned against him. He had been charged, along with his erstwhile comrades, with conspiring to commit acts of sabotage and other unlawful acts with a view to overthrowing the state. Now they were to give evidence against him. They would say that his real purpose in coming to South Africa was not to further his profession as a successful photographer, but to establish revolutionary cells. He had brought in a book, *The Anarchist's Cook Book,* and valuable equipment with which he planned to reproduce the book and distribute it among university students. His brother Henry was also involved but had left the country before he could be apprehended. There was ample evidence, said Coetzee, that Quentin had reconnoitred the gasworks in Johannesburg, the bridges along the road to Pretoria and the Union Buildings, the seat of government.

Although Jacobsen would admit that he did have social contacts with the persons mentioned in the indictment they were arranged mainly by his brother. He admitted possessing *The Anarchist's Cook Book* but said he had brought it in for no special reason. He did not intend duplicating or distributing it; and hadn't done so during the months he was in South Africa.

The State considered this a very important case. Deputy Attorney-General Nothling with Klaus von Lieres und Wilkau would be prosecuting. The presiding judge was Kobie Marais, who heard the matter in the Johannesburg Supreme Court. Highly sophisticated and apparently expensive photographic and printing equipment were placed in the courtroom as exhibits. Soon a young African man was brought into the witness box. The man, who'd been held in detention, was warned as an accomplice and promised indemnity if he told the truth. For the rest of the day, he gave evidence in support of practically every allegation in the indictment, often using its very words: 'incitement', 'conspiracy', and 'act of sabotage'. He repeatedly said that although he did not agree with Quentin, he eventually did 'because he incited me, he really did'.

The witness's demeanour was strange. He would not look at the judge or the prosecutor. He drank one glass of water after another, and periodically beckoned the investigating officer who would give him a pill which he eagerly swallowed. During the adjournments Quentin told us that this man, in common with his brother Henry, had a drug problem. He claimed to be a Sharpeville orphan, saying his father was killed by the police during the massacre. He was a student at Wits and faced financial and other problems. Out of pity Quentin had helped him. Now he was shocked to hear that he stood accused of persuading the witness to commit acts of sabotage. Further, the witness told the court that Quentin planned to use him to distribute the photostat copies of *The Anarchist's Cook Book*.

With Henry unavailable, we had meagre pickings on which to base our cross-examination. We left Quentin at the end of the first day with promises to see him early the next morning. I then asked Quentin's mother, who had come out especially for her son's trial, to get hold of Henry by phone and ask for details about the man now testifying against his brother. But our information eventually came from another source. Shortly before midnight my phone rang. The caller was speaking on behalf of a group of students with information which would show that the witness was lying. Half an hour later we met in my office with Morris Zimmerman.

The students were three men and two women in their early twenties. They knew both Quentin and the witness. After the two were detained the security police had called in this group of friends for questioning. When some of the allegations made against Quentin by the witness were put to them, they insisted that they were fabrications. Quentin never incited anyone nor attempted to recruit anyone. The group were told they were lying and would be called in again. It was in their interests to stay away from lawyers and the trial, especially if they were approached by Quentin's legal representatives.

As a result, they stayed away from court, but sent a friend to report on the trial's proceedings. What they heard appalled them. They had investigated the witness's background, and were convinced that he had reported them to the police. They discovered that the Sharpeville orphan story was false. His father was the owner of a number of buses, but the witness sponged on the brothers Jacobsen, and spent most of his time smoking dagga. He recited poems and listened to the music of dissident African-American activists, some of whom advocated violence. Several books and records belonging to him with his name on them in his own handwriting could be produced. He had also made inflammatory comments at protest meetings held at Wits university.

The group apologised for coming forward at the last minute. They'd been debating what to do since early evening after hearing their friend's report of the case. The information was vital and we praised them for their courage, but warned that while we would try to protect their identities, it might become necessary for them to give evidence if the witness denied some of the important matters that they had disclosed.

In the morning, I picked up Morris and he began pestering me with advice on how I was to attack the witness. I concentrated on the heavy traffic, deeply immersed in my own thoughts after only a couple of hours' sleep. His adamant arguments washed over me, and I said nothing. Morris noticed my lack of response. He launched into a story about his first match as coach of the Transvaal rugby team. He earnestly gave instructions on how they should attack, defend, scrum, arrange the line-outs and vary the position of the locks. He only stopped his instructions after the referee came to the door of the change room for the third time, and ordered the team out. They lined up behind their captain, Jan Lotz, who turned to his team-mates and shouted, '*Speel soos gewoonlik, kêrels*' – Play your usual game, guys. Morris chuckled. Clearly, he said, I was going to 'do a Jan Lotz' on him.

And so cross-examination of the witness began. After closing some of the possible avenues of escape, I adopted a frontal attack, starting with the falsehoods about his personal life and his political beliefs. His answers were evasive, unconvincing and betrayed a lack of confidence. Twice within the first hour he asked for a pill. Nobody asked him what the pill was or why he needed it. By midday he was punch-drunk. I asked if he remembered a large protest meeting in the Wits Great Hall where a 'brother' made a fiery speech.

BIZOS: Did you interrupt him and repeatedly shout out 'Tell it all, brother, tell it all'?

WITNESS: Yes, I did.

BIZOS: Would you agree that you were wallowing in your negritude?

WITNESS: I don't know the meaning of that word.

BIZOS: You believed that 'black was beautiful'?

WITNESS: Yeah, black is beautiful, black is beautiful, black is beautiful …

His incantation carried on as if he had been transferred to another sphere. Von Lieres couldn't restrain himself, and, in breach of the rule of practice that a junior does not participate unless instructed by his senior, he objected. He banged his fist on the bar and called on the judge to protect the witness from the 'most unfair cross-examination' that I was conducting. Judge Marais, a stickler for decorum, ignored Von Lieres, looked directly to me and nodded in the traditional manner, asking me to proceed.

Many photographs that Quentin had taken in South Africa, including those from his trip to Pretoria with the witness, had been sent to England for his friends to see. The hope was one day to publish a book. The negatives and prints were available at the trial. According to the witness, the photographs were for saboteurs to establish how best the structures could be destroyed. I led him on to say that Quentin had photographed nooks and crannies at a close distance. But I had not forgotten Vernon Berrangé's tutorial during my first political trial, that of photographer Eli Weinberg.

I asked the witness what had happened to the photographs. He said they'd been handed 'to an embassy of a hostile state'. The judge called the lunch adjournment, and I commented that that would be time enough to retrieve the photographs from the 'hostile embassy'.

The photographs of the gasworks were taken from at least a hundred metres away. The palm trees in the foreground were almost as high as the gas tanks: clearly a study in contrast. The picture of the Union Buildings showed a bride and groom and close relatives posing before this edifice. As the bridal party were disenfranchised coloured people, Quentin's photograph was a study in the ironies of South African life.

I asked for a further adjournment to prepare our case. I also wanted the photographic equipment kept in the courtroom so that I could consult with our clients about it. Colonel Coetzee refused to allow this. The equipment was to be taken back to his office and we could have our consultations there. I declined his invitation.

However successfully we had broken down the State's case on everything else, we could not deny Jacobsen's possession of *The Anarchist's Cook Book*. Nor could he reasonably explain why he bought it in the first place, and, most importantly, why he brought it to South Africa. Even if the court rejected the evidence that he intended distributing it, he could still be found guilty of possessing information that was of use to unlawful organisations, particularly the ANC, the Communist Party and MK.

Wendy Couzyn, a senior law student, had been assigned to me as a pupil. The three of us debated the sort of information that would fall foul of the Terrorism Act. Readily available information such as that contained in a train or plane time-table would surely not be 'information' of the sort envisaged by this law. Would our argument be enhanced if we could show that recipes for bombs using readily available materials could easily be found? Morris Zimmerman and I sent Wendy to the reference library. She came back with more than a dozen titles generally available to any curious reader. All these titles could have been used as reliable sources by the compiler of the 'cookbook'.

We subpoenaed the head of the library to produce these books in court. She thoroughly enjoyed the experience. The librarian steadfastly maintained that the library was for the use of 'the people'. She told the State's cross-examiner very firmly that it was not for the library to question how readers might use the knowledge they acquired from reading the books provided. Yes, there was a branch of the city library in Soweto, and, if requested, the books she had produced in court would be made available to any interested reader, even in Soweto. No, he or she would not be asked why they wanted a book on explosives.

We were fortunate that Judge Marais had more than a passing interest in the arts. He didn't share the prosecution's concerns about the availability of information. During the course of argument Nothling applied to amend the indictment. To meet our argument that 'possession' of the book was not 'an act', he wanted to insert the allegation that the accused had 'imported' the book into South Africa. Our objection to the amendment was upheld, the judge agreeing that it would be unfair to amend a charge so late in the day under an Act creating presumptions against an accused person.

In his closing argument, Nothling conceded the unreliability of their chief witness, but argued that the accused should be convicted on his own version. Surely he could give no rational explanation for bringing the book into South Africa.

The judge was critical of Jacobsen in his judgment, describing some of his explanations as fanciful and unbelievable. Nevertheless he found him not guilty and discharged him on all counts. Quentin's mother thanked me for my efforts, but said I was too harsh on her son Henry when cross-examining the witness.

I flippantly remarked that I only had one client. She plaintively reminded me that she had two sons.

After his acquittal Quentin hurriedly returned to the United Kingdom, where he wrote a book, *Solitary in Johannesburg*. After it was published, one of the investigating officers, a Captain van Rensburg, asked me: 'How do you feel, Mr Bizos, when with your help your clients are acquitted and then they write a book admitting even more than we tried to prove against them?'

The attempt by the security police to build up the significance of the 'Jacobsen group' and its activities failed. Anxious to explain Ahmed Timol's 'fall' from the tenth floor of their headquarters, they had said, before Quentin's trial, that Timol jumped when he heard that the white communists, Quentin's group, had been caught. This was nonsense. Quentin did not know Timol or anyone else in the Communist Party.

Judge Marais was not one of those regularly called upon to preside over political trials. Although a keen Afrikaner Nationalist he asserted his independence shortly after his appointment to the bench. Not long after the Jacobsen trial he resigned and became a member of an opposition political party. Judge Laurie Ackermann also resigned from the Bench some time later, no doubt partly because of the traumatic experience of hearing a terrorism trial. He became a professor of Human Rights Law at the University of Stellenbosch but later returned to the bench, this time as a judge of the new Constitutional Court.

As a result of criticism, particularly from academic lawyers, including John Dugard and Barend van Niekerk of Wits, Anthony Matthews of Natal and later Hugh Corder of Cape Town universities, the small circle of judges habitually presiding at political trials was widened. Some of the newcomers and even some among the veterans started questioning the role they were playing. There was soul-searching about the efficacy of harsh and compulsory sentences, particularly the death sentence. We would be called into chambers at the end of a trial to be told apologetically how saddened the judge was to send obviously intelligent and talented young people to prison.

Judge President Neville James of Natal sentenced Raymond Suttner to seven-and-a-half years' imprisonment for recruiting two of his colleagues at the university into banned organisations and posting thousands of pamphlets advocating the policies of the ANC and the Communist Party. But Judge James recognised the appeal of these policies among the black population and hoped that the government might soon improve the lives of the majority of the people. Judge Douglas Davidson sentenced senior journalist Anthony Holiday to six-and-a-half years for his underground activities, when he could have imposed a more severe sentence.

Judge Boshoff could identify with the sorrow of the parents of Robert Adam, a highly qualified scientist. The couple sat silently distraught throughout the trial. He passed a sentence of ten years. These sentences, long as they may seem now, would have been considered inappropriately short just a few years before they were handed down. Judge Frikkie Eloff, who heard more than his fair share of political trials, asked a PAC member found guilty on many counts of attempting to recruit young men for military training if he would do the same after he had served his sentence. The activist answered, 'If my country is in the sort of mess that it is now when I come out I would do the same and more, but I would be more careful not to be caught.' Such a defiant reply would have led some judges to increase the sentence. After passing sentence, Judge Eloff confided that he was impressed by the man's honesty and courage and had deducted a few years from his original intention.

CHAPTER 31

The Trial of the Nusas Five

It is not a question of age but of what is right and what is wrong.

– Sophocles, *Antigone*

In the early 1970s, Prime Minister John Vorster boasted that the struggle (he called it 'terrorism') had been smashed. His security police and army had to find new enemies in their bid to protect apartheid. The liberal universities, their teachers, their idealistic student bodies and the advocates of black consciousness became the new target.

The brunt was borne by the student organisations Saso and Nusas. Both were subjected to difficult and lengthy trials. David Soggott acted for the Saso leadership with Steve Bantu Biko as the main defence witness. Arthur Chaskalson, Denis Kuny and I appeared for the Nusas student leaders on trial during 1975 and 1976. We were briefed by Raymond Tucker, a senior Johannesburg attorney often used by students and academics in their political trials.

Five Nusas leaders were charged by the State: Glenn Moss, Charles Nupen, Eddie Webster (a lecturer at Wits University), Cedric de Beer and Karel Tip. Allegedly they'd conspired and committed acts to further the aims and objectives of communism together with Nusas and the student representative councils of the universities affiliated to Nusas. Specifically these charges related to calling for the release of political prisoners, encouraging black workers to form trade unions and aspiring to change South Africa into an egalitarian society.

The case was of particular importance because both the accused and their organisations, not to mention wider society, believed that what Nusas had done was perfectly legal. To prove that their actions were not legal, the State had a rather contorted argument, which went something like this. The aims of the ANC were illegal because the ANC was illegal. The aims of Nusas were similar to those of the ANC. Therefore the actions of the Nusas leaders in pursuing the aims of Nusas were undertaken to further the aims of the ANC. Thus the Nusas leaders were guilty of furthering the aims of the ANC.

We soon realised the significance of the trial. If the State made the charges stick, it would close down much political activity that was still permitted. Anyone, for example, urging that political prisoners be released was at risk of being successfully prosecuted just because the ANC had made a similar call.

Raymond Tucker's articled clerk, Geoff Budlender, was cited in the indictment. Raymond was concerned that it wouldn't be proper for Geoff to be involved professionally with us on the defence team. As a student leader at the University of Cape Town, Geoff had participated in the activities of both the local Student Representative Council and Nusas – activities which were under attack in the trial.

Arthur was an expert on difficult legal ethical questions. He had served as chairman of the Johannesburg Bar Council and as a member of the General Council of the Bar in South Africa. This experience steeped him in the theory and practice of legal ethics. To our delight, he sanctioned Geoff's participation in the defence. He accepted Geoff's assurance that he knew of no conspiracy and that he had done nothing unlawful. In Arthur's opinion, we should not waive Geoff's right (and those of the accused) to be presumed innocent. During lighter moments we referred to Geoff as Accused Number Six, but we were grateful that he was on the team. His personal knowledge, industry and judgment were invaluable throughout the trial.

Somewhat to our surprise, the Nusas trial was to be heard by Senior Regional Court Magistrate Gert Steyn. He seldom presided at political trials. The speculation in legal circles suggested that some kind of a statement of independence was being made by the chief magistrate. Apparently he had had enough of the criticism that security policemen were asking the control prosecutor to place cases before a magistrate with whom they agreed politically and from whom they could expect a sympathetic hearing. In reaction, the chief magistrate had to exercise his discretion about who would hear trials, particularly those with a high political profile.

The prosecution team was led by PB 'Flip' Jacobs, a relatively unknown prosecutor, although, as I told colleagues in the common room one day, I'd met him once or twice in Klerksdorp and thought he was competent in housebreaking and cheque fraud cases. In an imperious tone, Johann Kriegler said he was sick and tired of my cynicism and failure to acknowledge the worth of others. He knew the prosecutor well and wanted to assure us that Jacobs could also handle a stock theft case.

The second member of the team, Hymie Brandt, was one of the most senior and competent prosecutors in the regional court. He could have become a magistrate but wasn't interested as he enjoyed prosecuting. Without doubt he was the most professional and dangerous member of the prosecution team.

Completing their team was a comparatively inexperienced prosecutor, Theuns Verschoor. A former student leader, prominent in the Afrikaanse Studentebond and president of the SRC at the university where he studied, he had been brought into the case to supply background information. He was loyal to the regime, an enthusiastic supporter and promoter of its apartheid policies, the very antithesis of a Nusas proponent. If anyone had raised Geoff Budlender's association with

Nusas, we would have asked what Verschoor was doing on the other side. After all, as a student, he had locked horns with some of our clients or possible witnesses at meetings between the two organisations.

On the traditionally liberal campuses, students in general, and the Left in particular, eschewed the whites-only parliamentary elections. When Glenn Moss was president of the Wits SRC in 1974 he invited speakers from all the parliamentary political parties to explain their policies. They were given a hard time, particularly when students asked searching questions about the future of the disenfranchised. In conclusion, Glenn Moss told the students that the future of the black disenfranchised people was to be found in Nelson Mandela's statement from the dock. And he then read aloud extracts.

The SRC also published pamphlets which were distributed at the railway stations, taxi ranks and elsewhere in the centre of the city. Members of the security police, headed by Captain Arthur Benoni Cronwright, were ever present, monitoring student gatherings. At the end of one of these meetings Cedric de Beer said he would have liked students to distribute pamphlets stacked in boxes under the speaker's table, but he couldn't make the request because Captain Cronwright, standing under a tree on the fringe of the crowd, had served a warrant on him to seize the pamphlets. The angry students rushed at the security policeman, manhandled him and, according to the policeman's evidence, caused a serious injury to his back.

During the Nusas trial, he testified that Cedric de Beer had incited the violence against him. On another occasion, students had blocked the passage to the SRC office in an attempt to prevent the security police from searching the premises. Cronwright opened a docket and gradually added to it until he formulated the charges that the five faced.

Early in the trial of the Nusas leaders, the head of the Islamic Council was called as a witness for the State. The prosecution wanted to prove that Nusas lobbied for the release of political prisoners in answer to the ANC's call to release all political prisoners. To prove this, the head of the Islamic Council was asked to produce a Christmas and New Year card from the ANC for 1975, wishing him well during the 'year of the political prisoner'.

If the State had asked us for an admission of how the ANC had proclaimed 1975, we would readily have given it. But the temptation to embarrass the venerable leader of an oppressed minority and show that the eyes and ears of the security police were wide open, was not to be missed. The ever alert Geoff Budlender told us of a resolution passed by the Cape Town SRC. This called for the release of all political prisoners long before the ANC's year of dedication was announced. He undertook to acquire the minutes.

The State then called a Dr JZ Recsey to describe his personal experiences in Hungary under communist rule. He had escaped to South Africa, which by implication he considered an ideal democratic country. He was alarmed by the threat to democracy posed by an issue of *Wits Student* in which the Freedom Charter was reprinted. This document showed a dangerous socialist, if not a communist, attitude and in his view a university was duty bound not to publish such things. Nor should students be allowed to engage in political activities of the kind that was evident in the June 1974 issue of the *Wits Student* newspaper.

Recsey opposed the distribution of documents showing the conditions under which black people lived. When he came across these pamphlets he considered it his duty to take them to the security police. Arthur asked if Recsey regarded himself as an expert on communism. He answered in the negative. Arthur whispered that the evidence was inadmissible and that we should ask the magistrate to strike it off the record. I disagreed and no one could restrain me. I wanted to take on Dr Recsey.

I asked Recsey when he had been a student. In the mid-1930s, he replied. Was his country then a democracy or was it ruled by a tyrant? He wanted a definition of the word 'tyrant'. I suggested someone who came to power by unconstitutional means and was not answerable to the people. Reluctantly he agreed that this characterised the government of his country.

Was it during this period that he had learned the duty of a student to society? He said this was so.

Had he taken any steps to oppose the tyranny in his country?

No, he hadn't.

Starting from the time his country was liberated from the Austro-Hungarian Empire, for what period would he say that his country had been a democracy? For a brief period at the end of the Second World War.

Had he ever thought that the attitude to authority shown by himself and other students might have been responsible for this poor democratic record?

He had no real answer.

Did he know that many people in Hungary, including students, resisted the occupation of his country by the Soviet Union?

Yes, he did, but that was different.

Geoff passed me a booklet published by the Afrikaanse Studentebond containing a chapter entitled, 'Moral Grounds for Our Policy of Separate Development and the Urban African'. I asked Recsey if he would condemn it for representing student involvement in politics, just as he had condemned the *Wits Student*?

He said he had no time to read it, but that in any case, this too was 'different'.

I then wanted to know which provisions in the Freedom Charter led him to classify it an undemocratic document.

He took his time before saying, 'It contains nothing contrary to the principles of Western democracy.'

Then came another mini-victory with admissions extracted from him by Denis Kuny. It turned out that even the good doctor couldn't fault the formation of trade unions for black workers to protect their rights.

Our clients were pleased with what had been extracted from Dr Recsey. Even Brandt commented as he was walking out of court that they could have done without him.

Some ten years later Arthur phoned me to read a passage from a leading American magazine. The article quoted the president of Hungary, elected after the withdrawal of the Soviet forces, telling the United Nations about the difficulties experienced by his country because they did not have a democratic tradition.

Bartholomew Hlopane, who gave evidence in the Bram Fischer trial, spent the following ten years testifying in one political trial after another. Now he admitted spending eight months in detention and that while in solitary confinement he had bargained with the police for his release. Mostly this was because he feared being detained again if he did not do what the security police wanted.

In this instance it was to confess to being a member of the ANC and the Communist Party, and knowing that the Freedom Charter was the brainchild of the latter. In making this allegation he spoke of the role played by Mandela, Sisulu and Mbeki before the Rivonia trial.

For us this immediately signalled an opportunity to visit the prisoners on Robben Island. We asked that Hlopane should stand down until we had consulted with the three leaders. Permission was initially refused, then granted and then withdrawn again on the eve of our departure. So great was the furore when we complained that permission was again granted.

The three on the island were pleased to see us, and intrigued by the student publications, newspaper cuttings and other court evidence. We didn't spend much time on Hlopane's evidence, since we knew from previous trials that it was false. But did they have suggestions regarding cross-examination?

Our three clients reminded us that Hlopane was originally one of the accused in the treason trial. He knew that Professor ZK Matthews gave evidence before three judges of the Special Court that the Freedom Charter was his (Matthews') idea. Hlopane also knew that three judges found that the Freedom Charter was a document advocating democratic values.

Of course the three were willing to be called as witnesses for the defence, and greatly admired the dedication and courage of the young people on trial. I was to thank them for risking their freedom to call for the release of political prisoners.

In the meantime, Arthur and Denis had looked into the court records of trials in which Hlopane appeared. They found the important passage where Hlopane admitted giving contradictory and false evidence. When it came time for Arthur to cross-examine him, he raised one instance after another of Hlopane's lies and asked for an explanation. The man could give no proper reason for his inconsistencies.

Another bad witness was Professor Andrew Murray, former head of political philosophy at the University of Cape Town. No one took account of his poor performance in the treason trial some fifteen years earlier. Now he had been asked by the police to evaluate whether five documents from a 1973 Nusas seminar expressed extreme left-wing or Marxist-Leninist views. He believed they did.

The intention was to show that the accused had either written or associated themselves with the contents of the documents and were therefore guilty of furthering the objects of communism and the ANC. It will be recalled that his similar evidence at the treason trial had not been accepted by the three judges and the accused were acquitted.

Under cross-examination Arthur Chaskalson persuaded him to modify substantially, if not abandon, his opinion and, more importantly, make concessions helpful to our case. He agreed that the condemnation of South Africa's policies by non-communist states and international bodies was far stronger than that in the documents produced by the Nusas leaders. He accepted that the disenfranchised majority of the population had legitimate grievances that were not being addressed. Predictions in the documents that violence might break out if these problems were not addressed were no different to similar warnings made by many leaders both within and outside the country who were not communists. Then how, argued Arthur, did discussion about the emergence of the black consciousness movement and the role to be played by white students in understanding and accommodating its philosophy make them guilty of a crime?

The State had handed in as evidence seminar papers written by Webster, Nupen, Moss and Tip which, it claimed, showed their guilt. Murray conceded that if these were properly analysed and understood they were a legitimate exercise of the right to freedom of thought and speech. (Geoff Budlender also presented a paper that Murray analysed, and the professor made the same concessions about this document.)

In so far as these papers were critical of capitalism, Murray agreed that his published criticism of the system as practised in South Africa was stronger and more condemnatory than that of the accused. He fared far worse than at the treason trial and he was never again called to give evidence. From then on, the

State looked elsewhere for 'experts' on communism, terrorism and 'the determi-nants of revolutionary warfare' as detectable in the speeches and writings of some opponents of the apartheid regime.

The next witness for the prosecution was Colonel Johan Coetzee. He contended that the Freedom Charter was the brainchild and the creation of a clique of highly placed communists. In his opinion, publishing the charter in a student newspaper furthered the aims of these communists. We embarrassed him by pointing out that the students had copied it from an appendix to a book written by Gerard Ludi, the policeman who'd given evidence in the Bram Fischer and other trials.

We told Coetzee that Professor ZK Matthews and Chief Albert Luthuli had given evidence at the treason trial, accepted by the court, that the idea for the charter came from Matthews. Coetzee responded that the charter was then the biggest fraud ever perpetrated. For how could it reflect the demands of the people if it was one man's idea? What he couldn't understand was that the charter was both the idea of Matthews and the contribution of the people.

The morning after this exchange, the reporter from *Die Transvaler* came to me before court in great distress. She said she was not responsible for what had appeared in her paper that day. She thrust her notebook at me. Her notes would prove that it was not her fault. The cause for her concern was a report stating that I'd put it to Colonel Coetzee that I (George Bizos) had written the Freedom Charter. She pointed out the mistake to her editor, and he would print whatever apology I wanted. Would I sue? I told her not to worry. Though the report was not true, I did not think the contents of the story were defamatory. On the contrary, my reputation would no doubt be enhanced among the vast majority of the people of South Africa. The only pity was that hardly any of them read her paper.

Despite efforts to ensure that Nusas remained a non-racial organisation, black students had seceded from it under the leadership of Steve Biko. They formed their own body, the South African Students' Organisation – Saso. These students espoused black consciousness, confident that they were better off on their own rather than as a minority in a predominantly white student body. There was mutual respect and a desire to cooperate between the two student bodies, but some of the rank and file of Saso said, with justification, that Nusas was infiltrated by the security police, their agents and informers.

The exposure of a couple of such spies in earlier days, particularly Gerard Ludi, who was recruited while a student, lent credence to the Saso view. Their fears were again confirmed during the Nusas trial by the evidence of Sergeant Gerhardus Horak. He was not a registered student, but had loafed about on the Wits campus during 1974. Another example was JH Reyneke, a law student on the Pietermaritzburg campus of the University of Natal, who told the court that he had been an informer during 1974 and 1975. His task was to report on the work of the Nusas wages commission. Asked by Denis Kuny why he became an informer he said: 'Because it was a very patriotic deed.' Neither of these student 'spies' advanced the State's case.

Verschoor called Lieutenant Derek Brune, SRC vice-president at the time when Glenn Moss was president. He had worked for the police even before he registered as a regular student. By the time he was elected to the SRC, he was an old hand at living a double life. He diffidently admitted that he was well schooled in the art of deception and that he lied when necessary.

The image he projected in the witness box, from his combed short hair, neat suit and tie down to his black shoes, was every inch that of the officer and the gentleman. But we still feared he might falsely implicate our clients. Fortunately the reports that he produced and submitted to the police were in the main factually correct. The interpretation of these facts in his accompanying comment was occasionally neither accurate nor fair. But under cross-examination by Arthur Chaskalson, gentle persuasion would inevitably lead to the desired concession.

Brune identified numerous documents seized when the SRC office was raided. There was nothing secret or conspiratorial in them. By common account he was a good administrator and the finances of the council were well managed under his stewardship. He described the SRC under Moss as one of the most efficient to head the Wits student body. This aside, the SRC had been dominated by a radical clique led by Moss, and Wits, in turn, dominated Nusas. He readily conceded that if this was so, it was achieved by persuasion and not by secret or unfair means. It was clear from his evidence that he knew of no conspiracy to commit any crime.

Another regular spectator at the trial, Craig Williamson, had been a senior office bearer in the student movement. He was also a close friend of Charles Nupen. We considered consulting him as a defence witness, but Glenn Moss warned us off, claiming Williamson was a police spy. Charles was greatly disappointed. A few years later Williamson was exposed as a spy. By then much damage had been done to the movement. While a student spy, Williamson was also a policeman earning a comparatively high salary as an officer and confidant of the head of the security police, Johan Coetzee.

Finally the State closed its case and we made an application for the discharge of Eddie Webster as there was no evidence against him. One of the witnesses who supported this application was Jonathan Taylor. He had attended a seminar addressed by the accused in December 1973. At the time Taylor was president of the SRC of the Johannesburg College of Education. Although he was called by the State, his evidence exculpated the accused. He said that the call to free all political prisoners arose from a desire by students that violence be avoided and that negotiation was preferable to confrontation.

Taylor said the call by Nusas was no different from the prime minister's wish that Rhodesia's Ian Smith negotiate because 'the consequences [of not doing so] would be too ghastly to contemplate'. He added that most of the delegates at the seminar had a liberal English background and wanted a more egalitarian society. A number of papers, including one on black consciousness delivered by Webster, were discussed. The main focus, said Taylor, was how to bring about change while avoiding violent confrontation.

Arthur Chaskalson explained that our application was confined to Webster because he was not actively involved in the affairs of Nusas. Also he had left the seminar shortly after delivering his paper entitled, 'Black Consciousness and the White Left'. Nothing in the paper could remotely constitute an incitement or conspiracy to bring about social change by violent or unlawful means, nor could its sentiments give rise to racial hostility as alleged in the charge sheet. Moreover, the Suppression of Communism Act did not make it an offence to work for radical change or an egalitarian society. Although the views of the accused may be considered radical by some, they were views that every citizen was entitled to express in all but totalitarian states. The courts ought jealously to protect that right of the people. Calls for fundamental change were being made daily in South Africa. The court should reaffirm the right to do so.

Jacobs, in opposing the application, said that Webster 'accentuated' black leadership in his seminar paper, rejected the existing political parties, and was working for radical change and an egalitarian society. He contended that they were engaged in a conspiracy to overthrow the government and bring about black domination.

The magistrate rejected our application. His primary reason being that it was inadvisable to analyse the evidence relating to the alleged conspiracy against only one of the accused, as that would amount to piecemeal adjudication.

At that time the law allowed for defence witnesses to be called before the accused gave evidence. We decided to call Laurine Platsky, president of the SRC at the University of Cape Town and a Nusas executive during part of the period covered by the charge sheet. We wanted to know what had prompted her to call for the release of political prisoners. We were so impressed by the poignancy of her story that we asked her to repeat it in the witness box.

She told how, as a prepubescent she was being driven to school by her mother along the highway at the foot of Table Mountain. She asked if anyone lived on the

Laying the foundation stones for the Saheti Senior School, 1978. Today,
Saheti is recognised as one of the leading independent schools in the country.
Arethe, wearing dark glasses, stands to my left. *Nick Lakis/Bizos family archive*

With my mother Anastasia and my daughter-in-law Mary, preparing lunch at Kalogeriko, the family home near the village of Vasilitsi in Greece, early 1980. Below is my mother, whom I did not see for over twenty years. We were finally reunited in 1960 when she came to South Africa and remained for a few years. *Bizos family archive*

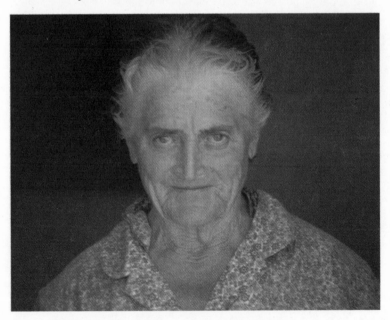

Damon, Kimon and Alexi on the bench, with Arethe and me standing behind them. The occasion was Kimon's wedding in 1994.

Bizos family archive

Making way for Nelson and Winnie Mandela to enter the Johannesburg Supreme Court for her trial on child kidnapping and assault charges, February 1991. © *Louise Grubb/Trace Images*

Talking over old times with Nelson Mandela in his Houghton garden, Johannesburg, 1995. © *Gisele Wulfson*

Port Elizabeth, 10 September 1997. Leaving the TRC amnesty hearing with Ntsiki Biko, wife of the murdered black consciousness leader Steve Biko, and her son Nkosinathi. Biko died in police custody in 1977.

© Adil Bradlow/Trace Images

Talking to Winnie Madikizela Mandela (right) and Limpho Hani, at the
TRC amnesty hearing in Pretoria, 20 August 1997. I represented the Hani
family at the hearing where Janusz Waluś and Clive Derby-Lewis sought a
pardon for the assassination of communist leader Chris Hani in 1993.

© Juda Ngwenya/Reuters/The Bigger Picture

With Nadine Gordimer at the Johannesburg Fort, now a museum and the seat of the South African Constitutional Court.
Photographer and occasion unknown

At the temple of Apollo at Sunion, Greece, 2004. *Bizos family archive*

At my seventy-fifth birthday party in 2003 at our Johannesburg home: Amina Cachalia (back to camera), Desmond Tutu, Jules Browde, Nelson Mandela and Arethe. *Alexi Bizos/Bizos family archive*

(Facing page) Being congratulated by Albertina and Walter Sisulu at my seventieth birthday party held at the Legal Resources Centre, Johannesburg. And (below) by my long-standing colleague Arthur Chaskalson at the same occasion. *Bizos family archive & LRC archive*

Celebrating my seventy-fifth birthday with the the Bizos clan. Left to right: Aspasia Daflos (Arethe's sister), Kimon, Anna, Nicholas (Damon and Anna's son), Eleni (Damon and Anna's daughter), Ana-Sophia (Alexi and Monique's

daughter), Damon, Monique, Sofia (Kimon and Mary's daughter) on my lap, Mary holding their oldest daughter, Lucia, Arethe and Joshua Gosher (Monique's son). The other children are not family. *Photographed by Alexi Bizos*

Among the vines in Greece, with Kalogeriko, the family home, in the background. *Bizos family archive*

Looking on while acclaimed Greek composer Mikis Theodorakis talks to Nelson Mandela at the signing of the call for Universal Peace, in preparation for the 2004 Athens Olympics. *Photographer unknown*

Handing the Olympic torch over to Dawn Hare in Rondebosch Main Road, Cape Town, on 12 June 2004. © *Denzil Maregele/Cape Argus/Trace Images*

Walking with the athletes behind the South African flag at the opening ceremony of the Athens Olympics, 13 August 2004.
© *Mike Blake/Reuters/Corbis*

island she could see beyond the harbour. Her mother said it was a prison. Who were the prisoners and what had they done? She listened closely to her mother's explanation, then asked how long the prisoners had been there and how much longer they would have to stay on the island.

Since then they had never been far from her thoughts. When she was elected to the SRC, she initiated a debate to call for their release. The motivation did not come from the ANC or anyone else but because of her long-standing interest in the welfare and activities of the prisoners on the island. Verschoor's cross-examination enhanced the value of her evidence. For one thing the minutes of the SRC, clearly indicating the date of the discussion, could hardly be challenged.

Much time was spent questioning her about that childhood conversation in the car. No, she and her mother were not alone, there were school friends in the car. Their mothers belonged to a school lift club and took it in turn to drive their children to and from school. Laurine occasionally patronised Verschoor by rephrasing his questions for the sake of clarity or to remind him to be more gender conscious. She denied knowledge of a conspiracy. The magistrate was favourably impressed by her evidence.

Denis Kuny, the most experienced member of our team in labour relations, also turned out to be a good detective. He traced a past member of the SRC in Pietermaritzburg, Brian Hackland, to a beach on the Natal south coast. Hackland was responsible for the Nusas wages commission. He too denied a conspiracy to overthrow the State by violence. The wages commission was about improving the position of many workers, mostly black, and to help them form trade unions.

Verschoor's cross-examination was based on the premise that the government would never allow blacks to establish trade unions. If black workers were encouraged to demand unions, violence would be the inevitable result. Hackland continued to deny a conspiracy or campaign to incite workers to strike.

To emphasise the prosecution's fallacious reasoning we called Professor Lawrence Schlemmer, the director of the Centre for Applied Social Sciences of the University of Natal in Pietermaritzburg. He had researched African labour and black consciousness. According to his research, only six per cent of the African people in Natal did not feel bitter, frustrated or discriminated against. To suggest that most African people needed to be conscientised about their grievances by a group of white students was unrealistic.

In his view, conflict between employers and employees was inevitable and this was accepted in most parts of the world. Structures such as trade unions and industrial courts were necessary to channel conflict and avoid strikes as well as violence or other unlawful behaviour. In addition, he was close to the student movement. He knew the work of the Nusas wages commission but he had never heard of a conspiracy. The students were doing nothing more than was generally acceptable in democratic states.

Called to the witness box, Eddie Webster emphatically denied the State's thesis that the only way to bring about change was by violence. He predicted that the 'New Man' would bring about a non-racial and harmonious society without violence. Webster regretted that the majority of whites were unable to liberate themselves from the need to dominate. This made them afraid and led to hatred and anxiety. The purpose of his paper, he confirmed, was to set out various alternative responses to black consciousness so that people could make an informed choice.

Lieutenant Brune accused Cedric de Beer of being part of the radical clique that dominated and controlled student affairs at Wits. De Beer denied this. On the contrary, there was free and open discussion among students. Meetings were held so that students could hear the views of the all-white parliamentary parties, criticise their policies and argue the policy of non-racialism offered by Nusas. The intention was to stimulate interest. Like Webster, de Beer wanted to live in a peaceful, democratic, non-racial society. He feared that apartheid would lead to violence. Like all the other accused he denied any conspiracy to commit violence or that any acts were performed on behalf of the ANC or the Communist Party. Everything they had done was prompted by their belief in democracy.

Jacobs' first question to de Beer in cross-examination drew gasps from the audience. Cedric's prompt answer drew a similar response.

JACOBS: Do you believe in God?
DE BEER: Yes. Do you?

Such trick questions were typically put to those charged under the Suppression of Communism Act. The prosecution hoped that the accused could be cornered into denying belief in God, or evade the question. This, the State imagined, was added proof of the correctness of the charge against the accused. One might have thought that Cedric was the wrong person for so bald a question, given that he was an office bearer in the University Christian Movement. His prompt response and challenging reply put an end to the use of that particular technique, not only by Jacobs but by all similarly minded prosecutors.

Glenn Moss was articulate, confident and forthright. He denied using the student organisation as a front to promote either the South African Communist Party or the ANC. He described himself as a democrat and a radical liberal. In his view, the release of all political prisoners, including communists, would be a gesture of good will opening the way for a new political climate in South Africa. He insisted that he had always been openly outspoken about his political beliefs and had never conspired to incite the black population or anyone else to illegal action against the government.

Moss had participated in the Nusas seminar at the end of 1973. He believed that the continued imprisonment of political prisoners increased the potential for eventual violent conflict. Full participation of all the people and their freely chosen representatives in a process of extended negotiations could avoid this. He was not seeking to secure black domination; he was against any form of domination.

In cross-examination he reiterated his earlier statements to the court and argued for freedom of speech.

Charles Nupen was the president of Nusas during most of the time covered by the charges. He thoughtfully and patiently explained what Nusas hoped to achieve and denied the allegations against his organisation and his co-accused. No conspiracy existed. He had never been a member of either the ANC or the Communist Party, nor was he an active supporter of either. Neither he nor his organisation advocated black domination or black racialism.

By the time Charles had finished his evidence we could see no point in calling Karel Tip. He had been an important student leader a few years earlier but his only involvement in the events relating to the charges was his participation at the seminar. There was already enough evidence on record denying any conspiracy and showing differences of opinion about the desirability or effectiveness of the proposed campaigns. Karel was anxious to give evidence, but accepted our view that it was not necessary.

To counter the views of the security police, Dr Recsey, Professor Murray and others regarding the proper role of students in society, we called Sir Richard Luyt, vice-chancellor and principal of the University of Cape Town. 'Sir Dick', as Geoff Budlender sometimes affectionately called him, described the atmosphere at his university as involving freedom for all members of the university to say, publish and criticise as long as it was done within the law. This had been part of university tradition for a long time: 'The years of being a student are those of vigorous intellectual and moral researching,' he told the court. 'It is an almost impatient searching for justice.'

He thought it natural that students talk about the sort of society they wanted. There was nothing wrong in campaigning for an egalitarian society in which people had equal opportunity. There was nothing wrong with protest. It was an acceptable way of making one's views known to society, and university protests went back to the nineteenth century. He saw nothing wrong in the work done by the Nusas wages commission. As far as the campaign for the release of political prisoners was concerned, he had some reservations concerning the need to distinguish between the true idealists and those who jumped on the bandwagon.

The magistrate did not appear interested in the vice-chancellor's evidence. In his final summing-up he said that the opinions expressed by Professor Schlemmer and Sir Richard Luyt were irrelevant.

The State handed in more than a hundred and thirty pages of written argument submitting in broad terms that the accused were guilty as charged, and should be convicted on all the charges.

Denis Kuny argued that there was no evidence that Nusas, through its wages commission, had done anything wrong. It had promoted a better deal for workers and encouraged their participation in trade unions. I drew attention to the contradictions and improbabilities in the evidence of the State's witnesses and the merits of those witnesses called for the defence. I also pointed to the lack of evidence that the ANC used Nusas as 'a front organisation' to call for the release of political prisoners. Attention was drawn to evidence given by Professor Murray that more than five years earlier the UN had recommended that there should be an international campaign for the release of political prisoners in South Africa.

The bulk of the argument was delivered by Arthur Chaskalson. He said there was an air of unreality about the prosecution of the five accused. 'If they are going to be found guilty, heaven help all of us.' It would mean that no one could advocate the vote for black people, criticise the policy of Bantustans or indeed any other policy of the government, or work for trade unions. No one could do any of this merely because the Communist Party and the ANC also did so.

The magistrate asked no questions, which in retrospect might have indicated his thinking. But at the time we feared that the Soweto uprising, the banning of trade union advisors and the frequent threats by the prime minister and his cabinet ministers to end the activities of white agitators might unduly influence the magistrate's decision. Eddie Webster's concerned father wrote to religious leaders to pray for a favourable judgment and asked the Bishop of Pretoria to arrange that a priest make regular visits to his son were he to be imprisoned.

A year after their arrest the five came to court for judgment. The absence of senior security police officers was a good omen. They almost invariably knew if there was to be a conviction. They claimed that they needed such information in advance so that they could make appropriate arrangements for transport and prison accommodation. For over five hours on the first day the magistrate recounted, analysed and evaluated the evidence led by the State. For more than half the next day he did the same.

He commented adversely on the lengthy evidence given by Lieutenant Brune, whom he described as an unconvincing witness. He found that our harsh criticism of his evidence was justified. Although he had some criticism of Sergeant Horak, much of what he said was not seriously challenged, was corroborated by other witnesses, including some of the evidence given by the accused, and it was acceptable. The evidence of Captain Cronwright and the other officers was accepted, despite Cedric de Beer's version, which the magistrate rejected.

For over four hours the next day, the magistrate dealt with the defence case. He was favourably impressed with the evidence of Charles Nupen, whom he described as a cheerful witness whose evidence could not be faulted either on his demeanour or any other ground. He could find no criticism in the evidence of Eddie Webster save that he was a bit of an egotist. He was impressed by the evidence of Glenn Moss which he said was given with great clarity and conviction.

He dealt with Arthur's lengthy argument on the proper interpretation of the Suppression of Communism Act, accepting our submission that the State had to prove that the accused had furthered a scheme for change by the promotion of disorder or unlawful acts or by the encouragement of a feeling of hostility between black and white. He found that the State had failed to prove its case against the five and discharged them a year and a day after they had been arrested.

Even before Magistrate Steyn rose from his chair, Webster's father shouted: 'Glory be to God!' The packed courtroom erupted into applause followed by embraces and expressions of gratitude to us.

In the years following their acquittal Charles Nupen and Karel Tip became lawyers and worked for the Legal Resources Centre, established not long after the trial by Arthur Chaskalson, Geoff Budlender and Felicia Kentridge. Eddie Webster is a professor at Wits where he helped transform that university into a non-racial institution. Glenn Moss has been a major figure in the publishing industry and Cedric de Beer in non-governmental organisations supporting democracy.

Charles Nupen and his wife Dren have played important roles as mediators in conflict resolution. They have helped organise elections, not only in South Africa but beyond its borders. None of them has sought political office. Geoff Budlender succeeded Arthur Chaskalson as national director of the Legal Resources Centre and is now a member of the Cape Town Bar.

Twenty-five years after the trial, the changes Nusas and the five accused had called for – along with so many others – became reality. I often wonder how much less suffering would have occurred, and how much more rapidly progress would have been made, if their elders in power had heeded their voices instead of trying to imprison them.

CHAPTER 32

The Soweto Uprising

When we passed the municipal office with the white man standing outside, he was an ordinary person to us, but when we came back he was an enemy.

– Dan Montsisi, student leader
(explaining the attack on Dr Leonard Melville Edelstein)

Unbridled violence broke out in Soweto during the morning of 16 June 1976 when police fired on school pupils protesting against the decree that half their subjects were to be taught in Afrikaans. The anger unleashed that day spread to other parts of the country, and went on for several years, during which many more people lost their lives. Most of those who died were killed by the police, although some were killed by pupils and unruly youths who targeted people they considered to be their enemies for not supporting the struggle.

In the view of many, Soweto 1976 and its aftermath was an important element in achieving liberation for South Africa. But it also showed the police – and sometimes the courts – at their worst.

The protest was four months old when, early in October 1976, more than a thousand students travelled surreptitiously into the centre of Johannesburg to hold a protest meeting in the Library Gardens. Of that group, a hundred and fifty-nine were arrested and charged with public violence and organising an unlawful gathering. They were also charged with other offences that had been committed by unknown persons in the city centre that day. At the instance of the South African Council of Churches, then headed by Desmond Tutu, legal representation was arranged for the arrested youths. They were kept in custody for months, visited regularly by attorney Sheila Camerer, now a member of Parliament and spokesperson on justice for the main opposition party. She helped prepare their defence and took care of their needs by, among other things, assisting their families to visit them and bringing food and reading material.

The students were separated from other prisoners because of their age. Arrangements had also been made for social welfare officers to interview their parents and some of their teachers. Their reports showed that most of the students were members of stable families and the children of caring, hardworking men and women, ambitious to provide for the education of their children in the hope that they would enjoy a better life. Many of their mothers disavowed any political motive for the presence of their children in the centre of the city. They maintained that the children were buying produce for their parents' hawker stalls.

Almost unanimously, our young clients told a different story. In statements to the police they said that they marched into Johannesburg to prove an important point. This being that in a white area police would neither shoot black protestors nor fire gas canisters at them, whereas in the townships they fired randomly, without concern about hitting bystanders.

Clearly a great shift had occurred in the thinking of the young; they were no longer prepared to be as docile and patient as their elders. In this they were encouraged by most of their teachers, who were critical of the syllabuses. For instance, they praised the kings that the colonialists demoted to chiefs, and described them as heroic leaders, who fought legendary battles with assegais against guns and cannons. In the classroom, on the school playgrounds and the makeshift football fields, in the church halls before and after choir practice and at informal gatherings at home, the schoolchildren would exchange banned books on the history of the ANC, carefully disguised copies of speeches by Nelson Mandela, Robert Sobukwe and Steve Biko, poems of black writers, and the writings of clerics on liberation theology.

The police killings during the uprising brought home to these youths the brutality of the police force and the army when it was deployed to re-establish the regime's law and order. The arrogant decision to impose Afrikaans, a strange and hated language to most of them and their teachers, propelled the pupils to action. Their seniors in Saso, Nusas, the SRCs and black groups at universities had protested against the government. Now they would do the same, even though they were still at school. They refused to be put off by claims that they were too young for involvement. Actually, many of these black pupils were as old as the students at white universities where protest was commonplace, even expected.

The regime's response to the uprising was to blame the ANC and 'agitators', and to crack down on activity in black areas. Schools were closed, groups of young people were dispersed, and the police used violence without hesitation. In reaction the schoolchildren posted lookouts on strategic corners to warn of approaching security vehicles. Inventively they gave each kind of vehicle a local name. Flying Squad cars were 'Zola Budds', named after a runner, while a slow, silent vehicle that crept along the streets was a 'mellow yellow', the name of a soft drink. Depending on the vehicle, the students might jump over the fence and meet it with a barrage of stones, or, in the face of the heavily armed *Buffel*, hastily retreat to the backyard of a friendly house.

The closure of schools, the disempowerment of students' parents, the arrest of the src leadership, the banning or imprisonment of leaders and their community organisations led a group of influential black Sowetan residents to form the Committee of Ten. This committee petitioned the authorities to reopen the schools, revoke the decree in relation to teaching through the medium of Afrikaans and stop the indiscriminate shootings.

For more than a year their voices fell on deaf ears. The regime wanted the riots to stop before they would revoke their crackdown; at this stubbornness the students coined a new slogan: 'liberation before education'. Their leaders, prominent among them Tsitsi Mashinini, went into hiding. Some were caught and tortured. Under torture some detainees implicated Mashinini in the death of Dr Melville Edelstein, a social scientist who had been killed even though he was well known in Soweto and had helped many people. Mashinini had a price on his head, but could not be found. It was said that a potion had made him invisible to the police.

Given the fraught climate, the police were in no mood for leniency and determined to press charges against our young clients for their audacious city centre protest. Sheila Camerer took me to the Cinderella prison at Boksburg, where some of the students were held. They admitted holding an unlawful meeting in central Johannesburg, but categorically denied the other charges.

One of the most articulate and confident in the group was eighteen-year-old Cyril Ndlovu, who had hoped to write his final school-leaving examination at the end of 1976. He had an important question for me. 'Can a prosecutor wear a gun in court?' I tried to get clarity. 'You mean in his inside pocket or on his belt covered by his jacket?' 'No, in a holster tied on his hip like cowboys in the films. He had it on when our case was postponed, in open court. The magistrate said nothing. What are you going to do about it?' Quite clearly, if he came to court wearing the gun again, he would have to be disarmed.

Our clients were keen to talk about themselves. Not only had they rejected the educational system but they were critical of many of their teachers and elders for not ending apartheid education long before. These young people were undergoing a crash course in political activism. They had attended the funerals of many of their peers, killed by police. At these funerals they were shot at by police and these gatherings became emotional political events. Once arrested, many of them were held in large prison cells and this further radicalised them. They aspired to become freedom fighters – joining the underground movement, fleeing the country on the pretext of seeking better schooling and then undergoing military training and returning to fight for freedom.

They used the slogans of the ANC, PAC and the Black Consciousness Movement indiscriminately, and did not discuss the ideological differences between them. It was not even clear if they understood these differences. They spent their time in prison writing and acting plays. They had also conducted 'trials' for 'crimes' such as uncomradely behaviour in not sharing with others the little that was brought by relatives on visiting days, or using provocative, insulting or foul language. Those found guilty were sentenced to wash everybody's tin dishes after a meal.

The trial was set to take place in the hall of a leading Catholic school closed down by the department of Bantu education. Later the school was converted into a police station that became notorious as a place of torture and police killings. Sheila Camerer and I arrived to find the gravelled courtyard full of mothers. They'd been prevented from speaking to their children by dozens of heavily armed policemen in uniform, who even questioned our presence there. That we were lawyers was not good enough for them; they insisted on identity documents. The officer in charge, Colonel Swanepoel, slowly walked over to us. I was well known to him and he told his men to let us through.

As we were greeted by the students, the tall, hefty, bearded prosecutor stared at us and I noticed the holster on his thigh and the handle of a six-shooter protruding from it. I didn't greet him but went directly to the senior public prosecutor and said I was not prepared to appear against a visibly armed prosecutor. Would he tell his junior colleague to remove his firearm? No, it had nothing to do with him. Would he accompany me to the magistrate? I was told to go on my own.

Senior Regional Magistrate van Dam was the kind of man who made his presence felt not only in the courtroom. He was conscious of his authority and insisted that judicial decorum be observed at all times. My complaint visibly upset him. I should remember that we were in Soweto, a dangerous place for whites. No doubt the prosecutor was armed to protect himself and, if need be, the magistrate while he presided in court. He added, 'He may even have to protect you, Mr Bizos.' I replied that I didn't need the prosecutor's protection. Security was a matter for the police and not officers of the court. I would discuss the matter with our clients. He shook his head in disbelief as we left his office. Obviously the problem we raised was a novel one for him.

Back in the courtroom I asked the prosecutor and the policemen to leave us while we consulted with our clients. Somewhat reluctantly they did. Our clients were overjoyed at the prospect of deliberately and on a matter of principle refusing to participate in the trial. We warned that it could have serious consequences for them and us. And before a decision was taken we needed to consult with their parents and senior legal practitioners.

While we stood talking in the courtyard, Ismail Mahomed arrived. He had been appointed senior counsel shortly before. Accompanying him was his junior, Clifford Mailer, and Ismail Ayob, his attorney. They had been retained by a number of the accused. For the previous twenty years Ismail Mahomed and I had done many a case together where I acted as his senior. I had not applied for silk status at that stage as I expected difficulties from John Vorster or Jimmy Kruger. As Ismail was the senior member of the Bar present, I deferred to him to handle the matter. He agreed that we should not appear unless the prosecutor removed his firearm and enthusiastically accepted the responsibility of protesting, if needs be by withdrawing from the case and letting our clients ask for a postponement to consider their position.

Ismail went to speak to van Dam and told him our decision. The magistrate was in no hurry to convene his court and must have alerted the chief magistrate of Johannesburg, who arrived shortly afterwards. He conferred with van Dam and instructed the prosecutor to remove his revolver. Although the prosecutor protested, the chief magistrate threatened to file a complaint against him with the Public Service Commission.

Ismail seized on the chief magistrate's presence to explain that our clients were not guilty of anything more than holding an unlawful gathering for which a caution and discharge was a proper punishment. Why indulge in a protracted trial on fanciful charges which were unlikely to be proved?

Again, I deferred to Ismail. He tested his negotiating skills with the two magistrates and the senior prosecutor while I explained the new developments. Ismail secured a caution and discharge for everyone under eighteen. The older students had to pay a minimal fine. The only exception was a sixteen-year-old boy charged with possession of a Molotov cocktail – an accusation he denied. The trial of this accused was postponed, but he had to remain in custody, as the senior prosecutor wouldn't allow bail. The outcome was welcomed by everyone but the mother of the sixteen-year-old. Her tearful plea for her son's release on bail succeeded. He eventually stood trial and was acquitted.

For these young people and their peers, their baptism of fire on the streets of Soweto, their imprisonment for months, their loss of at least a year of schooling and the anxiety of their parents was not in vain. While they were often called 'the lost generation', students and young political activists of this period saw themselves as freedom fighters.

Some ten years later I met Cyril Ndlovu, who'd raised the issue of the armed prosecutor. He was a bank teller at a branch in Innes Chambers. In the years before the Soweto uprising, the position of bank teller was reserved for whites only. A couple of years later, when I asked after Cyril Ndlovu at the bank, I learned that he had become a manager.

An early casualty of the Soweto uprisings was sociologist Dr Melville Edelstein. The police were most anxious to find his killers. Accordingly this led them to arrest the president of the Soweto Students' Representative Council, Tsitsi Mashinini, its secretary, Barney Makhatle, and the treasurer, Selby Semela. The conviction of these leaders would have discredited the student movement. And allowed the police to show that being sympathetic to the cause of the oppressed (as Dr Edelstein was) didn't make you immune from savage attacks.

For a while the three leaders operated underground, eventually surfacing in London where they denied responsibility for Dr Edelstein's death. They claimed that the statements implicating them in his death had been beaten out of their fellow students. Among supporters of the regime, Mashinini became a hated man. To the vast majority he was a charismatic young leader.

Almost everyone arrested on an offence arising out of the Soweto uprising was refused bail. The flight of the three youth leaders was used to justify this position. For example, Judge Irving Steyn asked during argument whether he was expected to grant bail so that the applicant could 'follow Mashinini' even though Mashinini's name was not mentioned in the papers before him. Pretending judicial ignorance, I asked who Mr Mashinini was. He replied that the likes of me did not know and did not care what was happening in the country.

The regime's propaganda claimed that the death of Dr Edelstein was planned and deliberate, orchestrated by the liberation movement through the student leadership. But if the three student leaders were beyond the reach of the police, someone else had to stand trial to prove that the regime's claim was true. That someone else was Dexter Ronnie Mosheshle, another student leader: convicting him and his co-accused was important to the State as that would validate its claims against the students and vindicate its subsequent crackdown.

Bowman, Gilfillan & Blacklock, a firm of attorneys established a century ago, usually acted for the captains of mining, industry and commerce, but the firm was not averse to allowing its younger partners, associates and candidate attorneys to do the occasional political trial. The firm's John Brand asked me to defend Mosheshle, whose family had approached the South African Council of Churches for help. He and his two co-accused would be tried by Judge Frikkie Eloff in the Springs Circuit Court. The other two accused were Kenneth 'Tiza' Dlamini, who would be defended by *pro Deo* counsel, and Lebegang John Matonkonyane, whose parents had engaged the services of their own attorney and of Sam Aarons as counsel.

Dexter's defence had been well prepared by John Brand. He denied any complicity in the attack on Dr Edelstein. Despite police pressure he had not confessed to the crime, nor were there reliable witnesses to give truthful evidence against him. Under the circumstances it was not surprising that merely days before the trial the prosecutor telephoned to say that he would be withdrawing the charges against Dexter.

I had set aside two weeks for the trial. This sudden development meant I had an unexpected fortnight of free time to clear my desk, something I cherished. But the next morning Errol Price, then a newcomer to the Bar, and Tiza Dlamini's *pro Deo* counsel showed me the indictment against his client. This amounted to a confession made by Tiza to a Captain Maree at the notorious Brixton Murder and Robbery Squad Police Station. Errol had gone to the leader of his group for assistance, and been referred to me as I had once cross-examined Captain Maree at an inquest. In that instance, the magistrate rejected the captain's claim that he acted in self-defence by shooting an arrested man. In fact he recommended to the attorney-general that the police officer be charged with murder.

Errol asked for a few tips for his cross-examination of Captain Maree in relation to Tiza's 'confession'. He was right at the beginning of preparations and had yet to see his client. In *pro Deo* cases, counsel had no help as attorneys were not appointed. To make matters even more difficult, Errol had never before challenged a confession. As he had no objection to my asking the Bar Council's *pro Deo* secretary to appoint me to lead him, I ended up back on the case. Lionel Weinstock, a friend of the minister of justice, was pleased with my offer. He intended asking the minister, Jimmy Kruger, to authorise an additional fee but I assured him that would be unnecessary.

Errol and I went to consult Tiza at the Johannesburg Fort. He was a short, undernourished eighteen-year-old who had dropped out of school, and relied financially on his mother and his sister. He admitted signing a document written by Captain Maree, but denied making a confession. He insisted that at the time of Dr Edelstein's death, which he fixed by a hovering helicopter that had came to rescue the fatally injured sociologist, he was in a local clinic having his septic hand treated. It had become swollen and infected after a shebeen fight and he needed urgent medical attention. His sister was with him because his mother feared he might spent the fifty cent fee on alcohol.

He was at the clinic for some time. First his septic hand was seen by a doctor, then cleansed and bandaged by a nurse. He had waited a further half an hour for confirmation that he was not allergic to the administered medicines. He spent more time at the hospital pharmacy while medicines were dispensed. Afterwards he had walked home and slept. Throughout this time his sister had been with him. Moreover, the clinic attendance card was on top of the kitchen cupboard at his home. The moment we heard this, it was obvious we needed the card, the clinic records and some witnesses.

Tiza had told the same story to the investigating officer but no one had bothered to ascertain his movements or retrieve the card. To save time, I asked our office messenger to fetch the card. John Brand asked Leon Goosen, his candidate attorney and a student at the then Rand Afrikaans University, to collect the all-important documents from the clinic. Although the clinic had closed down, the records were at Baragwanath Hospital. There Goosen had used his ingenuity. When the senior clerk demanded the authority of the superintendent before accessing the records, Goosen resorted to subterfuge. He folded his brown attorney's file so that it looked like a detective's docket, and told the superintendent in Afrikaans that he was investigating a murder case. This produced the desired results. Given carte blanche, Leon found and copied the records. They showed beyond any reasonable doubt that Tiza could not have participated in the attack of Dr Edelstein, and that the signed confession was false. Undoubtedly he had been forced or tricked into signing it.

On the first Monday of February 1977 Judge Frikkie Eloff called us into his chambers. He would not be sitting with assessors as he had decided that in the event of a conviction he would not impose the death sentence. The age of the accused and the circumstances of the crime had influenced his thinking.

The court convened. Our client was generally known by his nickname 'Tiza' – a tag commonly given to good soccer 'dribblers' who 'teased' their opponents. There were many Tizas in Soweto. It seemed that a suspect who had escaped from custody had mentioned a 'Tiza' in a statement to the police. Consequently when Sergeant Dempsey arrested 'our' Tiza he didn't push his investigations too far. Admittedly Dlamini told him he was at the clinic at the time of the murder, but the accused also told him that he had left the clinic by 9 a.m., two hours before the attack on Dr Edelstein.

The doctor and senior nurse confirmed the details recorded on the clinic card. In addition, Tiza's entire story about seeing the doctor, then the nurse, then queuing at the clinic pharmacy, was corroborated by his sister. Tiza himself then gave evidence that Captain Maree obtained his signature on blank pieces of paper. The policeman had also written out a 'confession', not a word of which was Tiza's. Tiza also described being tortured by the police.

The judge rejected this evidence, but did not admit the confession as having been freely and voluntarily made. The senior white officers were not criticised and their evidence was accepted. Both the two accused were found not guilty and discharged. The judge added that his finding did not exonerate the accused, it was merely that there was no proof beyond reasonable doubt that they had committed the killing.

Throughout the proceedings, Erona Edelstein sat anxious to learn by whom and why her husband had been killed. As a social scientist his reports showed that he was not indifferent to the plight of the oppressed. He had warned the authorities of the deeply felt frustration and anger of the people of Soweto and of the possibility of dire consequences. As often happens in criminal trials, there were no answers to her questions. I wanted to approach her but what could I say and how would she react? Now I very much regret not doing so. However disappointed she may have been, I am sure that she would not have wanted the wrong persons convicted.

Years later the Human Rights Violations Committee of the Truth and Reconciliation Commission heard evidence from some of those involved in the events of 16 June 1976. The Edelstein daughters, Janet and Shana, went to the hearing hoping to hear why their father was killed, what his last words were and how he was to be remembered.

At the hearings, Janet Edelstein had discussions with Dan Montsisi and others and appeared to accept that her father died at a time when the young people of Soweto were filled with rage. He was in the wrong place at the wrong time. She told the committee that she believed her father had 'died for a reason, he died for a cause ... I just feel that we should all make an effort to look after one another now because we are all one.' She added, 'He loved the people of Soweto almost like he did his own family.' Her younger sister, Shana, said, 'My father actually died a day before my birthday and so for me it has never ever been a happy birthday. It has always been a remembrance and a mourning, a day of mourning.' The sisters asked that their father, who 'had no personal fears of Soweto or the people because he worked so closely with them and that they were friendly with one another', should be remembered for his contribution to the struggle for change in South Africa.

In the late 1970s the detention provisions of the Terrorism Act were used extensively. Members of the Soweto Students' Representative Council were taken into custody shortly after the events of 16 June and brought to trial on a charge of sedition before Judge van Dyk. The prosecutor was KPCO von Lieres und Wilkau. The State relied heavily on archaic provisions of Roman-Dutch Law from which von Lieres argued that sedition had been committed by the accused even though their actions were non-violent. In the end, his advocacy prevailed against that of a prominent liberal and human rights lawyer, Ernie Wentzel.

The judge was unreceptive to the democratic rights of freedom of expression, the right to peaceful assembly, and the right to protest against the policies of a tyrannical government. Their trial started more than a year after the uprising. By the time it was completed and the sentences of the accused handed down, another year had passed. The harshest sentences were reserved for Dan Montsisi (eight years), Maffison 'Murphy' Morobe (seven years), Seth Mazibuko (six years) and Susan Sibongile Mthembu (four years). Parts of the sentences were suspended for five years. The four survived their ordeal, were eventually released and most of them today play an important role in public life.

Whatever the defects of Bantu education, students read documents of the liberation movement, those originating from within the country and those coming from outside. Nor could students be stopped from reading *Sechaba,* the official organ of the ANC, nor from listening to Radio Freedom broadcast from Lusaka. Exaggerated accounts of the nature and extent of the uprising reached Nelson Mandela and other political prisoners on Robben Island.

Even when matters were more accurately described to them during our visits and by those convicted and sent to Robben Island following the events of 16 June, the leaders were persuaded that the spirit of resistance had been revived. The prison population of Robben Island was substantially increased. Whatever ideological tendency they may have favoured when they arrived, the vast majority soon came under the influence of Nelson Mandela, Walter Sisulu, Govan Mbeki and Ahmed Kathrada. They emerged staunch supporters of the ANC and, on their release, played an important role in the formation of the United Democratic Front and its affiliated organisations.

One of those serving a prison term on Robben Island after 16 June was Linda Mario Mogale. His trial is notable as one of the worst examples of police duplicity and of procuring false evidence through torture. He appeared before Judge Fritz Steyn in a trial that was no more than a parody of justice. Linda was charged with three counts of murder, arson, malicious injury to property and terrorism. At least five of these charges carried a death sentence. He was convicted on all thirteen counts, but on the murder charges was found guilty of the lesser crime of culpable homicide, although neither the State nor the defence had advanced any argument to support such a finding.

Linda was a member of the Soweto Students' Representative Council and its chairman before the council was outlawed together with eighteen other organisations in October 1977. He then became a member of the Soweto Students' League. The security police hoped that if a student leader such as Linda was convicted of serious common-law crimes, this would not only remove him from the scene but would serve as a deterrent. Above all, they wanted to discredit the student movement.

Linda was kept in solitary confinement for months. At the time of his detention he had been assaulted in the presence of church elders. The assault continued at the Protea Police Station on the outskirts of Soweto. Linda wore a chain given him by his girlfriend. The police twisted it so violently that their action left scars – but that was the least of his troubles.

The State relied on two confessions by Linda. One was a tape-recording made to the police, the other was made to a magistrate. In the first confession, the State had the legal responsibility of proving that the tape-recording was freely and voluntarily made. With the second confession, the law had been changed. If a confession were made to a magistrate the accused would have to prove that it was not freely and voluntarily made. This meant we had to prove that the confessions had been forced out of Linda.

In his evidence, Linda explained why he had made the false confessions:

After some time one of the policemen came with a pair of pliers. While I was pinned down to the ground a black sergeant I know as Mohage had joined them in assaulting me and beating me up. I was told that they were going to soften me up. They were not going to play with me. I had given them a lot of, I had wasted a lot of their time. So a pair of pliers was taken by this chap Matthee. Sergeant Matthee, he took a pair of pliers and while I was pinned to the ground by Mohage an attempt was made to pull out two of my teeth. Then I struggled until both my teeth had broken down. After this I was hit continuously until I felt [sic] unconsciousness. On regaining consciousness I found some electrodes on my bed and a flow of electric current was flowing through my body, in other words, electrical shocks were applied to me. In fact I had a notion, a sort of hallucination of bad things happening. In other words my vision wasn't quite clear at the time so after some time I was visited by Mohage and thrown into the maroon Valiant.

Linda was the grandson of the founding editor of the *Bantu World*, the first daily newspaper devoted to the aspirations of African people. His mother was a teacher of English, a language Linda spoke fluently. He was an above average pupil at the Meadowlands High School. And yet he was recorded saying that he wanted to thank Lieutenant van Coller for showing him the light. For making him realise that he was a savage without a shirt on his back who had been misled by others to commit the crimes with which he was charged.

I was briefed to defend Linda by Raymond Tucker, who assigned his assistant, Kathleen Satchwell (now a High Court judge), to the case. She unearthed almost twenty witnesses to corroborate Linda's evidence that the confessions were the result of police assault and torture and were not freely and voluntarily made. Linda said that the version recorded on the tape was dictated to him bit by bit while the recorder was switched off – a claim denied indignantly by Lieutenant van Coller.

Once the trial began, Jan Swanepoel, the prosecutor, asked us to admit that the transcript of the taped confession was correct. We asked for the original tape so that our client could check it against the transcript. Soon after he began work on the tape, Linda asked to see us. Sergeant Mohage's voice could clearly be heard on the tape telling Linda in Setswana that if he wanted to help himself, he should say what he was told to say.

Before the hearing resumed I told Jan Swanepoel what we had heard on the tape. His pale face flushed bright red, but he said nothing. We suggested he ask the judge for time to consider his position, and that Simon Skosana, the official court interpreter, listen to the tape. If he confirmed our client's claim, we wanted an unequivocal admission placed on the record. The interpreter confirmed hearing the remarks by Sergeant Mohage. This admission was recorded in open court without any comment by the prosecutor or the judge.

The State's case alleged that the murders were committed by Linda and three others. We discovered that Lieutenant van Coller had obtained confessions to the crime from no fewer than eleven others. When asked in cross-examination how it was that he became the 'father confessor' of the people of Soweto, the lieutenant ventured that they had all volunteered their confessions to interfere with his investigation. Actually they had another story to tell, one of torture and suffering.

In preparation for the trial we asked Dr Chris Rachanis of the dental school at the University of the Witwatersrand to examine Linda's broken teeth. He had seen such injuries before, invariably they were inflicted by students performing extractions for the first time. Because of their lack of experience they did not push the extraction instruments far enough into the gum. A patient handled this way would jerk back and the teeth would break precisely as Linda's had done. Such untreated injuries would lead to excruciating pain for weeks followed by a period of progressively less pain for up to three months. Certainly initially, eating, drinking and even breathing would have been dreadfully painful. The prosecutor called a doctor from the Pretoria Dental School to rebut the evidence. He ventured some other possible explanations for the broken teeth, but could not deny that it probably happened in the manner described by Linda and Dr Rachanis.

One of Linda's co-accused was seventeen-year-old Sibusiso Tshabalala. Like

Linda he made a 'confession' of his involvement in the murder. And, like Linda, Sibusiso had harrowing tales of torture in detention. His story was important in emphasising the widespread police practice of assaulting prisoners and bringing to trial people that were not guilty. We hoped Sibusiso's story would throw more doubt on Linda's 'confessions'. After Sibusiso's detention, his father, who worked in Durban, travelled to Johannesburg to the security police headquarters at John Vorster Square. He wanted an explanation for his son's detention. He was told that his son had confessed to three counts of murder and would be brought to trial soon.

When were these murders committed, Tshabalala senior wanted to know. He was told on 19 February 1977. Impossible, replied the adamant father. At the beginning of that year Sibusiso had been enrolled at a good school in Newcastle. He was living with his grandfather and grandmother. The grandparents, the school principal and his teachers would corroborate his account. Newcastle was so far away that he could not possibly have been in Soweto on the night of the killings.

Lieutenant Heystek, the police officer who dealt with Mr Tshabalala, must have been impressed by the father's insistence on his son's innocence, for he took the trouble to visit Newcastle to verify the information. Sibusiso wasn't charged, but he wasn't released either. The police wanted to call him as a prosecution witness against Linda and for that reason he was kept in prison. When the case for the prosecution was closed, he was released. He had not testified for the State. By that time he had spent almost a year in detention. The evidence gathered by Heystek was suppressed and withheld even from the prosecutor. In presenting the defence case we called Sibusiso as a witness for Linda. Despite his youth and all that he had suffered he was an outstanding witness.

Why had he confessed to a murder he had not committed?

He explained: 'While I was talking to Sergeant Matthee and looking at him when next I felt something being pulled over my head. It was a sack, a bag and both my arms were taken to my back and held behind me. Water was poured onto this bag. I couldn't breathe. On that stage I was lying on the floor and I felt some burns, some shocks against my neck. Now they were saying throughout this process are you now going to tell the truth, are you now going to tell the truth? If you do, then nod with your head. I then nodded, indicating that I was going to tell the truth. Thereafter this bag was removed from my head and I told them.'

Obviously he told them what they wanted to hear, having been softened up by those experts in the field, Struwig, van Coller, Mohage and others.

Sibusiso eloquently described what happened in his cell at the Hillbrow Police Station where he was held in solitary confinement. Captain Struwig arrived with a cell sergeant who was ordered to leave. When they were alone Struwig said, 'Sibusiso, I thought that you were a clever boy.' Sibusiso recognised this as a bad omen. Being called 'clever' by a policeman never had good consequences. He asked Struwig what he had done. The police officer replied, 'What is this nonsense that you have been telling Lieutenant Heystek? How dare you tell him that you are innocent, that I took you to the house that was bombed, that I told you precisely where you were when the bombs were thrown? How dare you tell him that I got you to pose for photographs pointing things out even though you knew nothing about what happened?'

Sibusiso did some quick thinking. Standing in court, he recalled that moment very vividly. He turned to the judge and said, 'My Lord, I do not know whether you have seen Captain Struwig? Mark you, My Lord, he didn't touch me this time. But he had taken off his watch and his sunglasses and put them on my washbasin and glared at me whilst he was asking his questions. I thought that I must say something to satisfy him. I said, "You know, Captain Struwig, the problem is that Lieutenant Heystek and I don't understand one another so well." Captain Struwig then said, "Sibusiso, now you are talking like a clever boy. I will come and take you to Pretoria where you will meet the prosecutor. Promise me that you will tell him that you will give evidence as you said in your confession. Don't make any mention of what you told Heystek and then you will be released."'

Sibusiso agreed to do just that.

Jan Swanepoel must have decided that if he called Sibusiso it would do his case no good. Most other prosecutors would have kept Sibusiso in detention even after the prosecution case closed, so that we could neither consult with him nor call him as a witness. To his credit, Swanepoel allowed us to make good use of Sibusiso's testimony.

The young man said he had written a play which was performed at his school in Newcastle on the night the police had him throwing bombs in Johannesburg. It was called 'Mother, What Have I Done?' and was a teenage melodrama in Zulu, probably inspired by Shakespeare's *Romeo and Juliet*. The principal, the teachers, the actors, the local chief and his councillors were in the audience and could corroborate his evidence.

We called his grandfather. He was emphatic that on the night of 19 February the previous year, his grandson was at the school play and had returned to the grandparents' home when the play was over. In cross-examination the old man conceded that he had never been to school. How could he tell the date of the play? He said he could read a calendar. Swanepoel produced one. The octogenarian pointed to the month and date on which he was standing in court giving evidence.

The grandfather had another reason for remembering the date. Although Sibusiso occasionally went to Johannesburg over weekends to see his mother, it was always at the end of the month after pension day. The boy couldn't go before then as the money was needed to pay the train fare and to buy a chicken so that he would not go hungry on the long journey.

At the time, Debbie Dison, a young attorney in the prestigious firm of Bell, Dewar & Hall, was on record as the attorney representing Linda Mogale, even though the law did not allow legal representatives to visit detainees. Dison's firm became involved in the case at the request of the South African Council of Churches after the organisation was approached by Linda's mother. It is standard practice that police inform the attorney of record when and where the accused will be brought to court.

Debbie believed that the police were acting in good faith and in line with this accepted practice when they phoned the relevant information to her. She assumed that it would be in open court, which invariably sat from nine a.m. The next morning she discovered that Linda's case was not on the roll and the prosecutor knew nothing about it. Eventually she found out that he had been taken by the security police to a magistrate's office shortly after eight a.m. He had been remanded to the Johannesburg Fort to be kept as an awaiting-trial prisoner.

Debbie visited him. As a result of this underhand early morning 'appearance', Linda was deprived of the right to record what had happened to him during his detention. At the trial, Debbie testified about the injuries she had seen on his body and the horrific treatment he had described. Evidence was also given by the church elders who'd witnessed the assault at the time of his detention. Other detainees, who saw him in the police corridors, injured and obviously in pain, also testified.

Still the prosecution team would not give up. Although the taped 'confession' was a sham, they clung to the 'confession' made before the magistrate, arguing that Linda had not discharged the onus of proving on a balance of probabilities that it was not freely and voluntarily made. This despite Linda's evidence that after three weeks of solitary confinement, assault, indignity and torture he was taken to the magistrate by Captain Struwig. Even in the presence of the magistrate, Struwig still had him in thrall.

Captain Struwig then told me about the tape recorder on his desk. He told me he was going to give it to the magistrate, and if the magistrate asked if I minded it being switched on whilst I was making my statement, I was to tell the magistrate that I didn't mind at all. I should be clear that I should not mention the assaults by him and he told me that I shouldn't in any way try to be clever and trick him, because through this tape-recording he would know that I had tricked him and then he would give it to me. That is he would continue with the assaults on me.

When he came before the magistrate Linda tried to keep to the bargain. However, Struwig had forgotten that on the standard form there were a number of questions that had to be answered:

COUNSEL: Have you any injuries to your person?
MOGALE: Yes, I have two teeth missing. When I was interrogated I was manhandled. At Meadowlands I was nearly every day manhandled and interrogated.

The law required that when suggestions such as this were made by a detainee, the magistrate was obliged to find out what had happened. He should have asked, who manhandled you and why? Who were the interrogators and were they present when you were manhandled? Did you have any other injuries that are now not apparent after the lapse of three weeks? What sort of manhandling was it that caused your two teeth to be missing? None of these questions were asked, and the magistrate merely noted on the form: 'Two teeth broken, no other injuries visible.'

We thought that we'd proved beyond reasonable doubt that neither confession was freely or voluntarily made. Judge F S Steyn had other views. He held that the tape-recorded confession was inadmissible not for the obvious reasons but on the questionable grounds that it was not a written statement. In his ruling, the judge ignored Linda's evidence about the 'confession' being dictated to him by the police. Of course this evidence had been corroborated and vindicated by Mohage's audible instructions on the tape.

Worse still, the judge allowed the 'confession' made to the magistrate to be admitted to the record. In doing so, he indicated that he disbelieved Linda and believed the police officers. This bias he attributed to the good demeanour of the police officers and cited the 'high degree of improbability' that they would have behaved the way Linda described. Of Struwig, the judge made this flattering finding:

Lieutenant Struwig is bodily and spiritually a strong, impressive but quiet person. He as a witness made an impression that he was credible and honourable. In my view this conflicts with the reasonable probabilities that a person in his position and status in the special branch of the police would use bodily violence in order to intimidate a witness.

The judge had ordered that the evidence, particularly in relation to police brutality, should not be published before the end of the trial. This was to protect the good name of the South African Police against false and scurrilous allegations. The ruling was unprecedented. It was given late on a Friday afternoon and I could not resist letting Benjamin Pogrund know. The next morning the ruling was reported on the front page of the *Rand Daily Mail*. A reporter from the *Sunday Express* sought confirmation from the judge who denied it was the case. This was reported in a follow-up article.

Pogrund arrived at court early on the Monday morning and asked to listen to the tape of Friday afternoon's proceedings. This wasn't allowed. He asked the judge why the tape was embargoed, and whether his paper's report had been true. The judge confirmed its accuracy.

Needless to say, we appealed Linda's case. The matter went to the Appellate Division in Bloemfontein where it was heard by judges Pierre Rabie, André Botha and Hendrick van Heerden. It was set down for two days. Jan Swanepoel left the appeal to a junior member of his staff, probably knowing that he had no meaningful argument. Argument lasted no more than ninety minutes.

I submitted that the reduction of the murder charges to culpable homicide and the light sentences were inexplicable, having regard to the death of the three victims. Did this mean, Judge Rabie wondered, that if they confirmed the conviction, they should then increase the sentence? I was so shocked I couldn't speak. The judge quickly assured me I shouldn't take his remark seriously. Very early in the argument, when I mentioned the importance of the evidence of Sibusiso Tshabalala, the amiable Judge André Botha asked whether I was referring to Sibusiso 'Mark You My Lord' Tshabalala. I took this as a favourable sign for Linda Mogale, who had then been languishing on Robben Island for more than a year.

The judges then informed me that unless I had any important submissions to make, other than those contained in the heads of argument, it wouldn't be necessary for the court to hear me any further. Counsel for the State did not have much to say. She would no sooner start a point than one of the judges would say, 'But look at the evidence of ...' She sat down, and I was not called in reply.

The lengthy judgment was written by Judge Rabie. The Appellate Division set aside the convictions and sentences handed down by Judge Steyn. For some unknown reason the judgment was never reported in the South African Law Reports – perhaps because it concerned primarily an appeal on fact rather than law.

Whatever the reason, it was left to Julian Riekert, then a senior lecturer in law at the University of Natal, to analyse the judgment in the *South African Law Journal* of May 1982. He wrote:

The practical significance of this case is that it is the first, to the writer's knowledge, where the Appellate Division has formally recognised that the police have seriously assaulted a security-law detainee in order to compel him to confess. In that regard it is a matter for regret that one scans the judgment in vain for any rebuke, or even robust criticism, of the policemen concerned. This regret is heightened by the knowledge that no departmental action was, or will be, taken against Sergeant Matthee for his assaults on the appellant, because the Transvaal Attorney-General has declined to prosecute him.

However, this decision will serve to remind trial courts of their duties in regard to the assessment of credibility in cases where the accused has been held singly (as most security-law detainees are), and where there is no hope of corroboration of his allegations of police maltreatment because of that fact. It also contains an emphatic statement reiterating the requirement of a warning in terms of the Judges' Rules where suspects are being questioned by the police. And last, but not least, it has shown that the protective aura which surrounds a trial court's findings on credibility and demeanour is not impenetrable on appeal.

Linda Mogale was certainly not the only victim of improper police conduct and judicial partiality. Many other detainees and prisoners from other periods of the apartheid era were treated as badly. He was fortunate that his case was eventually heard by the Court of Appeal and that he was released from Robben Island. But he did not live long after regaining his freedom. A few years later he was involved in an argument at the gate of his home and shot dead.

CHAPTER 33

The Slow Turn of the Tide

The population of Robben Island increased significantly as hundreds of young activists were imprisoned there following trials in the wake of the Soweto uprising. These young political activists were sent to Robben Island so that they would not influence other prisoners on the mainland. The authorities had not foreseen the influence that Nelson Mandela and his colleagues would have on the newly convicted youths. The older activists fortified the resolve of the new prisoners to fight for freedom and urged them to study.

The University of South Africa, through which the islanders studied, was a well-established institution of tertiary learning. Many of the young prisoners followed the example of their elders and began to accept the discipline of higher education, cheerfully referring to themselves as attending the University of Robben Island. Registration and tuition fees for the Robben Island prisoners were usually paid out of Nelson Mandela's account. But something went wrong, and the young prisoners were alarmed to discover that their studies would be interrupted because the fees had not been paid. A telegraphic request by Nelson Mandela to Ismail Ayob to pay nearly R22 000 into his account, so that the prison authorities could settle with the university as a matter of urgency, upset the Department of Prisons. They decided to end Mandela's influence by removing him to Pollsmoor prison.

In mid-1982, Winnie sent Zindzi from Brandfort to see Ismail Ayob and me. We were to bring an urgent application to court to stop the prison authorities from keeping him in solitary confinement. Mother and daughter, together with millions of others, feared that the intention was to break his spirit. The move from Robben Island was to isolate him and induce him to agree to their plans. This would embarrass not only him but the ANC, and set back the organisation's struggle for freedom.

Realising the dangers of relying on second-hand reports we went to Pollsmoor to get instructions from him directly. The autumn leaves of the poplar, oak, peach, apricot, plum and pear trees were falling. So were the first leaves of the vines intermingled with the light green of the late-sprouting shoots. It was a scene reminiscent of areas around the Mediterranean. But in the heart of the beautiful valley, property developers had been beaten by the Department of Prisons. Instead of luxury townhouses, a mundane three-storey building stood in the midst of this beauty, surrounded by a tall wire fence with floodlights.

On Robben Island we could not see or be seen by any prisoner other than the one we came to visit. Here a few prisoners were milling around in the foyer. They had heard who I was and who I wanted to see. The obvious joy on their faces caused the chief warder to usher me into the office of the commanding officer. In due course I was taken up the steps to the third floor, where the world's best-known political prisoner was held. I waited in a small room with a couch, a table and chairs and a television set. Nelson was brought and the warder left us alone. He was as anxious as ever to learn what was happening outside. How was Winnie, the rest of his family? How were Arethe and our boys (he mentioned each of them by name)?

When I explained the purpose of the visit, he told me that he, Walter Sisulu and Andrew Mlangeni were in some respects better treated at Pollsmoor than they had been on the island. They had not been given reasons for their removal, although he believed it was an attempt to weaken the ANC's influence on the island. As he would write in his autobiography, *Long Walk to Freedom*: 'Robben Island itself was becoming a sustaining myth in the struggle, and they wanted to rob it of some of its symbolic import by removing us.'

I was to tell Winnie and the other families that he had regular contact with Walter; he was not isolated and was able to handle the government's proposals and the speculation about his release. He made it clear, even at that early stage, that he would insist on not being released before his comrades.

Brigadier Munro, the commanding officer of Pollsmoor, arranged visits more frequently and with less fuss than his counterparts on Robben Island. Locally and internationally the clamour grew for the release of all political prisoners, particularly Nelson Mandela. Leaders such as Kaizer Matanzima, Lucas Mangope and Mangosuthu Buthelezi put pressure on President Botha to release Mandela, perhaps hoping that these calls might lend legitimacy to their 'independent' territories. Even the Broederbond advised Botha to find a way of releasing Mandela.

Then it was announced that Mandela had a serious prostate problem requiring surgical intervention. When Winnie heard that Dr Willem Laubscher was to perform the operation, she again wanted us to make an urgent application to stop the procedure. She did not believe it should be performed by an Afrikaner at the instance of the prison authorities. Top physicians should be consulted. Although I understood her anxiety, I suggested we ascertain Nelson's opinion.

Nelson was impressed by Dr Laubscher. He was a competent surgeon and a man of honour. Equally, he did not want to appear mistrusting of the doctor, or of Afrikaners in general. At this stage in the struggle there was a need for trust. Winnie accepted his decision, but only after his own doctor suggested that a leading urologist in Johannesburg assist in the operation.

The operation was a success. For the lengthy period of recuperation Nelson was accommodated in a private nursing home in the centre of the city. He hadn't been there long when I was summoned to see him. I found him sitting in an easy chair wearing pyjamas and a dressing gown. He was well and was pleased to be having unrestricted visits from Winnie. He praised Dr Laubscher and the nursing staff and thanked Brigadier Munro, sitting opposite him, for facilitating the visits. Although we had important matters to discuss he wanted the brigadier to remain in the room. Our conversation was highly confidential, and came at the behest of the minister of justice, Kobie Coetsee. Coetsee had visited him in hospital and discussed the release of political prisoners, including himself.

Of more significance, they had broached the subject of a settlement of the conflict between the liberation movement and the government. This was the minister's initiative, a tentative first step. Nelson had confided in no one but Walter Sisulu, who had been brought from Pollsmoor Prison to visit him. Walter had encouraged him to carry on talking. They both knew that the movement in the country and in exile – concerned about his health and isolation – feared that he might compromise himself and them. Could I see Oliver Tambo in Lusaka as soon as possible to report the situation and the confidentiality? Tambo could raise the matter with Thabo Mbeki if necessary.

But before that I was to see the minister. The go-between here was a professor at UCT, HW van der Merwe. He came to my hotel room and telephoned the minister's secretary. And so it was arranged that on the flight back to Johannesburg I would sit with the minister in the business class section of the plane.

We talked for almost five hours because the plane could not land at the fog-bound Johannesburg airport. First we were diverted to Durban, then returned to Johannesburg. Coetsee asked many questions about Mandela. It became apparent that his knowledge of Nelson was not limited to reports compiled by the security police and intelligence services from days gone by, but included a more sympathetic analysis from the Department of Prisons and, more particularly, Brigadier Munro. Without saying so, he had been impressed by Mandela at their first interview.

Initially we were both cautious, but it soon became an earnest conversation about what ought to be done. The consequences of Mandela's release concerned him. Also, could he be talked into changing his attitude and accept release before the other political prisoners? I reminded him of Mandela's recent announcement, read out by his daughter Zindzi. Perhaps they could start by releasing Govan Mbeki. He had served more than twenty years and the practice of releasing prisoners after fourteen years was well established. Besides, there was Mbeki's age to consider. Coetsee did not respond, but I believed the suggestion had fallen on fertile ground. He then asked if Mandela, Sisulu and Mbeki would accept conditional release to the Transkei. I could see no merit in this. (Not long afterwards Govan Mbeki became the first of the Rivonia prisoners to be released.)

Coetsee also wanted an assessment of Oliver Tambo. Was he strong enough to withstand the communist influence of Joe Slovo and others? Would those in exile accept a fourth chamber to represent blacks as a first step towards a settlement of the conflict and the end of sanctions and the sports boycott? The answer to this was a clear, emphatic 'No'. I reminded him that the majority of coloured and Indian people had rejected the 1983 constitution. They would settle for nothing less than meaningful participation in the affairs of the country, universal suffrage, free and fair elections and a democratic constitution. He was visibly upset and told me not to preach to him.

As the plane neared Johannesburg the conversation took on a lighter note. We talked about legal practice, colleagues known to both of us and some recently appointed judges. We parted on good terms.

Earlier that afternoon, leaving the hospital in Cape Town, I had found Winnie Mandela, Zindzi and Ismail Ayob waiting for me, surrounded by television cameras and journalists. Would I confirm that I was there to arrange the release of Nelson Mandela directly from his hospital bed? What was wrong with him? How long would he remain in hospital? Was it true that he had agreed to go into exile? Did I intend to travel beyond the borders to make the necessary arrangements? I answered that what was said between us was both privileged and confidential. This didn't stop the questions or the widespread speculation.

On my drive home from the airport, through the midnight streets of Johannesburg, an uneasiness settled on me. If the minister was acting without the knowledge or authority of President PW Botha, then the security police and their agents in Lusaka would be unaware of the purpose of my visit. Would they be waiting for me when I returned? Judge Johann Kriegler had intervened on my behalf on at least two previous occasions, once when the police sought to ban me from seeing my clients in prison, and again when they subpoenaed me to give evidence against Barbara Hogan, a client I was to defend on a charge of treason. Now once more I confided in him. He advised that I get Ismail Ayob to accompany me. Being in the company of Mandela's attorney would prove that I was acting as a legal representative rather than as a conspirator.

At Lusaka airport Ismail and I were welcomed by three ANC officials, who cleared our entrance to Zambia. They behaved exactly like highly placed diplomats abroad receiving important guests from their country. At the hotel the three produced a letter with an ANC letterhead stating that we were their guests and agreeing to settle the account. In the past, such documents were used as evidence against those we defended. I could not help feeling that we might see this particular letter again if things went wrong.

Oliver Tambo came to my room at ten p.m. and remained until past three the next morning. By then his security men, who had been pacing up and down the passage, were worried that the meeting was becoming a security risk. We had much to talk about. It was February 1986. We had not seen, spoken or written to one another for twenty-six years, since the day in April 1960 when he hurriedly left the country. We embraced and remained silent for a while, looking intently into one another's eyes, fighting back tears of both joy and sorrow. Oliver was anxious to know the state of Nelson's health and how he was being treated. He asked what lay behind the rumours of his possible release. Would his illness and isolation lead to any embarrassing arrangement?

I reassured him that Nelson was not isolated but in touch with political developments in the country. He had access to the leaders of the UDF, and legal opinion. His conditions had improved. He enjoyed the gardening facilities provided for him on the roof, he was allowed much more reading material, and he could listen to the radio and watch television. There would be no early release. He stood by the speech Zindzi had read out in Soweto.

Oliver knew the speech well. He mentioned the references Nelson had made to him. He even wondered if it mightn't have been better if Nelson had gone into exile rather than him. I told him that he was undervaluing his contribution. I knew of no liberation movement that was as united in its resolve as the ANC had become under his leadership.

About my discussions with Kobie Coetsee, Oliver queried if I believed that the minister was acting without the president's knowledge. We agreed it was unlikely. Would he endanger his political career by allowing so many people to know of his discussions with Nelson, if they were taking place without the knowledge of President Botha? It seemed improbable. Our conclusion that Coetsee was acting on behalf of the government strengthened our belief that talks about talks might be in the offing.

Oliver was well informed about the positive popular response to the UDF. He believed that internal ungovernability, coupled with an intensification of the economic and sporting boycotts, were having an impact.

He reminded me that ever since the 1950s the ANC's policy had been to bring the government to the negotiating table. Oliver didn't regard Nelson's intentions as a departure from that policy and favoured exploratory talks remaining secret to avoid their floundering in public debate at that early stage. I was to assure Nelson that he had Oliver's full support; likewise that the national executive would support specific proposals when they were put on the table. However, Coetsee and his government must not be given the impression that the struggle would stop just because talks were in the air.

Next morning we were taken to the guest cottage within Government House grounds where Oliver lived. A meeting had been arranged with President Kenneth Kaunda. He embraced Oliver and shook hands warmly with Ismail and me. When I conveyed Nelson's greetings and gratitude for what Kaunda was doing for the people of South Africa, the president wiped away tears with his white handkerchief and said, 'Tell my friend Nelson that none of us in Africa feel free whilst he is in jail.'

As we sat down to lunch at the guest house, an aide brought a small transistor radio tuned to the BBC for Oliver to hear the news. Oliver waved him away. A few minutes later the aide returned to whisper in Oliver's ear. Obviously shocked, Oliver told us that Olaf Palme, the prime minister of Sweden, had been killed. Oliver ate hardly anything; our conversation came to an end. There were so many questions. Who had killed Palme? Why? Had a South African agent done it? Where was the ANC to find such a good friend again?

In the airport lounge, Oliver asked us not to divulge where he was living. South Africa's hit squads had assassinated ANC leaders in Botswana, Lesotho, Swaziland, Mozambique and Zimbabwe and unsuccessful attempts had also been made in Zambia. Like Oliver, we knew that he was the number one target on their list, and that every precaution should be taken.

On my return Winnie told me that Nelson was again separated from his comrades. What were we going to do about it? What I was going to do was visit Nelson for a report-back on my trip to Zambia.

He did not want to agitate to rejoin Walter, Kathy, Andrew and Raymond. He had been assured that the four would be brought together whenever he requested it. But he missed them as well as the roof-top garden and the fresh air.

Nelson was pleased with the message from KK, as he called the Zambian president, and even more so with Oliver's endorsement of his actions, although he cautioned me to be discreet in reporting to Kobie Coetsee. Once again I sought Johann Kriegler's advice. He arranged that we would meet at the minister's house. And he would drive me. Should someone recognise us, they would not think it unusual for a judge to see the minister of justice.

Johann Kriegler has a habit of finishing others' sentences, even if the pause is slight. When I saw the overbearing security arrangements before we could enter the minister's grounds, I started, 'The ANC-in-exile and the government ...' and he quickly filled in: 'They both live in military camps'. Kobie Coetsee was alone in his house. He brought a covered platter of snacks, KWV wine and glasses. He opened the bottle and served us himself. His patrician manners held him off asking any questions until we had half-emptied the platter and had finished the first glass of his excellent wine.

I then told him Tambo's attitude. Coetsee's responses were carefully phrased to ascertain whether Tambo was speaking for everyone associated with the ANC-in-exile. I knew that the Nationalist government, the security forces and the Broederbond believed that the communists dominated the ANC, so his question was to establish if the ANC's approval would be shared by the SACP. I reassured him that from what I knew of the ANC, it operated by consensus. Tambo was highly respected by the National Executive Committee and its various structures.

That the minister had sanctioned my visit to the president of the ANC-in-exile emboldened me. I travelled to Lusaka, London and Athens on behalf of Nelson to see Oliver, Albie Sachs and other members of the national executive, as well as various international leaders. Prime Minister Margaret Thatcher had her reservations about the ANC and about Nelson Mandela. Not so her ambassador, Sir Robin Renwick, or Under-Secretary for Africa, Linda Chalker. On Nelson's instructions I was to thank Chalker for her efforts, particularly in persuading her prime minister to put pressure on the apartheid government. Chalker made my task much easier by exclaiming, as I entered her office, 'How is dear Nelson?'

I also accepted invitations from an anti-apartheid group of parliamentarians to speak in various capitals about the South African struggle. The group was led by Jan Niko Scholtens from the Netherlands. After a conference in Athens we were taken to ancient Olympia where the mayor told me that his city had made Nelson Mandela an honorary citizen. They had written to inform him but had received no reply. When I told Nelson he was thrilled. He had not received the letter and presumed it had been withheld. We agreed that Greece would surely have the Olympics in 1996, the centenary year of the modern games, and that we would attend together. Undoubtedly, he would be free by then. He was, but Greece did not get the Olympic Games until 2004. By then we had already fulfilled our promise to visit Greece together.

Part Five: 1985–1989

CHAPTER 34

The Question of Human Rights

And we should recognise that the proper basis of our security is in good administration rather than in fear of legal penalties.

– Diodotus

More than fifty activists had died in detention before Steve Biko's body was found on the floor of a dark cell in Pretoria. Up till then the findings of compliant magistrates invariably exonerated the security police of all blame. The interrogators advanced the most implausible reasons and they were accepted. 'He slipped on a piece of soap'; 'He fell down a staircase'; 'He had been seriously injured before his arrest'; 'He attempted to escape through an open window several floors high'; 'He hanged himself after he betrayed his friends during our fair interrogation'. Those who survived detention and complained of assaults, suffocation, sleep deprivation, threats of indefinite detention and many other forms of torture were branded liars or enemies of the State. They were no more than 'propagandists' bent on besmirching the good name of the patriotic security police.

In terms of detention laws, doctors, lawyers and relatives could not visit those held by the security police. They would not be brought to court for months after a coerced confession was made, by which time bruises and wounds had often faded and healed. There were no visible injuries to corroborate their descriptions of torture during their period of isolation. Criticism of the police and the justice system in the local and foreign media were dismissed by the apartheid regime. The victims were referred to as 'terrorists' and 'communists'. Lawyers who appeared for the families of the victims were branded 'fellow travellers' or misguided liberals.

Of all the detainees who died in police custody, no one had as high a profile as Biko. Editor and journalist Donald Woods said of him,

> In the three years that I grew to know him, my conviction never wavered that this was the most important political leader in the entire country and quite simply the greatest man I ever had the privilege to know.

Woods wrote a book, *Cry Freedom*, later made into a movie under the same title by Richard Attenborough. The chairman of the US Senate Foreign Relations

Committee on Africa, Senator Dick Clark, called Biko's death an 'outrage', and Biko a 'remarkable man'. Percy Qoboza, the editor of *The World*, described him as 'one of South Africa's most articulate spokesmen of black consciousness, in many ways its spiritual father', adding that he hoped no stone would be left unturned to establish the cause of Biko's death.

Initially the police told the minister, Jimmy Kruger, that Biko had died from a hunger strike. Addressing his party's congress, Kruger uttered the now infamous words: 'The death of Biko leaves me cold.' To the amusement of the party faithful at the Pretoria City Hall, Kruger accepted their congratulations for being such a good democrat that he had allowed Biko the choice of dying of hunger.

The *Rand Daily Mail's* editor, Allister Sparks, published the post-mortem report given to him by Dr Jonathan Gluckman, the pathologist who attended the examination on behalf of the Biko family. The real cause of death, said Gluckman's report, was serious brain injury. Sparks was called before the government-appointed press council and admonished for publishing false information without taking reasonable steps to verify it.

The inquest was to take place, ironically enough, at the Old Synagogue in Pretoria where the treason trial had been held. The affidavits served on us were made by policemen, doctors who had failed to treat him properly and prison warders. The evidence established that the security police had made false and contradictory affidavits. Such documents as they chose to produce compounded the lies of the police. Equally, the doctors had not lived up to their Hippocratic oath because they did not want to disobey the security police.

The inquest began. A court crowded with members of the public, prominent foreign observers and the world's media heard the graphic detail of how a dying man was transported naked, in an ordinary vehicle, more than a thousand kilometres without any medical care despite his critical condition. In Pretoria he was reluctantly received by the head of the prison, who asked why the police were bringing a 'nearly dead man' for him to keep in custody. One thing emerged clearly: Biko had not lost any weight. So much for the initial false statement that he had died following a hunger strike.

Given all that emerged in the inquest, we felt confident that the policemen involved, and two of the three doctors who had 'treated' him, would be held criminally liable for his death.

In our final submissions Sydney Kentridge said:

It is difficult to comment on these facts in measured terms, certainly Colonel Goosen's statement, made after the death of Biko was made known to him, that everything was done for the comfort and health of Steve Biko, is as cynical a statement as any heard in a court of law.

The facts made public during the inquest told a different story from that given by Goosen: Biko had in fact 'died a miserable and lonely death on a mat on a stone floor in a prison cell.'

In conclusion Kentridge, speaking on behalf of all of us, in and out of court, said,

> The police felt confident that they could rely upon the doctors to support them. And their confidence was justified. Perhaps strengthened thereby, the police, with gross impertinence, presented to this court a totally implausible account of Mr Biko's death, starting with a fanciful description of a struggle, violent in the extreme, in which no blow was struck; a bizarre account of an alleged shamming when to any candid observer a man's progress to his death was being seen and described and all the while they refused to acknowledge the head injury … This inquest has exposed grave irregularity and misconduct in the treatment of a single detainee. It has incidentally revealed the dangers to life and liberty involved in the system of holding detainees incommunicado. A firm and clear verdict may help to prevent further abuse of the system. In the light of further disquieting evidence before this court, any verdict which can be seen as an exoneration of the Port Elizabeth security police will unfortunately be interpreted as a licence to abuse helpless people with impunity. This court cannot allow that to happen.

The chief magistrate of Pretoria, Marthinus Prins, was not persuaded. In less than thirty seconds, ignoring the facts, our arguments and the public outcry, he said:

> The available evidence does not prove that the death was brought about by any act or omission involving or amounting to an offence on the part of any person. That completes this inquest.

Steve Biko's mother, Alice, and his wife, Nontsikelelo (Ntsiki) were devastated. Ntsiki, in a state of disbelief, desperately tried to hold back her tears and kept asking: 'No one to blame?'

The inquest finding also left Sydney Kentridge with a despairing question. 'Is it worthwhile continuing to practise in the courts?' he asked Ernie Wentzel and me. I felt that although the magistrate had exonerated the police and the doctors, the world jury had convicted them. Ernie agreed, but it did not stop Sydney going to London where he soon established himself as one of the leading English barristers. Yet he and his wife Felicia Kentridge continued to play a leading role in the affairs of the Legal Resources Centre from their London base. Sydney also maintained his membership of the Johannesburg Bar and returned for a number of important cases. He accepted an acting appointment on South Africa's Constitutional Court soon after its establishment in February 1995.

In its first reports on Steve Biko's death, *The New York Times* reported that he had 'died mysteriously'. After the inquest it spoke for the international media by disregarding the magistrate's findings:

> The only mystery remaining after the lengthy magistrate's inquest, now concluded with a whitewash verdict, is which of the security officers who interrogated Mr Biko actually administered the fatal blows.

(That blows were struck was eventually admitted in their amnesty application by those involved. Their applications were refused, primarily because, twenty years later, they were still not prepared to tell the truth.)

Unlike *The New York Times*, *Die Vaderland*, the mouthpiece of die-hard Nationalist Afrikaners, commented:

> The South African judiciary remains a bastion of democracy … Our judicial system remains unscathed, a remarkable record when one bears in mind that we reside in Africa where there is very little respect for democracy.

In an attempt to influence international opinion their editorial was written in English.

Yet Afrikaner intellectuals, religious leaders, academics and other newspaper editors were uneasy about what had happened to Biko and was happening to detainees. Although they could not condemn detention without trial and torture, they called for safeguards to avoid a repetition of the 'Biko incident'. The government was unmoved. Not even the shame of the Biko revelations prevented the State from banning nineteen community organisations, detaining community leaders and intensifying its harassment of those who disagreed with its policies.

The government enjoyed greater popularity among the white electorate than ever before, but there were concerns about the apartheid state's future. Mozambique and Angola were no longer Portuguese colonies but independent states. They actively supported the ANC's liberation struggle by allowing Umkhonto we Sizwe to establish bases. At Mozambique's independence dinner celebration, Oliver Tambo was an honoured guest, although this went unreported in South Africa. Yet among the growing population on Robben Island it was common knowledge. When I visited Nelson at about the time of Mozambique's independence, he was surprised to hear that I knew nothing about it. He was proud of the ANC's diplomatic endeavours. He knew that Oliver Tambo and Thabo Mbeki had managed to establish more ANC offices throughout the world than the South African government had embassies or consulates.

To the north, Ian Smith's Rhodesia was hard hit by sanctions and hard pressed to come to terms with the liberation movements now operating within and outside his country. The United Nations' efforts to bring about Namibia's freedom from South Africa were having an impact. South Africa's support of Jonas Savimbi in Angola was countered by Cuban troops who were no pushover for South Africa's army. Some white men and many of their parents began questioning the border war.

Against this background, the idea of forming an organisation to advocate human rights was foolhardy. Prime Minister John Vorster had said that human rights in South Africa were 'getting out of hand'. An organisation promoting human rights would certainly be banned, as would its leaders. Despite this apparent certainty, Helen Suzman and a small number of others tried to use Parliament to advocate human rights. Academics, particularly at the universities of the Witwatersrand, Cape Town and Natal, also made known their views on the issue. The Bars in Cape Town, Johannesburg and Durban occasionally made statements in support of the rule of law and human rights, but the rest of the organised profession, advocates and attorneys, remained silent. It was not their function to concern themselves with 'political matters', they maintained. With rare exceptions the judiciary, too, remained silent.

Then, towards the end of 1978, Professor JD van der Vyver persuaded the Society of University Teachers of Law to call the first International Conference on Human Rights in South Africa. It would take place in Cape Town early the following year. Potchefstroom University had pushed out Johan van der Vyver for rejecting the university's ethos and espousing and promoting human rights for all. In response, the University of the Witwatersrand offered him a professorship. Wits had proved a place where academics were comparatively free to teach and publish on the South African government's rejection of human rights and the rule of law.

Calling such a conference was a brave step. There was no guarantee that visas would be granted to the invited human rights lawyers, particularly those from the

United States and the United Kingdom. Nor was the conference safe from being banned under the Suppression of Communism Act. Leading academic lawyers from the liberal universities, mindful of these dangers, requested a judge of the Appellate Division of the Supreme Court, Michael Corbett, to deliver the opening address. His subject: Human Rights: The Road Ahead. Judges did not readily accept invitations to speak on such 'controversial' matters, but Judge Corbett's acceptance saved the conference and encouraged some of the more timid lawyers to attend. Almost three hundred listened to twenty papers and ten panel discussions on almost every aspect of human rights throughout the world.

Judge Corbett warned that we might find his address insufficiently conclusive. If so it was due to the inhibitions and constraints of his office. Those living under tyrannical regimes sometimes feel safer quoting the words of others. Judge Corbett chose the words of Jan Smuts, though some of us thought that Smuts had not lived up to the lofty ideals he espoused.

> Freedom is the most ineradicable craving of human nature. Without it peace, contentment and happiness, even manhood itself, are not possible. The declaration of Pericles in his great funeral oration holds for all mankind: 'Happiness is freedom and freedom is courage'. This is the fundamental equation of all politics and all human government. Any system that ignores it is built on sand.

Judge Corbett then added his own view:

> At present and in the years to come prime consideration will be to achieve an accommodation between all the peoples of South Africa and to maintain the paramountcy of human rights.

He also spoke of the importance of an independent judiciary that could review the actions of the executive. In this he had been influenced by the United States Supreme Court, despite some of its inexplicable decisions relating to slavery, inequality and detention without trial during the Second World War. Knowing that Afrikaner academics were present, he appealed to them to embrace the principle of human rights and embed it in their students. Likewise he acknowledged the freedom of the press and, at the end, was given a standing ovation.

In summary, at the end of the conference, Sydney Kentridge echoed Judge Corbett and the other speakers, adding that, persuasive as they may have been, they were not going to change the political attitudes of the government.

What will change political attitudes in this country is the inexorable pressure of events, both abroad and within, and what we have to do is to see that among these pressures is the force of the arguments raised in this conference among other things. Change will come. When change comes let us try to see that there are institutions available that will as far as possible make that change beneficial and not retrogressive as far as human rights are concerned.

Sydney Kentridge's call did not fall on deaf ears. Professors van der Vyver and Dugard hosted a follow-up conference, which more than two hundred lawyers attended, at the University of the Witwatersrand in June 1979. From this came the Lawyers' Association for the Protection of Human Rights. An executive committee consisted of six professors of law, three attorneys and five members of the Bar, of which I was one. Professor van der Vyver was elected chairman and Johannesburg attorney Raymond Tucker drafted a constitution.

The association's two main objectives were to unite the legal profession in promoting the rule of law and human rights against increasing executive hegemony, and to act as a watchdog over the legislative and administrative activities of all levels of government. Some four hundred lawyers supported the association. Surprisingly so did seven judges. Among them, Judge John Didcott from Natal called on lawyers to speak out against violations of human rights and to question the social implications of the country's laws. At a later meeting the association was renamed Lawyers for Human Rights. Under the chairmanship of Judge Johann Kriegler, and later Jules Browde, it became a vibrant organisation with branches in most of the country's cities.

Some members of Lawyers for Human Rights joined the board of the Centre for Applied Legal Studies at the University of the Witwatersrand under the chairmanship of John Dugard. The centre was to concentrate on research and publications dealing with the rule of law and the promotion of human rights. The Black Lawyers' Association and the Black Attorneys' Association, in support of black consciousness, distanced themselves from the newly formed bodies. They believed that whites were unlikely to have an absolute commitment to the extension of human rights to black people. This did not prevent a number of black lawyers from joining the two new organisations and serving on their committees. Some time later, the Democratic Lawyers Association was established, a non-racial body more closely associated with the political struggle.

Despite some tensions between these organisations, substantial consensus was soon reached that lawyers had to actively bring about fundamental changes. The involvement of some judges, leading academic lawyers and top legal practitioners made the government cautious about banning them. The organisations were nevertheless carefully watched by the security police. They were infiltrated by informers and their offices monitored by hidden microphones.

Speaking out against the government's violation of fundamental human rights and the abrogation of the rule of law was no longer a subversive activity and something to be avoided by the rank-and-file members of our professions. As members of these organisations and as individuals we encouraged the Bar councils and the law societies to transform the judiciary and the governance of the bodies that controlled the legal profession.

The death of Steve Biko and other detainees before him, together with the regular publication of evidence of torture in the interrogation rooms, could not be ignored completely by government. Eventually Chief Justice Pierre Rabie was appointed to enquire into security legislation and its implementation. Through the new organisations and individually, we prepared to give evidence, as did some of those tortured in detention.

To my disappointment, Chief Justice Rabie announced that there would be no public hearings and he would invite only those whose evidence he wanted to hear. He listened to senior security officers and a number of magistrates favoured by the police to preside at political trials. Perhaps not surprisingly, the judge was persuaded by them that what we considered draconian powers were necessary for the safety of the State. He also approved the 'procedural safeguards' that they claimed had been introduced to avoid the unfortunate consequences of detention made public during the inquest into Steve Biko's death. As evidence of the efficacy of their standing orders relating to visits by magistrates and district surgeons, they said no deaths in detention had been reported for some time.

Among the bastions of apartheid were the universities of Pretoria, Stellenbosch, Port Elizabeth, Potchefstoom and the recently established Rand Afrikaans University in Johannesburg. With few exceptions their top administrators, professors, lecturers and students ardently supported the policy of segregation. They dismissed criticism of the security forces and considered gross violations of human rights as isolated incidents. They believed that apartheid was 'a necessary social experiment' within which the different racial and ethnic groups could enjoy group rights.

In the late 1970s and early 1980s, doubts were raised about the morality of apartheid. Was it just? Was it in keeping with Calvinist beliefs? A debate began in the Broederbond, the church, education, finance and big business. Those who controlled these various organisations were exclusively white adult males. But then younger lecturers, tutors and students from the Afrikaans universities showed an interest in Lawyers for Human Rights. Those of us on the national council were invited to speak at their universities as we had been doing on the English-speaking campuses. We were well received. Some had come as curious spectators, but we found a favourable response to the suggestion that we mark Human Rights Day on 10 December, and several professors and deans introduced discussions on human rights into their courses on jurisprudence and public international law.

I was regularly asked to speak to law students on the political trial. The struggle of Afrikaners against the British was documented and well known to the audience. My book knowledge had been enriched by numerous anecdotes related by Bram Fischer during the Rivonia trial and during the many days I spent with him after his arrest. I knew that the Boers had been called terrorists, that their guerrilla war tactics had led the British to justify detaining their mothers, wives, sisters and children in concentration camps. Their houses had been burned and their livestock commandeered. In my talks I would refer to judgments and sentences imposed on Boer rebels after the 1914 rebellion, and point to the comparatively light sentences imposed on those convicted of treason. I often referred to judgments which cautioned against harsh punishments for those who had committed crimes not for personal gain but to end oppression.

My audience understood what I was saying. I would refer to the Universal Declaration of Human Rights and speak of political and personal justice and draw attention to the provisions stipulating that everyone had the right to full citizenship, the right to vote, the right to be elected to high office. I stressed that everyone had the right to a democratic government with regular elections and a right to equality and dignity, and that when people were deprived of those rights they almost invariably rebelled. I would usually end by quoting Pericles from Thucydides' *History of the Peloponnesian War*, a passage highlighted by professors Tony Matthews and Ronald Albino in an article published in the *South African Law Journal*:

> Indeed it is true that in these acts of revenge on others men take it upon themselves to begin the process of repealing these general laws of humanity which are here to give a hope of salvation to all who are in distress, instead of leaving those laws in existence, remembering that there may come a time when they, too, will be in danger and will need their protection.

Then I observed that fundamental human rights were not a twentieth-century invention, but that history told us that we had a vital interest in promoting human rights and the rule of law. On one occasion, a student at the Rand Afrikaans University asked what disadvantages I had suffered by espousing unpopular causes. My response: 'I know of no unpopular cause that I have ever espoused!' Most of the audience smiled, but some took more than a few seconds to get my meaning.

Towards the end of 1981 more than sixty young men and women of all colours and ethnic origins were detained under the Terrorism Act by the security police. Many of them were post-graduate students actively involved in the struggle against apartheid. Close association between black and white activists was enough to elevate suspicion to proof of complicity in acts of terrorism. The more affluent parents among the affected families approached us to petition for their children's release, or, failing that, visitation rights or medical inspection. They struggled to accept that the court's jurisdiction was excluded and that there was nothing we could do for them. The Rabie Commission report was published during this period, on 3 February 1982, and Minister of Police Louis le Grange was well pleased with the finding. His security police had said that

> the information they obtained by means of interrogation in detention is the most powerful, and to a large extent their only, weapon of anticipating and combating activities endangering the State which are planned and organised outside the borders of the Republic, and that without it they would not be able to carry out the task which they have to perform in the interests of the security of the country.

In response, the minister told Parliament that

> the detainees in police cells or in prisons are being detained under the most favourable conditions possible ... All reasonable precautions are being taken to prevent any of them from injuring themselves or from being injured in some other way or from committing suicide. Surely honourable members are aware of the serious circumstances in the past [a reference to Steve Biko's death]. We were all faced with this, but during the past two-and-a-half years there has not been a single case of this nature.

Two days later Dr Neil Hudson Aggett was found hanging from the bars of the steel grille in his cell in John Vorster Square Police Station. The police quickly announced that Dr Aggett had committed suicide. Many disbelieved them. The media reported that Aggett was a doctor and a trade unionist. Although he had been in detention for seventy days already, he was an idealist and not likely to have committed suicide.

Aubrey Aggett believed that his son was killed by the security police. He approached a senior attorney, William Lane, who in turn phoned me. I advised him to ask Jonathan Gluckman to attend the post-mortem. Gluckman was not available and Dr Jan Botha observed the examination on behalf of the family. He reported some evidence of injuries but that the probabilities were that Neil had committed suicide.

To the surprise of his family, Neil's funeral became a high-profile political event taken over by activists, particularly from the university and the trade union in which he had held a senior position. Tens of thousands marched from the cathedral to the cemetery. Neil's death was an embarrassment to the government of President PW Botha. Having manipulated the departure of John Vorster whose colleagues were involved in the 'Information Scandal', President Botha declared that his government had to 'adapt or die'. At the same time he promised to end the 'total onslaught' against the country by using an iron fist.

When affidavits and documents regarding Neil's death were filed by the police, William Lane briefed Denis Kuny with me. Among the papers was a statement made by Neil to Sergeant Alletta Gertruida Blom the day before his death, complaining of ill-treatment. There was also evidence that he had been deprived of sleep for more than seventy hours at a stretch and that he was expecting another such session.

Together with Mohammed Navsa, Denis' pupil who now sits in the Supreme Court of Appeal, we discussed whether systematic torture that leads to suicide might be a crime. Our conclusion: an 'induced' suicide might well be an offence. In the past, relatives were reluctant to adopt such a line of attack. Few are prepared to accept that their loved one has committed suicide. We explained to the family the possible advantages of 'similar fact' evidence being led by other detainees tortured during the same period by the same interrogators as part of the same investigation.

Aubrey Aggett quickly realised the importance of following this course. If so many others had been tortured similarly, there was a strong probability that his son's statement of being tortured was true. And what mortal fears must have tormented him to make death preferable to continued mental and physical abuse? The affidavits by other detainees spoke of systematic torture. They also gave circumstantial detail corroborating the evidence in Neil's statement. Similarly, they supported the accounts of torture given in court by the accused, the allegations made by witnesses in indefinite detention and even the accounts of some State witnesses who had later rejected the statements forced out of them by the police.

Counsel for the police objected to our production of the affidavits, on the grounds that they were irrelevant. We persuaded the magistrate otherwise and he allowed us to cross-examine the team of interrogators on the content of the affidavits. Their bald denials were implausible and some of their explanations laughable. Their counsel accused us of turning the inquest into a commission of inquiry into police conduct. The details of these exchanges have been recorded elsewhere; suffice it here to record the response of Helen Joseph:

> The Aggett inquest was a mirror held up to reflect the unimagined depths of depravity, brutality and destruction employed by the security police.

We argued that the pathologists did not exclude the possibility that Dr Aggett was rendered unconscious by using a wet towel, and then hanged. The police evidence stated that he had been well treated and appeared and behaved normally before his death. This was contradicted by those who saw him in the corridors, obviously disorientated. They recalled a man acting in a way consistent with someone who had been tortured. All their evidence of his behaviour suggested that he had been deprived of sleep for long periods.

We expected that the police would be found culpable. The magistrate was surely not going to make the same mistake as his colleague in the Biko inquest. The Aggett magistrate gave a lengthy judgment, but he too disbelieved everything critical of the police, and accepted their fanciful stories. He theorised that the injuries of at least one detainee were probably self-inflicted. This person knew that he was to be detained and could use the self-inflicted wounds to falsely accuse the police. I must point out that the detainee was subjected to electric shock torture. The magistrate then found that one of the detainees was morally responsible for Aggett's death. This witness had given evidence that he saw his friend Aggett in an apparently suicidal state. Aggett's condition should have been reported, said the magistrate, blithely apportioning blame on the witness.

The long list of those disbelieved by Magistrate Petrus Kotze included Dr Liz Floyd, Neil Aggett's companion. She gave evidence of hearing others screaming while she was being interrogated. When she asked her interrogator why they were screaming, he protested that the police did not ill-treat people; rather, they used 'psychological methods'. Another interrogator was at pains to remind her that some people had jumped to their death through interrogation room windows. She said that this thought had never occurred to her before, but that she could not get it out of her mind afterwards. The magistrate disbelieved all her evidence. Why? Because she had admitted she was rude to her interrogator after he had threatened to hit her.

In the wake of Aggett's death, Minister of Justice Kobie Coetsee had been more careful than his predecessor, Jimmy Kruger. Ten days after Neil's death he said that '[t]he public would learn the full truth about the death in detention of Dr Neil Aggett, and that untested allegations of torture make no contribution to justice'. Judgment in the inquest was given three days before Christmas 1982. After she heard the magistrate's finding, Liz Floyd commented, 'If the security police say they dealt with Neil in the way they did, then why is he dead?' Even the government-supporting paper, *The Citizen*, commented 'Why indeed?' and added:

> The magistrate in the Aggett case exonerated the police. He could not exonerate a system. Thus, only the end of the system and a return to the normal proceedings of the law will suffice if we are to have no more Aggetts or Bikos or other detainees whose death shock all people who believe in the rule of law.

Michael Hornsby wrote in the London *Times*:

> The parade of ex-detainees, black and white, through the witness box to tell under oath their tales of beatings, strippings, electric shock torture, sleep deprivation, third-degree interrogation techniques and worse, gave the press a rare opportunity to report on conditions in security police custody. Rarer still was the spectacle of the policemen themselves, normally beyond the reach of the law, being cross-examined by counsel on their own interrogation techniques. By turns truculent, sheepish and evasive, they, too, had their day in court.

It must have become obvious that the police and the government could no longer afford cases such as the inquests into the deaths of Biko and Aggett. The partial judgments in their favour came across as neither credible nor legitimate to most of their supporters, much less to the majority of the people of South Africa and less still to the international community. So what were they to do? The answer was deeply disturbing. They formed covert police hit squads to kill their enemies and then put the blame for the deaths on alleged tribal factions or inter-political feuding. The police burned or buried the bodies of those they murdered and pretended that their victims had fled the country to join the armed struggle. This was why the activists did not communicate with their families. The advantages of the new strategy were many. For one thing, the police no longer had to appear in court to face hostile cross-examination.

We had to wait more than a decade for this conspiracy of silence to be broken before we could cross-examine members of the hit squads when they applied for amnesty for the crimes they committed. Even then, many wouldn't tell the whole truth. It often struck me at the amnesty hearings how the police were quite different: uncomfortable, even subdued, now that they were stripped of their unfettered powers.

The hit squads targeted those they suspected but did not have enough evidence to convict. Even some acquitted by the courts were murdered. Joe Gqabi, after serving time on Robben Island, was again charged. He was acquitted and left the country to become the ANC's representative in liberated Zimbabwe. But he did not escape the police for long and was gunned down. His counsel, Arthur Chaskalson, often muses about how much better it would have been if Gqabi had been sentenced to life imprisonment. On his release, he could have played an important role in democratic South Africa.

Then there was Dr Fabian Ribeiro, acquitted on a charge of terrorism. On his release, he continued his medical practice in Mamelodi. Both he and his wife, a close relative of Robert Sobukwe, were fatally shot at their home. He had insisted, during a consultation at the time of his trial, that his only 'crime' was to treat young people injured by the police. He neither charged a fee nor disclosed the identity of his young patients to the police when they wanted to arrest them. Or consider Griffiths Mxenge, stabbed innumerable times by a security police operative. He had frustrated the authorities because his associates would not give evidence against him.

Whenever I questioned the worth of defending people charged with political offences, my doubts were dispelled by the frequent requests for help from many organisations. Among them was the newly formed Detainees' Support Committee which focused on those in solitary detention and the difficulties of their families. We also helped the South African Council of Churches, numerous civic, women's and youth organisations and the trade unions. These bodies helped form the United Democratic Front, with Albertina Sisulu as patron.

Although Albertina Sisulu was no stranger to solitary detention without trial, Neil Aggett's death increased her fears for the safety of her son, Zwelakhe. He had been detained at the same police station as had Neil. She assumed that Walter would have heard of Zwelakhe's detention and Neil's death. I reassured her as best I could. Surely the outcry over Neil's death would restrain the security police in their treatment of Zwelakhe. Albertina hoped that I was right. I understood her need for contact with her husband over the danger threatening their son. I knew that if I asked to see Walter on Robben Island, I'd be refused, but I could try and see Nelson.

At the time I was defending a young woman, Masabatha Loate, on a charge of terrorism. She allegedly belonged to a little-known and offbeat organisation called Sayrco. Zwelakhe Sisulu was listed as one of the State witnesses. Masabatha assured me that Zwelakhe had nothing to do with their organisation. He had turned them away when she had gone to the Sisulu home requesting help. Loate had no defence on the merits. Not only did some of her friends give evidence against her, she was also found in possession of incriminating evidence. The case against her was watertight.

By chance I learned that Sisulu was in a cell below the courtroom. I tried to convince the prosecutor, Jan Swanepoel, that as the case against Loate was already proven, he would not need Sisulu's evidence. He knew that, as a matter of principle, Sisulu would not give evidence. He also knew that the police purpose was to imprison him for his refusal. Jan Swanepoel was an honourable man. He admitted being under pressure from the security police to call Zwelakhe. The police wanted him in prison at any cost. I warned him that if the State persisted, I would place the facts before the court and accuse the prosecution of abusing the process by needlessly exposing an innocent man to imprisonment. Could he and the security police live with the next day's headlines? Swanepoel promised to talk with the police. Ultimately, he closed his case without calling Zwelakhe.

Faced with evidence of growing black political dissent, *verligte* Afrikaners, under the leadership of the Broederbond, took what they considered a leap forward by creating two additional houses of parliament, one for Indians and one for coloureds. These appeared to extend political power, but continued white hegemony. The exclusion of Africans enraged not only Africans themselves, but also the majority of Indian and coloured citizens. They called for a complete boycott of the system, while some decided to participate to destroy these undemocratic structures from within.

The charismatic Allan Boesak had been elected president of the World Alliance of Reformed Churches. Boesak persuaded the alliance to declare apartheid a theological heresy. In January 1983 he called for the formation of a 'united front' to organise joint opposition to the new constitutional reforms. He was later accused of doing the bidding of the ANC. Mostly this was because Oliver Tambo had declared 1983 'The Year of United Action', with a directive from Robben Island and those leaders held at Pollsmoor that the call be supported. The launch of the UDF was always going to be dangerous for its new leaders. The organisation itself would inevitably be accused of fronting for the ANC, and its leaders were likely to be banned, detained and charged with furthering the objectives of the ANC, if they didn't face the more serious charges of sedition or treason. Nevertheless, Albertina Sisulu, whose banning order had recently expired, accepted a leading position in the organisation as it was important that the UDF be seen to enjoy the ANC's approval.

The agitation both within and outside South Africa against banning orders gave Albertina a brief respite. Her restrictions were not renewed immediately they expired and she had a taste of comparative freedom. But her role in the UDF was too much for the authorities. During preparations for the formal launch in Cape Town, Albertina and a young teacher, Thami Mali, were arrested. They were charged with furthering the aims of the ANC by participating in the funeral of ANC Women's League veteran Rose Mbele seven months earlier. Protestors claimed that Albertina's arrest so long after the event was a transparent strategy to prevent her from attending the UDF launch.

Johannesburg attorney Priscilla Jana asked me to defend Albertina. I discovered that the charges against the two arose from the songs they'd sung praising the ANC and its activities and lauding its leaders. At the same event, ANC flags were displayed, one of which was draped over the coffin. Although both had been in custody for some time, their case was remanded for a further two months without bail. This would prevent Albertina from addressing the thousands of people expected at the official inauguration of the UDF.

The funeral of Rose Mbele had been well attended by the security police. They joined the procession to the cemetery led by a horse-drawn cart, and had observed the coffin draped with the ANC colours. They had also seen the ANC colours on the programme and the cover of the obituaries. When the case against Sisulu and Mali reached court, the prosecutor called an 'expert witness', Isak de Vries from the Rand Afrikaans University. He was to explain how the funeral promoted the aims of the ANC and of its military wing, MK. Ironically, Albertina's speech had expressed her friendship and admiration for Rose Mbele during the time that the ANC was a lawful organisation.

I had hardly put my first question to de Vries when the problems began. He protested about my use of English, insisting that he be questioned in Afrikaans. His reasoning was that at an earlier trial he had been cross-examined by David Soggott and replied in English. As a result his evidence was rejected and adversely commented on in the press. Hearing the questions in one language and answering them in another had confused him. The magistrate, believing that I might be persuaded by flattery, said that he had often heard me cross-examining to good effect in Afrikaans. I replied that while I could ask police officers what had happened in interrogation rooms, this did not mean that I could do justice to my client's interests by dealing with Mr de Vries' convoluted political theories in Afrikaans. The magistrate, probably correctly, surmised that we were reluctant to use Afrikaans in political trials after the Soweto students' revolt against the compulsory use of Afrikaans in the classroom. To break the impasse he suggested that I provide an interpreter. While I didn't need the evidence of de Vries translated, my client did, so I suggested that the official court interpreter, who was quietly interpreting de Vries's evidence for Albertina's benefit, could also translate my questions to the witness.

This was too much for the magistrate. The idea of an African interpreter translating into Afrikaans the questions put in English by the cross-examiner, and doing so for the benefit of a supposedly leading academic, was extraordinary. In consternation, the magistrate adjourned the court for over an hour. When he returned, he made it clear that he did not take kindly to my uncooperative attitude. He declared that in the interests of the accused we could use the language of our choice. I had a copy of David Soggott's cross-examination of de Vries. This showed that he contradicted himself and admitted that his conclusions were groundless. Clearly language was not the problem but rather de Vries's lack of scholarship and deductive reasoning.

Nevertheless, the magistrate convicted Albertina Sisulu as charged on the basis of the evidence given by de Vries.

The magistrate was also not impressed by our plea that Albertina not be sent to prison as she had been in custody for months. He did admit that it must have been hard for her to lead such a lonely life, especially as her husband was serving a life sentence. However, as a deterrent to others and for the safety of the State, he felt obliged to impose a sentence of four years' imprisonment, two of which were conditionally suspended. Such was the outcry from inside and outside the country that the prosecution and the magistrate agreed to release her on bail pending an appeal.

A few weeks before the appeal she visited Walter to say goodbye, believing that she would not see him for some years as prisoners were not allowed to visit one another. Her message to me from Walter was that I would not lose the appeal. His exaggerated sense of confidence turned out to be correct, and judges Frikkie Eloff and Richard Goldstone acquitted her. This was not the end of her troubles. She was arrested on a charge of high treason together with the leaders who had helped form the UDF. They were all to be tried by Judge President John Milne of Natal in Pietermaritzburg.

CHAPTER 35

Delmas – The Longest Trial

Several of these defendants are highly regarded as spokespersons for peaceful black opposition to the injustices wrought by apartheid in South Africa ... It is inconceivable that their political activities would have qualified as treason or terrorism in this country or any other democracy.

– The US State Department

The South African judicial system is equal to many with a long-established tradition of impartiality, independence and integrity.

– Response by the Minister of Justice, Kobie Coetsee

For more than four years, from August 1985 to November 1989, I was engaged in a most difficult and unpleasant case before Judge Kees van Dijkhorst. We spent four hundred and twenty days in court and the rest of those four years involved preparation during the court vacations and then preparing and arguing two challenges to his judgment brought in the Appellate Division.

My involvement began in July 1985 as we were preparing for a trip to Greece during the school holidays. I was asked by four firms of attorneys acting for the accused in a treason trial to lead the defence, which at that stage consisted of Karel Tip and Zac Yacoob. Our clients were twenty-two men, among whom were three leaders of the United Democratic Front. A few days before my departure to Greece, a lengthy indictment was served on the accused and they were remanded in custody. Their trial was to take place in a small town hundreds of kilometres away from their homes.

The twenty-two were charged with treason, terrorism and furthering the objectives of unlawful organisations. It was alleged that the accused, together with hundreds of co-conspirators named in the indictment, including Bishop Desmond Tutu, the Rev Beyers Naudé, and the entire United Democratic Front and its leaders, had conspired with the ANC and the South African Communist Party to bring about a revolution. In pursuance of that conspiracy, violence had occurred in the Vaal Triangle and thirty-two other areas across the country. The UDF was said to have had a presence in all the areas where attacks occurred on councillors and their property, on schools, post offices, police vehicles and public transport. The intention of the conspirators was to render the country ungovernable.

My colleagues generously insisted that I take my holiday. Meanwhile they would prepare a request for further particulars. I thought that we needed Arthur Chaskalson's expertise and took the indictment to him. In his view, there were major defects and he agreed to cooperate with Karel and Zac in preparing the request for further particulars.

When I returned from Greece at the beginning of August that request – and the State's answers – were on my desk. Arthur believed the amplified indictment was worse than the original: the accused were not given precise allegations of what they had done in furtherance of the conspiracy or how they had associated themselves with the acts of each of the many conspirators. He felt the court should be asked to quash the indictment. Although Arthur was fully engaged as national director of the Legal Resources Centre, he agreed to draw the notice of exception and argue it.

Our clients were being held in the Pretoria Local Prison. The special consulting room for political prisoners used by us during the Rivonia and Bram Fischer trials was too small. Instead we had a room upstairs which was devoid of chairs or tables. We found our clients sitting on the floor. Among them were the secretary of the UDF, Popo Molefe, two other senior leaders, Patrick Lekota and Moss Chikane, along with Tom Manthata, who was a senior employee of the South African Council of Churches and personal assistant to Archbishop Tutu. The rest were residents of the Vaal townships Sebokeng, Sharpeville, Boipatong and Everton Small Farms. They were mostly members of the Vaal Civic Association, although two were members of the Azanian Peoples' Organisation (Azapo) and one, Father Geoff Moselane, was an Anglican minister and liberation theologian.

The magistrate had remanded the trial for hearing in a small town in the eastern Transvaal. The accused would be isolated from their families, friends and supporters and there was no accommodation for their legal representatives or adequate facilities for us to consult with our clients and witnesses. The attorneys intended applying to change the venue. If this was not granted, their clients would refuse to participate in the trial.

The State estimated that the trial would last six months. I heard that the judge president was having difficulty persuading any of his colleagues to become involved in such a lengthy matter away from Pretoria. Judge van Djikhorst had volunteered, bragging that no trial in which he presided would last so long.

He had two assessors. One was Professor Willem Joubert, a known opponent of the apartheid government's policies. The judge invited us to his chambers. We were courteously asked to sit while he made an important call. This turned out to be a lengthy discussion with an official in the Department of Bantu Affairs about the appointment of an additional teacher to the school which the judge ran on his farm for the benefit of his labourers' children. We took it as a good omen.

Once he had finished the call he told us that the registrar and the attorney-general informed him that the facilities at the Pretoria prison were inadequate for a trial involving so many accused. The resources of the court proposed by the State were equally inadequate. He assured us that he would move the trial. According to his information, a newly built and adequate circuit court in the little town of Delmas would have ample facilities both for the accused and for us. The accused could be kept in Modder B Prison where proper consultation facilities would be arranged. We agreed to put the proposal to our clients, and again felt that we could have done worse than have this judge hear our case.

But these apparently satisfactory arrangements with the judge counted for nothing when counsel for the prosecution, led by PP Jacobs, transported our clients to the original venue. This was done without our knowledge and we would have gone to the wrong place the next day had not a warder telephoned us at the request of our clients. There was no apology by the State for the lack of courtesy – an attitude which continued throughout the trial and which I paid back in kind from time to time. Jacobs had been lead counsel prosecuting the Nusas trial in which Karel Tip was an accused. Now Karel was a member of our team. This did not improve relations with Jacobs.

Once Arthur had agreed to argue the exception, I met with the accused before their first appearance. I introduced him as the leader of the defence team, which caused him to glare at me, but he didn't deny it. Then he shook hands warmly with each of our clients.

The first appearance before Judge van Djikhorst was a formality, but Arthur spoke at some length about the appalling way the defence team had been treated. He handed up a number of letters to the State in which our attorneys requested information, copies of video and audio tapes, documents and the right to inspect other evidence. A number of those letters were not even acknowledged. The judge first obtained an admission from Jacobs that Arthur was correct, then asked if Jacobs realised that failure to respond to letters by attorneys was a professional offence. Why did Jacobs consider that he was exempt from this rule? We considered these remarks yet another good omen. The presiding officer wasn't going to mollycoddle the prosecution.

While we failed to quash the indictment, we were given particulars of some of the allegations. We were also given volumes of documents found in the offices of the UDF and its hundreds of affiliates around the country, as well as videos of meetings, marches and funerals – and secretly recorded video and audio tapes.

Our clients were held in prison after the attorney-general issued a certificate overriding the court's jurisdiction in considering bail applications. All our consultations took place in jail. We decided to split the defence team to consult with our clients in small, more manageable groups. Our venue was a spacious room normally used as a prison garage and a safe holding place from which awaiting-trial prisoners were transported to court.

When our case started, a second trial involving the UDF was under way in Pietermaritzburg, where Albertina Sisulu and other members of the front's top leadership were appearing before Natal Judge President John Milne. We remained appraised of the Natal trial while preparing our defence. I had not worked with Zac before but knew that he had a successful practice despite his blindness. Judge Milne once told me that within half an hour of his appearance in court, people forgot that Yacoob couldn't see. Zac lived up to this reputation. In fact with his reader, his braille board and punch he was ahead of us.

During consultations our clients rejected the allegations of violence and denied that their activities furthered the aims of any unlawful organisation. Our defence was going to be similar to that in the mammoth treason trial. The accused would say that it was not treasonable to demand fundamental changes in your own country, including universal suffrage, political, economic and social rights, and the outlawing of discrimination on the grounds of race, ethnicity, gender or anything else. If the demands of the UDF and its affiliates as well as of our clients were similar to the demands and policies of unlawful organisations, this was in itself no proof that the UDF or the accused had acted on behalf of the unlawful organisations. This line of argument proved successful in several earlier political trials and we thought it was worth using again.

We hoped to show that the unbridled violence which had broken out at Sebokeng on 3 September 1984 as well as the violence in the thirty-two other areas was neither the result of the policies nor the actions of the UDF. Nor was it the result of the policies of the UDF's affiliated civic, women's or youth organisations. Rather we intended demonstrating that it was a spontaneous response to the discriminatory policies of the government, unlawful attacks by trigger-happy security forces, the removal of national and local leaders by detention without trial and the use of torture, as well as the corrupt practices of the Bantustan authorities and their puppet local councils.

The State planned to counter this defence by leading evidence at length of the killing of councillors in Sebokeng, Sharpeville and elsewhere. These murders, it said, were carried out in pursuance of the call made by Oliver Tambo in his annual address to the ANC for 1985 to be the year of 'ungovernability'. In a private conversation, Jacobs' senior assistant, P Fick, confidently claimed proof beyond a reasonable doubt that some of the accused, particularly Lekota and Malindi, were responsible for the death of councillors at Sharpeville and Sebokeng. He predicted that death sentences would be imposed.

We were forewarned of the State's thesis via the parallel trial in Pietermaritzburg. Indictments in both cases alleged that in the pamphlets and the speeches of the accused recorded on video and audio tapes, in their mass mobilisation marches and the 'political' funerals they arranged, they were acting for and on behalf of the ANC to create a revolutionary climate that would make the country ungovernable. The songs, slogans, poems and the rhythmic marching dance known as the *toyi-toyi* were intended to bring about the overthrow of the State. Although the accused didn't associate publicly with the ANC's violent struggle, and while they used supposedly legal and legitimate organisations, their propaganda incited the outbreak of violence.

At the time of these trials, the University of the Orange Free State and the Rand Afrikaans University in Johannesburg were conferring doctorates on the theory of 'revolutionary warfare'. These studies sought to explain why legitimate political activity elsewhere in the world was treated as treason or terrorism in South Africa. But apartheid prosecutors sometimes forgot the lessons they should have learned in their work for the State. One of these was how badly these expert witnesses often performed in court.

In the Pietermaritzburg trial, true to form, the prosecution called an expert witness on revolutionary warfare – none other than RAU's Isak de Vries. He faced Ismail Mahomed SC. A master of the English language, a student of philosophy, a great lawyer and formidable cross-examiner, he tore de Vries to shreds. The witness advanced theories about political bodies such as the ANC, UDF and the Transvaal and Natal Indian congresses of which he knew very little. For example, he wrongly assumed that the Natal Indian Congress was an unlawful organisation.

Asked by Ismail Mahomed about the history, aims and objects of the Natal Indian Congress, he confessed ignorance. Asked what its members had done during the period covered by the indictment he answered that they could have been making samoosas for all he knew. Ismail was at his best when he barely suppressed his anger, and this was such a moment. In response to the thinly disguised racism and contempt in de Vries's retort, Ismail repeatedly asked the witness: 'Why did you say that?' De Vries had no explanation. It was the beginning of the end.

Asked by the judge if, as an expert, he believed the organisations or individuals had committed themselves to violence, de Vries answered that he was undecided. Ismail was ready with the coup de grâce: 'M'lord, then I don't know the value of this witness and of the whole of his evidence.' 'That is why I am asking these questions,' agreed the judge. De Vries conceded that he didn't understand his brief and that he had no expertise to assess the correctness of statements or facts published in revolutionary literature.

As if that wasn't bad enough, the prosecution's case soon suffered further blows. The video and audio tape evidence was excluded for lack of proof of its provenance and authenticity. Witnesses interrogated in detention did not fare well and the prosecution finally withdrew all the charges against most of the accused. In the end, the remaining four were also acquitted.

The fate of de Vries in the Pietermaritzburg trial forewarned the Delmas prosecution and they tried to avoid this pitfall by abandoning the discredited witness. Instead, they retained André Pruis, another 'expert' in politics, this time from the University of the Orange Free State. He was to fare far worse than de Vries.

At the end of the Pietermaritzburg trial, Gilbert Marcus, one of several counsel in that matter, joined us. He was familiar with the documents produced by the State for both trials. They ran to thousands of pages, and his main task was to brief the defence team and the three UDF leaders as to their contents, both the favourable passages we could use to contradict adverse State witnesses and those that might need explanation on our part.

The judge was becoming impatient. He expected the defence to act in a way that would help the prosecution prove its case. Regarding documents produced by the State, he wanted us to admit who wrote them and on behalf of which organisation; he expected us to tell the court who distributed them and in whose possession each one was found. He came close to issuing an order, rather than a request, that one of the prosecution team work with Karel Tip on these documents. He wanted them to stay out of court and report regularly on the progress they were making in agreeing on this evidence. Frequently he queried their lack of progress.

There were some more social moments. The judge would invite us for tea and cake, baked by his wife. I reciprocated by providing rich Greek confectionery. On these occasions our talk ranged from the newspaper headlines to our personal lives and I was even congratulated on my part-time appointment to the Court of Appeal in Botswana. Interestingly, one of the newspapers regularly to be found on the judge's desk was the *Sowetan*, a newspaper most white people wouldn't bother to read. The judge read it to broaden his knowledge of the black community.

He was sympathetic when Peter Mokoena's mother died and allowed him to attend the funeral. The police objected, fearing that the police officers who accompanied him might be overpowered by the mob. Eventually they agreed that Mokoena could go when I offered to accompany him along with two plain-clothes black policemen. I promised to ensure that nothing untoward happened. The senior uniformed officer remained reluctant, as he put it, to entrust to me the safety of his men and the return of the accused to prison. But he, too, acquiesced.

Jacobs was much less cooperative than the police. Before I left for the funeral, he agreed not to call a major witness in my absence. Nevertheless, he called Colonel Gerrit Viljoen to implicate a number of the accused, particularly Father Geoffrey Moselane of the Anglican Church in Sharpeville. Karel objected, as we had agreed that I would cross-examine the police officer. The judge refused the request.

At the funeral, the police cars kept their distance from the hundreds of mourners. I was asked to speak at the family home after the customary washing of the hands and partaking of food, and our little group returned unscathed to the prison in the late afternoon. The next morning I learned of Jacobs' duplicity. Karel had detailed notes of the colonel's evidence, all of which was strongly denied by our clients.

What the prosecution didn't know was that we had a video from a foreign correspondent which contradicted much of what the colonel had said under oath. I arranged for a video operator to be present during my cross-examination of the colonel. When the prosecution wanted to know which of the videos I wanted to view, I fobbed them off. I decided my best strategy was to have the colonel specifically deny incidents on our tape. I wouldn't disclose that we had the video, but rather frame the questions in a manner that would gradually unnerve him into thinking there might well be one.

During the cross-examination I asked if he had been wearing specific items of clothing; if he held a red and white loud hailer; and if he was standing on a step or ledge on a particular part of a vehicle. I asked if his men carried sjamboks, if they'd attacked the passengers in the bus as well as some passengers on the roof, and if those on the roof, in trying to escape, had jumped off the top and out of the windows. The more detailed and graphic the description in my questions, the more worried and hesitant he became. In the end, he chose the way of most liars when they're caught out – 'I don't remember'.

Once he was settled into that mode I put to him what our clients had done even though these things did not appear on the video:

BIZOS: Did you shout to your men '*Slaan die kaffirs*' while they were busy indiscriminately beating people up as they were trying to get away at the end of the funeral?
VILJOEN: I don't remember.

BIZOS: Did you ask Accused Number One, Baleka, to kneel before you and then kick him on the chest?

VILJOEN: I don't remember. M'lord, I am not prepared to answer any more questions; I want to be legally represented.

I handed the video to the operator. The colonel could hardly look at it. The judge was angry but I couldn't make out whether his anger was with the witness who, despite his rank, was shown to be an outright liar, or with me for not having disclosed the video before the cross-examination. Either way he kept silent.

A few months into the trial, the judge asked me how much longer it was going to last. I told him that the State hoped to close its case before the end of the year, some six months ahead. He glanced at his desk where the morning paper lay open at a photograph of Judge Harry H Nestadt, whose elevation to the Court of Appeal in Bloemfontein had just been announced. Judge van Dijkhorst felt he was being left behind, a remark that betrayed his ambition. He wanted matters to come to a speedy end.

Tom Manthata, a senior employee of the South African Council of Churches and a close associate of Bishop Tutu, was accused of having addressed a meeting of residents at Geoff Moselane's church in Sharpeville shortly before the outbreak of violence in the Vaal Triangle. It was alleged that he had advocated violence. This Manthata denied – though he readily admitted speaking at the meeting. While a State witness implicated him and others, we had statements from a number of witnesses to contradict this evidence.

More importantly there was a videotape, shot by Kevin Harris as part of a documentary. It was made the Sunday after Tom had spoken and contradicted what the State witness said happened at church meetings. More particularly, it recorded a speaker complaining about what had happened since the meeting addressed by Tom. She bemoaned the lack of discipline in the youth. At the previous Sunday's meeting they had agreed that there should be no violence – but the youth had ignored this advice of their elders. To her great disappointment some youths had stoned buses. She pleaded with everyone to stick to the agreement of non-violence reached at the previous meeting.

The State's witness couldn't reconcile the two versions. I felt the video and other evidence had discredited the witness but this view wasn't shared by the judge.

Then the State called a girl in her late teens. She was unknown to the accused. Her task was to identify Patrick 'Terror' (a name earned as a soccer player) Lekota, a senior member of the UDF executive, as having addressed a group of young people in the nearby town of Parys. She said that he asked them to join the armed struggle and instructed them on how to make petrol bombs. Under cross-examination she admitted being detained in solitary confinement and that these were her circumstances when she made the statement. But she insisted that she spoke the truth. It was important for us to test her evidence as it was vital to the prosecution's case. The consequences for Terror Lekota as an individual would have been serious and, similarly, the repercussions for the UDF. Her evidence would have helped prove an 'organisational conspiracy' to commit acts of violence.

The judge was impatient with the time we took to cross-examine the witness about the precise date of the meeting in Parys. When she had decided on that, it was put to her that she was lying. Terror Lekota was in detention at the time. She considered this and we nervously awaited her reply. Were she to say that she had got the date wrong, her explanation was likely to be accepted. Instead, in a soft and trembling voice that was barely audible she said, 'But everything I have said about Mr Lekota is a lie.' Her words in the vernacular were greeted by a chorus of sighs among the accused and spectators. The excellent interpreter, Simon Skosana, invariably mimicked the tone and inflection of a witness to equally dramatic effect.

I asked the teenager, in my most sympathetic manner, how it had happened that she made a false statement to the police. She described in detail her detention, how she was coerced to agree with what the police told her about Mr Lekota. It was made clear to her that if she did not make a statement implicating him, she would be detained indefinitely. I noticed that the judge stopped making notes. I asked if she had had a consultation with the prosecutor who led her evidence in court. She had not met this man before, but had seen a white man in an office in the court building and told him that her statement was false. She had also told him her circumstances. He was not interested. He said that if she did not repeat her statement – a statement which she had made under oath – she would be charged with perjury and failure to give evidence and would go to prison for five years on each count.

She was asked to identify this person and his office at which point the judge broke in wanting to know why I was pursuing the matter as he had already struck her evidence from his notebook. I reminded him that procuring false evidence was a serious matter, one that should be investigated because an adverse inference could be drawn against a party knowingly making use of it. Reluctantly he let her continue. She was escorted out of court and returned a few minutes later: she had identified Jacobs' office and pointed him out as the person who had threatened her.

I wanted to know how she identified Lekota from all the others in the dock. She had been told his position in the group, and that he had a gap between his front teeth. The judge snapped that she couldn't possibly have seen the gap from the witness box. She insisted that she could. He placed on record that he could not. I then put on record that although I was further away from both the dock and the bench, I could see the gap clearly. His Lordship was not pleased.

The learned judge didn't pursue the irregularities with Jacobs. By contrast he lost no opportunity of complaining about members of the defence team. I had earlier offered my spectacles to a witness who couldn't read a document. He refused, saying he did not know what disease might be transmitted to him by the use of my glasses. The judge suggested myopia. The prosecution team and a few of its supporters giggled. I paused to glare at the judge, but said nothing.

The Congress of South African Students was one of the many organisations named as co-conspirators. Some of our clients from the Vaal Triangle had been members of this body. Policemen were called from various areas to describe the role that COSAS played in the conflict through protest action on school grounds, at funerals, mass meetings and marches. When the judge betrayed his bias by asking a policeman in Afrikaans, 'When you were observing this group of rioting students …' I immediately objected. What the policeman had described could not possibly be regarded as riotous behaviour. The students were marching and shouting slogans demanding a students' representative council at their school. If the judge considered that to be riotous behaviour we would have to consider our position. The judge said that I did not understand the meaning of the Afrikaans word he had used. We came back after the adjournment with an Afrikaans/English dictionary and I said that if we'd been wrong about the meaning of the word, then so was the dictionary.

The next round in the dispute over words concerned our use of the word 'chant' to describe the rhythmic *toyi-toyi*. The judge became increasingly upset when I drew attention to the French origin of the word, observing that it was commonly used in the expressions Byzantine and Gregorian chant. He didn't want the word 'chant' associated with *toyi-toying*. Later, when I used the word 'chant' again, the judge benevolently placed on record that he had found the dictionary definition and that I was right. As the case proceeded, the relationship between us, if not yet hostile, was at least unfriendly. No doubt he considered me truculent and uncooperative; certainly I thought of him as impatient and unresponsive, if not antagonistic to our defence.

At about this time, without any formal notice, an 'expert' from the University of the Orange Free State, André Pruis, was sprung on us as a substitute for the thoroughly discredited Isak de Vries. Pruis ran a programme at his university on the 'determinants of revolutionary warfare'. He spoke for hours without a single note, referring verbatim to various passages from a range of books, particularly those by Lenin and Régis Debray, the French intellectual who, before his imprisonment in Bolivia, advised Che Guevara.

Pruis made no reference to the allegations in the indictment, or to the documents, or even to the evidence. He spoke of how organisations professing to be non-violent brought about a revolutionary climate by criticising government, its policies and structures and by discrediting as collaborators those who served the government. Because he had been called in late, he was not asked if what the accused had said and done would bring about a revolutionary climate. Clearly, the State's intention was to establish 'norms' and then argue that as the facts fitted the theory the accused were guilty of treason, since they had aided and abetted the armed struggle by their propaganda.

We knew that Tom Lodge of the Department of Politics at the University of the Witwatersrand had consulted with Ismail Mahomed's team in Pietermaritzburg during that trial. We asked for the witness to stand down for a few days while we consulted with Lodge to prepare our cross-examination. The judge peremptorily ordered that the trial continue the next morning. We protested and he gave us a day's extension. I informed him in no uncertain terms that we would spend the limited time afforded by the court compiling affidavits of why we would be unable to cross-examine. We would file these papers and ask for a further adjournment.

Judge van Dijkhorst replied sarcastically that we required a lengthy adjournment because we did not know what questions to ask. I retorted that that was the reason exactly. This didn't amuse him. As he was about to refuse our application one of the assessors, Professor Joubert, put his hand on the judge's forearm and whispered in his ear. A short adjournment followed, after which we were granted our application.

During the adjournment we sought advice from Tom Lodge and Matthew Chaskalson. Both men supplied invaluable information. Matthew, a history student, produced numerous examples of political writings and speeches critical of the prevailing authorities – certainly as critical, and often more so, than the UDF documents. Generally the language was a great deal more intemperate, yet these works were not regarded as bringing about a revolutionary climate or as incitement to violence.

We studied two letters written by General Smuts shortly after the defeat of the Boers in 1902, one written to Lord Milner, who had offered Smuts and General Botha positions on the Transvaal Council established by the British to rule the defeated erstwhile Independent Republic of the Transvaal. The letter by Smuts rejecting the offer described the council and its members in the most derogatory terms. He told Milner that neither he nor General Botha were prepared to betray their people and take part in a puppet council appointed by those who'd conquered them. The other letter was written to John X Merriman, the last prime minister of the Cape Colony, who was opposed to the policies of Cecil Rhodes and regarded by the Boers as one of their friends. Smuts wrote to Merriman explaining why neither he nor Botha would be taking up the offer, using even stronger language than that used in the letter to Lord Milner.

In putting the document to André Pruis, and merely for the sake of completeness, I asked 'And who was John X Merriman?' The answer astounded the three Afrikaners presiding on the bench, the three Afrikaners in the prosecution team, the Afrikaner investigating officers and even the lower-rank Afrikaner policemen guarding the accused. The answer from the State's expert was 'I don't know'.

From then on, emboldened by Pruis's professed ignorance, I repeatedly made a point of asking if he knew who he was referring to. Questioned about the peaceful revolution that led to the independence of India and Pakistan, he confessed ignorance of Jawaharlal Nehru and Lord Mountbatten. I asked him about the authors indexed at the back of Debray's book – the one from which he had so fervently quoted. He recognised none of the authors on that list, not even Tito, who appeared there under his proper name Broz. The name of the newly elected president of the Philippines was likewise unknown to him. When asked who the loyal patriots, the moderates and the revolutionaries were in Vichy France, he said he did not know the place. The judge could take no more. He smiled and suggested that I possibly wait and ask such questions of a policeman in the witness box.

But the most humiliating scene was still to come. While in his Bolivian prison, Debray had time to rethink his views on revolution. On his release, he wrote a book contradicting everything he had told Che Guevara. The new book, freely available, was published a few years before Pruis entered the witness box. Tom Lodge brought it to our attention. He was astounded that the 'expert' witness hadn't referred to it. Perhaps he didn't know about the book, or maybe he had deliberately suppressed it. Either way this was a rare opportunity, the kind relished by a cross-examiner. When we put it to him, the witness conceded sheepishly that he was unaware that the guru of revolutionary theory, the expert on whom he had so heavily relied, had recanted.

The thorough discrediting of Pruis occurred only because we'd persisted in our demand for adequate time to consult with real experts. Gilbert Marcus, when lecturing on applied legal studies at Wits University, uses the record of this section of the trial to illustrate the importance of standing up to a judge and how beneficial it can be to seek advice from experts. Pruis is now the deputy commissioner of police. Lekota is the minister of defence and the national chairman of the ANC.

Daily, Karel Tip and I drove to and from Delmas. We used the travelling time every morning to review the previous day's events and to anticipate the coming session. Over and over again we listened to the music of Mikis Theodorakis and Yiannis Markopolous' 'Songs of Protest', Nikos Hadzidakis' 'Melodies' and the 'Rebetika' songs of joys and sorrows on the bouzouki. Caroline Nichols and Karel Tip wanted an explanation of the lyrics. From my loose translations and comments on the historical allusions, they were impressed by both the content and by what were to them unusual metaphors. We promised to visit Greece together at the end of the trial – at that stage we had no idea what lay before us.

The trial attracted attention both nationally and internationally. Bishop Tutu was a regular visitor. When he discovered that Lazarus More, at that stage still in custody, wanted to get married, he volunteered to officiate. On a day when the judge did not hold an afternoon session, he gave permission for the courtroom to be used. Little did he know that the bishop, the bride, the groom and their parents would all sit on the judges' bench during the event, as would the best man, Terror Lekota. The proceedings were televised and large colour photographs appeared on the front pages of the next day's newspapers. Although he said nothing in court, privately the judge expressed his displeasure that the bench had been used for such a purpose.

On another occasion, Caroline came into court agitated. She quickly scribbled a note to me although I was on my feet questioning a witness. Her note said that the police were insisting on carrying out a body search of the British ambassador and his companions who had come to observe the trial. She wrote, 'Tell the judge.' I ignored her message, partly because the judge might say that it was none of his business and partly because it would do our clients no harm for Her Britannic Majesty's envoy to be subjected to the sort of indignity that most of us were subjected to daily.

At this stage, many witnesses were giving evidence about a meeting held prior to the march on the town council's offices. Witnesses identified office-bearers of the Vaal Civic Association and its affiliates as being present, but we got them to admit that there was no talk of violence and that the march was to be peaceful. Evidence to the contrary was contradictory and implausible. Most of the State witnesses conceded that there were real grievances against the local councillors and administrators – they were perceived as puppets of the apartheid government who did not care about the plight of the people living in the area.

The State witnesses, much as they may have been programmed to condemn the accused, could hardly deny the legitimacy of the grievances of the vast majority. The government had asked a professor from Potchefstroom University to enquire into the causes of the outbreak of violence. He was unable to escape the obvious, and blamed police tactics and the continued general discontent against the inferior 'Bantu education system'. In addition, the exclusion of Africans from the tricameral system, the increase in rentals and the corruption of local councillors all helped lead to rejection of the whole system of government.

As part of our own research into local dissatisfaction with municipal corruption we established that the family of Mayor Esau Mahlatsi had been granted twelve of the twenty-five liquor licences in the township and had an interest in eight others. All the remaining licences went to other councillors. A councillor elected at a by-election had been granted a licence to operate a dry-cleaning business. Asked why he was not awarded a share in the profit of local liquor businesses, he replied that by the time he was elected the other councillors had taken everything.

As the time drew near for the State to close its case, Arthur Chaskalson and Gilbert Marcus prepared for the next stage of the trial. They worked on written argument calling for the accused to be discharged at the end of the State's case as, based on the facts and the law of treason, there was no case for them to meet. This was a matter of law so the two assessors had no say in the decision. The judge dismissed the application except regarding three of the accused. These three he found not guilty and discharged. The case was postponed. When it resumed we decided to begin with the accused from the Vaal Triangle area and leave the UDF leaders until the end. This would give us – and particularly Gilbert Marcus – an opportunity to prepare them in relation to the documents produced by the State.

Our first witness was Bavumile Vilakazi. He had chaired the meeting at which it was decided to march on the council offices. He spoke of the reasons for the formation of the Vaal Civic Association, described its peaceful policy and the reasons it affiliated to the UDF. He said that the association had no contact with any unlawful organisation; that it had not conspired with Azapo as alleged. There were in fact differences of policy and some hostility between the organisations. During Vilakazi's evidence the judge interrupted to ask if the association had had trouble getting permission to use the council's halls for their meetings. Bavumile said that it had.

JUDGE: You told us earlier that you passed a football ground. Why did you not hold your meetings there?
VILAKAZI: Because it was illegal to have open-air meetings, My Lord.
JUDGE: Then you knew that your march was illegal?
VILAKAZI: No, My Lord, there is a difference between a meeting and a march.
JUDGE: Mr Bizos, I like playing open cards. I have a notice prohibiting gatherings in various areas which I want to hand in as exhibit D.
BIZOS: No, My Lord. The letter D was intended for defence exhibits. What Your Lordship wants to put in is not a defence exhibit. Because we too want

to play open cards, we want to bring to Your Lordship's attention that the notice prohibiting gatherings you want to put in has been declared *ultra vires* by the full bench of the Transvaal Provincial Division. I will give Your Lordship the reference. May we say, My Lord, that you should leave it to the State to make out a case if it has one, and Your Lordship should not try and assist them to do so.

Judge van Dijkhorst did not take kindly to being told that he was wrong in relation to the notice. Nor did he like being chided about his interference on the side of the State. He gave the exhibit a different number. In his final judgment, he said that our belief that the declaration of the notice as invalid was a windfall had made no material difference to his judgment. That exchange over the notice prohibiting outdoor gatherings marked a sharp deterioration in an already unhappy relationship between us. Much worse was to follow.

We thought that Bavumile had given his evidence well, that he had easily dealt with the cross-examination and that there were no reasons to disbelieve him. It later emerged that although Professor Joubert agreed with us, the judge did not believe the witness.

Our next witness was Peter Mokoena. Peter's involvement was peripheral: he had allowed a table and a chair to be placed next to the entrance of his small grocery shop for people to sign the million-signature petition. This petition was a protest against the tricameral system and the exclusion of African people from the political process. At some point, Professor Joubert felt the cross-examination was too lengthy. During a short adjournment he told the judge the prosecutor was spending too much time on the petition. There was nothing wrong with it. He had signed it himself.

The judge came into court the next morning and placed on record what Professor Joubert had told him. In the presence of both assessors he declared Professor Joubert unfit to continue, then hurriedly adjourned the court. In doing so he ignored the professor, who wanted to say something. The three left and the judge came back minutes later accompanied by the remaining assessor.

We were all shocked and asked for a short adjournment to discuss matters with our clients. Terror passionately demanded that Joubert be reinstated because the remaining assessor was a member of the Broederbond. How could an assessor who had signed the million-signature campaign be dismissed while the Broederbonder remained?

When court reconvened we submitted that the dismissal of the assessor was irregular. We argued for a halt to the cross-examination in the absence of the professor. If the hearing went ahead without him, the trial would be irregular and any decision made in his absence would be a nullity. Our application for the matter to stand down so that we could prepare authority on which to argue was flatly rejected. The judge ordered the trial to continue. We could prepare whatever argument we wished to present and he would deal with it whenever we were ready. Once he had made his ruling, the prosecutor continued with his cross-examination of Peter Mokoena.

We met at the end of the day with Arthur and Gilbert who had not been in court. The judge's action was clearly wrong, but as the trial had continued in the absence of the assessor there was no point in asking the judge to set aside his decision. As Professor Joubert had not been allowed to speak, we thought he should file a document setting out what he would have said. We made this request through his lawyers, and once we received the document from them found that it revealed more than sufficient grounds to ask for the recusal of the judge and his assessor.

Joubert mentioned a conversation between himself and the judge concerning our application for the discharge of most of the accused. Judge van Dijkhorst had commented that we would not call our clients to give evidence – we were too clever for that – because we knew they were guilty and would not withstand cross-examination. Joubert had disagreed.

The judge had bet him a bottle of whisky that we would not lead our clients in evidence. The professor accepted the bet. On the morning that we called our first witness from among the accused, the judge's registrar delivered a bottle of whisky to Joubert. When the assessor disagreed with the judge's assessment of Vilakazi as a witness, the judge retorted that Joubert didn't understand the threat posed by people such as our clients. Joubert asserted that the million-signature campaign was nothing more than an exercise of citizens' democratic right to disagree with the policies of the government. He had signed it and this in no way disqualified him from making an impartial decision as to the guilt or innocence of the accused.

We prepared an application for the recusal of the judge and the second assessor, and annexed a copy of Joubert's statement. Our carefully drafted heads of argument were to be delivered by Arthur Chaskalson. In court we found I W D de Villiers s c with dozens of books spread out, briefed to oppose us. The judge was confident that there was no merit in the application. He made no statement admitting or denying what Professor Joubert had said before his exclusion, but he treated the application for recusal as though it were vexatious and not worthy of serious consideration. In fact he threatened to commit Arthur for contempt if he seriously pursued the applications. This caused the afternoon newspaper to carry the banner headline: 'Chaskalson threatened with contempt'. Arthur enjoyed such respect among most judges and members of the profession that the general conclusion was that the threat might have been justified against me, but against Arthur? Surely not.

The judge took some comfort from the State's contention that what the professor had said was not admissible and should be struck out. After all, discussions in a judge's chambers were confidential. This did not prevent the judge from setting out in his judgment a selection of the matters that were discussed there, arguing that it was in the interests of truth and justice.

The judge also spoke on behalf of the other assessor, W F Kruger, who admitted membership of the Afrikaner Broederbond. Kruger confessed to not knowing that the investigating officer, Major PEJ Kruger, was also a member. Nor could he see how his membership would in any way prevent him from being impartial. He regarded the organisation as a cultural and a political 'think-tank' that did not prescribe political beliefs. I was reminded of this exchange years later, when Judge van Dijkhorst, in another context, declared that members of secret organisations should not preside in court where they were involved in judging others.

After the judge ruled the Joubert report inadmissible, we asked for a short adjournment to discuss the matter with our clients. We confidently predicted that the judge was wrong. In our view he had erred both on the admissibility of the reports and in dismissing Joubert. We said that if the accused were convicted, the Court of Appeal would resolve either or both of these errors relating to the recusal issue. Our clients accepted this advice and resigned themselves to the continuation of an already lengthy trial. After four days of argument, the judge summarily dismissed the application and filed his reasons a week later in April 1987.

His written judgment concludes with a castigation of the defence team. 'It would not be unfair to suggest that to the knowledge of the defence team these applications for our recusal would do irreparable harm to the image of the administration of justice in South Africa.' Despite this knowledge, we proceeded with our application. In wilful ignorance of the facts we utilised inadmissible confidential information, and, in short, our conduct fell 'far short of the high standards set by this court for these honourable professions'.

When this judgment was published in the South African Law Reports, its editors added an editorial note to the judge's words:

Enquiries into the propriety of the conduct of defence counsel were held by the Bar Councils of the Bars of which they are members, and it was found that the conduct of counsel had not been improper and that they had complied with their duty as counsel.

Some time later, when the matter was eventually taken on appeal, Chief Justice Michael Corbett found the judge wrong in dealing with Professor Joubert as he had done. In a unanimous decision by the Appeal Court, delivered on 15 December 1989, the chief justice also cleared the legal team of any improper conduct. He wrote,

> Before I conclude this judgment there are two matters to which I feel myself impelled to refer. It is obvious from the reported judgment, and more particularly from the papers filed in the application for quashing and recusal, that after the events of 9/10 March 1987 there developed, unhappily, a bitter and acrimonious confrontation in public between the presiding judge and Dr Joubert. I think that this was largely due to tensions which had built up in the course of a long, wearying and politically charged trial. And I have no doubt that in the sober light of retrospect the protagonists in that confrontation sincerely regret some of the things that were said. I say no more.
>
> The second matter relates to the strictures passed by the learned judge on the conduct in the court apropos of counsel and attorneys acting for the accused. As appears from a footnote to the judgment inserted by the editors of the South African Law Reports, enquiries into the propriety of the conduct of defence counsel were held by the Bar Councils of the Bars of which they were members and it was found that the conduct of counsel had not been improper and that they had complied with their duty as counsel. The correctness of this information was confirmed to us from the Bar. We were also told by appellants' counsel that a similar enquiry by the appropriate Law Society had also exonerated the attorneys. In the circumstances it was, in my opinion, ill-judged and unfortunate that in argument presented to this court counsel for the State should have persisted in an attack upon the conduct and bona fides of the appellants' legal representatives. Moreover, the attack did not appear to have any substantial relevance to the issues which this court was called upon to decide.

However, that was for the future. Now the security police, the prosecutors and even Judge van Dijkhorst appeared anxious to question our professional integrity. One of the bitterest disputes between us and the judge concerned an instructing attorney in the case, Priscilla Jana. In the tense atmosphere of the time, attorneys were more vulnerable than advocates. They annoyed the security police by their persistent demands on where their detained clients were being held, and by delivering clean clothes, reading material, toiletries and chronic medication to these clients. Priscilla was a champion of the rights of her clients and their families. The security police, on the other hand, resented the volume of her work, the way she identified herself with the cause of her clients and her sharp tongue.

By this stage all the accused except the three UDF leaders had been granted bail. The State opposed bail for the three on several grounds. It was feared they might continue their treasonable activities by directing the activities of the UDF if released from custody, and that any conditions preventing them from doing so would be difficult to police. State President PW Botha issued a proclamation declaring the UDF an unlawful organisation. Gilbert Marcus and I, together with one of Priscilla's professional assistants, Caroline Nichols, prepared an application for bail relying on this new fact: there was no longer a UDF in whose affairs the three could involve themselves.

In response the State alleged that Priscilla Jana, in her capacity as legal adviser for persons other than the accused, had brought an application in the Cape Provincial Division of the Supreme Court for the proclamation to be declared invalid. This application was pending. The State's affidavit suggested that she explain to the judge her apparently unprofessional conduct. This misconduct, according to the State, related to an application for bail based on the content of a particular proclamation without disclosing that she was contesting the validity of this same proclamation.

The judge ordered her to appear before him the next morning. When we consulted with her that evening, her answer was simple. The application for bail was filed some time before she launched the challenge to the validity of the proclamation, a challenge brought on behalf of completely different clients. In court the next morning, Gilbert Marcus and I produced the notice of motion that had been filed in Cape Town and handed a copy to the prosecution team and the judge.

Gilbert and I submitted that surely this should be the end of the matter. While the judge let up in his persecution of her, his wrath now fell on us. Saying that we must have known about the Cape application, he demanded to know why we had not informed him. His questioning prompted me to ask on whose behalf he was now conducting the inquiry, the implication being that he had entered the arena on behalf of the State. My question angered him, but he said nothing.

A few days later Gilbert Marcus and I received copies of a lengthy letter from the judge to the chairman of the Bar Council charging us with untruthfulness on the basis that it was 'inconceivable' that what we had told him was true. We submitted a similarly lengthy response, explaining that Priscilla Jana attended hardly any of our planning sessions. She was usually represented by one of her professional assistants and this person had not reported the application launched in the Cape Town court. While we considered it unwise for the Bar Council to approach our ten colleagues to collect corroborating statements, we listed their names.

Our representations were sent on to the judge who indicated that he had nothing further to add. The Bar Council nevertheless appointed three members to inquire into our conduct. The judge was notified of the hearing. On the appointed day we asked for an early adjournment because of a 'private matter', not knowing that he too had been invited to attend.

We asked Jules Browde sc, a senior member and former chairman of the Bar Council, to represent us. In his view, the judge's speculation that we had withheld information from him was unfounded and he was surprised that once our statement was supplied he chose neither to deal with it nor to withdraw the complaint. The hearing before the council subcommittee was brief; we were exonerated. The committee did not respond to Jules Browde's request that it criticise the judge for his unfounded allegation against us.

Throughout we continued leading evidence by our clients and other witnesses in court. The testimony aimed at demonstrating that they had not acted for the ANC or any other unlawful organisation. Their protests were intended to gain freedom from oppression, a change from apartheid so that their citizenship would be recognised and they could enjoy the political and economic rights to which all were entitled. We asked our witnesses, clients included, to narrate the personal experience that led them to become activists.

Some told heart-rending stories. Gcina Malindi spoke of the shack in which his family lived at the back of a house in Everton. Although they had occupied the shack for many years, his father could not get permission to live and work in an urban area. The law provided that he could be there only as a visitor for not more than seventy-two hours at a time. Once, as his father was about to be arrested, his mother pleaded with the urban areas inspectors that he was a visitor from the countryside who had come the day before and was going to leave that day. The police asked nine-year-old Malindi who the man was. Wiping away tears with the palm of his hand, Malindi recalled his reply. 'I do not know him,' he told the police. The collective sigh in court bore testimony to the empathy felt by most people in the public gallery. In assessing Malindi's evidence, the judge described him as an embittered young man whose evidence he could not accept.

The defence team, both attorneys and counsel, split up in pairs to visit each of the thirty-two areas where violence had broken out, allegedly at the UDF's instigation. We found witnesses prepared to testify that this was untrue. The violence was caused by other factors: the unlawful conduct of the police at funerals and vigilante thuggery to which the police turned a blind eye. This thuggery was organised by town councillors who had been elected in a way that the residents regarded as illegitimate. On top of this there was the frustration created by authoritarian government officials and by action taken in terms of official political policies.

We led evidence of a funeral in a small town in the Eastern Province by way of illustration. In compliance with police regulations, the hundreds of mourners left the cemetery in small groups en route to the home of the deceased. On the pavement outside the house, plastic buckets and basins half filled with water were placed for the mourners to wash their hands. This is a time-honoured ritual observed after burying the dead. Tables at the home were laden with food brought by relatives and friends, also in accordance with the tradition of their ancestors.

Without warning or provocation, a police vehicle stopped nearby. On the back was a machine not seen by any of the mourners before. Out of the machine blew a dust that polluted the water, top-dressed the food and covered the faces of the mourners. They rubbed their eyes trying in vain to relieve the irritation caused by the dust. They continuously sneezed and gasped. In this manner, the grief of the mourners was turned to fury because of the callous disrespect with which the police and their collaborators treated them.

We decided not to call the many named co-conspirators on the charge sheet. To have done so would have extended the length of the trial beyond reasonable bounds. However, we seriously considered calling Dr Beyers Naudé, the Afrikaner theologian, former leader of the Dutch Reformed Church and once a member of the Broederbond. He had distanced himself from the Broederbond and was expelled from the church. Thanks to a radical change in the way he understood justice and the demands of the Bible he had become a prominent figure in the South African Council of Churches during the 1980s.

During the trial, an ANC turncoat gave damaging evidence against him. This witness said that he had gone to Dr Naudé's office at the Council of Churches to ask for money to commit acts of sabotage. Dr Naudé told us that he used some of his salary for those in urgent need, but that he never gave money to anyone to commit sabotage. During cross-examination we tied the witness to a specific date on which he alleged the visit to Dr Naudé had taken place and the money had been handed over. That date allowed us to prove conclusively that the man was lying, because Dr Naudé was abroad at the time.

For years he had been denied a passport and, when it was finally granted, after years of local and international pressure, he took a trip out of the country. His passport showed that he was away on the date when the meeting supposedly took place. We had no need to call him in person to refute the evidence.

To Gilbert Marcus fell the task of carefully examining the numerous UDF documents which the State was likely to categorise as treasonous, seditious, furthering the objects of communism and inciting the use of unlawful means. Once these had been analysed he had to brief the three leaders – Popo Molefe, Terror Lekota and Moss Chikane – to deal with the material during cross-examination. They needed to be able to refer to passages anywhere in the documents and not just those put to them by the prosecutors. For this purpose, Gilbert was out of court for many days and spent weekends consulting with the three. Arthur Chaskalson led Popo Molefe, Gilbert Marcus led Terror Lekota and Karel Tip led Moss Chikane. Zac Yacoob and I led the accused from the Vaal and other witnesses.

Gilbert consulted with them early in the morning before the hearings and during the midday lunch break. We assumed that these consultations would be bugged and so used the technique of writing down key words and pointing at them. In this way Gilbert produced comprehensive statements to lead the accused, and made detailed notes of their responses to particular topics. He also had to lead Popo Molefe through his evidence in chief. As the UDF secretary, Molefe was the author of many pamphlets, press statements and letters issued by the organisation.

Patrick 'Terror' Lekota was the UDF information secretary and one of that organisation's most popular speakers. He regularly addressed groups all over South Africa, eloquently condemning the policies of the government in English, Afrikaans and at least three indigenous languages. He articulated the aims of the UDF to large crowds and many of his speeches were secretly recorded on video or on audio tape. Sometimes he came close to calling for support for the ANC and this would have to be confronted on the witness stand.

'Terror' was no stranger to the courtroom. In the mid-seventies he had become a supporter of the Black Consciousness Movement led by Steve Biko. When black students withdrew from Nusas he was chosen as an office-bearer of the new, black South African Students' Organisation (Saso). During a government clampdown on black consciousness, Lekota and other leaders of Saso were charged under the widely defined Terrorism Act for advocating the liberation of black people. More particularly they were charged with organising an unlawful mass meeting to celebrate the independence of Mozambique from Portugal. After a lengthy trial they were sentenced to six years' imprisonment.

Lekota arrived on Robben Island during December 1976, fresh from the trial. He and the other new black consciousness arrivals shared facilities with the rank-and-file ANC prisoners from whom they were divided on ideological lines. When I visited Nelson Mandela I was told about the hostility between ANC and PAC prisoners, an enmity encouraged by the jailers. I also heard of the efforts made by the ANC leadership on the island to promote unity against the common apartheid enemy.

Despite the stringent steps taken by the authorities to isolate the ANC leadership from the rest of the prisoners, however, they kept in touch. Before long Lekota had established direct contact with Nelson Mandela and Walter Sisulu and, at some danger and cost to himself, he asked to join the ANC. He also influenced other black consciousness adherents to do the same. In Lekota's view, the ANC's programme of action within and outside the country was more likely to bring about liberation, so it made sense to change allegiance.

For his pains Lekota was assaulted by some of his former political colleagues. In the interests of unity he refrained from laying a charge. Our concern was whether the prosecution had learned about this assault and the reasons behind it. We suggested not calling him. He would have none of it. Faced with his determination, we thought to object to questions about the matter on the grounds that they were outside the period of the indictment. Also, no evidence on the subject had been led by the State, precluding the prosecution from putting questions on the issue during cross-examination. Lekota was anxious to defend his actions and the integrity of the UDF; he was confident that he could deal with the cross-examiner. We felt we could not stand in his way.

'Terror' was the leader of all those in the dock, irrespective of their age. He chaired the meetings of the accused with a firm hand, but like a good democrat he gave each an opportunity to be heard. He persuaded us to adopt the option favoured by our clients whenever difficult decisions had to be made. And he had enormous moral influence over all his colleagues. One of the accused, Simon Nkoli, was gay and made no secret of it. He received many messages of support from gay groups throughout the world. Some of his co-accused made unkind remarks about him and he complained to me about their behaviour. Eventually I requested Terror's help. The teasing stopped immediately.

Lekota was an excellent witness. He did not contradict himself or any other defence witness. He contextualised his comments at various meetings and defended the views expressed by other UDF leaders, particularly those who had been acquitted by Judge Milne in the Pietermaritzburg trial.

Judge van Dijkhorst didn't agree with our assessment of Lekota. He was visibly upset by some of Terror's arguments and justifications. Moreover, Terror was a good mimic and sometimes copied the voice and mannerisms of President PW Botha and other apartheid leaders – a touch that did not endear him to the judge. Also, despite our warnings, Terror occasionally lapsed into the manner he used on the political platform and this further irritated Judge van Dijkhorst.

Lekota was a most forthright witness. He attributed the formation of the UDF to the government's 1983 constitution excluding Africans from political rights, and not to an ANC initiative. The UDF was not intent on electing a black prime minister or a black government, but a government of all the people, who would be represented in Parliament. He described black people who collaborated with the government, particularly the Bantustan leaders, as rascals and scoundrels. The suggestion that the African people would be given rights similar to those limited rights granted to Indians and coloureds was unacceptable, he said.

Lekota defended statements that he had made in various speeches, including calling President PW Botha a tsotsi because he believed the president was dishonest. He became angry at the prosecution for encouraging witnesses in detention to give false evidence that he went about the country teaching people how to make petrol bombs.

When Moss Chikane, the Transvaal secretary of the UDF, was called to testify, he denied that the UDF wanted to destroy the existing education system in the black areas, take over control of schools and replace the syllabus. The main aim of the UDF was to bring about the end of apartheid by lawful means. He slowly and deliberately denied the allegations made against him and his organisation. The nearest the prosecutor got to contradicting Chikane was when he produced a document in Chikane's own handwriting that, in the prosecutor's words, advocated 'black power'. Chikane denied the allegation and asked to see the document. He apologised for his bad handwriting, and explained that the phrase he had written in the notes for his speech was 'person power', not 'black power'. As 'manpower' was politically incorrect he opted for the more inclusive alternative. Although this was accepted, it didn't change his position in the judge's eyes.

While the trial was in progress numerous extrajudicial steps were taken against the UDF, including, as mentioned, its banning. The forthright manner in which the three leaders expounded the UDF's aims and objectives again underlined that the witness box is often the last forum in which the oppressed may speak. In this trial at least, they did so to good effect. Diplomats, foreign media, politicians, religious leaders, trade unionists, artists and many others attended the trial and heard the accused eloquently defend their actions, their philosophy and their organisation.

It was bizarre running this case when the political reality was so at odds with the events within the courtroom. Despite continued oppression, the late 1980s was a time of meetings between representatives of the government and the ANC in Dakar and elsewhere. President PW Botha was ousted by FW de Klerk, who made ambiguous statements about the release of Nelson Mandela and other political prisoners. Against this background and the overwhelming national and international pressure for fundamental change, the Delmas trial continued as if in a vacuum.

Several prominent black community leaders agreed to testify on behalf of the accused, by speaking about the situation in Soweto. They blamed the government for the unrest and widespread dissatisfaction, and for the way it had exacerbated the situation by supporting the illegitimate local authorities which it created. Above all, they blamed the system of apartheid for depriving black people of political and economic rights.

We called Lybon Mabaso of Azapo to deny the State's contentions that his organisation was involved in a conspiracy with the UDF (or any other organisation) to overthrow the State by violence, to commit acts of terrorism, or to further the objects of any unlawful organisation. We also called Sheena Duncan, the leader of the Black Sash, to speak about the impact of discriminatory legislation. Given her organisation's involvement with the black community, she was able to testify about the effect that these laws had on family life. She explained that the hostile mood of the people was caused by these laws and by the corrupt practices of township bureaucrats, supported by the apartheid system.

By this stage our team was preparing detailed heads for concluding argument which had to deal with the thousands of pages of evidence and exhibits. The burden of analysing the facts as they emerged in the evidence was undertaken by Karel Tip, Zac Yacoob and Gilbert Marcus. We also prepared argument analysing the law in relation to the charges of treason, terrorism and furthering the objects of unlawful organisations. At a joint meeting of the advocates and attorneys we finalised what we believed to be unanswerable submissions for the acquittal of all the accused. We thought that we'd convincingly countered the State's argument. However, mindful of Professor Joubert's contention that the judge believed our clients were guilty, we were not overly optimistic.

As it turned out, this was a realistic assessment. The judge began his summing-up by criticising the manner in which we'd conducted the trial, blaming us for its inordinate length. He called for fundamental changes in the Criminal Procedure Act to avoid similar problems in future. For example, the accused should be compelled to disclose their defence before a trial started. Had his proposals been taken up, they would have removed the right of an accused person to remain silent, and this would indirectly have shifted the onus onto the accused to prove their innocence.

These ideas might have provoked response or comment from the Appeal Court, but when the case eventually got there, that court's attention was focused on his failure to observe important provisions of the Criminal Procedure Act by dismissing Professor Joubert. In the end, no one took much notice of his proposals. They were also untimely. By now the demise of apartheid was widely expected, even among members of the judiciary and the legal profession. The profession's interest was focused more on a bill of rights than his draconian, retrogressive proposals.

As part of his judgment he handed down what he called Annexure Z. This contained his supporting argument for finding the accused guilty of treason, terrorism or furthering the objects of unlawful organisations.

In the opening section, Judge van Dijkhorst set out some of the cautionary rules pertinent in criminal matters such as this. He enumerated the approach to witnesses held in solitary confinement for indefinite periods and inconsistencies in their statements to the police and what they had said in evidence. Then he evaluated the credibility and reliability of the witnesses. In the one hundred and twelve pages of Annexure Z, he reviewed the evidence of the sixteen accused, spending an average of seven pages on each, spelling out why neither he nor his remaining assessor believed them. He called each one of them a liar.

By contrast Pruis, the so-called expert, was described as 'an honest witness who was prepared to make concessions where necessary' – although we are told neither what these concessions were, nor that they were consistent with the accused's defence. Some of the accused were disbelieved because they professed ignorance of certain aspects of the UDF's policy or activities. Pruis, on the other hand, despite his shocking lack of knowledge in his field of 'expertise', was not criticised beyond a remark that he was out of his depth in some respects and did not keep up with the latest developments in his subject.

Colonel Viljoen was described as an impressive witness who answered questions forthrightly and who could express an opinion on whether riots were spontaneous or organised. In assessing the officer's evidence the judge made no reference to where we had discredited his testimony. Nor was there any judicial comment on the video we had produced that gave the lie to the colonel's evidence.

The judge and his assessor dismissed the evidence of Sheena Duncan, because the Black Sash was favourably disposed toward the UDF and she was in favour of the release of political prisoners. Also Duncan was a pacifist and not likely to know the covert aims and objects of the UDF. Similarly, the evidence of Ellen Kuzwayo, another witness who testified in favour of the accused, was not accepted. The judge found that she was 'a dignified lady' but 'naturally biased towards the freedom struggle' and therefore 'biased in her approach'.

By contrast hardly any policeman, town councillor or supporter of the government's policy was accused of bias in favour of the State. They appeared to have no 'natural bias' in their approach which might constitute a reason to disregard or even question their evidence. The Azapo leader, Lybon Mabaso, was described as 'a revolutionary and wholly untrustworthy witness'.

There was no criticism of the State for making unfounded allegations against the accused, such as the five counts of murder. Nor was there any reference to the young woman who gave false testimony against Lekota. She was one of the State witnesses who simply merited no attention.

Once the judge had convicted our clients we had to consider mitigating whatever sentence he imposed. During the Rivonia trial we had called author Alan Paton. This time among those we asked to give evidence in mitigation we called another writer, Nadine Gordimer.

She was cross-examined on her political beliefs and made no apology for being a supporter of the policies of the ANC and its armed wing, Umkhonto we Sizwe. She was also in favour of economic and other sanctions and an active supporter of the policies and actions of the UDF. Her endorsement of the use of force by Umkhonto we Sizwe was prominently reported. Although her husband, Reinhold Cassirer, was concerned that she might be visited by the security police and possibly arrested, they took no steps against her, no doubt fearing the worldwide protests that would follow.

But our witnesses in mitigation were not well received by the judge and his assessor. They may well have made little difference to the outcome. Lekota was to serve twelve years and Molefe ten. The judge had the grace to remark, when sentencing Molefe, that it was unfortunate that he had to send such a man to prison. He felt that if Molefe had followed a different path, he could have made a worthwhile contribution to the country. Moss Chikane was sentenced to ten years. Both Tom Manthata and Gcina Malindi were given five years. The rest received various terms of imprisonment wholly suspended on condition they did not commit a similar offence.

It was widely reported that Zac Yacoob and I could not keep back our tears when these sentences were imposed. Later, when arguing leave to appeal, the judge found it necessary to remark, 'Cowboys don't cry'. That prompted a stage whisper from me – which I made sure was quite audible to the judge – that we would not want to be known as 'cowboys'.

One of the grounds on which we applied for leave to appeal concerned the judge's bias in cross-examining the accused. He demanded details of this allegation. Karel Tip had searched the record and produced hundreds of references in support of our submission. During the course of argument we began to read these out, much to the judge's obvious embarrassment. He tried to stop me continuing. By now our exchanges were neither polite nor respectful. Anxious to end the ordeal, he insisted on concluding proceedings that day and the court sat well into the evening. Eventually the prosecutor asked for the court to adjourn, but the judge turned this down. Arthur Chaskalson wanted to make a similar request, but by now it was a matter of stamina. Eventually the judge gave in and we went home for the night.

During the argument for leave to appeal, the accused were not in court. They were already on Robben Island serving their sentences. We ensured that they were sent a transcript of proceedings. Lekota was most amused by the exchanges between the judge and me. His assessment: I was polite and restrained during the trial, but once the judge had done his worst I let him have it. He asked whether I had heard the wise Basotho proverb: 'Don't shout at the crocodile until you have crossed the river.'

I visited Gcina Malindi a couple of months after his imprisonment with news that his daughter was born on the same day I became a grandfather for the first time. There was another coincidence – the two mothers and their babies were in adjoining wards of the same hospital. To my delight, I was asked to be Lindiwe's godfather. Malindi started studying law in prison and he has become a successful advocate.

Almost a year after their conviction and sentence, all the accused were acquitted by the Appeal Court. We were confident of winning their acquittal on appeal, but although this proved correct, the decision reversing Judge van Dijkhorst's conviction and sentence was not as satisfying as it might have been. It was based on the higher court's finding that once the judge had sacked Professor Joubert, the trial court was no longer properly constituted. I found it disappointing that we had no opportunity to challenge his findings of fact against the accused, particularly his findings outlined in Annexure Z. I consoled myself with the thought that the appeal judges found the miscarriage of justice caused by the dismissal of the second assessor so flagrant that on its own this warranted overturning the outcome before they considered our other complaints.

There is a brief postscript. Some years later, after the change in government, Popo Molefe took office as the premier of the North West Province. He hosted an inaugural party at the football stadium in the provincial capital and invited members of the legal team, along with Judge van Dijkhorst. The judge accepted his invitation and we sat at adjoining tables. In a nice touch of irony, the judge, Arthur Chaskalson and I were asked to speak after Premier Molefe had welcomed the multitude with an address in which he appealed for reconciliation among the adversaries of the past.

CHAPTER 36

The Beginning of the End?

The four years of the Delmas treason trial coincided with a time of great political confusion and contradiction. Our clients spent years in the dock distancing themselves from the ANC to avoid conviction, yet the government was making tentative approaches to the imprisoned Nelson Mandela (and the ANC of which he was a recognised leader). While Broederbond chairman Pieter de Lange was meeting prominent exiled ANC official Thabo Mbeki in New York, the South African security forces were planning to assassinate Mbeki when he returned to Lusaka.

An eminent persons' group led by Olusegun Obasanjo (then a former Nigerian president) met Nelson Mandela in Pollsmoor Prison. They would also meet President de Klerk to start negotiations for a settlement of the conflict. At the same time Minister of Defence Magnus Malan ordered South African troops to attack refugee camps in Zambia, Botswana and Zimbabwe in a series of raids that killed many South Africans and citizens of neighbouring countries and undid any good achieved by the Obasanjo visit. Foreign Minister Pik Botha promised that President PW Botha would announce a major change in political course; instead, the South African leader – in what became known as the Rubicon speech – issued a defiant and uncompromising challenge to the world.

The times had also brought changes in the prisons. When we met with our clients in Pollsmoor we knew that our conversations were being recorded, but we rarely adopted our old methods of communicating. Nelson wanted to persuade his jailers, the minister of justice and the head of the National Intelligence Service that he could be trusted. The process of releasing the political prisoners began.

When Govan Mbeki was released in November 1987, he immediately took up a leadership role on behalf of the (still banned) ANC, moving about the country, addressing rallies and consulting with UDF leaders. He made public statements that flagrantly ignored the ANC's unlawful standing. Senior police officers publicly cursed the day he had been released. What were they to do about him? They could hardly detain him without trial as they had done to thousands of others; nor could they charge him. The police wanted him confined to Port Elizabeth under twelve-hour house arrest. This didn't happen.

It is arguable that the hectic political programme he followed may have delayed the release of the rest of the Rivonia trialists and other political prisoners by a couple of years. However, they never complained about his conduct; he did what was expected of a leader of the ANC.

The ideological justification for apartheid by some Afrikaner 'intellectuals' was that in a multiracial, multi-ethnic, multicultural, multi-religious society with groups having reached different beliefs and stages of development, individual rights were inappropriate. Instead, 'group rights' became the political buzzword. Kobie Coetsee appointed Judge Pierre Olivier, chairman of the South African Law Commission, to inquire into the matter. No doubt the minister believed that Judge Olivier, apparently one of their own, would favour group rights and so perpetuate justification of the apartheid doctrine. Separately, Judge Olivier and others had formed the Verligte Aksie Movement which quietly questioned apartheid orthodoxy. They were influenced by the ANC's Harare Declaration proposing a suspension of hostilities; by important conferences held near Oxford and at Columbia University; and by trips to Dakar and elsewhere in Africa conducted by leading Afrikaners.

The Oxford conference illustrates how peculiar were the prevailing political circumstances. Ronald Dworkin, a distinguished professor and writer on jurisprudence, initiated the conference, which he titled, 'The Concept of Law in South Africa'. Professor John Dugard canvassed some of us to accept invitations to the conference in the knowledge that representatives of the ANC would be present. The two professors, Dworkin and Dugard, even invited a number of senior judges. They too were informed of the ANC's presence. On hearing of their acceptance, Kobie Coetsee declared that it was improper for judges to attend a conference with members of an unlawful organisation. They were the upholders of the law. They should not do what writers, opposition politicians and professors had done (and were increasingly doing). The senior judge issued a short response that the group saw nothing wrong in attending the conference. In deference to the judges' possible predicament, Oliver Tambo, Thabo Mbeki and a couple of other senior members of the ANC kept in the background but met with some of the judges privately. The dilemma, however, was clear. If judges did not heed the request of the minister of justice, why should lawyers or anyone else be prohibited from contact with the ANC beyond South Africa's borders?

At about that time Jack Greenberg, a leading academic in the Faculty of Law at Columbia University, New York, initiated a course entitled Legal Responses to Apartheid. Arthur Chaskalson, Sydney Kentridge and others were invited to co-teach the course with Greenberg, one of the legends of American legal practice. Among his claims to fame was an appearance with Thurgood Marshall in the

United States Supreme Court for the almost legendary case of *Brown vs Board of Education*. This challenge to the prevailing 'separate but equal' doctrine, as it applied to education, led to the court holding that the doctrine was unconstitutional. Jack had helped Arthur Chaskalson, Felicia Kentridge and Geoff Budlender set up the Legal Resources Centre with the aim of doing similar work in South Africa. Greenberg was well aware of the South African situation.

At the conclusion of the Delmas trial, I was invited to Columbia in September 1989 to teach on the course. Some time before the Columbia invitation I'd advised on a film based on André Brink's novel *A Dry White Season*. Marlon Brando thought the original script too bland and the production team approached me through Nadine Gordimer for first-hand accounts of political cases.

I'd spent a couple of hours discussing the problems encountered before hostile judges, over-enthusiastic prosecutors and zealous investigating officers. I told them about programmed witnesses brought from the interrogation room, sometimes after a long period in solitary confinement, directly into the witness box with the interrogator sitting opposite as a reminder not to depart from the statement that they'd been coerced to sign. In short, I described the processes we'd gone through in trial after trial.

I later heard that the script, adapted after our discussions, found favour with Marlon Brando and the film went ahead.

While at Columbia University, I received an invitation to attend a premiere of the film. In one scene, Brando's cross-examination of a witness led dramatically to the vital question: 'Why did you make a false statement?' This was a situation I'd faced time after time. The witness lifted his shirt to reveal half-healed parallel wounds across his back. In the film nobody could hear what the witness said as his words were drowned by the predominantly African group of spectators at the back of the court shouting '*Amandla!*' And in the cinema, above all the on-screen noise, came the voice of Lindiwe Mabuza, the ANC's representative in New York, 'George! That's how George does it.' The cinema audience were mostly South African exiles and their close friends. After the premiere, word quickly spread that Marlon Brando had used me as his model. I never met him; like so many in the world I admired his talent and I don't think he needed a tutor. But I must add that my wife Arethe says that I am handsomer and I speak more clearly.

As a visiting scholar, I had ample time to enjoy a leisurely lifestyle, one that Arethe and I had never known before. We spent time with our old friend Professor Tom Karis and his wife Mary. We had become good friends since the long-ago days of the Rivonia trial. He was co-author with Gwendolen Carter and later Gail Gerhart of *From Protest to Challenge*, a monumental work described by the leading advocate Jules Browde sc as 'a definitive and immaculately researched documentary history of the national liberation struggle in South Africa'.

Tom and Mary, seasoned New Yorkers, knew how to get cheap tickets for Broadway shows and which museums and galleries to visit. These were things we had not done since Arethe was a student at the School of Art in the early 1950s and we had a wonderful time together. Gail and Tom interviewed me for a few days about the situation in South Africa and produced a lengthy transcript, which was distributed to various libraries in the United States, South Africa and elsewhere.

Jack Greenberg and his wife regularly invited us to dinner at their Westside apartment, where we discovered that Jack also wanted to be known as a chef. While dean of the college at Columbia, he and a colleague published *The Deans' Cookbook*. They named some of the dishes after their friends, for example, *Lorraine Chaskalson's Pilaf* and *Anchovies and Pickled Peppers a la Bizos*. His deputy, Ekatirine Yiatrakis, invited us to her traditional Sunday lunch. And on other occasions, Jack and Ekatirine together with Steven and Nancy Ellman and other friends enjoyed Greek food and music with us in Greek tavernas. (Fortunately we found tavernas where plate-breaking was not encouraged).

In New York I attended a conference at Columbia University at which Jack Greenberg, Tom Karis, Gail Gerhart, Albie Sachs, John Dugard, Johan van der Vyver, Laurie Ackermann and many others took part. They focused on what was likely to happen after liberation. There was little doubt that the apartheid regime would soon come to an end. During the opening sessions and in private conversations, Albie Sachs, who we knew to be close to Oliver Tambo and to the national executive of the ANC, reassured us that in the new dispensation, the struggle for freedom, democracy and an egalitarian society would be honoured.

On 10 October 1989 the United Nations marked the twenty-sixth anniversary of its call for the release of Mandela and the other Rivonia accused. The previous year, in December 1988, after Nelson Mandela had served more than six years at Pollsmoor Prison, he was transferred to Victor Verster Prison. There he was 'imprisoned' in the house of a senior prison officer. He had a key to the front door; he no longer wore prison clothes but double-breasted suits, starch-collared shirts and ties. He had a telephone and a fax machine; he could invite whoever he wished to. Together we ambled along the garden paths to have what we believed were confidential conversations. Little did we suspect that the bugging devices were hidden among the flowers.

Dullah Omar, a practising lawyer and a leader of the UDF in the Cape Province, saw Mandela regularly, and acted as a liaison between him and the political prisoners in Pollsmoor and on the island. Dullah arranged appointments for those Nelson wished to see. Permission was given by the authorities as a matter of course. Kobie Coetsee and others in the government allowed this for their own purposes; it enabled them to have more frequent secret meetings with Mandela. Nelson, for his part, ran what was virtually an ANC office.

The house at Victor Verster was fully furnished in the style of an early Holiday Inn. The linen on the large and comfortable bed was regularly changed by Nelson himself, despite the appointment of warder James Gregory and his son to minister to Nelson as housekeepers, cooks and waiters.

As we sat down for lunch one day, Nelson called on Gregory junior to bring the bottles of wine to the table so that I could make my choice. I fingered a chilled, well-known dry white to indicate my preference. Nelson smiled, then thanked the young man for having tipped him off that I would not drink the semi-sweet wines that he and most of his other guests enjoyed. With a chuckle Nelson warned me to be careful because the authorities appeared to know a fair amount about me.

Over lunch we discussed his release. He had made it clear he would not accept conditional release, and the other political prisoners had to be released before him. He was pleased that Oliver Tambo had persuaded the movement to adopt the Harare Declaration, suspending the armed struggle if all political prisoners were released, the ANC unbanned and defence force troops removed from the townships.

Nelson now had access to television and radio, local and international newspapers and magazines, so he was aware of PW Botha's failing health. Botha had voluntarily given up his leadership of the National Party and not long afterwards was removed as president. Once FW de Klerk was appointed president, he called an election in which both right-wing Afrikaners and progressives made some gains. Having won the election, FW claimed a mandate to negotiate with the recognised leaders of the black people. Nelson expected this to herald more talks between government leaders and the ANC.

Now, October 1998, the anti-apartheid committee of the UN, headed by Sotirious Moussouris, convened a special meeting in the UN plenary hall at which I was asked to speak. Ninety ambassadors and other dignitaries would attend. I arrived early to view a photographic exhibition. One exhibit displayed part of Toivo ja Toivo's statement from the dock predicting the independence of Namibia in the ringing words that had so upset Judge Joe Ludorf. Indeed, I thought, the world was right and apartheid South Africa was proved wrong.

Before we began, a small group of excited South African exiles told me that the

Pretoria government had announced the imminent release of Walter Sisulu and the other Rivonia accused held in Pollsmoor Prison and on the island. Nothing had been said about Nelson Mandela. The news was received with both joy and sorrow. I told them of Nelson's insistence that he be the last released and we all hoped that it would not take too long.

As I was led through the august assembly to the front row, I nervously put my hand into my inner jacket pocket to remove my speech. I wondered what to say about the news I had just received – it was obviously not yet widely known. The president of the UN assembly, Joseph Nanvem Garba, entered. He spoke about the intransigence of the South African government and its failure to release the political prisoners held in South Africa's jails, even though some had served inordinately long periods in jail. He expressed anger and despair that so little had been achieved over the years.

I put my speech aside and spoke off the cuff in praise of the United Nations and its efforts to bring about freedom, democracy, the rule of law and a human rights culture in South Africa. I related what had happened on 11 October 1963, when Bram Fischer came to our house at dawn with a copy of the *Rand Daily Mail*, its banner headlines proclaiming that the UN had called for the release of Mandela and others. I recalled Bram's instruction to show the newspaper to the accused in Pretoria prison and his message: 'They won't dare hang you after this!' Then I gave the news I had just received, and the auditorium broke into applause. Everyone shared the feeling that surely Nelson Mandela would not be left behind for too long.

The five-month period we spent at Columbia was quality time for both of us. Never before had Arethe and I spent so much time together, nor have we since. We read books, magazines and newspapers. We viewed programmes of high quality on television dealing with art, literature and history. We saw the world's best films; we took French lessons. I had access to excellent libraries from which I could choose biographies and even original documents to study.

I knew little about early American history and tried to familiarise myself with it by reading the Declaration of Independence, the Constitution of the United States, the letters written by federalists and republicans, the inaugural addresses of their early presidents and the decisions of their Supreme Court, particularly regarding the abolition of slavery. I realised that the lofty principles enunciated in a constitution or a bill of rights are no guarantee that these principles will be enforced or respected. Much work and courage is needed to ensure they are maintained despite an ever-changing history.

Some of the students in my class, particularly African Americans familiar with their own history and the failure of the courts to protect their ancestors, didn't believe that there could be effective or even appropriate legal responses to apartheid. At the end of the second session, a woman announced that she didn't know why she had enrolled for the course or continued on it as fundamental change by lawful means seemed remote. I advised her to consult the designated member of the faculty before she took any steps to drop out. She came back from that consultation, offered no explanation as to what had transpired, but continued to be an enthusiastic contributor to the debates.

Inevitably we discussed what sort of constitution and bill of rights South Africa should adopt. It was assumed that, as with the first amendment to the United States Constitution, we would not 'abridge the freedom of speech, or the press; or the right of the people peacefully to assemble and to petition the government for a redress of grievances'. A burning issue was whether, having regard to our racist past, we should limit the right by forbidding the use of racist speech. First amendment rights were deeply implanted in the minds of my students. They did not believe that anti-racism legislation in post-war Germany or the United Kingdom had any effect on racists. The young woman who wanted to give up the course insisted that racism could manifest itself even when nothing was said or written. It would be better to let it come out and confront it, she felt.

It was a strange experience, being with that class. They read the startling and brave decisions of judges Didcott, Goldstone, Ackermann, Friedman and a small number of others who found innovative ways to interpret security legislation in favour of the individual. But the students criticised them as no more than palliatives by the judges to salve their own consciences. Some even praised the pro-government, pro-executive judgments of Chief Justice Rabie and others. We could hardly get consensus as to who were political prisoners or what constituted a political trial.

Our time in the United States was spent mainly in snowbound New York. When we came home towards the end of January 1990, Johannesburg's sunshine was most welcome. But even more so was the expectation that momentous decisions were about to be announced concerning the future of our country.

CHAPTER 37

A Personal Footnote: the 1980s

In the mid-1980s I decided to build a family holiday home outside the village of Vasilitsi and within walking distance of the sea. My mother shed tears of joy when the foundation was laid. She invited the village priest to bless it and, in accordance with tradition, beheaded a rooster on the foundation and cooked it for the workmen.

A well was dug at the foot of the hill and a reservoir constructed at the top to supply the house with water, and to irrigate the citrus and other trees that my mother and sister planted. Kimon and Damon (both medical students) and Alexi (studying engineering) helped with planting the olive trees and vines, constructing the road and building the house, much to the surprise and approval of the locals. We also installed a wind-generator and solar panels to produce electricity which served for almost twenty years until the municipal infrastructure was upgraded.

My sons weren't the only ones with their sleeves rolled up. Relatives and friends came to see me working on the land, digging out thorny bushes, pruning olive trees, maintaining the retaining walls that had crumbled along the slopes. They laughed at me for wearing gloves and proudly held up their callused hands, joking that I should stop pretending I was a farmer.

The house was a statement, an emotional investment in the country of my birth. But it did not stop me worrying about my mother. She was alone there, my sister having married and emigrated to South Africa in the early 1970s. No matter how we tried to persuade her to uproot and move to South Africa, she refused. She said that the easy chairs of South Africa would be the end of her; she wanted to be buried where she was born.

Once my sons had graduated, Kimon and Alexi had to establish themselves in the United Kingdom to avoid national service. Damon had done his military service in the early 1970s before the war started on the border and in the townships. With Kimon and Alexi a good deal closer to Greece than the rest of the family they visited their grandmother whenever they could. I accepted the situation: she had a large family who saw her as often as possible.

My mother was remarkable. Despite her adherence to traditional values, she was prepared to dispense with customs when they became outdated. For instance, after decades of covering her head, she cut her hair, donned a costume and played with her grandchildren on the beach. She kept up with the times and wasn't shy. Sometimes she would slip off to the quieter part of the beach and sit there topless as some of the foreign tourists did. Her visits to South Africa and the visitors to the village from all over the world helped her emancipate herself from the restrictive practices of the past.

Another instance concerned Damon. He had fallen in love with a physiotherapist at Hillbrow Hospital, Anna Gordon, and they wanted to holiday in Greece. But mindful of the tradition that you did not take a woman to the village before you put a ring on her finger, Damon asked me to clear the path with his grandmother. It was much easier than I anticipated. Had Arethe and I accepted the relationship, my mother asked. Yes, we had. In her habitual way of answering questions by asking a question she said, 'Why then should I not accept it?'

Damon and Anna's trip coincided with the harvesting of the grape crop. This is hard work from sunrise to midday and then from late afternoon to sunset. When Anna left the vineyard an hour before sunset my mother was not surprised. How could this English girl (her father was Scottish and her mother Welsh, and Anna was unhappy at being called English) be as tough as the village girls? But when that day's session ended they returned home to find that Anna had cooked the meal. Here was clearly a good girl, grandmother advised grandson. Best to marry her than a girl not smart enough to divide a bale of hay for two donkeys.

The couple did marry not long afterwards and my mother came out for the wedding at the Greek Orthodox Church. Afterwards, at the reception, she sang traditional wedding songs and led the *kalamatiano*, the most popular Greek traditional dance. Eighteen months later, she had a wish fulfilled when a great-grandchild was born to wet her apron.

Part Six: 1999–2000

CHAPTER 38

Free at Last

President FW de Klerk's announcement at the opening of Parliament on 2 February 1990 that he would lift the ban on the ANC, PAC and SACP was applauded in the House. So did I, watching it on television. Along with those three organisations, thirty-three others were unbanned, a moratorium was placed on the death penalty, restrictions issued under emergency powers came to an end and indefinite detention without trial was limited to six months. The word on Nelson Mandela was that he would be released as soon as possible. I did no work during the rest of the day. Instead my colleagues and I discussed the motives for this move. Would the liberation movement put an end to the armed struggle? When would Oliver Tambo and the thousands of others return from exile?

The ANC networks buzzed. Delegations went to Victor Verster Prison to confer with Nelson Mandela. They asked him to delay his release to enable them to prepare for his reception. On the other hand, the government was anxious to let him out to avoid the large-scale gatherings that were inevitable and were likely to grow bigger with every day's anticipation by the excited populace.

Nelson firmly but politely told his jailers that he would not leave them for another nine days. As I was to be in a trial the day after his release, I could not go to Cape Town and had to watch this event, which I and so many others had longed for over the years, on State-controlled television.

Nelson timed his release for early afternoon to give people the opportunity to gather along the streets from the prison gates to the Grand Parade in Cape Town. From the balcony of the City Hall he greeted the tens of thousands in the square, declaring that the struggle would continue until everyone was free.

Back in Johannesburg at the home he and Winnie were to share, he was inundated with requests for appointments and interviews. Every political leader to the left of FW de Klerk's National Party, religious and community leaders, prominent businessmen, old friends and comrades – all queued in the street outside his house to pay homage to him.

I too telephoned and spoke to Winnie. She complained that the house was no longer her own and that despite her objections, the UDF leaders had taken over. She had put her foot down about Sunday's lunch which would be a traditional affair for family only. If I wanted to see Nelson I could come before lunch.

Hundreds of reporters from the print and electronic media were seeking interviews with him. To cater for this media onslaught, selected journalists were invited to a couple of press conferences. Mirela Kalostipi of ERT, the Greek national broadcaster, was desperate to interview Mandela. She asked me to facilitate an interview with him but I refused. However, when I mentioned in passing that my first meeting with him would be the next day, she asked to come along and film as I was entering the house.

While she knew there was no possibility of seeing Nelson, she wondered if Winnie couldn't receive me at the gate. Winnie obliged, but needed a few moments to dress for the occasion. Of course she welcomed me effusively and I was taken to a bench in the shade of a tree, where Nelson sat with the Sunday papers. We talked about our families. He inquired about his friends in the legal profession, particularly those who had acted for him (Arthur Chaskalson, Joel Joffe and Vernon Berrangé, who had since died) and of the prosecutors, magistrates and judges who had taken part in his trials. We reminisced about Bram Fischer.

Aware of his precious time, I stood up to go. He detained me. What was my hurry? I said that a reporter from Greece and a cameraman were waiting for me. Why had I kept them waiting outside? They were called in. Mirela's face glowed. She drew a small piece of paper from the pocket of her blouse, asked for permission to film and read out her initial question. How was he going to spend his first Sunday at home after twenty-seven years? The interview lasted more than fifteen minutes. Afterwards she hugged me and kissed my cheek, delighted that she had filmed one of the first exclusive interviews with Mr Mandela. Her interview was broadcast not only in Greece but also on other channels throughout the world.

A few days later, Arthur Chaskalson and I received glossy invitations to attend a mass rally welcoming Nelson Mandela. More than eighty thousand people crammed into Soweto's largest soccer stadium. We were lucky enough to have seats in the VIP section. Nelson arrived in a helicopter, and walked to the platform on which sat about a hundred heroes of the struggle against apartheid.

A few minutes later, union leader Cyril Ramaphosa called Arthur and me to the platform. The crowd applauded and a couple of ambassadors sitting nearby shook our hands. We were completely bewildered. How were we to get from the highest point of the stadium to the platform on the pitch?

We were led down by an ANC marshal. As we walked up the platform steps, Nelson embraced us warmly. The crowd shouted, 'Viva, Arthur Chaskalson, Viva! Viva, George Bizos, Viva!' and we felt both pleased and embarrassed at being so honoured in the presence of people such as Walter Sisulu, Govan Mbeki and Ahmed Kathrada, who had done and suffered so much.

Nelson Mandela's leadership of the ANC within the country was put to the test almost immediately. The regime wanted no 'known communists' in the ANC's delegation at the first formal talks. Mandela's strong rebuff won the day: the government had no say in the matter. Any insistence would jeopardise the meeting.

The release of political prisoners was a vital issue, one on which Mandela felt his good name depended. He wanted to be the last political prisoner released but this hadn't happened. It was an embarrassment for him, and thus a weapon for the regime. On this issue the government was still in control. Neither requests nor threats of mass action had any effect. Then matters were brought to a head. Political prisoners on Robben Island and in prisons in Pretoria and Johannesburg decided on a hunger strike until they were released.

Out of the blue, a senior official from the office of the commissioner of prisons let me know that the applications I had made to see political prisoners in Johannesburg and Pretoria had been granted. Though I had made no such application I thanked him. The telephone rang again almost as I put it down: Nelson Mandela calling from Zimbabwe. Arthur Chaskalson was to go to Robben Island and I was to meet with political prisoners in Johannesburg and Pretoria. We should tell them that the final decision over the hunger strike was theirs, but that negotiations for their release were well advanced. These talks were at a delicate stage and the threatened hunger strike could derail them.

Arthur and I discussed our strategy and I went off to Sun City, the ironic name given the newly built prison to distinguish it from the dungeon-like Fort. In a large hall I found about fifty young men sitting on the floor, bunched together in a corner. I recognised no one. I introduced myself, delivered my message and asked for a reply. They queried the presence of the warders and at my request the warders left.

From their questions it was clear that these young men did not trust me. Fortunately one of them, rather older than the rest, remembered me. Patrick Maqubela had been a candidate attorney with Griffiths and Victoria Mxenge. Maqubela had refused to give evidence in a trial of his colleagues and was sentenced to five years' imprisonment for his silence.

We embraced with obvious joy at meeting after many years. At this, the atmosphere changed. Patrick spoke to the young men in Zulu. They decided not to continue with the hunger strike. I was to convey their thanks and good wishes to Mr Mandela. There was no difficulty in achieving the same result with the older prisoners in Pretoria.

Arthur Chaskalson reported that on Robben Island the prisoners had held a rally, singing and making speeches. They declared victory as if they were no longer prisoners and the warders appeared unable and even unwilling to impose any discipline. Here too the political prisoners had acceded to Nelson Mandela's request.

Despite this pressure on de Klerk, no agreement was reached on a mass exodus from the jails. De Klerk used his presidential powers to release some high-profile political prisoners but, in order to mollify his white right-wing critics, he simultaneously released people convicted of racist murders.

In an attempt to give the process a semblance of legitimacy, a committee of three retired judges was established to rule on applications for indemnity. The process was slow, and lacked transparency and adequate guidelines. Throughout, prosecutors continued with pending cases, and the security police continued to detain witnesses for up to six months.

In the long run mass action on the streets and threats of work stayaways, together with international pressure, brought about the release of certain categories of political prisoners and, after a time, negotiations took care of the rest.

Despite the promise that the rule of law would be restored, the months after Mandela's release were highly volatile. The police still did not respect the right of people to march and demonstrate peacefully. Demonstrations called in celebration were broken up, as were protests against the rebel English cricket team when it arrived to play in defiance of the continuing sports boycott.

More seriously, at least eight people died and more than three hundred and fifty were injured when police fired on residents of the Vaal Triangle. A request for a protest march against local councils and high rentals was refused but more than fifty thousand ignored the ruling, believing that the times had changed. In this instance they hadn't. The police claimed that the crowd acted in a threatening manner, refused to disperse and surged forward clearly intent on an attack. To protect themselves, the police claimed they had no option but to open fire with live ammunition. The leaders of the protesters denied the provocation and the warnings to disperse.

Furious at what seemed a breach of good faith, the ANC threatened to suspend negotiations and called for an independent judicial inquiry. It was a measure of how things were changing that the government not only set up an inquiry but consulted the ANC about the presiding officer. All parties agreed on Judge Richard Goldstone, then a judge of the Appellate Division.

I led a team of lawyers acting for most of the relatives of those who had died or been injured. Some residents aligned to Azapo and the PAC were represented by Ismail Semenya and Vincent Maleka, office-bearers of the Black Lawyers' Association, who have since become leaders of the Johannesburg Bar. Johan 'JJ' du Toit led the evidence on behalf of the commission. He proved an honest and diligent prosecutor and later followed Judge Goldstone to The Hague when the judge was appointed by the UN as chief prosecutor for the International Criminal Court. The police for their part briefed those they had trusted to represent them in the past.

The hearings took place in the Vereeniging town hall. During the first sitting, Judge Goldstone introduced the members of the commission before referring to its terms of reference. I stood up to announce the members of our team and to identify our clients. The judge said that as this was not a court there was no need for me to stand when addressing him. I replied that I became tongue-tied when seated and asked for leave to stand. Benignly he told me to please myself.

(At a dinner not long after the commission opened I happened to sit at a table with the judge and his wife. Over the meal I delivered a spirited counter-opinion to one of the other guests, and the judge, assuming a most serious demeanour, wondered why I had been less than frank about my inability to speak when seated!)

Dozens of affidavits were filed in support of the police version of events. But things did not ring true. How was the absence of a senior police officer explained? Two comparatively junior commissioned officers headed the police at the scene. At the vital moment when the shooting began they retreated to their official vehicle to listen to the police in-house radio station. They had not given an order to shoot. Those who admitted firing shots had done so out of panic and not because they'd heard an order.

Then I had a lucky break. Over many years I have realised that journalists are reluctant to become witnesses. They are equally unwilling to make visual material available for use in court. Now someone anonymously came to our help with footage taken during the vital minutes of the protest march.

The film established that those in the forefront of the march were unarmed, peaceful protestors who were not threatening anyone. The police firing came as a complete surprise to them and continued for an unjustifiably long time. No one from the ranks of the police tried to stop the fatal spray of bullets into the backs of those who died or were wounded. The inference was irresistible that the two middle-ranking policemen had deliberately withdrawn from the scene and that no steps had been taken to prevent unauthorised shooting or to stop it.

The council chamber where we sat for the inquiry was packed, the crowd sang freedom songs before and after the hearing every day. A young man in an ANC volunteer's uniform stood in the middle of the VIP upper-circle of the chamber with a wooden AK47 on his shoulder. Counsel for the police described it as a provocation. The judge politely asked that it be removed.

For the white Afrikaners of Vereeniging the town was a symbol of both defeat and triumph. It was in Vereeniging that the Boer generals had surrendered to the English at the end of the Anglo-Boer War. It was there that their phoenix rose from the ashes in 1948 when they won the all-white election against the anglophile Jan Smuts and celebrated the return of their very own, beloved South Africa.

Now the only whites present at the hearings were a few spectators and a platoon of white policemen. What had happened to their separate entrances for blacks and whites? To the 'whites only' restaurants? Was their 'whites only' town now to be invaded by the hordes from neighbouring black townships? Would job reservation, intended to guarantee them employment, be abolished? Would black people get the vote and elect a black president to preside over the country?

The legal teams representing people from Vereeniging's townships included black and white lawyers. At lunch time we walked together to a nearby Italian pizzeria where we were welcomed by the owners, a middle-aged Italian couple. Their white customers were taken aback and they chose not to sit at the table adjacent to ours. Instead they looked furtively in our direction from the other side of the room. A couple even shook their heads when Khomotso Moroka, a confident young black female lawyer on our team, held the floor as we discussed the morning's proceedings.

Our favourite restaurant was closed on Mondays and we had to make other arrangements. Once, as we sought another eating place, we spotted an advert for a Portuguese establishment. The seven of us walked up the stairs to the first floor, Khomotso and I leading the way. The owner sternly told us that they were full. I pointed out to him that only one of the thirty or so tables was taken and I asked to see his booking list.

My demand was conveyed to his partner in the kitchen. The senior man came to the reception desk, looked at the four blacks and three whites in our party and said, 'Sorry, but I am not multiracial.' I told him to let us eat or it would not be the end of the matter. He would see me again as an objector when his licence was up for renewal. Convinced, he not only gave us a table, but he served us himself – and the food was excellent. One of our group jokingly wanted to know on what legal grounds I'd based my intimidating remark. We laughed it off. What counted was the result, as another colleague pointed out.

At the end of the hearing, the commission found sufficient evidence to charge some of the police with murder. The decision was welcomed by many as indicating that the days of a trigger-happy police force enjoying immunity from prosecution were over. While we waited for the murder trials, we sued for damages on behalf of a few hundred people. The minister of police wisely made payments. The prosecuting authorities, by contrast, dragged their feet and the wrongdoers were never charged. Eventually they were granted indemnity from prosecution.

During the course of the negotiations about a new dispensation, I was appointed to represent the ANC's legal and constitutional committee. I queried whether I would have to apply for a membership card, and was told I was one of the few who didn't need to go through that process. I was tasked with looking after all the legal aspects, but Cyril Ramaphosa, secretary-general of the organisation, said he would arrange an exemption from *toyi-toying*. I was never sure if this was granted. As a precaution I've refrained from the *toyi-toyi* in the presence of the media.

Our first task was to draft a constitution and bill of rights urgently. It was to be consistent with the Freedom Charter and the resolutions passed at the congresses of the ANC before the banning. There were other documents and statements we needed to consider, and the draft had to have special regard for universally accept-able democratic principles, particularly those in social democracies.

At one of our early drafting sessions in the small boardroom of a city centre hotel, Nelson Mandela came to speak to us. He stressed we were to draft a con-stitution that would be good for all South Africans, not only the ANC. Our group included lawyers, legal academics and legal activists. We discussed non-negotiable principles and tried to sort out which of the proposals by the National Party and some of the homeland leaders could be accepted and which should be rejected because they would undermine the will of the majority.

Once our basic principles were formulated, the National Party negotiators began worrying about majority rule. They formulated a twelve-point plan giving veto rights to minority groups concerning residential property ownership, schools, the security forces and the economy. Most striking of all was their proposal that 'Leaders who upheld appropriate values should represent their own minority grouping in the government.' On behalf of our committee, Albie Sachs acknowl-edged the difficulty in catering for cultural, linguistic and religious diversity while ensuring a common unity and equal rights for all, but argued that a constitution with guarantees of freedom of religion, language and culture should suffice.

For the next three years I spent much of my time attending meetings of Codesa (the Convention for a Democratic South Africa) and regional conferences where the proposed constitution was discussed. Among the participants were people from all walks of life, anxious to ask questions, participate in the debate and, often, to ridicule their absent political opponents.

Debate was lively and wide-ranging, the questions pertinent. How to elect a president? Certainly the United States model was a non-starter. Why spend millions electing a president who would be independent of Parliament? Nor was there favour for a system as in France with a prime minister and a president. For one thing they might quarrel. We wanted a president appointed by the majority of our democratically elected Parliament. So the debate continued, examining the issues around proportional representation, the governing of the provinces, socioeconomic rights, property rights, all the facets that had so long been denied the majority of South Africans.

While these discussions persisted, so did the blood feud between Chief Mangosuthu Buthelezi's Inkatha and supporters of the ANC and the UDF, particularly in Natal and KwaZulu. It was a matter of great concern to Nelson Mandela. After his release he lost no time in calling for peace between the two sides, and at a large rally of ANC supporters in Durban famously said,

> My message to those of you involved in this battle of brother against brother is this: Take your guns, knives and your pangas and throw them into the sea. Although there are fundamental differences between us, we commend Inkatha for their demand over the years for the unbanning and the release of political prisoners as well as their stand for refusing to participate in a negotiated settlement without the creation of the necessary climate. If we do not halt this conflict, we will be in grave danger of corrupting the proud legacy of our struggle. We endanger the peace process in the whole of the country. We recognise that in order to bring the war to an end, the two sides must talk.

Many of his supporters disagreed. They contended that Inkatha, the apartheid government, the army, the police and their hit squads were killing local leaders and many of their brothers and sisters to destabilise the region. Inkatha, it was felt, wanted a form of quasi-independence or it would not allow the ANC to govern.

Inkatha claimed the right to march in city streets with their 'traditional weapons'. After all, this was part of their cultural heritage. However, the 'traditional weapons' were not confined to the assegai or short spear, the knobkerrie and the leather shield, but included anything capable of inflicting grievous bodily harm, from axes to sugarcane cutters, knives, and metal pipes.

Pedestrians fled before an Inkatha march, shopkeepers closed their doors and traffic was forced to take alternative routes. The police stood by. Senior officers argued that they were unable to disarm the marchers. Any attempt to do so would lead to a bloodbath and, besides, they did not want to interfere with the rights of the Zulus to practise their culture. The prosecuting authorities took no steps, not even against the leaders who repeatedly incited their followers to acts of violence, who issued threats which could have been tried and punished as intimidation and who prevented free political activity in areas they considered their own.

Cyril Ramaphosa asked Arthur Chaskalson and me to draft a proclamation defining traditional weapons. We produced a draft to which none of the negotiators at Codesa had any serious objection. While Inkatha's representatives did not like it, they had no counterproposals.

Just six months before the 1994 elections, Nelson Mandela was incensed by television footage of armed Zulus rampaging through the main streets of Durban, breaking shop windows, looting, smashing cars and swearing vengeance against whoever stood in their way. He demanded a meeting with FW de Klerk and met him that evening. Why wasn't de Klerk exercising his powers as president to put an end to this violence? Somewhat to Mandela's bemusement de Klerk's replied, 'Mr Mandela, when you join my government after the election you will see how little power a president really has.'

That remark was no help in ending the violence, but it was a useful indication of de Klerk's thinking: he still saw Mandela as his future junior partner.

Violence spread to Johannesburg and the nearby towns: ANC supporters aligned against Inkatha supporters living in single-sex hostels originally intended for migrant workers. Judge Richard Goldstone, appointed to investigate the fighting, was kept busy. It was not always easy determining who had started the conflict and it became apparent that blame lay on both sides.

The violence was a complex mix of popular discontent, political expediency and individual power-mongers. Inkatha had formed an alliance with white extremists and black homeland leaders who hoped to retain their 'independence'. To many this explained the well-armed groups who murdered passengers indiscriminately on the trains. Although the attackers appeared to be black people, it was said that among them were white people in disguise, perhaps right-wingers or members of police hit squads, the existence of which was now acknowledged.

The ANC had acquired from an oil company a high-rise building, Shell House, near the railway station in Johannesburg as their headquarters. At the height of the conflict, the ANC's intelligence department received information that a march by Inkatha the following day would culminate in an attack on Shell House. The intention was to force entry and kill members of the ANC leadership.

The matter was reported to Nelson Mandela and forwarded to the commissioner of police. The information was treated lightly by the police, as only a few junior, not very well-trained policemen were dispatched to keep order. At Shell

House ANC security guards armed with AK47s were posted at the main entrance, on the pavement and on the parapet formed by the cantilever slab above.

During the march, two separate Inkatha groups converged on the building from different directions. According to the ANC guards, shots were fired at the building by the marchers. Then the mob surged forward.

The leader of the ANC guards fired a warning shot. It went unheeded: the marchers bore down. Believing themselves and their leaders under dire threat, the leader of the guards ordered his men to open fire. Nine were killed and many wounded.

Inkatha leaders declared that it was an unprovoked massacre and likened it to the killing of innocent protesters at Sharpeville more than thirty years before. They demanded justice and threatened revenge. The minister of justice announced a judicial inquest into the death of the nine, headed by Judge Robert Nugent.

Nelson Mandela, angered by the failure of the police to heed his warning and upset by what he considered false propaganda by Inkatha, asked me to represent the ANC and the guards. Our attorney, Caroline Nichols, asked Karel Tip, Khomotso Moroka and Danny Berger to join me. On the other side was a conservative attorney with a team of counsel from Pretoria. Each represented a couple of the victims, while a senior man represented Inkatha and its leaders. Their attorney had arranged with the Legal Aid Board for substantial fees. Much to my satisfaction, the judge ruled that, given their common interest, they appoint one person to cross-examine each witness.

It soon became clear that they hadn't consulted with their clients prior to the inquest. At least one of them eventually admitted that the deceased whose family he was representing was not killed outside Shell House. In fact he had died at a rally at the Library Gardens some distance from Shell House, where there had also been violence. In the affidavits filed by their lawyers, the marchers did not explain how they got to be at Shell House, so far from their intended destination.

Our team filed affidavits by Nelson Mandela, the intelligence personnel, the security guards and occupants of the building. Most importantly, we had the testimony of an erstwhile security policeman. He gave evidence that he and his colleague supplied Inkatha with caches of arms and that he was present when plans were hatched to attack Shell House.

In their affidavits the police admitted that they had been warned, but could not explain their failure to protect the ANC's headquarters. Ballistic evidence supported our clients' version but also showed that some of the bullet marks on the building were not from small arms fire from across the road, but the result of the uncontrolled firing of the guards' AK47s. Video evidence showed Inkatha leaders in the Transvaal threatening violence against the ANC on previous occasions and on that day.

The judge and his assessors found the ANC guards not culpable of the deaths of the nine marchers. They were critical of some of the evidence presented by both sides and careful to limit their findings to the bare minimum to prevent either side from claiming a political victory. For a number of years Inkatha held a service outside Shell House to commemorate the deaths. On our advice, the guards successfully applied for amnesty from prosecution and from civil liability, on the grounds that they responded to achieve the political objective of protecting the leadership of the ANC.

Because of our legal expertise, members of our committee were appointed advisors to the negotiators at Codesa. I was seconded to Zola Skweyiya. He was part of a group responsible for drafting agreements. I sat behind him and acted as ANC representative when he was absent. Leon Wessels headed the National Party's group and he and I enjoyed a good rapport. By gesture and eye contact we would check that consensus had been reached.

One difficult personality was the acerbic minister of education in KwaZulu, Lionel Mtshali, who represented the Inkatha Freedom Party. He would remain silent throughout the discussion, only to disrupt proceedings at the last moment. For example, when I proposed that we ask a subcommittee to draft an electoral law, everyone appeared to agree. Yet Mr Mtshali stood and, in the manner of a pedagogue, said that since Codesa was not going to agree about a constitution, there was no need for us to waste our time with an electoral law. He was backed by one of the homeland representatives, but to my surprise and that of Leon Wessels, also by the leader of the National Party in Natal, even though he had earlier supported the proposal. Mr Mtshali then declared that there was no consensus. He walked towards the door, then turned and said we could all go back to the desert.

Not long after Nelson's release he confided that his relationship with Winnie was strained, not only on a personal level but because of her public behaviour. She contradicted him while they were on a platform in Germany; she repudiated his call that the people of KwaZulu-Natal throw their weapons into the sea. He called for reconciliation but she advocated the continuation of the armed struggle. She refused to cooperate with or even acknowledge the ANC leadership. These matters weighed heavily on his mind, particularly since he had requested that she head the ANC's social welfare desk.

Matters were brought to a head before his release when the UDF accused her of abducting five young men from the home of a Methodist minister, Paul Verryn, later a bishop of that church. She contended that Verryn had sexually molested the youths and that she removed them for their own protection. This removal had been carried out by the coach and members of a soccer team, the Mandela United Football Club, who had attached themselves to her.

The youths were subsequently kept in an outhouse at the back of her home. There were allegations that the young men had been assaulted on her property and in her presence – which she denied – and one of the five, fourteen-year-old Stompie Seipei, was later found murdered. All of this added to Nelson's anxiety.

Winnie had distanced herself from me when her conflict began with Nelson and the high-powered committee he had asked to help her. I did not want to participate in a spat between her and the leaders of the UDF. But when the UDF issued a statement that no democratic lawyer should act for her regarding the allegations of abduction and assault, I felt compelled to contact her. I disagreed with the UDF and I invited her for a consultation.

She chose the middle of the afternoon and arrived overdressed, accompanied by a number of guards. This defiant gesture was for the benefit of members of the Bar in the lobby who would assume she was coming to see me. The reason I called her was partly to let Nelson know that, true to my undertaking at the end of the Rivonia trial, I had not abandoned her. Also I thought it wrong for some of my friends to declare that anyone was not worthy of being defended by a lawyer of her choice.

After Nelson's release she would have nothing to do with any of those who had criticised her. He, ever a loyal and disciplined member of the ANC, was working closely with them. She believed her husband had done enough. Now he belonged to her and their two children. She expected him to make her enemies his enemies. Instead, he invited them to meetings, let them keep his diary and organise his security. All this she found intolerable.

Reminding her of an admission to her German biographer that she would listen only to Nelson and George Bizos, I jokingly told her that she should follow the example of Prince Philip and not Evita. The Duke of Edinburgh always walked at least one step behind the queen. She laughed, but my advice fell on deaf ears.

The media continued to harangue the police and the deputy attorney-general to charge her with kidnapping, assault and even the murder of Stompie, of which the coach of her football club had by now been convicted. When she was charged with assault and abduction (she was never charged with Stompie's murder), Nelson called me. Would I lead a team to defend her? Despite the seriously strained relationship between them, he wanted me involved as I had defended her so often in the past. In addition, because of the friendship between us, the public perception that he was supporting her would be strengthened. He already knew from their children that she wanted me to defend her, but that she was too proud to ask him for help.

I took on the case at once. Two other counsel were appointed to work with me – Durban advocate Pius Langa, a man who had pulled himself up by his own shoestrings to become a successful member of the Bar, and his colleague from Pretoria, Dikgang Moseneke, imprisoned on Robben Island for twelve years when he was a mere fifteen-year-old schoolboy. They are now chief justice and deputy chief justice respectively.

The matter was heard in the Johannesburg High Court and Nelson attended the trial regularly, accompanied by leading members of the ANC. He arrived with her every morning, silently followed the proceedings and emerged with her at lunch time, as though they were a loving couple. He left with her in the afternoons while many hundreds of enthusiastic supporters applauded tumultuously and television cameras from throughout the world filmed his every gesture.

He drew the line at attending our consultations, primarily because these meetings were also attended by the young lawyer, Dali Mpofu, her lover during the latter part of Nelson's imprisonment and after he was released. He had never expected Winnie to be celibate while he was in prison, only that she be discreet. He couldn't accept that the relationship continued so openly after his release. Later, from the witness box in the divorce proceedings, he described this as the loneliest period of his life.

Three of the young men who had been abducted by the Mandela Football Club had given evidence against the coach, Jerry Richardson. My colleagues had gone carefully through the record and prepared notes for me to use in cross-examining the three youths. We wanted to establish whether the record showed any contradictions, improbabilities and behaviour inconsistent with their allegations of being assaulted in Mrs Mandela's presence and held at her house against their will.

They said that it was a common practice for the priest to sleep in the same bed with young men, and that it had happened before with one of the witnesses. He said Verryn had 'prickled' his lower back, which he found offensive and his complaints had reached Mrs Mandela. This prompted her co-accused, Verryn's housekeeper Xoliswa Falati, to remove them with the help of the football club to the Mandela house in Winnie's absence.

The witnesses fared so badly that the judge found he could not believe they were assaulted in Winnie's presence. However, he found her an accessory after the fact of the assault – an outcome which the Court of Appeal set aside. We led irrefutable evidence that she was in Brandfort when the assaults were carried out, and the trial judge could not reject this alibi. But she knew they were being held at her Soweto house against their will and thus was guilty of kidnapping. The Court of Appeal let this conviction stand, but qualified their findings in her favour.

The trial judge did not accept that she believed the youths were being molested. The appeal judges said there was evidence that had led her to the apprehension that they were in danger. Vital to this finding on appeal was that Winnie had approached Frank Chikane, secretary of the South African Council of Churches, some months before the event. Chikane, in turn, spoke to Verryn's bishop, Peter Storey, about the situation. The judges were persuaded that this chain of complaints indicated that Winnie had taken the allegations seriously, and had acted on them. In the light of this finding, the appeal judges set aside the six-year jail term. Instead she was given a fine and a suspended sentence.

In my view the media were hardly fair to Winnie Mandela in their coverage of the trial and the appeal. Their headlines spoke of 'The Stompie trial' and did not clarify that she faced no charges in connection with his death. In addition, they raised other allegations, details of which were published without regard for the *sub judice* rule.

The gay community and some editors accused us of mounting a homophobic defence. I believe our defence was justified by the finding of Chief Justice Michael Corbett and his four Appeal Court colleagues. And suppose Verryn had shared a bed with young women who had sought refuge in his house, what accusation would then have been made against us?

Later, Mrs Madikizela Mandela (as she was now known) appeared at the Truth and Reconciliation Commission before Archbishop Tutu. The accumulated allegations against her were discussed – allegations she categorically denied. This was not a judicial process. She could be neither convicted nor exculpated. The opportunities for cross-examination, calling witnesses, producing documents and arguing for and against were limited.

The evidence of the three witnesses who gave evidence against Richardson at his trial was clear and unambiguous: Richardson and another inflicted serious injuries on Stompie at a time that Winnie was not in Soweto but in Brandfort. Belated attempts by Richardson and Falati to implicate her were too self-serving to be given credence. Some speculated that I refused to appear for her before the commission. The truth is that I was not asked to do so.

Political trials were coming to an end. I found routine criminal and civil trials and appeals mundane, even though more lucrative. Arthur Chaskalson was spending much of his time drafting the interim constitution. The senior attorney at the Legal Resources Centre, Morris Zimmerman, had retired. Arthur asked me if I would make myself available on an informal basis to discuss cases with the younger people on the staff. Naturally I agreed.

Lee Bozalek of the Cape Town office, together with an advocate from the Cape Town Bar, John Whitehead, had prepared for an important case on behalf of a quadriplegic youth shot by police in Upington's Paballelo township. It was soon to be tried in the High Court at Kimberley. They thought that it was a case, in Arthur's words, 'right up my alley'.

The matter was well-pleaded and well-prepared. It was the story of Desmond Gudula, seventeen years old, and his slightly older friend who had been standing at the gate of a house belonging to Desmond's grandmother. A couple of hundred yards away police had blocked an intersection and were busy dispersing protesting youths. A gunshot was fired from the police vehicle. Desmond was hit in his upper shoulder and the side of his neck and collapsed 'like an empty sack', to use his description. His friend ran away, but was later apprehended and convicted of public violence in a subsequent trial on the evidence of the police officers. They testified that the shooting was justified because the two youths had stoned their vehicle. Because Desmond was languishing in hospital he was neither charged nor called as a witness.

The credibility of the police officer who fired the shot was destroyed by the young lawyer defending Desmond's friend. The policeman denied that he had used a heavy calibre SSG 18 cartridge, commonly used by hunters after large antelope. A judicial commission had strongly criticised the police for using this kind of cartridge on a crowd and we had a circular from the police commissioner instructing against its use.

Desmond underwent an operation to remove the bullet from his shoulder. In view of the denial appearing on the record of the criminal case it should not have been an SSG 18 pellet that was removed, yet this was what the doctors found. At a pretrial conference in Bloemfontein we produced the SSG pellet, kept safely in a tiny jewel box by Lee Bozalek. I opened the box and put it on the table. Our opponents wanted proof. I asked that this exchange be carefully noted in the minutes as they would be presented in court. In addition, it was noted that we would call six witnesses to prove that the pellet was removed from Desmond's body. The witnesses were the doctors and senior nurses at the public hospital where the operation was performed. They would have to be flown to Kimberley and accommodated in a hotel. Their testimony would account for handing the pellet to Lee Bozalek and he would tell of keeping it safe. After that we would call an expert to identify it as an SSG 18 pellet.

I went further. If they did not admit the main fact, the special note in the minutes would serve as notice of our intention to apply for a special order for costs against them for their obstructionist tactic. While they considered this, we adjourned. Outside the room, John joked that he now realised why counsel from Johannesburg had such a reputation for rough tactics. Lee said he shouldn't complain, as the tactics appeared likely to pay off. Back at the conference table the required admissions were made.

At the criminal trial of Desmond's friend, the police evidence stated that the two young men ran away from the scene. When the doctor treating Desmond heard this, she said it was impossible. The injury to Desmond's neck would instantly have prevented him taking a single step. On the doctor's advice the youth's defence had been taken up by the Legal Resources Centre in Cape Town.

For the trial we obtained the expert opinion of a doctor specialising in spinal injuries. He, likewise, stated categorically that Desmond couldn't have walked, let alone run. The injury had rendered him a quadriplegic by severing the main nerve. It was like cutting a telephone wire with a pair of pliers. Our opponent put it to the doctor that he was wrong. They would call a neurosurgeon to testify that this would not be the effect and he had textbooks to prove it. Our medical expert wondered if the books were on medicine or miracles. In the end, the court saw neither the neurologist nor any books.

Despite this evidence, which should have made it an open-and-shut case, our opponents made it a long and expensive trial. Their version of the facts was repeated parrot-like. They claimed that in terms of the Police Act and the emergency regulations, the police not only had the right to shoot in self-defence, but to shoot in the maintenance of law and order and for the ending of the state of emergency.

They couldn't explain why the statement made by the police officers was almost a verbatim copy of a passage in a reported judgment by one of the most conservative judges. They produced numerous witnesses to explain how an SSG cartridge might have inadvertently been loaded. Under cross-examination those responsible for issuing the ammunition were keener to defend themselves and their procedures than their trigger-happy colleague.

The judge studiously refrained from damning the policemen as liars, but, nevertheless, found that our client was entitled to compensation. The defendants' request for leave to appeal was granted on limited grounds. They could only contest the judge's interpretation of the law relating to the interpretation of the emergency regulations. These regulations indemnified them from liability if they acted in good faith.

The Appeal Court almost contemptuously dismissed their contentions. The matter reverted to the trial judge to determine the compensation Desmond should be paid. Black plaintiffs were generally inadequately compensated, so we took a different approach. Instead of relying only on doctors, we consulted with Neville Cohen who I'd known as a student during my university days. He had been involved in a collision, but went on to complete his engineering degree in a wheelchair. Since then he had been active in helping disabled people. He knew very well what a quadriplegic would need to live a full life, and how much it would cost.

When we began discussions with our opponents we let Neville Cohen do most of the talking. The judge was happy to wait for the outcome of the negotiations as he wanted to attend a cattle auction where he hoped to buy about a hundred heifers. His secretary would have him back at short notice to record any agreement that we might reach. After three days of haggling it was agreed that Desmond was entitled to R1,4 million, an amount unheard of for a black person.

Arthur tried tentatively to get me more involved with the LRC. He realised that the salary offered was hardly sufficient so we agreed that I could take 'outside' matters to supplement my income, just as he had done. I knew that I would be happier doing cases like Desmond's and the reopened inquest on the Cradock Four than merely routine matters. I am grateful to the Legal Resources Centre for that opportunity.

When Arthur Chaskalson stepped down as national director of the LRC he spoke at a party held in his honour. Among the guests, he said, were men and women of high political profile who would surely be senior members of the government in the near future. The Legal Resources Centre was a thorn in the flesh of the existing government, he reminded us. The new government would operate in terms of the fundamentally different values enshrined in the constitution and bill of rights still being drafted. But the new government shouldn't be surprised if the Legal Resources Centre watched them carefully and acted against them too, should the need arise. Everyone present applauded him. We have tried to live up to that promise.

One of the perks of being on the ANC's constitutional committee was the invitations by foreign foundations, governments and political parties to visit them. They offered us facilities to study their constitutions, electoral laws, judicial structures and to talk with their judges.

Those who went to France reported that the president of their constitutional court had said the one page of the rights of man was more than sufficient – our proposed bill of rights was much too long. He was surprised that we hadn't provided for the rubbish to be collected every Thursday morning. At this someone quipped that he now knew why rubbish collection in France was so irregular.

A number of us were invited to Germany. With the exception of Zola Skweyiya we cleared immigration and customs. I went back to find out where he was, only to be told it was none of my business. I suspected he might've been detained because of his black skin. Should I complain to our hosts? Eventually Zola joined us. He explained that he had spoken in fluent German as he handed over his documents, and the official suspected that his fluency might have resulted from his working illegally in Germany. Perhaps he was returning to work illegally again. Zola had to explain at length that he had been granted asylum, had studied law and returned to South Africa after his organisation was unbanned. But there was a racist tinge to the German visit. My black colleagues were told not to walk in the unlit part of the park over the road as neo-Nazi gangs might attack them.

On a guided bus tour of Berlin we were shown the remnants of the Wall and repeatedly told to note the marked differences between the wealth of the West and the poverty of the East where even gypsies were now allowed to squat on the pavements, something prohibited by the previous regime. Albie Sachs and I visited the museums. With a theatrical gesture he stood in front of a marble bust of one of the ancients and said he wanted to test my historical knowledge. With whom was he standing? Not wanting to be shown up, I stepped back to get a better view and almost knocked over a bust of Sophocles, earning a rebuke in German from the uniformed guard. Worse still, I failed Albie's test.

Our hosts had promised us lunch at the restaurant in Potsdam where Churchill, Roosevelt and Stalin dined at the end of the war, but to our disappointment we discovered that it would be closed on the appointed day.

Our trip was financed by the University of Hanover and the Friedrich Naumann Foundation, established by the president of the Weimar Republic after the First World War. The main purpose was to study the German fundamental law. It was deliberately not called a constitution because it was not entirely the people's choice. It was partly imposed by the victorious allies after they had defeated Hitler's Germany.

Of particular interest to us was the constitutional court in Karlsruhe. Two young German women, particularly well informed and fluent in English, acted as interpreters for us. Although many we interviewed were competent in English and easily understood us they insisted on speaking in German for the sake of absolute accuracy.

While the staff and facilities available to the judges of that court would be beyond South Africa's means, we were impressed by the ease with which citizens could register a complaint. Each complaint was investigated by competent lawyers and if well founded, would result in remedial action. I thought this admirable. So were the special provisions to secure the independence of the judges by limiting their term of office and prohibiting them from political, administrative or government appointments afterwards. And yet the honour of being appointed, the remuneration and the pleasant working conditions (not only at the court but in the historic town with its beautiful surroundings), attracted the most highly qualified and competent candidates.

Their well-considered judgments were generally accepted by the national and provincial governments and the vast majority of the people. We thought it a model which our negotiators and constitution drafters should seriously consider. Fortunately we did not have to rely on the cursory knowledge we acquired during our visit. Jurists such as Laurie Ackermann, Johan van der Westhuizen, Johan van der Vyver and others had carefully studied the system, and written and delivered lectures on its advantages.

We were most impressed by the administrative courts that operated on local, regional and national levels to review the decisions of government officials, boards, committees and other decision-making bodies. Equally impressive was the speed with which they were required to act. We considered recommending the establishment of a special administrative court but decided against this because of the well-developed principles of review by our superior courts, principles later enshrined in our constitution.

But it was a tempting proposition. There would be obvious advantages to a local administrative court with both investigating and reviewing powers, especially one that had to reach a decision within a few weeks about whether, say, a local authority acted justly in refusing an application for a licence to establish a small shopping centre.

The president of the administrative court told us that only twenty-seven lawyers were admitted to practise in his court. What did he consider the most important decision his court had made? They had stopped the construction of a nuclear power station at the instance of the Green Party and the local community until adequate precautions to prevent spillage were taken. The contractors complained that the delay would cost five million Deutschmarks a day. 'But what would the cost be if a Chernobyl-like event occurred?' asked the court.

Namibia's Swapo government repeatedly invited us to visit. They couldn't understand how we could go from Canada to Japan and yet not see our African neighbour. They had useful knowledge and experience of how the South African government had manipulated to its advantage the negotiations leading to Namibia's independence.

I had not seen Andimba Toivo ja Toivo for more than forty years. At the cocktail party held in our honour, I didn't recognise or remember the names of all those who came to remind me that I had defended them. Then Minister ja Toivo arrived and was applauded as he walked onto the platform. He saw me, came down to embrace me and then led me by the hand to the microphone. I was introduced and he overgenerously announced that if it were not for me, he and his colleagues would have been sentenced to death. He thanked me for saving their lives.

After the party we had a quiet chat about the other members of the team, particularly Ernie Wentzel, who, sadly, had passed away before the changes started taking place. We spoke about ja Toivo's heroic statement from the dock and particularly his prophecy that the nations of the world would be proved right about the future of Namibia and that the apartheid regime would be proved wrong.

The Swapo negotiators warned us to expect difficult demands from the government towards the end of the process. They predicted that the regime would want constitutional guarantees similar to those they had demanded in Namibia, for example that no civil servant or army officer could be removed, demoted or transferred, that no one would be prosecuted for any offence committed by any South African official during Pretoria's administration of the territory or the war against Swapo, that no contract entered into by any South African in relation to land ownership would be declared invalid by legislation, and that no indemnity granted by any South African president would be annulled. We remembered these warnings when indeed the government made similar demands.

I felt it inappropriate for me to remain a judge of the Court of Appeal in Botswana because of my involvement with Codesa, the high-profile Goniwe inquest and other prominent trials for the Legal Resources Centre. Thus, at the end of the second period of my appointment, it was not renewed. Neither was my membership of the Centre for Applied Legal Studies at the University of the Witwatersrand, nor did I stand for re-election to the National Council of Lawyers for Human Rights. I had mixed feelings about leaving all these bodies, but I knew it was necessary in the interests of my work at the centre.

Among my briefs was a political case offered to me by Kate Owen, an attorney from the well-established firm of Deneys Reitz. Its senior partners had established a human rights desk headed by Kate. Ever since her student days she had been passionate about the rights of the people and had obtained a postgraduate degree for her thesis on deaths in police detention. She wanted me to bring an action for damages against the Afrikaner Weerstandsbeweging (AWB) and its commandant,

Eugene Terre'Blanche, in the magistrate's court in Ventersdorp. This town was the headquarters of Terre'Blanche's 'army' and of its leader who was inspired by the Nazis and modelled himself on them.

The AWB boasted thousands of official members and many more secret supporters in the national army and police force. They defied authority with impunity, asserting that no Afrikaner policeman or soldier would ever point a gun at them. They called themselves the only true Afrikaner patriots, dedicated to saving white South Africa from the peril of the black masses after the betrayal by the cowardly President FW de Klerk. They made plain their hatred of de Klerk's unbanning of the ANC and had chased him out of their town and district when he campaigned there for support for the negotiation process.

They were an unruly organisation. For instance, at the complex outside Johannesburg where the Codesa negations were taking place, they drove an armed vehicle through the glass doors, chasing away delegates. They met no resistance and, their mission accomplished, they held a party on the grounds.

Kate explained that on a farm called Goedgevonden, not far from Terre'Blanche's own farm, lived a small community of about a hundred people. During the apartheid years they had been removed and dumped in Bophuthatswana, the 'independent' Bantustan. Like so many others, the Goedgevonden people resented the forced removal from the graves of their ancestors and the land on which they were born, where they had built their homes, where they grew crops and where their cattle grazed.

They'd never really settled on the 'dumping ground' and soon after Nelson Mandela's release they returned to Goedgevonden and built makeshift homes. This was an unbearable provocation to Terre'Blanche, his army and the white farmers of the district. They called on the government to remove the community lest they serve as an example to millions of others to invade white-owned farms elsewhere in the country. The government failed to act.

One day at sunset, dozens of heavy lorries driven by farmers from the area surrounded Goedgevonden, except the strip where a tall, rich crop of maize awaited harvesting. After dark they switched on the bright beams of the lorries to light up the shacks of Goedgevonden. Their hooters blaring, they shouted intimidating slogans and threats that if the people did not leave they would be overrun. The residents took cover and hoped for the best. All that stood between them and the belligerent AWB was a small contingent of policemen. The police were under the command of a colonel and had split into two groups, some near the lorries and some on the other side of the farm.

In the middle of the night the police colonel heard a noise from the maize fields and the nearby shacks. He sent a young lieutenant to investigate. The lieutenant and his men heard the unmistakable booming voice of Terre'Blanche shouting, 'Wie gaan daar?' (Who goes there?) as he emerged on his horse through the maize.

The lieutenant politely introduced himself. He was told there were some two hundred AWB members hiding in the maize field and among the tall gum trees serving as a windbreak. They were to ensure that the kaffirs went away. The police officer realised he was out of his depth and appealed to the great man to allow him to call his colonel to deal with the situation. Terre'Blanche acquiesced. A number of AWB men wearing black hoods and the uniform and insignia of the AWB joined them.

What the lieutenant did not know was that the noises he had heard were made by an attack by similarly dressed men on the returnees of Goedgevonden. They smashed their huts, their furniture, kitchen utensils, plates, cups and saucers, their battery-operated radios and tape recorders and anything else they could find. Those who'd hidden under beds were dragged outside and whipped, before lorries were used to bulldoze some homes. In the early hours of the morning, the attackers withdrew.

But the people of Goedgevonden would not be intimidated. They sought legal advice from Kate Owen. An investigation and criminal charge followed, but the police and the prosecutors were not anxious to bring the matter to trial. Kate was inspired by the actions brought by victims of Ku Klux Klan attacks in the southern states of the US, some of which were successful and financially crippled the Klan. She issued a summons on behalf of nineteen plaintiffs claiming what by the standards of the United States was the very modest sum of about R100 000. In deciding to limit the claim, she was probably realistic, for the courts rarely awarded adequate damages to black plaintiffs for pain and suffering and loss of dignity.

We consulted with our clients in the shade of a tall blue-gum tree on the very edge of Goedgevonden where the AWB had gathered on the night of 10 May 1991. Kate and I were accompanied by Happy Masondo, a newly qualified attorney fluent in Setswana, the language of our clients. In their plea, the defendants (Terre'Blanche and his organisation) denied responsibility for the attack. Our clients described their attackers as wearing balaclavas and with their hands painted black, but their voices and threats in Afrikaans betrayed their disguise. Their khaki uniforms with the distinctive, slightly distorted swastika on the sleeves and the epaulettes also gave them away.

Attempts to obtain access to the police docket had failed. It was more than two years since the event and no action had been taken. Despite this, the police claimed that there might yet be a criminal prosecution. The statements taken by them were thus privileged, a status that they were not prepared to waive.

We decided to go over the heads of the local police and visited the regional police headquarters at Potchefstroom. There the senior commander was both courteous and cooperative. He was familiar with the work I had done in Lichtenburg, Zeerust and Rustenburg in years gone by and was glad to meet me. He made the docket available to us, offered copies of the statements that we required and promised to instruct any policemen that we might want as witnesses to cooperate. What a marked contrast to the mistrust of the past. And to the obstructionism we had met in Ventersdorp.

In the docket we found the statement of the police lieutenant about his maize-field meeting with Terre'Blanche in the middle of the night. It would prove vital for our case.

However small a farming town in the former Transvaal and Orange Free State may be, one of its main streets will be named after a revered member of the Voortrekker leadership and there will be monuments dedicated to them and to brave Boer War generals. On our arrival at Ventersdorp to start the trial, we found that while no statue had yet been erected to Eugene Terre'Blanche, he and his 'army' had been granted the freedom of the town, an example followed by a number of other towns in the area.

Directly opposite the courthouse there was a monument commemorating the death of four of Terre'Blanche's men who had been shot by the police while chasing President FW de Klerk from the town. When his meeting was stormed by the AWB, the police had opened fire in defence of the president.

Recalling all this racist violence we wondered about the safety of our clients and ourselves, and whether justice could be done in that environment. Of course, Happy Masondo and our clients had more reason to be fearful than Kate and I. Members of the AWB were wont to take pot shots at Africans. We discussed instituting special security arrangements during the trial, but decided against this.

Eugene Terre'Blanche arrived in court surrounded by an entourage of uniformed AWB men. Our clients, mostly elderly men and women, were accompanied by very few of their friends and relatives. There was no police presence.

We knew that our opponent would be Danie Bischoff, better known as a politician of the far Right than as an advocate. We were told that the chief magistrate of Potchefstroom had appointed Magistrate Ben Bester to hear the trial. Friends from Potchefstroom University, who considered Eugene Terre'Blanche and his 'army' an insult to Afrikanerdom, informed us that Bester was an experienced civil court magistrate who would give us a fair hearing. Still, we wondered if he would be able to withstand pressure from the majority of the community to which he belonged.

Less than a month before the attack, Terre'Blanche's incendiary statements to his supporters were reported in *Beeld*. The journalist had come to give evidence but made no secret of her fear of the consequences. She had been threatened before by right-wingers. She produced her report which she read out and confirmed as correct.

The vital portion for us was Terre'Blanche's statement that 'if the coward de Klerk did not remove the kaffirs from Goedgevonden within a month he and his men would remove them by force'. She reported further that the audience had heartily approved of the threat. Some stood on their chairs to hail the leader's brave words. According to this report, among those sitting on the platform was the Conservative Party MP for Ventersdorp, Fanie van Vuuren, whose party professed to be against violence.

Our opponent was taken by surprise by the report and by our witness. His cross-examination of her was ineffective. We had gone a long way towards establishing an intention to commit the attack.

Cross-examination of the police lieutenant who met with Terre'Blanche and the AWB that night was equally ineffective. Our clients described the AWB insignia on the uniforms worn by their attackers. As they were mostly illiterate they could not speak of a swastika. One of them referred to it as three upside-down sevens. She had earlier said that she hadn't been to school, and following this description was accused of lying. She explained that she had gone to school for a year. When given paper and a pen she accurately reproduced the swastika-like design of the AWB.

The court heard detailed descriptions of the meagre belongings destroyed in the attack. Our clients painstakingly produced receipts showing how much they had paid for each item, explaining the age and condition of each and what they had done with the broken pieces. The trial was not continuous. It lasted for seven weeks but took almost a year to complete. Most of the time was taken up by the plaintiffs' testimony about their goods and the evidence of an insurance assessor who had to estimate the cost of replacing the dwellings and the goods destroyed.

At the start of the defendants' case, Terre'Blanche did not turn up. His counsel had no explanation for the man's absence. When he did arrive, his counsel shouted at him that he lacked discipline, that he did not listen and that he embarrassed his counsel by his inexplicable behaviour.

Sunday Times journalist Chris Barron wrote a blow-by-blow account of the humiliation meted out to the folk hero by his own counsel. The dressing-down was symptomatic of Terre'Blanche's diminishing reputation. Already, on the magistrate's initiative, the trial had been shifted from Ventersdorp to Potchefstroom, which was more convenient for the magistrate and the lawyers, but not for our clients and particularly not for Terre'Blanche. Fewer and fewer of his guard of honour came to court. Often he came alone. Shortly before the elections he had suffered a humiliating defeat at the hands of the Bophuthatswana army whose members killed some of his senior commanders. This had cracked the morale of the AWB.

The humiliating election defeat of his right-wing allies was a further blow to AWB morale. Affluent farmers who had bankrolled him and his 'army' cancelled their stop orders. By the time he came to the witness box he was grossly overweight, unfit and breathing heavily. More to the point, he was bleary-eyed and had been drinking far too heavily. Long gone was the man who could spellbind audiences and challenge the legal order, confident that he was untouchable.

Terre'Blanche surprised us all by admitting that he was present with his men near the scene where the crimes were committed. But he took our breath away with the audacity of the lie that followed. He was there because he had learned of a plan by ANC and PAC terrorists to attack the Tswana women and children at Goedgevonden. He and his men wanted to protect the vulnerable people. His army's council had not authorised any attack; his men were disciplined and none of them would have attacked anyone without his authority.

Terre'Blanche blamed the attack on the Boere-Aksie Komitee (BAK), an organisation he detested. Although he may have threatened to attack within a month, the BAK pre-empted his threat to steal the AWB's thunder.

It was not difficult to discredit him in cross-examination. He maintained that his presence on the scene was coincidental and not by arrangement with the two thousand farmers who had brought their heavy vehicles. There certainly was no common purpose between them and him. They must have been organised by the BAK.

Who was the president of the BAK – this organisation that no one had heard about? He did not know. He dismissed the suggestion that if the BAK was involved there was common purpose between him, his army and BAK. He would not even hold a school picnic with them, he said. He held them in contempt. He did not know a single one of its office bearers. No, he did not tell the lieutenant or the colonel or any other policeman that he had information that terrorists planned to attack the community and that he was there to protect them. Nor did he ask the police to cooperate with him to achieve this noble result. He could give no reason for not doing so. He agreed that there hadn't been a 'terrorist attack' on the people at Goedgevonden.

When I wanted to know what he and the lieutenant had said, he couldn't remember. In his sworn statement, the lieutenant stated that Terre'Blanche appeared under the influence of liquor. Was this possibly why he couldn't remember? I asked. Terre'Blanche glared at me and emphatically denied the suggestion. The next morning's headline in a leading Afrikaans newspaper was too much for him. It said that according to a police lieutenant he had been drunk.

From the witness box he put on a performance worthy of his best. As if on a political platform with an enthusiastic audience of thousands, he lashed out at the newspapers for trying to discredit him and his noble cause of Afrikaner unity and self-determination. He accused me of using the court for the benefit of the ANC. The magistrate sharply interrupted him. Turning to Terre'Blanche's counsel, he said that he would not let the witness box be used as a forum to berate the newspapers and senior counsel. The court would adjourn while counsel advised their client how to behave. When we reconvened, Terre'Blanche said that he had prayed hard for the Lord's guidance to help him answer my questions nicely and he was confident that his prayer would be answered.

During the mid-morning session he asked for water. Happy Masondo sitting with me stretched for the water bottle. As she was about to pour water into my half-filled glass I put my hand on it and indicated that she should use hers. Surprised, she filled her almost empty glass, haltingly walked the few paces to the witness box and put it in front of Terre'Blanche.

He looked desperately at his counsel and the magistrate hoping they would intervene. When no help was forthcoming, and as I was about to ask the next question, he raised the glass, threw back his head, opened his mouth and slowly poured in the water so that his lips did not touch the glass.

Would any of his AWB generals present at Goedgevonden that night come to give evidence? No, they were no longer available. They had gone to Uruguay to avoid being governed by blacks. Instead, Conservative Party MP Fanie van Vuuren gave evidence in court. His version was that the hundred and fifty vehicles involved in the face-off at Goedgevonden and the two thousand farmers inside the vehicles formed nothing more than a protest meeting against the government's failure to evict the unlawful occupiers on the farm. He had joined them. The meeting was peaceful. There was a friendly relationship between the farmers and the police who were offered grilled meat and liquor by the farmers, which they accepted. There was no intention by the AWB to attack the residents. The attack was organised by the BAK whose leaders he did not know and could not identify.

He too fared poorly in cross-examination. For one thing, he could hardly explain why, as a member of Parliament and a practising attorney, he remained on the platform in the Ventersdorp Town Hall when Terre'Blanche threatened to use violence. If the gathering of farmers was a protest meeting, why was it not held during the day? Why were the media not informed about it? Why were the lights of the vehicles on and the hooters blaring? No satisfactory answers to these questions were forthcoming. Why were a number of the farmers' vehicles involved in ramming some of the dwellings? This he agreed had been wrong. He had told the police colonel but his men did nothing to stop the farmers.

Shortly before Christmas 1994, judgment was given in favour of the plaintiffs against both the AWB and Terre'Blanche. The compensation was a comparatively paltry total of R45 000 plus costs. The AWB then brought an unsuccessful appeal after which the costs of the trial, the appeal and the award amounted to about R250 000. A warrant of execution was issued and Terre'Blanche's tractor and motor vehicle were attached, but they hardly satisfied the debt. We were then advised by friendly colleagues in Potchefstroom to issue a warrant of attachment against the AWB. The organisation owned the ox-wagon used in the 1938 symbolic re-enactment of the 1838 Great Trek. The faithful two thousand would not allow the attachment of this sacred ox-wagon. Our colleagues were correct. The debt was paid.

The AWB subsequently disintegrated and its leader has served terms of imprisonment for acts of violence against black people. He claims to have become a born-again Christian, but I am still uncertain whether he would be prepared to put his lips on a communion cup after a black person had drunk from it.

There is no evidence that Terre'Blanche was personally responsible for instigating the murder of the leader of Umkhonto we Sizwe, Chris Hani, despite his various public declarations that, given the opportunity, he would have killed Hani himself. Terre'Blanche said Hani needed to be removed because he was the anti-Christ, a communist, a terrorist and generally enemy number one of the God-loving white people of South Africa. This was also the reason given by Janusz Walus and Clive Derby-Lewis, who murdered Hani over the Easter weekend of 1993.

According to their applications for amnesty, they expected his murder to lead black people to attack white civilians. In the resulting chaos, the army, the police and right-wing political leaders would take over. They would declare total war against the black population, a war which the whites were bound to win, thereby saving South Africa from black domination.

Their objective was thwarted by the swift arrest of Walus as a result of the report made to the police by an Afrikaner woman who lived next door to the Hani family in Boksburg. The situation was calmed by the intervention of Nelson Mandela and Tokyo Sexwale on television and radio and in the print media. They urged people not to commit acts of revenge or take part in mass action against the government's tardiness in agreeing to an interim constitution or setting an election date. There was an overwhelming response to their call. Commerce and industry, financial institutions and many politicians also called for an end to work stoppages and marches, simultaneously urging the parties negotiating at Codesa to proceed.

I had met Chris Hani in Lusaka on the occasion I reported to Oliver Tambo about the secret negotiations between Kobie Coetsee and Nelson Mandela. We didn't talk about the armed struggle, nor did I discuss the real purpose of my mission. But I learned that he was something of a classical scholar, familiar with the works of the Greek philosophers, historians, poets and dramatists. This was why he and his wife Mpho enrolled their daughters at Saheti School. The girls regularly attended services in the Greek Orthodox Church, particularly during the Holy Week after their father was murdered.

The murder of a top ANC leader and the response by the vast majority of the people weakened the regime. The government realised that it could no longer stall the negotiation process, nor could it put off agreeing to a timetable for adopting the interim constitution. At last these were finalised: December 1993 for the constitution and April 1994 for the first democratic election.

Right-wing factions, each aspiring to form an independent Afrikaner homeland in a different part of the country, made common cause with a couple of homeland leaders who wanted to retain their independence. Even Buthelezi's Inkatha Freedom Party flirted with the right wing, hoping to secure special powers and privileges for KwaZulu-Natal. Wide provincial powers, stopping short of independence, were also favoured by members of the National Party living in the Western Cape, a province they expected to govern with the electoral support of the coloured people.

How best to respond to this push towards federalism, even perhaps an incipient threat of Balkanisation? The legal and constitutional committee of the ANC examined all the proposals critically and showed that the federalism of Switzerland or the United States or elsewhere was unsuitable. South Africa needed a strong central government to secure the unity of the country and avoid tribal and ethnic divisions such as prevailed in Nigeria and elsewhere. This study drew attention to the problems created by secessionist movements in south-eastern Europe, Canada and other countries.

According to agreements reached at Codesa, the constitution would have to comply with thirty-four democratic principles in which provision was made for the inclusion of some federal-type powers. The ANC eventually proposed that other major political parties and not simply the overall winner would participate in a government of national unity for five years after the first election. This broke the deadlock. The stage was then set for an interim constitution to be drafted by the political parties. It was passed by the tricameral Parliament without any amendments. However, as the Namibians had predicted, towards the end of negotiations the regime raised difficult issues. These related to amnesty for acts committed by the security forces and to the tenure of civil servants, not only their own but also those in the homelands. Under no circumstances would the ANC agree to a blanket amnesty. A compromise was reached which led to the Truth and Reconciliation Commission.

There was still unacceptable violence occurring, particularly in KwaZulu-Natal, Johannesburg and some surrounding towns, but South Africans and their leaders were praised by the world for their efforts. Then the Nobel Peace Prize was awarded jointly to Nelson Mandela and FW de Klerk. Should Mandela accept the prize?

Mandela had called de Klerk the head of an illegitimate, discredited minority regime, secretly financing violent organisations, particularly Inkatha. He had said he did not believe that de Klerk didn't know about a third force indiscriminately killing innocent people. But Mandela had also praised de Klerk for taking bold steps forward towards a settlement, which his predecessor PW Botha would not have done.

Nelson decided to accept the shared prize. His delegation to Oslo included his daughter Zenani and other members of the family, the ANC publicity secretary Carl Niehaus, Nobel literature laureate Nadine Gordimer, and myself. FW de Klerk was accompanied by his wife Marike, his foreign minister, Pik Botha, and other prominent members of his political party. Both groups were booked into the Grand Hotel. All was well until a journalist reported Zenani saying of the shared prize, 'My father deserved it'. The laconic remark led an angry Pik Botha to tell Carl Niehaus that the proposed joint shopping spree arranged by our host was off, cancelled by Mrs de Klerk. This was not a matter of great concern to Zenani. But worse was to follow.

Nelson expected that in his acceptance speech, President de Klerk would acknowledge the evils of apartheid and the suffering of the majority of the people. Instead the president said that both sides had made mistakes – an approach which infuriated Mandela. At the prime minister's dinner that evening, Nelson spoke off the cuff, making a scathing attack on the regime treatment of political prisoners, the murders by hit squads both within and outside South Africa, the apartheid policy of forced removals and the oppression of black people. At the end, Pik Botha told us that de Klerk would in future insist on speaking last so that he could answer in kind.

The two recipients called on the king of Norway, both accompanied by three members of their entourage. After a private audience with the two laureates, he emerged with them into the antechamber where we were waiting. De Klerk introduced Pik Botha as the longest-serving foreign minister of all democratic countries. Nelson, as he often did, introduced me as his lawyer who was responsible for his twenty-seven-year imprisonment. Respectfully bowing towards His Majesty I said that perhaps Mr de Klerk was more directly responsible. De Klerk in turn assured His Majesty that he was not even at nursery school at the time. A quick calculation would have proved that he was being less than frank.

As the short winter day ended we were invited to a room behind the balcony of the Grand Hotel. On the balcony, the prizewinners and their companions would stand to acknowledge the cheers of the symbolic torch bearers and those members of the public who had gathered on the ice-covered road, pavement and park. Everywhere we could see placards and banners, and hear the slogans and freedom songs in praise of Mandela. There was hardly anything lauding his co-recipient.

When the vanguard of the torchbearers arrived, the Norwegians sang 'Nkosi Sikelel' iAfrika' with greater ease and gusto than most South African whites do today. At this stage Mr and Mrs de Klerk were busy talking, their breath turning to mist in the below-zero temperature. Then they hurriedly left the balcony leaving Nelson and Zenani behind to acknowledge the adulation of the people.

De Klerk's delegation complained to the media that the ANC had hijacked the event, but the reporters reminded them that, in Norway at least, the people were free to applaud whoever they pleased. The de Klerk delegation left without saying goodbye.

We left for the Swedish capital of Stockholm where our welcome was as warm as it had been in Oslo. Religious groups, businessmen, NGOs and the media invited us to speak about our interim constitution, the forthcoming elections, and various other issues. They sang the praises of Nelson Mandela, welcomed his confidence in the future of South Africa and promised to help us as they had done during the battle against apartheid.

CHAPTER 39

The New Country

I will go down on my knees to beg those who want to drag our country into bloodshed.

– Nelson Mandela

Before the first democratic polls I attended an ANC election rally in the ballroom of a posh hotel to which captains of industry, mining, commerce and finance had been invited. A journalist asked why I was there. I told her that I trusted the ANC as a democratic organisation. I had defended many of its members over the previous forty years. I'd known the last five presidents and I knew many of its leaders, ordinary members and supporters. I was confident that, as our elected representatives, members of this party would promote and protect democracy, the rule of law and fundamental human rights. Sound bites of what I said appealed to those managing the ANC campaign and my words were broadcast as an advert.

I was often asked to attend election meetings addressed by Nelson, particularly those expected to draw white audiences. Nelson would tell the crowd that the ANC would be true to the opening words of the Freedom Charter: that South Africa belonged to all, black and white. He praised Father Trevor Huddleston, Helen Joseph, Beyers Naude, Joe Slovo and many other white people who'd contributed significantly to the struggle for justice. He also assured whites that, despite propaganda to the contrary, they had nothing to fear from an ANC majority.

Then I was approached about standing for election. A sufficient number of branches had nominated me, and the ANC wanted my consent so that my name could be put forward. I thanked them for the honour but I wanted to continue the work I'd done throughout my professional life. I wanted to retain my independence so that, with my colleagues in the Legal Resources Centre, we could try to protect the rights of the people.

Nelson Mandela heard of my refusal and asked if I would join the government or seek a judicial appointment. I wasn't interested in either. He expressed concern about the administration of justice. My seniority, experience and personal knowledge of those on the bench would help bring about the necessary transformation of the judiciary. I reminded him that there would be a Judicial Service Commission.

If appointed to the commission I would be more than happy to serve. I would in the meantime be available to the ANC as counsel.

Despite Nelson's occasional warnings to the party faithful that they should not take electoral victory for granted, I had no doubt that he would soon be president. Judge Johann Kriegler's Independent Electoral Commission assured us all was ready for the poll that would take place over two days.

Thousands of international observers began arriving to monitor the elections. At the last minute, when Inkatha decided to participate, Chief Mangosuthu Buthelezi's photograph as leader of the IFP was added at the bottom of the ballot paper which, by then, had already been printed. The Electoral Court worked overtime to deal with complaints about the conduct of one or other of the political parties, including the ANC, and substantial fines were imposed for overzealous behaviour. The leaders of the security forces promised to be ruthless if anyone interfered with the elections. Nelson Mandela's efforts to make it an almost all-inclusive election had succeeded.

Anxiety prevented tranquil sleep in our household during the night before the elections. We left the radio on, hoping against hope that there would be no bombings or other acts of violence at any polling booths, and no violent demonstrations in KwaZulu-Natal. There were none. Instead, hours before polls were to open on 27 April 1994 many joined long queues to vote. The early news on television showed Nelson Mandela casting his vote outside Durban near the grave of John Dube, one of the founders of the ANC. He had chosen to vote at this polling station in honour of all those who'd struggled for freedom but not lived to see this day. Behind him stood Gay MacDougal, a human rights lawyer from the United States, a member of our Independent Electoral Commission and a long-time supporter of those who'd defended political prisoners in Namibia and South Africa.

Images of thousands waiting in long queues throughout the country, most of them about to vote for the first time in their lives, prompted me to dress hurriedly and rush to the nearby school. Since Arethe is a late riser, I went on my own. There I found a queue ten-deep, almost around the block. Black and white voters stood solemnly silent as if they had joined a church procession. Gardeners and chauffeurs, cooks and domestic servants waited, interspersed among their masters and madams.

Hardly anyone complained about the delay. No one campaigned. Occasionally someone remarked on the pleasant autumn weather. A few people who lived nearby brought out garden chairs for the elderly and disabled. After three hours my row in the queue turned the corner and I saw that there was still a couple of hundred meters to go. I asked a bored police sergeant leaning on a parked car where the nearest toilet was? In the school where we were to vote, he replied.

In the hall I was recognised and welcomed by the electoral officer. She told me that as I was over sixty I could go to the head of the queue. I thanked her but said that my immediate need was more urgent. I also explained that as I had been in the queue for some time I didn't want to take advantage of the special 'over sixty' privilege. Relieved, I went back to the queue. It moved even more slowly than before. I had not breakfasted and it was almost lunch time. I weakened, physically and morally, and eventually took advantage of the privilege offered by the electoral officer.

The long colourful ballot paper, with the logos and photographs of the leaders of the numerous parties emphasised that it was an all-embracing election. The next day when I accompanied Arethe to cast her ballot, we walked directly into the hall. There was no queue. Everyone wanted to vote on the first day.

The election was certified free and fair by practically all the observers. There were complaints about incidents in KwaZulu-Natal by both the IFP and the ANC. The wisdom and leadership of Judge Kriegler prevailed and the results were accepted. The ANC's failure to get a two-thirds majority gave some comfort to its political opponents. They had feared that if the ANC achieved a two-thirds majority it would write the constitution without regard to the rights of others, a claim which the ANC denied.

The National Party and the IFP fared even worse than they had anticipated. The National Party, having come second, had the right to participate in the government of national unity, and de Klerk became one of the two vice-presidents. MPS were appointed on a proportional basis and the ANC proposed Nelson Mandela for president. The inauguration was to be held at the Union Buildings.

On the day we parked at a sports ground some twenty-five kilometres away from the Union Buildings and were driven in by coach. Among the passengers was Judge Richard Goldstone and his wife. She and Arethe sat together while Richard and I moved to the back to discuss the future of the judiciary.

Many of his fellow judges on the Court of Appeal were wary of the Constitutional Court that was soon to be established. If the Appeal Court judges were to hear constitutional cases, their judgments could be set aside by the new court, and this would diminish their status – a difficult reality to accept as this court had until then been the apex forum. Chief Justice Michael Corbett's term of office was about to end. The new president would have to appoint someone to head the Constitutional Court as well as a new chief justice at the Appeal Court. We discussed the prospect of Chief Justice Corbett accepting an extension of his term of office. If he did, it would not be necessary for the president to appoint a new chief justice at this stage.

Nelson was aware of the chief justice's record. He knew that Judge Corbett had been marginalised under his predecessor, Chief Justice Pierre Rabie. Chief Justice Rabie had a small coterie of judges on whom he relied to hear security cases during the state of emergency when a pro-executive outcome was required. Nelson was also aware of a significant speech Judge Corbett had made in the late 1970s about the importance of a bill of rights in South Africa. Richard agreed to sound out the chief justice about an extended term. He would let me know what transpired.

We arrived early and took our seats near the stage. The centre section was slowly filling up with royalty accompanied by entourages larger than expected, presidents, prime ministers, foreign ministers and ambassadors, leaders of political parties and senior civil servants. Winnie Mandela, now estranged from Nelson, was ushered to a seat to the side and behind us. She greeted neither Arethe nor me, nor those around her. Instead she glared unhappily into space. Fortunately a senior official soon escorted her to a seat on the platform. We could not see the real crowd, but we heard the freedom songs of the tens of thousands gathered in the park below who were to witness the ceremony on large screens.

The ceremony was late in starting, mainly because some of the VIPs insisted on being driven to the main entrance in their own vehicles, instead of using the shuttle buses. While waiting I thought of the many poignant moments in Nelson's life to which I had been a witness and the great impact they had made on both my personal and professional life. Though the inauguration ceremony was organised by the apartheid government, Barbara Masekela, an ANC stalwart and personal assistant to Nelson Mandela, was in charge of the proceedings.

When she announced his arrival we all stood to applaud. Women ululated and the multitude behind the stage shouted 'Viva!' Mandela was accompanied by his daughter Zenani, Chief Justice Corbett, who was to administer the oath, outgoing President de Klerk, Archbishop Tutu and other religious leaders. But there were also half a dozen generals in their ceremonial uniforms, each with numerous decorations earned in campaigns specifically aimed at preventing exactly what we were gathered there to witness.

There was something odd about the commissioner of police and the head of the army, both zealous servants of an illegitimate regime, standing next to Nelson Mandela. I could not help wondering whether they and the men and women under them would be loyal to the new president.

In the distance helicopters slowly flew towards us, passing over the Voortrekker Monument, the edifice glorifying white Afrikaner hegemony. Suddenly fighter jets thundered between them and as they dipped their wings to salute the new president the great mass of people repeatedly exclaimed, 'Viva the South African Air

Force, Viva!' No matter that these planes had once flown over Soweto, Sebokeng, Khayelitsha or our neighbouring countries with hostile intent. They were no longer the enemy; they belonged to the people. Our new president said never, never and never again would what had happened under apartheid be repeated.

The ceremony over, we soon met in the president's office at the Union Buildings and then for breakfast in the nearby presidential residence. Nelson found the accommodation there far less comfortable than his private home in Johannesburg, where he could enjoy the company of his grandchildren and his friends.

The matter of the judiciary was a concern that Nelson raised with me from time to time, even though Nicholas 'Fink' Haysom, a young constitutional and human rights lawyer, was his personal legal advisor on a full-time basis. He was worried about the administration of justice and how to deal with dissent by those from different political parties within the government of national unity, particularly Deputy President FW de Klerk. Well versed in achieving consensus in the ANC, Nelson used these methods to good effect by avoiding a vote whenever possible.

A good example was the death penalty. Fundamental differences emerged within the government over the official attitude to be presented at the Constitutional Court hearing into the death penalty. To retain the unity of the government, de Klerk and his party, who wanted capital punishment retained, agreed that the government brief counsel to argue for its abolition. On the other hand, it was agreed that the attorneys-general could exercise their independence and support its retention if they so wished. The consensus method proved useful for the better part of his presidency until de Klerk and his party withdrew from the government in anticipation of another general election.

I received a not-unexpected letter appointing me to the Judicial Service Commission, whose task it is to recommend the appointment and promotion of judges. This appointment was later renewed by President Mbeki. Transforming the judiciary in relation to race and gender has been a difficult task. Nevertheless, more than half the judges we have appointed are black, among them nine of the eleven heads of superior courts and eight of the eleven justices on the Constitutional Court, including the chief justice and the deputy chief justice. (An amendment to the constitution has made the head of the Constitutional Court, previously known as the president of that court, the chief justice. The head of the Appeal Court has now become the president of the Supreme Court of Appeal.)

We have not been nearly as successful regarding gender equality, mainly because there are so few women in the legal profession. In my view women have been sidelined for too long. Although much work needs to be done on these issues,

I believe the commission has helped fulfil the demands of the constitution, namely that when judges are appointed, the commission must consider 'the need for the judiciary to reflect broadly the racial and gender composition of South Africa'.

Another of the issues Nelson wanted advice on was the question of mixed cabinets. How many heads of government had handled such cabinets? I remembered reading how the French leader, Georges Clemenceau, dealt with the problems during and shortly after the First World War. He would canvas opinion then announce his decision as a cabinet decision, simultaneously asking if there were any resignations. He hardly ever asked for a vote to be taken.

CHAPTER 40

Judging the Judges

The interim constitution made provision for the establishment of a powerful new court. It was this court, together with the move from parliamentary to constitutional sovereignty, that represented the most significant change in the way the law operated.

The Constitutional Court was to be the court of final instance over all matters relating to the interpretation, protection and enforcement of the provisions of the constitution. Its role would be crucial, guarding the bill of rights contained in the constitution and ensuring the protection of the individual in relation to the State. The court would consist of a president and ten other justices. As a mark of how different and important this body was, its members would be chosen in a way never seen before. The president of the court was to be appointed by the president of the country in consultation with the cabinet and after consultation with the chief justice.

Once President Nelson Mandela had carried out the required discussions, he appointed Arthur Chaskalson to this top post. Four of the remaining justices were required to be judges already serving on one of the existing superior courts. Again there was a complex series of consultations before justices Richard Goldstone, Laurie Ackermann, Tholakele Madala and Ismail Mahomed were appointed.

The appointment of the remaining six involved a measure of public participation, in that the Judicial Service Commission held open hearings at which candidates were interviewed. As required by the constitution, the commission then gave President Mandela its shortlist of ten names and he chose six.

The Judicial Service Commission consisted of twenty-three members representing several constituencies, including the judiciary, the executive (through the minister of justice), parliamentarians, representatives of the legal profession and appointees of the president. I was one of the four appointed by President Nelson Mandela. In drawing up our shortlist of ten recommendations for the president, we were directed by the constitution to consider 'the need for the judiciary to reflect broadly the racial and gender composition of South Africa'. This is also one of the guidelines which the commission must constantly consider in its ongoing work of interviewing and recommending judges for appointment to all the superior courts.

At the time the Constitutional Court was being finalised, this whole procedure was regarded as a radical departure from the manner in which judges had been appointed previously. In the past, the minister of justice invariably appointed male white senior counsel practising at the Bar. Attorneys and academic lawyers were excluded. The minister's appointees were usually graduates of Afrikaans-speaking universities, members of the National Party or the secret Afrikaner Broederbond – and supporters of the apartheid regime. Most were politically powerful.

Despite their background, some of them had a strong sense of justice. To the surprise of those who appointed them, some delivered judgments checking the excesses of the securocrats, the harsh decisions of administrators and the cruel and inhuman behaviour of officials. A few even questioned the morality of the laws they were compelled to enforce. But for all that, the appointment process lacked transparency while the pool from which judges were drawn was exclusive, homogenous and urgently required broadening. The establishment of a Judicial Service Commission was a strong reaction to apartheid practices.

There were fears that candidates would not make themselves available for public hearings – such interviews were unheard of in the profession and individuals might be concerned that their privacy was being invaded. All the commissioners felt that in the interests of transparency and accountability the interviews for vacancies on the Constitutional Court had to be public. Despite strong arguments by Professor Etienne Mureinik we excluded the electronic media with their cameras and microphones, as this would be too intrusive. We followed the established practice in the courts – journalists could report, but without cameras or microphones. This is still the practice and policy at commission hearings.

Prerequisites for appointment to the new court were that a candidate be a South African citizen and a 'fit and proper person'. He or she must have been an advocate, attorney or teacher of law at a university for at least ten years and have expertise in the field of constitutional law. Dozens applied. Many were excluded in a sifting process before the ten were selected for the president's shortlist.

The hearings took place at the Civic Theatre in Johannesburg, not far from where the Constitutional Court was to be established. Proceedings were chaired by Chief Justice Michael Corbett. His style was to ask a number of non-controversial questions to put candidates at ease. These concerned their personal, academic and professional background, and what skills each would bring to the court. The more difficult and at times controversial questions were left to other members of the commission.

And they were often taxing and difficult – even embarrassing – for some candidates: What political, community or social organisations did you belong to during the apartheid regime? Did you belong to a secret organisation? Were women, or members of any ethnic group or faith, excluded from membership? Did you personally or through your association with any organisation overtly or covertly support the apartheid regime?

And by way of contrast: Did you overtly dissociate yourself from apartheid structures? Did you participate in any non-racial organisation? Did you promote the wellbeing of disadvantaged people? If you did not do any of these things was it because you were only interested in promoting your own affairs?

Those who admitted being part of apartheid structures had to explain how they would interpret and apply the bill of rights, which underwrote an approach to society that was the antithesis of their past beliefs and actions. A few ascribed their transformation to experiences akin to that of the apostle Paul on his journey to Damascus. But this questioning was important. Those able to show us a change of political heart were not excluded because of their earlier lives.

Those involved in the liberation struggle also faced close questioning. How, for example, would they overcome their bias in favour of the government which would now consist mainly of their comrades in the struggle? The usual answer was that such candidates would resign from the party that had won the election. After that, their integrity and respect for the rule of law and an impartial and independent judiciary would guide them in dispensing justice without fear or favour.

The hearings were not without incident. Students from nearby Wits university gathered at the entrance with placards protesting against two professors of law who were candidates for the court, but who were involved in a dispute on the campus. Chief Justice Corbett met the students and received their memorandum, then invited them into the hearings. Without their posters, but won over by his non-confrontational manner, the students complied, entered the room in a dignified manner and quietly followed proceedings.

Of the six appointed by President Mandela from our shortlist, two were already judges, though of another court – Johann Kriegler and John Didcott. The others, Pius Langa, Yvonne Mokgoro, Kate O'Regan and Albie Sachs were either practising lawyers or legal academics.

Once all the appointments were announced, the Constitutional Court and its new personnel moved into a temporary home in a hastily renovated office building.

Seven of the judges were white and four black. Two were women. This hardly fulfilled the constitutional injunction for the judiciary to reflect, in broad terms, race and gender. But so soon after the dismantling of apartheid, which had excluded black lawyers from appointment to the bench and prevented their proper advancement as lawyers, it was not yet possible to fulfil the requirement as fully as the commission would have liked.

Although most of the justices took their oath in English, others did it in their own languages: a powerful statement of the constitutional right for everyone to do the same in court. On the day the new court was inaugurated, members of the Judicial Service Commission, the Bar in their black gowns, attorneys, prominent jurists from beyond our borders, the media, the Minister of Justice Dullah Omar, members of Parliament and of provincial authorities, judges of the lower courts and others packed the courtroom. Beside President Mandela, dressed in a suit, sat the eleven judges. They presented a striking contrast to their colleagues in the other superior courts. While judges traditionally wear crimson robes for criminal matters and black for other cases, judges of the Constitutional Court wear gowns of an unusual shade of green. Was this, I wondered, to show that they intended to be somewhat different from other judges?

Addressing the head of the new court, President Mandela's opening words were: 'The last time I appeared in court was to hear whether or not I was going to be sentenced to death.' This was no mere light-hearted remark; it reminded us all of the reality experienced by his comrades, their families and their lawyers – including of course Arthur Chaskalson – just over thirty years previously.

While he delivered his short speech I could not help pondering what might have happened had he been put to death, or if he had emerged bitter and uncompromising from his long imprisonment. What if these experiences and the indignity imposed on him, his family and the vast majority of the people had caused him to seek revenge rather than reconciliation? But he did not speak about these matters. He looked ahead.

The future of democracy in South Africa hinged on the work of the Constitutional Court, he said. The task of the court was to ensure that the values of freedom and equality were nurtured and protected so that they would endure. The court should guard not only against direct assault on the principles of the constitution but also against insidious corrosion. The eleven judges were not expected to act as a rubber stamp, but rather to be creative and independent, true to their oath of office. All of us, he said, owed allegiance to the same supreme law and its principles, whether we were black or white, male or female, young or old, rich or poor, irrespective of the language we spoke and whether we wore a uniform. He promised that the government would support the new court in its work and concluded:

Judge Arthur Chaskalson and other members of the Constitutional Court, let me say the following: Yours is the most noble task that could fall to any legal person. In the last resort, the guarantee of the fundamental rights and freedoms for which we fought so hard, lies in your hands. We look to you to honour the constitution and the people it represents. We expect from you, no, demand of you, the greatest use of your wisdom, honesty and good sense – no shortcuts, no easy solutions. Your work is not only lofty, it is also lonely.

In the end you only have the constitution and your conscience on which you can rely. We look upon you to serve both without fear or favour.

Judge Richard Goldstone was absent. The secretary general of the United Nations had asked President Mandela to grant him a temporary absence so that he could take up the post of chief prosecutor of the International Criminal Court which dealt with charges of genocide and other serious violations of fundamental human rights during the conflict in the former Yugoslavia.

President Mandela always had the highest regard for the United Nations and was anxious that the new South Africa should be seen as contributing to its endeavours. In turn, Justice Chaskalson, as president of the court, released Justice Goldstone and requested the minister of justice to give a temporary appointment to Sydney Kentridge.

After the official opening, the court adjourned. It would begin work the next day on a matter about which Justice Sachs said, 'This court is unlikely to get another case which is emotionally and philosophically more elusive, and textually more direct.'

For my part, it would be the most significant case I have ever argued.

CHAPTER 41

Thou Shalt Not Kill

The measure of a country's greatness is its ability to retain compassion in time of crisis.

– Justice Thurgood Marshall of the US Supreme Court

Certainly the first case heard by the new Constitutional Court was the most important and the most controversial the court has yet heard. In South Africa few issues are as divisive as the death penalty. Public interest was exceptionally high, both because of the topic and because this was the new court's first matter. Everyone wanted to see how things would be handled.

The seating capacity of the court's temporary premises was inadequate and video screens were installed in the lobby. The passage leading to the small robing room was packed with counsel who made up the many legal teams arguing the matter.

The case was not argued in the abstract. Although it would have wide-reaching consequences whatever the outcome, it focused on two convicted criminals sitting on death row. Themba Makhwanyane and Mavusa Mchunu had been convicted on four counts of murder without extenuating circumstances and sentenced to death some time before. Their attempt to challenge the outcome before the Appeal Court had been dismissed. The constitutional issue could not be argued because at that stage it had no jurisdiction in constitutional issues. The men had not been executed because of a moratorium imposed on the death penalty by de Klerk. If the court ruled that capital punishment was compatible with the constitution, Makwanyane and Mchunu would face their sentences.

These two prisoners were appellants in the case and they and their counsel accepted the assistance of the Legal Resources Centre. Senior attorneys Geoff Budlender and Thandi Orleyn were assigned to help with Wim Trengove SC and Gilbert Marcus appearing *pro bono*.

The divisions caused by the death penalty were clear not only on the streets, they were evident in court. The cabinet had briefed counsel to support the appellants and I was approached. So it came about that for the first time in my life I had a government brief. The cabinet also recognised the independence of the attorneys-general who wished to oppose the appeal. They argued that the death penalty was constitutional, that it should be declared a valid punishment, that the moratorium be lifted and hangings resumed forthwith.

As counsel gathered in the robing room and the corridors outside, the registrar invited the leaders of all the teams into the chambers of the president of the court. Arthur, smiling a little nervously, greeted each of us by first names. We had each been allotted time and a red light on the podium would indicate its end. He would tolerate requests for short extensions. Despite this curtailment, Arthur emphasised that our written submissions had been read and considered. He informed us that members of the court did not want us to address them as 'Milord' or 'Milady' as we did in other courts, but as 'Justice Such and Such'. Although he did not ask for this courtesy, I decided to call him President Chaskalson and there appeared to be no objection when I did so in court.

Representing the prosecution or the State (as distinct from the government) there was a team of no fewer than ten prosecutors from the various provinces. These were led by KPCO von Lieres und Wilkau SC, deputy attorney-general of the Witwatersrand Local Division. This division of the court had imposed the death sentence on the two accused whose fate was now being considered. The prosecutors were supported in their position by Johannesburg advocate Emanuel Zar SC acting on behalf of his individual client, Ian Glauber, a member of the public with such strong views on the subject that he was willing to retain counsel.

Representatives of the Black Advocates Forum, FE Davis and GM Makhanya, associated themselves in part with our argument, but asked that the decision should be deferred for further investigations. They argued that there was insufficient information about the provisions of customary law and the matter should not be decided until such research was carried out – a suggestion not accepted by the court.

Wim Trengove began with a brief sketch of the history of capital punishment in South Africa from the middle of the seventeenth century when the Dutch East India Company established a colony at the Cape. At that time the punishment was carried out by decapitation, hanging, slow strangulation, burning alive, impaling and other equally horrible means. These were gradually abandoned except for hanging behind closed doors.

Capital punishment was obligatory for those convicted of murder unless the president or the governor-general exercised the prerogative of mercy and imposed a prison sentence instead. In 1935 a discretion was conferred on the courts to impose a lesser sentence if extenuating circumstances were proved. In the first half of the twentieth century the number of executions diminished, influenced by the international trend away from capital punishment. This was abruptly reversed after 1948 with the advent of the apartheid regime. There were twenty-one executions during the thirty-six years from 1911 to 1947, but in the first seven months of 1948 no fewer than thirty-seven people were hanged. By 1987 the annual toll had reached a hundred and eighty-one.

As the day progressed, it became clear that the judges had indeed read the submissions in the heads of argument of all parties. More than that, they had mastered the contents of the voluminous bundles handed in containing copies of judgments, legislative provisions, articles in law journals, extracts from textbooks, essays in philosophical books and journals, newspaper and magazine articles.

It also quickly became apparent that the justices of the Constitutional Court would be a highly participatory audience. Justices Ismail Mahomed, John Didcott and Johann Kriegler almost vied with one another, springing questions on counsel even when we were in mid-sentence. They would not accept simple answers. If you agreed with a proposition made by Justice Mahomed, for example, he would tell you that he was 'not interested in your vote', but that he wanted cogent reasons why you thought there was merit in his idea.

Unlike some of us, Wim would not be sidetracked nor speculate. When asked why Parliament had not expressly abolished capital punishment he said simply, 'I don't know'. What he did know was that a number of the justices had been part of Codesa – Justice Mahomed was the co-chairman – and so any speculation would have been pointless before people who possibly had inside knowledge. Wim worked methodically through his ninety pages of argument, confidently answering questions and dealing with submissions contained in the argument of the other side.

The argument for the appellants stated that the death penalty violated a number of fundamental rights. It infringed the rights to life, respect for and protection of the dignity of human beings, the prohibition on physical, mental and emotional torture and on cruel, inhuman and degrading treatment and punishment. Furthermore, this infringement could not be justified and therefore could not be condoned. (Under the constitution there is a test that limitations of the right must pass before the infringement they commit can be held to be justified.) We argued that the death penalty fails the justification test because it 'negates the essential content' of the rights to life and dignity, it is 'not necessary' and is 'not reasonable and justifiable in an open and democratic society based on freedom and equality'.

When you argue a case, you look for judicial or other acceptable authority to support your contention. If you find it, you can do no better than use their words. Wim's team found the words they wanted from the pen of Judge John Sopinka of Canada:

At the very heart of this appeal is a conflict between two concepts. On one side is the concept of human dignity and the belief that this concept is of paramount importance in a democratic society. On the other side is the concept of retributive justice and the belief that capital punishment is necessary to deter murderers. A historical review reveals an increasing tendency to resolve this tension in favour of human dignity.

To give substance to this tendency in favour of human dignity, Wim made reference to the preamble of the United Nations' Charter of October 1945. This was developed further when, in 1983, the European Union abolished the death penalty and member states agreed not to extradite anyone to countries where the death penalty could be imposed.

Instruments expressing similar intentions were adopted by the American Declaration of the Rights and Duties of Man at the Ninth International Conference of American States in 1948, and the Charter on Human and Peoples' Rights adopted by the Organisation of African Unity in Kenya during 1981.

Another example was the parliamentary assembly of the Council of Europe, which resolved to

[call] on the parliaments of all member states of the council of Europe and of all states whose legislative assemblies enjoy special guest status at the assembly which retain capital punishment for crimes committed in peacetime and/or in wartime to strike it from their statute books completely.

Finally it urges all heads of state and all parliaments in whose countries death sentences are passed to grant clemency to the convicted.

It was argued that if the death penalty was not considered a reasonable, viable penalty in open and democratic societies based on freedom and equality such as all of these, we should follow their example and similarly refuse to permit it in South Africa.

Wim also argued, with examples, that the death penalty was arbitrary, biased and fallible. During the course of argument Von Lieres interrupted us, triumphantly handing in a fax from the South African consul general in New York to the effect that Governor George Pataki had signed a statute legalising the death penalty of the state of New York. With this, he said, how could we argue that there was a trend in democratic countries against abolition?

Von Lieres and the rest of the prosecution also found comfort in the views of Lord Denning:

Punishment is the way in which a society expresses its denunciation of wrong-doing: And in order to maintain respect for law it is essential that the punishment inflicted for grave crimes should adequately reflect the revulsion felt by the great majority of citizens. It is a mistake to consider the objects of punishments as being deterrent or reformative or preventive and nothing else … The truth is that some crimes are so outrageous that society insists on adequate punishment because the wrongdoer deserves it, irrespective of whether it is a deterrent or not.

Although these words had been uttered more than fifty years earlier it was argued that they were as valid today. The State also handed in a bundle of newspaper cuttings reporting gruesome murders, and including editorials and letters in support of Lord Denning's views. This was intended to show that South African public opinion was in favour of retaining capital punishment. Under the moratorium no one had been hanged for five years – the State said the citizenry of South Africa blamed the increase in serious crime on this moratorium.

We countered by handing in a bundle almost as thick as theirs in favour of abolition. We pointed out that retentionist views were usually expressed in inappropriate language, as unsubstantiated generalisations with racist undertones. We argued that calls to 'hang them high' could not be said to prove public opinion. The express constitutional wording providing for the right to life should be the dominant factor in the debate: this wording in the interim constitution had been approved by more than twenty political parties and other groups represented at Codesa and by the majority of those elected to the tricameral parliament. With this backing, the right-to-life provision could safely be said to have the support of the public through their representatives.

We produced evidence showing it was wrong that the courts were infallible when they passed the death penalty. As for those who relied on the biblical injunction of 'an eye for an eye' we said this was an injunction for proportionality. In any case, direct biblical authority to the contrary was God's demand that no one touch Cain on whom he had placed his mark for the murder of Abel.

We cautioned that while the views of the majority ought to be considered, the matter was complex. A number of judgments from various countries (to some of which we referred) held that when it came to fundamental rights the court's function was more than merely giving effect to the transient opinions of the majority.

We submitted that individuals or groups of people often required the protection of constitutional guarantees against the prevalent opinion of the majority. In this regard, Attorney-General von Lieres und Wilkau was irritated by our example that Hitler had obtained a ninety-nine per cent majority in greater Germany for his 1938 annexation of Austria and a portion of Czechoslovakia. We also referred to the judgment of the United States Supreme Court in relation to the internment of Japanese residents of the United States during the Second World War. We quoted the words of Justice Lewis Franklin Powell: 'The assessment of popular opinion is essentially a legislative, not a judicial function.'

The attorney-general's bundle referred to a number of judgments in which South African judges said that the death penalty was necessary because of its deterrent effect. In our argument we mentioned as many judges with dissenting views on the question of deterrence. Among them was Judge Dante Cloete. He had no hesitation in advocating the abolition of the death penalty because it did not act as a deterrent and that even the most experienced judges could make grave mistakes in imposing it. Judge Isie Maisels said in the 1960s: 'I do not believe that it acts as a deterrent and I have always had a personal loathing of it.' The judge president of Natal, John Milne, had said in the 1980s that he was often troubled by the memory of the men he had sent to the gallows. He thought that the death penalty should be abolished. It had never been proven to be an effective deterrent to crime. A serious criticism was the punishment's finality. What if a man were hanged in error? In Milne's words:

The mechanics of it are particularly repellent to me. The notion that you take a man in cold blood and take his life. I concede that that is an emotional feeling. But I hold to it.

In the mid-1920s Judge Frederick Krauss had said:

I have it on the best authority of those who have had an opportunity of investigating the matter that approximately ten per cent of the natives executed for murder were actually innocent of the crime ...

Legal academics at South Africa's liberal universities had a reputation for being opposed to capital punishment and one of them, Dennis Davis (now a judge of the High Court in Cape Town), together with Danny Berger from the Johannesburg Bar represented Lawyers for Human Rights, the Centre for Applied Legal Studies, and the Society for the Abolition of the Death Penalty in South Africa at the hearing. Over the years, these organisations at the universities of Cape Town, the Witwatersrand and Natal had studied the subject. Eminent among them were professors Ellison Kahn and Barend van Niekerk, both of whom regularly wrote articles in the academic journals and popular media calling for the abolition of the death penalty. Barend even had to face criminal charges arising out of his opposition to capital punishment.

Among the submitted papers was a lengthy memorandum supporting the abolition of the death penalty signed by Jack Greenberg of the Columbia University School of Law, Anthony G Amsterdam of New York University's School of Law, Steven W Hawkins of the us-based National Association for the Advancement of Coloured People's Legal Defence and Educational Fund, and Kenneth Roth and Juan Mendez of the Human Rights Watch.

When he rose to argue the position of retention, Attorney-General von Lieres faced a barrage of questions. At some point he said he would answer a question 'in due course', and the judge said he should deal with it there and then. Justice Sydney Kentridge came to his rescue. 'Speaking for myself, Mr von Lieres, I would like to hear your argument in the order in which you want to present it.'

This was not the end of the difficulties for Von Lieres. When he made a statement more appropriate for a populist politician than a senior counsel in court, he was told by Justice Kriegler to argue the matter 'in an honest manner'.

Argument on the death penalty lasted for three days. It took the court more than three months to hand down its judgment. The judges were unanimous – the death penalty was unconstitutional.

Eleven years later Professor Hugh Corder, one of South Africa's leading legal academics, wrote about the significance of the case selected by the court as the first it would hear. Both the choice of the case and the ultimate decision he said, were

a powerful indication of [the court's] intention to mark a parting of the ways from the old order. It duly unanimously declared the death penalty to be unconstitutional chiefly for the reason that it amounted to 'cruel, inhuman or degrading punishment', allied with reliance on the rights to dignity, equality and life.

[This case] laid the basis of so many of the subsequent policies and principles observed by the [Constitutional Court] that it must go down as the single most significant case of the first decade, in my view. For example, the judges all concurred in the leading judgment of [President] Chaskalson, yet each judge also delivered a separate concurrence, which lent great weight to the decision and allowed each member of the court the opportunity to signal their own particular approach to matters constitutional for the future.

He added:

> Much more could be written about [this case] but ... it suffices to say that the
> series of judgments delivered in this case constitutes perhaps the single most
> substantial cornerstone of the [Constitutional Court's] jurisprudence from
> which, in a sense, all other decisions flow. Perhaps most vital of all the les-
> sons to be learned from this case is the confirmation of the supremacy of the
> constitution in governmental life in South Africa, as well as the pivotal role of
> the [Constitutional Court] in giving final meaning and life to it.

Corder's critique included the following important observations:

> Many of the [individual judgments making up the decision] provided detailed
> analysis of comparative jurisprudence, both international and national in
> origin and explored in a transparent and refreshing way the value system
> underlying any process of interpretation. These have become features of most
> of the subsequent decisions of the court. In the process the court raised the
> relevance of African approaches to justice, in the form of *ubuntu*, which had
> hitherto not found its place in the pages of the law reports. Even the fact that
> the court was prepared to be seized of the matter of determining the ques-
> tion was significant, as the death penalty was undoubtedly a punishment
> which evoked strong popular sentiments, [and] which a more cautious court
> may have elected to leave for decision to the newly constituted democratic
> Parliament.

Though many of us welcomed the decision, strident voices were raised against
the court and those who had drafted the interim constitution in terms of which
the death penalty was declared unlawful. Some, purporting to speak on behalf of
the majority of the people, insist to this day that a referendum should be called to
canvass popular opinion on the subject. They confidently predict that the majority
would vote in favour of reinstating capital punishment. Most of them have not
read the court's judgments consisting of more than a hundred pages in which
arguments such as these were rejected. Perhaps the reasons given by the judges
would not convince those who would retain the death penalty.

I have long associated myself with the hope that the international campaign
for abolition will succeed and I am an office-bearer of Don't Touch Cain – an
Italian-based NGO campaigning for abolition throughout the world. Many people
do not have access to the decision of the Constitutional Court and so here are

some of the opinions expressed by the judges. I lose no opportunity of setting out these arguments whenever I can.

Arthur Chaskalson, writing as president of the court and on behalf of his unanimous colleagues, said:

Most accused facing a possible death sentence are unable to afford legal assistance, and are defended under the *pro Deo* system. The defending counsel is more often than not young and inexperienced, frequently of a different race to his or her client, and if this is the case, usually has to consult through an interpreter. *Pro Deo* counsel are paid only a nominal fee for the defence, and generally lack the financial resources and the infrastructural support to undertake the necessary investigations and research, to employ expert witnesses to give advice, including advice on matters relevant to sentence, to assemble witnesses, to bargain with the prosecution, and generally to conduct an effective defence. Accused persons who have the money to do so are able to retain experienced attorneys and counsel, who are paid to undertake the necessary investigations and research, and as a result they are less likely to be sentenced to death than persons similarly placed who are unable to pay for such services.

The attorney-general argued that what is cruel, inhuman or degrading depends to a large extent upon contemporary attitudes within society, and that South African society does not regard the death sentence for extreme cases of murder as a cruel, inhuman or degrading form of punishment ... The question before us, however, is not what the majority of South Africans believe a proper sentence for murder should be. It is whether the constitution allows the sentence.

Those who are entitled to claim this protection include the social outcasts and marginalised people of our society. It is only if there is a willingness to protect the worst and the weakest amongst us, that all of us can be secure that our own rights will be protected.

We would be deluding ourselves if we were to believe that the execution of the few persons sentenced to death during this period, and of a comparatively few other people each year from now onwards will provide the solution to the unacceptably high rate of crime. There will always be unstable, desperate and pathological people for whom the risk of arrest and imprisonment provides no deterrent, but there is nothing to show that a decision to carry out the death sentence would have any impact on the behaviour of such people, or that there will be more of them if imprisonment is the only sanction. No information was placed before us by the attorney-general in regard to the rising crime rate other than the bare statistics and they alone prove nothing, other than that we are living in a violent society in which most crime goes unpunished – something that we all know.

The greatest deterrent to crime is the likelihood that offenders will be apprehended, convicted and punished. It is that which is presently lacking in our criminal justice system; and it is at this level and through addressing the causes of crime that the State must seek to combat lawlessness.

In the debate as to the deterrent effect of the death sentence, the issue is sometimes dealt with as if the choice to be made is between the death sentence and the murder going unpunished. That is of course not so. The choice to be made is between putting the criminal to death and subjecting the criminal to the severe punishment of a long term of imprisonment, which, in an appropriate case, could be a sentence of life imprisonment. Both are deterrents and the question is whether the possibility of being sentenced to death, rather than being sentenced to life imprisonment, has a marginally greater deterrent effect and whether the constitution sanctions the limitation of rights affected thereby.

In the course of his argument the attorney-general contended that if sentences imposed by the courts on convicted criminals are too lenient, the law will be brought into disrepute and members of society will then take the law into their own hands. Law is brought into disrepute if the justice system is ineffective and criminals are not punished. But if the justice system is effective and criminals are apprehended, brought to trial and in serious cases subjected to severe sentences, the law will not fall into disrepute. We have made the commitment to 'a future founded on the recognition of human rights, democracy and peaceful co-existence … for all South Africans.' Respect for life and dignity lies at the heart of that commitment. One of the reasons for the prohibition of capital punishment is 'that allowing the State to kill will cheapen the value of human life and thus [through not doing so] the State will serve in a sense as a role model for individuals in society.' Our country needs such role models.

The attorney-general contended that it is common sense that the most feared penalty will provide the greatest deterrent, but accepted that there is no proof that the death sentence is in fact a greater deterrent than life imprisonment for a long period … A punishment as extreme and as irrevocable as death cannot be predicated upon speculation as to what the deterrent effect might be …

Retribution is one of the objects of punishment, but it carries less weight than deterrence. The righteous anger of family and friends of the murder victim, reinforced by the public abhorrence of vile crimes, is easily translated into a call for vengeance. But capital punishment is not the only way that society has of expressing its moral outrage at the crime that has been committed. We have long outgrown the literal application of the biblical injunction of 'an eye for an eye, and a tooth for a tooth'.

In the balancing process, deterrence, prevention and retribution must be weighed against the alternative punishments available to the State, and the factors which taken together make capital punishment cruel, inhumane and degrading: the destruction of life, the annihilation of dignity, the elements of arbitrariness, inequality and the possibility of error in the enforcement of the penalty.

The rights to life and dignity are the most important of all human rights, and the source of all other personal rights in Chapter Three [of the constitution]. By committing ourselves to a society founded on the recognition of human rights we are required to value these two rights above all others. And this must be demonstrated by the State in everything that it does, including the way it punishes criminals. This is not achieved by objectifying murderers and putting them to death to serve as an example to others in the expectation that they might possibly be deterred thereby.

Justice Laurie Ackermann wrote:

Apart from deterring others, one of the goals of punishment is to prevent the convicted prisoner from committing crimes again. Both the preventative and reformative components of punishment are directed towards this end, although reformation obviously has the further commendable aim of the betterment of the prisoner. Society as a whole is justifiably concerned that this aim of punishment should be achieved and society fears the possibility that the violent criminal, upon release from prison, will once again harm society. Society is particularly concerned with the possibility of this happening in the case of an unreformed recidivist murderer or rapist if the death penalty is abolished.

The president has rightly pointed out in his judgment that in considering the deterrent effect of the death sentence the evaluation is not to be conducted by contrasting the death penalty with no punishment at all but between the death sentence and 'severe punishment of a long term of imprisonment which, in an appropriate case, could be a sentence of life imprisonment'.

Justice John Didcott:

A very large proportion of murderers were in no mood or state of mind at the time to contemplate or care about the consequences of their killings which they might personally suffer. Those rational enough to take account of them gambled by and large on their escape from detection and arrest, where the odds in their favour were often rather high. The prospect of conviction and punishment was much less immediate and seldom entered their thinking.

It is unnecessary, however, to go so far. The protagonists of capital punishment bear the burden of satisfying us that it is permissible under section 33(1). To the extent that their case depends upon the uniquely deterrent effect attributed to it, they must therefore convince us that it indeed serves such a purpose. Nothing less is expected from them in any event when human lives are at stake, lives which may not continue to be destroyed on the mere possibility that some good will come of it. In that task they have failed and, as far as one can see, could never have succeeded.

South Africa has experienced too much savagery. The wanton killing must stop before it makes a mockery of the civilised, humane and compassionate society to which the nation aspires and has constitutionally pledged itself and the State must set the example by demonstrating the priceless value it places on the lives of all its subjects, even the worst.

Acting Justice Sydney Kentridge felt that he had to deal with some of the specific arguments of Von Lieres:

Capital punishment is an issue on which many members of the public hold strong and conflicting views. To many of them it may seem strange that so difficult and important a public issue should be decided by the eleven appointed judges of this court. It must be understood that we undertake this task not because we claim a superior wisdom for ourselves but, as President Chaskalson has explained in his judgment, because the framers of the constitution have imposed on us the inescapable duty of deciding whether the death penalty for murder is consistent with Chapter Three of the constitution. It should not be overlooked that a decision holding the death penalty to be constitutional would have been just as far-reaching an exercise of judicial power as the decision to strike it down.

But that does not mean that the State should respond to the murderer's cruelty with a deliberate and matching cruelty of its own. As Simon Jenkins said in a recent article on the death penalty in *The Times* (London), that would imply that punishment must not merely fit the crime, but repeat the crime ... [T]he striking down of the death penalty entails no sympathy whatsoever for the murderer, nor any condonation of his crime. What our decision does entail is a recognition that even the worst and most vicious criminals are not excluded from the protections of the constitution.

Justice Johann Kriegler found emphatically that

[n]o empirical study, no statistical exercise and no theoretical analysis has been able to demonstrate that capital punishment has any deterrent force greater than that of a really heavy sentence of imprisonment. That is the ineluctable conclusion to be drawn from the mass of data so thoroughly canvassed in the written and oral arguments presented to us.

Justice Pius Langa, with his experience at a personal level and as counsel defending those in danger of being sentenced to death, wrote:

The emphasis I place on the right to life is, in part, influenced by the recent experiences of our people in this country. The history of the past decades has been such that the value of life and human dignity have been demeaned. Political, social and other factors created a climate of violence resulting in a culture of retaliation and vengeance. In the process, respect for life and for the inherent dignity of every person became the main casualties. The State has been part of this degeneration, not only because of its role in the conflicts of the past but also by retaining punishments which did not testify to a high regard for the dignity of the person and the value of every human life.

An outstanding feature of *ubuntu* in a community sense is the value it puts on life and human dignity. The dominant theme of the culture is that the life of another person is at least as valuable as one's own. Respect for the dignity of every person is integral to this concept. During violent conflicts and times when violent crime is rife, distraught members of society decry the loss of *ubuntu*. Thus heinous crimes are the antithesis of *ubuntu*. Treatment that is cruel, inhuman or degrading is bereft of *ubuntu*.

We have all been affected, in some way or other, by the 'strife, conflict, untold suffering and injustice' of the recent past. In sum, there is hardly anyone who has not been a victim in some way or who has not lost a close relative in senseless violence. Some of the violence was perpetrated through the machinery of the State, in order to ensure the perpetuation of a status quo that was fast running out of time. But all this was violence on human beings by human beings. Life became cheap, almost worthless.

That is why, during argument, a tentative proposition was made that a person who has killed another has forfeited the right to life. Although the precise implications of this suggestion were not thoroughly canvassed, this cannot be so. The test of our commitment to a culture of rights lies in our ability to respect the rights not only of the weakest, but also of the worst among us. A person does not become 'fair game' to be killed at the behest of the State, because he has killed.

The protection afforded by the constitution is applicable to every person. That includes the weak, the poor and the vulnerable. It includes others as well who might appear not to need special protection; it includes criminals and all those who have placed themselves on the wrong side of the law. The constitution guarantees them their right, as persons, to life, to dignity and to protection against torture or cruel, inhuman or degrading punishment or treatment.

Justice Thole Madala dealt with the argument advanced by counsel for the Black Advocates Forum by referring to *ubuntu* and traditional law.

The constitution in its post-amble declares: 'There is a need for understanding but not vengeance, and for reparation but not for retaliation, a need for *ubuntu* but not victimisation.'

The concept *ubuntu* appears for the first time in the post-amble, but it is a concept that permeates the constitution generally and more particularly Chapter Three which embodies the entrenched fundamental human rights. The concept carries in it the ideas of humaneness, social justice and fairness.

It was argued by Mr Bizos, on behalf of the government, that the post-amble enjoins the people of South Africa to open a new chapter which envisages the country playing a leading role in the upholding of human rights. He submitted, further, that the government favoured the abolition of the death penalty because it believed that such punishment could not be reconciled with the fundamental rights contained in the constitution, and that its application diminished the dignity of our society as a whole.

From the statistics supplied by the attorney-general and from what one gleans daily from the newspapers and other media, we live at a time when the high crime rate is unprecedented, when the streets of our cities and towns rouse fear and despair in the heart, rather than pride and hope, and this in turn robs us of objectivity and personal concern for our brethren. But, as [Judge] Marshall put it in *Furman v Georgia* (*supra*) at 371: 'The measure of a country's greatness is its ability to retain compassion in time of crisis.'

This, in my view, also accords with *ubuntu* – and calls for a balancing of the interest of society against those of the individual, for the maintenance of law and order, but not for dehumanising and degrading the individual.

We must stand tallest in these troubled times and realise that every accused person who is sent to jail is not beyond being rehabilitated – properly counselled – or, at the very least, beyond losing the will and capacity to do evil.

A further aspect which I wish to mention is the question of traditional African jurisprudence and the degree to which such values have not been researched for the purposes of the determination of the issue of capital punishment.

Ms Davids, who appeared on behalf of the Black Advocates Forum, in its capacity as *amicus curiae*, touched on, but did not fully argue, this matter.

She submitted that we could not determine the question of the constitution-ality or otherwise of the death sentence without reference to further evidence which would include the views, aspirations and opinions of the historically disadvantaged and previously oppressed people of South Africa, who also constitute the majority of our society.

As I understood her argument, the issue of capital punishment could not be determined in an open and democratic society without the active participation of the black majority. This, in my view, would be tantamount to canvassing public opinion among the black population for the decisions of our courts. I do not agree with this submission, if it implies that this court or any other court must function according to public opinion.

In order to arrive at an answer as to the constitutionality or otherwise of the death penalty or any enactment, we do not have to canvass the opinions and attitudes of the public. Ours is to interpret the provisions of the constitu-tion as they stand and if any matter is in conflict with the constitution, we have to strike it down.

For purposes of the determination of the question of the constitutionality of the death penalty, however, it is, in my view, not necessary or even desirable that public opinion should be sought on the matter in the manner she suggests.

In his typical style, Justice Ismail Mahomed said:

The post-amble to the constitution gives expression to the new ethos of the nation by a commitment to 'open a new chapter in the history of our coun-try', by lamenting the transgressions of 'human rights' and 'humanitarian principles' in the past and articulating a 'need for understanding, but not for vengeance, a need for reparation but not retaliation, a need for *ubuntu* but not for victimisation.'

The need for *ubuntu* expresses the ethos of an instinctive capacity for and enjoyment of love towards our fellow men and women; the joy and the fulfilment involved in recognising their innate humanity; the reciprocity this generates in interaction within the collective community; the richness of the creative emotions which it engenders and the moral energies which it releases both in the givers and the society which they serve and are served by.

We were not furnished with any reliable research dealing with the relationship between the rate of serious offences and the proportion of successful apprehensions and convictions following on the commission of serious offences. This would have been a significant enquiry. It appears to me to be an inherent probability that the more successful the police are in solving serious crimes and the more successful they are in apprehending the criminals concerned and securing their convictions, the greater will be the perception of risk for those contemplating such offences. That increase in the perception of risk, contemplated by the offender, would bear a relationship to the rate at which serious offences are committed. Successful arrest and conviction must operate as a deterrent and the State should, within the limits of its undoubtedly constrained resources, seek to deter serious crime by adequate remuneration for the police force; by incentives to improve their training and skill; by augmenting their numbers in key areas; and by facilitating their legitimacy in the perception of the communities in which they work.

On a judicial application of all the relevant considerations and the facts made available to us, I therefore cannot conclude that the State has successfully established that the death penalty per se had any deterrent effect on the potential perpetrators of serious offences.

Justice Yvonne Mokgoro wrote:

The described sources of public opinion can hardly be regarded as scientific. Yet even if they were, constitutional adjudication is quite different from the legislative process, because the court is not a politically responsible institution to be seized every five years by majoritarian opinion. The values intended to be promoted by section 35 are not founded on what may well be uninformed or indeed prejudiced public opinion. One of the functions of the court is precisely to ensure that vulnerable minorities are not deprived of their constitutional rights.

Generally, *ubuntu* translates as humaneness. In its most fundamental sense, it translates as personhood and morality. Metaphorically it expresses itself in *umuntu ngumuntu ngabantu*, describing the significance of group solidarity on survival issues so central to the survival of communities. While it envelops the key values of group solidarity, compassion, respect, human dignity, conformity to basic norms and collective unity, in its fundamental sense it denotes humanity and morality. Its spirit emphasises respect for human dignity, marking a shift from confrontation to conciliation. In South Africa *ubuntu* has become a notion with particular resonance in the building of a democracy. It is part of our rainbow heritage, though it might have operated and still operates differently in diverse community settings. In the Western cultural heritage, respect and the value for life, manifested in the all-embracing concepts of humanity and *menswaardigheid* are also highly priced ['prized' meant]. It is values like these that section 35 requires to be promoted. They give meaning and texture to the principles of a society based on freedom and equality.

Once the life of a human being is taken in the deliberate and calculated fashion that characterises the described methods of execution the world over, it constitutes the ultimate cruelty with which any living creature could ever be treated. This extreme level of cruel treatment of a human being, however despicably such person might have treated another human being, is still inherently cruel. It is inhuman and degrading to the humanity of the individual, as well as to the humanity of those who carry it out.

Taking the life of a human being will always be reprehensible. Those citizens who kill deserve the most severe punishment, if it deters and rehabilitates and therefore effectively addresses deviance of this nature. Punishment by death cannot achieve these objectives. The high rate of crime in this country is indeed disturbing and the State has a duty to protect the lives of all citizens – including those who kill. However, it should find more humane and effective integrated approaches to manage its penal system and to rehabilitate offenders.

Justice Kate O'Regan:

The values urged upon the court are not those that have informed our past. Our history is one of repression not freedom, oligarchy not democracy, apartheid and prejudice not equality, clandestine not open government.

The right to life is, in one sense, antecedent to all the other rights in the Constitution.

The new constitution stands as a monument to this society's commitment to a future in which all human beings will be accorded equal dignity and respect.

Justice Albie Sachs wrote:

> The unqualified statement that 'every person has the right to life', in effect outlaws capital punishment. Instead of establishing a constitutional framework within which the State may deprive citizens of their lives, as it could have done, our constitution commits the State to affirming and protecting life.

In relation to customary law he said:

> Thus, if these sources are reliable, it would appear that the relatively well-developed judicial processes of indigenous societies did not in general encompass capital punishment for murder. Such executions as took place were the frenzied, extra-judicial killings of supposed witches, a spontaneous and irrational form of crowd behaviour that has unfortunately continued to this day in the form of necklacing and witch burning. In addition, punishments by military leaders in terms of military discipline were frequently of the harshest kind and accounted for the lives of many persons. Yet, the sources referred to above indicate that, where judicial procedures were followed, capital punishment was in general not applied as a punishment for murder.
>
> In seeking the kind of values which should inform our broad approach to interpreting the constitution, I have little doubt as to which of these three contrasted aspects of tradition we should follow and which we should reject.
>
> Accordingly, the idealism that we uphold with this judgment is to be found not in the minds of the judges, but in both the explicit text of the constitution itself, and the values it enshrines. I have no doubt that even if, as the president's judgment suggests, the framers subjectively intended to keep the issue open for determination by this court, they effectively closed the door by the language they used and the values they required us to uphold. It is difficult to see how they could have done otherwise. In a founding document dealing with fundamental rights, you either authorise the death sentence or you do not. In my view, the values expressed by section 9 are conclusive of the matter. Everyone, including the most abominable of human beings, has the right to life and capital punishment is therefore unconstitutional.

Abolitionists throughout the world welcomed the decision. We hoped that what we believed to be the persuasive and convincing reasons given by our judges would silence the retentionists. They were, however, highly critical of the court and accused its members of bias. They said the decision should have been left to Parliament and not to a group of liberal judges.

They challenged the government to a referendum, which they confidently expected would show that the majority disagreed with them. They also called for an amendment to the constitution. Although editorial comment was supportive of the court's decision, the media went on to urge that government take steps to reduce serious crime lest public opinion encouraged vigilantism.

Most critics have been white conservatives, staunch supporters of the apartheid regime. They assert that their farming community needs protection against blacks, and that this could only be provided by the death penalty.

I would answer by reminding them of their demand that their land should not be taken away from them. This was acceded to by the new government. In fact it was entrenched as a right by the constitution. Then I ask if they would support a referendum to abolish that right so that justice could be done to over seventy-five per cent of the population who were deprived of their land because they were black.

My opponents answer that this is a different matter and then they change the subject. On the land issue they expect their rights as a minority to be protected against the will of the majority. Apparently they agree with the Constitutional Court that the will of the majority (at least on this matter) should not be allowed to ride roughshod over the minority. This is exactly our position on the question of a referendum about capital punishment.

Despite such dissenting voices as these, the death penalty is at long last no more in South Africa. May it be so forever; that is my fervent wish.

CHAPTER 42

The Constitution

The Constitution of South Africa speaks of both the past and the future.

[It] permits us to build a nation based on the democratic values of human dignity, equality and freedom, through constitutionalism and the rule of law. [It] describes the mechanisms and institutions which we have created to ensure that we achieve this. There are no shortcuts on the road to freedom. The constitution describes the path which we must and shall follow.

[It] is a living document. Our understanding of its requirements will and must adapt over time. But the fundamental principles are and must be unchanging. Full understanding of how and why those principles were adopted will help us to ensure that we remain true to the solemn undertakings which we have made to each other and to those who will follow us.

– Nelson Mandela, April 2001

Wednesday, 8 May 1996 was a momentous day for constitutionalism in the new South Africa. Senators and members of the National Assembly, elected in the country's first free polls two years before, came together to vote on the Constitution of the Republic of South Africa Bill. Of the four hundred and thirty-five members present, four hundred and twenty-one voted to adopt the Bill. Two opposed it and twelve abstained. The senators had to vote separately on the clauses of the Bill relating to the boundaries, powers and functions of the provinces. Of the eighty-three present, eighty voted to pass the Bill. No one voted against it and there were three abstentions.

But although the Bill had been approved by such an overwhelming majority this was not enough. The Constitutional Court still had to certify that the text complied with the thirty-four constitutional principles that had been agreed during the constitutional negotiations and that were now annexed in a schedule to the interim constitution. If the text did not comply it would be sent back to the Constitutional Assembly for revision before this draft could be submitted once more. The procedure was not simply unusual, it was unique. It had been designed to pacify the minority parties which feared that previously disenfranchised voters might treat them as the oppressed had been treated for almost four centuries.

The application for the court's approval was brought in the name of the Constitutional Assembly and a large team of advocates was to argue the case for certification on behalf of the assembly. Wim Trengove SC, Marumo Moerane SC, Nono Goso and Khomotso Moroka all appeared with me as part of this team. Five of the individual political parties that had participated in the assembly were represented by counsel as they wanted to oppose certification for various reasons. Some of the problems they raised concerning the Bill had been considered during the drafting process and in debate, but they were dissatisfied because their views had not been incorporated into the text. They hoped the certification process would provide another opportunity for their views to be heard, accepted and incorporated into the final text.

Many others, however, had applied to be heard on the question of certification even though they had not been part of the assembly. Those wanting to comment on the draft constitution formed such a broad cross-section of society that it seemed the judges were being asked to hear the 'people's voices' directly, as well as through their elected representatives via the Constitutional Assembly's draft text.

Among those who asked for audience were the South African Police, the senior attorney-general, representatives of traditional leaders, employers' associations and trade unions, campaigners in favour of reinstating the death penalty, those who favoured the prohibition of abortion and those who defended new legislation that permitted legal abortion. Those who opposed the incorporation of socio-economic rights wanted an audience. So did magistrates who were concerned that their judicial status was not acknowledged in the draft constitution. And several NGOs concerned with the protection of human rights and a number of individuals with special interests also wanted to be heard.

There were those who wanted provisions analogous to a provincial right to secede and who opposed the unitary nature of the state. These objectors wanted some form of confederation. They complained that the provincial powers were unduly limited and that the provisions in relation to the functioning of local government were insufficient. Arthur Chaskalson, the president of the Constitutional Court, announced that all the letters and memoranda that had been sent to the court had been considered even though not all those who wrote them had been invited to make oral submissions to the court.

Sitting behind us in court were Cyril Ramaphosa, leader of the Constitutional Assembly, and Fink Haysom, President Mandela's chief law advisor. They needed to be there for a number of reasons. If the court refused certification, they had to understand the reasons so that they could work with us in advising the Constitutional Assembly as to the necessary changes.

Every seat in court was taken by leaders of political parties, ministers, MPs, and community and religious leaders. For those who could not find a place the proceedings were televised on a large screen in the lobby. Usually, the oral argument is not recorded in our apex courts, but on this occasion video tapes were made, although they were not made available. Fortunately Carmel Rickard, then legal editor of *The Sunday Times*, made detailed notes throughout the two weeks of the hearing, recording the issues, the argument, and the atmosphere. These subsequently became the basis of her LLM thesis which analyses and provides a useful record of the entire process of certification, a politico-legal strategy unique in world history. Historians, political scientists and lawyers will no doubt find her work on this question as useful as I have done, particularly in writing this chapter. There is also an authoritative account by Hassen Ebrahim, *The Soul of a Nation: Constitution Making in South Africa*.

When I was at university the subjects I found most interesting were history and political theory and government. I avidly read biographies of political leaders, particularly those who tried to bring about fundamental change within their own countries and beyond. During the apartheid years, little of this knowledge proved useful. But now the time had come to make something of it.

The five of us in our team compared the constitutional principles with the text produced by the Constitutional Assembly and drafted more than two hundred and fifty pages of argument and schedules that we hoped would show conclusively that the proposed constitution complied with the principles. We filed copies of our argument with the court almost a month before the hearing. From the submissions made by other parties we knew that once the oral argument began we would have a lot of work to do.

Among those whose submissions we would have to counter were groups that had voted to adopt the constitutional draft when it was considered in Parliament, but who now claimed that it did not satisfy the constitutional principles. I believe that one of the many areas in which we were successful was this: we persuaded the judges that the court could not be used as a forum for interest groups to lobby for amendments to the text on issues where the text already complied with the principles.

There was, of course, an inherent problem in the whole notion of an unelected court being required to certify a draft constitution that was plainly the will of the majority of the democratically elected representatives of the majority of the people. But there were many other problems as well. Suppose a constitutional principle were capable of being complied with in more than one way? And suppose that the requisite majority in the Constitutional Assembly chose a way of complying which was then reflected in the draft? What would the court's attitude be to parties arguing that another interpretation, another way of complying, ought to be preferred?

Surely the Constitutional Assembly's decision about how to satisfy that particular constitutional principle should be accepted by the objectors instead of the other, minority, interpretation that they wanted to prevail and surely, too, the Constitutional Assembly's interpretation should be respected by the court as the will of the people? We submitted that the Constitutional Assembly should be given generous latitude.

Argument was often lively:

JUSTICE CHASKALSON: What troubles me is understanding how we are to approach inherently political questions.

BIZOS: Leave it to the politicians.

JUSTICE MAHOMED: I am not sure. There may be one man opposed to it. But he may be right.

Justice Mahomed, not one to keep out of an argument, usually had the last word, adding: 'The constitutional principles are the lights of the runway within which you operate the plane. You can choose the speed and the angle but it must be between its lights.'

The court was anxious to hear argument about when it was entitled to substitute its opinion for that of the will of Parliament. Could it afford to be accused of having elevated itself into a *dikastocracy*, rule by judges, in conflict with a democratically elected Parliament, its president and ministers?

I was used as a sounding board, particularly by justices Chaskalson, Ackermann, Kriegler and Goldstone, concerning what should happen where a provision was capable of more than one meaning, one which complied with the principles and one that didn't. We submitted that if the provision was capable of an interpretation that would comply, the court should spell this out, and then certify the constitution. This did not satisfy Justice Didcott or Justice Kriegler.

What if, in the near or distant future, a differently constituted Constitutional Court thought otherwise? Could a future court go back to the principles and reinterpret them? And if a future court were to do so, what would happen if the draft, now become law, was found not to comply?

Justice Goldstone was of the view that a future Constitutional Court, '... sitting in ten or three hundred years' time, would have to refer to the constitutional principles. They do not disappear. They would be a primary source of interpretation.' My response was that, 'Even in a deep freeze they would be there forever.'

Justice Kriegler was then concerned about how the 'solemn pact' reached between the previously hostile parties could be honoured and maintained if changes were made to the interpretation of the principles and if the text were changed. To which Justice Chaskalson added a complexity. 'It is more difficult when you have multiple choices. Could we say that as long as the constitution stands, all future matters must be construed in the light of the constitutional principles?' It seemed the justices were anxious to debate the difficult problems they predicted the court was likely to face in establishing its jurisprudence for the future.

In relation to the plethora of written submissions made to the court we contended that many of them were of little assistance. They were mainly alternative ways in which the principles could be complied with. The country should not be kept waiting for its constitution. There was, however, a most important issue on which there was no consensus: the question of provincial powers.

FW de Klerk's National Party and Mangosuthu Buthelezi's Inkatha Freedom Party contended that the draft did not comply with the principles requiring meaningful provincial powers. One of the principles provided that, under the final constitution, provincial powers were not to be 'substantially less than, or substantially inferior to' their powers in the interim constitution. The two opposition parties had in fact demanded a federal state but this was rejected during the negotiations. Then they insisted that at least there should be provision for a strongly decentralised government. The ANC feared the secessionist tendencies of the IFP, which had won a majority in KwaZulu-Natal. It was also concerned about the establishment of a white, National Party-controlled enclave in the Western Cape. These were the two provinces out of the nine where the ANC did not get more than fifty per cent of the vote. The party did not want to lose the provinces altogether, by secession or other means.

Wim Trengove had the arduous task of trying to convince the court that the provincial powers provided in the draft constitution satisfied the constitutional principles. I was happy to leave this to him. Although some of the provincial powers granted in the interim constitution had been taken away, others had been given and we believed the package of powers was not substantially less than or substantially inferior to that in the interim constitution.

Wim was the director of the Constitutional Litigation Unit of the Legal Resources Centre. Despite his comparative youth he was considered one of the top litigators at the Bar, a worthy successor of Isie Maisels, Sydney Kentridge and Arthur Chaskalson. Like Arthur, Wim used his skills to ensure the law was an instrument of justice.

Under the new political dispensation he used the law to promote the development of a fully democratic society based on the principle of substantive equality. Before the Constitutional Court on the highly contentious question of provincial powers he knew that his was the most important part of the argument. Yet when I stepped down from the podium, he quipped that I had left him to check the laundry list! This referred to the lengthy process he was about to begin, of comparing the provincial powers in the draft text and those powers granted under the interim constitution, against the framework required by the constitutional principles.

He submitted that it was permissible for the provincial powers to be different from those set out in the interim constitution but that they were not to be substantially less. The powers should not be looked at individually but as two separate baskets. As he dealt with the details, Justice Kriegler made one of his Delphic admonitions: 'Look not at the trimmings, but at the substance.'

At the end of the first day we met with Cyril Ramaphosa and his legal advisors. It was apparent that the justices were anxious to be seen as independent of any political influence and would give serious consideration to the arguments of opposition parties who claimed that provincial powers had been diminished.

The opposition parties argued that greater legislative and executive powers were needed for the provinces. They relied on the constitutional principles, emphasising that provincial powers were to be conducive to financial viability and effective public administration, but they ignored the requirement that there should be national unity and *legitimate autonomy*. The powers of the provinces had been deliberately limited to avoid the possibility that one or other of the provinces might seek a level of autonomy bordering on independence.

What could lie ahead by way of demand for autonomy was illustrated by the hurriedly constructed provincial constitution for KwaZulu-Natal adopted by the IFP and submitted to the Constitutional Court. This showed no regard for consistency with the provisions of the interim constitution and the constitutional principles. It claimed the widest possible powers in relation to the security services, the administration of justice and the establishment of its own constitutional court. It was intent on providing for a Zulu kingdom within a republican democratic state.

There was little doubt that the IFP wanted more than the *legitimate autonomy* to which the province was entitled in terms of the constitutional principles. It was also doubtful whether the majority of its citizens, who lived in one of the poorest of the nine provinces, would want to forfeit their fair share of South Africa's wealth.

Similar demands for greater levels of autonomy were made by small conservative white Afrikaner groups. They produced maps showing various pockets of land where they wanted to establish enclaves that would form a discontinuous, fragmented, white Afrikaner homeland. The very idea of a 'homeland' – for any group – was reminiscent of apartheid structures and completely contrary to the policy of the ANC. Limitations on provincial powers were intended to put an end to such plans.

The national unity versus federalism debate was one that greatly interested me. Once, shortly before there was to be a referendum in Quebec on the possible independence of that Canadian province, I was asked to address the Canadian Bar Association at their annual general meeting in Winnipeg. I believe that the invitation came as a result of a discussion I had had with former Prime Minister Pierre Trudeau at a luncheon given in his honour by the University of the Witwatersrand. When he pertinently asked, 'In whom will sovereignty vest in your country?' I glibly repeated the liberation movement's slogan: 'The people shall govern in a united South Africa.'

He was well pleased with the answer and advised that we try to avoid Canada's age-old problem between Anglophone and Francophone and the possible secession and independence of Quebec. 'Do not be seduced by the alleged advantages of a federal system, for it could encourage secessionist tendencies', he said. Influenced by Trudeau's view I deliberately avoided any reference to Quebec's impending referendum, but I emphasised the reasons why we wanted a strong central government and limited provincial powers.

The Canadian lawyers were divided. The Anglophone majority applauded but most of the Francophones were not so happy. I was told that the Canadian Broadcasting Corporation aired my speech more than once.

During the certification hearing it became increasingly apparent from the judges' questions that they had serious doubts whether sufficient powers had been given to the provinces. They were beginning to ask questions about what might happen if they did not certify the constitutional text. The ANC was short of a two-thirds majority in Parliament and it would require some support from the opposition benches to amend any clauses that the court found objectionable. What if the opposition parties decided that they would not support a new draft? Would that be the end of the 'solemn pact'? Would new elections have to be held? Would negotiations have to start from the beginning again?

In the interests of stability and finality we hoped this would not happen. We advised Ramaphosa and his team of our growing suspicion that we might not succeed this time round, but they seemed less worried than we were about the consequences of a rejection. We wondered whether the justices would accept the submission of Jan Heunis of the National Party who said that 'the constitutional principles were designed to enhance political autonomy and thus ensure the participation of interested groups which value political autonomy', or whether the court would endorse our view that 'the other parties to the solemn pact entered into it with a somewhat different perspective.'

Among the provisions to which the federalists objected strongly was one that gave the national commissioner of police power to appoint provincial police commissioners. We countered that power to appoint a provincial head of police was not a legitimate power for a province since national safety and security could be jeopardised by a poor choice. We said, 'There is within the principles an area which is a matter for political judgment by the majority. It is not a function of the court to decide fundamental questions such as how national unity should be brought about.' And added, 'A substantial part of the negotiating parties insisted on a unitary state: it was part of the pact which they entered. The majority of the people of South Africa did not abdicate the right of sovereignty through their elected representatives. This is why, poignant as the call [by Heunis] is, for the minority to have their rights respected, we must remember that after all, the majority also have rights.'

When outsiders hear that our constitution provides for eleven official languages they raise an eyebrow. White-ruled South Africa recognised only two official languages, English and Afrikaans. The other nine indigenous languages, Sepedi, Sesotho, Setswana, siSwati, Tshivenda, Xitsonga, isiNdebele, isiXhosa and isiZulu were considered less important, were taught at black schools at an elementary level and to a limited extent at the tertiary level. We were urged to follow the example of some erstwhile multilingual British colonies and adopt English as the only official language.

Even the Afrikaners conceded that English was South Africa's lingua franca but they insisted that Afrikaans remain an official language. There was some statistical justification for the claim, particularly as Afrikaans is spoken by about eight million South Africans and is a first language for many of them. Also Afrikaans is a developed language with a rich literary tradition. At least four leading universities offer it not only as a language in itself, but also as a medium of instruction in the arts, law, medicine and the sciences.

Many of those who wanted Afrikaans to remain an official language maintained that the indigenous languages were much less developed – without admitting that these languages had been neglected, and in some cases suppressed, for over three centuries. There was consensus among the negotiators that if Afrikaans were to be an official language then so should the other nine, so that the spoken languages of the people of South Africa could be developed. To facilitate the implementation, provinces could promote at least two out of the eleven within their boundaries.

The draft constitution provided for the creation of a Pan-South African Language Board. It had to ensure the conditions necessary for the development and use of the official languages as well as the Khoi, Nama and San languages and sign language. In addition, the board had to 'promote and ensure respect for' all languages commonly used by communities in South Africa including German, Greek, Gujarati, Hindi, Portuguese, Tamil, Telugu and Urdu. Arabic, Hebrew, Sanskrit and other languages used for religious purposes were to be similarly regarded.

Many South Africans of Indian origin had been prominent in the freedom struggle. Some were intimately involved in drafting the interim constitution. Others were cabinet ministers and members of the Constitutional Assembly. None of them suggested that any of the Indian languages should be accorded a higher status by being made an official language. This idea and its propagation were left to Beema Naidoo, a retired former headmaster who had formed the Concerned South African Indians to lobby on a matter about which they felt so strongly.

His organisation collected many signatures asking for the Indian languages to be included as official languages, pointing out that the Indian people and their languages had also been victims of white supremacy. We wondered why his group was not represented by counsel. Surely one of our colleagues would have appeared for his organisation, even without a fee. Anyone wanting to argue in favour of Beema Naidoo's position could start by mentioning Mahatma Gandhi, the lawyer who had pioneered the struggle for freedom and equality almost a hundred years earlier.

But Beema Naidoo did better than any lawyer could have done. He handed in a letter on a single sheet written by a child in a script unknown to us, appealing to the court to make it possible for him to speak, read and write the language of his ancestors. Beema Naidoo asked that there should be no discrimination against his community and their languages. His argument was patiently received by the court and his presence symbolised the right of everyone with a just cause to appear before that august body of eleven judges. Justice Sachs was quick to assure him that there was surely no intention to discriminate against anyone, but that the exclusion of the Indian languages could be explained on the basis that there would have been just too many if they were added.

We for our part, defending the text as it stood, attempted to justify the differentiation between the various languages on the basis that reasonable limitations to the equality clause were sometimes necessary. It was not possible for the State to cater for all the needs and aspirations of every community, we said. Language groups had the right to association, and community structures supported by their members would have to cater for any special needs. This was always provided that they did not exclude those outside the group on grounds such as race, which were not permitted by the constitution.

With a faint smile Justice Mahomed asked me why Tamil, the oldest language in the world, should be in a lower category. Through his phrasing of this question he was reminding me of our discussions which had continued over many years, in which he chided me because he contended that Greeks wrongly claimed the distinction of having the oldest language. We submitted that, sympathetic as the court might be to the objections of Beema Naidoo and his supporters, this was no reason to refuse to certify the constitution.

Another issue concerned African kings and queens whose standing had been demoted to that of mere 'paramount chiefs' by those who conquered them. To their subjects they continued to be known as *Inkosi* and *Inkosikazi*. The colonisers diminished their powers, and those powers left them were in the main subject to the approval of commissioners, high commissioners or ministers of native affairs. The traditional leaders and at least some of their subjects wanted their status and dignity restored, and their powers and privileges defined in the new constitution.

The Congress of Traditional Leaders of South Africa (Contralesa) represented the interests of this leadership and two of its senior members, *Inkosi* Mwelo Nonkonyana and *Inkosi* Sango Patekile Holomisa were also lawyers. I met the urbane *Inkosi* Holomisa at various regional conferences called to introduce and debate the constitution.

He had to face a barrage of questions at these meetings, particularly from women who did not accept Contralesa's proposals. The traditional leaders wanted provision to be made in the bill of rights or elsewhere in the constitution, entrenching the patriarchal practices of customary law.

On the day they were to argue their position at the certification hearing, the two Contralesa members came to court in snappy suits, well-polished shoes and fashionable ties. But during lunch they changed into traditional ceremonial attire, in animal skins and barefoot. When they stood to address the court they made it clear that they were not doing so as advocates, but as traditional leaders.

In days gone by this would have been regarded as a contempt of court, but nobody raised any objection. *Inkosi* Holomisa quipped that as this was not his court he did not expect the judges to stand up and salute him. We later learned that they had first discussed the matter with the president of the court, Arthur

Chaskalson, and asked whether they could appear dressed in this way if they did not address the court in their capacity as counsel.

They complained that although there was a chapter in the constitution headed 'Recognition of Traditional Authorities and Indigenous Law', there was little in it that would enable them to participate in government. At best there was the Provincial House of Traditional Leaders, which in their view was nothing more than an advisory body.

They conceded that everyone was entitled to the protection of the bill of rights and the constitution, but they argued that the position of women could be protected by the development of the common law. And, they submitted further, some of the provisions of customary law, if understood properly, were favourable to women. Two members of our team representing the Constitutional Assembly were Khomotso Moroka and Nono Goso. As women they did not agree with this view; nor did the vast majority of the women in the country.

Difficult questions were put to members of our team towards the end of the week, which did not augur well for the position we were defending. The Judicial Service Commission had the task of appointing judges, but fifteen of its twenty-three members were politicians. Could politicians be trusted to appoint independent judges? the court asked. Furthermore, if the auditor-general, the public protector and the governor of the Reserve Bank could all be fired by a simple majority in the assembly, what confidence would the public have in their independence? Our arguments did not appear to find favour with the court.

During the hearing, the Congress of South African Trade Unions (Cosatu) defended the constitutional protection of strikes and the omission from the text of the right of employers to lockout. This right had been guaranteed in the interim constitution, but was removed from the draft text of the final constitution as a result of Cosatu's vehement protests. Not only was the Constitutional Assembly persuaded to omit the right, but it also proposed to immunise the Labour Relations Act against constitutional review, giving mere statutory legislation constitutional status.

Martin Brassey SC, arguing on behalf of Cosatu that management's 'right to lockout' should be scrapped, explained the history of black worker disempowerment as slaves or as victims of job reservation. Business South Africa was sufficiently sensitive not to use the phrase 'right to lockout' and instead spoke of management's right to exercise economic power in pursuit of collective bargaining. They claimed a constitutional protection equal to that of their employees so that they could counter aggressive behaviour by workers.

Chris Loxton SC, for Business South Africa, claimed that if Cosatu's argument prevailed it would establish a special constitutional shield for the labour law. From the questions asked by the judges it appeared that they might accept a text that granted the workers the right to strike while withholding employers' right to lockout. They would not, however, be prepared to grant Cosatu's request for constitutional protection for the Labour Relations Act. The justices indicated that they believed there could be only one supreme law – the constitution.

The judges also preferred higher majorities in Parliament before amendments to certain parts of the constitution could be made. In particular they were concerned about whether the bill of rights would be sufficiently protected if it could be amended by a two-thirds majority. Should the majority required not be higher? During the course of this debate, justices Mahomed and Sachs questioned whether 'the basic structure of the constitution could be changed by an amendment'. Justice Mahomed emphasised that there was a difference between an 'amendment' – even if all the formalities were properly observed – and 'tearing up the constitution', something which could not be done by any majority.

Wim Trengove also got involved in a lively debate with the judges as to the justiciability, the enforcement, of socioeconomic rights. Justice Sachs had been the chief proponent of the inclusion of socioeconomic rights during the drafting process of the interim constitution, but now, as a justice of the Constitutional Court, he wanted persuasion about this position. He debated the issue with Margie Victor, who represented the Legal Resources Centre, and who argued in support of justiciable socioeconomic rights. His main concern was 'that the court could end up usurping the role of the legislature. There are all kinds of choices which belong to the legislature and not to the court. When should it be Parliament that makes this choice and when should it be the courts? There is a danger that government in South Africa could become a 'dichostocracy' – rule by judges.

I reminded him that the correct word was *dikastocracy.*

The debate went on probing the desirability of the court dealing with matters traditionally viewed as better left to the legislature. What would happen if the legislature did not act in response to orders of court? What powers would the court have to direct democratically elected representatives to do what the court thought should be done? In other words, how could the court enforce the orders it made? In their debate, the justices anticipated many of the problems that they have had to deal with in the past ten years, particularly in relation to socioeconomic rights affecting housing and health.

On the eleventh and final day of the argument, the question of the sufficiency of provincial powers was argued once more. The searching questions asked by the judges again indicated they had some serious concerns about the draft. In particular they seemed worried that the powers of the provinces might well have been 'substantially less' than in the interim constitution. They also found unacceptable the elevation of the Labour Relations Act and the Promotion of National Unity and Reconciliation Act into effective subsections of the constitution.

During the drafting one of the issues concerned emergency powers. There was considerable discussion about this. Those who had been detained under emergency regulations in 1960s and in the 1980s and those of us who had so often and with so little success tried to have them released, felt strongly that there should be a complete bar on any undemocratic security powers.

On the other hand, the more pragmatic felt that were a future government to declare an emergency, the absence of any controls in the constitution might permit unbridled presidential or executive power. It would be better, they argued, to have safety nets to prevent such misuse. The safety nets would take the form of safeguards built into the bill of rights, limiting what could be done in the name of an emergency. There was substantial consensus that this view should prevail. A draft section with appropriate safeguards was hurriedly drawn, following which the Constitutional Assembly made a number of changes and then incorporated it into the text.

During certification only one objection was filed to this section of the draft, and it appeared of no particular importance. As no one was to appear to argue the objection we didn't give the matter much attention. I took responsibility for its confirmation – little knowing what I had let myself in for.

It was virtually the closing stages of the lengthy hearing and we were tired after almost two full weeks in court. But instead of ending with the quiet exchanges that characterise the closure of many cases and sometimes leave participants with a let-down feeling, this one was to end with a mighty bang. And at my expense. The last scene has been recorded by Carmel Rickard in a chapter she contributed to *The Post-Apartheid Constitutions*:

> [p]erhaps the deepest irony of the entire [hearing] was that it was Bizos, with his untarnished reputation as a fighter against the injustice perpetrated by the previous government, who had to face the ire of the judges over the emergency provisions proposed in the new constitutional text'

There I stood, arguing a position that was the opposite of my instincts. At one point I referred to the oppressive emergency legislation of the apartheid state and mentioned that several safeguards in the draft were designed to prevent a repetition of the past. She continued:

Bizos: 'The constitution lays down a simple majority by Parliament for the first declaration of emergency and sixty per cent majority for any extension. There is nothing wrong with sixty per cent' ...

Then Justice Kriegler set the cat among the pigeons with some criticism of the proposed table of rights which could not be affected (derogated) during an emergency. His main concern was with the rights left off the list and he gave some examples: 'Section 37, read with the table of non-derogable rights, makes it possible to impose higher penalties for an offence [than would have obtained at the time an offence was committed]. This is because one of the rights which can be derogated is s 35(3)(n). And s 35(5) can be scrubbed during an emergency: you can have an unfair trial. Everyone gives [the right to a fair trial] a standing ovation when it is passed, and then it becomes derogable in an emergency.'

Justice Didcott: Apparently forced labour is also permissible during an emergency.

Justice Mahomed: How can you ever permit, even during an emergency, an unfair trial? If it is unfair – tough luck. I think we had enough of that during the apartheid years.

Bizos: There might be circumstances that arise during an emergency that require great urgency.

Justice Mahomed: And allow an unfair trial?

Bizos: Let us take a more benign example. Suppose during an emergency a police officer has broken down a door without a warrant and seizes a cache of arms. Why shouldn't this be admissible?

Justice Mahomed: If the particular evidence would ordinarily have made a trial unfair, in an emergency – tough luck. Why?

Bizos: The difficulties of emergency situations ...

Justice Didcott: Even if it relates to an unfair trial for an offence committed when there was no emergency? [Justice] Mahomed is pointing out that s 35(5) does not necessarily apply only during an emergency – the trial could be related to an offence committed six months before the emergency was declared.

Bizos: A court has wide discretion to exclude evidence.

Justice Mahomed: But there is no *right*. The answer is – tough luck.

Bizos: If a door is broken down and a cache of arms found, the person should not be able to say, 'This evidence cannot be used against me because I acquired the cache before the state of emergency was declared.' One must, however great the dislike of any person may be to a state of emergency, agree that – I do not want to utter the words of [former President] PW Botha – it may be necessary effectively to restore law and order.

Justice Mahomed and Didcott in chorus: I do not understand why we need unfair trials.

Justice Didcott: I cannot see any reason why it should be there in a state of emergency. It creates a minefield of uncertainty.

Bizos: In an appropriate case, evidence will be excluded.

Justice Mahomed: Naturally if they knock the hell out of me at the police station and get a confession it would be inadmissible. But now they can do it because it is an emergency. We had it so often under apartheid; so many abuses. We must be particularly careful.

Bizos: Torture is not allowed …

Justice Mahomed: But you can get inadmissible evidence.

Judge Kriegler, coming at last to the rescue of Bizos, invited him to put in a note on the issue. Having agreed to do so, Bizos went on to suggest that some of the arguments heard during the day 'should be ignored'. In an obvious reference to the IFP submissions he added, 'Your function is not to give a party that chose not to take part in the formation of the text another opportunity, or to give them an invitation to participate.'

Then he closed with a reference to the image with which the case had begun. 'This is the end – or it ought to be – of a long and difficult process. There is a grave responsibility on this court to see whether the front wheel of the plane is dead centre or whether, on landing, the fringes of the wings have gone over the limits.'

Next day the posters of a leading Johannesburg newspaper read: 'Bizos clashes with judges.' Some of my friends wanted to know how I felt about it. Part of the job, I said.

As we had begun to suspect, we lost the first round. Despite the enormous amount of work involved in reaching its conclusion, judgment took just two months to be handed down. The justices followed a different approach to that in the death penalty case. There, each had written a separate judgment. In this case there was a lengthy single decision handed down in the name of 'The Court' to which all members of the court contributed. The headnote, summarising the court's findings on all the matters argued, was not left to the editors of the law reports to finalise, as is usually the case. Instead the court provided an official summary of its findings that ran to more than thirty pages, as well as an index to the findings.

We had known that the most challenging aspect was proving that the powers and functions of the provinces were not 'substantially less than or inferior to' the powers and functions accorded them in the interim constitution. There was also dissatisfaction with the majority requirements prescribed for amending certain sections of the bill of rights, the appointment and removal of the public protector, the auditor-general and the Public Service Commission. Certain provisions relating to local government were also found to be inadequate. And as my exchange with the judges had anticipated, the emergency provisions were criticised.

The court held that although the overwhelming majority of the clauses satisfied the constitutional principles, those nine that did not were of sufficient importance for the text to be sent back to the Constitutional Assembly. Although the court was careful not to dictate to the Constitutional Assembly, helpful guidance was provided on the thinking behind the adverse findings.

The Constitutional Assembly lost no time in producing a new draft. Again we were briefed for the certification process. This time it was a much easier task and although both the Democratic Party and the Inkatha Freedom Party, among others, objected to the new version the court was not persuaded to refuse certification a second time.

In deciding to adopt the entirely novel system of having the Constitutional Court 'certify' the Constitutional Assembly's draft text as a way of allaying the fears of the minority parties, South Africa's negotiators had taken a significant risk. For example, if the court rejected the text there was a risk that the public might not accept its ruling. In turn this might seriously harm the court which had quickly proved itself a crucial element in the new dispensation.

We had now come to the end of the process, how had it worked? During the first certification hearing, Justice Mahomed employed an aviation metaphor which I thought fitting. More than that, I extended it by contending that the plane was on a test flight operating on new instruments, in a manoeuvre never before attempted. Although the pilots had failed the first attempted landing, the second attempt came down successfully within the lights of the runway. It had been a bumpy ride and the court probably didn't want to go through such an experience again, but for the negotiators the risk had paid off.

CHAPTER 43

Zimbabwe's Treason Trial

The reason for the rule requiring two witnesses to prove treason is plain enough. As the eighteenth-century jurist Sir William Blackstone explained, it is to 'secure the subject from being sacrificed to fictitious conspiracies which have been the engines of profligate and crafty politicians in all ages'.

'Profligate' has a number of meanings but surely 'shamelessly vicious' would most appositely describe the conduct of President Robert Mugabe of Zimbabwe along with his government and security services in the charges brought against the leader of the opposition, Morgan Tsvangirai, in 2003.

During the freedom struggle against Ian Smith's illegitimate Rhodesian government, Robert Gabriel Mugabe emerged as its leader. On the eve of Zimbabwe's independence in 1980, Mugabe, then the prime minister-elect, was widely acclaimed as one of the great sons of Africa. In a speech that won him even more support as a statesman he said,

> If yesterday I fought you as an enemy, today you have become a friend and an ally with the same national interest, loyalty, rights and duties as myself ... The wrongs of the past must now stand forgiven and forgotten. If we ever look to the past, let us do so for the lesson the past has taught us, namely that oppression and racism are inequalities that must never find scope in our political and social system. It could never be a correct justification that because the whites oppressed us yesterday when they had power, the blacks must oppress them today because they have power. An evil remains an evil, whether practised by white against black or black against white.

At that time Morgan Richard Tsvangirai was twenty-five years old. He regarded Mugabe as his hero. He would even have laid down his life for his leader. Yet twenty years later he was the leader of an opposition party, the Movement for Democratic Change (MDC), and had fallen out with Mugabe so completely that he faced charges of treason and the death penalty.

Tsvangirai held a comparatively good job as a foreman at a nickel mine. He and his wife Susan were the proud parents of a year-old son, Edwin. Morgan was active in the Mine Workers' Union and tried to help improve the lives of his fellow workers. But Mugabe did not want an independent trade union movement, nor did he want active non-governmental organisations advocating constitutional reform, or a free press.

By the end of the second decade of his rule, the president was no longer universally regarded as an angel. Serious allegations had emerged against him concerning violent suppression of the Matabele people, thousands of whom lost their lives in the early 1980s. Corruption was rampant and the economy in decline. In September 1999, the opposition forces came together to form the MDC and Tsvangirai was elected its president. The MDC announced that it would contest the parliamentary elections called for 2000.

To ensure he would stay in power Mugabe, now executive president, had established a constitutional commission, answerable to him alone. It was to draft constitutional amendments, one of which would allow Mugabe to serve two further terms as president. Afterwards other presidents would be limited to two terms. To sweeten this pill another amendment was proposed that would allow for the expropriation of land without due process or compensation. A referendum was to be held before the election of 2000 to test the popular response to these changes. Mugabe was certain that no loyal Zimbabwean would reject his proposals.

But the president misread the mood of the people and underestimated the efficiency of the MDC under Tsvangirai's leadership. He lost the referendum. MDC supporters, who had gained a comfortable majority in the referendum, now believed that they could win the parliamentary elections to be held nine months later.

Mugabe's Zanu-PF Party had won the 1990 and 1995 elections with overwhelming majorities, but the setback in the referendum was considerable and the MPS and high-ranking supporters of the party were afraid of worse to come. They worried that they would lose their seats. To avoid this prospect some Zanu-PF leaders quietly proposed that Mugabe resign at the forthcoming party congress and that another leader take over. This Mugabe was not prepared to do. Although he ostensibly accepted the result of the referendum, he now embarked on a campaign that indicated that this was far from the truth.

He began a strategy of demonising white Zimbabwean farmers and the MDC along with them. The upstart political party would lead Zimbabwe back to its colonial past, he said. Mugabe formed an alliance with the disaffected veterans of the liberation movement, particularly those who had been excluded from benefits and perks after independence. One method he used to win over these ex-soldiers was to pay them with money provided by the International Monetary Fund and the World Bank, something that the lending organisations, not surprisingly, found unacceptable. Then the veterans were told to seize and occupy white-owned farms.

For their part, the police had instructions to acquiesce; they should not accept any complaints nor protect the white farmers. When orders of court were obtained against the leaders of these lawless groups or against the commissioner of police for not taking any action, they were simply ignored.

Reports of violence and intimidation grew. Of particular interest to judges and lawyers throughout the world were accounts of attacks on Chief Justice Anthony Gubbay and other judges of the Supreme and High Courts. These attacks came from the minister of justice, the minister of land and agriculture, the minister of information and one Joseph Chinotimba. Chinotimba was the leader of a group that invaded the Supreme Court and threatened that if Chief Justice Gubbay did not vacate his office then the war veterans would declare war on him.

The Human Rights Institute of the International Bar Association (IBA) asked Lord Goldsmith QC, a former chairman of the Bar Council of England and Wales, the co-chairman of the IBA's Human Rights Institute and later the Lord Chancellor of the United Kingdom, to put together a group of experienced judges and lawyers from around the world to visit Zimbabwe. The delegation consisted of Justice AM Ahmadi, a former chief justice of India, Chief Justice Sir Dennis Byron of the Eastern Caribbean Supreme Court, Judge André Davis, a federal district judge of Maryland in the USA, Ezer Hosea Tala Angula, a leading attorney in Namibia, and Ashwin Trikamjee, a former president of the Association of Law Societies of South Africa. I was invited to join the group.

During March 2001 we spent six days in Zimbabwe. We met with practically every judge of the High Courts of Bulawayo and Harare as well as the judges of the Supreme Court of Zimbabwe, all but two of whom had been appointed by President Mugabe himself. We saw the attorney-general and his assistant and the leaders of the legal profession. Not without difficulty we even managed a meeting with the minister of justice and President Mugabe, though it took an appeal from our group to the South African minister of justice, Penuell Maduna, to assist us.

The minister and the president emphatically denied that they were party to any threat against judges. They also shrugged off allegations that they incited the veterans to commit unlawful acts. In their view, the Western powers were to blame for the problems Zimbabwe was facing and they kept us for several hours as they expanded on this claim. President Mugabe, in particular, seemed not to differentiate between the rule of law and rule by law. He told us that everything done in Zimbabwe was carried out in terms of a law or would be validated by a law to be passed in the future.

Outside the president's conference room we found Minister of Information Jonathan Moyo waiting for us with cameras and journalists from the State television station. The minister then interrogated us in a loud voice about why his office had not been informed of our visit. How could we reach any conclusions about Zimbabwe without spending time in the countryside? We had to gauge the problems in relation to the restitution of land and to question ordinary people about it. We assured him that we well knew the nature and extent of the land question in Zimbabwe. However, our primary purpose was to report on the rule of law and the extent to which it was compromised by improper conduct towards the judges, and then to make recommendations for their protection.

We received many assurances during our visit: from the attorney-general to the effect that there would not be selective prosecutions; from the minister of justice that there would be no threats against judges; and then from the president that he was not about to increase the number of the judges on the Supreme Court bench in order to pack that court with compliant judges. None of these undertakings was honoured.

We made a number of recommendations as to what steps ought to be taken to restore the rule of law. More particularly, we recommended the execution of court orders. Everything we said was ignored, and an amendment passed during 2005 ousted the jurisdiction of the courts in relation to land restitution. At the end of our meeting with the president he invited us to return to Zimbabwe with our families to enjoy the country's national resources and hospitality, an invitation which none of us accepted.

Almost eighteen months later I did return to Harare, but it was hardly for a holiday – I had been requested to defend Tsvangirai and two other top MDC leaders. They were charged with treason and faced the death penalty.

Mugabe's party won the March 2000 parliamentary election, but the MDC had made inroads, despite the government's tactics. In all, fifty-seven of the hundred and twenty elective seats went to the MDC. The election's validity was contested on the grounds that the polls were neither free nor fair and a number of election petitions were filed. If these challenges were allowed by the courts, then the future of Zanu-PF and of President Mugabe himself looked precarious. A presidential election was scheduled for March 2002 with Mugabe and Tsvangirai as the candidates. The MDC was confident that if the election was free and fair Tsvangirai would become president.

But the same thing happened in that election. According to claims by Tsvangirai, the MDC, the legal community in Zimbabwe and a substantial section of the international community, neither the poll itself nor the re-election of Robert

Mugabe was fair, let alone free. Tsvangirai filed an election petition on 12 April 2002 contesting the outcome.

By December 2006, the courts of Zimbabwe had still not determined this challenge to the legitimacy of Mugabe's election – even though he had served most of his term of office. In those cases where the MDC succeeded in contesting the results of individual seats, the Zanu-PF candidates whose election was set aside, simply noted an appeal. This effectively suspended the order that a by-election be held. In the end these candidates served their full term without the appeals being heard. Much of the blame for this serious failure of justice must be borne by Judge President Pennington Garwe and the new Chief Justice Godfrey Chidyausiku, who were apparently unconcerned about these unprecedented delays.

All this I gathered from the media and my new friends in Zimbabwe. Then suddenly it all became far more real when a letter from the offices of the attorneys Atherstone and Cooke reached me at our holiday home in Greece during mid-August 2002. The letter, written by Innocent Chagonda, asked whether I would accept a brief in a treason trial. The accused were the MDC president, Morgan Tsvangirai, its general secretary, Welshman Ncube, and the shadow minister of agriculture, Renson Gasela.

It was alleged that they had planned to assassinate President Mugabe and stage a military coup. I was told that already advocates Chris Anderson SC and Eric Matinenga had been briefed but they and their clients had decided that, in view of my seniority and experience, I should be asked to lead them. They did not expect any difficulty in obtaining the necessary permission from the Zimbabwean minister of justice.

There were other factors I needed to take into consideration before accepting the case. The request came at a time when my family was urging me to take it easy. I would also need leave of absence from the Legal Resources Centre if I were to take on the case in my private capacity. However, both the LRC's national director, Bongani Majola, and the executive committee of the organisation thought that the case was germane to the LRC's mission of promoting and defending human rights in the region. Arethe, our sons and their wives were always supportive of whatever work I was doing, they merely advised that I should be careful. They did not say that I should refuse the brief. When Innocent Chagonda announced in Harare that I had accepted the brief, there was general approval of my decision among colleagues, judges, politicians and journalists in South Africa and elsewhere.

The allegations in the indictment read like a particularly poor movie script. According to the State, the three accused met Ari Ben-Menashe of the company Dickens & Madson at Heathrow Airport outside London on 22 October 2001 and requested that he organise the assassination of President Mugabe. They also wanted him to arrange a military coup. The next day, Ncube faxed Dickens & Madson a 'memorandum of understanding' which was a cover for the unlawful plot to overthrow the government. During the following month Tsvangirai met with Ben-Menashe at the Royal Automobile Club in London and made the same request. The MDC agent in London then sent US$97 400 as an initial deposit against the previously promised fee for the assassination and coup. Tsvangirai again repeated his request to Ben-Menashe in December.

In the further particulars and the summary of the State's case, to which statements were annexed, it appeared that the prosecution's case would be based on the evidence of Ben-Menashe, Tara Thomas, his personal assistant, an audiotape secretly made by Thomas at the request of Ben-Menashe and a videotape made at the third meeting. Our clients denied that any such illegal request was made by any of them at any of the meetings. They said that they had been persuaded by Ben-Menashe and his co-director, one Rupert Johnson, that Dickens & Madson could collect millions of US dollars for the MDC. They believed that the contract signed on MDC's behalf by Ncube, and by Johnson on behalf of Dickens & Madson, was a genuine agreement to secure this assistance for the party and its work.

South Africa's common law was transplanted into Rhodesia. Similarly our Criminal Procedure and Evidence Act was copied by Rhodesia, and with minor differences it continues to be applicable in Zimbabwe. Before going to Harare I found a transcript of the argument advanced by HC 'Nick' Nicholas before the criminal court in the late 1950s on the meaning of treason and how it ought to be proved. Nicholas was later to become a High Court judge and thereafter a judge in the Appellate Division. I recall discussing his argument on the treason issue with Sydney Kentridge. He believed the argument was the best he had ever heard in any court.

At the time Nicholas argued the issue, the 'two witness' rule was the law of South Africa, but Parliament quietly amended the Criminal Procedure Act by providing that one witness was sufficient to convict any person on any charge. Shortly after my arrival in Harare, while we were having lunch in a public dining room, my colleagues told me that neither Rhodesia nor Zimbabwe had followed suit and so the 'two witness' rule still applied. As we were concerned that the rooms in which we were to consult might be bugged, we agreed not to discuss the matter any further in the hope that we could take the prosecution by surprise when we raised the point.

My colleagues and clients had already put together a bundle of articles published in reputable newspapers and magazines asserting that Ben-Menashe was a fraudulent operator holding himself out as a friend of many heads of state. Some of these leaders had paid deposits to him against promises that he failed to deliver. He held himself out as a former Mossad agent from Israel, a well-connected arms dealer, a commodity merchant and an influence peddler, all of which our clients had naively believed was true.

A copy of the videotape and a transcript of the dialogue were handed over to the defence. I was assured by my colleagues that nowhere on the tapes did Tsvangirai make any of the requests alleged by the State. On the contrary, bad as the video was, it contained enough to corroborate Tsvangirai's allegations. According to Tsvangirai, Ben-Menashe tried to trap him by suggesting that requests for help with assassinating Mugabe had been made at previous meetings. On the video Tsvangirai was seen and heard denying these suggestions and he walked out of the meeting when Ben-Menashe persisted in using the word 'elimination'. There was also more than sufficient evidence on the video that Tsvangirai attended the meeting to meet an 'American representative'. Ben-Menashe had suggested that Tsvangirai persuade this person (who turned out to be an impostor) to contribute money to the MDC. There was also evidence on the tape that, far from a coup, Tsvangirai's political strategy was via constitutional changes and an interim government. The army should be kept out of any political involvement, he maintained.

The audiotape made at the second meeting was handed over to Zimbabwe's Air Vice Marshal Robert Mhlanga with what was purported to be a transcript. It was not given to us because, so the prosecution said, it was inaudible and of no use. We nevertheless demanded both the tape and the transcript. We also wanted to know the precise relationship between Ben-Menashe and the Zimbabwean security services. More particularly, we asked how much money he had been paid by them to secure the audiotape and video for their purposes.

Towards the end of 2001, before charges were laid and before the accused knew anything about Ben-Menashe's secret audiotape and video, the film was handed to the Australian Broadcasting Corporation. Both the ABC and the Zimbabwe Broadcasting Corporation aired selected passages purporting to show that Tsvangirai had asked Ben-Menashe to kill Mugabe and arrange a coup. The MDC leaders denied the plot and sceptical journalists queried whether the grainy video supported the allegations.

Day after day, Zimbabwe's television showed Ben-Menashe backing Zanu-PF's election campaign – a campaign in which Mugabe and Tsvangirai were the only candidates. Ben-Menashe assured the viewers that the video was not his only evidence. He also had an audiotape of a second meeting, which fully corroborated his allegations about the MDC leaders. Impatiently and rudely he dismissed questions about his motives and his unsavoury past. He used intemperate language about the MDC leaders, accusing them of treachery and claiming that they wanted to return Zimbabwe to the British colonists. On the other hand, he, Ben-Menashe, was a real friend of the people of Zimbabwe, and it was for their benefit that he became involved in this matter.

Jury trials had long been abolished in Zimbabwe. Judge President Garwe was to preside in our trial along with two assessors. According to local lawyers, the assessors were men of substance and of sufficiently independent mind that, if they were convinced it was the correct thing to do, based on the facts, would outvote the judge and acquit the accused.

Officers of the department of national security were in charge at the main entrance of the court building slowly checking everyone who wanted to come into court and either turning them away or issuing written permits. Relatives, friends and supporters of the accused were denied access and I was only exempt from this time-consuming procedure after a few days of thorough scrutiny. I was politely greeted by the prosecution team, warmly greeted by the judge's registrar and glared at by the security officers. Before the first day's hearing began, counsel for the prosecution and the defence paid the usual courtesy call to the presiding officer's chambers, where Judge Garwe received us politely.

We continued to ask for the information we had requested, particularly the audiotape and transcript. The deputy attorney-general promised to let us have it as soon as possible. The first words in his opening address stated that this was 'a political trial', a statement of which we reminded him frequently.

Ben-Menashe was the first witness for the prosecution. It was not long before he began behaving as he had done on television – as a propagandist for Zanu-PF. He did not answer questions but made speeches. He did not address the judge but rather the gallery and he used insulting language when he referred to the accused. I objected to his behaviour and to what he said. The judge politely asked him to behave properly, but to no avail.

When he repeated one of his most objectionable utterances I rose to say that the witness was clowning and requested that the judge deal with him. Again he was asked to refrain and he agreed to do so, but not for long. He resented being called a clown, even more so when the cartoonist of a leading opposition newspaper depicted him in clown's attire. During cross-examination he lost no opportunity of making personal attacks on me, some of which amounted to contempt of court. I repeatedly appealed to the judge whose requests to Ben-Menashe were repeatedly ignored. The judge was obviously reluctant to commit him for contempt but he criticised Ben-Menashe's behaviour in his judgment. Then he softened the blow against the witness by saying that I had provoked him on occasion.

It was not difficult to show in cross-examination that Ben-Menashe had lied about himself, his business and his motives. He wanted the court to believe that he had gone to all the trouble and expense involved in procuring evidence on tapes simply for the sake of the previously colonised people of Zimbabwe, and that he had no expectations of receiving any money as a reward.

When he admitted, albeit reluctantly, that the maker of the video had been paid US$5 000 it became clear that the prosecution had not questioned its witnesses on these vital aspects of its case. Three of the State's own witnesses gave evidence that Ben-Menashe had claimed US$30 000 as expenses incurred for the making of the video, and their testimony showed that he had been untruthful about important elements of his own evidence, for he had simply pocketed US$25 000 of the money claimed on behalf of the video makers.

He presented himself as a philanthropist acting out of a deep feeling for the people of Zimbabwe, but he was unable to mention a single act of philanthropy performed by him or his business at any time in his life. Once again, through the mouths of the State's own witnesses, we discovered further damning evidence. Despite his protestations, he had been paid US$200 000 a few days after he had delivered the tape. With this payoff, he had received a total of US$615 000 from the Harare government. In addition, he told the court, he was owed a further US$400 000 and a contract to act on behalf of the Zimbabwe government for another year.

To hide the truth he maintained that all the money was for work whose nature he refused to disclose. In collaboration with the security services and the prosecution he produced a ministerial certificate purporting to back this claim, but the court set it aside as invalid. Confronted with these and other contradictions in his evidence, he made no reasonable attempt to explain them but simply launched into lengthy tirades: he did not know what all this questioning was about because the accused were guilty and I knew it.

Ben-Menashe admitted that highly defamatory attacks on his reputation had been made in numerous publications, but could not explain why he had taken no steps against any of them. Initially we had indicated that we would call the authors of some of these articles. But in the end we didn't as we believed that our other evidence more than proved the correctness of our contention.

At the end of the trial, Judge Garwe was to note that we had not called any witness to prove Ben-Menashe's bad reputation. Although we had called a witness specifically for this purpose, we did prove through cross-examination of Ben-Menashe and other prosecution witnesses that he was a corrupt liar. It was unnecessary for us to call any witnesses to testify specifically on the question of Ben-Menashe's character and reputation.

He admitted, for example, that in discussions with the MDC he had held himself out as a leading lobbyist and a successful fundraiser, well connected with many heads of state, security and funding agencies. In court he conceded that none of this was true. He had further lied to them when he represented his company as capable of supplying aeroplanes worth millions of US dollars from its own resources.

In Chris Anderson's cross-examination of Ben-Menashe's personal assistant, Tara Thomas, he established beyond any doubt that Ben-Menashe was nothing more than a confidence trickster. His previous company had gone into liquidation owing millions of US dollars and had a number of judgments entered against it. She was the only employee – and a poorly paid one – in this allegedly flourishing company. Although Ben-Menashe claimed it was financially sound, the company was short of cash and the MDC was in fact its only client.

Chris also established that Ben-Menashe's partner was a fugitive from justice in the United States. What about the person who had held himself out as a senior US state department representative and who Ben-Menashe promised would make funds available to the MDC? Ben-Menashe would not identify him – probably because he was no more than an out-of-work actor, hired to play a crucial role in the trap set by Ben-Menashe.

Ten other witnesses were called whose evidence did not take the case much further. At this stage we made an application for the discharge of all three accused, relying heavily on the two-witness rule. The judge acquitted Ncube and Gasela without hearing any evidence from the defence, but found that Tsvangirai had a case to answer.

We called all three of our clients as witnesses for the defence. Their version of events and their demeanour was satisfactory in every respect. It was obvious, we contended, whose witnesses – ours or the State's – the court should believe. Under lengthy cross-examination, Tsvangirai did not contradict himself and emerged unscathed.

As we worked through each painstaking stage of our case, the MDC called a national stay-away in protest against the government's policies and actions. This prompted the prosecution to apply for the cancellation of Tsvangirai's bail. As leader of the MDC he had now committed another act of treason by calling for the stay-away which, they claimed, would inevitably lead to violence. We opposed the rescinding of his bail and somewhat to our surprise the judge found for us, saying that bail was intended to secure the presence of the accused in court, not to stop him taking part in political activity.

Nevertheless, Tsvangirai and Ncube were arrested. Once again the charge was treason. When he was taken before a magistrate, Ncube, a professor of law and member of the Bar, successfully argued that the charge sheet disclosed no offence and he was released. Tsvangirai was remanded in custody and brought to the High Court from police cells for his trial. Yet while he was held in the basement of the court, his wife was not allowed to see him, nor would the orderlies take the change of clothing she had brought so that he could dress appropriately for the trial.

We asked the deputy attorney-general to intervene. He refused. We advised Tsvangirai not to come into court until we could raise the matter with the judge in open court. The deputy attorney-general insisted that the prisoner come up; we insisted even more firmly that the judge should be called to hear our complaint. When the judge took his seat we explained that it was at our insistence that our client was not in the dock. We submitted that the prosecution was behaving in an inappropriate and callous manner by insisting that Tsvangirai appear publicly in the prison garb reserved for convicted prisoners. We requested an order that our client's wife be allowed to see him and hand over his clothes. This the judge granted.

Trials in a foreign city are always difficult. Although my colleagues were friendly and hospitable, I led a lonely life. There was no flight from Harare to Johannesburg on Friday evenings. I flew early on Saturday and back on Sunday evenings. Although Meikle's Hotel in the city centre is near the courts, I chose to stay at the Sheraton because of the spacious grounds where I walked before breakfast and after dinner. I was warned that the Sheraton was owned by people close to ZANU-PF and that the room and telephone may be bugged and that copies of documents duplicated on their machines may be passed on to the secret police. But I decided that if one hotel spied on its guests, then another could as easily.

During the early days of the trial, one of my colleagues fetched me by car but then the fuel crisis started and fuel ran out. Welshman Ncube had the use of an MDC vehicle and could get extra petrol. His driver would often transport me but I took taxis to the airport. On one Saturday morning, thieves smashed the taxi's side window and stole my briefcase with documents relating to the trial. The taxi driver insisted I report the robbery to the police although I didn't want the press putting a political interpretation to the event. I was fairly certain the thieves were opportunist. Afterwards a bulletproof MDC vehicle was put at my disposal. The driver had a sense of humour and joked that he had paid Zim$600 lobola for his wife but now you couldn't buy four slices of bread with that.

At the restaurant where I often had supper I was told another story of the ordinary Zimbabwean's plight. The waitress had a secondary education but considered herself lucky to have a job. Her salary was hardly enough to buy a bag of mealie meal which did not last the whole month, and pay for the transport to get her daughters to and from school. For the rest she depended on her parents, who farmed a smallholding, and on the tips left by the few guests staying at the virtually empty hotel. She used her parents' savings to fly to London in the hopes of getting a job. Immigration wouldn't let her through.

While the government-controlled television and the *Herald* newspaper were biased against the accused, the *Daily News* was critical of the prosecution and its main witnesses. As for the citizens, they praised my efforts. Some white Zimbabweans betrayed their attitudes when they thanked me for 'what I was doing for Rhodesia.' They blamed South Africa for not helping to topple Mugabe's regime. I avoided this debate.

On the day appointed for judgment, there were no fewer than five uniformed prison officials surrounding the dock. We again protested to the deputy attorney-general. Security within the court was the responsibility of police and not prison officials. Why were they surrounding the dock? And why was one of them standing next to the accused in the dock itself? The prosecution team again told us that they saw nothing wrong with this. Again we gave notice that we would raise the matter with the judge. Moments before he entered, a junior member of the prosecution team ordered the prison officials to move away.

Tsvangirai was acquitted more than a year after he was charged. When I accepted the brief I was told that the trial would last a few weeks, but I hardly did anything else for a whole year. I did not regret the time it took and it was not the first time suggestions were made that I had dragged out a trial. I have never apologised for taking the time that is needed in cases such as this.

When you defend someone charged with political crimes in a dispensation where the administration of justice is already under stress, it is not enough to confine yourself to the technical argument that there is a 'reasonable doubt' concerning the guilt of the accused. I would consider it my duty to take as long as necessary to destroy the prosecution's case and prove that my client was not only 'not guilty', but innocent.

As one of South Africa's foremost legal figures commented, 'In a high-profile case like this one, with the leader of the opposition being defended on a capital charge by a world-renowned human rights advocate, Mandela's lawyer and friend, and with the diplomatic community and the world media watching closely, a verdict of guilty would have called for convincing or, at the very least, credible reasons.'

That legal figure was retired Constitutional Court judge Johann Kriegler. He had followed the Tsvangirai trial at the time of the judgment as an independent observer on behalf of the General Council of the Bar of South Africa. Justice Kriegler's comments form a valuable assessment of the case.

Kriegler found that although the rule of law had been debased in Zimbabwe for some time, there was no trace of judicial corruption evident in the case, nor was the judgment anything other than the 'judge's genuine expression of the reasoning and conclusions of the court'. He found the prosecution's case 'inherently preposterous', and symptomatic of Zimbabwe's 'slide into anarchy'. Of Ben-Menashe he remarked that he cut a 'sorry figure' and that his evidence was unreliable. For the prosecution Kriegler reserved harsh words and criticism that it had behaved in an obstructionist manner and placed doubtful evidence before the court.

'To my mind,' he concluded, 'it is clear that the man who goes under the name Ben-Menashe and claims to be an Israeli living in Canada, had in all probability at all times been a tool of the Zimbabwean state security apparatus, though it is just possible that it too was hoodwinked. In either event, the prosecution case was eventually shown to be quite insupportable. There was no credible evidence to support the allegations in the indictment. There is therefore no reason to believe that any of the accused were guilty of the conduct alleged against them. The verdict of not guilty was undoubtedly correct.'

Despite some blustering that the State would appeal, it never did. The second treason charge against Tsvangirai arising from the mid-trial stay-away organised by the MDC was also abandoned.

Life for the vast majority in Zimbabwe has not become any easier and the abrogation of the rule of law continues. It is estimated that more than two million Zimbabweans live in South Africa as refugees from the consequences of oppression, hunger and the destruction of their homes. President Mugabe still reigns on the strength of a mandate obtained through elections that were neither free nor fair. He has promised that he will destroy the MDC. Perhaps he will fulfil this promise, but if he does so it will be thanks to his illegitimate electoral excesses that have inflicted as much damage on the unity of the MDC leadership as they have on the rest of the country.

To be candid, I am disappointed about our government's handling of Zimbabwe. On the other hand, what could the government do? People in Zimbabwe don't want comprehensive sanctions. We could cut off their electricity. We could cut off their fuel. But I don't think it would help.

CHAPTER 44

A Personal Footnote: the 1990s

The 1990s I remember as bringing great joy but also deep sorrow. The joy came with the marriages in 1994 of both Kimon and Alexi.

Kimon, in London, had met Mary Beal although they had both studied at Wits university. Mary was an historian and anti-apartheid activist and very soon an earnest Graecophile. She determinedly learned the language, 'decorating' the objects in their apartment with tags of Greek words. Also they visited the village and my mother regularly.

Mary would sit at the foot of my mother's bed and question her about growing up at the beginning of the twentieth century. They spoke about the poems and freedom songs that honoured the generals and soldiers who won Greece's freedom from the Turks. These my mother had learned from her brothers and parents and grandparents while working in the fields. Did she not go to school? Mary asked. No, in those days girls did not go to school for fear they would form relationships with boys. With a smile she would add: 'Little did they know how much easier it was to do that if they sent their girls out alone to look after sheep.'

Meanwhile Alexi was in a relationship with a Wits graduate in physiotherapy, Monique van Oosterhout. Monique had a young son, Joshua, who soon called Arethe Yiayia, and me Papou. They too visited the village and were given my mother's blessing.

Kimon and Mary married in London, and Alexi and Monique were to be married at Vasilitsi a week later. Then, after a particularly happy and poignant reception in London, I received a phone call from Yianni to say that our brother Stavros had died of a heart attack at the very hour when the marriage ceremony was taking place. Yianni had delayed the call until the reception was over. Alexi and Monique postponed their wedding and we flew back for the funeral via Vasilitsi. On the day that the couple should have married we held a memorial service for Stavros at the village. I was told by his friends that as a teenager and young man he had done much to provide for the family in the absence of my father and me. Stavros was not one to praise himself and these spontaneous eulogies filled me with admiration for him. His death hit my sister and mother particularly badly. My mother covered her head with a black shawl, wore black clothes. The laughter had gone out of her and for the next six years until her death she no longer sang freedom or love songs or tried to dance. Why, she demanded, had Charon taken her son before he came for her?

My mother was in her late nineties and becoming very frail. Kimon tried to persuade her to walk with a walking stick, warning of the danger of broken bones at her age. But she did not take the warning seriously and fell one night, breaking her hip. She underwent an operation and Arethe and I flew over to visit her. True to form, when she came round after the operation and was told that Yianni was on the phone she demanded to speak with him and asked if he had eaten properly.

With her usual tenacity and courage, my mother weathered the final months of her life and died in mid-2001, just fourteen months short of her hundredth birthday.

Part Seven: 2004

CHAPTER 45

The Seven New Zealanders

Whenever I went home for the summer holiday I visited the scene of my escape from Nazi-occupied Greece. I walked on the beach from which we left, stood on the rock I leapt from into the boat and looked across at the uninhabited island of Venetiko.

Always the memory of that voyage and our rescue was startlingly clear. Decades had gone by and despite various efforts I'd never managed to track down the seven New Zealanders, last glimpsed only by chance near the refugee camp in Cairo. But that did not stop me remembering and wondering about them. Each time I went home I would drive the short distance to Vromovrisi, the watering hole near which the New Zealanders hid, now overgrown by bamboo because shepherds no longer lead flocks to drink there at midday.

Usually I visited the village council office to read the letter of thanks written to the people of the village after the war by the prime minister of New Zealand and the head of the army in his country. I had a copy made. I was about to reach my seventy-fifth year and wanted to show this letter to my family. It was written on the prime minister's letterhead and proudly bore the emblem of a Maori with a spear on the right and a queen holding the Union Jack on the left. In English the letter reads:

To the community of Vasilitsi, Province of Messinia:
I am addressing this brief message to tell you how grateful the government and people of New Zealand are to the Greek people. We remember all you did to help the New Zealand soldiers who remained behind when the German Army occupied your country in April 1941. We have a deep sense of New Zealand's debt towards the brave Greeks for their courage and self-sacrifice.

I wish to say to you personally that we will never forget what you did. We know that you clothed and fed our men when you were deprived and that in so doing you suffered and exposed yourselves to danger.

For all this we are deeply grateful. I am sending our most sincere best wishes for the happiness and wellbeing of your country from your friends and colleagues in New Zealand.

[Signed]
P. Fraser – Prime Minister
B. Freyberg – Commander of the Second Expeditionary Force

Shortly after making this translation I was asked to give an interview to the BBC World Service. During this I referred to the letter and our vain efforts to find the men we had rescued. At the end of the programme, the interviewer expressed the hope that someone might be able to help me.

A call did come from Antwerp in Belgium, from Alex van Heeren, the honorary consul of New Zealand. He suggested I write to the prime minister's office, and that he would help expedite matters. He also believed that he might get access to the HMS Kimberley's logbook which my daughter-in-law, Mary Beale, had discovered was sealed. In the end his efforts were in vain on both scores.

Mary then elicited help from the Kimberley Association. They referred her to a former sailor, Richard (Rick) Wakelin. Among his papers was a newspaper cutting of a photograph taken from the bridge of the Kimberley showing men on the deck looking down at a small boat in the water. The photograph was grainy but it excited Mary. Did our boat have a mast? How many people were on it? There was an image of a person smaller than the others, could this be me? They faxed the photograph from the United Kingdom, but it was hopelessly indistinct. Nevertheless I was convinced that this was a photograph of us.

Mary, being an historian, wanted corroboration, not just my gut feelings. How did we know that the Kimberley had not come across a boat other than ours? She put this question to the long-serving sailor. He was certain there'd been only one such incident. But Mary was still doubtful. Also, why had her efforts to obtain information from ex-servicemen's organisations in New Zealand failed? And why was there no response to the letters she had written to newspapers?

The old photograph was captioned: 'With a sixpenny compass and a map torn from an atlas, a little party of men set out from Crete in a rowing boat. They were soldiers who had been in hiding on the island since the Allied evacuation in May. This British official picture was taken from the destroyer Kimberley which sighted the boat adrift.' Some of the information was clearly wrong, but it didn't necessarily mean the boat was not ours.

The inaccuracies could be explained. When we left the mainland we had intended sailing to Crete. At the time we met the ship, we were nearer Crete than the mainland, and perhaps the caption writer simply made an assumption that turned out to be wrong. Whatever the explanation, Alex van Heeren, Mary Beale and I were not going to give up the search.

In March 2004, to mark fifty years at the Johannesburg Bar, its council made me an honorary member. Soon afterwards the General Council of the Bar in South Africa conferred the Sir Sydney and Lady Felicia Kentridge Award on me for my contribution to human rights. I was advised by some of my colleagues and best friends not to retire. Then came a letter from the International Bar Association awarding me its Bernhard Simon Memorial Award citing an 'Outstanding contribution to human rights in South Africa'. The award would be handed over at the association's general meeting in Auckland, New Zealand in October 2004.

In accepting the honour I disclosed to the organisers the other important reason for wishing to visit New Zealand – my passion to find the seven soldiers. Tim Hughes and Fiona Patterson, who were arranging the association event, circulated details to the media before I arrived. Alex van Heeren had two lawyers, Brigadier David MacGregor and Rebecca Macky, meet and assist me. But best of all, and unrelated to the great search, he invited the three of us to stay in his Huka Lodge located on the Waikato River near Taupo.

As I emerged from New Zealand customs on Saturday 23 October, I saw a couple holding the *Herald* newspaper high above their heads. There on the front page was a large colour photograph of me. The couple turned out to be Rebecca and David. Pointing to the photograph on the front page they said that there was no need for me to identify myself.

At the hotel I took a call from a senior reporter on the *Herald,* Bernard Orsman. The family of John Lewis, the soldier who led the group of New Zealanders, were in the *Herald'*s office and wanted to see me. I asked them to come to the hotel.

The reporter and a photographer led the sprightly ninety-five-year-old widow of John Lewis towards me. Freena Lewis was accompanied by their daughter, Bronwyn, and her grandchild, Michaela. They were certain that there was no mistake and that put my mind at ease. We embraced and each of us shed a tear. Bronwyn was the first to speak. The headline and the large photograph had attracted her attention early that morning.

Long before she finished reading the story, she realised that this was the tale of escape that her father had told the family so often. She said meeting me was like having a precious heirloom, which you pass from generation to generation. Michaela, who had also been told the story many times by her grandfather, described our meeting as a surreal event. Freena Lewis did not say much. We held hands and looked deeply into one another's eyes.

Bronwyn produced a family photo album. There was an empty space under the heading, 'Escape from Greece'. Six names appeared at the bottom of the page, presumably the names of the people who would have been in that missing photograph. The media, particularly Bernard Orsman of the *Herald*, worked overtime during the weekend to track down other sources. The six names were published, as was a picture of John Lewis and one of the group originally in the photograph, his friend Don Gladding. An appeal was made to anyone who might have information. By Tuesday morning 26 October all seven had been identified.

Don Gladding, a staff sergeant, served in Greece and Africa, and was awarded the Military Medal for bravery. After the war, he had worked as an accountant in Oakland. He died in 1981. Mick Karup was a seaman before and after the war and lived in Mangere with his parents. He moved to Cairns where he died in 1990, aged eight-four. Private Syd Hey, a farmer, served with the 24th Battalion and was killed at Sidi Rezegh in the Western Desert at the end of November 1941, aged thirty-two.

Before the war Peter Martin had worked in Fiji with Tom Freeman, another member of our escape party. At the outbreak of hostilities they returned to New Zealand and joined the 24th Battalion. Peter continued his military career after the war and died in 1999, aged eighty-two. Little was known of Tom Freeman, bar that he had been a policeman in Whangarei in 1958, and he couldn't be traced. Jim Simpson had been a farmer, but there was no information about him after the war.

And then, of course, there was the leader of the group, John Lewis, a sergeant in the 24th Battalion at the time our paths crossed. He rose to a higher rank by the end of the war and then returned to become a successful sheep and cattle farmer in Cambridge. He had died in 1996.

My search had come too late to meet with the men themselves, but I met some of their relatives. Ruth Allen and her sister Jeanette Harrison, the nieces of Mick Karup, came to see me, and said that their uncle had told them much about me. Ruth kept touching me and repeating, 'I can't believe that you are real.' John Moss and his wife Kim were happy to make contact with me and the families of other members of the group.

Each had poignant details of those long-ago events. Jeanette Harrison, whose uncle Mick Karup was the experienced seaman who'd rigged up two blankets when the sail of our fishing boat blew out, told me how lovingly her grandmother had knitted a cardigan for the thirteen-year-old boy whose father saved them. She sent it off together with some money for my education after the war. The cardigan and money were returned. We agreed that there was no point in looking for the cardigan, for even if it were to be found it would surely not fit me.

I told them how sorry I was that I hadn't accepted an invitation to a conference in Australia in the late 1980s. I might've gone on to New Zealand. How much happier the occasion would have been as Mick Karup, John Lewis and Peter Martin were still alive then.

The president of the International Bar Association, Emilio Cardenas, arranged a lunch for all of us, including his senior assistants, at a waterfront restaurant in

Auckland. At the end of the meal, Bernard Orsman of the *Herald* handed me copies of two letters.

One was brief but made me proud of my father all over again. It was from him to the New Zealanders and had been found in the archives. As it was in English, it was probably written on his behalf by one of the brothers Bouzales, American residents whose families were trapped in Greece by the war. It read: 'We bought a sail-boat, we will go together, the boat is big enough, it needs a little repair and it will be ready soon, do not worry and don't be afraid, we will take care of you until we leave together, all expenses of food, boat etc is ours, because we think it is our duty and obligation. Good luck, sincerely yours, Anthony Bizos.'

The other letter was much longer, five long pages typed in single spacing and written by Sergeant Don Gladding, number 23129, A Company, 24th Battalion, New Zealand Expeditionary Force in the Middle East. It began:

> My dear Mother and Sister Betty … I know you must be worried. However let's get on with the story. On March 17th we left Alexandria after experiencing in camp a frightful sand storm in which quite honestly one could not see his own feet. We arrived at Athens after travelling in a famous war ship and a few days later I left the city for the north of Greece. We received great acclamation in the march through the city receiving flowers and kisses from the big crowd.

It relates how his company got to Salonika, then describes how the 'Hun' routed them following the collapse of the Greek forces. They eventually reached Kalamata on 28 April. 'Being heavily outnumbered both in men and ammunition and no tanks or artillery and no air support, my officer instructed the men, totalling about a hundred to divide themselves into sections under NCOs and do their best to get off Greece.'

He records how various villagers helped them with food, clothes and guides as they fled southwards in the hope of getting a boat to Crete. He tells of being cheated by a man who proclaimed himself a hero from the First World War. The man took their money and, promising to come back with a boat, went to get drinking water for the trip. He never returned. They walked on to Vasilitsi where we lived. His own words echoed my memories.

> We were discovered again. Again extreme luck, this man took us to a better hiding place, and he proved a very fine man indeed. He and his family were poor, yet he risked hiding us for 6 days, and fed us magnificently. We found the poorer the man, the more freely they gave. During this period he was

raising money to buy us a boat – as I said he was very poor, he and his family subscribed £28, and bought an old sailing boat. This had to be repaired and painted on the bottom – eventually, the Hun fortunately not seeing the boat, the night of the 18th May, we departed, after kissing and embracing which we genuinely reciprocated. They were a very fine charactered people, risking their all for us, and we owe them much indeed – our escape.

It was very rough, and the two Greek seamen anchored off an island, saying it was too rough to take the boat any further, so all the next day we again hid; we being nervous as the island was well in sight of the Germans, and their motor boats were patrolling around. That night we ditched our two Greek seamen, and away we went in a howling wind and a heavy sea. We had on board seven, and eight Greek civilians who wanted to get away. We left Greece on May 19th. The boat was about 16 feet with a good wide beam; she had a heavy solid hull with two long sweeps, her sail riggings were rotten however, having the Greek style of low thick masts, and just one sail with the boom on top.

During the night various stays snapped, and at 3 in the morning the sail blew out at the peak and split across the back. I meant to say that one of our boys, Karup, was a seaman having spent some years in sail, and that also we had procured a map, and with the aid of our compass intended making for Crete, not of course knowing there was fighting there. Anyway we had great difficulty in getting the sail down, and also keeping the boat head onto the wind; Karup rigged up two blankets, and we sailed before the wind until dawn, when believe it or not, we mended the hole in the peak with our last remaining face towel, and sewed the long tear both with an ordinary needle and cotton, that is what the sail was like.

We hauled the sail up; it jammed, and the rope broke; another rope, the sail went up another few more inches; three quarters way up the mast and the rope broke again; another rope and this broke – the sail had jammed so Karup by some method lashed the boom to the pulley, trusted to luck; all this in a howling wind and raging sea. I myself thought all was up, and was I sick; later on I was so sick I just laid in 6 inches of water, and took no heed of the waves splashing over me into the boat. She was of course an open boat – by great sailing on Karup's and the boys' parts, the sail held and we sailed all day until 3pm when we saw German planes on the horizon, with heavy anti-aircraft fire concentrated on them, and about half an hour later smoke appeared, and then our Navy – marvellous sight, appeared crossing our bows.

We made frantic efforts to draw their attention, and eventually a destroyer dashed off towards us, and at 5pm on the 20th May, after one of the boys signalled s.o.s. with a shaving mirror we were picked up by it – no one can possibly describe our relief. That night our squadron were in action when they intercepted German convoys from Greece to Crete, blowing and ramming them off the sea, besides getting a transport and a destroyer.

Our destroyer let go all she had, and I saw her ram one German boat – it being weird hearing the cries all round the boat of drowning Germans, screaming "Kamerad" in the pitch dark – needless to say none were picked up. There was that night a few less Germans our boys had to fight in Crete. Next day more patrolling with dive-bombing attacks from German planes. The day after having turned for Egypt to refuel, we landed at Alexandria on May 23rd, and back to Helwan May 25th. Had a great reception from the boys, and our Brigadier was kindly interested in the story.

I found on return that another Sergeant had returned with about 7 men – therefore so far only 15 have returned, of the 100 cut off. Incidentally our [battalion] being the last to leave Greece, did not go to Crete. It was a really miraculous escape, especially as there are hundreds from other units still hiding in Greece besides many more taken prisoner. I truthfully suffered no injury, and honestly feel none the worse. The tension whilst trying to escape was keen and we got, at times, very nervy, but that is now over.

I don't mind saying I prayed pretty hard, because at times things did look black, though I am sure it was your prayers which pulled me through. Honestly, we seemed to be guided, everything turned out for the best and I am convinced that a Higher Power, God, must have watched over us. To me it was miraculous, as it was to the other boys who are certainly not Bible students, and they eventually thought as I did. Your continual prayers did the trick.

When I came back I had 21 letters and 8 parcels waiting for me and have detailed them in Stella's letter.

With much love
From Son and Brother
Don

p.s. Hope you yourself are much better in health. I won't say "and brighter" knowing of course that you are always bright. By the way I often could not understand your hospitality to comparative strangers, but after experiencing the sacrificing hospitality and help given unstintedly and happily and enjoying doing so by these Greek people, I begin to understand.

Love Don

P.S. Another lucky break – a strong wind proved a blessing in disguise as, if we had been sighted by the Navy at night, we would have been blown up. The navy were patrolling there, knowing that German sailing boats were coming from Greece to Crete and were there to prevent all boats from reaching Crete. At night their searchlights would have picked us up, no questions asked – we would have been blown sky high.

Don

This letter explained why the admiralty kept the logbook sealed. Presumably the authorities decided to cover up the questionable act of war described by Gladding.

As a thirteen-year-old I regarded the incident as a great adventure. The letter brought home to me the reality of that war, the fate of those who shouted 'Kamerad' but found no help, and for the first time I thought about what might have happened to us on that little boat had the Allied ships mistaken us for Germans.

The New Zealand Infantry Battalion Association responded to the publicity. Suddenly there was a widespread resurgence of public interest in how New Zealand's soldiers had fought in Greece, more particularly in the battles of Mount Olympus, Elasson and Mollos; and how, although they had escaped from Greece, they did not return home, but went on to fight against the Nazi and fascist armies in North Africa and Italy.

The association presented me with gifts bearing the name and insignia of the battalion and with literature recording the heroic acts and sacrifice of its members. I learned that the battalion's first encounter on the battlefield was in Greece – but in a campaign intended to serve political rather than military ends. The Greeks had repulsed the invading Italian armies and pushed them back into Albania. This was a moral victory too, because of the confident prediction by the Italians that they would march down the streets of Athens within days after the invasion of 28 October 1940.

Once the Italian army retreated the Allies agreed there should be a presence of New Zealand, Australian and British forces in Greece to show Allied support for the first of the European nations to stand up to the enemy with success. A special message to the 24th Battalion from General Bernard Freyberg was read out on the ship taking them from Alexandria to Piraeus, the port town of Athens. He said:

In the course of the next few days we may be fighting in defence of Greece, the birthplace of culture and of learning. We shall be meeting our real enemy, the Germans, who have set out with the avowed object of smashing the British Empire. It is clear that wherever we fight them we shall be fighting not only for Greece, but also in defence of our own homes.

The Germans came to the assistance of their inept Italian allies. They were preparing Operation Barbarossa against the Soviet Union, but couldn't expose their south-eastern flank while they advanced against Leningrad, Moscow and Stalingrad. Consequently, they had to occupy Greece and expel the Allies. Many historians believe that the delay involved in dealing with Greece deprived the Germans of the early victory they expected in Russia before the snow and sub-zero temperatures helped the Soviet Union turn them back.

During my visit to New Zealand, David and Rebecca absented themselves from their legal practices and devoted much of their time to me. We visited the military museum, where I was moved by the realistic reconstructions of the campaigns and battles in which New Zealanders took part during the two world wars. And of course of what happened at Gallipoli, where the lives of so many New Zealanders were lost. The roll of honour of those who died in Europe appeared very long for a small country whose forces were fighting so far away from home.

Then came our all-too-brief stay at Alex van Heeren's Huka Lodge. En route to the lodge we stopped at a number of the small towns. Almost invariably a ceno-taph or memorial plaque in the town square and near the church commemorated those who had died in various wars fought in far-off lands.

When I received the Bernard Simons Memorial Award for the Advancement of Human Rights I said, 'I am glad to receive this award in New Zealand, where democracy is well rooted and freedom of speech and other human rights are protected ... If you need an example for our people to follow, I say look to New Zealand.'

I have idealised New Zealanders ever since I saw pictures of them in Greek newspapers mingling with boys of my age in the streets of Athens. And then our special seven soldiers were gentle yet heroic figures for me as a teenager. Also their fate caused my family to end up in South Africa. Now, as I reflect on the significance to my family of our leaving Greece at that time, I have strong doubts whether my father would have survived if he had stayed. Inevitably, he would have taken up arms against the German occupation or during the civil war that followed it.

What I said in Auckland to my colleagues from all over the world is a sum-mary of what I have stood for during my life:

The war that was to end all wars was responsible for my journey from the land of my birth, Greece, to South Africa, which received me as an adopted son. We believed what we were told, about the reasons for fighting that war. That influenced the road that I took. I was fortunate to cross the path of many brave men and women who had the courage to say 'No' to tyranny and who yearned for democratic governments, the rule of law and the promotion of fundamental human rights.

Tyrants use political trials to remove their opposition without acknowledging that they are merely political opponents. They find ugly names to call them by – murderers, terrorists, traitors, or, at the very least, agitators.

Where there is absolute tyranny, there is very little, if anything, that a lawyer can do. There are, however, many who are not democrats, have no respect for the rule of law, nor for the promotion of fundamental human rights, but nevertheless, would like to be known as such.

That allows sufficient room for lawyers to be of some assistance to those whom they would execute, imprison, torture, exile, silence. It is the function, I dare say the duty, of lawyers to unapologetically represent clients who come into conflict with the man-made laws of overambitious politicians, who want to retain power.

We in South Africa, by opposing the laws of the apartheid regime, defending those accused of offences against those laws, and exposing the excesses of their security forces, were accused even by some of our friends of doing nothing more than lending legitimacy to an illegitimate regime. Our answer was that those holding the knife by its cutting edge were not interested in logically correct philosophical notions; it was for the accused and their loved ones to decide whether they wanted to be defended or not.

Our task was not an easy one. The judiciary was neither representative nor conscious of the suffering of the oppressed. Particular judges were chosen to do political trials. The prosecution blindly followed the instructions of the security police. There were no juries, and the specially chosen judges hardly ever took lay assessors to assist them in the determination of the facts.

It was not easy to cross-examine witnesses who were programmed whilst held in solitary confinement, on how to implicate the accused. Their complaints that confessions were extracted from them by torture, threat of further indefinite detention, and other unlawful means, could hardly ever be corroborated because no one had access to them until their wounds were healed. There were harsh minimum sentences. The right to appeal was limited.

Those of us at the Bar who habitually took political trials did not receive work from large successful firms of attorneys. Those firms that did brief us, large or small, were threatened by their corporate clients that they would be abandoned, for fear that the government might refuse to give them contracts. Despite all this, there was a considerable number of advocates and attorneys in South Africa who made themselves available to those in distress.

The legal profession's insistence on defending people against tremendous odds did help on occasion to secure the release of the obviously innocent. Criticism by academic lawyers of patent injustices put at least some judges on their guard.

However inadequate the judicial system may have been, it remained intact as a structure. However few lawyers may have become involved, the honour of the legal profession was not entirely impugned.

It has been authoritatively stated that the survival of the system assisted in bringing about the transition to and the settlement between the adversaries who did not trust one another. This was achieved by the establishment of a Constitutional Court to guarantee the freedom of the fundamental rights of every individual, even against a majority of the voters and the members of Parliament.

The Constitutional Court is now generally accepted amongst the vast majority of the South African people of whatever race, colour or creed, as the upper guardian of the rights of all of us.

What happened in South Africa in the past is now taking place in a number of southern African states.

I believe that it is the duty of every one of us, as individuals, and particularly the International Bar Association and its constituent Bars, to lend moral and material support to our colleagues who are engaged in the establishment of democracy, the rule of law and the human rights contract in their countries.

It is not only in southern Africa that human rights culture is in decline. Even established democracies, when under actual or supposed danger, find it convenient to abrogate the laws of humanity, forgetting that they too may one day be in distress and that the laws may not be there to protect them.

What we expected as young idealists more than 50 years ago did not come to pass. The Cold War, as a result of great power antagonism, exacerbated local conflicts into major civil wars, violent secession movements and tyrannical methods to suppress them. Far from being the war ending all wars, the promises of the Atlantic Charter, the Universal Declaration of Human Rights and other continental and regional declarations, have not stopped the blood feud.

There can be no peace, development or the enjoyment of fundamental rights whilst international conventions are treated as dead letters, where interests considered vital to powerful countries are concerned. Nor can this happen when the chasm between the very rich and the very poor is so great in so many parts of the world.

During the futile Gallipoli campaign against the Turks at the beginning of the First World War, New Zealanders paid proportionally the highest price. Regular pilgrimages are held in memory of those who lost their lives in that terrible campaign. Some of those who go to Gallipoli in the Dardanelles also visit places in Greece that are the scenes of other battles involving their loved ones. Our new friends, the families of the seven, agreed that they should visit Kalamata and Vasilitsi. Some of them came to the airport to say goodbye to me when I returned to South Africa, and they brought mementos for me to take back.

Many letters were written to the New Zealand newspapers to welcome what the writers described as the good news of our successful search. The president of the International Bar Association wrote to the *Herald*:

LAWYERS' HEARTS TOUCHED

After these extraordinary few days for George Bizos and the families of the New Zealand soldiers with whom he escaped from Greece in 1941, I wanted to let you know how much we appreciate what the *Herald* and your wonderful readers have done in making our time in Auckland so special.

Your reporters Eugene Bingham, Bernard Orsman and Alan Perrott told this amazing story superbly. It has been a privilege for us to meet family members like Freena Lewis, her daughter Bronwyn and her three grandchildren.

We learned that Mrs Lewis' war was at least as remarkable as that of her late husband. These events have added a whole extra dimension to our honouring of George for his lifetime's work in fighting oppression.

While the story has such a special resonance in New Zealand, we know from the more than 100 nationalities attending our conference here in Auckland that it touches hearts all across cultures. One day, perhaps, we will be able to look forward to seeing the movie – filmed, let us all hope, in New Zealand.

Emilio Cardenas, president,
International Bar Association

CHAPTER 46

My Two Ithacas

Greece is the Mother of Democracy and South Africa, its youngest daughter.

– Nelson Mandela

Nelson Mandela considered his honorary citizenship of Ancient Olympia one of the most important awards bestowed on him. And he always regretted that the sports boycott excluded young South Africans from the Olympic Games. It was a pity, he felt, that there would never be a photograph of Jake Ntuli, the champion boxer during the apartheid years, arm in arm with Zola Budd, the long-distance runner, coming back in triumph from the Olympics. What a symbol that would have been of the unity of South Africa's people, black and white.

There was to be a special centenary celebration of the Olympic Games in 1996 and we assumed it would be held in Athens for historic reasons. While our confidence that Nelson would be free by then proved correct, to our sorrow it wasn't Athens but Atlanta that hosted the games.

Thanks to the political negotiations, South Africa participated in the 1992 Barcelona Olympics and Nelson was able to witness Derartu Tulu, the Ethiopian gold medallist, and the South African silver medallist Elana Meyer with their arms linked in comradeship, performing a lap of honour at the end of the ten-thousand-metre race, all those in the stadium rising to cheer them in a wave of emotion.

Greece, through its foreign minister, George Papandreou, was anxious to restore the spirit of the ancient games. To enhance that spirit, Greece called on the nations of the world to adopt what was in antiquity known as *Ekeheiria*, the Olympic Truce. Under this truce, all hostilities had to cease seven days before the start of the games. The truce would hold throughout the games and continue for a further seven days so that athletes, artists, officials and spectators could travel to Olympia, participate in the games and return home in safety.

George Papandreou asked me if Nelson Mandela would support this effort so that his name could appear as a sponsor together with Kofi Annan, the secretary general of the United Nations, Jacques Rogge, the president of the International Olympic Committee, Juan Antonio Samaranch, the former president of the committee, the president of Greece and many others. Papandreou believed that if the

Olympic Truce were in place during the games it would eloquently demonstrate the positive influence that sport could make to global peace and the upliftment of young people in particular.

His call was enthusiastically received internationally, with high-level support. The initiative was officially announced during the flame-lighting ceremony for the Olympic Winter Games in November 2001 in Olympia. In December 2001 the United States took the initiative by passing a resolution co-sponsored by a hundred and seventy member states in the United Nations General Assembly.

While all these things were taking place in the world of Olympic sport, the South African ambassador to Greece, Jannie Momberg, and his counterpart in South Africa, Yiannis Economides, were keen to arrange a visit to Greece by South Africa's most famous couple, to be hosted by the minister of foreign affairs, George Papandreou.

In 1996 after his divorce from Winnie, Nelson had led a lonely life. His most precious personal companionship was with a couple of young great-grandchildren. Then a loving relationship developed between him and Graça Machel, widow of President Samora Machel of Mozambique who'd died in a plane crash on the border between his country and South Africa. Initially Nelson was coy about the relationship and reluctant to make a public announcement about their intentions. In July 1998, I knew that a marriage was imminent because he mentioned to me, as though in passing, that Graça's relatives were arriving the following weekend. Respectful of his desire for privacy I refrained from further questions. The next weekend they married in a private ceremony on the lawn of his home.

The companionship between them and the care she takes of him is of great importance and comfort to Nelson. Whenever he is asked to do anything, he jokes that he will have to get permission from his wife first. Graça has promoted the unity of his family as a whole, including Winnie, who is often given pride of place at family gatherings. A recent example was the wedding of Nelson's eldest grandson, Mandla Mandela. Graça also pays special attention to Nelson's friends, warmly welcoming his close comrades to their home.

Now they were to be official guests in Greece and Arethe and I were to join them on the trip. Included in the itinerary was a voyage on a luxury yacht past the Aegean and Ionian islands and including a stop in the Venetian-built harbour of Koroni, near Vasilitsi.

Arethe and I flew ahead and moved into the top floor of a leading hotel on Athens's Constitution Square. From our window the view extended to Parliament to our left, the Acropolis and below it the Plaka, favourite haunt of the young in search of restaurants and night life. To the right lay the Parthenon.

We joined George Papandreou and the two ambassadors in welcoming Nelson and Graça at the airport. The guests of honour occupied the hotel's presidential suite one floor below us. Within minutes Nelson asked me to come down.

The heavy curtains of their suite were drawn to keep out the afternoon sun and increase the effectiveness of the air conditioner. Nelson was sitting on a sofa and invited me to sit next to him. Instead I went to the curtains, drew them wide open and suggested he take a look. He fixed his eyes on the Parthenon and remained silent for a while. Without looking away he said, 'George, are you sure that I have not been here before?'

The next morning, 19 June 2002, there was a function in Nelson's honour. It was held to acknowledge his role in the advancement of universal peace and for his support for the Olympic Truce campaign. The function took place at the Megaro Mousikis of Athens, the largest concert hall and indoor theatre in the country. As part of his party we were seated in the area reserved for diplomats. Ambassador Stavros Lambrinidis, director of the International Olympic Truce Centre, asked us to stand as George Papandreou and Nelson Mandela appeared on the stage.

Nelson sat between Lambrinidis and Papandreou. To my embarrassment he said in a firm, clearly audible voice, 'Where is George? Let him come here.' I was ushered to a seat next to Nelson. Speeches were made in English and Greek. I whispered short summaries of the Greek into Nelson's ear in the hope that my sudden elevation would be seen as his need of a translator and not be misconstrued by those who preferred strict adherence to protocol.

Over a hundred signatures of support for the truce were reproduced on the programme: presidents, prime ministers, ministers of foreign affairs, speakers and members of parliaments, heads of international organisations and religious leaders from every continent. Ambassador Lambrinidis read out the final paragraph of the statement:

Humanity's quest is for a world free of hatred, terrorism and war, where ideals of peace, goodwill, and mutual respect form the basis of relations among people and countries. The goal may still remain elusive, but if the Olympic Truce can help us bring about even a brief respite from conflict and strife, it will send a powerful message of hope to the international community … We pledge to support and disseminate, individually and collectively, the symbolic call for the Olympic Truce throughout all future Olympic Games and beyond, and to exercise our best efforts within our communities, countries, and relevant international organisations to achieve its recognition and observance.

Nelson was to sign the declaration in person. As he took his pen from his inside jacket pocket, he received a standing ovation. Next, Mikis Theodorakis was called to the table. The world-renowned composer came forward, a man who had survived the German occupation, civil war, detention without trial, torture and exile, whose songs had inspired those who struggled in Greece and elsewhere against tyranny. He stretched out his hand to Nelson, who grasped it firmly to enthusiastic applause as he signed the declaration. After George Papandreou had signed, he invited me to do the same. A number of academics, intellectuals, writers and artists added their signatures. The few among them who spoke, addressed themselves to Nelson Mandela, describing him as hero, icon, world leader, peacemaker, reconciler and – could there be higher praise from such an audience? – a committed philhellene.

Prime Minister Costas Simitis gave a lunch in Mandela's honour. Among those present were members of the cabinet and other dignitaries, including the head of the Olympic Committee, Gianna Angelopoulou-Daskalaki. Nelson had many questions about ancient Greece, the four-hundred-year occupation of Greece by the Ottoman Empire, its heroic fight against fascism, the suffering of its people during the occupation and the regrettable civil war. He wanted to know about the country's electoral system, the strength of the parties and the role played by opposition parties to the left and right of the socialist government.

A further function was arranged by President Constantine Stephanopolos, who expressed his regret that Nelson Mandela had not managed to visit Greece while he was president of South Africa despite the efforts of both ministers of foreign affairs and the ambassadors of the two countries. President Stephanopolos assured the former president that in the eyes of the Greeks, if not the whole world, he was still President Mandela whatever the rules of protocol provided. Ambassadors Momberg and Economides had been busy arranging a visit by President Stephanopolos to South Africa and a return visit by President Mbeki to Greece. Both ambassadors saw the fulfilment of their work not long after our visit to Greece and say these visits were the pinnacle of their diplomatic careers.

There was only one other official engagement which Nelson had to fulfil. This was a visit the following day to the trustees of the Alexander Onassis Foundation. Then Nelson, Graça, Arethe, our son Kimon, my sister Vaso and I were to board the yacht and sail the Aegean Sea together with Ambassador Economides and his wife Athena. In the middle of this anticipation came a call from Zelda la Grange, Mandela's personal assistant, asking me down to the presidential suite. Madiba was not well.

The doctor from Number One Military Hospital, who had accompanied him, was not sure of the precise problem, although it appeared to be a stomach ailment, but believed that the appointment with the trustees of the Onassis Foundation should be postponed and the yacht trip cancelled. The doctor conferred with Kimon, who is a Fellow of the Royal College of Surgeons. They could not safely say when his condition would improve or whether there would be a recurrence. The yacht trip would certainly have been most uncomfortable for him.

A journalist got a distorted version of the situation from a source unknown to us and the electronic media broadcast that Nelson Mandela had been admitted to the Onassis Cardiac Hospital and that his condition was serious. We assured the ambassador that the information was incorrect and a press conference was called in the foyer of the hotel to put the record straight.

Arrangements were made to leave the hotel. Instead of the cruise, we would go to an east-side resort where Madiba and Graça could enjoy a quiet holiday. The hotel adjoined a protected beach with well-wooded gardens and a panoramic view of the sea.

This was the first time in our fifty-four-year friendship that Nelson and I had spent a holiday together. His stomach ailment cleared up in less than two days and he was in good spirits, welcoming the privacy and relaxed atmosphere.

Madiba and Graça would breakfast in their suite but we lunched and dined together every day. After breakfast we relaxed at the shaded tables and garden chairs close to the fine white sand constantly washed by the gentle waves of the Aegean Sea. It looked so cool and inviting that Graça, Zelda la Grange and I couldn't resist swimming. Sometimes our conversation was interrupted by parents asking if their children could be photographed with Nelson Mandela. His security people were unhappy about these requests but he invariably posed for the photograph. He would shake hands and ask how old the children were and how they were getting on with school. The hotel staff took it in turns to serve us with refreshments so that they, too, could be photographed with him. Even the chef came to find out if Mr Mandela wanted him to prepare a special dish.

Such solicitousness included the hotel's general manager. Were we comfortable and enjoying our stay? Taking our answers for granted, he began to enumerate the kings, queens and presidents who had occupied the suite made available to President Mandela. Madiba asked whether King Constantine of Greece had ever stayed in the suite. Consistent with the local practice the manager answered that the "ex-king" had indeed also stayed there.

Nelson was bemused by the number of kings, queens and princes he had met who deferred to his actually rather humble royal lineage and requested that he call them by their first names rather than Your Majesty or Royal Highness.

I reminded him that he had referred to his warders on Robben Island as his 'guard of honour'. Hadn't he also given permission for his daughter to marry a Swazi prince? I'd conveyed his message to the Swazis to remember that they were getting a Tembu princess.

A short while after we'd been at the hotel, I realised that there was no South African flag flying above the main entrance, and reported this immediately to Ambassador Economides. He was surprised but had it rectified immediately. A couple of hours later, what should I see but the flag so dear to the apartheid regime fluttering next to the Greek flag. The usually unflappable Ambassador Economides, anxious to avoid even a minor diplomatic incident, rushed to secure the removal of that symbol of oppression and to have the six-coloured banner of freedom, equality and justice raised, without anyone else having noticed the slip-up.

Nelson is fond of quoting the advice of an eastern philosopher: you should have a hearty breakfast, share your lunch with a friend and make a present of your dinner to your enemy. He nevertheless joined us after sunset when the bright August moon appeared on the horizon. We preferred to eat at the open-air restaurant almost on the edge of the cliff where the breeze was cool and fresh.

Unfortunately, the Aegean cruise was not the only event that had to be cancelled. For example, we did not get to Ancient Olympia, where Nelson was an honorary citizen and where his portrait hung in the council chamber. While he was able to visit the Acropolis and the Temple of Apollo on Cape Sounion, there were many things left undone, so many more places still to see. We agreed we would return together to Athens in 2004 for the Olympic Games.

CHAPTER 47

My Odyssey

Immortal spirit of antiquity,
Father of the true, beautiful and good,
Descend, appear, shed over us thy light
Upon this ground and under this sky
Which has first witnessed thy unperishable flame.
Give life and animation to those noble games!
Throw wreaths of fadeless flowers to the victors
In the race and in the strife!
Create in our breasts, hearts of steel!
In thy light, plains, mountains and seas
Shine in a roseate hue and form a vast temple
To which all nations throng to adore thee,
Oh immortal spirit of antiquity!

– Kostis Palamas
early 20th century national poet of Greece

Nelson Mandela is revered by the Greek people, not only as a world statesman but as a friend of Greece and its people. He acknowledges that he was influenced by the writings of the classical historians, philosophers and moderate rulers who used their power wisely.

When both Cape Town and Athens wanted to host the Olympic Games he won even greater admiration in Greece because of his response once Cape Town was eliminated from the race: he canvassed members of the Olympic Committee, particularly the Africans, to use their votes in favour of Athens. It was ultimately this generous gesture that helped bring the Olympics home to Athens. Not long afterwards, he was visited by Gianna Angelopoulou-Daskalaki, head of the Greek Olympic Committee, and it was fully expected that he would be a guest of honour at the Athens Olympics in 2004.

While she was in South Africa, Gianna attended a dinner at which it was announced that I had been invited to be part of the South African Olympic Committee's delegation to Athens. This was an honour beyond my wildest dreams. More than ever it felt as though my two worlds were coming closer. I had a sense that I should prepare myself spiritually for the journey. I reread the *Iliad*, particularly the section that graphically describes the games ordered by Achilles in memory of his closest friend, Protoclos. I was even tempted to suggest to sports commentators how it should be done.

I read the history of the games in both the ancient and modern days and spoke about them to whoever was prepared to listen. I asked schools to collect signatures in support of the Olympic Truce and I requested journalists to write and broadcast about the forthcoming event.

Traditionally, in the modern era the Olympic flame is ignited in Olympia some time before the event. This is done by means of a glass prism during a staged theatrical performance, after white-clad maidens offer a prayer to Zeus. The flame is then transferred to torches and these are taken all over the world by specially appointed men and women. On this occasion and for the first time, Africa was to be included in these preparatory events with the torch being lit and carried during special festivities in Cape Town.

To my surprise I was chosen as one of the two hundred who would bear the flame. I queried my participation with Sam Ramsamy. Surely the honour would be confined to young athletes? What could a septuagenarian contribute? He replied that people from all walks of life would take part in the South African section of the ceremony. As to my age, a man of over a hundred would be participating.

The maximum distance was five hundred meters. I could do less if I wished. Similarly I could run, jog or walk. I decided that I would jog the required distance and members of the family, particularly my two doctor sons, told me that I was being stubborn as usual and should be careful. I started training by covering the distance on our long driveway and lawn almost daily. In the process I even lost a couple of kilograms, so determined was I to be fit enough to participate.

The Olympic committee invited nominations for additional participants for the preliminary torch ceremonies. They wanted young and old athletes; men and women who had volunteered their services to the community; the disabled who had courageously overcome their handicaps. They even accepted the nomination of street children who chose to entertain by singing, dancing, gymnastic turns or playing home-made musical instruments.

The torch we were to carry was modelled on the one that was to rise above the roof of the arena in Athens. We gathered on the appointed morning at a stadium in one of Cape Town's less affluent areas. There we were met by officials who had flown in from Greece, most of them volunteers. These were young men and women from various parts of the world who accompanied the flame from one city to another throughout the preliminary ceremonies.

The leader of our group was a young Swede. We were a diverse group. There was a girl in her mid-teens whose parents had died; with the help of small social grants and her neighbours, she managed to care for her siblings in a shack. Another young man was a dancer who had returned from the United Kingdom to train street children as dancers and gymnasts. There were sports administrators from rural areas, and a woman who had established a clinic for people with HIV-Aids.

Next to me sat Natalie du Toit, a top swimmer. She had lost a leg in a scooter accident during 2001 and walked with a prosthesis. She was to participate in the Athens Paralympics. Natalie was apprehensive that she might fall if she tried to run.

I mentioned that I feared not being able to jog the whole distance, but that I had been assured I could go more slowly if I wanted. No one would think any less of her if she did not run. After her turn, which went without a hitch, she said she had been thrilled by the applause and the encouragement she received from the crowd and those on the vehicle manning the camera.

When it came to my turn, I started at a trot. What I hadn't anticipated was the gradual incline towards the University of Cape Town. I had to reduce my pace. As I approached the crossroads to turn right towards the city, a large group had gathered waving South African and Greek flags. They called my name, prompting me to quicken my pace and run up the hill, holding the torch high, while they shouted, "*Viva* South Africa! *Viva* Hellas! *Viva* George Bizos, *viva!*"

My run ended behind a wheelchair in which sat an elderly woman. I lit her torch, and her helper and I pushed the chair forward so that the flame could continue its all-day journey to the Grand Parade. The last runner was Lucas Radebe, former captain of South Africa's national soccer team Bafana Bafana and of Leeds United. Radebe was to run onto the Parade and use his torch to light the cauldron, specially made and erected there.

Ambassador Yiannis Economides had invited me to a party at Cape Town's Hellenic Club that evening, but I asked to be excused. I wanted to join the people of Cape Town and celebrate with them as the last runner arrived. I reached the square well before Radebe, but by then such a vast crowd had gathered that it was impossible to get near the cauldron or the platform from which Sam Ramsamy had invited me to watch. But I was happy simply to be among the people in the square: some raised their children on their shoulders; others held hands tightly lest they separated in the crowd. A few even recognised me from our 'torch run' and offered their congratulations.

The controlled explosion of the fire in the cauldron caused an almost frenzied response – exclamations, ululating and applause – as if everyone there wanted the rest of Cape Town to hear them. We guessed there would be a like spirit in the other cities holding similar ceremonies. The prophetic words of Baron Pierre de Coubertin, the Frenchman who revived the Olympic Games more than a century before, came to my mind: 'Olympism is not a system, it is a state of mind. It can permeate a wide variety of modes of expression and no single race or era can claim to have the monopoly on it.' It is such a pity that the leaders of the apartheid State did not share de Coubertin's joy at being surrounded by men, women and children of all colours.

Sam Ramsamy asked me to write a message for the *Olympian Pursuit*, an educational book on the Olympic Games. I wrote:

As we are preparing to go to Athens let us be inspired by the words of George Seferis, the modern Greek poet and Nobel Laureate for literature, who spent a few years in Pretoria:

Just a little more
And we shall see the
Almond trees in blossom
The marbles shining in the sun
The sea, the curling waves.
Just a little more
Let us rise just a little higher.

Let our athletes remember these words whilst they are training; just a little more effort may lead to an extra medal. Let Nocsa, our coaches and our administrators do a little more to help the athletes do better.

Let our heads of government, our sponsors, our fellow citizens, our supporters do a little more to show the athletes that we are fully behind them. So, united, we will surely rise much more than a 'little higher'.

South Africa plunged in earnest into the Olympic Games almost immediately after the demise of apartheid. Our exclusion for over thirty years at the instance of our liberation movement created a burning desire that led us to bid for the 2004 Olympics to be staged in Cape Town.

After we were excluded, Athens won the vote to host the games. Nelson Mandela, then president of South Africa, immediately congratulated Athens. He no doubt did so mindful of the values to which he has dedicated his life and which had their origin in the Olympic spirit enunciated by the ancient Greeks almost three thousand years ago. Freedom, human dignity, equality and the advancement of human rights – all values entrenched in our Constitution – were then not accorded to all men nor to any women, but they formed the basis of the Olympian ideal.

There was also a personal reason. When President Mandela was in prison the ancient city of Olympia conferred honorary citizenship on him. The letter informing him of this award was not handed to him by his jailers. When he was told later he was overjoyed. He said that he valued it as one of the greatest honours bestowed on him.

For this and so many other reasons the people of Gréece love him and South Africa. Our presence in Greece will surely enhance the already excellent relations between South Africa and Greece.

Nelson Mandela was one of the first leaders of the world to urge support for the 'Olympic Truce'. Let all of us support the call. Ending even one conflict may inspire others in the future to put an end to wars.

Be ready to hear '*Kalos ilthate*' – You are welcome – over and over again in Athens in August 2004.

I asked the teachers of Greek at the Saheti School to compile an English-Greek Olympic dictionary to be given to each of the almost one hundred and fifty people going to Athens. The whole school also enacted the lighting of the Olympic flame and the opening and closing ceremonies with the head boy and head girl of the school handing over the Olympic flag to a group of Chinese students. These students sang the Chinese national anthem and then invited everyone present to be in Beijing in 2008.

The South African team gathered at the Advanced Sports Centre of the University of Pretoria for final training. I met some of them and spoke about ancient and modern Greece, and how the games had taken place long ago and in more recent times. We were fitted out with clothing in the South African national colours and insignia. Hundreds of guests from government, various sports federations, sponsors of the team, leading athletes from days gone by and others gathered in Johannesburg to bid us farewell. At this late stage I was disappointed to learn that Nelson Mandela and Graça Machel would not be coming: his doctors had advised that the heat and strain might adversely affect his health.

We flew in to the newly built airport in Athens. Waiting for us were Sam Ramsamy, his wife Helga and South Africa's ambassador to Greece, Jannie Momberg, with his wife Trinnie. The halls and corridors were crowded with national sports teams and specially trained young women and men from all over the world in their distinctive volunteers' uniforms. I noticed some from South

Africa. The athletes, their trainers, doctors, physiotherapists and others boarded buses to go to the Olympic village. Arethe and I were taken to a hotel within walking distance of the stadium that was built with white marble for the first Olympic Games of the modern era held in 1906 near the centre of Athens. The newly built highway halved the time it previously took to reach the city. Everywhere we saw recently planted olive trees, cypresses, broom and multicoloured oleanders. Athens had been spruced up in honour of the games.

Our large hotel was fully occupied by what seemed to be representatives of every country on earth. The larger than usual accreditation card around our necks with 'South Africa' prominently printed at the top led many delegates to greet us warmly. Mostly they wanted to know if Mr Mandela was expected. Sam Ramsamy knew practically everyone by name as well as the country they represented. He was sought out by those from the other African countries. They asked his advice or reminisced about the past when they had together promoted the exclusion of South Africa from the Olympic Games and from other international sporting events. Although Jannie Momberg and Sam Ramsamy were on opposite sides at that time they were now reconciled. The two men had become good friends and worked together to promote the interests of South Africa.

We were driven by one of the volunteers to the Olympic village on the outskirts of Athens. Those entrusted with the planning, designing and building of urgently required mass housing could learn much from what had been done there in such a short time. Most striking was the absence of uniformity; the number of open spaces; the variation of colour – although most of the roofs were terracotta. The balconies and the little gardens added to the charm. The small, unfenced units spoke of quiet and relaxed living. The larger contingents, such as South Africa's, had a unit for themselves and our flag hung from all levels of the building. Smaller delegations shared buildings, and you could sometimes see a unit flying three or four different flags.

Even while the leaders of the South African team, under Hajera Kajee, began allocating rooms, unpacking equipment, medical supplies and books and documents, workmen were putting finishing touches to the place, carpeting the cement floor or adjusting the air-conditioning system.

Hajera seemed to be on top of the situation, but I was concerned because the media, particularly in the United States, the United Kingdom and Australia, had stated categorically that Greece was not ready. Australia had even suggested that the games should be switched to Sydney where they'd been held four years previously. Humorists predicted that Beijing would be ready in 2008 – and so would Athens. The Americans asserted that Greece was incapable of arranging adequate security and insisted that their own armed services provide protection. There were even suggestions that the US team would withdraw from the event. Greece stood firm; she would not succumb to these threats.

When we next visited the village practically all the teams had arrived. The village square, containing some two hundred flagpoles, waited for the national flags to be raised, the national anthems to be played and a member of each team to take the oath on behalf of their team-mates:

> In the name of all the competitors, I promise that we shall take part in these Olympic Games, respecting and abiding by the rules which govern them, committing ourselves to a sport without doping and without drugs, in the true spirit of sportsmanship, for the glory of sport and the honour of our teams.

Two extra-large dining halls provided well-stocked food counters for officials, athletes and their guests. Service was speedy and the food abundant, varied and healthy. There were long tables to sit at, and as if by arrangement most sought a place next to someone not from their own country and engaged in animated conversation.

We were invited by President Constantine Stephanopolos to the Megaron of Music, where more than a thousand representatives were to be welcomed to Athens. Some time before this, the president had paid an official visit to South Africa and addressed a combined sitting of Parliament, emphasising how important South Africa's democracy was to Africa, the world and the United Nations.

During his visit he also addressed gatherings of the Hellenic communities in South Africa, and praised us for being good ambassadors for the country of our origin and that of our ancestors. He spent time at the Saheti School, finding favour in the open-door policy, and the promotion of the Greek language and the Hellenic culture, ancient and modern.

At the Megaron there was a special place for South Africa's first lady, Zanele Mbeki. President Thabo Mbeki was too involved in the affairs of state and elsewhere in Africa to attend the Olympic Games. The hosts were disappointed that neither he nor former president Nelson Mandela could be there.

President Stephanopolos warmly welcomed kings, queens, presidents, prime ministers and other dignitaries from throughout the world. Despite his gentility and impeccable diplomatic manners he could not resist referring to the doubts expressed by many that Greece would not be able to stage the games. He indulged in some not-too-gentle irony on the subject, which earned him good coverage by the local media.

One commentator, tongue-in-cheek, put the blame on the Greeks themselves. How would the media have been able to criticise Greece if her language had not provided journalists with words such as 'chaos' and 'catastrophe'? The comedians had their moment too. President George W Bush was shown stepping up to a podium to address the athletes before they left for the games. He glanced at the pages placed before him and read, 'O, O, O ...' His aide rushed up and whispered that he was looking at the emblem of the Olympic Games on the front cover, his speech was on the next page.

Sylvia Dale and Tombi Mothei, senior employees of the National Olympic Committee of South Africa, went out of their way to help us reach the fields where our teams were playing. They made special arrangements for Arethe, who was using crutches after two hip operations. In the late 1940s she had played hockey at St Mary's School in Johannesburg and we learned that Ross Howell, coach of the women's team, was a senior teacher at St Mary's. Not surprisingly, perhaps, three of the players on the Olympic hockey team learned their game at the same school. A close bond developed between Arethe and this team and we attended all their games.

On the day of the opening ceremony we dressed in the national uniform. Sylvia Dale arranged for Arethe to go directly to the stadium while the South African squad went by coach. The notorious traffic congestion of Athens was under control and we had no trouble getting there on time, partly because a section of the road was reserved for Olympic vehicles.

Together with other teams we were taken to a large hall within the main stadium where the indoor events would take place. This acted as a kind of holding area from which we were to march into the arena. While we waited for our turn a large screen projected the outside ceremony. Our flag bearer was Mbulaeni Mulaudzi, considered among the top three eight-hundred-metre runners, and someone from whom a gold medal was expected. At the last minute, Hajera Kajee invited me to march immediately behind the flag, an unexpected, wonderful honour.

We were given a tumultuous reception as we approached the podium and took our place in the middle of the field. It was a dignified spectacle, steeped in the spirit of the ancient games. And to the gratification of the Greeks, CNN publicly apologised for the doubts it had expressed about the ability of Greece to stage the games.

The Americans and Australians were expected to take top honours in the 4 × 100 metre swimming relay, one of the first big contests. Then the South African team of Roland Schoeman, Lindon Ferns, Johannes Zandberg and Ryk Neethling won their heat in the morning and we wondered if we were about to witness something exciting. This race is one of the most prestigious events and the spectators in the packed stadium were on their feet as the swimmers powered through the water during the final. The race was so close that the crowd couldn't determine who'd won. When the score-board showed the astonishing result: 'RSA – Olympic Record – World Record' there was some confusion as not everyone knew what 'RSA' stood for. Then came thunderous applause when the result was announced in full: 'First, Republic of South Africa'.

It was an extraordinary moment when the four stepped onto the podium where olive crowns were placed on their heads. As they stood with their gold medals, each holding a bunch of flowers, attentive as our national anthem was played and the flag was raised, I found it difficult to hold back tears of joy. A gold medal for these four athletes so early in the games and for such an important event put South Africa on the map at the start. Many in the stadium, on the streets and in restaurants would stop us once they noticed our accreditation cards, congratulate us and wish us well.

One of the last events was the shot-put and it was held in the Olympic stadium where the ancient games took place. We sat on the grass banks together with tens of thousands of others as the ancients had done, and I wished that at least some track and field events had been held there during these games as well.

The closing ceremony was a joyous occasion. The athletes no longer kept to their national groups, but intermingled, embraced, sang and danced together. President of the International Olympic Committee, Jacques Rogge, delivered a speech in which he used some Greek, gracefully thanking Greece for the successful games.

The president of the Athens 2004 Organising Committee for the Olympic Games, Gianna Angelopoulou-Daskalaki, was given a standing ovation for the theme of the closing celebration. It took on the appearance of a massive traditional village wedding party with one feisty song and one regional dance after another, every attempt being made to ensure it was all-inclusive. There was a particularly amusing and touching moment when Gypsies, often regarded as outcasts in Europe, were also brought into the spectacle. An open vehicle filled with watermelons and with an old-style scale hanging on the side was wheeled into the stadium; exuberant Romany men and women followed the vehicle, falling on would-be customers to buy their wares.

The finale was the handing over of the Olympic flag by Athens to Beijing. The oriental splendour displayed by the Chinese augured well for another great Olympic Games in 2008.

During the latter half of 2006 I was appointed an Ambassador of Hellenism. I was invited to Greece to join two other appointees at the Megaron Musikis in Athens to receive the honour from the president of Greece. Unfortunately I was unable to attend and an alternative function was held instead at the embassy in Pretoria.

The ambassador explained that the first Ambassador of Hellenism was Melina Mercouri in the early 1980s. I was the fortieth to be appointed. He went on:

> Ambassadors of Hellenism are personalities who have a vision for an open, free and universal society devoid of discrimination, racism and injustice, and who work conscientiously and voluntarily in the spirit of ecumenical Hellenism. They establish institutions harmoniously tying local and Greek traditions and spread Greek civilisation, culture and education to the younger generations. They contribute to the creation of movements for the protection of human rights and the promotion of democracy; they cooperate with international organisations combating poverty, suppression, hunger and diseases, and they strive for the elimination of the scourge of war. They also offer their good services to sports and Olympism.
>
> During his lifetime George Bizos has demonstrated great courage and determination in pursing with conviction all those principles, values and ideals that first appeared in the land of the Greeks: protection of human rights and basic freedoms, justice and equality for all, promotion of democracy, non-discrimination, humanism. At the same time, never forgetting that he is a Greek by birth, he has been instrumental in establishing the famous Saheti School, where Greek language, culture and civilisation are taught to all South Africans. I firmly believe that George Bizos, this world-renowned and respected champion of human rights, is the most significant link in the human chain linking our two nations.

My duties, it turned out, were to help in the endeavour to get the Parthenon marbles in the British Museum returned to Greece and the newly built Acropolis Museum. This is something desired by Greeks and Philhellenes throughout the world and a cause I was only too happy to become involved in. Subsequently I was also invited to join the British Committee for the Reunification of the Parthenon Marbles.

There are always touchstones in our lives, and mine, very literally, is a particular rock on a particular beach near my village. Many times over the years I have sat on the rock from which I had jumped into the boat with the New Zealanders.

I went back there after the 2004 Olympic Games in an attempt to understand the overwhelming experience of the games and its meaning to me. And I have sat there frequently since.

From that rock I look at the north-western horizon beyond which lies Ithaca, that island kingdom for which Odysseus sought and for which he longed all those many years. I know it is there, even though it is far away and out of sight.

On this occasion I had with me a copy of Kimon Friar's *Translations of Modern Greek Poetry*, and read aloud that wonderful poem *Ithaca*, by CP Cavafy:

> *When you set out on the voyage to Ithaca,*
> *pray that your journey may be long,*
> *full of adventures, full of knowledge.*
> *Of the Laestrygones and the Cyclopes*
> *and of furious Poseidon, do not be afraid,*
> *for such on your journey you shall never meet*
> *if your thought remain lofty, if a select*
> *emotion imbue your spirit and your body.*
> *The Laestrygones and the Cyclopes*
> *and furious Poseidon you will never meet*
> *unless you drag them with you in your soul,*
> *unless your soul raises them up before you.*
>
> *Pray that your journey may be long,*
> *that many may those summer mornings be*
> *when with what pleasure, what untold delight*
> *you enter harbours you've not seen before;*
> *that you stop at Phoenician market places*
> *to produce the goodly merchandise,*
> *mother of pearl and coral, amber and ebony,*
> *and voluptuous perfumes of every kind,*
> *as lavish an amount of voluptuous perfumes as you can;*
> *that you venture on to many Egyptian cities*
> *to learn and yet again to learn from the sages.*
>
> *But you must always keep Ithaca in mind.*
> *The arrival there is your predestination.*
> *Yet do not by any means hasten your voyage.*
> *Let it best endure for many years,*

until grown old at length you anchor at your island
rich with all you have acquired on the way.
You never hoped that Ithaca would give you riches.

Ithaca has given you the lovely voyage.
Without her you would not have ventured on the way.
She has nothing more to give you now.

Poor though you may find her, Ithaca has not deceived you.
Now that you have become so wise, so full of experience,
you will have understood the meaning of an Ithaca.

I pondered those last lines in particular. Was my Odyssean journey at an end? How much longer would it last? Had I really understood the meaning of this voyage? Can there be more than one Ithaca at which to cast anchor in a single life? I saw that I straddled both the country that gave me birth and the other that adopted me. I have made them both my Ithaca. I have shared their joys and sorrows.

The journey, my odyssey to freedom, has been long with many steps, many waves to crest. But I have always kept both Ithacas in mind. Perhaps I have become wise; I have surely gained much experience. And this I can now say with certainty: these Ithacas have not deceived me.

INDEX OF PERSONS

GENERAL INDEX